THE COLLECTED WORKS

OF

C. G. JUNG

VOLUME 5

EDITORS

SIR HERBERT READ

MICHAEL FORDHAM, M.D., M.R.C.P.

GERHARD ADLER, PH.D.

WILLIAM McGUIRE, *executive editor*

The Ostian head of Mithras
Roman

SYMBOLS

OF

TRANSFORMATION

AN ANALYSIS OF THE PRELUDE TO A CASE OF SCHIZOPHRENIA

C. G. JUNG

SECOND EDITION

TRANSLATED BY R. F. C. HULL

ROUTLEDGE & KEGAN PAUL

LONDON

FIRST PUBLISHED IN ENGLAND BY
ROUTLEDGE & KEGAN PAUL, LTD.
BROADWAY HOUSE, 68–74 CARTER LANE,
LONDON E. C. 4
1956

Second edition, with corrections, 1967
Second printing, with corrections, 1970

THIS EDITION IS BEING PUBLISHED BY ROUT-
LEDGE & KEGAN PAUL, LTD., IN ENGLAND,
AND BY PRINCETON UNIVERSITY PRESS IN
THE UNITED STATES OF AMERICA. THE PRES-
ENT VOLUME IS NUMBER 5 OF THE COL-
LECTED WORKS, AND WAS THE FIFTH TO
APPEAR.

Translated from *Symbole der Wandlung*
(4th edition, rewritten, of *Wandlungen
und Symbole der Libido*), published by
Rascher Verlag, Zurich, 1952.

ISBN 0 7100 1636 0

MANUFACTURED IN THE U.S.A.

EDITORIAL NOTE

As the author's Foreword indicates, the volume from which the present translation has been made is an extensive revision, published in 1952, of *Wandlungen und Symbole der Libido,* published in 1912.* The reasons for this revision and its extent are explained by Dr. Jung and need no further comment here.

The present translation differs in certain respects from the revised Swiss edition. First of all, the number of illustrations has been reduced. In the Swiss edition, these had been inserted to amplify the text rather than to illustrate. It seemed to the Editors that the illustrations sometimes had the disadvantage of interrupting the text unduly, and after careful consideration it was decided that only those having a direct relevance to the text should be included. Among these, some new photographs and substitutions have been used. Secondly, an appendix containing the complete Miller fantasies has been added. Since these were available only in a French text published in 1906 in the *Archives de psychologie,* a translation by Philip Mairet has been provided. The textual quotations are also from this translation. Other differences from the Swiss edition result from bringing the volume into conformity with the general plan for the Collected Works. A bibliography has been added, and accordingly the references in the footnotes have been somewhat shortened.

In respect to the quotations from various languages, special mention must be made of the work of Dr. A. Wasserstein and Dr. Marie-Louise von Franz in checking and translating some of the Latin and Greek texts. The philological material has been checked over by Dr. Leopold Stein.

---

* First published in two parts in the *Jahrbuch für psychoanalytische und psychopathologische Forschungen* (Leipzig), III–IV (1911–12), and republished the same year as a book by Deuticke Verlag, Leipzig and Vienna. An English translation, by Dr. Beatrice M. Hinkle, entitled *Psychology of the Unconscious,* was published in 1916 by Moffatt Yard and Co., New York, and in 1917 by Kegan Paul, London. Translations have also appeared in Dutch, French, and Italian.

EDITORIAL NOTE TO THE SECOND EDITION

For this edition, appearing ten years after the first, bibliograph-
ical citations and entries have been revised in the light of subsequent publications in the *Collected Works* and in the Standard
Edition of Freud's works, some translations have been substituted in quotations, and other essential corrections have been
made, but there have been no changes of substance in the text.

TRANSLATOR'S NOTE

During the preparation of this volume, the text of the original
English translation by Beatrice M. Hinkle, first published in
America in 1916 under the title *Psychology of the Unconscious,*
was freely consulted. Certain of the quotations of poetry there
rendered by Louis Untermeyer have been taken over into the
present edition, sometimes with slight modifications. For some
of the quotations from *Faust,* I am indebted to Philip Wayne,
both for extracts from his published version of Part 1 and for
passages from Part 2 specially translated for this volume. Quotations from Latin and Greek sources are taken when possible
from existing translations, but mostly they are of a composite
nature, resulting from comparison of the existing translations
with the original texts and with the German versions used by
the author, who in some cases translated direct from the orig-
inals. For the purpose of comparison, reference is sometimes
made, in square brackets, to an existing translation although it
has not been quoted.

NOTE OF ACKNOWLEDGMENT

Grateful acknowledgment is made to the following publishers and others for the reproduction of illustrations or for permission to quote:

Allen and Unwin, London, for a passage from Freud's *The Interpretation of Dreams;* O. W. Barth, Munich: a plate from Wachlmayr, *Das Christgeburtsbild der frühen Sakralkunst;* Professor W. Norman Brown: passages from his translation of the Rig-Veda; Bruckmann Verlag, Munich: an illustration from J. J. Bernoulli, *Die erhaltenen Darstellungen Alexanders des Grossen;* Clarendon Press, Oxford: a passage from John Todhunter's translation of Heine and an illustration from the catalogue of the Palazzo dei Conservatori, Rome, edited by H. S. Jones for the British School at Rome; Diederichs Verlag, Düsseldorf: a plate from Wirth, *Der Aufgang der Menschheit;* Dodd, Mead and Co., New York: for the use of material originally appearing in Beatrice Hinkle's translation of Jung's *Psychology of the Unconscious;* Folkwang Verlag, Hagen i. W.: a plate from Fuhrmann, *Reich der Inka;* Friedrichsen Verlag, Hamburg: figures from Danzel, *Symbole, Dämonen, und heilige Türme;* Harcourt, Brace and Co.: passages from Untermeyer's translation of Heine and Cornford's translation of Plato's *Timaeus;* Harvard University Press: passages from the Loeb Classical Library editions of Ovid, Seneca, Virgil, and the Homeric Hymns; William Heinemann, London: passages from the Thomas and Guillemard translation of Rostand's *Cyrano de Bergerac;* Hoepli, Milan: a plate from Prampolini, *La Mitologia nella vita dei popoli;* The Hogarth Press; quotations from the Standard Edition of the Works of Sigmund Freud and the Collected Papers of Sigmund Freud; Houghton Mifflin Co., Boston: passages from Longfellow's *Hiawatha;* H. Keller Verlag, Berlin: a plate from Deubner, *Attische Feste;* Librairie Larousse, Paris: two plates from Guirand, *Mythologie générale;* Macmillan and Co., New York: a quotation from Baldwin, *Thoughts and Things,* and translations from Nietzsche's works, and figs. 28 and 33, from *The Mythology of All Races,* II; The Medici Society, London, for an illustration from Budge's *Osiris and the Egyptian Resurrection,* I; Methuen and Co., London: figs. 5, 24, and 27 and Pl. XLI*b,* from Budge, *Gods of the Egyptians;* Oxford University Press, New York: passages from Louis Mac-Neice's translation of *Faust;* Penguin Books: passages from Rieu's translation of the Iliad and the Odyssey, de Selincourt's translation of Herodotus, Wayne's translation of *Faust,* and Hamilton's translation of Plato; Princeton University Press: passages from E. A. Speiser's translations in *Ancient Near Eastern Texts;* Reimer Verlag, Berlin: a plate from LeCoq, *Die Buddhistische Spätantike in Mittelasien;* Schwann Verlag, Düsseldorf: a plate from Clemen, *Die romanische Wandmalerei des Rheinlands;* Seeman Verlag, Cologne: a plate from Cohn, *Buddha in der Kunst des Ostens;* Sheed and Ward, New York: passages from F. J. Sheed's translation of the *Confessions* of St. Augustine; Stubenrauch Verlag, Berlin: a plate from Spiess, *Marksteine der Volkskunst;* Editions Tel, Paris: a photograph of Strasbourg Cathedral, by Marc Foucault; Mr. Philip Wayne: passages from his unpublished translation of *Faust,* Part II.

TABLE OF CONTENTS

LIST OF PLATES

(following page 274)

For full documentation of sources, see the Bibliography. P = photograph.

Frontispiece.   The Ostian head of Mithras
Roman. Museo Laterano, Rome. P: Museum, courtesy of Torgil Magnusson.

I*a*. Expulsion of the demons
Anonymous engraving, 17th century. P: Courtesy of Dr. Jolande Jacobi.

I*b*. Sun-god
Shamanistic Eskimo idol, Alaska. P: From Wirth, *Der Aufgang der Menschheit,* Pl. XI, fig. 1.

II. Romulus and Remus with the She-Wolf
Painted wood, northern Italian, medieval. Victoria and Albert Museum, London. P: Museum, Crown copyright.

III. Christ in the Virgin's womb
Upper Rhenish Master, Germany, *c.* 1400. Formerly Staatliche Gemäldegalerie, Berlin. P: From Wachlmayr, *Das Christgeburtsbild,* p. 4.

IV*a*. Boar-headed mother goddess: shakti of boar-headed Vishnu
Relief, northern India, 7th century. British Museum. P: Museum.

IV*b*. Scenes from the Eleusinian Mysteries
From a burial urn, Rome, 1st century A.D. Formerly in the Kircher Museum, Rome. Reconstructed drawing from *Bullettino della Commissione Archeologica Comunale di Roma,* VII (1879), 2nd series, Pls. II–III.

V*a*. Veneration of the Buddha's teachings as a sun-wheel
Stupa of Amaravati, India, 2nd century A.D. Government Museum, Madras. P· Guirand, *Mythologie générale,* p. 330.

V*b*. The Son of Man between the Seven Candlesticks
Universitätsbibliothek, Tübingen: Beatus Commentary, Theol. Lat. fol. 561, fol. 3^V. P: E. Surkamp, courtesy of the Bibliothek.

xi

LIST OF TEXT FIGURES

FOREWORD TO THE FOURTH SWISS EDITION [1]

I have long been conscious of the fact that this book, which was written thirty-seven years ago, stood in urgent need of revision, but my professional obligations and my scientific work never left me sufficient leisure to settle down in comfort to this unpleasant and difficult task. Old age and illness released me at last from my professional duties and gave me the necessary time to contemplate the sins of my youth. I have never felt happy about this book, much less satisfied with it: it was written at top speed, amid the rush and press of my medical practice, without regard to time or method. I had to fling my material hastily together, just as I found it. There was no opportunity to let my thoughts mature. The whole thing came upon me like a landslide that cannot be stopped. The urgency that lay behind it became clear to me only later: it was the explosion of all those psychic contents which could find no room, no breathing-space, in the constricting atmosphere of Freudian psychology and its narrow outlook. I have no wish to denigrate Freud, or to detract from the extraordinary merits of his investigation of the individual psyche. But the conceptual framework into which he fitted the psychic phenomenon seemed to me unendurably narrow. I am not thinking here of his theory of neurosis, which can be as narrow as it pleases if only it is adequate to the empirical facts, or of his theory of dreams, about which different views may be held in all good faith; I am thinking more of the reductive causalism of his whole outlook, and the almost complete disregard of the teleological directedness which is so characteristic of everything psychic. Although Freud's book *The Future of an Illusion* dates from his later years, it gives the best possible account of his earlier views, which move within the confines of the outmoded rationalism and scientific materialism of the late nineteenth century.

As might be expected, my book, born under such conditions, consisted of larger or smaller fragments which I could only string together in an unsatisfying manner. It was an attempt,

[1] [The edition here translated.—EDITORS.]

only partially successful, to create a wider setting for medical psychology and to bring the whole of the psychic phenomenon within its purview. One of my principal aims was to free medical psychology from the subjective and personalistic bias that characterized its outlook at that time, and to make it possible to understand the unconscious as an objective and collective psyche. The personalism in the views of Freud and Adler that went hand in hand with the individualism of the nineteenth century failed to satisfy me because, except in the case of instinctive dynamisms (which actually have too little place in Adler), it left no room for objective, impersonal facts. Freud, accordingly, could see no objective justification for my attempt, but suspected personal motives.

Thus this book became a landmark, set up on the spot where two ways divided. Because of its imperfections and its incompleteness it laid down the programme to be followed for the next few decades of my life. Hardly had I finished the manuscript when it struck me what it means to live with a myth, and what it means to live without one. Myth, says a Church Father, is "what is believed always, everywhere, by everybody"; hence the man who thinks he can live without myth, or outside it, is an exception. He is like one uprooted, having no true link either with the past, or with the ancestral life which continues within him, or yet with contemporary human society. He does not live in a house like other men, does not eat and drink like other men, but lives a life of his own, sunk in a subjective mania of his own devising, which he believes to be the newly discovered truth. This plaything of his reason never grips his vitals. It may occasionally lie heavy on his stomach, for that organ is apt to reject the products of reason as indigestible. The psyche is not of today; its ancestry goes back many millions of years. Individual consciousness is only the flower and the fruit of a season, sprung from the perennial rhizome beneath the earth; and it would find itself in better accord with the truth if it took the existence of the rhizome into its calculations. For the root matter is the mother of all things.

So I suspected that myth had a meaning which I was sure to miss if I lived outside it in the haze of my own speculations. I was driven to ask myself in all seriousness: "What is the myth you are living?" I found no answer to this question, and had to

xxiv

admit that I was not living with a myth, or even in a myth, but rather in an uncertain cloud of theoretical possibilities which I was beginning to regard with increasing distrust. I did not know that I was living a myth, and even if I had known it, I would not have known what sort of myth was ordering my life without my knowledge. So, in the most natural way, I took it upon myself to get to know "my" myth, and I regarded this as the task of tasks, for—so I told myself—how could I, when treating my patients, make due allowance for the personal factor, for my personal equation, which is yet so necessary for a knowledge of the other person, if I was unconscious of it? I simply had to know what unconscious or preconscious myth was forming me, from what rhizome I sprang. This resolve led me to devote many years of my life to investigating the subjective contents which are the products of unconscious processes, and to work out methods which would enable us, or at any rate help us, to explore the manifestations of the unconscious. Here I discovered, bit by bit, the connecting links that I should have known about before if I was to join up the fragments of my book. I do not know whether I have succeeded in this task now, after a lapse of thirty-seven years. Much pruning had to be done, many gaps filled. It has proved impossible to preserve the style of 1912, for I had to incorporate many things that I found out only many years later. Nevertheless I have tried, despite a number of radical interventions, to leave as much of the original edifice standing as possible, for the sake of continuity with previous editions. And although the alterations are considerable, I do not think one could say that it has turned into a different book. There can be no question of that because the whole thing is really only an extended commentary on a practical analysis of the prodromal stages of schizophrenia. The symptoms of the case form the Ariadne thread to guide us through the labyrinth of symbolistic parallels, that is, through the amplifications which are absolutely essential if we wish to establish the meaning of the archetypal context. As soon as these parallels come to be worked out they take up an incredible amount of space, which is why expositions of case histories are such an arduous task. But that is only to be expected: the deeper you go, the broader the base becomes. It certainly does not become narrower, and it never by any chance ends in a point—in a psychic trauma, for instance. Any such theory presupposes a knowledge of the traumatically affected psyche which no human being possesses, and which can only be laboriously acquired by investigating the workings of the unconscious. For this a great deal of comparative material is needed, and it cannot be dispensed with any more than in comparative anatomy. Knowledge of the subjective contents of consciousness means very little, for it tells us next to nothing about the real, subterranean life of the psyche. In psychology as in every science a fairly wide knowledge of other subjects is among the requisites for research work. A nodding acquaintance with the theory and pathology of neurosis is totally inadequate, because medical knowledge of this kind is merely information about an illness, but not knowledge of the soul that is ill. I wanted, so far as lay within my power, to redress that evil with this book—then as now.

This book was written in 1911, in my thirty-sixth year. The time is a critical one, for it marks the beginning of the second half of life, when a metanoia, a mental transformation, not infrequently occurs. I was acutely conscious, then, of the loss of friendly relations with Freud and of the lost comradeship of our work together. The practical and moral support which my wife gave me at that difficult period is something I shall always hold in grateful remembrance.

September, 1950   C. G. JUNG

FOREWORD TO THE THIRD SWISS EDITION

The new edition of this book appears essentially unaltered, except for a few textual improvements which hardly affect its content.

This book has to perform the thankless task of making clear to my contemporaries that the problems of the human psyche cannot be tackled with the meagre equipment of the doctor's consulting-room, any more than they can be tackled with the layman's famous "understanding of the world and human nature." Psychology cannot dispense with the contribution made by the humane sciences, and certainly not with that made by the history of the human mind. For it is history above all that today enables us to bring the huge mass of empirical material into ordered relationships and to recognize the functional significance of the collective contents of the unconscious. The psyche is not something unalterably given, but a product of its own continuous development. Hence altered glandular secretions or aggravated personal relationships are not the sole causes of neurotic conflicts; these can equally well be caused by historically conditioned attitudes and mental factors. Scientific and medical knowledge is in no sense sufficient to grasp the nature of the soul, nor does the psychiatric understanding of pathological processes help to integrate them into the totality of the psyche. Similarly, mere rationalization is not an adequate instrument. History teaches us over and over again that, contrary to rational expectation, irrational factors play the largest, indeed the decisive, role in all processes of psychic transformation.

It seems as if this insight were slowly making headway with the somewhat drastic assistance of contemporary events.

November, 1937   C. G. JUNG

FOREWORD TO THE SECOND SWISS EDITION

In this second edition the text of the book remains, for technical reasons, unaltered. The reappearance of this book after twelve years, without alterations, does not mean that I did not consider certain emendations and improvements desirable. But such improvements would have affected details only, and not anything essential. The views and opinions I expressed in the book I would still maintain, in substance and in principle, today. I must ask the reader to bear patiently with a number of minor inaccuracies and uncertainties of detail.

This book has given rise to a good deal of misunderstanding. It has even been suggested that it represents my method of treatment. Apart from the fact that such a method would be a practical impossibility, the book is far more concerned with working out the fantasy material of an unknown young American woman, pseudonymously known as Frank Miller. This material was originally published by my respected and fatherly friend, the late Théodore Flournoy, in the *Archives de psychologie* (Geneva). I had the great satisfaction of hearing from his own lips that I had hit off the young woman's mentality very well. Valuable confirmation of this reached me in 1918, through an American colleague who was treating Miss Miller for the schizophrenic disturbance which had broken out after her sojourn in Europe. He wrote to say that my exposition of the case was so exhaustive that even personal acquaintance with the patient had not taught him "one iota more" about her mentality. This confirmation led me to conclude that my reconstruction of the semi-conscious and unconscious fantasy processes had evidently hit the mark in all essential respects.

There is, however, one very common misunderstanding which I feel I ought to point out to the reader. The copious use of comparative mythological and etymological material necessitated by the peculiar nature of the Miller fantasies may evoke the impression, among certain readers, that the purpose of this book is to propound mythological or etymological hypotheses. This is far from my intention, for if it had been, I would have

xxviii

undertaken to analyse a particular myth or whole corpus of myths, for instance an American Indian myth-cycle. For that purpose I would certainly not have chosen Longfellow's *Hiawatha,* any more than I would have used Wagner's *Siegfried* had I wished to analyse the cycle of the younger Edda. I use the material quoted in the book because it belongs, directly or indirectly, to the basic assumptions of the Miller fantasies, as I have explained more fully in the text. If, in this work, various mythologems are shown in a light which makes their psychological meaning more intelligible, I have mentioned this insight simply as a welcome by-product, without claiming to propound any general theory of myths. The real purpose of this book is confined to working out the implications of all those historical and spiritual factors which come together in the involuntary products of individual fantasy. Besides the obvious personal sources, creative fantasy also draws upon the forgotten and long buried primitive mind with its host of images, which are to be found in the mythologies of all ages and all peoples. The sum of these images constitutes the collective unconscious, a heritage which is potentially present in every individual. It is the psychic correlate of the differentiation of the human brain. This is the reason why mythological images are able to arise spontaneously over and over again, and to agree with one another not only in all the corners of the wide earth, but at all times. As they are present always and everywhere, it is an entirely natural proceeding to relate mythologems, which may be very far apart both temporally and ethnically, to an individual fantasy system. The creative substratum is everywhere this same human psyche and this same human brain, which, with relatively minor variations, functions everywhere in the same way.

Küsnacht/Zurich, November, 1924   C. G. JUNG

I

Therefore theory, which gives facts their value and significance, is often very useful, even if it is partially false, because it throws light on phenomena which no one has observed, it forces an examination, from many angles, of facts which no one has hitherto studied, and provides the impulse for more extensive and more productive researches. . . .

Hence it is a moral duty for the man of science to expose himself to the risk of committing error, and to submit to criticism in order that science may continue to progress. A writer . . . has launched a vigorous attack on the author, saying that this is a scientific ideal which is very limited and very paltry. . . . But those who are endowed with a mind serious and impersonal enough not to believe that everything they write is the expression of absolute and eternal truth will approve of this theory, which puts the aims of science well above the miserable vanity and paltry *amour propre* of the scientist.

—Ferrero, *Les Lois psychologiques du symbolisme,* p. viii

I

INTRODUCTION

1   Anyone who can read Freud's *Interpretation of Dreams* without being outraged by the novelty and seemingly unjustified boldness of his procedure, and without waxing morally indignant over the stark nakedness of his dream-interpretations, but can let this extraordinary book work upon his imagination calmly and without prejudice, will not fail to be deeply impressed at that point [1] where Freud reminds us that an individual conflict, which he calls the incest fantasy, lies at the root of that monumental drama of the ancient world, the Oedipus legend. The impression made by this simple remark may be likened to the uncanny feeling which would steal over us if, amid the noise and bustle of a modern city street, we were suddenly to come upon an ancient relic—say the Corinthian capital of a long-immured column, or a fragment of an inscription. A moment ago, and we were completely absorbed in the hectic, ephemeral life of the present; then, the next moment, something very remote and strange flashes upon us, which directs our gaze to a different order of things. We turn away from the vast confusion of the present to glimpse the higher continuity of history. Suddenly we remember that on this spot where we now hasten to and fro about our business a similar scene of life and activity prevailed two thousand years ago in slightly different forms; similar passions moved mankind, and people were just as convinced as we are of the uniqueness of their lives. This is the impression that may very easily be left behind by a first acquaintance with the monuments of antiquity, and it seems to me that Freud's reference to the Oedipus legend is in every way comparable. While still struggling with the confusing impressions of the infinite variability of the individual psyche, we suddenly catch a glimpse of the simplicity and grandeur of the

[1] *The Interpretation of Dreams,* pp. 260–61.

Oedipus tragedy, that perennial highlight of the Greek theatre. This broadening of our vision has about it something of a revelation. For our psychology, the ancient world has long since been sunk in the shadows of the past; in the schoolroom one could scarcely repress a sceptical smile when one indiscreetly calculated the matronly age of Penelope or pictured to oneself the comfortable middle-aged appearance of Jocasta, and comically compared the result with the tragic tempests of eroticism that agitate the legend and drama. We did not know then—and who knows even today?—that a man can have an unconscious, all-consuming passion for his mother which may undermine and tragically complicate his whole life, so that the monstrous fate of Oedipus seems not one whit overdrawn. Rare and pathological cases like that of Ninon de Lenclos and her son [2] are too remote from most of us to convey a living impression. But when we follow the paths traced out by Freud we gain a living knowledge of the existence of these possibilities, which, although too weak to compel actual incest, are yet sufficiently strong to cause very considerable psychic disturbances. We cannot, to begin with, admit such possibilities in ourselves without a feeling of moral revulsion, and without resistances which are only too likely to blind the intellect and render self-knowledge impossible. But if we can succeed in discriminating between objective knowledge and emotional value-judgments, then the gulf that separates our age from antiquity is bridged over, and we realize with astonishment that Oedipus is still alive for us. The importance of this realization should not be underestimated, for it teaches us that there is an identity of fundamental human conflicts which is independent of time and place. What aroused a feeling of horror in the Greeks still remains true, but it is true for us only if we give up the vain illusion that we are *different,* i.e., morally better, than the ancients. We have merely succeeded in forgetting that an indissoluble link binds us to the men of antiquity. This truth opens the way to an understanding of the classical spirit such as has never existed before—the way of inner sympathy on the one hand and of intellectual comprehension on the other. By penetrating into the blocked subterranean passages of our own psyches we grasp the living meaning

[2] He is supposed to have killed himself when he heard that his adored Ninon was really his mother.

4

of classical civilization, and at the same time we establish a firm foothold outside our own culture from which alone it is possible to gain an objective understanding of its foundations. That at least is the hope we draw from the rediscovery of the immortality of the Oedipus problem.

2   This line of inquiry has already yielded fruitful results: to it we owe a number of successful advances into the territory of the human mind and its history. These are the works of Riklin,[3] Abraham,[4] Rank,[5] Maeder,[6] and Jones,[7] to which there has now been added Silberer's valuable study entitled "Phantasie und Mythos." Another work which cannot be overlooked is Pfister's contribution to Christian religious psychology.[8] The *leitmotiv* of all these works is to find a clue to historical problems through the application of insights derived from the activity of the unconscious psyche in modern man. I must refer the reader to the works specified if he wishes to inform himself of the extent and nature of the insights already achieved. The interpretations are sometimes uncertain in particulars, but that does not materially detract from the total result. It would be significant enough if this merely demonstrated the far-reaching analogy between the psychological structure of the historical products and those of modern individuals. But the analogy applies with particular force to the symbolism, as Riklin, Rank, Maeder, and Abraham have shown, and also to the individual mechanisms governing the unconscious elaboration of motifs.

3   Psychological investigators have hitherto turned their attention mainly to the analysis of individual problems. But, as things are at present, it seems to me imperative that they should broaden the basis of this analysis by a comparative study of the historical material, as Freud has already tried to do in his study of Leonardo da Vinci.[9] For, just as psychological knowledge furthers our understanding of the historical material, so, conversely, the historical material can throw new light on individual psychological problems. These considerations have led me to direct my attention more to the historical side of the picture, in the hope of gaining fresh insight into the foundations of

3 *Wishfulfilment and Symbolism in Fairy Tales.*   4 *Dreams and Myths.*
5 *The Myth of the Birth of the Hero.*   6 "Die Symbolik in den Legenden."
7 *On the Nightmare.*   8 *Die Frömmigkeit des Grafen Ludwig von Zinzendorf.*
9 Also Rank, "Ein Traum, der sich selbst deutet."

psychology. In my later writings [10] I have concerned myself chiefly with the question of historical and ethnological parallels, and here the researches of Erich Neumann have made a massive contribution towards solving the countless difficult problems that crop up everywhere in this hitherto little explored territory. I would mention above all his key work, *The Origins and History of Consciousness*,[11] which carries forward the ideas that originally impelled me to write this book, and places them in the broad perspective of the evolution of human consciousness in general.

[10] [I.e., after 1912, the date of the original publication of the present work.—EDITORS.]

[11] His subsequent publications, *Umkreisung der Mitte* and *The Great Mother*, may also be included in this category. [Three of the essays in the former work were translated in *Art and the Creative Unconscious*.—EDITORS.]

II

TWO KINDS OF THINKING

4   As most people know, one of the basic principles of analytical psychology is that dream-images are to be understood symbolically; that is to say, one must not take them literally, but must surmise a hidden meaning in them. This ancient idea of dream symbolism has aroused not only criticism, but the strongest opposition. That dreams should have a meaning, and should therefore be capable of interpretation, is certainly neither a strange nor an extraordinary idea. It has been known to mankind for thousands of years; indeed it has become something of a truism. One remembers having heard even at school of Egyptian and Chaldaean dream-interpreters. Everyone knows the story of Joseph, who interpreted Pharaoh's dreams, and of Daniel and the dream of King Nebuchadnezzar; and the dream-book of Artemidorus is familiar to many of us. From the written records of all times and peoples we learn of significant and prophetic dreams, of warning dreams and of healing dreams sent by the gods. When an idea is so old and so generally believed, it must be true in some way, by which I mean that it is *psychologically true.*

5   For modern man it is hardly conceivable that a God existing outside ourselves should cause us to dream, or that the dream foretells the future prophetically. But if we translate this into the language of psychology, the ancient idea becomes much more comprehensible. The dream, we would say, originates in an unknown part of the psyche and prepares the dreamer for the events of the following day.

6   According to the old belief, a god or demon spoke to the sleeper in symbolic language, and the dream-interpreter had to solve the riddle. In modern speech we would say that the dream is a series of images which are apparently contradictory and meaningless, but that it contains material which yields a clear meaning when properly translated.

7

7   Were I to suppose my readers to be entirely ignorant of
dream-analysis, I should be obliged to document this statement
with numerous examples. Today, however, these things are so
well known that one must be sparing in the use of case-histories
so as not to bore the public. It is an especial inconvenience that
one cannot recount a dream without having to add the history
of half a lifetime in order to represent the individual foundations of the dream. Certainly there are typical dreams and
dream-motifs whose meaning appears to be simple enough if
they are regarded from the point of view of sexual symbolism.
One can apply this point of view without jumping to the conclusion that the content so expressed must also be sexual in
origin. Common speech, as we know, is full of erotic metaphors
which are applied to matters that have nothing to do with sex;
and conversely, sexual symbolism by no means implies that the
interests making use of it are by nature erotic. Sex, as one of the
most important instincts, is the prime cause of numerous affects
that exert an abiding influence on our speech. But affects cannot be identified with sexuality inasmuch as they may easily
spring from conflict situations—for instance, many emotions
spring from the instinct of self-preservation.

8   It is true that many dream-images have a sexual aspect
or express erotic conflicts. This is particularly clear in the motif
of *assault*. Burglars, thieves, murderers, and sexual maniacs figure prominently in the erotic dreams of women. It is a theme
with countless variations. The instrument of murder may be a
lance, a sword, a dagger, a revolver, a rifle, a cannon, a fire-
hydrant, a watering-can; and the assault may take the form of a
burglary, a pursuit, a robbery, or it may be someone hidden in
the cupboard or under the bed. Again, the danger may be represented by wild animals, for instance by a horse that throws the
dreamer to the ground and kicks her in the stomach with his
hind leg; by lions, tigers, elephants with threatening trunks,
and finally by snakes in endless variety. Sometimes the snake
creeps into the mouth, sometimes it bites the breast like Cleo-
patra's legendary asp, sometimes it appears in the role of the
paradisal serpent, or in one of the variations of Franz Stuck,
whose snake-pictures bear significant titles like "Vice," "Sin,"
or "Lust" (cf. pl. x). The mixture of anxiety and lust is perfectly

expressed in the sultry atmosphere of these pictures, and far more crudely than in Mörike's piquant little poem:

Girl's First Love Song

What's in the net? I feel
Frightened and shaken!
Is it a sweet-slipping eel
Or a snake that I've taken?

Love's a blind fisherman,
Love cannot see;
Whisper the child, then,
What would love of me?

It leaps in my hands! This is
Anguish unguessed.
With cunning and kisses
It creeps to my breast.

It bites me, O wonder!
Worms under my skin.
My heart bursts asunder,
I tremble within.

Where go and where hide me?
The shuddersome thing
Rages inside me,
Then sinks in a ring.

What poison can this be?
O that spasm again!
It burrows in ecstasy
Till I am slain.[1]

9   All these things seem simple and need no explanation to be intelligible. Somewhat more complicated is the following dream of a young woman. She dreamt that she saw *the triumphal Arch of Constantine. Before it stood a cannon, to the right a bird, to the left a man. A cannon-ball shot out of the muzzle and hit her; it went into her pocket, into her purse. There it remained, and she held the purse as if there were something very precious inside it. Then the picture faded, and all she could see was the*

[1] Mörike, *Werke*, I, p. 33.

stock of the cannon, with Constantine's motto above it: "In hoc signo vinces." The sexual symbolism of this dream is sufficiently obvious to justify the indignant surprise of all innocent-minded people. If it so happens that this kind of realization is entirely new to the dreamer, thus filling a gap in her conscious orientation, we can say that the dream has in effect been interpreted. But if the dreamer has known this interpretation all along, then it is nothing more than a repetition whose purpose we cannot ascertain. Dreams and dream-motifs of this nature can repeat themselves in a never-ending series without our being able to discover—at any rate from the sexual side—anything in them except what we know already and are sick and tired of knowing. This kind of approach inevitably leads to that "monotony" of interpretation of which Freud himself complained. In these cases we may justly suspect that the sexual symbolism is as good a *façon de parler* as any other and is being used as a dream-language. "Canis panem somniat, piscator pisces." Even dream-language ultimately degenerates into jargon. The only exception to this is in cases where a particular motif or a whole dream repeats itself because it has never been properly understood, and because it is necessary for the conscious mind to reorient itself by recognizing the compensation which the motif or dream expresses. In the above dream it is certainly a case either of ordinary unconsciousness, or of repression. One can therefore interpret it sexually and leave it at that, without going into all the niceties of the symbolism. The words with which the dream ends—"In hoc signo vinces"—point to a deeper meaning, but this level could only be reached if the dreamer became conscious enough to admit the existence of an erotic conflict.

10   These few references to the symbolic nature of dreams must suffice. We must accept dream symbolism as an accomplished fact if we wish to treat this astonishing truth with the necessary degree of seriousness. It is indeed astonishing that the conscious activity of the psyche should be influenced by products which seem to obey quite other laws and to follow purposes very different from those of the conscious mind.

11   How is it that dreams are symbolical at all? In other words, whence comes this capacity for symbolic representation, of which we can discover no trace in our conscious thinking? Let us examine the matter a little more closely. If we analyse a train of thought, we find that we begin with an "initial" idea, or a

"leading" idea, and then, without thinking back to it each time, but merely guided by a sense of direction, we pass on to a series of separate ideas that all hang together. There is nothing symbolical in this, and our whole conscious thinking proceeds along these lines.[1a] If we scrutinize our thinking more closely still and follow out an intensive train of thought—the solution of a difficult problem, for instance—we suddenly notice that we are *thinking in words,* that in very intensive thinking we begin talking to ourselves, or that we occasionally write down the problem or make a drawing of it, so as to be absolutely clear. Anyone who has lived for some time in a foreign country will certainly have noticed that after a while he begins to think in the language of that country. Any very intensive train of thought works itself out more or less in verbal form—if, that is to say, one wants to express it, or teach it, or convince someone of it. It is evidently directed *outwards,* to the outside world. To that extent, directed or logical thinking is reality-thinking,[2] a thinking that is adapted to reality,[3] by means of which we imitate the successiveness of objectively real things, so that the images inside our mind follow one another in the same strictly causal sequence as the events taking place outside it.[4] We also call this "thinking with directed attention." It has in addition the peculiarity of causing fatigue, and is for that reason brought

[1a] Cf. Liepmann, *Über Ideenflucht;* also my "Studies in Word Association" (1918/-19 edn., p. 124). For thinking as subordination to a ruling idea, cf. Ebbinghaus, in *Kultur der Gegenwart,* pp. 221ff. Kuelpe (*Outlines of Psychology,* p. 447) expresses himself in a similar manner: in thinking "we find an anticipatory apperception, which covers a more or less extensive circle of individual reproductions, and differs from a group of accidental incentives to reproduction only in the consistency with which all ideas outside the circle are checked or suppressed."

[2] In his *Psychologia empirica,* ch. II, § 23, p. 16, Christian Wolff says simply and precisely: "Cogitatio est actus animae quo sibi sui rerumque aliarum extra se conscia est" (Thinking is an act of the soul whereby it becomes conscious of itself and of other things outside itself).

[3] The element of adaptation is particularly stressed by William James in his definition of logical thinking (*Principles of Psychology,* II, p. 330): "Let us make this ability to deal with *novel* data the technical differentia of reasoning. This will sufficiently mark it out from common associative thinking."

[4] "Thoughts are shadows of our feelings, always darker, emptier, and simpler than these," says Nietzsche. Lotze (*Logik,* p. 552) remarks in this connection: "Thinking, if left to the logical laws of its own movement, coincides once more at the end of its correct trajectory with the behaviour of objectively real things."

11

into play for short periods only. The whole laborious achievement of our lives is adaptation to reality, part of which consists in directed thinking. In biological terms it is simply a process of psychic assimilation that leaves behind a corresponding state of exhaustion, like any other vital achievement.

12   The material with which we think is *language* and *verbal concepts*—something which from time immemorial has been directed outwards and used as a bridge, and which has but a single purpose, namely that of communication. So long as we think directedly, we think *for* others and speak *to* others.[5] Language was originally a system of emotive and imitative sounds —sounds which express terror, fear, anger, love, etc., and sounds which imitate the noises of the elements: the rushing and gurgling of water, the rolling of thunder, the roaring of the wind, the cries of the animal world, and so on; and lastly, those which represent a combination of the sound perceived and the emotional reaction to it.[6] A large number of onomatopoeic vestiges remain even in the more modern languages; note, for instance, the sounds for running water: *rauschen, rieseln, rûschen, rinnen, rennen, rush, river, ruscello, ruisseau, Rhein.* And note *Wasser, wissen, wissern, pissen, piscis, Fisch.*

13   Thus, language, in its origin and essence, is simply a system of signs or symbols that denote real occurrences or their echo in the human soul.[7] We must emphatically agree with Anatole France when he says:

What is thinking? And how does one think? We think with words; that in itself is sensual and brings us back to nature. Think of it! a metaphysician has nothing with which to build his world system except the perfected cries of monkeys and dogs. What he calls profound speculation and transcendental method is merely the stringing together, in an arbitrary order, of onomatopoeic cries of hunger,

5 Cf. Baldwin's remarks quoted below. The eccentric philosopher Johann Georg Hamann (1730–88) actually equates reason with language. (See Hamann's writings, pub. 1821–43.) With Nietzsche reason fares even worse as "linguistic metaphysics." Friedrich Mauthner goes the furthest in this direction (*Sprache und Psychologie*); for him there is absolutely no thought without speech, and only speaking is thinking. His idea of the "word fetishism" that dominates science is worth noting.   6 Cf. Kleinpaul, *Das Leben der Sprache.*

7 My small son gave me an explicit example of the subjectivity of such symbols, which originally seem to belong entirely to the subject: He described everything he wanted to take or eat with an energetic "stô lô!" (Swiss-German for "leave it!").

fear, and love from the primeval forests, to which have become attached, little by little, meanings that are believed to be abstract merely because they are loosely used. Have no fear that the succession of little cries, extinct or enfeebled, that composes a book of philosophy will teach us so much about the universe that we can no longer go on living in it.[8]

14   So our directed thinking, even though we be the loneliest thinkers in the world, is nothing but the first stirrings of a cry to our companions that water has been found, or the bear been killed, or that a storm is approaching, or that wolves are prowling round the camp. There is a striking paradox of Abelard's which intuitively expresses the human limitations of our complicated thought-process: "Speech is generated by the intellect and in turn generates intellect." The most abstract system of philosophy is, in its method and purpose, nothing more than an extremely ingenious combination of natural sounds.[9] Hence the craving of a Schopenhauer or a Nietzsche for recognition and understanding, and the despair and bitterness of their loneliness. One might expect, perhaps, that a man of genius would luxuriate in the greatness of his own thoughts and renounce the cheap approbation of the rabble he despises; yet he succumbs to the more powerful impulse of the herd instinct. His seeking and his finding, his heart's cry, are meant for the herd and must be heeded by them. When I said just now that directed thinking is really thinking in words, and quoted that amusing testimony of Anatole France as drastic proof, this might easily give rise to the misunderstanding that directed thinking is after all "only a matter of words." That would certainly be going too far. Language must be taken in a wider sense than speech, for speech is only the outward flow of thoughts formulated for communication. Were it otherwise, the

---

[8] Le Jardin d'Epicure, p. 80.

[9] It is difficult to estimate how great is the seductive influence of primitive word meanings on our thinking. "Everything that has ever been in consciousness remains as an active element in the unconscious," says Hermann Paul (Prinzipien der Sprachgeschichte, p. 25). The old word-meanings continue to have an effect which is imperceptible at first and proceeds "from that dark chamber of the unconscious in the soul" (ibid.). Hamann states emphatically (Schriften, VII, p. 8): "Metaphysics misuses all the verbal signs and figures of speech based on empirical knowledge and reduces them to empty hieroglyphs and types of ideal relationships." Kant is supposed to have learnt a thing or two from Hamann.

deaf-mute would be extremely limited in his thinking capacity, which is not the case at all. Without any knowledge of the spoken word, he too has his "language." Historically speaking, this ideal language, this directed thinking, is derived from primitive words, as Wundt has explained:

A further important consequence of the interaction of sound and meaning is that many words come to lose their original concrete significance altogether, and turn into signs for general ideas expressive of the apperceptive functions of relating and comparing, and their products. In this way abstract thought develops, which, because it would not be possible without the underlying changes of meaning, is itself the product of those psychic and psychophysical interchanges in which the development of language consists.[10]

¹⁵   Jodl [11] rejects the identity of language and thought on the ground that the same psychic fact can be expressed in different ways in different languages. From this he infers the existence of a "supra-linguistic" type of thinking. No doubt there is such a thing, whether one elects to call it "supra-linguistic" with Jodl or "hypological" with Erdmann. Only, it is not logical thinking. My views coincide with those of Baldwin, who says:

The transition from pre-judgmental to judgmental meaning is just that from knowledge which has social confirmation to that which gets along without it. The meanings utilized for judgment are those already developed in their presuppositions and implications through the confirmations of social intercourse. Thus the personal judgment, trained in the methods of social rendering, and disciplined by the interaction of its social world, projects its content into that world again. In other words, the platform for all movement into the assertion of individual judgment—the level from which new experience is utilized—is *already and always socialized;* and it is just this movement that we find reflected in the actual result as the sense of the "appropriateness" or synnomic character of the meaning rendered. . . .
     Now the development of thought, as we are to see in more detail, is by a method essentially of trial and error, of experimentation, of *the use of meanings as worth more than they are as yet recognized to be worth.* The individual must use his old thoughts, his established knowledge, his grounded judgments, for the embodiment of

10 *Grundriss der Psychologie,* pp. 363–64.
11 *Lehrbuch aer Psychologie,* II, ch. 10, par. 26, p. 260.

his new inventive constructions. He erects his thought as we say "schematically"—in logical terms, problematically, conditionally, disjunctively—projecting into the world an opinion still personal to himself, as if it were true. *Thus all discovery proceeds.* But this is, from the linguistic point of view, still to use the current language, still to work by meanings already embodied in social and conventional usage.

By this experimentation both thought and language are together advanced. . . .

Language grows, therefore, just as thought does, *by never losing its synnomic* or dual reference; its meaning is both personal and social. . . .

Language is the register of tradition, the record of racial conquest, the deposit of all the gains made by the genius of individuals. . . . The social "copy-system" thus established reflects the judgmental processes of the race, and in turn becomes the training-school of the judgment of new generations. . . .

Most of the training of the self, whereby the vagaries of personal reaction to fact and image are reduced to the funded basis of sound judgment, comes through the use of speech. When the child speaks, he lays before the world his suggestion for a general or common meaning; the reception it gets confirms or refutes him. In either case he is instructed. His next venture is from a platform of knowledge on which the newer item is more nearly convertible into the common coin of effective intercourse. The point to notice here is not so much the exact mechanism of the exchange—secondary conversion—by which this gain is made, as the training in judgment that the constant use of it affords. In each case, effective judgment is the common judgment. . . . Here the object is to point out that it is secured by the development of a function *whose rise is directly* ad hoc . . . *—the function of speech.*

In language, therefore, to sum up the foregoing, we have the tangible—the actual and historical—instrument of the development and conservation of psychic meaning. It is the material evidence and proof of *the concurrence of social and personal judgment.* In it synnomic meaning, judged as "appropriate," becomes "social" meaning, held as socially generalized and acknowledged.[12]

16   Baldwin's argument lays ample stress on the limitations imposed on thought by language,[13] which are of the greatest

[12] Baldwin, *Thought and Things,* II, pp. 145 ff.
[13] In this connection I would mention the experimental "investigations into the linguistic components of association" (1908) made by Eberschweiler [q.v., Bibliog-

importance both subjectively and objectively, i.e., psychologically and socially—so great, indeed, that we must ask ourselves whether the sceptical Mauthner [14] was not right in his view that thinking is speech and nothing more. Baldwin is more cautious and reserved, but at bottom he is plainly in favour of the primacy of speech.

[17]   Directed thinking or, as we might also call it, *thinking in words,* is manifestly an instrument of culture, and we shall not be wrong in saying that the tremendous work of education which past centuries have devoted to directed thinking, thereby forcing it to develop from the subjective, individual sphere to the objective, social sphere, has produced a readjustment of the human mind to which we owe our modern empiricism and technics. These are absolutely new developments in the history of the world and were unknown to earlier ages. Inquiring minds have often wrestled with the question of why the first-rate knowledge which the ancients undoubtedly had of mathematics, mechanics, and physics, coupled with their matchless craftsmanship, was never applied to developing the rudimentary techniques already known to them (e.g., the principles of simple machines) into a real technology in the modern sense of the word, and why they never got beyond the stage of inventing amusing curiosities. There is only one answer to this: the ancients, with a few illustrious exceptions, entirely lacked the capacity to concentrate their interest on the transformations of inanimate matter and to reproduce the natural process artificially, by which means alone they could have gained control of the forces of nature. What they lacked was training in directed thinking.[15] The secret of cultural development is the *mobility and disposability of psychic energy.* Directed thinking, as we know it today, is a more or less modern acquisition which earlier ages lacked.

raphy] at my request, which disclose the remarkable fact that during an association experiment the intrapsychic association is influenced by phonetic considerations.   [14] See n. 5, above.

[15] There was as a matter of fact no external compulsion which would have made technical thinking necessary. The labour question was solved by an endless supply of cheap slaves, so that efforts to save labour were superfluous. We must also remember that the interest of the man of antiquity was turned in quite another direction: he reverenced the divine cosmos, a quality which is entirely lacking in our technological age.

18   This brings us to a further question: What happens when we do not think directedly? Well, our thinking then lacks all leading ideas and the sense of direction emanating from them.[16] We no longer compel our thoughts along a definite track, but let them float, sink or rise according to their specific gravity. In Kuelpe's view,[17] thinking is a sort of "inner act of the will," and its absence necessarily leads to an "automatic play of ideas." William James regards non-directed thinking, or "merely associative" thinking, as the ordinary kind. He expresses himself as follows:

> Much of our thinking consists of trains of images suggested one by another, of a sort of spontaneous revery of which it seems likely enough that the higher brutes should be capable. This sort of thinking leads nevertheless to rational conclusions both practical and theoretical.
>
> As a rule, in this sort of irresponsible thinking the terms which come to be coupled together are empirical concretes, not abstractions.[18]

19   We can supplement James's definitions by saying that this sort of thinking does not tire us, that it leads away from reality into fantasies of the past or future. At this point thinking in verbal form ceases, image piles on image, feeling on feeling,[19]

---

[16] So at least it appears to the conscious mind. Freud (*The Interpretation of Dreams*, II, p. 528) says in this connection: "For it is demonstrably untrue that we are being carried along a purposeless stream of ideas when, in the process of interpreting a dream, we abandon reflection and allow involuntary ideas to emerge. It can be shown that all we can ever get rid of are purposive ideas that are *known* to us; as soon as we have done this, *unknown*—or, as we inaccurately say, 'unconscious'—purposive ideas take charge and thereafter determine the course of the involuntary ideas. No influence that we can bring to bear upon our mental processes can ever enable us to think without purposive ideas; nor am I aware of any states of psychical confusion which can do so."

[17] *Outlines*, p. 448.   [18] *Principles*, II, p. 325.

[19] This statement is based primarily on experiences derived from the field of normal psychology. Indefinite thinking is very far removed from "reflection," particularly where readiness of speech is concerned. In psychological experiments I have frequently found that subjects—I am speaking only of cultivated and intelligent people—whom I allowed to indulge in reveries, as though unintentionally and without previous instruction, exhibited affects which could be registered experimentally, but that with the best will in the world they could express the underlying thought only very imperfectly or not at all. More instructive are experiences

and there is an ever-increasing tendency to shuffle things about and arrange them not as they are in reality but as one would like them to be. Naturally enough, the stuff of this thinking which shies away from reality can only be the past with its thousand-and-one memory images. Common speech calls this kind of thinking "dreaming."

20   Anyone who observes himself attentively will find that the idioms of common speech are very much to the point, for almost every day we can see for ourselves, when falling asleep, how our fantasies get woven into our dreams, so that between day-dreaming and night-dreaming there is not much difference. We have, therefore, two kinds of thinking: directed thinking, and dreaming or fantasy-thinking. The former operates with speech elements for the purpose of communication, and is difficult and exhausting; the latter is effortless, working as it were spontaneously, with the contents ready to hand, and guided by unconscious motives. The one produces innovations and adaptation, copies reality, and tries to act upon it; the other turns away from reality, sets free subjective tendencies, and, as regards adaptation, is unproductive.[20]

---

of a pathological nature, not so much those arising in the field of hysteria and the various neuroses, which are characterized by an overwhelming transference tendency, as experiences connected with introversion neurosis or psychosis, which must be regarded as constituting by far the greater number of mental disturbances, at any rate the whole of Bleuler's schizophrenic group. As already indicated by the term "introversion" (which I cursorily introduced in 1910, in my "Psychic Conflicts in a Child," pp. 13 and 16 [*Coll. Works,* Vol. 17]), this type of neurosis leads to an isolated inner life. And here we meet with that "supralinguistic" or pure "fantasy thinking" which moves in "inexpressible" images and feelings. You get some idea of this when you try to find out the meaning of the pitiful and muddled expressions used by these people. As I have often observed, it costs these patients endless trouble and effort to put their fantasies into ordinary human speech. A highly intelligent patient, who "translated" such a fantasy system for me piecemeal, used to say to me: "I know quite well what it's all about, I can see and feel everything, but it is quite impossible for me to find the right words for it."

20 Similarly James, *Principles,* II, pp. 325–26. Reasoning is productive, whereas "empirical" (merely associative) thinking is only reproductive. This opinion, however, is not altogether satisfying. It is no doubt true that fantasy-thinking is not immediately productive, i.e., is unadapted and therefore useless for all practical purposes. But in the long run the play of fantasy uncovers creative forces and contents, just as dreams do. Such contents cannot as a rule be realized except through passive, associative, and fantasy-thinking.

21   As I have indicated above, history shows that directed thinking was not always as developed as it is today. The clearest
expression of modern directed thinking is science and the techniques fostered by it. Both owe their existence simply and solely
to energetic training in directed thinking. Yet at the time when
the forerunners of our present-day culture, such as the poet
Petrarch, were just beginning to approach nature in a spirit of
understanding,[21] an equivalent of our science already existed
in scholasticism.[22] This took its subjects from fantasies of the
past, but it gave the mind a dialectical training in directed
thinking. The one goal of success that shone before the thinker
was rhetorical victory in disputation, and not the visible transformation of reality. The subjects he thought about were often
unbelievably fantastic; for instance, it was debated how many
angels could stand on the point of a needle, whether Christ
could have performed his work of redemption had he come into
the world in the shape of a pea, etc., etc. The fact that these
problems could be posed at all—and the stock metaphysical
problem of how to know the unknowable comes into this category—proves how peculiar the medieval mind must have been,
that it could contrive questions which for us are the height of

21 Cf. the impressive description of Petrarch's ascent of Mt. Ventoux, in Burckhardt, *The Civilization of the Renaissance in Italy,* pp. 180–81: "A description
of the view from the summit would be looked for in vain, not because the poet
was insensible to it, but, on the contrary, because the impression was too overwhelming. His whole past life, with all its follies, rose before his mind; he remembered that ten years ago that day he had quitted Bologna a young man,
and turned a longing gaze towards his native country; he opened a book which
was then his constant companion, the 'Confessions of St. Augustine,' and his eye
fell on the passage in the tenth chapter: 'and men go forth, and admire lofty
mountains and broad seas, and roaring torrents, and the ocean, and the course
of the stars, and turn away from themselves while doing so.' His brother, to whom
he read these words, could not understand why he closed the book and said
no more."

22 Wundt gives a short account of the scholastic method in his *Philosophische
Studien* (XIII, p. 345). The method consisted "firstly, in regarding as the chief
aim of scientific investigation the discovery of a firmly established conceptual
scheme capable of being applied in a uniform manner to the most varied problems; secondly, in laying an inordinate value upon certain general concepts, and
consequently upon the verbal symbols designating these concepts, as a result of
which an analysis of the meanings of words or, in extreme cases, a vapid intellectual subtlety and splitting of hairs comes to replace an investigation of the real
facts from which the concepts are abstracted."

absurdity. Nietzsche glimpsed something of the background of this phenomenon when he spoke of the "glorious tension of mind" which the Middle Ages produced.

22   On a historical view, the scholastic spirit in which men of the intellectual calibre of St. Thomas Aquinas, Duns Scotus, Abelard, William of Ockham, and others worked is the mother of our modern scientific method, and future generations will see clearly how far scholasticism still nourishes the science of today with living undercurrents. It consisted essentially in a dialectical gymnastics which gave the symbol of speech, the word, an absolute meaning, so that words came in the end to have a substantiality with which the ancients could invest their Logos only by attributing to it a mystical value. The great achievement of scholasticism was that it laid the foundations of a solidly built intellectual function, the *sine qua non* of modern science and technology.

23   If we go still further back into history, we find what we call science dissolving in an indistinct mist. The culture-creating mind is ceaselessly employed in stripping experience of everything subjective, and in devising formulas to harness the forces of nature and express them in the best way possible. It would be a ridiculous and unwarranted presumption on our part if we imagined that we were more energetic or more intelligent than the men of the past—our material knowledge has increased, but not our intelligence. This means that we are just as bigoted in regard to new ideas, and just as impervious to them, as people were in the darkest days of antiquity. We have become rich in knowledge, but poor in wisdom. The centre of gravity of our interest has switched over to the materialistic side, whereas the ancients preferred a mode of thought nearer to the fantastic type. To the classical mind everything was still saturated with mythology, even though classical philosophy and the beginnings of natural science undeniably prepared the way for the work of "enlightenment."

24   Unfortunately, we get at school only a very feeble idea of the richness and tremendous vitality of Greek mythology. All the creative power that modern man pours into science and technics the man of antiquity devoted to his myths. This creative urge explains the bewildering confusion, the kaleidoscopic changes and syncretistic regroupings, the continual rejuvenation, of

myths in Greek culture. We move in a world of fantasies which, untroubled by the outward course of things, well up from an inner source to produce an ever-changing succession of plastic or phantasmal forms. This activity of the early classical mind was in the highest degree artistic: the goal of its interest does not seem to have been how to understand the real world as objectively and accurately as possible, but how to adapt it aesthetically to subjective fantasies and expectations. There was very little room among the ancients for that coldness and dis-illusionment which Giordano Bruno's vision of infinite worlds and Kepler's discoveries brought to mankind. The naïve man of antiquity saw the sun as the great Father of heaven and earth, and the moon as the fruitful Mother. Everything had its demon, was animated like a human being, or like his brothers the animals. Everything was conceived anthropomorphically or therio-morphically, in the likeness of man or beast. Even the sun's disc was given wings or little feet to illustrate its motion (pl. 1b). Thus there arose a picture of the universe which was completely removed from reality, but which corresponded exactly to man's subjective fantasies. It needs no very elaborate proof to show that children think in much the same way. They too animate their dolls and toys, and with imaginative children it is easy to see that they inhabit a world of marvels.

25   We also know that the same kind of thinking is exhibited in dreams. The most heterogeneous things are brought together regardless of the actual conditions, and a world of impossibili-ties takes the place of reality. Freud finds that the hallmark of waking thought is *progression:* the advance of the thought stim-ulus from the systems of inner or outer perception through the endopsychic work of association to its motor end, i.e., innervation. In dreams he finds the reverse: regression of the thought stimulus from the pre-conscious or unconscious sphere to the perceptual system, which gives the dream its peculiar at-mosphere of sensuous clarity, rising at times to almost hallucina-tory vividness. Dream-thinking thus regresses back to the raw material of memory. As Freud says: "In regression the fabric of the dream-thoughts is resolved into its raw material." [23] The reactivation of original perceptions is, however, only one side of regression. The other side is regression to infantile memories,

23 *The Interpretation of Dreams*, II, p. 543.

and though this might equally well be called regression to the original perceptions, it nevertheless deserves special mention because it has an importance of its own. It might even be considered as an "historical" regression. In this sense the dream can, with Freud, be described as a modified memory—modified through being projected into the present. The original scene of the memory is unable to effect its own revival, so has to be content with returning as a dream.[24] In Freud's view it is an essential characteristic of dreams to "elaborate" memories that mostly go back to early childhood, that is, to bring them nearer to the present and recast them in its language. But, in so far as infantile psychic life cannot deny its archaic character, the latter quality is the especial peculiarity of dreams. Freud expressly draws attention to this:

Dreams, which fulfil their wishes along the short path of regression, have merely preserved for us in that respect a sample of the psychical apparatus's primary method of working, a method which was abandoned as being inefficient. What once dominated waking life, while the mind was still young and incompetent, seems now to have been banished into the night—just as the primitive weapons, the bows and arrows, that have been abandoned by adult men, turn up once more in the nursery.[25]

26   These considerations [26] tempt us to draw a parallel between the mythological thinking of ancient man and the similar think-

24 Ibid., p. 546.   25 Ibid., p. 567.
26 The passage in *The Interpretation of Dreams* that follows immediately afterwards has since been confirmed through investigation of the psychoses. "These methods of working on the part of the psychical apparatus, which are normally suppressed in waking hours, become current once more in psychosis and then reveal their incapacity for satisfying our needs in relation to the external world" (ibid., p. 567). The importance of this sentence is borne out by the views of Pierre Janet, which were developed independently of Freud and deserve mention here because they confirm it from an entirely different angle, namely the biological side. Janet distinguishes in the function a firmly organized "inferior" part and a "superior" part that is in a state of continuous transformation: "It is precisely on this 'superior' part of the functions, on their adaptation to existing circumstances, that the neuroses depend. . . . Neuroses are disturbances or checks in the evolution of the functions. . . . Neuroses are maladies dependent on the various functions of the organism and are characterized by an alteration in the superior parts of these functions, which are checked in their evolution, in their adaptation to the present moment and the existing state of the external world and

ing found in children,[27] primitives, and in dreams. This idea is not at all strange; we know it quite well from comparative anatomy and from evolution, which show that the structure and function of the human body are the result of a series of embryonic mutations corresponding to similar mutations in our racial history. The supposition that there may also be in psychology a correspondence between ontogenesis and phylogenesis therefore seems justified. If this is so, it would mean that infantile thinking [28] and dream-thinking are simply a recapitulation of earlier evolutionary stages.

27   In this regard, Nietzsche takes up an attitude well worth noting:

In sleep and in dreams we pass through the whole thought of earlier humanity. . . . What I mean is this: as man now reasons in dreams, so humanity also reasoned for many thousands of years when awake; the first cause which occurred to the mind as an explanation of anything that required explanation was sufficient and passed for truth. . . . This atavistic element in man's nature still manifests itself in our dreams, for it is the foundation upon which the higher reason has developed and still develops in every individual. Dreams carry us back to remote conditions of human culture and give us a ready means of understanding them better. Dream thinking comes so easily to us now because this form of fantastic and facile explanation in terms of the first random idea has been drilled

---

of the individual, while there is no deterioration in the older parts of these same functions. . . . In place of these superior operations some degree of physical and mental disturbance develops—above all, emotionality. This is nothing but the tendency to replace the superior operations by an exaggeration of certain inferior operations, and particularly by gross visceral disturbances." (*Les Névroses*, pp. 386ff.) The "older parts" are the same as the "inferior parts" of the functions, and they replace the abortive attempts at adaptation. Similar views concerning the nature of neurotic symptoms are expressed by Claparède (p. 169). He regards the hysterogenic mechanism as a "tendance à la reversion," a kind of atavistic reaction.

27 I am indebted to Dr. Abraham for the following story: "A small girl of three and a half had been presented with a baby brother, who soon became the object of well-known childish jealousy. One day she said to her mother: 'You are two Mamas. You are my Mama, and your breast is little brother's Mama.' " She had just been observing with great interest the act of suckling. It is characteristic of the archaic thinking of the child to call the breast "Mama" [so in the original— EDITORS]. *Mamma* is Latin for 'breast.'

28 Cf. particularly Freud's "Analysis of a Phobia in a Five-year-old Boy" and my "Psychic Conflicts in a Child."

into us for immense periods of time. To that extent dreaming is a recreation for the brain, which by day has to satisfy the stern demands of thought imposed by a higher culture. . . .

From this we can see how *lately* the more acute logical thinking, the strict discrimination of cause and effect, has been developed, since our rational and intellectual faculties still involuntarily hark back to those primitive forms of reasoning, and we pass about half our lives in this condition.[29]

28   Freud, as we have seen, reached similar conclusions regarding the archaic nature of dream-thinking on the basis of dream-analysis. It is therefore not such a great step to the view that myths are dreamlike structures. Freud himself puts it as follows: "The study of constructions of folk-psychology such as these is far from being complete, but it is extremely probable that myths, for instance, are distorted vestiges of the wishful phantasies of whole nations, the [age-long] dreams of youthful humanity." [30] In the same way Rank [31] regards myth as the collective dream of a whole people.[32]

29   Riklin has drawn attention to the dream mechanism in fairy-tales,[33] and Abraham has done the same for myths. He says: "The myth is a fragment of the superseded infantile psychic life of the race"; and again: "The myth is therefore a fragment preserved from the infantile psychic life of the race, and dreams are the myths of the individual." [34] The conclusion that the myth-makers thought in much the same way as we still think in dreams is almost self-evident. The first attempts at myth-making can, of course, be observed in children, whose games of make-believe often contain historical echoes. But one must certainly put a large question-mark after the assertion that myths spring from the "infantile" psychic life of the race. They are on the contrary the most mature product of that young humanity. Just as those first fishy ancestors of man, with their gill-slits, were not embryos, but fully developed creatures, so the myth-making and myth-inhabiting man was a grown reality and not a four-year-old child. Myth is certainly not an infantile

29 *Human, All-Too Human,* trans. by Zimmern and Cohn, I, pp. 24–27, modified.
30 "Creative Writers and Day-Dreaming," p. 152, mod.   31 *Der Künstler,* p. 36.
32 Cf. also Rank, *The Birth of the Hero.*
33 *Wishfulfilment and Symbolism in Fairy Tales.*
34 Abraham, *Dreams and Myths,* pp. 36 and 72, modified.

phantasm, but one of the most important requisites of primitive life.

30   It might be objected that the mythological proclivities of children are implanted by education. This objection is futile. Has mankind ever really got away from myths? Everyone who has his eyes and wits about him can see that the world is dead, cold, and unending. Never yet has he beheld a God, or been compelled to require the existence of such a God from the evidence of his senses. On the contrary, it needed the strongest inner compulsion, which can only be explained by the irrational force of instinct, for man to invent those religious beliefs whose absurdity was long since pointed out by Tertullian. In the same way one can withhold the material content of primitive myths from a child but not take from him the need for mythology, and still less his ability to manufacture it for himself. One could almost say that if all the world's traditions were cut off at a single blow, the whole of mythology and the whole history of religion would start all over again with the next generation. Only a very few individuals succeed in throwing off mythology in epochs of exceptional intellectual exuberance—the masses never. Enlightenment avails nothing, it merely destroys a transitory manifestation, but not the creative impulse.

31   Let us now turn back to our earlier reflections.

32   We were speaking of the ontogenetic recapitulation of phylogenetic psychology in children, and we saw that archaic thinking is a peculiarity of children and primitives. We now know that this same thinking also occupies a large place in modern man and appears as soon as directed thinking ceases. Any lessening of interest, or the slightest fatigue, is enough to put an end to the delicate psychological adaptation to reality which is expressed through directed thinking, and to replace it by fantasies. We wander from the subject and let our thoughts go their own way; if the slackening of attention continues, we gradually lose all sense of the present, and fantasy gains the upper hand.

33   At this point the important question arises: How are fantasies made, and what is their nature? From the poets we learn much, from scientists little. It was the psychotherapists who first began to throw light on the subject. They showed that fantasies go in typical cycles. The stammerer fancies himself a great

orator, which actually came true in the case of Demosthenes, thanks to his enormous energy; the poor man fancies himself a millionaire, the child a grown-up. The oppressed wage victorious war on the oppressor, the failure torments or amuses himself with ambitious schemes. All seek compensation through fantasy.

34   But just where do the fantasies get their material? Let us take as an example a typical adolescent fantasy. Faced by the vast uncertainty of the future, the adolescent puts the blame for it on the past, saying to himself: "If only I were not the child of my very ordinary parents, but the child of a rich and elegant count and had merely been brought up by foster-parents, then one day a golden coach would come and the count would take his long-lost child back with him to his wonderful castle," and so on, just as in a Grimms' fairy-story which a mother tells to her children. With a normal child the fantasy stops short at the fleeting idea, which is soon over and forgotten. There was a time, however, in the ancient world, when the fantasy was a legitimate truth that enjoyed universal recognition. The heroes—Romulus and Remus (pl. II), Moses, Semiramis, and many others—were foundlings whose real parents had lost them.[35] Others were directly descended from the gods, and the noble families traced their descent from the heroes and gods of old. Hence the fantasy of our adolescent is simply a re-echo of an ancient folk-belief which was once very widespread. The fantasy of ambition therefore chooses, among other things, a classical form which at one time had real validity. The same is true of certain erotic fantasies. Earlier on we mentioned the dream of sexual assault: the robber who breaks in and does something dangerous. That too is a mythological theme and in days gone by was undoubtedly a reality.[36] Quite apart from the fact that rape was a common occurrence in prehistoric times, it was also a popular theme of mythology in more civilized epochs. One has only to think of the rape of Persephone, of Deianira, Europa, and of the Sabine women. Nor should we forget that in many parts of the earth there are

[35] Rank, *The Birth of the Hero;* also Kerényi, "The Primordial Child," in Jung and Kerényi, *Science of Mythology*, pp. 38f. (1963 edn., pp. 27ff.).
[36] For the mythological rape of the bride, cf. id., "Kore," pp. 170ff. (122ff.).

marriage customs existing today which recall the ancient marriage by capture.

35   One could give countless examples of this kind. They would all prove the same thing, namely that what, with us, is a subterranean fantasy was once open to the light of day. What, with us, crops up only in dreams and fantasies was once either a conscious custom or a general belief. But what was once strong enough to mould the spiritual life of a highly developed people will not have vanished without trace from the human soul in the course of a few generations. We must remember that a mere eighty generations separate us from the Golden Age of Greek culture. And what are eighty generations? They shrink to an almost imperceptible span when compared with the enormous stretch of time that separates us from Neanderthal or Heidelberg man. I would like in this connection to call attention to the pointed remarks of the great historian Ferrero:

It is a very common belief that the further man is separated from the present in time, the more he differs from us in his thoughts and feelings; that the psychology of humanity changes from century to century, like fashions or literature. Therefore, no sooner do we find in past history an institution, a custom, a law, or a belief a little different from those with which we are familiar, than we immediately search for all manner of complicated explanations, which more often than not resolve themselves into phrases of no very precise significance. And indeed, man does not change so quickly; his psychology at bottom remains the same, and even if his culture varies much from one epoch to another, it does not change the functioning of his mind. The fundamental laws of the mind remain the same, at least during the short historical periods of which we have knowledge; and nearly all the phenomena, even the most strange, must be capable of explanation by those common laws of the mind which we can recognize in ourselves.[37]

36   The psychologist should accept tnis view without qualification. The Dionysian phallagogies, the chthonic mysteries of classical Athens, have vanished from our civilization, and the theriomorphic representations of the gods have dwindled to mere vestiges, like the Dove, the Lamb, and the Cock adorning our church towers. Yet all this does not alter the fact that in childhood we go through a phase when archaic thinking and

[37] Ferrero, *Les Lois psychologiques*, p. vii.

27

feeling once more rise up in us, and that all through our lives we possess, side by side with our newly acquired directed and adapted thinking, a fantasy-thinking which corresponds to the antique state of mind. Just as our bodies still retain vestiges of obsolete functions and conditions in many of their organs, so our minds, which have apparently outgrown those archaic impulses, still bear the marks of the evolutionary stages we have traversed, and re-echo the dim bygone in dreams and fantasies.

37   The question of where the mind's aptitude for symbolical expression comes from brings us to the distinction between the two kinds of thinking—the directed and adapted on the one hand, and the subjective, which is actuated by inner motives, on the other. The latter form, if not constantly corrected by adapted thinking, is bound to produce an overwhelmingly subjective and distorted picture of the world. This state of mind has been described in the first place as infantile and autoerotic, or, with Bleuler, as "autistic," which clearly expresses the view that the subjective picture, judged from the standpoint of adaptation, is inferior to that of directed thinking. The ideal instance of autism is found in schizophrenia, whereas infantile autoeroticism is more characteristic of neurosis. Such a view brings a perfectly normal process like non-directed fantasy-thinking dangerously close to the pathological, and this must be ascribed less to the cynicism of doctors than to the circumstance that it was the doctors who were the first to evaluate this type of thinking. Non-directed thinking is in the main subjectively motivated, and not so much by conscious motives as—far more —by unconscious ones. It certainly produces a world-picture very different from that of conscious, directed thinking. But there is no real ground for assuming that it is nothing more than a distortion of the objective world-picture, for it remains to be asked whether the mainly unconscious inner motive which guides these fantasy-processes is not itself an *objective fact*. Freud himself has pointed out on more than one occasion how much unconscious motives are grounded on instinct, which is certainly an objective fact. Equally, he half admitted their archaic nature.

38   The unconscious bases of dreams and fantasies are only apparently infantile reminiscences. In reality we are concerned with primitive or archaic thought-forms, based on instinct,

which naturally emerge more clearly in childhood than they do later. But they are not in themselves infantile, much less pathological. To characterize them, we ought therefore not to use expressions borrowed from pathology. So also the myth, which is likewise based on unconscious fantasy-processes, is, in meaning, substance, and form, far from being infantile or the expression of an autoerotic or autistic attitude, even though it produces a world-picture which is scarcely consistent with our rational and objective view of things. The instinctive, archaic basis of the mind is a matter of plain objective fact and is no more dependent upon individual experience or personal choice than is the inherited structure and functioning of the brain or any other organ. Just as the body has its evolutionary history and shows clear traces of the various evolutionary stages, so too does the psyche.[38]

39   Whereas directed thinking is an altogether conscious phenomenon,[39] the same cannot be said of fantasy-thinking. Much of it belongs to the conscious sphere, but at least as much goes on in the half-shadow, or entirely in the unconscious, and can therefore be inferred only indirectly.[40] Through fantasy-thinking, directed thinking is brought into contact with the oldest layers of the human mind, long buried beneath the threshold of consciousness. The fantasy-products directly engaging the conscious mind are, first of all, waking dreams or daydreams, to which Freud, Flournoy, Pick, and others have devoted special attention; then ordinary dreams, which present to the conscious mind a baffling exterior and only make sense on the basis of indirectly inferred unconscious contents. Finally, in split-off complexes there are completely unconscious fantasy-systems that have a marked tendency to constitute themselves as separate personalities.[41]

38 See my paper "On the Nature of the Psyche," pars. 398ff.
39 Except for the fact that the contents entering consciousness are already in a high state of complexity, as Wundt has pointed out.
40 Schelling (*Philosophie der Mythologie*, II) regards the "preconscious" as the creative source, just as Fichte (*Psychologie*, I, pp. 508ff.) regards the "preconscious region" as the birthplace of important dream contents.
41 Cf. Flournoy, *From India to the Planet Mars*. Also my "On the Psychology and Pathology of So-called Occult Phenomena," "The Psychology of Dementia Praecox," and "A Review of the Complex Theory." Excellent examples are to be found in Schreber, *Memoirs of My Nervous Illness*.

40   All this shows how much the products of the unconscious have in common with mythology. We should therefore have to conclude that any introversion occurring in later life regresses back to infantile reminiscences which, though derived from the individual's past, generally have a slight archaic tinge. With stronger introversion and regression the archaic features become more pronounced.

41   This problem merits further discussion. Let us take as a concrete example Anatole France's story of the pious Abbé Oegger.[42] This priest was something of a dreamer, and much given to speculative musings, particularly in regard to the fate of Judas: whether he was really condemned to everlasting punishment, as the teaching of the Church declares, or whether God pardoned him after all. Oegger took up the very understandable attitude that God, in his supreme wisdom, had chosen Judas as an instrument for the completion of Christ's work of redemption.[43] This necessary instrument, without whose help humanity would never have had a share in salvation, could not possibly be damned by the all-good God. In order to put an end to his doubts, Oegger betook himself one night to the church and implored God to give him a sign that Judas was saved. Thereupon he felt a heavenly touch on his shoulder. The next day he went to the archbishop and told him that he was resolved to go out into the world to preach the gospel of God's unending mercy.

42   Here we have a well-developed fantasy-system dealing with the ticklish and eternally unresolved question of whether the legendary figure of Judas was damned or not. The Judas legend is itself a typical motif, namely that of the mischievous betrayal of the hero. One is reminded of Siegfried and Hagen, Baldur and Loki: Siegfried and Baldur were both murdered by a perfidious traitor from among their closest associates. This myth is moving and tragic, because the noble hero is not felled in a fair fight, but through treachery. At the same time it is an event that was repeated many times in history, for instance in the case of Caesar and Brutus. Though the myth is extremely old it is still

[42] *Le Jardin d'Épicure.*

[43] The Judas-figure assumes great psychological significance as the sacrificer of the Lamb of God, who by this act sacrifices himself at the same time (suicide). See Part II.

a subject for repetition, as it expresses the simple fact that envy does not let mankind sleep in peace. This rule can be applied to the mythological tradition in general: it does not perpetuate accounts of ordinary everyday events in the past, but only of those which express the universal and ever-renewed thoughts of mankind. Thus the lives and deeds of the culture-heroes and founders of religions are the purest condensations of typical mythological motifs, behind which the individual figures entirely disappear.[44]

43   But why should our pious Abbé worry about the old Judas legend? We are told that he went out into the world to preach the gospel of God's unending mercy. Not long afterwards he left the Catholic Church and became a Swedenborgian. Now we understand his Judas fantasy: *he* was the Judas who betrayed his Lord. Therefore he had first of all to assure himself of God's mercy in order to play the role of Judas undisturbed.

44   Oegger's case throws light on the mechanism of fantasies in general. The conscious fantasy may be woven of mythological or any other material; it should not be taken literally, but must be interpreted according to its meaning. If it is taken too literally it remains unintelligible, and makes one despair of the meaning and purpose of the psychic function. But the case of the Abbé Oegger shows that his doubts and his hopes are only apparently concerned with the historical person of Judas, but in reality revolve round his own personality, which was seeking a way to freedom through the solution of the Judas problem.

45   Conscious fantasies therefore illustrate, through the use of

44 Cf. Drews' remarks in *The Christ Myth*. Intelligent theologians, like Kalthoff (*The Rise of Christianity*), are of the same opinion as Drews. Thus Kalthoff says: "The documents that give us our information about the origin of Christianity are of such a nature that in the present state of historical science no student would venture to use them for the purpose of compiling a biography of an historical Jesus" (ibid., p. 10). "To look behind these evangelical narratives for the life of a natural historical human being would not occur to any thoughtful men today if it were not for the influence of the earlier rationalistic theologians" (p. 13). "In Christ the divine is always most intimately one with the human. From the God-man of the Church there is a straight line back, through the Epistles and Gospels of the New Testament, to the apocalypse of Daniel, in which the ecclesiastical conception of Christ makes its first appearance. But at every single point in this line Christ has superhuman features; he is never what critical theology would make him—a mere natural man, an historical individual" (p. 11). Cf. also Schweitzer, *The Quest of the Historical Jesus*.

mythological material, certain tendencies in the personality which are either not yet recognized or are recognized no longer. It will readily be understood that a tendency which we fail to recognize and which we treat as non-existent can hardly contain anything that would fit in with our conscious character. Hence it is mostly a question of things which we regard as immoral or impossible, and whose conscious realization meets with the strongest resistances. What would Oegger have said had one told him in confidence that he was preparing himself for the role of Judas? Because he found the damnation of Judas incompatible with God's goodness, he proceeded to think about this conflict. That is the *conscious* causal sequence. Hand in hand with this goes the *unconscious* sequence: because he wanted to be Judas, or had to be Judas, he first made sure of God's goodness. For him Judas was the symbol of his own unconscious tendency, and he made use of this symbol in order to reflect on his own situation—its direct realization would have been too painful for him. There must, then, be typical myths which serve to work out our racial and national complexes. Jacob Burckhardt seems to have glimpsed this truth when he said that every Greek of the classical period carries in himself a little bit of Oedipus, and every German a little bit of Faust.[45]

46   The problems with which the simple tale of the Abbé Oegger confronts us will meet us again when we examine another set of fantasies, which owe their existence this time to the exclusive activity of the unconscious. We are indebted to a young American woman, known to us by the pseudonym of Miss Frank Miller, for a series of fantasies, partly poetical in form, which

---

[45] Cf. Burckhardt's letter (1855) to his student Albert Brenner (trans. by Dru, p. 116, modified): "I have no special explanation of *Faust* ready prepared and filed away. And in any case you are well provided with commentaries of every kind. Listen: take all those second-hand wares back to the library from which they originally came! (Perhaps in the meanwhile you have already done so.) What you are destined to discover in *Faust,* you will have to discover intuitively (*N.B.* I am only speaking of the first part). *Faust* is a genuine myth, i.e., a great primordial image, in which every man has to discover *his* own being and destiny in his own way. Let me make a comparison: whatever would the Greeks have said if a commentator had planted himself between them and the Oedipus saga? There was an Oedipus chord in every Greek that longed to be directly touched and to vibrate after its own fashion. The same is true of *Faust* and the German nation."

Théodore Flournoy made available to the public in 1906, in the *Archives de psychologie* (Geneva), under the title "Quelques faits d'imagination créatrice subconsciente." [46]

[46] [See the Appendix for the full Miller account, translated into English.— EDITORS.]

III

THE MILLER FANTASIES: ANAMNESIS

47   Experience has taught us that whenever anyone tells us his fantasies or his dreams, he is concerned not only with an urgent and intimate problem but with the one that is most painful for him at the moment.[1] Since, in the case of Miss Miller, we have to do with a complicated fantasy system, we shall have to give attention to details which I can best discuss by keeping to Miss Miller's own account. In the first section, entitled "Phenomena of Transitory Suggestion or of Instantaneous Autosuggestion," she gives a number of examples of her unusual suggestibility, which she herself regards as a symptom of her nervous temperament. She seems to possess an extraordinary capacity for identification and empathy; for instance she identifies herself to such

[1] There is an example of this in C. A. Bernoulli, *Franz Overbeck und Friedrich Nietzsche*, I, p. 72. Bernoulli describes Nietzsche's behaviour at a party in Basel: "Once at a dinner he said to the young lady seated next to him, 'I dreamed a short while ago that my hand, lying before me on the table, suddenly had a skin like glass, shiny and transparent; in it I saw distinctly the bones, the tissues, the play of the muscles. All at once I saw a fat toad sitting on my hand and I felt at the same time an irresistible compulsion to swallow the creature. I overcame my terrible loathing and gulped it down.' The young lady laughed. 'Is that a thing to laugh at?' Nietzsche asked, dreadfully serious, his deep eyes fixed on his companion, half questioning, half sorrowful. She then knew intuitively, even though she did not quite understand it, that an oracle had spoken to her in a parable, and that Nietzsche had allowed her to glimpse, as through a narrow crack, into the dark abyss of his inner self." Bernoulli makes (p. 166) the following observation: "One can perhaps see that behind the faultless exactitude of his dress there lay not so much a harmless pleasure in his appearance, as a fear of defilement born of some secret, tormenting disgust."

Nietzsche came to Basel very young; he was just at the age when other young people are contemplating marriage. Sitting beside a young woman, he tells her that something terrible and disgusting has happened to his transparent hand, something he must take completely into his body. We know what disease caused the premature ending of Nietzsche's life. It was precisely this that he had to tell his young lady, and her laughter was indeed out of tune.

a degree with the wounded Christian de Neuvillette in *Cyrano de Bergerac* that she feels a piercing pain in her own breast, the very place where the hero receives his death wound.

48   One might describe the theatre, somewhat unaesthetically, as an institution for working out private complexes in public. The enjoyment of comedy, or of the blissful dénouement of the plot, is the direct result of identifying one's own complexes with those personified by the actors, while the enjoyment of tragedy lies in the thrilling yet satisfying feeling that what is happening to somebody else may very well happen to you. The palpitations of our author at the sight of the dying Christian mean that there is a complex in her awaiting a similar solution, which whispers a soft "today to you, tomorrow to me"; and lest there should be any doubt as to the critical moment, Miss Miller adds that she felt the pain in her breast "when Sarah Bernhardt throws herself upon him to stanch the bleeding of his wound." The critical moment, therefore, is when the love between Christian and Roxane comes to a sudden end. If we examine Rostand's play as a whole, we shall be struck by certain passages whose effect it is not so easy to escape, and which we must emphasize here because they are of importance for everything that follows. Cyrano de Bergerac of the long ugly nose, on account of which he undertakes innumerable duels, loves Roxane, who is in love with Christian, because she thinks he is the author of the beautiful verses which really come from Cyrano's pen. Cyrano is the misunderstood one whose passionate love and noble soul no one suspects, the hero who sacrifices himself for others and, in the evening of life, with his dying breath, reads her once more Christian's last letter, the verses of which he has composed himself:

> Roxane, adieu! I soon must die!
> This very night, beloved; and I
> Feel my soul heavy with a love untold.
> I die! No more, as in the days of old,
> My loving, longing eyes will feast
> On your least gesture—ay, the least!
> I mind me of the way you touch your cheek
> So softly with your finger, as you speak!
> Ah me! I know that gesture well!
> My heart cries out! I cry "Farewell!

My life, my love, my jewel, my sweet,
My heart was yours in every beat!" [2]

49   Whereupon Roxane recognizes him as the true beloved. But
it is already too late, death comes, and in an agonized delirium
Cyrano rouses himself, draws his sword:

Why, I do believe
He dares to mock my nose! Ho! insolent!
(*He raises his sword*)
What say you? It is useless? Ay, I know!
But who fights ever hoping for success?
I fought for lost cause, and for fruitless quest!
You there, who are you?—You are thousands! Ah!
I know you now, old enemies of mine!
Falsehood!
(*He strikes the air with his sword*)
Have at you! Ha! and Compromise!
Prejudice! Treachery! . . .
(*He strikes*)
Surrender, I?
Parley? No, never! You too, Folly, you?
I know that you will lay me low at last;
Let be! Yet I fall fighting, fighting still!
You strip from me the laurel and the rose!
Take all! Despite you there is yet one thing
I hold against you all; and when tonight
I enter Christ's fair courts, and lowly bowed,
Sweep with doffed casque the heavens' threshold blue,
One thing is left that, void of stain or smutch,
I bear away despite you—my *panache*! [3]

50   Cyrano, who beneath his hideous exterior hides a soul so
much more beautiful, is full of misunderstood yearnings, and
his final triumph lies in his departing with a clean shield—"void
of stain or smutch." The author's identification with the dying
Christian, who in himself is not a very inspiring figure, tells us
that a sudden end is destined for her love, just as for Christian's.
But, as we have seen, the tragic intermezzo with Christian is
played against a background of far wider significance, namely

2 Rostand, *Cyrano de Bergerac,* trans. by Thomas and Guillemard, p. 282.
3 Ibid., p. 293.

Cyrano's unrequited love for Roxane. The identification with Christian is probably only a cover. That this is so will become clear in the course of our analysis.

51   The identification with Christian is followed by an extraordinarily plastic memory of the sea, evoked by a photograph of a steamer plunging through the waves. ("I felt the throb of the engines, the heave of the waves, the roll of the ship.") We may here hazard the conjecture that the sea-voyages of our author were associated with particularly impressive memories which bit deep into her soul and, through unconscious sympathy, threw the screen memory into particularly vivid relief. We shall see later how far these conjectured memories hang together with the problem touched on above.

52   The example that now follows is remarkable: Once, while she was having a bath, Miss Miller wound a towel round her hair to prevent it from getting wet. At that moment she had the following vivid impression: ". . . it seemed to me, for one moment and with an almost breath-taking clarity, that I was on a pedestal, a veritable Egyptian statue with all its details; stiff-limbed, one foot forward, holding insignia in my hand, etc." So Miss Miller is now identifying herself with an Egyptian statue, obviously on the basis of an unrecognized similarity. What she means is: I am like an Egyptian statue, just as stiff, wooden, sublime, and impassible, qualities for which the Egyptian statue is proverbial.

53   The next example lays stress on the personal influence she wields over a certain artist:

However, I succeeded in making him draw landscapes, such as those of Lake Geneva, where he had never been, and he used to pretend that I could make him depict things that he had never seen and give him the sense of a surrounding atmosphere that he had never felt; in short, that I was using him as he himself used his pencil; that is, simply as an instrument.

54   This remark stands in abrupt contrast to the fantasy of the Egyptian statue. Miss Miller evidently has an unspoken need to emphasize her almost magical influence over another person. This, too, could not have happened without an inner compulsion, such as is particularly noticeable in one who often does *not* succeed in establishing a real emotional relationship. She

37

will then solace herself with the idea of her almost magical powers of suggestion.

55   With that, we come to the end of the examples illustrating the autosuggestibility and suggestive influence of our author. The examples are neither particularly striking nor particularly interesting in this respect, but are all the more valuable from the psychological point of view because they allow us to glimpse some of her personal problems. Most of the examples show how liable Miss Miller was to succumb to the powers of suggestion, how the libido gained control of certain impressions and intensified them, which would naturally not have been possible but for the free-floating energy placed at her disposal by her lack of relation to reality.

IV

THE HYMN OF CREATION

56   The second section in the Miller material bears the title:
" 'Glory to God': A Dream Poem."

57   In 1898, as a girl of twenty, Miss Miller went on a long
journey through Europe. We leave the description to her:

After the long and rough voyage from New York to Stockholm, then
to St. Petersburg and Odessa, it was a real pleasure [*une véritable
volupté*] [1] to leave the world of cities, of roaring streets, of business—
in short, of the earth—and enter the world of waves, sky, and silence.
. . . I spent hours on end on the deck of the ship, dreaming,
stretched out in a deck chair. All the histories, legends, and myths of
the different countries I saw in the distance came back to me confusedly, dissolved in a kind of luminous mist in which real things
seemed to lose their being, while dreams and ideas took on the
aspect of the only true reality. At first I even avoided all company
and kept to myself, lost in my reveries, where everything I had ever
known that was truly great, beautiful, and good came back to mind
with renewed life and vigour. I also spent a good part of my days
writing to absent friends, reading, or scribbling little bits of poetry
in remembrance of the various places we visited. Some of these
poems were of a rather serious character.

58   It may perhaps seem superfluous to go into all these details
more closely. But if we remember what we said above, that
when people let their unconscious speak it always blurts out the
most intimate things, then even the smallest detail often has a
meaning. Miss Miller is here describing a "state of introversion": after the life of the cities, with their many impressions,
had absorbed her interest (with that suggestive power which, as

1 The choice of words and comparisons is always significant. [The words "a real
pleasure," however, may not be precisely those which Miss Miller originally wrote
in English and which Flournoy rendered as "une véritable volupté," the phrase
being remarked on here.—Editors.]

we have seen, forcibly produced the impression), she breathed freely again on the sea and became wholly engrossed in her inner world, deliberately cutting herself off from the environment, so that things lost their reality and dreams became truth. We know from psychopathology that there is a certain mental disturbance [2] which is initiated by the patient's shutting out reality more and more and sinking into his fantasies, with the result that as reality loses its hold, the determining power of the inner world increases. This process leads up to a climax when the patient suddenly becomes more or less conscious of his dissociation from reality: in a sort of panic he begins making pathological efforts to get back to his environment. These attempts spring from the compensating desire for re-association and seem to be the psychological rule, valid not only for pathological cases but also, to a lesser degree, for normal people.

59   One might therefore expect that after this prolonged introversion, which even impaired her sense of reality for a time, Miss Miller would succumb to a new impression of the external world, and one whose suggestive influence would be at least as great as that of her reveries. Let us proceed with her narrative:

But as the voyage drew near its end, the ship's officers outdid themselves in kindness and amiability [*se montrèrent tout ce qu'il y a de plus empressés et aimables*], and I passed many an amusing hour teaching them English.

Off the coast of Sicily, in the port of Catania, I wrote a sea-chanty, which, however, was little more than an adaptation of a well-known song about the sea, wine and love ("Brine, wine and damsels fine"). The Italians are all good singers, as a rule; and one of the officers,

[2] This illness had until recently the not altogether suitable name given it by Kraepelin: dementia praecox. Bleuler later called it schizophrenia. It is the particular misfortune of this illness that it was discovered by the psychiatrists, for its apparently bad prognosis is due to this fact, dementia praecox being synonymous with therapeutic hopelessness. How would hysteria appear if judged from the standpoint of psychiatry! The psychiatrist naturally sees only the worst cases in his asylum, and because of his therapeutic helplessness he is bound to be a pessimist. Tuberculosis would indeed be in a deplorable situation if it were described solely on the basis of experiences acquired in a Home for Incurables. The chronic cases of hysteria who slowly degenerate into idiots in lunatic asylums are no more characteristic of real hysteria than schizophrenia is characteristic of the early forms of the disease, so frequently met with in practice, that hardly ever come under the supervision of the institutional psychiatrist. "Latent psychosis" is an idea that the psychotherapist knows and fears only too well.

singing at night as he stood watch on deck, had made a great impression on me and had given me the idea of writing some words that could be fitted to his melody.

Soon afterwards, I nearly did what the proverb says, "See Naples and die," for in the port of Naples I began by being very ill (though not dangerously so); then I recovered sufficiently to go ashore and visit the principal sights of the city in a carriage. This outing tired me extremely; and as we were intending to visit Pisa the next day, I soon returned on board and went to bed early, without thinking of anything more serious than the good looks of the officers and the ugliness of Italian beggars.

60   One is slightly disappointed at meeting here, instead of the powerful impression one expected, an apparently insignificant episode, a mere flirtation. Nevertheless one of the officers, a singer, had evidently made a considerable impression on her. The concluding remark—"without thinking of anything more serious than the good looks of the officers"—does, it is true, tone it down somewhat. Even so, the assumption that this impression had no little influence on her mood is supported by the fact that a poem in honour of the singer was immediately forthcoming. One is only too ready to make light of such an experience and to accept the assurance of those concerned that everything is quite simple and not at all important. I am inclined to pay rather more attention to it, because experience has shown that an impression which comes after an introversion of that kind has a profound effect and may possibly have been underestimated by Miss Miller herself. The sudden, passing attack of sickness requires psychological explanation, though this is not possible for lack of data. But the phenomena about to be described can only be understood as arising out of a convulsion that reaches into the very depths of her being:

From Naples to Leghorn is one night by boat, during which I slept moderately well—my sleep is rarely deep or dreamless—and it seemed to me that my mother's voice woke me up just at the end of the following dream, which must, therefore, have taken place immediately before waking.

First, I was vaguely conscious of the words "when the morning stars sang together," which served as the prelude, if I may so put it, to an involved idea of creation and to mighty chorales reverberating through the universe. But, with the confusion and strange contradiction characteristic of dreams, all this was mixed up with choruses from oratorios given by one of the leading musical societies of New York, and with indistinct memories of Milton's *Paradise Lost*. Then, slowly, out of this medley, words appeared, and a little later they arranged themselves in three stanzas, in my handwriting, on a sheet of ordinary blue-lined writing-paper, in a page of my old poetry album that I always carry about with me: in short, they appeared to me exactly as they did in reality, a few minutes later, in my book.

61   Miss Miller then wrote down the following poem, which she rearranged slightly a few months later, in order to make it more nearly, in her opinion, like the dream original:

First Version	*Second Version (more exact)*
When God had first made Sound,	When the Eternal first made Sound
A myriad ears sprang into being	A myriad ears sprang out to hear,
And throughout all the Universe	And throughout all the Universe
Rolled a mighty echo:	There rolled an echo deep and clear:
"Glory to the God of Sound!"	"All glory to the God of Sound!"
When beauty (light) first was given by God,	When the Eternal first made Light,
A myriad eyes sprang out to see	A myriad eyes sprang out to look,
And hearing ears and seeing eyes	And hearing ears and seeing eyes,
Again gave forth that mighty song:	Once more a mighty choral took:
"Glory to the God of Beauty (Light)!"	"All glory to the God of Light!"
When God has first given Love,	When the Eternal first gave Love,
A myriad hearts lept up;	A myriad hearts sprang into life;
And ears full of music, eyes all full of Beauty,	Ears filled with music, eyes with light,
Hearts all full of love sang:	Pealed forth with hearts with love all rife:
"Glory to the God of Love!"	"All glory to the God of Love!"

62   Before we examine her attempts to get at the roots of this subliminal creation through her own associations, let us take a quick look at the material already in hand. The impression of the ship has already received due emphasis, so it ought not to

be difficult to lay hold of the dynamic processes responsible for this poetic revelation. It was suggested further back that Miss Miller may have considerably underestimated the scope of the erotic impression she had received. This assumption is the more probable in that experience has shown that relatively weak erotic impressions are often underestimated. One can see this most clearly in cases where an erotic relationship is regarded as impossible on social or moral grounds (for instance between parents and children, brothers and sisters, older and younger men, etc.). If the impression is comparatively slight, it does not exist at all for the persons concerned; if it is strong, then a tragic dependence develops which can lead to all sorts of trouble. This lack of judgment can go unbelievably far—a mother who sees her small son having an erection in her own bed; a sister who half-playfully embraces her brother; a twenty-year-old daughter who still sits herself in her father's lap and then has "strange" sensations in her "tummy." And yet they are all highly indignant when anyone speaks of "sexuality." There is a certain kind of education that tacitly aims at knowing as little as possible about these unmentionable facts in the background, and which shrouds them in the deepest ignorance.[3] No wonder, then, that most people's judgment in regard to the scope of erotic impressions is precarious and inadequate. Miss Miller was, as we have seen, quite prepared for a *deep* impression. But not many of the feelings it aroused seem to have come to the surface, for the dream had to repeat the lesson over again. We know from analytical experience that the initial dreams of patients at the beginning of an analysis are of especial interest, not least because they often bring out a critical evaluation of the doctor's personality which previously he would have asked for in vain. They enrich the patient's *conscious* impression of the doctor, often on very important points, and they frequently contain erotic comments which the unconscious had to make in order to counterbalance the patient's underestimation and uncertain appraisal of the impression. Expressed in the drastic and hyperbolic manner peculiar to dreams, the impression often appears in almost unintelligible form owing to the incongruity of the symbolism. A further peculiarity, which seems due to the

[3] The reader must remember that these lines were written before the first World War. Much has changed since then.

43

historical stratification of the unconscious, is that when an impression is denied conscious recognition it reverts to an earlier form of relationship. That explains why young girls, at the time of their first love, have great difficulty in expressing themselves owing to disturbances brought about by regressive reactivation of the father-imago.[4]

63   We may suppose that something similar has happened to Miss Miller, for the idea of a masculine Creator-God is apparently derived from the father-imago,[5] and aims, among other things, at replacing the infantile relation to the father in such a way as to enable the individual to emerge from the narrow circle of the family into the wider circle of society. Naturally this is far from exhausting the meaning of the dream-image.

64   In the light of these reflections, the poem and its prelude appear as the religiously and poetically formulated product of an introversion that has regressed back to the father-imago. Despite inadequate apperception of the operative impression, its essential ingredients have been built into the substitute product, as marks of its origin, so to speak. The operative impression was the handsome officer singing in the night-watch—"When the morning stars sang together"—whose image opened out a new world to the girl ("Creation").

65   This "creator" created first Sound, then Light, and then

4 Here I purposely give preference to the term "imago" rather than to "complex," in order to make clear, by this choice of a technical term, that the psychological factor which I sum up under "imago" has a living independence in the psychic hierarchy, i.e., possesses that *autonomy* which wide experience has shown to be the essential feature of feeling-toned complexes. This is brought out by the term "imago." (Cf. my "Psychology of Dementia Praecox," chs. 2 and 3.) My critics have seen in this view a return to medieval psychology and have therefore repudiated it. This "return" was made consciously and deliberately on my part, because the psychology of ancient and modern superstition furnishes abundant evidence for my point of view. Valuable insight and confirmation is also given us by the insane Schreber in his autobiography. My use of "imago" has close parallels in Spitteler's novel of the same name, and also in the ancient religious idea of the "imagines et lares." In my later writings, I use the term "archetype" instead, in order to bring out the fact that we are dealing with impersonal, collective forces.

5 The idea that the masculine deity is derived from the father-imago need be taken literally only within the limits of a personalistic psychology. Closer investigation of the father-imago has shown that certain collective components are contained in it from the beginning and cannot be reduced to personal experiences. Cf. my essay, "The Relations between the Ego and the Unconscious," pars. 211ff.

Love. That Sound should be the first thing created has parallels in the "creative word" in Genesis, in Simon Magus, where the voice corresponds to the sun,[6] in the sounds or cries of lamentation mentioned in *Poimandres*,[7] and in God's laughter at the creation of the world ($\kappa o \sigma \mu o \pi o \iota \alpha$) in a Leiden Papyrus.[8] Hence we may hazard the conjecture, which will be amply confirmed later on, that there was the following chain of association: the singer—the singing morning star—the God of Sound—the Creator—the God of Light—of the sun—of fire—and of Love. Most of these expressions are also characteristic of the language of love and are found wherever speech is heightened by emotion.

66   Miss Miller has tried to understand this unconscious creation by means of a procedure which agrees in principle with the methods of psychological analysis and therefore leads to the same results. But, as is usually the case with laymen and beginners, she gets stuck at associations which bring the underlying complex to light only in an indirect way. Nevertheless, a simple procedure, a mere matter of carrying the thought to its logical conclusion, is enough to help one find the meaning.

67   Miss Miller finds it astonishing, first of all, that her unconscious fantasy does not, like the Biblical account of the Creation, put light in the first place, but sound. There now follows a truly *ad hoc* theoretical explanation. She says:

It may be of interest to recall that Anaxagoras, too, makes the cosmos arise out of chaos by means of a whirlwind[9]—which does not normally occur without producing a noise. But at that time I had not yet made a study of philosophy and I knew nothing either of Anaxagoras or of his theories about the $\nu o \tilde{\upsilon} s$ which I found I had

6 "But the voice and the name [are] sun and moon." Hippolytus, *Elenchos*, VI, 13.—Max Müller, in his foreword to the *Sacred Books of the East*, I, p. xxv, says of the sacred syllable *Om:* "He therefore who meditates on Om, meditates on the spirit in man as identical with the spirit . . . in the sun."

7 Schultz, *Gnosis*, p. 62. Text in Scott, *Hermetica*, I, p. 115: Lib. I, 4.

8 Pap. J 395, in Dieterich, *Abraxas*, p. 17: "And God laughed seven times Cha Cha Cha Cha Cha Cha Cha, and as God laughed, there arose seven gods."

9 In Anaxagoras, the living primal power of $\nu o \tilde{\upsilon} s$ imparts movement to inert matter. There is, of course, no mention of noise. Also, Miss Miller stresses the wind nature of $\nu o \tilde{\upsilon} s$ more than is warranted by ancient tradition. On the other hand, this $\nu o \tilde{\upsilon} s$ is related to the $\pi \nu \epsilon \tilde{\upsilon} \mu \alpha$ of late antiquity and to the $\lambda \acute{o} \gamma o s \ \sigma \pi \epsilon \rho \mu \alpha \tau \iota \kappa \acute{o} s$ of the Stoics. In the incest fantasy of one of my patients, her father covered her face with his hands and blew into her open mouth—an allusion to *inspiration*.

been unconsciously following. I was in equally complete ignorance of the name of Leibniz and consequently of his doctrine "dum Deus calculat fit mundus."

The allusions to Anaxagoras and Leibniz both refer to creation through thought, so that divine thought alone is held capable of producing a new material reality—a reference which seems unintelligible at first, but will soon become more understandable.

68   We come now to the associations from which Miss Miller mainly derives her unconscious creation:

In the first place, there is Milton's *Paradise Lost,* of which we had a fine edition at home, illustrated by Gustave Doré, and which I have known well since childhood. Then the Book of Job, which has been read aloud to me ever since I can remember. Now, if you compare my first line with the first words of *Paradise Lost,* you find it is in the same metre ($\smile$ — / $\smile$ — / $\smile$ — / $\smile$ —):
     Of man's first disobedience . . .
     When the Eternal first made sound.
Moreover, the general idea of my poem is slightly reminiscent of various passages in Job, and also of one or two places in Handel's [10] oratorio *The Creation* (which appeared in the confusion at the beginning of the dream).

69   So the "lost paradise," which is as we know closely associated with the beginning of the world, is defined more precisely through the line "Of man's first disobedience"—a clear reference to the Fall, which in this connection is not without significance. I know the objection which everyone will raise here, namely that Miss Miller could just as well have chosen any other line as an example, that she picked on the first suitable one purely by accident, and that its content was equally accidental. The criticism levelled at the association method generally operates with arguments of this kind. The misunderstanding arises from the fact that the law of psychic causality is never taken seriously enough: there are no accidents, no "just as wells." It *is* so, and there is a very good reason why it is so. It is a fact that Miss Miller's poem is associated with the Fall, and this focuses our attention on the very same problem whose existence we have already surmised. Unfortunately, the author neglects to tell us

[10] Probably Haydn's *Creation* is meant.

which passages in Job came into her mind, so we can only make broad conjectures. First of all, the analogy to *Paradise Lost:* Job loses everything he has, because Satan made God doubt his integrity. In the same way, paradise was lost through the temptation of the serpent, and mankind was cast out into a life of earthly travail. The idea, or rather the mood, expressed by this recollection of *Paradise Lost* is Miss Miller's feeling of having lost something which was somehow connected with Satanic temptation. Like Job, she is an innocent victim because she did not succumb to the temptation. Job's sufferings are not understood by his friends;[11] none of them knows that Satan has a hand in the game and that Job is really innocent. Indeed, he never wearies of protesting his innocence. Does this, perhaps, give us a clue? We know that certain neurotics and mentally diseased people continually defend their innocence against nonexistent attacks; but on closer inspection one discovers that in defending their innocence apparently without cause they are simply indulging in a self-deceiving manoeuvre, which derives its energy from those very impulses whose unpleasant character is plainly revealed by the content of the alleged accusations and calumnies.[12]

70   Job suffers doubly, firstly through the loss of his fortune, secondly through the lack of understanding of his friends, a theme that can be traced all through the book. The misery of being misunderstood reminds us of the figure of Cyrano de Bergerac: he too suffers doubly—on one side through unrequited love, on the other through misunderstanding. He falls, as we have already seen, in the last hopeless struggle against "Falsehood, Compromise, Prejudice, Treachery, and Folly":

You strip from me the laurel and the rose!

71   Job laments:

God hath delivered me to the ungodly,
and turned me over into the hands of the wicked.
I was at ease, but he hath broken me asunder:

11 See Job 16 : 1–11.
12 I remember the case of a crazy young girl of 20, who continually imagined that her innocence was suspected despite all my efforts to talk her out of it. Gradually her indignant defence developed into a correspondingly aggressive erotomania.

he hath also taken me by my neck, and shaken me to pieces,
and set me up for his mark.
His archers compass me round about,
he cleaveth my reins asunder, and doth not spare;
he poureth out my gall upon the ground.
He breaketh me with breach upon breach,
he runneth upon me like a giant.[13]

72   The emotional analogy lies in having to suffer a hopeless
struggle against overwhelming odds. It is as if this struggle were
accompanied from afar by the clangour of "creation," as if it
constellated in the unconscious a wonderful and mysterious
image that has not yet forced its way into the light of the
upper world. We surmise, rather than know, that this struggle
has got something to do with creation, with the unending battle
between affirmation and negation. The allusions to Rostand's
Cyrano through the identification with Christian, to Milton's
Paradise Lost, to the sorrows of Job, misunderstood by his
friends, plainly betray that in the soul of the poet there is
something that identifies with these ideas. She too has suffered
like Job, has lost paradise, and dreams of "creation"—creation
through thought—and of fructification through the rushing
wind of the pneuma.

73   We submit ourselves once more to Miss Miller's guidance:

I remember that, at the age of fifteen, I was very much excited by an
article my mother had read to me, about "the Idea spontaneously
creating its own object," and I passed almost the whole night without sleep, wondering what it could all mean.—From the age of nine
to sixteen, I used to go on Sundays to a Presbyterian church, where
the pastor was a highly cultivated man, now president of a well-
known college. And in one of the earliest memories I have of him, I
see myself, still quite a little girl, sitting in our large pew in church
and struggling to keep myself awake, without being able to understand what in the world he meant when he spoke to us of "Chaos,"
"Cosmos," and "the Gift of Love."

74   There are, then, fairly early memories of the awakening of
puberty (nine to sixteen), which connect the idea of the cosmos
born of chaos with the "Gift of Love." The medium in which
this happy connection took place is the memory of a much-
respected ecclesiastic who spoke those dark words. From the

13 Job 16 : 11f.

same period comes the memory of her excitement over the "Idea spontaneously creating its own object." Two ways of creation are here hinted at: creative thought, and the mysterious reference to the "Gift of Love."

75   During the latter part of my medical studies I had an opportunity of gaining, through long observation, a deep insight into the soul of a fifteen-year-old girl. I then discovered, to my astonishment, what the contents of unconscious fantasies are like, and how far removed they are from what a girl of this age shows in her outward demeanour and from what an outsider would suspect. They were far-reaching fantasies of a positively mythical nature: the girl saw herself, in her split-off fantasy, as the racial mother of uncounted generations of men.[14] Even allowing for the markedly poetic cast of her imagination, there still remained elements that are probably common to all girls of her age, for the unconscious is infinitely more common to all men than are the contents of their individual consciousnesses. The unconscious is, in fact, the condensation of the average run of historical experience.

76   Miss Miller's problem at this age was the common human problem: How am I to be creative? Nature knows only one answer to that: Through a child (the gift of love). But—how does one get a child? Here arises the problem which, as experience has shown, is connected with the father,[15] so that it cannot be tackled properly because too much preoccupation with the father at once brings up the incest-barrier. The strong and natural love that binds the child to the father turns away, during the years when the child is outgrowing the family circle, to the higher forms of the father, to authority, to the "Fathers" of the Church and to the father-god visibly represented by them, where there is even less possibility of coming to grips with the problem. Nevertheless, mythology is not lacking in consolations. Did not the Word become flesh? And did not the divine pneuma enter into the Virgin's womb? (pl. III.) The whirlwind of Anaxagoras was that same divine *nous* which produced the world out of itself. Why do we cherish the image of

14 The case is published in my "On the Psychology and Pathology of So-called Occult Phenomena."
15 Cf. Freud, "Analysis of a Phobia in a Five-year-old Boy," and my "Psychic Conflicts in a Child," pars. 46ff.

the Immaculate Mother even to this day? Because it is still comforting and speaks without words or noisy sermons to the comfortless, saying, "I too have become a mother"—through the "Idea spontaneously creating its own object." I believe there would be reason enough for a sleepless night if those adolescent fantasies once got hold of this idea—the consequences would indeed be incalculable.

77   Everything psychic has a lower and a higher meaning, as in the profound saying of late classical mysticism: "Heaven above, Heaven below, stars above, stars below, all that is above also is below, know this and rejoice." [16] Here we lay our finger on the secret symbolical significance of everything psychic. We would be doing less than justice to the intellectual originality of our author if we were content to trace back the excitement of that sleepless night simply and solely to the sexual problem in its narrower sense. That would be only one half of the meaning, and the lower half at that. The other half is ideal creation as a substitute for real creation.

78   With personalities who are obviously capable of intellectual effort, the prospect of spiritual fruitfulness is something worthy of their highest aspirations, and for many people it is actually a vital necessity. This other side of the fantasy also explains the excitement, for we are concerned here with a thought that contains a presentiment of the future—one of those thoughts which, to quote Maeterlinck,[17] spring from the "inconscient supérieur," from the "prospective potency" of a subliminal synthesis.[18] I have had occasion to observe, in the course of my daily profes-

16 οὐρανὸς ἄνω, οὐρανὸς κάτω, ἄστρα ἄνω, ἄστρα κάτω, πᾶν τοῦτο ἄνω, πᾶν τοῦτο κάτω, τοῦτο λαβὲ καὶ εὐτύχει.—An old paraphrase of the *Tabula smaragdina* of Hermes, and of the text mentioned by Athanasius Kircher (*Oedipus Aegyptiacus*, Part 2, p. 414). I have quoted the latter text in my "Psychology of the Transference," par. 384.
17 *Wisdom and Destiny*.
18 This time I shall hardly escape the charge of mysticism. But perhaps the facts should be considered further: there is no doubt that the unconscious contains psychological combinations which do not reach the threshold of consciousness. Analysis dissolves these combinations back into their historical determinants. It works backwards, like the science of history. Just as a large part of the past is so remote as to be beyond the reach of historical knowledge, so too the greater part of these unconscious determinants is unreachable. History, however, knows nothing either of that which is hidden in the past or of that which is hidden in the future. Both might be reached with some degree of probability, the first as a postulate, the second as a political prognosis. Thus, in so far as tomorrow is al-

sional work (though this is an experience about whose certainty I must express myself with all the caution which the complexity of the material enjoins), that in certain cases of long-standing neurosis a dream, often of visionary clarity, occurs about the time of the onset of the illness or shortly before, which imprints itself indelibly on the mind and, when analysed, reveals to the patient a hidden meaning that anticipates the subsequent events of his life.[19] I am inclined to attribute a similar meaning to the excitement of that restless night, because the later events, so far as Miss Miller consciously or unconsciously reveals them to us, are entirely of a nature to confirm our supposition that we must take that moment as foreshadowing a future life-aim.

79   Miss Miller ends her string of associations with the following comment:

> It [the dream] seems to me to result from a mixture in my mind of *Paradise Lost, Job,* and *The Creation,* with notions like the "Idea spontaneously creating its own object," the "Gift of Love," "Chaos," and "Cosmos."

80   Thus, like little bits of coloured glass in a kaleidoscope, fragments of philosophy, aesthetics, and religion are blended together in her mind, so she tells us—

---

ready contained in today, and all the threads of the future are already laid down, a deeper knowledge of the present might render possible a moderately far-sighted prognosis of the future. If we apply this reasoning to the realm of the psychic we necessarily come to the same result. Just as memories that have long since fallen below the threshold are still accessible to the unconscious, so also are certain very fine subliminal combinations that point forward, and these are of the greatest significance for future events in so far as the latter are conditioned by our psychology. But no more than the science of history bothers itself with future combinations of events, which are rather the object of political science, can the forward-pointing psychological combinations be the object of analysis; they would be much more the object of a refined psychological syntheticism that knew how to follow the natural currents of libido. This we cannot do, or only badly; but it happens easily enough in the unconscious, and it seems as if from time to time, under certain conditions, important fragments of this work come to light, at least in dreams, thus accounting for the prophetic significance of dreams long claimed by superstition. Dreams are very often anticipations of future alterations of consciousness. [Cf. Jung, "General Aspects of Dream Psychology," pars. 492ff. —Editors.]

19 Dreams seem to remain spontaneously in the memory for just so long as they correctly sum up the psychological situation of the individual.

. . . under the stimulation of the voyage and of countries fleetingly seen, coupled with the vast silence and impalpable charm of the sea —to produce this beautiful dream. There was only this and nothing more. "Only this, and nothing more!"

81   With these words Miss Miller shows us politely but emphatically out. Her parting words of negation make one curious to know exactly what position they are intended to negate. "There was only this and nothing more" must refer to "the impalpable charm of the sea"; so presumably the handsome young officer who sang so melodiously during the watches of the night is long since forgotten, and nobody is to know, least of all the dreamer, that he was a star of the morning who heralded the dawning of a new day.[20] One should, however, avoid pacifying oneself or the reader with soothing phrases like "There was only this," for something might easily give them the lie the next moment. This is what happens to Miss Miller, who immediately adds, "Only this, and nothing more!" but without giving the source. The quotation comes from Poe's poem "The Raven," and the operative stanza runs:

While I nodded, nearly napping, suddenly there came a tapping,
As of some one gently rapping, rapping at my chamber door.
" 'Tis some visitor," I muttered, "tapping at my chamber door—
Only this, and nothing more."

82   A spectral raven knocks nightly at his door and reminds the poet of his irrevocably lost "Lenore." The raven's name is "Nevermore," and he croaks his horrible "Nevermore" as a refrain to every verse. Old memories come back tormentingly,

20 How collective the elements in such an experience are can be seen from the following love-song. Of its many variants, I quote a modern Greek version from Epirus (*Zeitschrift des Vereins für Volkskunde*, XII, 1902, p. 159):

> O maiden, when we kissed, it was night. Who saw us?—
> A bright star saw us, and the moon saw us,
> And it leaned down to the sea and whispered the tidings,
> And the sea told the rudder, and the rudder told the sailor,
> The sailor made a song, then the neighbours heard it,
> Then the priest heard it too and told it to my mother,
> From her my father heard it and was livid with anger,
> They nagged me and scolded me and now have forbidden me
> Ever to go to the door or look out of the window,
> And yet I will go to the window as if to my flowers,
> And never will I rest until my beloved is mine.

and each time the spectre repeats inexorably: "Nevermore." In vain the poet seeks to frighten away the dismal guest, shouting at the raven:

"Be that word our sign of parting, bird or fiend!" I shrieked upstart-
    ing—
"Get thee back into the tempest and the Night's Plutonian shore!
Leave no black plume as a token of the lie thy soul hath spoken!
Leave my loneliness unbroken!—quit the bust above my door!
Take thy beak from out my heart, and take thy form from off my
    door!"
            Quoth the raven, "Nevermore!"

83   The words "Only this and nothing more!," which apparently skip so lightly over the situation, are taken from a poem which depicts in an affecting manner the poet's despair over a lost love.[21] Their quotation gives the show away completely. Miss Miller evidently underestimated the impression which the night-watching singer had made upon her, and its far-reaching consequences. This under-estimation is precisely the reason why the problem was not worked out consciously and why it produced those "psychological riddles." [22] The impression goes on working in the unconscious and throws up symbolical fantasies. First it is the "morning stars [that] sang together," then *Paradise Lost,* then the yearning clothes itself in ecclesiastical garb, speaks darkly of "World Creation" and finally rises to a religious hymn, where it at last finds its way to freedom. But the hymn bears in its own peculiarities the marks of its origin: by the devious route of the father-imago relationship, the night-watching singer becomes the Creator, the God of Sound, of Light and of Love. This is not to say that the idea of God derives from the loss of a lover and is nothing but a substitute for

21 The atmosphere of the poem is very reminiscent of Gérard de Nerval's *Aurelia,* a book that anticipates the same fate that befell Miss Miller: spiritual benighted-ness. Cf. the significance of the raven in alchemy, where it is a synonym for the *nigredo (Psychology and Alchemy,* pars. 333ff.).   ·

22 This again is decidedly reminiscent of Gérard de Nerval's attitude towards Aurelia, whose significance he refuses to admit. He would not believe that a "femme ordinaire de ce monde" could have the glamour his unconscious endowed her with. Today we know that a powerful impression of this kind is due to the projection of an archetype, i.e., that of the anima or animus. See "The Relations between the Ego and the Unconscious," pars. 296ff., and my "Psychological Aspects of the Kore," pars. 356ff.

the human object. What is evidently in question here is the displacement of libido on to a *symbolical* object, with the result that the latter is turned into a sort of substitute. It is in itself a perfectly genuine experience, though, like everything else, it can be put to improper use.

84   The winding path of the libido seems to be a *via dolorosa;* at any rate, *Paradise Lost* and the parallel reference to Job lead one to that conclusion. The initial hints of identification with Christian, which really points to Cyrano, prove that the long way round is a way of suffering, just as it was when mankind, after the Fall, had to bear the burden of earthly life, or when Job suffered under the power of God and Satan and became the unsuspecting plaything of two superhuman forces. *Faust* offers the same spectacle of a wager with God:

MEPHISTOPHELES: What do you wager? You will lose him yet,
    Provided *you* give *me* permission
    To steer him gently in the course I set.[23]

85   Compare with this the passage in Job, where Satan says:

But put forth thine hand now, and touch all that he hath, and he will curse thee to thy face.[24]

86   While in Job the two great forces are characterized simply as good and evil, the immediate problem is a definitely erotic one in *Faust,* where the devil is aptly characterized by the appropriate role of tempter. This aspect is lacking in Job, but at the same time Job is not conscious of the conflict within his own soul, and he never ceases to inveigh against the arguments of his friends who want to convince him of the evil in his heart. To that extent, one could say that Faust is the more conscious in that he openly admits his psychic conflicts.

87   Miss Miller acts like Job: she admits nothing, and pretends that good and evil come from outside. Hence her identification with Job is significant in this respect also. But there is another, very important analogy still to be mentioned: the procreative urge—which is how love must be regarded from the natural standpoint—remains the essential attribute of the God whom Miss Miller apparently derives from the erotic impression, for

23 Trans. by MacNeice, p. 15, modified.
24 Job 1 : 11. [Cf. these pars. with Jung, "Answer to Job."—EDITORS.]

which reason he is praised in the hymn as Creator. We see the same thing in Job. Satan is the destroyer of Job's fruitfulness, but God is the All-Fruitful: therefore, at the end of the book, he addresses a paean filled with lofty poetic beauty to his own creative power, but it is curious to note that he gives chief consideration to two highly unsympathetic representatives of the animal kingdom, Behemoth and Leviathan, both expressive of the crudest force conceivable in nature.

88   Miss Miller uses the text of the Authorized Version, which, like Luther's version, is very suggestive:

> Behold now behemoth, which I made with thee;
>   he eateth grass as an ox.
> Lo now, his strength is in his loins,
>   and his force is in the navel of his belly.
> He moveth his tail like a cedar:
>   the sinews of his stones are wrapped together.
> His bones are as strong pieces of brass;
>   his bones are like bars of iron.
> He is the chief of the ways of God. . . .
>
> Canst thou draw out leviathan with an hook?
>   or his tongue with a cord which thou lettest down?
> Canst thou put an hook into his nose?
>   or bore his jaw through with a thorn?
> Will he make many supplications unto thee?
>   will he speak soft words unto thee?
> Will he make a covenant with thee?
>   wilt thou take him for a servant for ever? [25]

89   God speaks thus in order to parade his power and omnipotence forcibly before Job's eyes. God is as Behemoth and Leviathan: [26] the fruitfulness and abundance of Nature, the ungovernable wildness and licentiousness of Nature, the overwhelming danger of unchained power.[27] What was it that destroyed Job's earthly paradise? The unchained power of Nature.

[25] Job 40 : 15–19; 41 : 1–4.

[26] Cf. Schärf, "Die Gestalt des Satans im Alten Testament," in Jung, *Symbolik des Geistes,* pp. 288ff.

[27] Job 41 : 19–20:

> Out of his mouth go burning lamps, and sparks of fire leap out.
> Out of his nostrils goeth smoke, as out of a seething pot or cauldron.
> His breath kindleth coals, and a flame goeth out of his mouth.
> In his neck remaineth strength, and sorrow is turned into joy before him

 [continued]

God, so the poet gives us to understand, has simply shown his
other side for once, the side we call the Devil, and let loose all
the terrors of Nature upon the unfortunate Job. The God who
created such monstrosities, at the very thought of which we poor
weak mortals stiffen with fear, must certainly harbour within
himself qualities which give one pause. This God dwells in the
heart, in the unconscious.[28] That is the source of our fear of the
unspeakably terrible, and of the strength to withstand the terror.
Man, that is to say his conscious ego, is a mere bagatelle, a
feather whirled hither and thither with every gust of wind,
sometimes the sacrificed and sometimes the sacrificer, and he
cannot hinder either. The Book of Job shows us God at work
both as creator and destroyer. Who is this God? An idea that
has forced itself upon mankind in all parts of the earth and in
all ages and always in similar form: an otherworldly power
which has us at its mercy, which begets and kills—an image of
all the necessities and inevitablenesses of life. Since, psychologically speaking, the God-image is a complex of ideas of an
archetypal nature, it must necessarily be regarded as representing a certain sum of energy (libido) which appears in projection.[29] In most of the existing religions it seems that the
formative factor which creates the attributes of divinity is the

---

The flakes of his flesh are joined together: they are firm in themselves;
they cannot be moved.

His heart is as firm as a stone; yea, as hard as a piece of the nether mill-
stone.

When he raiseth up himself, the mighty are afraid: by reason of breakings
they purify themselves.

The sword of him that layeth at him cannot hold: the spear, the dart, nor
the habergeon.

He esteemeth iron as straw, and brass as rotten wood.

The arrow cannot make him flee: slingstones are turned with him into
stubble.

Darts are counted as stubble: he laugheth at the shaking of a spear.

28 These expressions are all anthropomorphisms whose source is primarily psychological.

29 This proposition has caused much offence, because people have failed to see
that it is a *psychological* view and not a metaphysical statement. The psychic fact
"God" is a typical autonomism, a *collective archetype,* as I later called it. It is
therefore characteristic not only of all higher forms of religion, but appears
spontaneously in the dreams of individuals. The archetype is, as such, an unconscious psychic image, but it has a reality independent of the attitude of the conscious mind. It is a psychic existent which should not in itself be confused with

father-imago, while in the older religions it was the mother-imago. These attributes are omnipotence, a sternly persecuting paternalism ruling through fear (Old Testament), and a loving paternalism (New Testament). In certain pagan conceptions of divinity the maternal element is strongly emphasized, and there is also a wide development of the animal or theriomorphic element.[30] (Pl. IVa.) The God-concept is not only an image, but an elemental force. The primitive power which Job's Hymn of Creation vindicates, absolute and inexorable, unjust and super-human, is a genuine and authentic attribute of the natural power of instinct and fate which "leads us into life," which makes "all the world become guilty before God" (Romans 3 : 19) and against which all struggle is in vain. Nothing remains for mankind but to work in harmony with this will. To work in harmony with the libido does not mean letting oneself drift with it, for the psychic forces have no uniform direction, but are often directly opposed to one another. A mere letting go of oneself leads in the shortest space of time to the most hopeless confusion. It is often difficult, if not impossible, to feel the ground-current and to know the true direction; at any rate collisions, conflicts, and mistakes are scarcely avoidable.

90   As we have seen, the religious hymn unconsciously produced by Miss Miller appears in the place of the erotic problem. It derives its material for the most part from reminiscences which were reactivated by the introverted libido. Had this "creation" not come off, Miss Miller would inevitably have yielded to the erotic impression, either with the usual consequences, or else with a negative result which would have replaced the lost happiness by a correspondingly strong feeling of regret. Opinions, as we know, are deeply divided over the value of solving an erotic conflict like Miss Miller's in this way. It is thought to be much more beautiful and noble to let an erotic tension resolve

---

the idea of a metaphysical God. The existence of the archetype neither postulates a God, nor does it deny that he exists.

30 Theriomorphic elements are lacking in Christianity, except for remnants like the dove, the fish, and the lamb, and the beasts representing the Evangelists. The raven and the lion symbolized definite degrees of initiation in the Mithraic mysteries. Since Dionysus was represented, among other things, as a bull, his female worshippers wore horns, as though they were cows. (I owe this information to Professor Kerényi. The female worshippers of the bear goddess Artemis were called ἄρκτοι, 'bears.' Cf. pl. Lb.)

itself unnoticed into the sublime feelings of religious poetry, in which perhaps other people can find joy and consolation, and that it is a kind of unjustified fanaticism for truth to complain about the unconsciousness of such a solution. I would not like to decide this question one way or the other, but would prefer to find out the meaning and purpose of the apparently devious path followed by the libido, and of the apparent self-deception, in the case of a so-called unnatural and unconscious solution. There are no "purposeless" psychic processes; that is to say, it is a hypothesis of the greatest heuristic value that the psyche is essentially purposive and directed.

91   That the root-cause of the poem has been shown to be the love-episode is an explanation that does not amount to very much at present, for the question of purpose still remains to be settled. Only the discovery of the purpose can provide a satisfactory answer to psychological questions. Were there not a secret purposiveness bound up with the supposedly devious path of the libido or with the supposed *repression,* it is certain that such a process could not take place so easily, so naturally, and so spontaneously. Also, it would hardly occur so frequently in this form, or in some other like it. There is no doubt that this transformation of libido moves in the same direction as, broadly speaking, the cultural modification, conversion, or displacement of natural drives. It must be a well-trodden path which is so habitual that we hardly notice the conversion ourselves, if at all. Between the normal psychic transformation of instinctual drives and the present case there is, however, a certain difference: we cannot rid ourselves of the suspicion that the critical experience—the singer—was assiduously overlooked; in other words, that there was a certain amount of "repression." This latter term should really be used only when it is a voluntary act of which one cannot help being conscious. Nervous persons can successfully hide voluntary decisions of this kind from themselves up to a point, so that it looks as if the act of repression were completely unconscious. The context [31] of associations provided by the author herself is so impressive that she must have felt this background in a fairly lively fashion, and must therefore have transformed the situation through a more or less conscious act of repression.

[31] See my "On the Nature of Dreams," pars. 542ff.

92 Repression, however, is an illegitimate way of evading the conflict, for it means pretending to oneself that it does not exist. What then becomes of the repressed conflict? Clearly, it continues to exist, even though not conscious to the subject. As we have seen already, the repression leads to regressive reactivation of an earlier relationship or type of relatedness, in this case the reactivation of the father-imago. "Constellated" (i.e., activated) unconscious contents are, so far as we know, always projected; that is, they are either discovered in external objects, or are said to exist outside one's own psyche. A repressed conflict and its affective tone must reappear *somewhere*. The projection caused by repression is not something that the individual consciously does or makes; it follows automatically and, as such, is not recognized unless there are quite special conditions which enforce its withdrawal.

93 The "advantage" of projection consists in the fact that one has apparently got rid of the painful conflict once and for all. Somebody else or external circumstances now have the responsibility. In the present case, the reactivated father-imago gives rise to a hymn addressed to the deity in his specifically paternal aspect—hence the emphasis on the Father of all things, Creator, etc. The deity thus takes the place of the human singer; and earthly love is replaced by the heavenly. Although it cannot be proved from the material available, it is nevertheless highly improbable that Miss Miller was so unaware of the conflicting nature of the situation that the apparently effortless transformation of the erotic impression into feelings of religious exaltation cannot be explained as an act of repression. If this view is correct, then the picture of the father-god is a projection and the procedure responsible for this a self-deceiving manoeuvre undertaken for the illegitimate purpose of *making a real difficulty unreal*, that is, of juggling it out of existence.

94 If, however, a product like the hymn came into being *without* an act of repression, i.e., unconsciously and spontaneously, then we are confronted with an entirely natural and automatic process of transformation. In that case the creator-god who emerges from the father-imago is no longer a product of repression or a substitute, but a natural and inevitable phenomenon. Natural transformations of this kind, without any semi-conscious elements of conflict, are to be found in all genuine acts

of creation, artistic or otherwise. But to the degree that they are causally connected with an act of repression they are coloured by complexes which neurotically distort them and stamp them as *ersatz* products. With a little experience it would not be difficult to determine their origin by their character, and to see how far their genealogy is the result of repression. Just as in natural birth no repression is needed to bring or "project" a living creature into the world, so artistic and spiritual creation is a natural process even when the figure projected is divine. This is far from being always a religious, philosophical, or even a denominational question, but is a universal phenomenon which forms the basis of all our ideas of God, and these are so old that one cannot tell whether they are derived from a father-imago, or vice versa. (The same must be said of the mother-imago as well.)

95   The God-image thrown up by a spontaneous act of creation is a living figure, a being that exists in its own right and therefore confronts its ostensible creator autonomously. As proof of this it may be mentioned that the relation between the creator and the created is a *dialectical* one, and that, as experience shows, man has often been the person who is addressed. From this the naïve-minded person concludes, rightly or wrongly, that the figure produced exists in and for itself, and he is inclined to assume that it was not he who fashioned it, but that it fashioned itself in him—a possibility which no amount of criticism can disprove, since the genesis of this figure is a natural process with a teleological orientation in which the cause anticipates the goal. As it is a natural process, it cannot be decided whether the God-image is created or whether it creates itself. The naïve intellect cannot help taking its autonomy into account and putting the dialectical relationship to practical use. It does this by calling upon the divine presence in all difficult or dangerous situations, for the purpose of unloading all its unbearable difficulties upon the Almighty and expecting help from that quarter.[32] In the psychological sense this means that complexes weighing on the soul are *consciously* transferred to the God-image. This, it should be noted, is the direct opposite of an act of repression, where the complexes are handed over to an unconscious authority, inasmuch as one prefers to forget them.

[32] Cf. I Peter 4 : 7; and Philemon, vv. 4 and 6.

But in any religious discipline it is of the highest importance
that one should remain conscious of one's difficulties—in other
words, of one's sins. An excellent means to this end is the
mutual confession of sin (James 5 : 16), which effectively prevents one from becoming unconscious.[33] These measures aim at
keeping the conflicts conscious, and that is also a *sine qua non*
of the psychotherapeutic procedure. Just as medical treatment
appoints the person of the doctor to take over the conflicts of
his patients, so Christian practice appoints the Saviour, "in
whom we have redemption through his blood, the forgiveness
of sins." [34] He is the deliverer and redeemer of our guilt, a God
who stands above sin, who "committed no sin, no guile was
found on his lips," [35] who "himself bore our sins in his body on
the tree." [36] "So Christ was once sacrificed to take away the sins
of many." [37] This God is characterized as being himself innocent
and a self-sacrificer. The conscious projection at which Christian
education aims therefore brings a double psychic benefit: firstly,
one keeps oneself conscious of the conflict ("sin") of two mutually opposing tendencies, thus preventing a known suffering
from turning into an unknown one, which is far more tormenting, by being repressed and forgotten; and secondly, one lightens
one's burden by surrendering it to God, to whom all solutions
are known. But, as we have said, the divine figure is in the first
place a psychic image, a complex of archetypal ideas which faith
equates with a metaphysical entity. Science has no competence
to pass judgment on this equation: on the contrary, it must pursue its explanations without resorting to any such hypostasis. It
can only establish that instead of an objective human being
there appears an apparently subjective figure, i.e., a complex of
ideas. This complex, as experience has shown, possesses a certain
functional autonomy and has proved itself to be a psychic existent. That is what psychological experience is primarily concerned with, and to that extent this experience can be an object
of science. Science can only establish the existence of psychic
factors, and provided that we do not overstep these limits with

33 Cf. I John 1 : 8: "If we say we have no sin, we deceive ourselves, and the truth
is not in us" (RSV; also nn. 34–36).
34 Ephesians 1 : 7 and Colossians 1 : 14. Isaiah 53 : 4: "Surely he has borne our
griefs and carried our sorrows."   35 I Peter 2 : 22.
36 I Peter 2 : 24.   37 Hebrews 9 : 28 (ZB).

professions of faith, in all so-called metaphysical problems we find ourselves confronted exclusively with psychic existents. These, in accordance with their nature, are intimately interwoven with the individual personality and are therefore subject to all manner of variations, unlike the postulates of faith whose uniformity and permanence are guaranteed by tradition and by institutional religion. The epistemological boundaries set by the scientific standpoint make it inevitable that the religious figure appears essentially as a psychic factor which can only be separated theoretically from the individual psyche. And the more it is so separated, the more it loses its plasticity and concreteness, since it owes its explicit form and vitality precisely to its intimate connection with the individual psyche. The scientific approach makes the divine figure, which faith posits as being the supreme certainty, into a variable and hardly definable quantity, although it cannot cast doubt on its actuality (in the psychological sense). Science therefore puts, in place of the certainty of faith, the uncertainty of human knowledge. The resultant change of attitude is not without serious consequences for the individual: his conscious mind sees itself isolated in a world of psychic factors, and only the utmost caution and conscientiousness can prevent him from assimilating them and from identifying them with himself. This danger is all the greater because, in his immediate experience of dreams, visions, etc., the religious figures show a marked tendency to appear in the most varied forms; they often clothe themselves so convincingly in the stuff of the individual psyche that it remains a moot point whether they are not in the last resort produced by the subject himself. That is an illusion of the conscious mind, but a very common one.[38] In reality all inner experience springs from the unconscious, over which we have no control. *But the unconscious is nature, which never deceives: only we deceive ourselves.* Thus, inasmuch as the scientific approach disregards metaphysics, basing itself entirely on verifiable experience, it plunges us straight into the uncertainty which is conditioned by the variability of everything psychic. It emphasizes outright the subjectivity of religious experience, thereby offering an open

[38] As I have shown above, it is not always an illusion, for the subject himself can be the main source of these figures, as is particularly the case in neuroses and psychoses.

62

threat to the solidarity of faith. This long-felt and ever-present danger is countered by the institution of the Christian community, whose psychological significance is best expressed in the command in the Epistle of James: "Confess your sins to one another." [39] Again, it is emphasized as being especially important to preserve the community through mutual love; the Pauline commands leave no doubts on this score:

> Through love be servants of one another. [40]
> Let brotherly love continue. [41]
> And let us consider how to stir up one another to love and good works, not neglecting to meet together. . . . [42]

96   Fellowship in the Christian community appears to be a condition of salvation, or however one chooses to describe the desired state. The First Epistle of John expresses similar views:

> He who loves his brother abides in the light. . . . But he who hates his brother is in the darkness. . . . [43]
> No man has ever seen God; if we love one another, God abides in us and his love is perfected in us. [44]

97   We have already referred to the mutual confession of sin and the transference of psychic difficulties to the divine figure. Between it and man there thus arises an intimate bond. Yet man should be bound through love not to God alone, but also to his fellows. The latter relation, indeed, seems to be just as essential as the former. If God dwells in us only when we love our brother, we might be led to suppose that love is even more important than God. This is not so absurd when we consider the words of Hugh of St. Victor:

> You have great power, O Love; you alone could draw God down from heaven to earth. O how strong is your bond with which even God could be bound. . . . You brought him bound with your bonds, you brought him wounded with your arrows, . . . you wounded him who was invulnerable, you bound him who was invincible, you drew down him who was immovable, the Eternal you made mortal. . . . O Love, how great is your victory! [45]

39 James 5:16. And Galatians 6:2: "Bear one another's burdens." (RSV; and nn. 40–44.)   40 Galatians 5:13.   41 Hebrews 13:1.
42 Hebrews 10:24f.   43 I John 2:10f.   44 I John 4:12.
45 "Magnam ergo vim habes, caritas, tu sola Deum trahere potuisti de caelo ad terras. O quam forte est vinculum tuum, quo et Deus ligari potuit. . . . Adduxisti illum vinculis tuis alligatum, adduxisti illum sagittis tuis vulneratum. . . . Vul-

Accordingly, love would seem to be no trifling thing: it is God himself.[46] But, on the other hand, "love" is an extreme example of anthropomorphism and, together with hunger, the immemorial psychic driving-force of humanity. It is, psychologically considered, a function of relationship on the one hand and a feeling-toned psychic condition on the other, which, as we have seen, practically coincides with the God-image. There can be no doubt that love has an instinctual determinant; it is an activity peculiar to mankind, and, if the language of religion defines God as "love," there is always the great danger of confusing the love which works in man with the workings of God. This is an obvious instance of the above-mentioned fact that the archetype is inextricably interwoven with the individual psyche, so that the greatest care is needed to differentiate the collective type, at least conceptually, from the personal psyche. In practice, however, this differentiation is not without danger if human "love" is thought of as the prerequisite for the divine presence (I John 4 : 12).

98   No doubt this presents those who would like to keep the man-to-God relationship free from psychology with no small problem. But for the psychologist the situation is not so complicated. "Love," in his experience, proves to be the power of fate par excellence, whether it manifests itself as base *concupiscentia* or as the most spiritual affection. It is one of the mightiest movers of humanity. If it is conceived as "divine," this designation falls to it with absolute right, since the mightiest force in the psyche has always been described as "God." Whether we believe in God or not, whether we marvel or curse, the word "God" is always on our lips. Anything psychically powerful is invariably called "God." At the same time "God" is set over against man and expressly set apart from him. But love is common to both. It belongs to man in so far as he is its master, and to the daemon if ever he becomes its object or its victim. This means, psychologically, that the libido, regarded as the force of desire and aspiration, as psychic energy in the widest sense,

---

nerasti impassibilem, ligasti insuperabilem, traxisti incommutabilem, aeternum fecisti mortalem. . . . O caritas quanta est victoria tua!"—*De laude caritatis,* cols. 974f.

46 I John 4 : 16: "God is love, and he who abides in love abides in God, and God abides in him" (RSV).

stands in part at the disposal of the ego, and in part confronts the ego autonomously, sometimes influencing it so powerfully that it is either put in a position of unwilling constraint, or else discovers in the libido itself a new and unexpected source of strength. Since the relation of the unconscious to the conscious mind is not merely mechanical or complementary, but rather compensatory, taking its cue from the anfractuosities of the conscious attitude, the intelligent character of this unconscious activity can hardly be denied. Experiences like these make it immediately understandable why the God-image is so often regarded as a personal being.

99 Now, since a man's *spiritual vocation* in the widest sense has been thrust upon him to an increasing degree by the unconscious,[47] this naturally gave rise to the view that the God-image was a spirit who required man's spirit. This is not an invention of Christianity or of philosophy, but a common human experience to which even the atheist bears witness. (The important thing is *what* he talks about, not whether he agrees with it or not.) The other definition of God therefore asserts: "God is spirit." [48] The pneumatic God-image has been further attenuated as the Logos, and this gives the "love of God" that peculiarly abstract quality which is also apparent in the idea of "Christian love."

100 It is this "spiritual love," which is actually far more appropriate to the God-image than to man, that is supposed to hold the human community together:

Welcome one another, therefore, as Christ has welcomed you, for the glory of God.[49]

101 It is obvious that, since Christ "welcomed" men with "divine" love, men's love for one another should also have, and indeed *can* have, a "spiritual" and "divine" quality. However, it is not so obvious from the psychological point of view, since, as a rule, the energy of an archetype is not at the disposal of the conscious mind. Hence the specifically human forms of love are, very rightly, not regarded as either "spiritual" or "divine." The energy of an archetype communicates itself to the ego only

47 One cannot of one's own free will choose and desire something that one does not know. Hence a spiritual goal cannot consciously be striven for if it does not yet exist.   48 John 4 : 24 (RSV).   49 Romans 15 : 7 (RSV).

when the latter has been influenced or gripped by an autonomous action of the archetype. From this psychological fact one would have to conclude that the man who practises a spiritual form of love has already been gripped by something akin to a *donum gratiae,* for he could hardly be expected to be capable of usurping, on his own resources, a divine action such as that love is. But by virtue of the *donum amoris* he becomes capable of taking God's place in this respect. It is a psychological fact that an archetype can seize hold of the ego and even compel it to act as it—the archetype—wills. A man can then take on archetypal dimensions and exercise corresponding effects; he can appear in the place of God, so that it is not only possible, but quite sensible, for other men to act towards him as they act towards God. We know that, in the Catholic Church, this possibility has become an institution whose psychological efficacy cannot be doubted. From this intimate relationship there arises a community of an archetypal order which is distinguished from all other communities by the fact that its aim or purpose is not immanent in mankind and not directed to utilitarian ends, but is a transcendental symbol whose nature corresponds to the peculiarity of the ruling archetype.

102   The closer relations between men thus made possible by such a community produce a psychological intimacy which touches on the personal instinctual sphere of "human" love and therefore harbours certain dangers. Above all, the power and sex instincts are inevitably constellated. Intimacy creates various short-cuts between people and is only too likely to lead to the very thing from which Christianity seeks to deliver them, namely to those all-too-human attractions and their necessary consequences, which had already been the bane of the highly civilized man at the beginning of our Christian era. Religious experience in antiquity was frequently conceived as bodily union with the deity,[50] and certain cults were saturated with sexuality of every

---

[50] Cf. Reitzenstein, *Die hellenistischen Mysterienreligionen,* p. 20: "To the various forms in which primitive peoples have envisaged the supreme religious sacrament, union with God, there necessarily belongs that of sexual union, through which man takes into himself the innermost essence and power of a god, his semen. What is at first a wholly sensual idea becomes, independently in different parts of the world, a sacred act, where the god is represented by a human deputy or by his symbol the phallus." Further material in Dieterich, *Eine Mithrasliturgie,* pp. 121ff.

66

kind. Sexuality was all too close to the relations of people with one another. The moral degeneracy of the first centuries of the Christian era produced a moral reaction which then, in the second and third centuries, after germinating in the darkness of the lowest strata of society, expressed itself at its purest in the two mutually antagonistic religions, Christianity and Mithraism These religions strove after precisely that higher form of social intercourse symbolized by a projected ("incarnate") idea (the Logos), whereby all the strongest impulses of man—which formerly had flung him from one passion to another and seemed to the ancients like the compulsion of evil stars, *Heimarmene*,[51] or like what we psychologists would call the *compulsion of libido* [52]—could be made available for the maintenance of so-

[51] Cf. the prayers in the so-called Mithras liturgy (published in 1910 by Dieterich, ibid.). There we find such characteristic passages as: τῆς ἀνθρωπίνης μου ψυχικῆς δυνάμεως ἥν ἐγὼ πάλιν μεταπαραλήμψομαι μετὰ τὴν ἐνεστῶσαν καὶ κατεπείγουσάν με πικρὰν ἀνάγκην ἀχρεοκόπητον (my human soul-force, which I shall recover again undiminished after the present bitter necessity that presses upon me), and ἕνεκα τῆς κατεπειγούσης καὶ πικρᾶς ἀπαραιτήτου ἀνάγκης (because of the bitter inexorable necessity that oppresses me). The speech of the high priest of Isis (Apuleius, *The Golden Ass*, XI, 15) reveals a similar train of thought. The young philosopher Lucius was changed into an ass, that ever-rutting animal hateful to Isis. Later he was released from the spell and initiated into the mysteries. (Cf. pl. VI.) During his disenchantment, the priest says: "On the slippery path of your lusty youth you fell a prey to servile pleasures, and won a sinister reward for your ill-fated curiosity. . . . But hostile fortune has no power over those who have devoted their lives to serve the honour and majesty of our goddess. . . . Now, you are safe, and under the protection of that fortune which is not blind, but can see." In his prayer to Isis, Queen of Heaven, Lucius says (XI, 25): ". . . thy saving hand, wherewith thou unweavest even the inextricably tangled web of fate, and assuagest the tempests of fortune, and restrainest the baleful orbits of the stars." Altogether, the purpose of the mysteries (pl. IVb) was to break the "compulsion of the stars" by magic power.

The power of fate makes itself felt unpleasantly only when everything goes against our will, that is to say, when we are no longer in harmony with ourselves. The ancients, accordingly, brought εἱμαρμένη into relation with the "primal light" or "primal fire," the Stoic conception of the ultimate cause, or all-pervading warmth which produced everything and is therefore fate. (Cf. Cumont, *The Mysteries of Mithra*, p. 114.) This warmth, as will be shown later, is a libido-image (cf. fig. 4). Another conception of Ananke (Necessity), according to Zoroaster's book Περὶ Φύσεως ("On Nature"), is air, which in the form of wind is again connected with the fertilizing agent.

[52] Schiller says in *Piccolomini*, II, 6: "The stars of thine own fate lie in thy breast." "A man's fortunes are the fruits of his character," says Emerson, in his essay "Fate," in *The Conduct of Life* (*Works*, VI, p. 41).

ciety. As one example among many others, I would cite St. Augustine's description of the fate of Alypius, in his *Confessions:*

But at Carthage the maelstrom of ill morals—and especially the passion for idle spectacles—had sucked him in, his special madness being for gladiatorial shows. . . . As a result of what he had heard me say, he wrenched himself out of the deep pit in which he had chosen to be plunged and in the darkness of whose pleasures he had been so woefully blinded. He braced his mind and shook it till all the filth of the Games fell away from it and he went no more. . . .

In pursuit of the worldly career whose necessity his parents were always dinning into his ears, he had gone before me to Rome to study Law; and there he had been, incredibly, carried away again by an incredible passion for gladiatorial shows. He had turned from such things and utterly detested them. But it happened one day that he met some friends and fellow students coming from dinner: and though he flatly refused and vigorously resisted, they used friendly violence and forced him along with them to the amphitheatre on a day of these cruel and murderous Games. He protested: "Even if you drag my body to the place, can you force me to turn my mind and my eyes on the show? Though there, I shall not be there, and so I shall defeat both you and it."

Hearing this his companions led him on all the faster, wishing to discover whether he could do as he had said. When they had reached the Arena and had got such seats as they could, the whole place was in a frenzy of hideous delight. He closed up the door of his eyes and forbade his mind to pay attention to things so evil. If only he could have stopped his ears too! For at a certain critical point in the fight, the vast roar of the whole audience beat upon him. His curiosity got the better of him, and thinking that he would be able to treat the sight with scorn—whatever the sight might be— he opened his eyes, and was stricken with a deeper wound in the soul than the man he had opened his eyes to see suffered in the body. He fell more miserably than the gladiator whose fall had set the crowd to that roar—a roar which had entered his ears and unlocked his eyes, so that his soul was stricken and beaten down. But in truth the reason was that its courage had so far been only audaciousness, and it was weak because it had relied upon itself when it should have trusted only in You. Seeing the blood he drank deep of the savagery. He did not turn away but fixed his gaze upon the sight. He drank in all the frenzy, with no thought of what had happened to him, revelled in the wickedness of the contest, and was drunk with lust for

68

blood. He was no longer the man who had come there but one of the crowd to which he had come, a fit companion for those who had brought him.

What more need I say? He continued to gaze, shouted, grew hot, and when he departed took with him a madness by which he was goaded to come back again, not only with those who at first took him there, but even more than they and leading on others.[53]

103   One can take it as certain that man's domestication cost him the heaviest sacrifices. An age which created the Stoic ideal must doubtless have known why and against what it was set up. The age of Nero provides an effective foil for the celebrated passage from the forty-first letter of Seneca to Lucilius:

We push one another into vice. And how can a man be recalled to salvation, when he has none to restrain him, and all mankind to urge him on? . . .

If you see a man who is unterrified in the midst of dangers, untouched by desires, happy in adversity, peaceful amid the storm, who looks down upon men from a higher plane, and views the gods on a footing of equality, will not a feeling of reverence for him steal over you? Will you not say: "This quality is too great and too lofty to be regarded as resembling this petty body in which it dwells. A divine power has descended upon that man." When a soul rises superior to other souls, when it is under control, when it passes through every experience as if it were of small account, when it smiles at our fears and at our prayers, it is stirred by a force from heaven. A thing like this cannot stand upright unless it be propped by the divine. Therefore, a greater part of it abides in that place from whence it came down to earth. Just as the rays of the sun do indeed touch the earth but still abide at the source from which they are sent, even so the great and hallowed soul, which has come down in order that we may have a nearer knowledge of divinity, does indeed associate with us, but still cleaves to its origin; on that source it depends, thither it turns its gaze and strives to go, and it concerns itself with our doings only as a being superior to ourselves.[54]

104   The men of that age were ripe for identification with the word made flesh, for the founding of a community united by

[53] *The Confessions of St. Augustine*, VI, 7–8, trans. by Sheed, pp. 88–91, slightly modified.
[54] Seneca, *Ad Lucilium epistulae morales*, trans. by Gummere, I, pp. 278f., 274f.

an idea,[55] in the name of which they could love one another and call each other brothers.[56] The old idea of a μεσίτης, of a mediator in whose name new ways of love would be opened, became a fact, and with that human society took an immense stride forward. This was not the result of any speculative, sophisticated philosophy, but of an elementary need in the great masses of humanity vegetating in spiritual darkness. They were evidently driven to it by the profoundest inner necessities, for humanity does not thrive in a state of licentiousness.[57] The meaning of these cults—Christianity and Mithraism—is clear: moral subjugation of the animal instincts.[58] The spread of both these religions betrays something of that feeling of redemption which animated their first adherents, and which we can scarcely appreciate today. We can hardly realize the whirlwinds of brutality and unchained libido that roared through the streets of Imperial Rome. But we would know that feeling again if

[55] The ascent to the "idea" is described in Augustine, *Confessions,* Book X, ch. 6ff. The beginning of ch. 8 reads: "I shall mount beyond this power of my nature, still rising by degrees towards Him who made me. And so I come to the fields and vast palaces of memory." (Trans. by Sheed, p. 172.)

[56] The followers of Mithras also called themselves brothers. In philosophical language, Mithras was the Logos emanated by God (Cumont, *Mysteries,* p. 140).

[57] Augustine, who was close to that period of transition not only in time but intellectually too, writes in his *Confessions* (Book VI, ch. 16; Sheed trans., pp. 99–100): "And I put the question, supposing we were immortals and could live in perpetual enjoyment of the body without any fear of loss, why should we not then be happy, or what else should we seek? I did not realize that it belonged to the very heart of my wretchedness to be so drowned and blinded in it that I could not conceive the light of honour, and of beauty loved for its own sake, which the eye of the flesh does not see but only the innermost soul. I was so blind that I never came to ask myself what was the source of the pleasure I found in discussing these ideas (worthless as they were) with friends, and of my inability to be happy without friends, even in the sense of happiness which I then held, no matter how great the abundance of carnal pleasure. For truly I loved my friends for their own sake, and I knew that I was in turn loved by them. O tortuous ways! Woe to my soul with its rash hope of finding something better if it forsook Thee! My soul turned and turned again, on back and sides and belly, and the bed was always hard. For thou alone art her rest."

[58] Both religions teach a distinctly ascetic morality and a morality of action. The latter is particularly true of Mithraism. Cumont (p. 147) says that Mithraism owed its success to the value of its morality, "which above all things favoured action." The followers of Mithras formed a "sacred army" in the fight against evil (p. 148), and among them were *virgines,* 'nuns', and *continentes,* 'ascetics' (p. 165).

ever we understood, clearly and in all its consequences, what is happening under our very eyes. The civilized man of today seems very far from that. He has merely become neurotic. For us the needs of the Christian community have gone by the board; we no longer understand their meaning. We do not even know against what it is meant to protect us.[59] For enlightened people, the need for religion is next door to neurosis.[60] It must be admitted that the Christian emphasis on spirit inevitably leads to an unbearable depreciation of man's physical side, and thus produces a sort of optimistic caricature of human nature. He gets too good and too spiritual a picture of himself, and becomes too naïve and optimistic. In two world wars the abyss has opened out again and taught us the most frightful lesson that can be imagined. We now know what human beings are capable of, and what lies in store for us if ever again the mass psyche gets the upper hand. Mass psychology is egoism raised to an inconceivable power, for its goal is immanent and not transcendent.

105   Let us now turn back to the question from which we started, namely, whether or not Miss Miller has created anything of value with her poem. If we bear in mind the psychological and moral conditions under which Christianity came to birth, in an age when the crudest brutality was an everyday spectacle, we can understand the religious convulsion of the whole personality and the value of a religion that protected people living in the Roman sphere of culture from the visible onslaughts of wickedness. It was not difficult for those people to remain conscious of

59 I have intentionally let these sentences stand from the earlier editions, as they typify the false *fin de siècle* sense of security. Since then we have experienced abominations of desolation of which Rome never dreamed. As regards the social conditions in the Roman Empire I would refer the reader to Pöhlmann (*Geschichte des antiken Kommunismus und Sozialismus*) and Bücher (*Die Aufstände der unfreien Arbeiter 143–129 B.C.*). The fact that an incredibly large proportion of the people languished in the black misery of slavery is no doubt one of the main causes of the singular melancholy that reigned all through the time of the Caesars. It was not in the long run possible for those who wallowed in pleasure not to be infected, through the mysterious working of the unconscious, by the deep sadness and still deeper wretchedness of their brothers. As a result, the former were driven to orgiastic frenzy, while the latter, the better of them, fell into the strange *Weltschmerz* and world-weariness typical of the intellectuals of that age.

60 Unfortunately Freud, too, has made himself guilty of this error.

71

sin, for they saw it every day spread out before their eyes. Miss Miller not only underestimates her "sins," but the connection between the "bitter inexorable necessity" and her religious product has altogether escaped her. The poem thus loses the living value of a religious work of art. It seems to be not much more than a sentimental rehash of an erotic experience, slyly working itself out on the fringe of consciousness and having about the same ethical value as a dream, which is also none of our doing.

106   To the degree that the modern mind is passionately concerned with anything and everything rather than religion, religion and its prime object—original sin—have mostly vanished into the unconscious. That is why, today, nobody believes in either. People accuse psychology of dealing in squalid fantasies, and yet even a cursory glance at ancient religions and the history of morals should be sufficient to convince them of the demons hidden in the human soul. This disbelief in the devilishness of human nature goes hand in hand with the blank incomprehension of religion and its meaning. The *unconscious* conversion of instinctual impulses into religious activity is ethically worthless, and often no more than an hysterical outburst, even though its products may be aesthetically valuable. Ethical decision is possible only when one is conscious of the conflict in all its aspects. The same is true of the religious attitude: it must be fully conscious of itself and of its foundations if it is to signify anything more than unconscious imitation.[61]

107   Through centuries of educational training, Christianity subdued the animal instincts of antiquity and of the ensuing ages of barbarism to the point where a large amount of instinctual energy could be set free for the building of civilization. The effect of this training showed itself, to begin with, in a fundamental change of attitude, namely in the alienation from reality, the otherworldliness of the early Christian centuries. It was an age that strove after inwardness and spiritual abstraction.

[61] A theologian, who accuses me of being anti-Christian, has completely overlooked the fact that Christ never said "Unless ye *remain* as little children," but, most emphatically, "Unless ye *become* as little children." His accusation is proof of a remarkable dulness of religious sensibility. One cannot, after all, ignore the whole drama of rebirth *in novam infantiam*!

Nature was abhorrent to man. One has only to think of the passage in St. Augustine quoted by Jacob Burckhardt:

And men go forth, and admire lofty mountains and broad seas, . . . and turn away from themselves.[62]

108   But it was not only the aesthetic beauty of the world that distracted their senses and lured them away from concentrating on a spiritual and supramundane goal. There were also daemonic or magical influences emanating from nature herself.

109   The foremost authority on the Mithraic cult, Franz Cumont, describes the classical feeling for nature as follows:

The gods were everywhere, and they mingled in all the events of daily life. The fire that cooked the food and warmed the bodies of the faithful, the water that allayed their thirst and cleansed them, the very air they breathed, and the light that shone for them, all were objects of their adoration. Perhaps no other religion has ever offered to its votaries, in so high a degree as Mithraism, opportunities for prayer and motives for veneration. When the initiate betook himself in the evening to the sacred grotto concealed in the solitude of the forest, at every step new sensations awakened in his heart some mystical emotion. The stars that shone in the sky, the wind that whispered in the foliage, the spring or brook that hastened murmuring to the valley, even the earth which he trod under his feet, were in his eyes divine, and all surrounding nature evoked in him a worshipful fear of the infinite forces that swayed the universe.[63]

110   This religious oneness with nature is beautifully described by Seneca:

When you enter a grove peopled with ancient trees, higher than the ordinary, and shutting out the sky with their thickly intertwining branches, do not the stately shadows of the wood, the stillness of the place, and the awful gloom of this domed cavern then strike you as with the presence of a deity? Or when you see a cave penetrating into the rock at the foot of an overhanging mountain, not made by human hands, but hollowed out to a great depth by nature, is not your soul suffused with a religious fear? We worship the sources of great rivers, we erect altars at the place where a sudden rush of water bursts from the bowels of the earth, warm springs we adore, and

62 *Confessions*, X, 8, cited in Burckhardt, *The Renaissance in Italy*, p. 181.
63 Cumont, *The Mysteries of Mithra*, p. 149, modified.

73

certain pools we hold sacred on account of their sombre darkness or their immense depth.[64]

111   Sharply contrasting with this ancient nature worship is the Christian aversion from the world, as described in the most poignant language in the *Confessions* of St. Augustine:

What do I love when I love my God? Not the beauty of any bodily thing, not the graciousness of the times, nor the splendour of the light that rejoices the eye, nor the sweet melodies of richly varied songs; not the fragrance of flowers and sweet-smelling ointments and spices, not manna and honey, nor the fair limbs whose embraces are pleasant to the flesh. None of these do I love when I love my God; and yet I love a kind of light, and a kind of melody, and a kind of fragrance, and a kind of savour, and a kind of embracement when I love my God, who is the light and the melody and the fragrance and the savour and the embracement of my inner man; where that light shines into my soul which no space can contain, that melody sounds which no time takes away, that fragrance smells which no wind scatters, that savour tastes which no gluttony diminishes, and that embracement is enjoyed which no satiety can put apart. That is what I love when I love my God.[65]

112   The world and its beauty had to be shunned, not only because of their vanity and transitoriness, but because love of created nature soon makes man its slave. As St. Augustine says (X, 6): ". . . they love these things too much and become subject to them, and subjects cannot judge." [66] One would certainly think it possible to love something, to have a positive attitude towards it, without supinely succumbing to it and losing one's power of rational judgment. But Augustine knew his contemporaries, and knew furthermore how much godliness and godlike power dwelt in the beauty of the world.

Since you alone govern the universe, and without you nothing rises into the bright realm of light, and nothing joyous or lovely can come to be. . . .[67]

64 [Cf. Gummere trans., pp. 272–75.]
65 *Confessions*, X, 6, trans. based on Sheed, p. 170.
66 Trans. by Sheed, p. 171.
67 Lucretius, *De rerum natura*, I, 21–24 [cf. Rouse trans., pp. 4–5]:
    "Quae quoniam rerum naturam sola gubernas,
    Nec sine te quicquam dias in luminis oras
    Exoritur, neque fit laetum neque amabile quicquam."

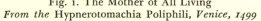

ΠΑΝΤΩΝ ΤΟΚΑΔΙ

Fig. 1. The Mother of All Living
From the Hypnerotomachia Poliphili, *Venice, 1499*

113   Thus Lucretius extols "alma Venus" as the ruling principle
of nature. To such a *daimonion* man falls an abject victim unless he can categorically reject its seductive influence at the outset. It is not merely a question of sensuality and of aesthetic
corruption, but—and this is the point—of paganism and nature-
worship. (Fig. 1.) Because gods dwell in created things, man

75

falls to worshipping them, and for that reason he must turn away from them utterly lest he be overwhelmed. In this respect the fate of Alypius is extremely instructive. If the flight from the world is successful, man can then build up an inner, spiritual world which stands firm against the onslaught of sense-impressions. The struggle with the world of the senses brought to birth a type of thinking independent of external factors. Man won for himself that *sovereignty of the idea* which was able to withstand the aesthetic impact, so that thought was no longer fettered by the emotional effect of sense-impressions, but could assert itself and even rise, later, to reflection and observation. Man was now in a position to enter into a new and independent relationship with nature, to go on building upon the foundations which the classical spirit had laid,[68] and to take up once more the natural link which the Christian retreat from the world had let fall. On this newly-won spiritual level there was forged an alliance with the world and nature which, unlike the old attitude, did not collapse before the magic of external objects, but could regard them in the steady light of reflection. Nevertheless, the attention lavished upon natural objects was infused with something of the old religious piety, and something of the old religious ethic communicated itself to scientific truthfulness and honesty. Although at the time of the Renaissance the antique feeling for nature visibly broke through in art [69] and in natural philosophy,[70] and for a while thrust the Christian principle into the background, the newly-won rational and intellectual stability of the human mind nevertheless managed to hold its own and allowed it to penetrate further and further into depths of nature that earlier ages had hardly suspected. The more successful the penetration and advance of the new scientific spirit proved to be, the more the latter—as is usually the case with the victor—became the prisoner of the world it had conquered. At the beginning of the present century a Christian writer could still regard the modern spirit as a sort of second incarnation of the Logos. "The deeper comprehension of the spirit of nature in modern painting and poetry,"

68 Cf. Kerényi, "Die Göttin Natur," pp. 50ff.
69 Cf. Hartlaub, *Giorgiones Geheimnis.*
70 Particularly in alchemy. See my "Paracelsus as a Spiritual Phenomenon," pars. 184, 198f., 228f.

writes Kalthoff, "the living intuition which science is no longer willing to dispense with even in its most arduous endeavours, demonstrate how the Logos of Greek philosophy, which gave to the early Christ-ideal its cosmic position, is divesting itself of its transcendental character and entering upon a new incarnation." [71] It did not take us long to realize that it was less a question of the incarnation of the Logos than of the descent of the Anthropos or Nous into the dark embrace of Physis. The world had not only been deprived of its gods, but had lost its soul. Through the shifting of interest from the inner to the outer world our knowledge of nature was increased a thousandfold in comparison with earlier ages, but knowledge and experience of the inner world were correspondingly reduced. The religious interest, which ought normally to be the greatest and most decisive factor, turned away from the inner world, and the great figures of dogma dwindled to strange and incomprehensible vestiges, a prey to every sort of criticism. Even modern psychology has the greatest difficulty in vindicating the human soul's right to existence, and in making it credible that the soul is a mode of being with properties that can be investigated, and therefore a suitable object for scientific study; that it is not something attached to an outside, but has an autonomous inside, too, and a life of its own; that it is not just an ego-consciousness, but an existent which in all essentials can only be inferred indirectly. To people who think otherwise, the myths and dogmas of the Church are bound to appear as a collection of absurd and impossible statements. Modern rationalism is a process of sham enlightenment and even prides itself morally on its iconoclastic tendencies. Most people are satisfied with the not very intelligent view that the whole purpose of dogma is to state a flat impossibility. That it could be the symbolic expression of a definite idea with a definite content is something that occurs to hardly anybody. For how can one possibly know what that idea really is! And what "I" do not know simply does not exist. Therefore, for this enlightened stupidity, there is no non-conscious psyche.

114   *Symbols* are not allegories and not signs: they are images of contents which for the most part transcend consciousness. We have still to discover that such contents are real, that they are

71 Kalthoff, *The Rise of Christianity*, p. 200 (trans. modified).

agents with which it is not only possible but absolutely necessary for us to come to terms.[72] While making this discovery, we shall not fail to understand what dogma is about, what it formulates, and the reason for its existence.[73]

[72] See my "Relations between the Ego and the Unconscious," pars. 353ff.

[73] When I wrote this book, these things were still completely dark to me, and I knew no other counsel but to quote to myself the following passage from the 41st letter of Seneca to Lucilius (Gummere trans., pp. 272–73): "You are doing an excellent thing, one which will be wholesome for you, if . . . you persist in your effort to attain sound understanding; it is foolish to pray for this when you can acquire it from yourself. We do not need to uplift our hands towards heaven, or to beg the keeper of a temple to let us approach his idol's ear, as if in this way our prayers were more likely to be heard. God is near you, he is with you, he is within you. This is what I mean, Lucilius; a holy spirit indwells within us, one who works our good and bad deeds, and is our guardian. As we treat this spirit, so we are treated by it. Indeed, no man can be good without the help of God. Can one rise superior to fortune unless God helps him to rise? He it is that gives noble and upright counsel. In each good man 'a god doth dwell, but what god we know not.' "

V

THE SONG OF THE MOTH

115   Shortly after the events described above, Miss Miller travelled from Geneva to Paris. She says:

My fatigue on the train was such that I hardly slept an hour. It was horribly hot in the ladies' compartment.

116   At four o'clock in the morning she noticed a moth fluttering round the light in the carriage. She then tried to go to sleep again. Suddenly the following poem sprang into her mind:

The Moth to the Sun

I longed for thee when first I crawled to consciousness.
My dreams were all of thee when in the chrysalis I lay.
Oft myriads of my kind beat out their lives
Against some feeble spark once caught from thee.
And one hour more—and my poor life is gone;
Yet my last effort, as my first desire, shall be
But to approach thy glory; then, having gained
One raptured glance, I'll die content,
For I, the source of beauty, warmth, and life
Have in his perfect splendor once beheld!

117   Before we go into the material which Miss Miller offers for an understanding of the poem, we will again cast a glance over the psychological situation in which the poem arose. Some weeks or months appear to have elapsed since the last direct manifestation of the unconscious. About this period we have no information; we know nothing of her moods and fantasies during the interval. If any conclusion is to be drawn from this silence, it is that nothing of real importance has happened during the time between the two poems, and that the new poem is another verbalized fragment reflecting the unconscious working out of

79

the complex that had been going on for months. It is highly probable that it is concerned with the same conflict as before.[1] The earlier product, the Hymn of Creation, bears, however, little resemblance to the present poem. This has a truly hopeless and melancholy character: moth and sun, two things that never meet. But, we must ask, is a moth really expected to reach the sun? We all know the proverbial saying about the moth that flies into the flame and burns its wings, but we know of no legend about a moth that strives towards the sun. Evidently there is a condensation here of two things that do not really belong together: firstly the moth which flies round the light till it burns its wings; secondly the image of a tiny ephemeral being, the May-fly perhaps, which in pathetic contrast to the eternity of the stars longs for the imperishable light. This image is reminiscent of Faust, where he says:

> Mark, now, the glimmering in the leafy glades
> Of dwellings gilded by the setting sun.
> Now slants the fiery god towards the west,
> Hasting away, but seeking in his round
> New life afar: I long to join his quest,
> On tireless wings uplifted from the ground.
> Then should I see, in deathless evening light,
> The world in cradled stillness at my feet . . .
> And now at length the sun-god seems to sink,
> Yet stirs my heart with new-awakened might,
> The streams of quenchless light I long to drink,
> Before me day and, far behind, the night,
> The heavens above me, and the waves below:
> A lovely dream, but gone with set of sun.
> Ah me, the pinions by the spirit won
> Bring us no flight that mortal clay can know.[2]

118   A little later, Faust sees the "black dog scampering through corn and stubble"—the poodle who is the devil himself, the Tempter in whose hellish fires Faust will soon singe his wings. Believing that he was expressing his great longing for the beauty

1 Complexes are usually of great stability even though their outward manifestations change kaleidoscopically. Experimental researches have entirely convinced me of this fact. See my "Studies in Word Association."
2 Part I, trans. by Wayne, pp. 66–67.

of sun and earth, he "turned away from himself" and fell into the hands of the Evil One.

> Spurn this terrestrial sun,
> Leave, resolute, its loveliness,[3]

Faust had said to himself but a little while before, in true recognition of his danger—for the worship of Nature and her beauties leads the medieval Christian to pagan thoughts which stand in antagonistic relationship to his conscious religion, just as Mithraism was once the threatening rival of Christianity.[4]

119   Faust's longing became his ruin. His longing for the other world brought in its train a loathing of life, so that he was on the brink of self-destruction.[5] And his equally importunate longing for the beauties of this world plunged him into renewed ruin, doubt and wretchedness, which culminated in the tragedy of Gretchen's death. His mistake was that he made the worst of both worlds by blindly following the urge of his libido, like a man overcome by strong and violent passions. Faust's conflict is a reflection of the collective conflict at the beginning of the Christian era, but in him, curiously enough, it takes the opposite course. The fearful powers of seduction against which the Christian had to defend himself with his absolute hope in a world to come can be seen from the example of Alypius, to which we have already referred. That civilization was foredoomed, because humanity itself revolted against it. We know that, even before the spread of Christianity, mankind was seized

3 Ibid., p. 54, modified.

4 As the reader will be aware, the last notoriously unsuccessful attempt to conquer Christianity with a nature religion was made by Julian the Apostate.

5 This solution of the problem had its parallel in the flight from the world during the first few centuries after Christ (cities of the anchorites in the desert). The Desert Fathers mortified themselves through spirituality in order to escape the extreme brutality of the decadent Roman civilization. Asceticism occurs whenever the animal instincts are so strong that they need to be violently exterminated. Chamberlain (*Foundations of the Nineteenth Century*) saw asceticism as a biological suicide caused by the enormous amount of racial interbreeding among the Mediterranean peoples at that time. I believe that miscegenation makes rather for a coarsened *joie de vivre*. To all appearances the ascetics were ethical people who, disgusted with the melancholy of the age which was merely an expression of the disruption of the individual, put an end to their lives in order to mortify an attitude that was itself obsolete.

by wild, eschatological hopes of redemption. This mood may well be reflected in Virgil's eclogue:

Now has come the last age foretold in the song of the Cumaean Sibyl; the great cycle of centuries begins anew. Now the Virgin [6] returns, and the reign of Saturn is restored. Now a new generation comes down from high heaven. Only do thou, chaste Lucina, favour the birth of the child, through whom the iron brood shall cease to be, and a golden race arise throughout the world. Thine own Apollo now is king. . . . Under thy governance any lingering traces of our guilt shall be wiped out, and the earth shall be freed from its perpetual fear. He shall have the gift of divine life, shall see heroes consort with gods and shall himself be seen mingling with them; he shall rule over a world to which his father's virtues have brought peace.[7]

120   For many, the cult of asceticism that followed the wholesale expansion of Christianity denoted a new adventure: monasticism and the life of the anchorite. Faust takes the opposite road; for him the ascetic ideal is sheer death. He struggles for liberation and wins life by binding himself over to evil, thereby bringing about the death of what he loves most: Gretchen. He tears himself away from his grief and sacrifices his life in unceasing work, thus saving many lives.[8] His double mission as saviour and destroyer had been hinted at from the beginning:

WAGNER: With what emotion must your noble soul
        Receive the acclamations of the crowd! . . .
FAUST: So, with a nostrum of this hellish sort,
        We made these hills and valleys our resort,
        And ravaged there more deadly than the pest.
        These hands have ministered the deadly bane

[6] Δίκη, Justice, daughter of Zeus and Themis, who after the Golden Age forsook the degenerate earth.

[7] Bucolica, Eclogue IV. Trans. based on Fairclough, I, pp. 28–31. (Cf. Norden, Die Geburt des Kindes.) Thanks to this eclogue, Virgil was later honoured as a quasi-Christian poet. To this position he also owes his function as psychopomp in Dante.

[8]   "Below the hills a marshy plain
        Is poisoning all that we have won;
        This pestilential swamp to drain
        Would crown the work I have begun,
        Give many millions room to live." [Cf. MacNeice trans., p. 287.]

To thousands who have perished; I remain
To hear cool murderers extolled and bless'd.[9]

121   What makes Goethe's *Faust* so profoundly significant is that
it formulates a problem that had been brewing for centuries,
just as *Oedipus* did for the Greek sphere of culture: how to
extricate ourselves from between the Scylla of world-renuncia-
tion and the Charybdis of its acceptance.

122   The hopeful note struck in the hymn to the Creator-God
cannot long be sustained by our author. It is a pose that prom-
ises, but does not fulfil. The old longing will come back again,
for a peculiar feature of all complexes that are simply left to
work themselves out in the unconscious is that they lose nothing of their original affectivity, though their outward manifestations can change almost endlessly. One can therefore take
the first poem as an unconscious attempt to solve the conflict
by adopting a religious attitude, in much the same way as in
earlier centuries people decided their conscious conflicts by the
criterion of religion. This attempt fails. There now follows a
second attempt, which is decidedly more worldly in tone, and
unequivocal in meaning: "one raptured glance," and then—to
die. From the supramundane sphere of religion her gaze turns,
as in *Faust*,[10] to "this terrestrial sun." And already there is
mingled in it something with another meaning—the moth that
flutters round the light until it burns its wings.

123   We now pass to what Miss Miller says about the poem:

This little poem made a profound impression on me. I could not at
first find a sufficiently clear and direct explanation of it. But a few
days afterwards, having again taken up a philosophical article that
I had read in Berlin the previous winter, which had delighted me
extremely, and reading it aloud to a friend, I came upon these words:
"The same passionate longing of the moth for the star, of man for
God. . . ." I had completely forgotten them, but it seemed to me
quite obvious that these were the words that had reappeared in my

9 Part I, trans. by Wayne, pp. 64–65, modified.
10 "FAUST: I long to join his quest
   On tireless wings uplifted from the ground.
   Then should I see, in deathless evening light,
   The world in cradled stillness at my feet. . . .
   Yet stirs my heart with new-awakened might,
   The streams of quenchless light I long to drink. . . ."
                    (Part I, trans. by Wayne, p. 66.)

hypnagogic poem. Moreover, a play entitled *The Moth and the Flame*,[11] which I saw a few years ago, also came back to me as another possible source of my poem. You see how often the word *moth* has been impressed upon me!

124 The profound impression the poem made on the author means that it expresses a correspondingly intense psychic content. In the "passionate longing" we meet the profound yearning of the moth for the star, and of man for God—in other words, the moth is Miss Miller herself. Her final remark that the word "moth" had often been impressed upon her shows how often she had noticed the "moth" as being a suitable name for herself. Her longing for God resembles the longing of the moth for the "star." The reader will remember that this word has already occurred in the earlier material: "When the morning stars sang together," with reference to the ship's officer singing in the night-watch. The passionate longing for God is like that longing for the singing morning star. We pointed out in the previous chapter that this analogy was only to be expected—*si parvis componere magna solebam.*

125 It is, if you like, shameful and degrading that the more exalted longings of humanity, which alone make us what we are, should be so directly connected with an all-too-human passion. One is therefore inclined, despite the undeniability of the facts, to dispute the connection. What? A helmsman with bronzed skin and black mustachios, and the loftiest ideas of religion? Impossible! We do not doubt the incommensurability of these two objects, but one thing at least they have in common: both are the object of a passionate desire, and it remains to be seen whether the nature of the object alters the quality of the libido, or whether it is the same desire in both cases, i.e., the same emotional process. It is not at all certain psychologically—to use a banal comparison—whether appetite as such has anything to do with the quality of the object desired. Outwardly, of course, it is of some importance *which* object is desired, but inwardly it is at least as important to know what kind of desire it is. Desire can be instinctual, compulsive, uninhibited, uncontrolled, greedy, irrational, sensual, etc., or it may be rational, considered, controlled, co-ordinated, adapted, ethical, reflective, and so on.

11 [For a note on this play, see Appendix, pp. 456f.—EDITORS.]

As regards its psychological evaluation the *how* is more important than the *what—si duo faciunt idem, non est idem.*

126   The quality of the desire is important because it endows its object with the moral and aesthetic qualities of goodness and beauty, and thus influences our relations with our fellow men and the world in a decisive way. Nature is beautiful because I love it, and good is everything that my feeling regards as good. Values are chiefly created by the quality of one's subjective reactions. This is not to deny the existence of "objective" values altogether; only, their validity depends upon the consensus of opinion. In the erotic sphere, it is abundantly evident how little the object counts, and how much the subjective reaction.

127   Apparently Miss Miller did not think much of the officer, which is understandable enough from the human point of view —though it did not prevent the relationship from having a deep and lasting effect which even dragged in the Deity. The moods apparently produced by such dissimilar objects can hardly spring from them in reality, but must spring from the subjective experience of love. So when Miss Miller praises God or the sun, she really means her love, the instinct most deeply rooted in human nature.

128   The reader will remember the chain of associations we adduced in the previous chapter: the singer—the singing morning star—the God of Sound—the Creator—the God of Light—of the sun—of fire—of Love. With the changing of the erotic impression from positive to negative there is a predominance of *light* symbols for the object. In the second poem, where the longing comes out into the open, the object is the terrestrial sun. The libido having turned away from the concrete object, its object has become a psychic one, namely God. Psychologically, however, God is the name for a complex of ideas grouped round a powerful feeling; the feeling-tone is what really gives the complex its characteristic efficacy,[12] for it represents an emotional tension which can be formulated in terms of energy. The light and fire attributes depict the intensity of the feeling-tone and are therefore expressions for the psychic energy which manifests itself as libido. If one worships God, sun, or fire (cf. fig. 4), one is worshipping intensity and power, in other words the phe-

12 Cf. my "Psychology of Dementia Praecox," pars. 77ff., and my "Review of the Complex Theory," pars. 200ff.

nomenon of psychic energy as such, the libido. Every force and every phenomenon is a special form of energy. Form is both an image and a mode of manifestation. It expresses two things: the energy which takes shape in it, and the medium in which that energy appears. On the one hand one can say that energy creates its own image, and on the other hand that the character of the medium forces it into a definite form. One man will derive the idea of God from the sun, another will maintain that it is the numinous feelings it arouses which give the sun its godlike significance. The former, by attitude and temperament, believes more in the causal nexus of the environment, the latter more in the spontaneity of psychic experience. I fear it is the old question of which came first, the chicken or the egg. For all that, I incline to the view that in this particular case the psycho-energic phenomenon not only takes precedence, but explains far more than the hypothesis of the causal primacy of the environment.

129   I am therefore of the opinion that, in general, psychic energy or libido creates the God-image by making use of archetypal patterns, and that man in consequence worships the psychic force active within him as something divine. (Pl. va.) We thus arrive at the objectionable conclusion that, from the psychological point of view, the God-image is a real but subjective phenomenon. As Seneca says: "God is near you, he is with you, he is within you," or, as in the First Epistle of John, "He who does not love does not know God; for God is love," and "If we love one another, God abides in us." [13]

130   To anyone who understands libido merely as the psychic energy over which he has conscious control, the religious relationship, as we have defined it, is bound to appear as a ridiculous game of hide-and-seek with oneself. But it is rather a question of the energy which belongs to the archetype, to the unconscious, and which is therefore not his to dispose of. This "game with oneself" is anything but ridiculous; on the contrary, it is extremely important. To carry a god around in yourself means a great deal; it is a guarantee of happiness, of power, and

[13] I John 4 : 8 and 12 (RSV). "Caritas" in the Vulgate corresponds to ἀγάπη. This New Testament word derives, like ἀγάπησις (love, affection), from ἀγαπᾶν, 'to love, esteem, praise, approve, etc.' Ἀγάπη is, therefore, an unmistakably psychic function.

even of omnipotence, in so far as these are attributes of divinity. To carry a god within oneself is practically the same as being God oneself. In Christianity, despite the weeding out of the most grossly sensual ideas and symbols, we can still find traces of this psychology. The idea of "becoming a god" is even more obvious in the pagan mystery cults, where the neophyte, after initiation, is himself lifted up to divine status: at the conclusion of the consecration rites in the syncretistic Isis mysteries [14] he was crowned with a crown of palm leaves, set up on a pedestal, and worshipped as Helios. (Pl. vi.) In a magic papyrus, published by Dieterich as a Mithraic liturgy, there is a ἱερὸς λόγος in which the neophyte says: "I am a star wandering together with you and shining up from the depths." [15]

131   In his religious ecstasy the neophyte makes himself the equal of the stars, just as the saint in the Middle Ages put himself, through the stigmata, on a level with Christ. St. Francis of Assisi carried the relationship even further by speaking of his brother the sun and his sister the moon.[16]

132   Hippolytus insists on the future deification of the believer: "You have become God, you will be a companion of God and co-heir in Christ." He says of the deification: "That is the 'Know thyself.' " [17] Even Jesus proved his divine Sonship to the Jews by appealing to Psalm 82 : 6: "I have said, Ye are gods" (John 10 : 34).

133   This idea of becoming a god is age-old. The old belief relegates it to the time after death, but the mystery cults bring it about in this world. An ancient Egyptian text represents it, very beautifully, as the triumphal song of the ascending soul:

I am the god Atum, I who alone was.
I am the god Ra at his first appearing.

14 Apuleius, *The Golden Ass*, XI: "In my right hand I carried a torch blazing with flames; my head was garlanded with a fair crown of white palm, with the leaves standing out like rays. Thus I was adorned like the sun and set up as an image."

15 Dieterich, *Mithrasliturgie,* pp. 8–9. ('Εγώ εἰμι σύμπλανος ὑμῖν ἀστὴρ καὶ ἐκ τοῦ βάθους ἀναλάμπων.)

16 In the same way, the Sassanid kings styled themselves "brothers of the sun and moon." In ancient Egypt the soul of every Pharaoh was a split-off from the Horus-sun.

17 *Elenchos,* X, 34, 4. (Γέγονας γὰρ θεὸς ἔσῃ δὲ ὁμιλητὴς θεοῦ καὶ συγκληρονόμος Χριστοῦ./ Τοῦτ' ἔστι τὸ γνῶθι σεαυτόν.)

I am the great god who created himself,
The lord of the gods, to whom no other god is equal.
I was yesterday and know tomorrow; the battle-ground of the gods
was made when I spoke.
I know the name of that great god who dwells there.
I am the god Min at his coming forth, whose feathers I place upon
my head.[18]
I am in my country, I come into my city. I am daily together with
my father Atum.
My impurity is driven out, and the sin which was in me is trodden
under foot.
I washed myself in the two great pools which are in Heracleopolis,
in which the sacrifices of men are purified for that great god who
dwells there.
I go on my way, where I wash my head in the water of the righteous.
I reach this land of the glorified and enter in at the splendid
portal.
You who stand before me, reach me your hands, it is I, I am become
one of you. I am daily together with my father Atum.[19]

134   When man becomes God, his importance and power are
enormously increased.[20] That seems to have been its main purpose: to strengthen the individual against his all-too-human
weakness and insecurity in personal life. But the strengthening
of his power-consciousness is only the outward effect of his becoming God; far more important are the deeper lying processes
in the realm of feeling. For whoever introverts libido, i.e., withdraws it from the external object, suffers the necessary consequences of introversion: the libido which is turned inwards, into

18 Cf. the coronation rite mentioned above. Feathers symbolize power. The feather
crown = crown of sun rays, halo. Crowning is in itself an identification with the
sun. For instance the spiked crown appeared on Roman coins from the time
when the Caesars were identified with the *Sol invictus. Solis invicti comes:* 'companion of the unconquerable sun.' The halo means the same thing; it is an image
of the sun, as is the tonsure. The priests of Isis had smooth-shaven heads that
shone like stars (Apuleius).
19 "The Coming Forth by Day from the Underworld," in Erman, *Life in Ancient
Egypt,* p. 343 (trans. modified).
20 The text of the Mithraic liturgy reads: Ἐγώ ἐ'ιμι σύμπλανος ὑμῖν ἀστήρ καὶ ἐκ τοῦ
βάθους ἀναλάμπων . . . ταῦτά σου εἰπόντος εὐθέως ὁ δίσκος ἀπλωθήσεται (I am a star wandering with you and shining up from the depths. . . . When you have said this,
the disc of the sun will immediately unfold). Through his prayer, the celebrant
has the divine power to make the sun come out.

the subject, reverts to the individual past and digs up from the treasure-house of memory those images glimpsed long ago, which bring back the time when the world was a full and rounded whole. First and foremost are the memories of childhood, among them the imagos of father and mother. These are unique and imperishable, and in adult life not many difficulties are needed to reawaken those memories and make them active. The regressive reactivation of the father- and mother-imagos plays an important role in religion. The benefits of religion are equivalent, in their effects, to the parental care lavished upon the child, and religious feelings are rooted in unconscious memories of certain tender emotions in early infancy—memories of archetypal intuitions, as expressed in the above hymn:

> I am in my country, I come into my city. I am daily together with my father Atum.[21]

135   The visible father of the world is the sun, the heavenly fire, for which reason father, God, sun, and fire are mythologically synonymous. The well-known fact that in worshipping the sun's strength we pay homage to the great generative force of Nature is the plainest possible evidence—if evidence were still needed—that in God we honour the energy of the archetype. This symbolism is expressed very plastically in the third logos of the Dieterich papyrus: after the second prayer, stars float down towards the neophyte from the disc of the sun—"five-pointed, in great numbers and filling the whole air." "When the sun's disc has opened, you will see an immense circle, and fiery doors which are closed." The neophyte then utters the following prayer:

> Give ear to me, hear me, Lord, who hast fastened the fiery bolts of heaven with thy spirit, double-bodied, fire-ruler, creator of light, fire-breathing, fiery-hearted, shining spirit, rejoicing in fire, beautiful light, Lord of light, fiery-bodied, giver of light, sower of fire, confounding with fire, living light, whirling fire, mover of light, hurler

---

21 Cf. the sayings in John: "I and the Father are one" (10 : 30). "He who has seen me has seen the Father" (14 : 9). "Believe me that I am in the Father and the Father in me" (14 : 11). "I came from the Father and have come into the world; again, I am leaving the world and going to the Father" (16 : 28). "I am ascending to my Father and your Father, to my God and your God" (20 : 17). (All RSV.)

of thunderbolts, glorious light, multiplier of light, holder of fiery light, conqueror of the stars, etc.[22]

136   The invocation is an almost inexhaustible catalogue of light and fire attributes, and for sheer extravagance can only be compared with the endless vociferations about "love" in Christian mysticism. Among the many texts which might be cited I select this passage from Mechthild of Magdeburg (1212–77):

> Ah Lord! love me greatly, love me often and long! For the more continuously Thou lovest me, the purer I shall be; the more fervently Thou lovest me, the more lovely I shall be; the longer Thou lovest me the more holy I shall become, even here on earth.

137   God answers:

> That I love thee continuously is My Nature
> For I Myself am Love;
> That I love thee fervently is My Desire
> For I long to be greatly loved.
> That I love thee long comes from My Eternity
> For I am everlasting and without end.[23]

138   Religious regression makes use of the parental imago, but only as a symbol—that is to say, it clothes the archetype in the image of the parents, just as it bodies forth the archetype's energy by making use of sensuous ideas like fire, light, heat,[24] fecundity, generative power, and so on. In mysticism the inwardly perceived vision of the Divine is often nothing but sun or light, and is rarely, if ever, personified. (Fig. 2.) For example, there is this significant passage in the Mithraic liturgy: "The path of the visible gods will appear through the disc of the sun, who is God my father." [25]

139   Hildegarde of Bingen (1100–1178) declares:

22 Ἐπάκουσόν μου, ἄκουσόν μου κύριε ὁ συνδήσας πνεύματι τὰ πύρινα κλεῖθρα τοῦ οὐρανοῦ, δισώματος, πυρίπολε, φωτὸς κτίστα . . . πυρίπνοε, πυρίθυμε, πνευματόφως, πυριχαρῆ, καλλίφως, φωτοκράτωρ, πυρισώματε, φωτοδότα, πυρισπόρε, πυρικλόνε, φωτόβιε, πυριδῖνα, φωτοκινῆτα, κεραυνοκλόνε, φωτὸς κλέος, αὐξησίφως, ἐνπυρισχησίφως, ἀστροδάμα, κτλ
23 The Revelations of Mechthild of Magdeburg, trans. by Menzies, p. 14.
24 Renan, Dialogues, p. 168, says: "Avant que la religion fût arrivée à proclamer que Dieu doit être mis dans l'absolu et l'ideal, c'est-à-dire hors du monde, un seul culte fût raisonnable et scientifique, ce fût le culte du soleil."
25 Dieterich, p. 6: Ἡ δὲ πορεία τῶν ὁρωμένων θεῶν διὰ τοῦ δίσκου, πατρός μου, θεοῦ φανήσεται.

But the light I see is not local, but is everywhere, and brighter far than the cloud which supports the sun. I can in no way know the form of this light, just as I cannot see the sun's disc entire. But in this light I see at times, though not often, another light which is called by me the living light, but when and in what manner I see

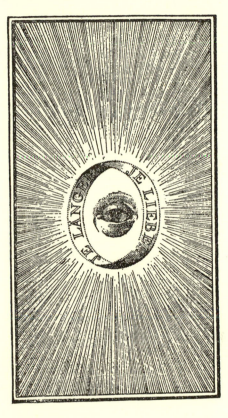

Fig. 2. The Eye of God
Frontispiece to Jakob Böhme,
Seraphinisch Blumengärtlein,
Amsterdam, 1700

this I do not know how to say. And when I see it all weariness and need is lifted from me, and all at once I feel like a simple girl and not like an old woman.[26]

140   Symeon, the "New Theologian" (970–1040), says:

My tongue lacks words, and what happens in me my spirit sees clearly but does not explain. It sees the Invisible, that emptiness of all forms, simple throughout, not complex, and in extent infinite. For it sees no beginning, and it sees no end, and is entirely uncon-

[26] In Pitra, *Analecta sacra*, VIII, p. 333. Cited from Buber, pp. 51f.

91

scious of any middle, and does not know what to call that which it sees. Something complete appears, it seems to me, not indeed with the thing itself, but through a kind of *participation*. For you enkindle fire from fire, and you receive the whole fire; but this thing remains undiminished and undivided as before. Similarly, that which is imparted separates itself from the first, and spreads like something corporeal into many lights. But this is something spiritual, immeasurable, indivisible, and inexhaustible. For it is not separated when it becomes many, but remains undivided, and is in me, and rises in my poor heart like a sun or circular disc of the sun, like light, for it is a light.[27]

Fig. 3. The Voyage of the Sun: The Western Goddess in the Barge of Evening gives the Sun-disc to the Eastern Goddess in the Barge of Morning
Late Egyptian

⟨41   That the thing perceived as an inner light, as the sun of the other world, is an emotional component of the psyche, is clear from Symeon's words:

And questing after it, my spirit sought to comprehend the splendour it had seen, but found it not as a creature and could not get away from created things, that it might embrace that uncreated and uncomprehended splendour. Nevertheless it wandered everywhere and strove to behold it. It searched through the air, it wandered over the heavens, it crossed the abysses, it searched, so it seemed, to the ends of the world.[28] But in all that it found nothing, for all was

[27] "Love-songs to God," in Buber, p. 40. There is a related symbolism in Carlyle ("Heroes and Hero Worship," p. 280): "The great fact of Existence is great to him. Fly as he will, he cannot get out of the awful presence of this Reality. His mind is so made; he is great by that, first of all. Fearful and wonderful, real as Life, real as Death, is this Universe to him. Though all men should forget its truth, and walk in a vain show, he cannot. *At all moments the Flame-image glares in upon him.*" One could take any amount of examples from literature. For instance, S. Friedländer says, in *Jugend* (1910), p. 823: "Her longing demands only

the purest from the beloved. Like the sun, she burns to ashes with the flame of her immense vitality anything that does not desire to be light. This sun-like eye of love," etc.

28 This image contains the psychological root of the "heavenly wanderings of the soul," an idea that is very old. It is an image of the wandering sun (fig. 3), which from its rising to its setting travels over the world. This comparison has been indelibly imprinted on man's imagination, as is clear from the poem "Grief" of Mathilde von Wesendonck (1828–1902):

> The sun, every evening weeping,
> Reddens its beautiful eyes for you;
> When early death seizes you,
> Bathing in the mirror of the sea.
>
> Still in its old splendour
> The glory rises from the dark world;
> You awaken anew in the morning
> Like a proud conqueror.
>
> Ah, why then should I lament,
> When my heart, so heavy, sees you?
> Must the sun itself despair?
> Must the sun set?
>
> And does death alone bear life?
> Do griefs alone give joys?
> O, how grateful I am that
> Such pains have given me nature!

There is another parallel in a poem by Ricarda Huch (1864–1947):

> As the earth, separating from the sun,
> Withdraws in quick flight into the stormy night,
> Starring the naked body with cold snow,
> Deafened, it takes away the summer joy.
> And sinking deeper in the shadows of winter,
> Suddenly draws close to that which it flees,
> Sees itself warmly embraced with rosy light
> Leaning against the lost consort.
> Thus I went, suffering the punishment of exile,
> Away from your countenance, into the ancient place.
> Unprotected, turning to the desolate north,
> Always retreating deeper into the sleep of death;
> And then would I awake on your heart,
> Blinded by the splendour of the dawn.

[Both poems as trans. in the Hinkle edn. (1916).]

The heavenly journey is a special instance of the journeys of the hero, a motif that was continued as the *peregrinatio* in alchemy. The earliest appearance of this motif is probably the heavenly journey of Plato (?) in the Harranite treatise "Platonis liber quartorum" (*Theatrum chemicum*, V, p. 145). See also my *Psychology and Alchemy*, par. 457.

created. And I lamented and was sorrowful, and my heart burned, and I lived as one distraught in mind. But it came as it was wont, and descending like a luminous cloud, seemed to envelop my whole head, so that I cried out dismayed. But flying away again it left me alone. And when I wearily sought it, I realized suddenly that it was within me, and in the midst of my heart it shone like the light of a spherical sun.[29]

142   In Nietzsche's "Glory and Eternity" we meet with essentially the same symbolism:

> Hush!
> I see vastness!
> And of vasty things
> One should not speak—
> Save in vast words! Well then:
> Grandiloquize, charmed wisdom mine!
>
> Look up:
> There roll the star-strewn seas,
> Night, stillness, deathly silent roar!
> Behold, a sign:
> Slowly, from endless space.
> A glittering constellation floats towards me.[30]

143   It is not surprising that Nietzsche's great solitude should have called awake certain images which the old cults had exalted as religious ideas. In the visions of the Mithraic liturgy we move among ideas of a very similar kind, which can now be understood without difficulty as ecstatic libido-symbols:

> But after you have said the second prayer, where silence is twice commanded, then whistle twice and click twice with the tongue, and immediately you will see stars coming down from the disc of the sun, five-pointed, in large numbers and filling the whole air. But say once again *Silence! Silence!* [31]

144   The whistling and clicking with the tongue are archaic devices for attracting the theriomorphic deity. Roaring has a similar significance: "You are to look up at him and give forth a long roar, as with a horn, using all your breath and pressing your sides, then kiss the amulet" etc.[32] "My soul roars with the

---

[29] Buber, p. 45.   [30] *Werke*, VIII, p. 427.
[31] Dieterich, pp. 8f.   [32] Ibid., p. 13.

94

voice of a hungry lion," says Mechthild of Magdeburg. "As the hart panteth after the water brooks, so panteth my soul after thee, O God" (Psalm 42 : 1). As so often happens, the ceremony has dwindled to a mere figure of speech. Schizophrenia, however, infuses new life into the old usage, as in the case of the "bellowing miracle" [33] described by Schreber, who in this way gave God, sadly uninformed about the affairs of humanity, notice of his existence.

145   Silence is commanded, then the vision of light is revealed. The similarity between the situation of the neophyte and Nietzsche's poetic vision is very striking. Nietzsche says "constellation"; but constellations, as we know, are mainly theriomorphic or anthropomorphic. The papyrus has ἀστέρας πενταδακτυλιαίους (literally, 'five-fingered stars,' similar to the 'rosy-fingered Dawn'), which is a pure anthropomorphic image. Hence, if one looked long enough, one would expect that a living being would form itself out of the fiery image, a "constellation" in the form of a man or animal—for libido-symbols do not stop at sun, light, and fire, but have a whole range of other expressions at their disposal. I leave Nietzsche to speak for himself:

The Beacon

Here, where the island grew amid the seas,
Like a high-towering sacrificial rock,
Here under the darkling heavens
Zarathustra lights his mountain-fires. . . .

This flame with its grey-white belly
Hisses its desire into the chill distances,
Stretching its neck to ever purer heights—
A snake upreared in impatience:

This emblem I set up before me.
This flame is my own soul,
Insatiable for new distances,
Sending upwards its blaze of silent heat. . . .

To all the lonely I now throw my fishing-rod:
Give answer to the flame's impatience,
Let me, the fisher on high mountains,
Catch my seventh, last solitude! [34]

[33] *Memoirs*, pp. 4, 162ff.   [34] From *Ecce Homo*, trans. based on A. M. Ludovici's.

Fig. 4. Germanic sun-idol
From the Sachsisch Chronicon, *1596*

146   Here the libido turns into fire, flame, and a snake. The
Egyptian symbol of the "living sun-disc"—a disc with the two
intertwined Uraeus serpents (pl. VII)—is a combination of both
these libido analogies. And the sun-disc with its fructifying
warmth is analogous to the fructifying warmth of love. The comparison of libido with sun and fire is essentially a "comparison
by analogy." There is also a "causative" element in it, because

96

sun and fire, as beneficent forces, are objects of human love (for instance the sun-hero Mithras is called the "well-beloved"). In Nietzsche's poem the comparison is also a causative one, but this time in the opposite sense: the snake comparison is unmistakably phallic. The phallus is the source of life and libido, the creator and worker of miracles, and as such it was worshipped everywhere. We have, therefore, three ways of symbolizing the libido:

1. *Comparison by analogy:* as sun and fire (fig. 4).

2. *Causative Comparisons:* (*a*) with objects. The libido is characterized by its object, e.g., the health-giving sun. (*b*) with the subject. The libido is characterized by its instrument or by something analogous to it, e.g., the phallus or its analogue, the snake.

147   To these three fundamental forms of comparison there must be added a fourth: the *functional comparison,* where the "tertium comparationis" is *activity*. For instance, the libido is fertile like the bull, dangerous like the lion or boar (because of the fury of its passion), and lustful like the ever-rutting ass, and so on. These comparisons represent so many possible ways of symbolization, and for this reason all the infinitely varied symbols, so far as they are libido-images, can be reduced to a common denominator—the libido and its properties. This psychological simplification is in accord with the historical attempts of civilization to unify and simplify, in a higher synthesis, the infinite number of gods. We come across this attempt even in ancient Egypt, where the boundless polytheism of local demon-worship finally made simplification necessary. The various local gods, such as Amon of Thebes, Horus of the East, Horus of Edfu, Khnum of Elephantine, Atum of Heliopolis, etc., were all identified with the sun-god, Ra.[35] In the hymns to the sun, the composite deity Amon-Ra-Harmachis-Atum was invoked as "the only god, in truth, the living one." [36] Amenophis IV (XVIIIth Dynasty) went the furthest in this direction: he replaced all former gods by the "great living disc of the sun," whose official title was: "Lord of the Two Horizons, exulting on the horizon in his name: Glittering Splendour, which is in the sun-disc." "In fact," adds Erman,[37] "it was not a sun-god who was adored, but

[35] Even the water-god Sobk, who appeared as a crocodile, was identified with Ra.
[36] Erman, *Life in Ancient Egypt,* p. 261.   [37] Ibid., p. 262.

the material sun itself, which, by the hands of his beams,[38] bestowed upon living beings that 'eternal life' which was in him." (Fig. 5; cf. also fig. 7 and pl. 1*b*.)

148   Amenophis IV achieved, by his reforms, a psychologically valuable work of interpretation. He united all the bull,[39] ram,[40] crocodile,[41] and pile-dwelling [42] gods into the sun-disc, and

Fig. 5. The life-giving Sun: Amenophis IV on his throne
Relief, Egypt

made it clear that their various attributes were compatible with those of the sun.[43] A similar fate overtook Hellenic and Roman polytheism as a result of the syncretistic strivings of later cen-

[38] Cf. the "five-fingered stars" mentioned above.
[39] The Apis-bull as manifestation of Ptah.
[40] Amon.   [41] Sobk of the Fayum.
[42] The god of Dedu, in the Delta, who was worshipped as a wooden post.
[43] This reformation was initiated with a great deal of fanaticism but soon collapsed.

turies. An excellent illustration of this is the beautiful prayer of Lucius to the Queen of Heaven (the moon):

Queen of heaven, whether thou be named Ceres, bountiful mother of earthly fruits, or heavenly Venus, or Phoebus' sister, or Proserpina, who strikest terror with midnight ululations . . . , thou that with soft feminine brightness dost illume the walls of all cities. . . .[44]

149   These attempts to reunite the basic archetypes after polytheism had multiplied them into countless variants and personified them as separate gods prove that such analogies must forcibly have obtruded themselves at a fairly early date. Herodotus is full of references of this kind, not to mention the various systems known to the Greco-Roman world. But the striving for unity is opposed by a possibly even stronger tendency to create multiplicity, so that even in strictly monotheistic religions like Christianity the polytheistic tendency cannot be suppressed. The deity is divided into three parts, and on top of that come all the heavenly hierarchies. These two tendencies are in constant warfare: sometimes there is only one God with countless attributes, sometimes there are many gods, who are simply called by different names in different places, and who personify one or the other attribute of their respective archetype, as we have seen in the case of the Egyptian gods. This brings us back to Nietzsche's poem "The Beacon." The flame was there used as a libido-image, theriomorphically represented (fig. 6) as a snake (and at the same time as an image of the soul: [45] "This flame is

44 Apuleius, XI, 2. ("Regina coeli, sive tu Ceres, alma frugum parens, seu tu coelestis Venus . . . seu Phoebi soror . . . seu nocturnis ululatibus horrenda Proserpina . . . ista luce feminea conlustrans cuncta moenia.") It is worth noting that the Humanists too (I am thinking of a passage in Mutianus Rufus) developed the same syncretism and maintained that there were really only two gods in antiquity, a masculine and a feminine.

45 The light or fire-substance was ascribed not only to divinity but also to the soul, as for instance in the system of Mani, and again with the Greeks, who thought of it as a fiery breath of air. The Holy Ghost of the New Testament appeared to the apostles in the form of flames, because the pneuma was believed to be fiery (cf. Dieterich, p. 116). The Iranian conception of Hvareno was similar: it signified the "Grace of Heaven" through which the monarch ruled. This "Grace" was understood as a sort of fire or shining glory, something very substantial (cf. Cumont, *Mysteries*, p. 94). We come across ideas of the same type in Kerner's *Seeress of Prevorst*.

Fig. 6. The mercurial serpent, alchemical symbol of psychic
transformation
From Barchusen, Elementa chemiae, *1718*

my own soul"). We saw, however, that the snake is to be taken
not only in the phallic sense, but as an attribute of the sun's
image (the Egyptian uraeus) and as a libido-symbol. It is therefore possible for the sun-disc to be equipped not only with
hands and feet (fig. 7; cf. also pl. 1*b*), but also with a phallus.
We find proof of this in a strange vision in the Mithraic liturgy:
"And likewise the so-called tube, the origin of the ministering
wind. For you will see hanging down from the disc of the sun
something that looks like a tube." [46]

150   This remarkable vision of a tube hanging down from the sun
would be absolutely baffling in a religious text were it not that
the tube has a phallic significance: the tube is the origin of the
wind. The phallic significance of this attribute is not apparent
at first sight, but we must remember that the wind, just as much
as the sun, is a fructifier and creator.[47] There is a painting by an

[46] Dieterich, pp. 6–7: Ὁμοίως δὲ καὶ ὁ καλούμενος αὐλός, ἡ ἀρχὴ τοῦ λειτουργοῦντος
ἀνέμου · ὄψει γὰρ ἀπὸ τοῦ δίσκου ὡς αὐλὸν κρεμάμενον.
[47] According to ancient superstition, the mares of Lusitania and the Egyptian
vultures were fertilized by the wind.

early German artist which depicts the fructification of Mary in the following manner: a sort of tube or hose-pipe comes down from heaven and passes under the robe of the Virgin, and we can see the Holy Ghost flying down it in the form of a dove to fecundate the Mother of God.[48] (Cf. pl. VIII; cf. also pl. III.)

151   I once came across the following hallucination in a schizophrenic patient: he told me he could see an erect phallus on the sun. When he moved his head from side to side, he said, the sun's phallus moved with it, and *that was where the wind came from.* This bizarre notion remained unintelligible to me for a long time, until I got to know the visions in the Mithraic liturgy. The hallucination, it seems to me, also throws light on a very obscure passage in the text which comes immediately after the one quoted above:

εἰς δὲ τὰ μέρη τὰ πρὸς λίβα ἀπέραντον οἷον ἀπηλιώτην. Ἐὰν ᾖ κεκληρωμένος εἰς τὰ μέρη τοῦ ἀπηλιώτου ὁ ἕτερος, ὁμοίως εἰς τὰ μέρη τὰ ἐκείνου ὄψει τὴν ἀποφορὰν τοῦ ὁράματος.

152   Mead translates as follows:

And towards the regions Westward, as though it were an infinite East-Wind. But if the other wind, toward the regions of the East, should be in service, in like fashion shalt thou see, toward the regions of that (side), the converse of the sight.[49]

Fig. 7. The Sun's hands
Relief, Spitalkirche, Tübingen

48 St. Jerome (*Adversus Jovinianum*, I, 7, in Migne, *P.L.*, vol. 23, col. 219) says of Mithras, who was born in a miraculous manner from a rock (cf. fig. 9), that his birth was caused "solo aestu libidinis"—by the sole heat of libido. (Cumont, *Textes*, I, p. 163.)
49 Mead, *A Mithraic Ritual*, p. 22.

153   Basing ourselves on Dieterich, we would say:

And towards the regions westward it is as though there were an
infinite east wind. But if the other wind should prevail towards the
regions of the east, you will in like manner see the vision veering
in that direction.[50]

154   Ὅραμα is the vision, the thing seen; ἀποφορά really means a
carrying away, or taking away. The probable meaning is that
the vision moves or is carried hither and thither according to
the direction of the wind. The thing seen is the tube, the
"origin of the wind," which turns now to the east, now to
the west, and presumably generates the corresponding wind.
The vision of our schizophrenic tallies in the most astonishing
way with this movement of the tube.[51] This remarkable case
prompted me to undertake various researches on mentally de-
ranged Negroes.[52] I was able to convince myself that the well-
known motif of Ixion on the sun-wheel (cf. pl. XLVI*b*) did in fact
occur in the dream of an uneducated Negro. These and other
experiences like them were sufficient to give me a clue: it is not
a question of a specifically racial heredity, but of a universally
human characteristic. Nor is it a question of *inherited ideas,* but
of a functional disposition to produce the same, or very similar,
ideas. This disposition I later called the *archetype.*[53]

155   The various attributes of the sun appear one after another in
the Mithraic liturgy. After the vision of Helios, seven maidens
appear with faces like snakes, and seven gods with the faces of
black bulls. The maiden can easily be understood as a causative
libido analogy. The serpent in Paradise is usually thought of as
feminine, as the seductive principle in woman, and is represented as feminine by the old painters.[54] (Fig. 8.) Through a

[50] Dieterich, p. 7.

[51] I am indebted to my late colleague Dr. Franz Riklin for the following case,
which presents an interesting symbolism. It concerns a paranoid woman patient
who developed the stage of manifest megalomania in the following way: She
suddenly saw a *strong light,* a *wind blew upon her,* she felt as if her "heart
turned over," and from that moment she knew that God had visited her and
was in her.

[52] Permission for me to do this was kindly given by Dr. William Alanson White,
late superintendent of the St. Elizabeth's Hospital, in Washington, D.C.

[53] Further material in my "Psychology of the Child Archetype," pars. 26off., and
my "On the Nature of the Psyche," pars. 388ff.

[54] See my "Psychology and Religion," pars. 104f.

similar change of meaning the snake in antiquity became a symbol of the earth, which has always been considered feminine. The bull is a notorious fertility-symbol. In the Mithraic liturgy, the bull-gods are called κνωδακοφύλακες, 'guardians of the world's axis,' who turn the "axle of the wheel of heaven." The same attribute falls also to Mithras: sometimes he is the *Sol invictus* itself, sometimes the companion and ruler of Helios (cf. pls. xxiv*a*, xl); in his right hand he holds "the constellation of the Bear, which moves and turns the heavens round." The bull-headed deities, ἱεροὶ καὶ ἄλκιμοι νεανίαι, 'sacred and valorous youths' like Mithras himself, who is also given the attribute νεώτερος, 'the younger one,' are merely aspects of the same divinity. The chief god of the Mithraic liturgy is himself divided into Mithras and

Fig. 8. The Tempting of Eve
From the Speculum humanae salvationis, *Augsburg,*
1470

Helios (cf. pl. xxiv*a*), both of whom have closely related attributes. Speaking of Helios, the text says:

You will see a god, young, comely, with glowing locks, in a white tunic and a scarlet cloak, with a fiery crown.[55]

And of Mithras:

You will see a god of enormous power, with a shining countenance, young, with golden hair, in a white tunic and a golden crown, with

[55] Dieterich, p. 11: ὄψει θεὸν νεώτερον εὐειδῆ πυρινότριχα ἐν χιτῶνι λευκῷ καὶ χλαμύδι κοκκίνῃ, ἔχοντα πύρινον στέφανον.

wide trousers, holding in his right hand the golden shoulder of a young bull. This is the constellation of the Bear, which moves and turns the heavens round, wandering upwards and downwards according to the hour. Then you will see lightnings leap from his eyes, and from his body, stars.[56]

156   If we equate gold and fire as essentially similar, then there is a large measure of agreement in the attributes of the two gods. To these mystical pagan ideas we must add the visions of the Johannine Apocalypse, which are probably not much older:

And I turned to see the voice that spake with me. And being turned, I saw seven golden candlesticks; and in the midst of the seven candlesticks one like unto the Son of man, clothed with a garment down to the foot, and girt about the paps with a golden girdle. His head and his hairs were white like wool, as white as snow; and his eyes were as a flame of fire; and his feet like unto fine brass, as if they burned in a furnace; and his voice as the sound of many waters. And he had in his right hand seven stars:[57] and out of his mouth went a sharp two-edged sword:[58] and his countenance was as the sun shineth in his strength. [Rev. 1 : 12ff.]

And I looked, and behold a white cloud, and upon the cloud one sat like unto the Son of Man, having on his head a golden crown,[59] and in his hand a sharp sickle. [Rev. 14 : 14.]

His eyes were as a flame of fire, and on his head were many crowns. . . . And he was clothed with a vesture dipped in blood. . . .[60] And the armies which were in heaven followed him upon white horses, clothed in fine linen, white and clean.[61] [Rev. 19 : 12ff.]

[56] Ibid., p. 15: ὄψει θεὸν ὑπερμεγέθη, φωτινὴν ἔχοντα τὴν ὄψιν, νεώτερον, χρυσοκόμαν, ἐν χιτῶνι λευκῷ καὶ χρυσῷ στεφάνῳ καὶ ἀναξυρίσι, κατέχοντα τῇ δεξιᾷ χειρὶ μόσχου ὦμον χρύσεον, ὅς ἐστιν ἄρκτος ἡ κινοῦσα καὶ ἀντιστρέφουσα τὸν οὐρανόν, κατὰ ὥραν ἀναπολεύουσα καὶ καταπολεύουσα. ἔπειτα ὄψει αὐτοῦ ἐκ τῶν ὀμμάτων ἀστραπὰς καὶ ἐκ τοῦ σώματος ἀστέρας ἀλλομένους.   [57] The Great Bear consists of seven stars.

[58] Mithras is frequently represented with a short sword in one hand and a torch in the other (fig. 9). The sword as sacrificial instrument plays a considerable role in the Mithraic myth and also in Christian symbolism. See my "Transformation Symbolism in the Mass," pars. 324, 357ff.

[59] στέφανον χρυσοῦν, lit. 'golden wreath.'

[60] Cf. the scarlet mantle of Helios. An essential feature in the rites of many different cults was that the worshippers dressed themselves in the bloody pelts of the sacrificed animals, as at the Lupercalia, Dionysia, and Saturnalia. The last of these lingers on in the Carnival; in Rome the typical Carnival figure was the priapic Punchinello.

[61] Cf. the linen-clad retinue of the god Helios. The bull-headed gods wore white περιζώματα (aprons?).

157   There is no need to assume any direct connection between the Apocalypse and Mithraic ideas. The visionary images in both texts are drawn from a source not limited to any one place, but found in the souls of many people. The symbols it produces are far too typical to belong to any one individual.

Fig. 9. Mithras with sword and torch
Roman sculpture

158   I mention these images in order to show how the light-symbolism gradually develops,[62] as the intensity of the vision increases, into the figure of the sun-hero, the "well-beloved." [63]

[62] The development of the sun-symbolism in *Faust* (Part I, Scene 1) does not go as far as an anthropomorphic vision; it stops in the suicide scene (Wayne, p. 54) at the chariot of Helios ("As if on wings, a chariot of fire draws near me"). The fiery chariot comes to receive the dying or departing hero, as in the ascension of Elijah or Mithras (and also with St. Francis of Assisi). Faust in his flight passes over the sea, just as Mithras does; the early Christian paintings of the ascension of Elijah are based partly on the corresponding Mithraic representations, where the horses of the sun-chariot mounting up to heaven leave the solid earth behind them and gallop away over the figure of a water-god—Oceanus—lying at their feet. Cf. Cumont, *Textes*, I, p. 178.
[63] Title of Mithras in the Vendidad, XIX, 28, cited by Cumont, *Textes*, I, p. 37.

These visionary processes are the psychological roots of the sun-coronations in the mystery religions. (Pl. VI.) The religious experience behind the ritual had congealed into liturgy, but it was a regular enough occurrence to be accepted as a valid outward form. In view of all this it is evident that the early Church stood in a special relationship to Christ as the *Sol novus,* and on the other hand had some difficulty in shaking off the pagan symbol. Philo Judaeus saw in the sun the image of the divine Logos, or even the deity itself.[64] And in a hymn of St. Ambrose, Christ is invoked with the words "O sol salutis," etc. At the time of Marcus Aurelius, Melito, in his treatise Περὶ λούτρου, called Christ "The sun of the East. . . . As the only sun he rose in the heavens." [65]

159 Even more explicit is a passage from Pseudo-Cyprian:

O how wonderful is Providence, that Christ should be born on the same day on which the sun was created, the 28th of March! Therefore the prophet Malachi said to the people concerning him: "The Sun of righteousness shall rise, with healing in his wings." This is the sun of righteousness in whose wings healing was foreshown.[66]

160 In a treatise attributed to St. John Chrysostom, "De solstitiis et aequinoctiis," it is said:

But the Lord, too, was born in wintertime, on the 25th of December, when the ripe olives are pressed in order to produce the oil for anointing, the chrism. They also call this day the birthday of the Unconquerable One. Yet who is as unconquerable as our Lord, who overthrew and conquered death itself? As for their calling it the birthday of the sun, he himself is the sun of righteousness of whom the prophet Malachi spoke.—He is the Lord of light and darkness,

---

64 *De somniis,* I, 85.

65 Ἥλιος ἀνατολῆς . . . μόνος ἥλιος οὗτος ἀνέτειλεν ἀπ' οὐρανοῦ. Cf. Pitra, *Analecta sacra,* II, p. 5, cited in Cumont, *Textes,* I, p. 355.

66 *De Pascha Computus,* in Migne, *P.L.,* 4, col. 964. Cited in Usener, *Weihnachtsfest,* p. 5.—"O quam praeclara . . . providentia ut in illo die quo factus est sol, in ipso die nasceretur Christus, v. Kal. Apr. feria IV. Et ideo de ipso merito ad plebem dicebat Malachias propheta: 'Orietur vobis sol iustitiae et curatio est in pennis ejus,' hic est sol iustitiae cuius in pennis curatio praeostendebatur." The passage occurs in Malachi 4:2: "But unto you that fear my name shall the Sun of righteousness arise, with healing in his wings." This image recalls the winged sun-disc of ancient Egypt. (Pl. IXa; cf. also pl. VII.)

the creator and separator, who is called by the prophet the sun of righteousness.[67]

161   According to the testimony of Eusebius of Alexandria, Christians, too, shared in the worship of the rising sun until well into the fifth century:

Woe to those who prostrate themselves before the sun and the moon and the stars! For I know of many who prostrate themselves and pray to the sun. At sunrise they address their prayers to him, saying: "Have pity on us!" And this is done not only by sun-worshippers and heretics, but by Christians too, who forget their faith and mix with heretics.[68]

162   Augustine remonstrated with his Christian followers, telling them emphatically: "Christ the Lord has not been made [like unto] the sun, but is he through whom the sun is made." [69]

163   Not a few traces of sun-worship are preserved in ecclesiastical art,[70] for instance the nimbus round the head of Christ, and the haloes of the saints. Numerous fire- and light-symbols are attributed to the saints in Christian legend.[71] The twelve apostles, for example, were likened to the twelve signs of the zodiac and were therefore represented each with a star over his head.[72] No wonder the heathen, as Tertullian reports, took the

67 "Sed et dominus nascitur mense Decembri hiemis tempore, VIII. kal. Januarias, quando oleae maturae premuntur ut unctio, id est chrisma, nascatur—sed et Invicti natalem appellant. Quis utique tam invictus nisi Dominus noster qui mortem subactam devicit? Vel quod dicant Solis esse natalem, ipse est sol iustitiae, de quo Malachias propheta dixit.—Dominus lucis ac noctis conditor et discretor qui a propheta Sol iustitiae cognominatus est." Cumont, *Textes*, p. 355.

68 Οὐαὶ τοῖς προσκυνοῦσι τὸν ἥλιον καὶ τὴν σελήνην καὶ τοὺς ἀστέρας. Πολλοὺς γὰρ οἶδα τοὺς προσκυνοῦντας καὶ εὐχομένους εἰς τὸν ἥλιον. Ἤδη γὰρ ἀνατείλαντος τοῦ ἡλίου, προσεύχονται καὶ λέγουσιν " Ἐλέησον ἡμᾶς " καὶ οὐ μόνον Ἡλιογνῶσται καὶ αἱρετικοὶ τοῦτο ποιοῦσιν ἀλλὰ καὶ χριστιανοὶ καὶ ἀφέντες τὴν πίστιν τοῖς αἱρετικοῖς ἀναμίγνυνται.— Oratio VI: Περὶ ἀστρονόμων, cited in Cumont, p. 356.

69 "Non est Dominus Christus sol factus, sed per quem Sol factus est."—*In Johannis Evang.*, Tract. XXXIV, 2. [Trans. from author's version.]

70 The pictures in the catacombs likewise contain a good deal of sun symbolism. For instance there is a swastika (sun-wheel) on the robe of Fossor Diogenes in the cemetery of Peter and Marcellinus. The symbols of the rising sun—bull and ram—are found in the Orpheus frescoes in the cemetery of Domitilla; also the ram and peacock (a sun-symbol like the phoenix) on an epitaph in the Callistus catacomb.   71 Numerous examples in Görres, *Die Christliche Mystik.*

72 Le Blant, *Sarcophages de la Gaule.* In the Homilies of Clement of Rome (*Homil.* II, 23, cited in Cumont, *Textes*, I, p. 356) we read: Τῷ κυρίῳ γεγόνασιν

sun for the God of the Christians! "Some, in a more human and probable way, believe the Sun to be our god." [73] Among the Manichees the sun actually was God. One of the most remarkable records of this period, an amalgam of pagan-Asiatic, Hellenistic, and Christian beliefs, is the Ἐξήγησις περὶ τῶν ἐν Περσίδι πραχθέντων, [74] a book of fables which affords deep

Fig. 10. Serpent representing the orbit of the moon
Assyrian boundary stone, Susa

insight into syncretistic symbolism. There we find the following magical dedication: Διὶ Ἡλίῳ θεῷ μεγάλῳ βασιλεῖ Ἰησοῦ. [75] In certain parts of Armenia, Christians still pray to the rising

δώδεκα ἀπόστολοι τῶν τοῦ ἡλίου δώδεκα μηνῶν φέροντες τὸν ἀριθμὸν (The Lord had twelve apostles, bearing the number of the twelve months of the sun) (trans. by Roberts and Donaldson, p. 42). This image evidently refers to the sun's course through the zodiac. The course of the sun (like the course of the moon in Assyria; cf. fig. 10) was represented as a snake carrying the signs of the zodiac on its back (like the *Deus leontocephalus* of the Mithraic mysteries; cf. pl. XLIV). This view is supported by a passage from a Vatican Codex edited by Cumont (190, 13th cent., p. 229; in *Textes*, I, p. 35): Τότε ὁ πάνσοφος δημιουργὸς ἄκρῳ νεύματι ἐκίνησε τὸν μέγαν δράκοντα σὺν τῷ κεκοσμημένῳ στεφάνῳ, λέγω δὴ τὰ ιβ′ ζῴδια, βαστάζοντα ἐπὶ τοῦ νώτου αὐτοῦ (Then the all-wise Demiurge, by his highest command, set in motion the great dragon with the spangled crown, I mean the twelve signs of the zodiac which are borne on his back). In the Manichaean system, the symbol of the snake, and actually the snake on the tree of Paradise, was attributed to Christ. Cf. John 3 : 14: "And as Moses lifted up the serpent in the wilderness, so must the Son of man be lifted up." (Pl. IXb.)

[73] *Apologia* 16: "Alii humanius et verisimilius Solem credunt deum nostrum."
[74] "Report on the Happenings in Persia," from an 11th-cent. MS. in Munich: Wirth, ed., *Aus orientalischen Chroniken*, p. 151.
[75] "To the great God Zeus Helios, King Jesus" (p. 166, § 22).

sun, that it may "let its foot rest on the face of the worshipper." [76]

164   Under the symbol of "moth and sun" we have dug deep down into the historical layers of the psyche, and in the course of our excavations have uncovered a buried idol, the sun-hero, "young, comely, with glowing locks and fiery crown," who, forever unattainable to mortal man, revolves round the earth, causing night to follow day, and winter summer, and death life, and who rises again in rejuvenated splendour to give light to new generations. For him the dreamer longs with her very soul, for him the "soul-moth" burns her wings.

165   The ancient civilizations of the Near East were familiar with a sun-worship dominated by the idea of the dying and resurgent god—Osiris (cf. fig. 23), Tammuz, Attis-Adonis,[77] Christ, Mithras,[78] and the phoenix. The beneficent as well as the destroying power was worshipped in the fire. The forces of nature are always two-faced, as is plainly the case with the God of Job. This ambivalence brings us back to Miss Miller's poem. Her recollections as to its antecedents bear out our earlier supposition that the image of the moth and the sun is a condensation of two ideas, one of which we have just discussed. The other is the idea of the moth and the flame. As the title of a play, about whose contents the author tells us absolutely nothing, "The Moth and the Flame" could easily have the hackneyed meaning of flying round the flame of passion until one's wings are burned. This passionate longing has two sides: it is the power which beautifies everything, but, in a different set of circumstances, is quite as likely to destroy everything. Hence a violent desire is either accompanied by anxiety at the start, or is remorselessly pursued by it. All passion is a challenge to fate, and what it does cannot be undone. Fear of fate is a very understandable phenomenon, for it is incalculable, immeasurable, full of unknown dangers. The perpetual hesitation of the neurotic to launch out into life

---

[76] Abeghian, Der armenische Volksglaube, p. 43.

[77] Attis was later assimilated to Mithras, and like him was represented with the Phrygian cap (cf. fig. 9). Cumont, Mysteries, p. 87. According to the testimony of St. Jerome (Ep. 58 ad Paulinum), the birth-cave at Bethlehem was originally a sanctuary (spelaeum) of Attis-Adonis (Usener, Weihnachtsfest, p. 283).

[78] Cumont (pp. iv–v) says: "The two adversaries discovered with amazement, but with no inkling of their origin, the similarities which united them."

is readily explained by his desire to stand aside so as not to get involved in the dangerous struggle for existence. But anyone who refuses to experience life must stifle his desire to live—in other words, he must commit partial suicide. This explains the death-fantasies that usually accompany the renunciation of desire. Miss Miller had already given vent to these fantasies in her poem, and she now comments:

I had been reading a selection of Byron's poems that pleased me greatly and that I often dipped into. Moreover, there is a great similarity of rhythm between my two last lines, "For I, the source, etc." and these two of Byron's:
"Now, let me die as I have lived in faith
Nor tremble tho' the Universe should quake!"

166   This reminiscence, the last link in her chain of associations, corroborates the death-fantasies born of renunciation. The quotation comes—a point not mentioned by Miss Miller—from an unfinished poem of Byron's called "Heaven and Earth." The passage reads:

Still blessed be the Lord,
For what is past,
For that which is:
For all are his,
From first to last—
Time, space, eternity, life, death—
The vast known and immeasurable unknown,
He made, and can unmake;
And shall *I*, for a little gasp of breath,
Blaspheme and groan?
No; let me die, as I have lived, in faith,
Nor quiver, though the universe may quake! [79]

167   These words form part of a panegyric or prayer spoken by a "mortal" who is in headlong flight before the oncoming Deluge. Quoting them, Miss Miller puts herself in a similar situation: she hints that her own feelings are very like the hopeless despair of the unfortunates who saw themselves threatened by the rising waters. She thus allows us to peer into the dark abyss of her longing for the sun-hero. We see that her longing is in vain, for she too is a mortal, momentarily upborne on the wings of her

[79] *Works*, p. 559.

longing into the light and then sinking down to death—or should we perhaps say, *driven by deadly fear* to climb higher and higher, like the people in the flood, and yet despite the most desperate struggles irretrievably doomed to destruction. One is forcibly reminded of the closing scene in *Cyrano de Bergerac:*

> CYRANO: But since Death comes,
> I meet him still afoot, and sword in hand! . . .
> What say you? It is useless? Ay, I know!
> But who fights ever hoping for success?
> I fought for lost cause, and for fruitless quest! . . .
> I know that you will lay me low at last.[80]

168   Her human expectations are futile, because her whole longing is directed towards the Divine, the "well-beloved," who is worshipped in the sun's image. The existing material makes it clear that there is no question of any conscious decision or choice on her part: it is rather that she is confronted, against her will and inclinations, with the disquieting fact that a divine hero has stepped into the shoes of the handsome officer. Whether this betokens a good thing or a bad remains to be seen.

169   Byron's "Heaven and Earth" is a "mystery, founded on the following passage in Genesis: 'And it came to pass . . . that the sons of God saw the daughters of men, that they were fair; and they took them wives of all which they chose.' " [81] Besides that, Byron used as a motto for his poem the following words from Coleridge: "And woman wailing for her demon-lover." [82] The poem is composed of two major episodes, one psychological, the other telluric: a passion that breaks down all barriers, and the terrors of the unleashed forces of Nature. The angels Samiasa and Azaziel burn with sinful love for the beautiful daughters of Cain, Anah and Aholibamah, and thus break through the barrier between mortals and immortals. Like Lucifer, they rebel against God, and the archangel Raphael raises his voice in warning:

> But man hath listen'd to his voice,
> And ye to woman's—beautiful she is,

---

[80] Trans. by Thomas and Guillemard, p. 293.   [81] Genesis 6 : 2.
[82] [Cf. "Kubla Khan," *Poems*, p. 297.—EDITORS.]

> The serpent's voice less subtle than her kiss.
> The snake but vanquish'd dust; but she will draw
> A second host from heaven, to break heaven's law.[83]

170   The power of God is menaced by the seductions of passion; heaven is threatened with a second fall of angels. If we translate this projection back into the psychological sphere from whence it came, it would mean that the good and rational Power which rules the world with wise laws is threatened by the chaotic, primitive force of passion. Therefore passion must be exterminated, which means, in mythological projection, that the race of Cain and the whole sinful world must be wiped out, root and branch, by the Flood. That is the inevitable result of a passion that sweeps away all barriers. It is like the sea breaking through its dykes, like the waters of the deep and the torrential rains,[84] the creative, fructifying, "motherly" waters, as Indian mythology calls them. Now they depart from their natural courses and surge over the mountain-tops and engulf all living things. As a power which transcends consciousness the libido is by nature daemonic: it is both God and devil. If evil were to be utterly destroyed, everything daemonic, including God himself, would suffer a grievous loss; it would be like per-

[83] Byron, p. 556.

[84] Nature, the object par excellence, reflects all those contents of the unconscious which as such are not conscious to us. Many nuances of pleasure and pain perceived by the senses are unthinkingly attributed to the object, without our pausing to consider how far the object can be made responsible for them. An example of direct projection can be seen in the following modern Greek folksong:

> "Down on the strand, down on the shore,
> A maiden washed the kerchief of her lover . . .
> And a soft west wind came sighing over the shore,
> And lifted her skirt a little with its breath,
> So that a little of her ankles could be seen,
> And the seashore grew bright as all the world."

(Sanders, *Das Volksleben der Neugriechen*, p. 81, cited in the *Zeitschrift des Vereins für Volkskunde*, XII, 1902, p. 166.) Here is a Germanic variant, from the *Edda*:

> "In Gymir's farm I saw
> A lovely maid coming towards me.
> With the glory of her arm glowed
> The sky and all the everlasting sea."

(Gering, p. 53, cited in the *Zeitschrift*, p. 167.) Projection also accounts for all the miraculous reports of "cosmic" events at the birth and death of heroes.

forming an amputation on the body of the Deity. Raphael's lament over the rebel angels, Samiasa and Azaziel, suggests as much:

> Why
> Cannot this earth be made, or be destroy'd,
> Without involving ever some vast void
> In the immortal ranks?

171 Passion raises a man not only above himself, but also above the bounds of his mortality and earthliness, and by the very act of raising him, it destroys him. This "rising above himself" is expressed mythologically in the building of the heaven-high tower of Babel that brought confusion to mankind,[85] and in the revolt of Lucifer. In Byron's poem it is the overweening ambition of the race of Cain, whose strivings make the stars subservient and corrupt the sons of God themselves. Even if a longing for the highest is legitimate in itself, the sinful presumption and inevitable corruption lie in the very fact that it goes beyond the fixed human boundaries. The longing of the moth is not made pure by reaching for the stars, nor does it cease to be a moth on account of such noble aspirations. Man continues to be man. Through excess of longing he can draw the gods down into the murk of his passion.[86] He seems to be raising himself up to the Divine, but in so doing he abandons his humanity. Thus the love of Anah and Aholibamah for their angels becomes the ruin of gods and men. Their impassioned invocation of the angels is an exact parallel to Miss Miller's poem:

> ANAH: [87] Seraph!
> From thy sphere!
> Whatever star [88] contain thy glory;
> In the eternal depths of heaven
> Albeit thou watchest with "the seven";
> Though through space infinite and hoary
> Before thy bright wings worlds be driven,
>   Yet hear!

[85] Cf. the mythical heroes, who after their greatest deeds fall into spiritual confusion. [86] The history of religion is full of such aberrations.
[87] Anah is the beloved of Japhet, the son of Noah. She deserts him for the seraph.
[88] The one invoked is actually a star. Cf. Miss Miller's "morning stars," par. 60 above.

Oh! think of her who holds thee dear!
And though she nothing is to thee,
Yet think that thou art all to her. . . .

Eternity is in thine ears,
Unborn, undying beauty in thine eyes;
With me thou canst not sympathize,
Except in love, and there thou must
Acknowledge that more loving dust
Ne'er wept beneath the skies.
Thou walk'st thy many worlds,[89] thou see'st
The face of him who made thee great,
As he hath made of me the least
Of those cast out from Eden's gate;
Yet, Seraph dear!
    Oh hear!
For thou hast loved me, and I would not die
Until I know what I must die in knowing,
That thou forgett'st in thine eternity
Her whose heart death could not keep from o'erflowing
For thee, immortal essence as thou art!
Great is their love who love in sin and fear;
And such, I feel, are waging in my heart
A war unworthy: to an Adamite
Forgive, my Seraph! that such thoughts appear,
For sorrow is our element. . . .

    The hour is near
Which tells me we are not abandon'd quite.
    Appear! Appear!
    Seraph!
My own Azaziel! be but here,
And leave the stars to their own light. . . .

AHOLIBAMAH: I call thee, I await thee, and I love thee. . . .
Though I be form'd of clay,
And thou of beams
More bright than those of day
On Eden's streams,
Thine immortality cannot repay
With love more warm than mine
My love. There is a ray [90]

89 This is an attribute of the "wandering sun."
90 The light substance of her own psyche.

In me, which, though forbidden yet to shine,
I feel was lighted at thy God's and thine.[91]
It may be hidden long: death and decay
Our mother Eve bequeath'd us—but my heart
Defies it: though this life must pass away,
Is *that* a cause for thee and me to part? . . .

I can share all things, even immortal sorrow;
For thou hast ventured to share life with *me*,
And shall *I* shrink from thine eternity?
No! though the serpent's sting should pierce me thorough,
And thou thyself wert like the serpent, coil
Around me still! [92] and I will smile,
And curse thee not; but hold
Thee in as warm a fold.
. . . descend, and prove
A mortal's love
For an immortal. . . .

172   The apparition of both angels which follows the invocation
is, as always, a glorious vision of light:

AHOLIBAMAH: The clouds from off their pinions flinging,
As though they bore tomorrow's light.

ANAH: But if our father see the sight!

AHOLIBAMAH: He would but deem it was the moon
Rising unto some sorcerer's tune
An hour too soon. . . .

ANAH: Lo! they have kindled all the west,
Like a returning sunset; lo!
On Ararat's late secret crest
A mild and many-colour'd bow,
The remnant of their flashing path,
Now shines!

173   At the sight of this rainbow-hued vision both women are
filled with longing and expectation, and Anah makes use of a

91 The bringing together of the two light substances shows their common origin:
they are libido images. According to Mechthild of Magdeburg (*Das fliessende
Licht der Gottheit*), the soul is compounded of "Minne" (love).
92 Cf. the paintings by Stuck—"Sin," (pl. x), "Vice," and "Sensuality"—where a
woman's naked body is encircled by a huge snake. At bottom it portrays the fear
of death.

pregnant simile. Once more the abyss opens, and we catch a brief but terrifying glimpse of the theriomorphic nature of the mild god of light:

> . . . and now, behold! it hath
> Return'd to night, as rippling foam,
> Which the leviathan hath lash'd
> From his unfathomable home,
> When sporting on the face of the calm deep,
> Subsides soon after he again hath dash'd
> Down, down, to where the ocean's fountains sleep.

174   Leviathan—we remember this prize exhibit that tips the scales of Yahweh's justice so heavily against Job. There, where the deep fountains of the ocean are, dwells Leviathan; from there the all-destroying flood ascends, the tidal wave of animal passion. The choking, heart-constricting surge of instinct is projected outwards as a mounting flood to destroy everything that exists, so that a new and better world may arise from the ruins of the old:

> JAPHET: The eternal Will
> Shall deign to expound this dream
> Of good and evil; and redeem
> Unto himself all times, all things;
> And, gather'd under his almighty wings,
> Abolish hell!
> And to the expiated Earth
> Restore the beauty of her birth. . . .
>
> SPIRITS: And when shall take effect this wondrous spell?
>
> JAPHET: When the Redeemer cometh; first in pain,
> And then in glory. . . .
>
> SPIRITS: New times, new climes, new arts, new men; but still
> The same old tears, old crimes, and oldest ill,
> Shall be amongst your race in different forms;
> But the same moral storms
> Shall oversweep the future, as the waves
> In a few hours the glorious giants' graves.[93]

175   Japhet's prognostications have an almost prophetic meaning for our poetess and must therefore be understood on the "sub-

[93] Byron, p. 551.

jective level." [94] With the death of the moth in the light the danger has been removed for the time being, though the problem is still far from solved. The conflict must begin again from the beginning; but this time there is a promise in the air, a premonition of the redeemer, the "well-beloved," who mounts to the zenith with the sun and then sinks again into night and the cold darkness of winter—the young dying god, who has ever been our hope of renewal and of the world to come.

[94] Interpretation of the products of the unconscious, for instance of a person in a dream, has a double aspect: what that person means in himself (the "objective level") and what he means as a projection ("subjective level"). Cf. "On the Psychology of the Unconscious," *Two Essays*, par. 130.

II

I

INTRODUCTION

176   Before I enter upon the contents of this second part, it seems
necessary to cast a backward glance over the singular train of
thought which the analysis of the poem "The Moth to the Sun"
has revealed. Although this poem is very different from the preceding "Hymn of Creation," closer investigation of the longing
for the sun has led us into a realm of mythological ideas that
are closely related to those considered in the first poem: the
Creator God, whose dual nature was plainly apparent in the
case of Job, has now taken on an astromythological, or rather
an astrological, character. He has become the sun, and thus finds
a natural expression that transcends his moral division into
a Heavenly Father and his counterpart the devil. The sun, as
Renan has observed, is the only truly "rational" image of God,
whether we adopt the standpoint of the primitive savage or of
modern science. In either case the sun is the father-god from
whom all living things draw life; he is the fructifier and creator,
the source of energy for our world. The discord into which the
human soul has fallen can be harmoniously resolved through
the sun as a natural object which knows no inner conflict. The
sun is not only beneficial, but also destructive; hence the zodiacal sign for August heat is the ravaging lion which Samson [1]
slew in order to rid the parched earth of its torment. Yet it is
in the nature of the sun to scorch, and its scorching power seems
natural to man. It shines equally on the just and the unjust, and
allows useful creatures to flourish as well as the harmful. Therefore the sun is perfectly suited to represent the visible God of
this world, i. e., the creative power of our own soul, which we
call libido, and whose nature it is to bring forth the useful and
the harmful, the good and the bad. That this comparison is not

1 Samson as a sun-god. See Steinthal, "Die Sage von Simson." The killing of the
lion, like the Mithraic bull-sacrifice, is an anticipation of the god's self-sacrifice.

just a matter of words can be seen from the teachings of the mystics: when they descend into the depths of their own being they find "in their heart" the image of the sun, they find their own life-force which they call the "sun" for a legitimate and, I would say, a *physical* reason, because our source of energy and life actually *is* the sun. Our physiological life, regarded as an energy process, is entirely solar. The peculiar nature of this solar energy as inwardly perceived by the mystic is made clear in Indian mythology. The following passages, referring to Rudra,[2] are taken from the Shvetashvatara Upanishad:

There is one Rudra only, they do not allow a second, who rules all the worlds by his powers. Behind all creatures he stands, the Protector; having created them, he gathers all beings together at the end of time.

He has eyes on all sides, faces on all sides, arms on all sides, feet on all sides. He is the one God who created heaven and earth, forging all things together with his hands and wings.

You who are the source and origin of the gods, the ruler of all, Rudra, the great seer, who of old gave birth to the Golden Seed— give us enlightenment! [3]

177   Behind these attributes we can discern the All-Creator, and behind him the sun, who is winged and scans the world with a thousand eyes.[4] (Cf. fig. 11.) This is confirmed by the following passages, which bring out the important point that God is contained in the individual creature:

Beyond this is Brahma, the highest, hidden in the bodies of all, encompassing all. Those who know him as the Lord become immortal.

[2] Rudra, properly—as father of the Maruts (winds)—a wind- or storm-god, appears here as the sole creator-god, as the text shows. The role of creator and fertilizer naturally falls to him as a wind-god. Cf. my comments on Anaxagoras in pars. 67 and 76, above.

[3] Trans. of this and the following passages (Shvet. Up. 3. 2–4; 7, 8, 11; 12–15) based on Hume, *The Thirteen Principal Upanishads*, pp. 399–401; and Max Müller, *The Upanishads*, II, pp. 244ff.

[4] Similarly, the Persian sun-god Mithras is equipped with an immense number of eyes. It is possible that Loyola's vision of the snake with multiple eyes is a variant of this motif. See my "On the Nature of the Psyche," par. 395.

I know this mighty Person (purusha), who is like to the sun, transcendent over darkness. Those who know him truly pass beyond death; by no other road can they go.

He is the face, the head, the neck of all, he dwells in the heart of all things, all-pervading, bountiful, omnipresent, kindly.

178   The all-powerful God, who is "like to the sun," is in every one of us, and whoever knows him is immortal.[5] Following the

Fig. 11. Bes, with Horus-eyes
Bronze figure, Egypt, c. 6th century B.C.

text, we come upon further attributes which tell us in what form Rudra dwells in man:

A mighty Lord is Purusha, spurring on the highest in us to purest attainment, inexhaustible light.

That Person, no bigger than a thumb, the inner Self, seated forever in the heart of man, is revealed by the heart, the thought, the mind. They who know That, become immortal.

Thousand-headed, thousand-eyed, thousand-footed is Purusha. He encompasses the earth on every side and rules over the ten-finger space.

That Person is this whole world, whatever has been and what will be. He is Lord of immortality, he is whatever grows by food.

5 Whoever has God, the sun, in himself is immortal like the sun. Cf. Part I, ch. 5, above.

¹79   There is a famous parallel passage in the Katha Upanishad:

> That Person in the heart, no bigger than a thumb, burning like flame without smoke, maker of past and future, the same today and tomorrow, that is Self.⁶

¹8o   We know that Tom Thumbs, dactyls, and Cabiri have a phallic aspect, and this is understandable enough, because they are personifications of creative forces, of which the phallus, too, is a symbol. It represents the libido, or psychic energy in its creative aspect. The same is true of many other sexual images which are found not only in dreams and fantasies but in everyday speech. In neither case should they be taken literally, for they are not to be understood semiotically, as *signs* for definite things, but as *symbols*. A symbol is an indefinite expression with many meanings, pointing to something not easily defined and therefore not fully known. But the sign always has a fixed meaning, because it is a conventional abbreviation for, or a commonly accepted indication of, something known. The symbol therefore has a large number of analogous variants, and the more of these variants it has at its disposal, the more complete and clear-cut will be the image it projects of its object. The same creative force which is symbolized by Tom Thumb, etc., can also be represented by the phallus or by numerous other symbols (pl. xi*b*), which delineate further aspects of the process underlying them all. Thus the *creative dwarfs* toil away in secret; the *phallus,* also working in darkness, begets a living being; and the *key* unlocks the mysterious forbidden door behind which some wonderful thing awaits discovery. One thinks, in this connection, of "The Mothers" in *Faust:*

> MEPHISTOPHELES: Congratulations, before you part from me!
> You know the devil, that is plain to see.
> Here, take this key.
>
> FAUST: That little thing! But why?
>
> MEPHISTOPHELES: First grasp it; it is nothing to decry.

⁶ 4, 13; trans. by Purohit Swami and Yeats, p. 34. [Or, in René Guénon's trans., *Man and His Becoming according to the Vedanta,* p. 45: "This Purusha, of the size of a thumb, is of a clear luminosity like a smokeless fire; it is the Lord of the past and of the future; it is today, and it will be tomorrow, such as it is." —TRANS.]

FAUST: It glows, it shines, increases in my hand! [7]

MEPHISTOPHELES: How great its worth, you soon shall understand.
The key will smell the right place from all others:
Follow it down, it leads you to the Mothers! [8]

181   Here the devil again puts into Faust's hand the marvellous tool, as once before when, in the form of the black dog, he introduced himself to Faust as:

> Part of that power which would
> Ever work evil, but engenders good.[9]

182   What he is describing here is the libido, which is not only creative and procreative, but possesses an intuitive faculty, a

Fig. 12. The birth-giving orifice
From a Mexican lienzo

strange power to "smell the right place," almost as if it were a live creature with an independent life of its own (which is why it is so easily personified). It is purposive, like sexuality itself, a favourite object of comparison. The "realm of the Mothers" has not a few connections with the womb (fig. 12), with the matrix, which frequently symbolizes the creative aspect of the unconscious. This libido is a force of nature, good and bad at once, or morally neutral. Uniting himself with it, Faust succeeds in accomplishing his real life's work, at first with evil results and then for the benefit of mankind. In the realm of the Mothers he finds the tripod, the Hermetic vessel in which the "royal marriage" is consummated. But he needs the phallic

---

[7] The light symbolism in the etymology of φαλλός is discussed in pars. 321f., below.   [8] *Faust*, Part II, trans. based on MacNeice, p. 177.
[9] Ibid., Part I, trans. by Wayne, p. 75, modified.

wand in order to bring off the greatest wonder of all—the creation of Paris and Helen.[10] The insignificant-looking tool in
Faust's hand is the dark creative power of the unconscious,
which reveals itself to those who follow its dictates and is indeed
capable of working miracles.[11] This paradox appears to be very
ancient, for the Shvetashvatara Upanishad (19, 20) goes on to
say of the dwarf-god, the cosmic *purusha:*

> Without feet, without hands, he moves, he grasps; eyeless he sees,
> earless he hears; he knows all that is to be known, yet there is no
> knower of him. Men call him the Primordial Person, the Cosmic
> Man.
> Smaller than small, greater than great. . . .

183   The phallus often stands for the creative divinity, Hermes
being an excellent example. It is sometimes thought of as an
independent being, an idea that is found not only in antiquity
but in the drawings of children and artists of our own day. So
we ought not to be surprised if certain phallic characteristics
are also to be found in the seers, artists, and wonder-workers of
mythology. Hephaestus, Wieland the Smith, and Mani (the
founder of Manichaeism, famous also for his artistic gifts), had
crippled feet. The foot, as I shall explain in due course, is supposed to possess a magical generative power. The ancient seer
Melampus, who is said to have introduced the cult of the
phallus, had a very peculiar name—Blackfoot,[12] and it also
seems characteristic of seers to be blind. Ugliness and deformity
are especially characteristic of those mysterious chthonic gods,
the sons of Hephaestus, the Cabiri,[13] to whom mighty wonder-
working powers were ascribed. (Fig. 13.) Their Samothracian
cult was closely bound up with that of the ithyphallic Hermes,
who according to Herodotus was brought to Attica by the
Pelasgians. They were called μεγάλοι θεοί, 'great gods.' Their
near relatives were the Idaean dactyls (fingers or else Tom

10 *Psychology and Alchemy,* index, s.v. "coniunctio." For a psychological account
of the problem, see my "Psychology of the Transference."
11 Goethe is here referring to the "miracle" of the Chrysopoea, or gold-making.
12 It is also said that, out of gratitude to him for having buried the mother of
the serpents, the young serpents cleaned his ears, so that he became clairaudient.
13 Cf. the vase painting from the Cabirion at Thebes (fig. 14), where the Cabiri
are depicted in a noble as well as a caricatured form (Roscher, *Lexikon,* s.v.
"Megaloi Theoi"). Cf. also Kerényi, "The Mysteries of the Kabeiroi."

Thumbs [14]), to whom the mother of the gods had taught the blacksmith's art. ("Follow it down, it leads you to the Mothers!") They were the first Wise Men, the teachers of Orpheus, and it was they who invented the Ephesian magic formulae and the musical rhythms.[15] The characteristic disparity which we noted in the Upanishads and *Faust* crops up again here, since the giant Hercules was said to be an Idaean dactyl. Also the colossal Phrygians, Rhea's technicians,[16] were dactyls. The two Dioscuri are related to the Cabiri; [17] they too wear the queer little pointed hat, the pileus,[18] which is peculiar to these mysterious gods and was thenceforward perpetuated as a secret mark of identification. Attis and Mithras both wore the pileus. (Cf. figs. 9, 20.) It has become the traditional headgear of our infantile chthonic gods today, the pixies and goblins.

184   The dwarf motif brings us to the figure of the divine boy, the *puer aeternus*, παῖς, the young Dionysus, Jupiter Anxurus, Tages, etc. In the Theban vase-painting already mentioned (fig. 14), there is a bearded Dionysus who is designated as ΚΑΒΙΡΟΣ, together with the figure of a boy labelled ΠΑΙΣ, followed by a caricatured boy's figure labelled as ΠΡΑΤΟΛΑΟΣ, and then another bearded caricature labelled ΜΙΤΟΣ.[19] Μίτος really means 'thread,' but in Orphic speech it stands for semen. It is conjectured that this group corresponded to a set of cult-images in the sanctuary. The conjecture is supported by what we know of the history of the cult, which is supposed to have been originally a Phoenician cult of father and son,[20] an old and a young Cabir who were more or less assimilated to the Greek gods. The double figure of the adult and infant Dionysus lends

14 Justification for calling the dactyls "Thumblings" may be found in a note in Pliny (VII, 57; Bostock and Riley trans., II, p. 225), where he says that in Crete there were precious stones, iron-coloured and shaped like a thumb, which were known as Idaean dactyls.

15 Hence the dactylic metre in poetry.   16 Roscher, s.v. "Daktyloi."

17 Varro identifies the μεγάλοι θεοί with the *penates*. He says the "simulacra duo virilia Castoris et Pollucis" in the harbour of Samothrace were Cabiri.

18 Statues only a foot high, with caps on their heads, were found at Prasiae, on the Laconian coast, and at Pephnos.

19 Next to him is a female figure labelled ΚΡΑΤΕΙΑ, orphically interpreted as "she who brings forth."

20 Roscher, s.v. "Megaloi Theoi." Today an ancient Mediterranean, pre-Grecian origin is regarded as more probable. Cf. Kerényi, *Die Geburt der Helena*, p. 59.

itself particularly well to this assimilation. One might also call it the cult of the big and little man. Now Dionysus, under his various aspects, is a god in whose cult the phallus occupied a prominent position, as for instance in the worship of the Argive Dionysus-bull. Moreover the phallic herm of the god gave rise to a personification of the phallus of Dionysus in the form of the god Phales, who was nothing but a Priapus. He was called ἑταῖρος or σύγκωμος Βακχίου.[21] The paradox of great and small, giant and dwarf in the Upanishadic text is expressed less dras-

Fig. 13. Odysseus as a Cabiric dwarf, with Circe
From a bowl by the Cabiri Painter (?), c. 400 B.C.

tically here as man and boy, or father and son. The motif of deformity (cf. fig. 13), which constantly appears in the Cabiric cult, is also present in the vase-painting, where the parallel figures to Dionysus and Παῖς are the caricatured Μίτος and Πρατόλαος.[22] Just as formerly the difference in size led to their separation, so now they are separated by deformity.

185   All this goes to show that though the term "libido," intro- duced by Freud, is not without a sexual connotation,[23] an exclu-

21 "Companion and fellow-reveller of Bacchus." Roscher, s.v. "Phales."
22 Illustrated in Kerényi, "The Mysteries of the Kabeiroi," fig. 1 (and our fig. 14).
23 Freud, in "Notes on . . . a Case of Paranoia," pp. 78f., which appeared simul- taneously with Part I of this book (1st [1912] edition), makes an observation that closely parallels my own remarks concerning the "libido theory" based on the fantasies of the insane Schreber: "Schreber's 'rays of God,' which are made up of a condensation of the sun's rays, of nerve-fibres, and of spermatozoa, are in reality nothing else than a concrete representation and projection outwards of libidinal cathexes; and they thus lend his delusions a striking conformity with our theory. His belief that the world must come to an end because his ego was

sively sexual definition of this concept is one-sided and must therefore be rejected. Appetite and compulsion are the specific features of all impulses and automatisms. No more than the sexual metaphors of common speech can the corresponding analogies in instinctual processes, and the symptoms and dreams to which they give rise, be taken literally. The sexual theory of psychic automatisms is an untenable prejudice. The very fact that it is impossible to derive the whole mass of psychic phenomena from a single instinct forbids a one-sided definition of "libido." I

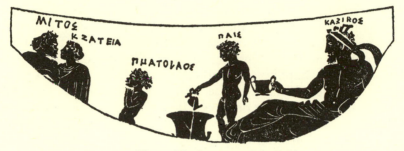

Fig. 14. The banquet of the Cabir
From a bowl by the Cabiri Painter, c. 435 B.C.

use this term in the general sense in which it was understood by the classical authors. Cicero gives it a very wide meaning:

They hold that from two kinds of expected good arise desire and delight, in the sense that delight is concerned with present good, and desire with future good . . . since desire, being tempted and enflamed, is carried away towards what seems good. . . . For all men naturally pursue those things that seem good and shun their opposites. Wherefore, as soon as anything presents itself that seems good, nature herself impels them to obtain it. If this is done with moderation and prudence, the Stoics call that kind of striving βούλησις, and we call it *will*. In their opinion this is found only in the wise man, and they define it as follows: will is a rational desire, but when it is

attracting all the rays to itself, his anxious concern at a later period, during the process of reconstruction, lest God should sever his ray-connection with him, —these and many other details of Schreber's delusional formation sound almost like endopsychic perceptions of the processes whose existence I have assumed in these pages as the basis of our explanation of paranoia."

divorced from reason and is too violently aroused, that is "libido," or unbridled desire, which is found in all fools.[24]

186   Here *libido* means a 'want' or a 'wish,' and also, in contradistinction to the 'will' of the Stoics, 'unbridled desire.' Cicero uses it in this sense when he says: "[Gerere rem aliquam] libidine, non ratione" (to do something from wilful desire and not from reason).[25] Similarly Sallust: "Iracundia pars est libidinis" (rage is a part of desire), or, in a milder and more general sense which comes closer to our use of the word: "Magisque in decoris armis et militaribus equis, quam in scortis atque conviviis libidinem habebant" (they took more pleasure in fine weapons and war-horses than in whores and drinking parties).[26] Or again: "Quod si tibi bona libido fuerit patriae" (if you have a proper concern for your country).[27] The use of *libido* is so general that the phrase "libido est scire" merely means 'I like,' 'it pleases me.' [28] In the phrase "aliquam libido urinae lacessit," *libido* has the meaning of 'urge.' It can also have the nuance of 'lasciviousness.' St. Augustine aptly defines *libido* as a "general term for all desire" and says:

There is a lust for revenge, which is called rage; a lust for having money, which is called avarice; a lust for victory at all costs, which is called stubbornness; a lust for self-glorification, which is called boastfulness. There are many and varied kinds of lust, some of which are specifically named, others not. For who could easily give a name to the lust for domination, which, as we know from the civil wars, is nevertheless very powerful in the minds of tyrants? [29]

24 Cicero, *Tusculan Disputations*, Book IV, vi, 12. ([volunt ex duobus opinatis] bonis [nasci] . . . libidinem et laetitiam, ut sit laetitia praesentium bonorum, libido futurorum . . . cum libido ad id, quod videtur bonum, illecta et inflammata rapiatur . . . natura enim omnes ea quae bona videntur, sequuntur, fugiuntque contraria; quam ob rem simul obiecta species est cuiuspiam, quod bonum videatur, ad id adipiscendum impellit ipsa natura. Id cum constanter prudenterque fit, eiusmodi appetitionem Stoici βούλησιν appellant, nos appellemus voluntatem; eam illi putant in solo esse sapiente, quam sic definiunt: voluntas est quae quid cum ratione desiderat; quae autem a ratione aversa incitata est vehementius, ea libido est, vel cupiditas effrenata, quae in omnibus stultis invenitur.)

25 *Pro Quinctio*, 14.

26 *The War with Catiline*, VII, trans. by Rolfe, pp. 14–15.

27 *Letter to Caesar*, XIII, trans. ibid., pp. 488–89.

28 In this sense the word *libidine* is still commonly used in Tuscany today.

29 *De Civitate Dei*, XIV, xv. (Est igitur libido ulciscendi, quae ira dicitur; est libido habendi pecuniam, quae avaritia; est libido quomodocumque vincendi, quae per-

187   For him libido denotes an appetite like hunger and thirst, and so far as sexuality is concerned he says: "Pleasure is preceded by an appetite that is felt in the flesh, a kind of desire like hunger and thirst." [30] This very wide use of the term in the classics coincides with the etymological context:

188   *Libido* or *lubido* (with *libet*, formerly *lubet*), 'it pleases'; *libens* or *lubens*, 'gladly, willingly'; Skr. *lúbhyati*, 'to experience violent longing,' *lôbhayati*, 'excites longing,' *lubdha-h*, 'eager,' *lôbha-h*, 'longing, eagerness'; Goth. *liufs*, OHG. *liob*, 'love.' Also associated with Goth. *lubains*, 'hope,' and OHG. *lobôn, loben, lob*, 'praise, glory'; OBulg. *ljubiti*, 'to love,' *ljuby*, 'love,' Lith. *liáupsinti*, 'to praise.' [31]

189   We can say, then, that the concept of libido in psychology has functionally the same significance as the concept of energy in physics since the time of Robert Mayer.[32]

---

vicacia; est libido gloriandi, quae iactantia nuncupatur. Sunt multae variaeque libidines, quarum nonnullae habent etiam vocabula propria, quaedam vero non habent. Quis enim facile dixerit, quid vocetur libido dominandi, quam tamen plurimum valere in tyrannorum animis, etiam civilia bella testantur?)

[30] Ibid. (Voluptatem vero praecedit appetitus quidam, qui sentitur in carne quasi cupiditas eius, sicut fames et sitis.)

[31] Walde, *Wörterbuch*, p. 426, s.v. "libet." *Liberi*, 'children,' is grouped with *libet* by Nazari (pp. 573f.). If this is correct, then Liber, the ancient Italian god of procreation, who is most certainly connected with *liberi*, would also be related to *libet*. Libitina, the goddess of the dead, is supposed to have nothing to do with Lubentina or Lubentia (an attribute of Venus), which is related to *libet*. The name is as yet unexplained.

[32] See my "On Psychic Energy," par. 37.

II

THE CONCEPT OF LIBIDO

190   Freud introduced his concept of libido in his *Three Essays on the Theory of Sexuality*,[1] and there, as we have said, he defined it *sexually*. The libido appears subject to displacement, and in the form of "libidinal affluxes" can communicate itself to various other functions and regions of the body which in themselves have nothing to do with sex. This fact led Freud to compare the libido with a stream, which is divisible, can be dammed up, overflows into collaterals, and so on.[2] Thus, despite his definition of libido as sexuality, Freud does not explain "everything" in terms of sex, as is commonly supposed, but recognizes the existence of special instinctual forces whose nature is not clearly known, but to which he was bound to ascribe the faculty of taking up these "libidinal affluxes." At the back of all this lies the hypothetical idea of a "bundle of instincts," [3] in which the sexual instinct figures as a partial instinct. Its encroachment into the sphere of other instincts is a fact of experience.[4] The resultant Freudian theory, which held that the instinctual forces of a neurotic system correspond to the libidinal affluxes taken up by other, non-sexual, instinctual functions,[5]

1 [Originally *Drei Abhandlungen zur Sexualtheorie*, 1905.—EDITORS.]
2 "Three Essays on the Theory of Sexuality," pp. 135ff.
3 An idea which Möbius tried to resuscitate. Fouillée, Wundt, Beneke, Spencer, and Ribot are among the more modern writers who recognize the psychological primacy of the instincts.
4 But the same is also true of hunger. I once had a patient whom I had freed pretty well from her symptoms. One day she suddenly turned up with what looked like a complete relapse into her earlier neurosis. I was unable to explain it at first, until I discovered that she was so engrossed in a lively fantasy that she had forgotten to eat lunch. A glass of milk and a slice of bread successfully removed the "hunger afflux."
5 Freud ("Essays on the Theory of Sexuality," p. 163) says: "I must first explain . . . that all my experience shows that these psychoneuroses are based on sexual in-

has become the keystone of the psychoanalytical theory of neurosis and the dogma of the Viennese school. Later, however, Freud was forced to ponder whether libido might not in the end coincide with *interest* in general. (Here I would remark that it was a case of paranoid schizophrenia that gave rise to these considerations.) The operative passage, which I set down word for word, runs:

A third consideration which arises from the views that have been developed in these pages is as follows. Are we to suppose that a general detachment of the libido from the external world would be an effective enough agent to account for the "end of the world"? Or would not the ego-cathexes which still remained in existence have been sufficient to maintain *rapport* with the external world? To meet this difficulty we should either have to assume that what we call libidinal cathexis (that is, interest emanating from erotic sources) coincides with interest in general, or we should have to consider the possibility that a very widespread disturbance in the distribution of the libido may bring about a corresponding disturbance in the ego-cathexes. But these are problems which we are still quite helpless and incompetent to solve. It would be otherwise if we could start out from some well-grounded theory of instincts; but in fact we have nothing of the kind at our disposal. We regard instinct as being the concept on the frontier-line between the somatic and the mental, and see in it the psychical representative of organic forces. Further, we accept the popular distinction between ego-instincts and a sexual instinct; for such a distinction seems to agree with the biological conception that the individual has a double orientation, aiming on the one hand at self-preservation and on the other at the preservation of the species. But beyond this are only hypotheses which we have taken up—and are quite ready to drop again—in order to help us to find our bearings in the chaos of the obscurer processes of the mind. What we expect from the psycho-analytic investigations of pathological mental processes is precisely that they shall drive us to some conclusions on questions connected with the theory of instincts. These investigations, however, are in their infancy and are only

---

stinctual forces. By this I do not merely mean that the energy of the sexual instinct makes a contribution to the forces that maintain the pathological manifestations (the symptoms). I mean expressly to assert that that contribution is the most important and only constant source of energy of the neurosis and that in consequence the sexual life of the persons in question is expressed—whether exclusively or principally or only partly—in these symptoms."

being carried out by isolated workers, so that the hopes we place in them must still remain unfulfilled.[6]

191   Nevertheless, Freud finally decides that the paranoidal alteration is sufficiently explained by the recession of sexual libido. He says:

It therefore appears to me far more probable that the paranoic's altered relation to the world is to be explained entirely or in the main by the loss of his libidinal interest.[7]

192   In this passage Freud broaches the question of whether the well-known loss of reality in paranoia and schizophrenia,[8] to which I have drawn attention in my *Psychology of Dementia Praecox*,[9] is to be traced back solely to the recession of the "libidinal condition," or whether this condition ordinarily coincides with "objective interest." It can hardly be supposed that the normal "fonction du réel," to use Janet's term,[10] is maintained only through affluxes of libido or erotic interest. The fact is that in very many cases reality disappears entirely, so that the patient shows no trace of psychological adaptation. (In these states, reality has been buried under the contents of the unconscious.) One is compelled to admit that not only the erotic interest, but all interest whatsoever, has completely disappeared except for a few feeble flickers, and with it the man's whole relation to reality. If the libido were really nothing but sexuality, what would happen in the case of eunuchs? In their case it is precisely the "libidinal" interest that has been cut off, but they do not necessarily react with schizophrenia. The term "afflux of libido" connotes something that is highly questionable. Many apparently sexual contents and processes are mere metaphors and analogies, as for instance "fire" for passion, "heat" for anger, "marriage" for a bond or union, etc. Presumably no one imagines that all plumbers who connect up male and female pipe-joints, or all electricians who work with

6 "Notes on a Case of Paranoia," pp. 73ff.
7 Ibid., p. 75.
8 Schreber's case, which Freud is here discussing, is not a pure paranoia. See Schreber, *Memoirs of My Nervous Illness*.
9 Pp. 30ff. Also see "The Content of the Psychoses."
10 Cf. "The Psychology of Dementia Praecox," pars. 19, 195.

male and female outlets, are blessed with particularly potent "affluxes of libido"?

193 Earlier, in *The Psychology of Dementia Praecox,* I made use of the term "psychic energy," because what is lacking in this disease is evidently more than erotic interest as such. If one tried to explain the loss of relationship, the schizophrenic dissociation between man and world, purely by the recession of eroticism, the inevitable result would be to inflate the idea of sexuality in a typically Freudian manner. One would then be forced to say that every relationship to the world was in essence a sexual relationship, and the idea of sexuality would become so nebulous that the very word "sexuality" would be deprived of all meaning. The fashionable term "psychosexuality" is a clear symptom of this conceptual inflation. But in schizophrenia far more is lacking to reality than could ever be laid at the door of sexuality in the strict sense of the word. The "fonction du réel" is absent to such a degree as to include the loss of certain instinctual forces which cannot possibly be supposed to have a sexual character, for no one in his senses would maintain that reality is nothing but a function of sex! And even if it were, the introversion of libido in the neuroses would necessarily be followed by a loss of reality comparable with that which occurs in schizophrenia. But that is far from being the case. As Freud himself has pointed out, introversion and regression of sexual libido leads, at the worst, to neurosis, but not to schizophrenia.

194 The attitude of reserve which I adopted towards the sexual theory in the preface to *The Psychology of Dementia Praecox,* despite the fact that I recognized the psychological mechanisms pointed out by Freud, was dictated by the general position of the libido theory at that time. The theory as it then stood did not permit me to explain functional disturbances which affect the sphere of other instincts just as much as that of sex, solely in the light of a one-sided sexual theory. An interpretation in terms of energy seemed to me better suited to the facts than the doctrine set forth in Freud's *Essays on the Theory of Sexuality.* It allowed me to identify "psychic energy" with "libido." The latter term denotes a desire or impulse which is unchecked by any kind of authority, moral or otherwise. Libido is appetite in its natural state. From the genetic point of view it is bodily needs like hunger, thirst, sleep, and sex, and emo-

tional states or affects, which constitute the essence of libido. All these factors have their differentiations and subtle ramifications in the highly complicated human psyche. There can be no doubt that even the highest differentiations were developed from simpler forms. Thus, many complex functions, which today must be denied all trace of sexuality, were originally derived from the reproductive instinct. As we know, an important change occurred in the principles of propagation during the ascent through the animal kingdom: the vast numbers of gametes which chance fertilization made necessary were progressively reduced in favour of assured fertilization and effective protection of the young. The decreased production of ova and spermatozoa set free considerable quantities of energy which soon sought and found new outlets. Thus we find the first stirrings of the artistic impulse in animals, but subservient to the reproductive instinct and limited to the breeding season. The original sexual character of these biological phenomena gradually disappears as they become organically fixed and achieve functional independence. Although there can be no doubt that music originally belonged to the reproductive sphere, it would be an unjustified and fantastic generalization to put music in the same category as sex. Such a view would be tantamount to treating of Cologne Cathedral in a text-book of mineralogy, on the ground that it consisted very largely of stones.

195   Consequently, to speak of libido as the urge to propagation is to remain within the confines of a view which distinguishes libido from hunger in the same way that the instinct for the preservation of the species is distinguished from the instinct for self-preservation. In nature, of course, this artificial distinction does not exist. There we see only a continuous life-urge, a will to live which seeks to ensure the continuance of the whole species through the preservation of the individual. Thus far our conception of libido coincides with Schopenhauer's Will, inasmuch as a movement perceived from outside can only be grasped as the manifestation of an inner will or desire. This throwing of psychological perceptions into material reality is known in philosophy as "introjection." [11] Through introjection one's world picture becomes subjectivized, and it is to this same

11 Ferenczi's use of the term "introjection" denotes the exact opposite: taking the external world into oneself. Cf. his "Introjection and Transference," p. 47.

process that the physical concept of force owes its existence. As Galileo aptly remarked, its origin is to be sought in the subjective perception of our own muscular power. Similarly, the concept of libido as desire or appetite is an *interpretation* of the process of psychic energy, which we experience precisely in the form of an appetite. We know as little about what underlies it as we know about what the psyche is *per se*.

196   Having once made the bold conjecture that the libido which was originally employed in the production of ova and spermatozoa is now firmly organized in the function of nest-building, for instance, and can no longer be employed otherwise, we are compelled to regard every striving and every desire, including hunger and instinct however understood, as equally a phenomenon of energy.

197   This view leads to a conception of libido which expands into a conception of *intentionality* in general. As the above quotation from Freud shows, we know far too little about the nature of human instincts and their psychic dynamism to risk giving priority to any one instinct. We would be better advised, therefore, when speaking of libido, to understand it as an energy-value which is able to communicate itself to any field of activity whatsoever, be it power, hunger, hatred, sexuality, or religion, without ever being itself a specific instinct. As Schopenhauer says: "The Will as a thing-in-itself is quite different from its phenomenal manifestation, and entirely free from all forms of phenomenality, which it assumes only when it becomes manifest, and which therefore affect its objectivity only, and are foreign to the Will itself." [12]

198   Numerous mythological and philosophical attempts have been made to formulate and visualize the creative force which man knows only by subjective experience. To give but a few examples, I would remind the reader of the cosmogonic significance of Eros in Hesiod,[13] and also of the Orphic figure of Phanes (pl. XII), The Shining One, the First-Created, the "Father of Eros." Orphically, too, he has the significance of Priapus; he is bisexual and equated with the Theban Dionysus Lysius.[14] The Orphic significance of Phanes is akin to that of the Indian Kama, the god of love, who is likewise a cosmogonic

12 *The World as Will and Idea*, trans. by Haldane and Kemp, I, p. 145, modified.
13 *Theogony*, 120.   14 Cf. Roscher, *Lexikon*, III, 11, 2248ff.

principle. To the Neoplatonist Plotinus, the world-soul is the energy of the intellect.[15] He compares the One, the primordial creative principle, with light, the intellect with the sun (♂), and the world-soul with the moon (♀). Or again, he compares the One with the Father and the intellect with the Son.[16] The One, designated as Uranos, is transcendent; the Son (Kronos) has dominion over the visible world; and the world-soul (Zeus) is subordinate to him. The One, or the *ousia* of existence in totality, is described by Plotinus as hypostatic, and so are the three forms of emanation; thus we have μία οὐσία ἐν τρισὶν ὑποστάσεσιν (one being in three hypostases). As Drews has observed, this is also the formula for the Christian Trinity as laid down at the councils of Nicaea and of Constantinople.[17] We might add that certain early Christian sects gave a maternal significance to the Holy Ghost (world-soul or moon). According to Plotinus, the world-soul has a tendency towards separation and divisibility, the *sine qua non* of all change, creation, and reproduction. It is an "unending All of life" and wholly energy; a living organism of ideas which only become effective and real in it.[18] The intellect is its progenitor and father, and what the intellect conceives the world-soul brings to birth in reality.[19] "What lies enclosed in the intellect comes to birth in the world-soul as Logos, fills it with meaning and makes it drunken as if with nectar."[20] Nectar, like soma, is the drink of fertility and immortality. The soul is fructified by the intellect; as the "oversoul" it is called the heavenly Aphrodite, as the "undersoul" the earthly Aphrodite. It knows "the pangs of birth."[21] It is not without reason that the dove of Aphrodite is the symbol of the Holy Ghost.

199   The energic standpoint has the effect of freeing psychic energy from the bonds of a too narrow definition. Experience shows that instinctual processes of whatever kind are often intensified to an extraordinary degree by an afflux of energy, no matter where it comes from. This is true not only of sexuality, but of hunger and thirst too. One instinct can temporarily be depotentiated in favour of another instinct, and this is true of psychic activities in general. To assume that it is always and

[15] Drews, *Plotin*, p. 127.   [16] Ibid., p. 132.   [17] Ibid., p. 135.
[18] Plotinus, *Enneads*, II, 5, 3.   [19] Ibid., IV, 8, 3.   [20] Ibid., III, 5, 9.
[21] Drews, p. 141.

only sexuality which is subject to these depotentiations would be a sort of psychic equivalent of the phlogiston theory in physics and chemistry. Freud himself was somewhat sceptical about the existing theories of instinct, and rightly so. Instinct is a very mysterious manifestation of life, partly psychic and partly physiological by nature. It is one of the most conservative functions in the psyche and is extremely difficult, if not impossible, to change. Pathological maladjustments, such as the neuroses, are therefore more easily explained by the patient's attitude to instinct than by a sudden change in the latter. But the patient's attitude is a complicated psychological problem, which it would certainly not be if his attitude depended on instinct. The motive forces at the back of neurosis come from all sorts of congenital characteristics and environmental influences, which together build up an attitude that makes it impossible for him to lead a life in which the instincts are satisfied. Thus the neurotic perversion of instinct in a young person is intimately bound up with a similar disposition in the parents, and the disturbance in the sexual sphere is a secondary and not a primary phenomenon. Hence there can be no sexual theory of neurosis, though there may very well be a psychological one.

200   This brings us back to our hypothesis that it is not the sexual instinct, but a kind of neutral energy, which is responsible for the formation of such symbols as light, fire, sun, and the like. The loss of the reality function in schizophrenia does not produce a heightening of sexuality: it produces a world of fantasy with marked archaic features.[22] This is not to deny that, particularly at the beginning of the illness, violent sexual disturbances may sometimes occur, though they occur just as often in any intensive experience, such as panic, rage, religious mania, etc. The fact that an archaic world of fantasy takes the place of reality in schizophrenia proves nothing about the nature of the reality function as such; it only demonstrates the well-known biological fact that whenever a more recent system suffers deterioration it is likely to be replaced by a more primitive and therefore obsolete one. To use Freud's simile, one begins firing with bows and arrows instead of with guns. A loss of the latest

22 Cf. Spielrein, "Über den psychologischen Inhalt eines Falles von Schizophrenie," p. 329.

acquisitions of the reality function (or adaptation) must of necessity be replaced, if at all, by an earlier mode of adaptation. We find this principle in the theory of neurosis which holds that any failure of adaptation is compensated by an older one, that is, by a regressive reactivation of the parental imagos. In neurosis the substitute product is a fantasy of individual origin and scope with hardly a trace of those archaic features which are characteristic of the fantasies of schizophrenics. Again, in neurosis there is never an actual loss of reality, only a falsification of it. In schizophrenia, on the other hand, reality has all but disappeared. I must thank my erstwhile pupil J. Honegger, whose work [23] was unfortunately cut short by an early death, for a simple illustration of this: A paranoid patient of good intelligence, who knew very well that the earth was a sphere and rotated round the sun, superseded all our modern views of astronomy by an elaborate system of his own devising, where the earth was a flat disc over which the sun travelled. Spielrein, too, gives some interesting examples of archaic definitions which, in the course of the illness, begin superimposing themselves on the meanings of words. Thus, one of her women patients declared that the mythological analogue of alcohol was an "emission of seed," i.e., soma.[24] She also hit upon a symbolism of cooking which parallels the alchemical vision of Zosimos, who saw, in the "bowl" of the altar, people being transformed in boiling water.[25] The patient substituted earth,[26] and also water,[27] for "mother." (Cf. pls. xiva, xxvi.)

201   What I said above about a disturbed reality function being replaced by an archaic substitute is supported by a remark of Spielrein's: "I often had the illusion that the patients might simply be victims of a deep-rooted folk superstition." [28] As a matter of fact, patients do set up, in place of reality, fantasies very like certain archaic ideas which once had a reality function. But, as the vision of Zosimos shows, the old superstitions were

23 It was never published. [He committed suicide in 1911.—EDITORS.]
24 Spielrein, pp. 338, 353, 387. See par. 246, n. 41, below, for soma as "seminal fluid."
25 Berthelot, Collection, III, I, 2ff. (Textes, pp. 107–12; Traductions, pp. 117–21). [Cf. "The Visions of Zosimos," par. 86.—EDITORS.]
26 Spielrein, p. 345.   27 Ibid., p. 338.
28 Ibid., p. 397.

symbols [29] that sought to give adequate expression to the unknown in the world (and in the psyche). The "conception" (*Auffassung*) gives us a "handle" (*Griff*) by which to "grasp hold" of things (*fassen, begreifen*), and the resultant "concept" (*Begriff*) enables us to take possession of them. Functionally, the concept corresponds to the *magically powerful name* which gets a grip on the object. This not only renders the object harmless, but incorporates it into the psychic system, thus increasing the meaning and power of the human mind. (Compare the primitive respect for name-giving in the Alvissmal of the Elder Edda.) Spielrein evidently thinks symbols have a similar significance when she says:

> Thus a symbol seems to me to owe its origin to the striving of a complex for dissolution in the common totality of thought. . . . The complex is thus robbed of its personal quality. . . . This tendency towards dissolution or transformation of every individual complex is the mainspring of poetry, painting, and every form of art.[30]

202   If, for "complex," we substitute the idea of "energy value," i.e., the total affectivity of the complex, it is clear that Spielrein's views fall into line with my own.

203   It seems as if this process of analogy-making had gradually altered and added to the common stock of ideas and names, with the result that man's picture of the world was considerably broadened. Specially colourful or intense contents (the "feeling-toned" complexes) were reflected in countless analogies, and gave rise to synonyms whose objects were thus drawn into the magic circle of the psyche. In this way there came into being those intimate relationships by analogy which Lévy-Bruhl fittingly describes as "participation mystique." It is evident that this tendency to invent analogies deriving from feeling-toned contents has been of enormous significance for the development of the human mind. We are in thorough agreement with Steinthal when he says that a positively overwhelming importance attaches to the little word "like" in the history of human thought. One can easily imagine that the canalization of libido into analogy-making was responsible for some of the most important discoveries ever made by primitive man.

[29] Here I might also mention those American Indians who believe that the first human beings arose from the union of a sword-hilt and a shuttle.
[30] Spielrein, p. 399.

III

THE TRANSFORMATION OF LIBIDO

204   In what follows I should like to give some concrete examples of this canalization of libido. I once had to treat a woman patient who suffered from catatonic depressions. As there was a mild degree of psychosis, I was not surprised by the numerous hysterical symptoms she exhibited. At the beginning of the treatment, while she was telling me of a very painful experience, she fell into an hysterical dream-state in which she showed all the signs of sexual excitement. (It was abundantly evident that during this state she was completely unaware of my presence.) The excitement culminated in an act of masturbation. This act was accompanied by a singular gesture: she kept on making a violent rotary movement with the forefinger of the left hand against the left temple, as though she were boring a hole there. Afterwards there was complete amnesia for what had happened, and nothing could be elicited about the singular gesture with the hand. Although this performance could easily be recognized as an act of thumb-sucking, or of nose- or ear-picking, transferred to the temple, and hence as an analogy of the masturbatory act, it nevertheless struck me as somehow significant, though at first I did not know why. Weeks later I had an opportunity of speaking with the patient's mother, and she told me what a very exceptional child her daughter had been. When only two years old she would sit for hours with her back to an open cupboard door, rhythmically banging it shut with her head [1] and driving the whole household distracted. A little later, instead of playing like the other children, she began boring holes in the plaster of the wall with her finger. She did this with little turning and scraping movements, which she would

[1] I have seen this pendulum movement of the head in a catatonic patient, gradually building itself up from what Freud has termed the "upward displacement" of coitus movements.

142

keep up for hours on end. To her parents she was a complete mystery. From about her fourth year she began to masturbate. So it is clear that in the earlier infantile occupation we have the preliminary stage of the later activity.

205   The boring with the finger, then, can be traced back to a very early stage of childhood which antedates the period of masturbation. That period is very obscure psychologically, because there were no individual memories. Such a peculiar mode of behaviour is highly remarkable in a child of that age. We know from her subsequent history that her development—which was, as always, bound up with parallel external events—led to a mental illness which is well known for the individuality and originality of its products, namely schizophrenia. The peculiarity of this disease lies in the startling emergence of an archaic psychology. That accounts for the innumerable points of contact with mythological material, and what we take to be original and individual creations are mostly products which can only be compared with those of antiquity. We have to apply this criterion to probably all the products of this remarkable illness, including perhaps this odd symptom of boring. As we have seen, it dates from a very early period, and it was revived from the distant past only when the patient, after several years of marriage, fell back into her early masturbatory habits following the death of her child, with whom she had identified herself through an over-indulgent love. When the child died, the infantile symptoms again inflicted themselves on the still healthy mother in the form of fits of masturbation, accompanied by this same act of boring. The primary boring, as we have said, appeared some time before the infantile masturbation. This fact is important inasmuch as the boring is seen to be distinct from a similar and later habit which supervened after she began masturbating.

206   We know that in infants the libido first manifests itself exclusively in the nutritional zone, where, in the act of sucking, food is taken in with a rhythmic movement. At the same time there develops in the motor sphere in general a pleasurable rhythmic movement of the arms and legs (kicking, etc.). With the growth of the individual and development of his organs the libido creates for itself new avenues of activity. The primary model of rhythmic movement, producing pleasure and satisfac-

tion, is transferred to the zone of other functions, with sexuality as its ultimate goal. This is not to say that the rhythmic activity derives from the act of nutrition. A considerable part of the energy supplied by nutrition for growth has to convert itself into sexual libido and other forms of activity. This transition does not take place suddenly at the time of puberty, as is commonly supposed, but only very gradually during the course of childhood. In this transitional period there are, so far as I am able to judge, two distinct phases: the phase of sucking, and the phase of rhythmic activity in general. Sucking still belongs to the sphere of the nutritive function, but outgrows it by ceasing to be a function of nutrition and becoming an analogous rhythmic activity without intake of nourishment. At this point the hand comes in as an auxiliary organ. It appears even more clearly as an auxiliary organ in the phase of rhythmic activity, which then leaves the oral zone and turns to other regions. Numerous possibilities now present themselves. As a rule, it is the other body openings that become the main object of interest; then the skin, or special parts of it; and finally rhythmic movements of all kinds. These, expressed in the form of rubbing, boring, picking, and so forth, follow a certain rhythm. It is clear that this activity, once it reaches the sexual zone, may provide occasion for the first attempts at masturbation. In the course of its migrations the libido carries traces of the nutritional phase into its new field of operations, which accounts for the many intimate connections between the nutritive and the sexual function. Should this more developed activity meet with an obstacle that forces it to regress, the regression will be to an earlier stage of development. The phase of rhythmic activity generally coincides with the development of mind and speech. I therefore propose to call the period from birth up to the time of the first clear manifestations of sexuality the "presexual stage." As a rule it falls between the first and the fourth year, and is comparable to the chrysalis stage in butterflies. It is characterized by a varying mixture of elements from the nutritional and sexual phases. Certain regressions go right back to the presexual stage: so far as one can judge from experience, this seems to be the rule with regressions in schizophrenia and epilepsy. I will give two examples. One is the case of a young girl who developed a catatonic state during her engagement.

144

The first time she saw me she suddenly came up to me and gave me a kiss, saying, "Papa, give me something to eat!" The other case concerns a young servant-girl who complained that people were pursuing her with electricity, and that this caused a queer feeling in her genitals, "as if it ate and drank down there."

207   These things show that the earlier phases of libido are capable of regressive reactivation. It is a road that is easily travelled, and has often been travelled in the past. If this assumption is correct, it is very likely that in earlier stages of human development this way of transformation was not just a pathological symptom, but a frequent and normal occurrence. It would therefore be interesting to see whether it has left any historical traces.

208   We are indebted to Abraham [2] for drawing attention to the ethnological connection between boring and fire-making. The latter subject has been elaborated in the work of Adalbert Kuhn.[3] From these investigations we learn that the fire-bringer Prometheus may possibly be brother to the Indian *pramantha*, the masculine fire-stick. The Indian fire-bringer was called Matarisvan, and the activity of fire-making is always referred to in the sacred texts by means of the verb *manthāmi*,[4] 'to shake, to rub, to bring forth by rubbing.' Kuhn relates this verb to Gr. μανθάνω, 'to learn,' and has also explained the conceptual relationship between them.[5] The *tertium comparationis* may lie in the rhythm, the movement to and fro in the mind. According to Kuhn, the root *manth-* or *math-* leads, via μανθάνω (μάθημα, μάθησις) and προ-μηθέομαι, to Προμηθεύς, the well-known Greek fire-robber. He points out that just as the Thuric Zeus bore the especially interesting cognomen Προ-μανθεύς, so Προ-μηθεύς might be not an original Indo-European word related to the Skr. *pramantha*, but only a cognomen. This view is supported by a gloss of Hesychius, explaining the name Ἰθάς as ὁ τῶν Τιτάνων κῆρυξ Προμηθεύς (Prometheus, the herald of the titans). Another gloss of Hesychius explains ἰθαίνομαι (ἰαίνω, 'to heat, melt') as θερμαίνομαι,

---

2 *Dreams and Myths.*
3 *Mythologische Studien*, I: *Die Herabkunft des Feuers und des Göttertranks.* (Cf. pl. xv.) A résumé of the contents is to be found in Steinthal, "Die ursprüngliche Form der Sage von Prometheus," and in Abraham, *Dreams and Myths.*
4 Also *mathnāmi* and *māthāyati*. The root is *manth* or *math.*
5 Kuhn, in *Zeitschrift für vergleichende Sprachforschung*, II, p. 395 and IV, p. 124.

'to grow hot,' so that 'Ιθάς acquires the meaning 'Flaming One,' similar to Αἴθων or Φλεγύας.[6] The relation of Prometheus to *pramantha* is therefore questionable. On the other hand, Προμηθεύς is highly significant as a cognomen for 'Ιθάς, since the "Flaming One" is the "Forethinker." [7] (*Pramati*, 'precaution,' is also an attribute of Agni, the god of fire, although *pramati* is of different derivation.) Prometheus, however, belongs to the line of Phlegians whom Kuhn puts into incontestable relationship with the Indian priestly family of Bhrigu.[8] The Bhrigu, like Matarisvan ("he who swells in the mother"), were also fire-bringers. Kuhn cites a passage to show that the Bhrigu arose from the fire like Agni. ("Bhrigu arose in the flame; Bhrigu roasted, but did not burn.") This idea leads to a root cognate with Bhrigu: Skr. *bhrāy*, 'to shine,' Lat. *fulgeo*, Gr. φλέγω (Skr. *bhargas*, 'splendour,' Lat. *fulgur*). Bhrigu therefore appears as the "Shining One." Φλεγύας denotes a certain species of eagle distinguished for its burnished yellow colour. The connection with φλέγειν, 'to burn,' is obvious. Hence the Phlegians were fiery eagles.[9] Prometheus, too, was a Phlegian. The line from *pramantha* to Prometheus does not go via the word, but more probably through the idea or image, so that Prometheus may in the end have the same meaning as *pramantha*.[10] Only, it would

[6] K. Bapp, in Roscher, *Lexikon*, III, 3034.

[7] ["The one who thinks ahead" is the meaning of Prometheus now accepted as philologically correct.—EDITORS.] An interesting parallel is the Balinese fire-god, who has his seat in man's brain and is always represented as dancing on a fiery wheel (a sun-symbol). He is regarded as the highest and most popular god of the Balinese. (Pl. XIIIa.)

[8] *Bhrigu* = φλέγυ, an accepted phonetic equivalence. See Roscher, III, 3034, 54.

[9] For the eagle as a fire-totem among the Indians, see Roscher, III, 3034, 60.

[10] According to Kuhn the root *manth* becomes in German *mangeln* (Eng. 'to mangle'). *Manthara* is the stick used for churning butter. (Cf. pl. xv.) When the gods produced the *amrita* (drink of immortality: ambrosia) by churning the ocean round, they used Mt. Mandara as a churning-stick (Kuhn, *Mythologische Studien*, I, pp. 16ff.). Steinthal calls attention to Lat. *mentula*, a poetic expression for the male organ, presumably derived from *ment* or *manth*. I would add that *mentula* can be taken as a diminutive of *menta* or *mentha* (μίνθα), 'mint.' In antiquity mint was called "Aphrodite's crown" (Dioscorides, II, 154). Apuleius calls it "mentha venerea," because it was held to be an aphrodisiac. Hippocrates ("On Diet," II, 54) gives it the opposite meaning: "Si quis eam saepe comedat, eius genitale semen ita colliquescit, ut effluat, et arrigere prohibet et corpus imbecillum reddit" (If one eats of it often, the genital seed becomes so liquid that it flows out; it prevents erection and renders the body weak), and accord-

be an *archetypal* parallel and not a case of linguistic transmission.

209   For some time it was believed that Prometheus took over the meaning "Forethinker" (as the figure of Epimetheus, the "After-thinker," testifies) only quite late, and that the word was originally connected with *pramantha, manthāmi, mathāyati* and had, etymologically, nothing to do with προμηθέομαι, μάθημα, μανθάνω. Conversely, *pramati,* 'precaution,' which is associated with Agni, has no connection with *manthāmi.* Lately, however, there has been a tendency to derive Prometheus from μανθάνω after all.[11] The only thing that can be established with any certainty in this complicated situation is that we find thinking, precaution, or foresight somehow connected with fire-boring, without there being any demonstrable etymological connections between the words used for them. In considering the etymology, therefore, we have to take into account not only the migration of the root-words, but the autochthonous revival of certain primordial images.

210   The *pramantha,* or instrument of the *manthana* (fire-sacrifice), is conceived under a purely sexual aspect in India, the fire-stick being the phallus or man, and the bored wood underneath the vulva or woman. The fire that results from the boring is the child, the divine son Agni. (Pl. XIII*b*.) The two pieces of wood are ritually known as *pururavas* and *urvasi,* and, when personified, are thought of as man and woman. The fire is born [12] from the genitals of the woman. Weber gives the following account of the fire-producing ceremony:

---

ing to Dioscorides (III, 34) mint is a contraceptive (cf. Aigremont, *Volkserotik,* I, p. 127). But the ancients also said: "Menta autem appellata, quod suo odore mentem feriat . . . mentae ipsius odor animum excitat" (It is called *menta* because it strikes the mind [*mentem*] with its smell . . . the smell of the mint excites the mind). This leads us to the root *ment,* as in *mens* (mind), so that the development of the parallel to *pramantha* would be complete. One might also add that a strong chin was called *mento* or *mentum.* As we know, the priapic figure of Punchinello was given a powerfully developed chin, and the pointed beards (and ears) of the satyrs and other priapic demons have a similar meaning, just as in general all the protruding parts of the body can be given a masculine, and all its concavities a feminine, significance.   11 Cf. Kerényi, *Prometheus,* p. 36.

12 "What is named the gulya (pudendum) means the yoni (the birthplace) of the god; the fire that is born there is called beneficent": *Katyayanas Karmapradipa,* I, 7 (Kuhn, *Mythol. Studien,* I, p. 67). Kuhn's suggestion of an etymological con-

A sacrificial fire is kindled by rubbing two fire-sticks together. One of the fire-sticks is taken up with the words: "Thou art the birth-place of fire," and two blades of grass are placed upon it: "Ye are the two testicles." The priest then places on them the *adhararani* (the underlying piece of wood), saying: "Thou art Urvasi," and anoints the *uttararani* (uppermost piece) with butter: "Thou art the power" (semen). This is then placed on the *adhararani,* with the words: "Thou art Pururavas." Rubbing them together three times the priest says: "I rub thee with the Gayatrimetrum: I rub thee with the Trishtubhmetrum: I rub thee with the Jagati-metrum." [13]

211   The sexual symbolism is unmistakable. We find the same idea and symbolism in a hymn of the Rig-Veda:

Here is the gear for friction, here tinder is made ready for the spark.
Bring the mistress of the people: [14] we will rub Agni in ancient fashion forth.
In the two fire-sticks lies Jatavedas, safe as the seed in pregnant women;
Daily let Agni be praised by men who watch and worship with oblations.
Let this (staff) enter into her as she lies there outstretched, O you skilled ones;
Straightway she conceives, has given birth to the fructifier:
With his red pillar lighting his path, the son of Ila is born from the precious wood.[15]

212   It is to be noted that in this hymn the *pramantha* is also Agni, the begotten son: the phallus is the son, or the son is the phallus. In colloquial German today there are distant echoes of

nection between G. *bohren,* 'to bore,' and *geboren,* 'born,' is very unlikely. According to him, G. *boron (bohren)* is primarily related to Lat. *forare* and Gr. φαράω, 'to plough.' He conjectures an Indo-European root **bher,* meaning 'to bear,' Skr. *bhar-,* Gr. φερ-, Lat. *fer-,* whence OHG, *beran,* 'to bear'; Lat. *fero, fertilis,* and *fordus,* 'pregnant'; Gr. φορός, 'pregnant.' Walde, in *Lateinisches Wörterbuch* (s.v. *ferio*), however, definitely relates *forare* to the root *bher.* Cf. the plough symbolism, below, par. 214, n. 22, and fig. 15.

13 Weber, *Indische Studien,* I, p. 197, cited in Kuhn, p. 71.

14 Or of mankind in general. *Vispatni* is the feminine fire-stick; *vispati,* an attribute of Agni, the masculine.

15 Rig-Veda, III, 29, 1–3, trans. based on Griffith, II, p. 25. For wood as a mother-symbol, see Freud, *The Interpretation of Dreams,* p. 355. "The son of Ila": Ila was the daughter of Manu, the Indian Noah, who with the help of his fish survived the deluge and then begat a new race of human beings with his daughter.

this primitive symbolism: a lout or urchin is known as a *Bengel,* 'club, cudgel,' and in the Hessian dialect as a *Stift,* 'peg,' or *Bolzen,* 'bolt.' [16] The plant *Artemisia abrotanum,* called in German *Stabwurz,* 'stick-root,' is known in English as "boy's-love." The vulgar designation of the penis as "boy" was remarked even by the brothers Grimm. Ceremonial fire-making lingered on in Europe as a superstitious custom until well into the nineteenth century. Kuhn mentions one such case which occurred in Germany in 1828. This magical rite, practised with due ceremony, was called the "Nodfyr" (need-fire),[17] and the charm was used mainly against cattle epidemics. Kuhn quotes from the Chronicles of Lanercost, in the year 1268, a particularly interesting case of "Nodfyr" which plainly reveals the sexual symbolism of the ceremonies:

> In order to safeguard the integrity of divine faith, let the reader remember that when the herds of cattle in Laodonia were ravaged this year by the pest called lung-sickness, certain cattle-breeders, monastery folk by habit or dress but not by disposition, taught the ignorant rustics to make fire by rubbing pieces of wood together, and to set up an image of Priapus, and in this wise to help their animals. After a Cistercian lay brother had done this near Fenton in front of the courtyard, he dipped the testicles of a dog in holy water and sprinkled the animals with it. . . .[18]

213   These examples, coming from different periods of history and from different peoples, prove the existence of a widespread tendency to equate fire-making with sexuality. The ceremonial or magical repetition of this age-old discovery shows how persistently the human mind clings to the old forms, and how deep-rooted is the memory of fire-boring. One might be inclined to

16 Cf. Hirt, *Etymologie,* p. 348.

17 The capitulary of Charlemagne in 942 expressly forbids "illos sacrilegos ignes quos niedfyr vocant" (those sacrilegious fires which are called Niedfyr). Cf. Grimm, *Teutonic Mythology,* II, p. 604, where similar fire ceremonies are described.

18 *Mythologische Studien,* I, p. 43. (Pro fidei divinae integritate servanda recolat lector, quod cum hoc anno in Laodonia pestis grassaretur in pecudes armenti, quam vocant usitate Lungessouth, quidam bestiales, habitu claustrales non animo, docebant idiotas patriae ignem confrictione de lignis educere et simulacrum Priapi statuere, et per haec bestiis succurrere. Quod cum unus laicus Cisterciensis apud Fentone fecisset ante atrium aulae, ac intinctis testiculis canis in aquam benedictam super animalia sparsisset.)

see the sexual symbolism of fire-making simply as a gratuitous addition to priestly lore. That may be true of certain ritualistic elaborations of the fire mystery, but the question remains whether fire-making originally had a deeper connection with sex. We know that similar rites are practised among primitives from studies of the Wachandi, of Australia,[19] who in spring perform the following piece of fertility-magic: They dig a hole in the ground, so shaping it and setting it about with bushes that it looks like a woman's genitals. Then they dance round this hole all night, holding their spears in front of them in imitation of an erect penis. As they dance round, they thrust their spears into the hole, shouting: "Pulli nira, pulli nira, wataka!" (Not a pit, not a pit, but a c——!). Obscene dances of this kind are found among other tribes as well.[20]

214   In this rite of spring [21] there is enacted a sacramental mating, with the hole in the earth representing the woman, and the

[19] Preuss, "Der Ursprung der Religion und Kunst," p. 358.

[20] Cf. Schultze, *Psychologie der Naturvölker*, pp. 161f.

[21] This primitive play leads to the phallic plough symbolism of higher cultures. Ἀροῦν means 'to plough' and possesses in addition the poetic meaning of 'to impregnate.' The Latin *arare* means simply 'to plough,' but the phrase "fundum alienum arare" is the equivalent of 'plucking cherries in your neighbour's garden.' There is an excellent picture of the phallic plough on a vase in [or once in] the Museo Archeologico in Florence: it portrays a row of six naked ithyphallic men carrying a plough which is represented ithyphallically (fig. 15). (Cf. Dieterich, *Mutter Erde*, pp. 107ff.) The "carrus navalis" (Carnival) of our spring festivals during the Middle Ages was occasionally a plough. (Hahn, *Demeter und Baubo*, p. 40, cited in Dieterich, p. 109.) Prof. Emil Abegg, of Zurich, has drawn my attention to the work of Meringer, "Wörter und Sachen," which demonstrates a far-reaching fusion of libido-symbols with external materials and external activities, and lends the strongest support to the views I have outlined above. Meringer bases his argument on two Indo-European roots, *uen* and *ueneti*. IEur. *uen*, OInd. *vân*, *vána*, = 'wood.' Agni is called *garbhas vanâm*, 'fruit of the womb of the woods.' IEur. *ueneti* = 'he ploughs' (*er ackert*)—piercing the ground and tearing it up with a sharp piece of wood. The verb itself is not verified, because the primitive method of agriculture it denoted—a sort of hoeing—died out at a very early date. When a better method of tillage was discovered, the designation for the primitive ploughed field was transferred to pastureland and meadows; hence Goth. *vinja*, Gr. νομή, OIcel. *vin*, 'pasture, meadow.' Also perhaps the Icel. *Vanen*, gods of agriculture. Also IEur. *uenos*, 'enjoyment of love,' Lat. Venus. From the emotional significance of *uenos* comes OHG. *vinnan*, 'to rage'; also Goth. *vens*, Gr. ἐλπίς, OHG. *wân*, 'expectation, hope'; Skr. *van*, 'to want, desire'; G. *Wonne*, 'ecstasy'; OIcel. *vinr*, 'beloved, friend.' From the connotation *ackern* arose G. *wohnen*, 'to dwell,' OE. *won*, 'dwelling,' a transition found

spear the man. The *hieros gamos* was an essential component of many cults and played an important part in various sects.[22]

215   One can easily imagine that just as the Australian bushmen perform a sort of *hieros gamos* with the earth, so the same or a similar idea could be represented by producing fire from two pieces of wood. The ritual coitus is enacted, not by two people, but by two simulacra, Pururavas and Urvasi, the male and female fire-sticks. (Cf. pl. xiii*b*.)

Fig. 15. The phallic plough
From a Greek vase

216   Of all the components of the psyche, sex is undoubtedly the one with the strongest affective tone. Certain persons are therefore inclined to assume that everything which bears an obvious analogy to sex must of necessity be derived from it, on the

only in the Germanic languages. From *wohnen* comes *gewöhnen*, 'to get accustomed, to be wont'; OIcel. *vanr*, 'accustomed.' From *ackern*, again, comes *sich mühen, plagen*, 'to take trouble or pains'; OIcel. *vinna*, 'to work,' OHG. *winnan*, 'to toil or drudge'; Goth. *vinnan*, Gr. πάσχειν, 'to suffer,' *vunns*, πάθημα, 'suffering.' On the other hand, from *ackern* comes *gewinnen, erlangen*, 'to win, attain,' OHG. *giwinnan;* but also *verletzen*, 'to wound,' Goth. *vunds*. 'Wound' in the original sense, therefore, meant the ground torn up by hoeing. From *verletzen* come *schlagen*, 'to strike,' *besiegen*, 'to conquer'; OHG. *winna*, 'strife'; Old Saxon *winnan*, 'to battle.' (Fig. 16.)

22 The old custom of the "bridal bed" in the field, to make the field fruitful, expresses the analogy in the clearest possible way: as I make this woman fruitful, so I make the earth fruitful. The symbol canalizes the libido into cultivating and fructifying the earth. (Cf. pl. xi*b*.) Cf. Mannhardt, *Wald- und Feldkulte*, I, for exhaustive evidence.

hypothesis that the sexual libido comes up against some sort of barrier which compels it to seek a substitute activity in the form of a ritual analogy. In order to account for the partial conversion and transformation of libido, Freud assumed that the barrier was the *incest-taboo*. Strictly speaking, however, the incest-taboo is a check on the endogamous tendency in man. For an instinct to be forcibly converted into something else, or even partially checked, there must be a correspondingly higher energy on the opposite side. Freud rightly supposed that this

Fig. 16. The twirling-stick
From an Aztec hieroglyph-painting

energy came from *fear,* and in order to explain the fear, he had to resort to the more or less plausible hypothesis of the primal horde, which, like a herd of gorillas, was tyrannized over by a ferocious patriarch. To complete the picture, we would have to add an equally awe-inspiring matron who instils fear into the daughters, just as the primordial father compels the savage respect of the sons. We would then have a patrilineal and a matrilineal source of anxiety to match the primitive conditions. I can well imagine that the more neurotic among the troglodytes "thought" in this manner.

217   Such a derivation of the motive for checking the instincts seems to me somewhat doubtful, to say the least of it, for the simple reason that the tensions inside a primitive group are never greater than those involved in the struggle for existence of the group as a whole. Were it otherwise, the group would speedily perish. What does constitute a serious threat to the primitive group is the endogamous tendency, which has to be checked in order to exorcize the danger. The best means to this end seems to be the widespread custom of cross-cousin-mar-

riage,[23] because it keeps the endogamous and exogamous tendencies balanced. The danger that then threatens the group comes from the very advantages it has gained through checking the endogamous tendency to which the incest-taboo applies. The group acquires an inner stability, opportunities for expansion, and hence greater security. That is to say, the source of fear does not lie inside the group, but in the very real risks which the struggle for existence entails. Fear of enemies and of hunger predominates even over sexuality, which is, as we know, no problem at all for the primitive, as it is far simpler to get a woman than it is to get food. Fear of the consequences of being unadapted is a compelling reason for checking the instincts. Confronted with disaster, one is obliged to ask oneself how it is to be remedied. The libido that is forced into regression by the obstacle always reverts to the possibilities lying dormant in the individual. A dog, finding the door shut, scratches at it until it is opened, and a man unable to find the answer to a problem rubs his nose, pulls his lower lip, scratches his ear, and so on. If he gets impatient, all sorts of other rhythms appear: he starts drumming with his fingers, shuffles his feet about, and it will not be long before certain distinctly sexual analogies manifest themselves, such as masturbation gestures. Koch-Grünberg, writing on South American rock-paintings, tells us how the Indians sit on the rocks and scratch lines on them with sharp stones while waiting for their canoes to be transported round the rapids.[24] In the course of time there have arisen chaotic drawings or scribbles that might perhaps be compared with doodling on blotting-pads. This makes it easier to understand what Maeterlinck tells us in his *Blue Bird:* [25] the two children who are looking for the blue bird in the Land of the Unborn find a boy who *picks his nose.* It is said that one day he will discover a new *fire* when the earth has grown cold. Spielrein's patient [26] associated the act of boring with fire and procreation. She said: "You need iron to bore through the earth. With iron you can make cold people out of stone. With a hot iron you can bore through the mountain. The iron becomes red-hot when it is pushed into a stone."

23 Cf. "The Psychology of the Transference," pars. 433ff.
24 *Südamerikanische Felszeichnungen*, p. 17.
25 Teixeira de Mattos trans., p. 100.   26 P. 371.

218   Now when the libido is forced back by an obstacle, it does not necessarily regress to earlier sexual modes of application, but rather to the rhythmic activities of infancy which serve as a model both for the act of nutrition and for the sexual act itself. The material before us does not seem to preclude the possibility that the invention of fire-making came about in the manner suggested, that is, through the regressive reawakening of rhythm.[27] This hypothesis seems to me psychologically possible, though I would not maintain that this is the only way in which the discovery of fire could have been made. It could just as well have been made from striking flints together. All I am concerned with here is the psychological process, whose symbolisms suggest that fire-making may possibly have been discovered in this way.

219   Even if these rhythmic activities give one the impression of a game, one is nevertheless impressed by the intentness and energy with which this alleged game is conducted. It is well known that such rites (for that is how we must regard them) are performed with great seriousness and an uncommon display of energy, which is in marked contrast to the notorious laziness of primitive man. The so-called game takes on the character of purposeful effort. If certain tribes can dance all night long to a monotonous tune of three notes, then, to our way of thinking, the play-element is entirely lacking: it is more like an exercise with a set purpose. This is in fact the case, for rhythm is a classic device for impressing certain ideas or activities on the mind, and what has to be impressed and firmly organized is the canalization of libido into a new form of activity. Since the rhythmic activity can no longer find an outlet in the act of feeding after the nutritional phase of development is over, it transfers itself not only to the sphere of sexuality in the strict sense, but also to the "decoy mechanisms," such as music and dancing, and finally to the sphere of work. The close connection which work always has with music, singing, dancing, drumming, and all manner of rhythms in primitive societies, indeed its absolute dependence on these things, is very striking. This connection forms the bridge to sexuality, thus giving the primitive an opportunity to sidetrack and evade the task in hand. Because diversions of this kind are a frequent occurrence, and are to be

27 For evidence of this, see Bücher, *Arbeit und Rhythmus*.

found in all spheres of culture, people have been led to believe that there is no differentiated achievement that is not a substitute for some form of sexuality. I regard this as an error, albeit a very understandable one considering the enormous psychological importance of the sexual instinct. I myself once held similar views, at least in so far as I assumed that the various forms of attraction and protection of the young came from the splitting and differentiation of an originally sexual libido, or of the reproductive instinct in its widest sense, and were therefore the preliminary stages of all cultural activities, so far as these are by nature instinctive. One reason for this error was the influence of Freud; the other, and more cogent, reason was the element of rhythm which often attaches to these functions. Only later did I realize that the rhythmic tendency does not come from the nutritional phase at all, as if it had migrated from there to the sexual, but that it is a peculiarity of emotional processes in general. Any kind of excitement, no matter in what phase of life, displays a tendency to rhythmic expression, perseveration, and repetition, as can easily be seen from the repetition, assonance, and alliteration of complex-toned reaction-words in the association experiment.[28] Rhythmic patterns therefore offer no ground for assuming that the function they affect originated in sexuality.

220   The psychological importance of sexuality and the existence of plausible sexual analogies make a deviation into sex extremely easy in cases of regression, so that it naturally seems as if all one's troubles were due to a sexual wish that is unjustly denied fulfilment. This reasoning is typical of the neurotic. Primitives seem to know instinctively the dangers of this deviation: when celebrating the *hieros gamos,* the Wachandi, of Australia, may not look at a woman during the entire ceremony. Among a certain tribe of American Indians, it was the custom for the warriors, before setting out on the warpath, to move in a circle round a beautiful young girl standing naked in the centre. Whoever got an erection was disqualified as unfit for military operations. The deviation into sex is used—not always, but very frequently—as a means of escaping the real problem. One makes oneself and others believe that the problem is purely

28 Eberschweiler, "Untersuchungen über die sprachlichen Komponenten der Assoziation."

sexual, that the trouble started long ago and that its causes lie in the remote past. This provides a heaven-sent way out of the problem of the present by shifting the whole question on to another and less dangerous plane. But the illicit gain is purchased at the expense of adaptation, and one gets a neurosis into the bargain.

221   In an earlier paragraph we traced the checking of the instincts back to fear of the very real dangers of existence in this world. But external reality is not the only source of this instinct-inhibiting fear, for primitive man is often very much more afraid of an "inner" reality—the world of dreams, ancestral spirits, demons, gods, magicians, and witches. Although we, with our rationalism, think we can block this source of fear by pointing to its unreality, it nevertheless remains one of those psychic realities whose irrational nature cannot be exorcized by rational argument. You can free the primitive of certain superstitions, but you cannot talk him out of his alcoholism, his moral depravity, and general hopelessness. There is a psychic reality which is just as pitiless and just as inexorable as the outer world, and just as useful and helpful, provided one knows how to circumvent its dangers and discover its hidden treasures. "Magic is the science of the jungle," a famous explorer once said. Civilized man contemptuously looks down on primitive superstitions, which is about as sensible as turning up one's nose at the pikes and halberds, the fortresses and tall-spired cathedrals of the Middle Ages. Primitive methods are just as effective under primitive conditions as machine-guns or the radio are under modern conditions. Our religions and political ideologies are methods of salvation and propitiation which can be compared with primitive ideas of magic, and where such "collective representations" are lacking their place is immediately taken by all sorts of private idiocies and idiosyncrasies, manias, phobias, and daemonisms whose primitivity leaves nothing to be desired, not to speak of the psychic epidemics of our time before which the witch-hunts of the sixteenth century pale by comparison.

122   Notwithstanding our rationalistic attempts to argue it out of existence, psychic reality is and remains a genuine source of anxiety whose danger increases the more it is denied. The biological instincts then meet not only with outer obstacles but

with an internal resistance. The same psychic system which, on one side, is based on the concupiscence of the instincts, rests on the other side on an opposing will which is at least as strong as the biological urge.

223   Except when motivated by external necessity, the will to suppress or repress the natural instincts, or rather to overcome their predominance (*superbia*) and lack of co-ordination (*concupiscentia*), derives from a spiritual source; in other words, the determining factor is the numinous primordial images. These images, ideas, beliefs, or ideals operate through the specific energy of the individual, which he cannot always utilize at will for this purpose, but which seems rather to be drawn out of him by the images. Even the authority of the father is seldom powerful enough to keep the spirit of the sons in permanent subjection. This can only happen when the father appeals to or expresses an image which, in the eyes of humanity, is numinous, or at any rate backed up by the consensus of opinion. The suggestive power of the environment is itself a consequence of the numinosity of the image and intensifies it in turn. If there is no such suggestion, the collective effect of the image will be negligible, or non-existent, even though it may be extremely intense as an individual experience. I mention this circumstance because it is a controversial point whether the inner images, or collective representations, are merely suggested by the environment, or whether they are genuine and spontaneous experiences. The first view simply begs the question, because it is obvious that the content suggested must have come into existence somehow and at some time. There was a time when the utterances of mythology were entirely original, when they were numinous experiences, and anyone who takes the trouble can observe these subjective experiences even today. I have already given one example [29] of a mythological statement (the solar phallus) coming alive again under circumstances which rule out any possibility of direct transmission. The patient was a small business employee with no more than a secondary school education. He grew up in Zurich, and by no stretch of imagination can I conceive how he could have got hold of the idea of the solar phallus, of the vision moving to and fro, and of the origin of the wind. I myself, who would

29 [See pp. 100ff., above.]

have been in a much better position, intellectually, to know about this singular concatenation of ideas, was entirely ignorant of it and only discovered the parallel in a book of Dieterich's which appeared in 1910, four years after my original observation (1906).[30]

224   This observation was not an isolated case: it was manifestly not a question of inherited ideas, but of an inborn disposition to produce parallel thought-formations, or rather of identical psychic structures common to all men, which I later called the archetypes of the collective unconscious. They correspond to the concept of the "pattern of behaviour" in biology.[31]

225   The archetype, as a glance at the history of religious phenomena will show, has a characteristically numinous effect, so that the subject is gripped by it as though by an instinct. What is more, instinct itself can be restrained and even overcome by this power, a fact for which there is no need to advance proofs.

226   Whenever an instinct is checked or inhibited, it gets blocked and regresses. Or, to be more precise: if there is an inhibition of sexuality, a regression will eventually occur in which the sexual energy flowing back from this sphere activates a function in some other sphere. In this way the energy changes its form. Let us take as an example the Wachandi ceremony: in all probability the hole in the earth is an analogy of the mother's genitals, for when a man is forbidden to look at a woman, his Eros reverts to the mother. But as incest has to be avoided at all costs, the hole in the earth acts as a kind of mother-substitute. Thus, by means of ceremonial exercise, the incestuous energy-component becomes as it were desexualized, is led back to an infantile level where, if the operation is successful, it attains another form, which is equivalent to another function. It is to be assumed, however, that the operation is accomplished only with difficulty, for the primary instinct is composed of an endogamous ("incestuous") tendency and an exogamous one, and must therefore be split into two. This splitting is connected with consciousness and the process of becoming conscious. The regression is always attended by certain difficulties because the energy clings with specific force to its object, and on being

30 Further details of this case in "The Concept of the Collective Unconscious," pars. 104ff.
31 [Cf. "On the Nature of the Psyche," pars. 397ff.—EDITORS.]

changed from one form carries something of its previous character into the next form.[32] So although the resultant phenomena have the character of a sexual act, it is not a sexual act any longer. In the same way fire-boring is only an analogy of the sexual act, just as the latter often has to serve as a linguistic analogy for all sorts of other activities. The presexual, early infantile stage to which the libido reverts is characterized by numerous possibilities of application, because, once the libido has arrived there, it is restored to its original undifferentiated polyvalency. It is therefore understandable that the libido which regressively "invests" this stage sees itself confronted with a variety of possible applications. Since, in the Wachandi ceremony, the libido is bound to its object—sexuality—it will carry at least part of this function into the new form as an essential characteristic. The result is that an analogous object is "invested" and takes the place of the one thrust into the background. The ideal example of such an object is the nurturing earth-mother. (Pl. xiva; cf. also fig. 1.) The psychology of the presexual stage accounts for her nourishing character, and sexuality for her most typical form of worship, the *hieros gamos*. From this arise the age-old symbols of agriculture. In the work of tilling and sowing the fields hunger and incest intermingle. The ancient cults of Mother Earth saw in this the fertilization of the mother. But the aim of the action is to bring forth the fruits of the field, and it is magical rather than sexual. Here the regression leads to a reactivation of the mother as the goal of desire, this time as a symbol not of sex but of the giver of nourishment.

227   It is just possible that we owe the discovery of fire to some such regression to the presexual stage, where the model of rhythmic activity can co-operate effectively. The libido, forced into regression by the checking of instinct, reactivates the infantile boring and provides it with objective material to work on—fittingly called "material" because the object at this stage is the mother (*mater*). As I have pointed out above, the act of boring requires only the strength and perseverance of an adult man and suitable "material" in order to generate fire. Consequently,

32 Known as the "factor of extensity" in the older physics. Cf. von Hartmann, *Die Weltanschauung der modernen Physik*, p. 5.

the production of fire may have originally occurred as the objective expression of a quasi-masturbatory activity analogous to the aforementioned case of masturbatory boring. Though we can never hope to advance any real proof of our contention, it is at least thinkable that some traces of these first exercises in fire-making may have been preserved. I have succeeded in finding a passage in a monument of Indian literature which describes this conversion of libido into fire-making. It occurs in the Brihadaranyaka Upanishad: [33]

He (*Atman* [34]) was as big as a man and woman joined together; he divided himself into two, and thus husband and wife were born. . . .[35] He joined himself to her, and thus men were born.

She thought: "How should he lie with me after having produced me? I will hide myself." She became a cow, he became a bull; they joined and cattle were born. She became a mare, he a stallion; she became a she-ass, he an ass; they joined and the hoofed animals were born. She became a she-goat, he a goat; she became a ewe, he a ram; they joined and goats and sheep were born. Thus he created everything down to the ants, male and female. . . .

Then he knew: "I am this creation, for I produced it all from myself." Such was creation. He who possesses this knowledge creates his own being in that creation.

Thereupon he rubbed thus [holding his hands before his mouth]. From his mouth, the fire-hole (*yoni*), and from his hands, he brought forth fire.[36]

[33] The Upanishads expound the theology of the Vedic writings and contain the speculative, theosophical part of the teachings. The Vedic writings are mostly of very uncertain age, and since for a long time they were handed down only orally, they may date back to the very remote past.

[34] The primordial universal being, a concept which in psychological terms coincides with that of the libido.

[35] The atman is thus thought of as originally bisexual or hermaphroditic. The world was created by desire: cf. Brih. Up. 1, 4, 1–3: "In the beginning this world was Self alone in the form of a Person (*purusha*). He looked round and saw nothing but himself. . . . He became afraid; therefore one who is alone is afraid. He thought: 'Why should I be afraid, since there is nothing but myself? . . . .' He had no joy; therefore one who is alone has no joy. He desired a second." Then follows the description of his division into two, quoted above. Plato's idea of the world-soul comes very close to this Indian image: "It had no need of eyes, for there was nothing outside it to be seen; nor of ears, for there was nothing outside it to be heard. . . . Nothing went out from or came into it anywhere, for there was nothing." (*Timaeus*, 33, trans. based on Cornford, p. 55.)

[36] Brih. Up. 1, 4, 3–6, trans. based on Hume, pp. 81–82.

228   I once observed a year-old baby making a very peculiar gesture: it held one hand before its mouth and kept rubbing it with the other. It lost this habit after some months. Such cases show that there is some justification for interpreting a mythologem like the above as being based on a very early infantile gesture.

229   The baby's gesture is interesting in another respect, too: it lays emphasis on the mouth, which at this early age still has an exclusively nutritive significance. The pleasure and satisfaction it finds in feeding is localized in the mouth, but to interpret this pleasure as sexual is quite unjustified. Feeding is a genuine activity, satisfying in itself, and because it is a vital necessity nature has here put a premium on pleasure. The mouth soon begins to develop another significance as the organ of speech. The extreme importance of speech doubles the significance of the mouth in small children. The rhythmic activities it carries out express a concentration of emotional forces, i.e., of libido, at this point. Thus the mouth (and to a lesser degree the anus) becomes the prime place of origin. According to the Brihadaranyaka Upanishad, the most important discovery ever made by primitive man, the discovery of fire, came out of the mouth. As we might expect, there are texts which draw a parallel between fire and speech. The Aitareya Upanishad says:

Then he drew forth a Person (purusha) from the waters and shaped him. He brooded upon him, and when he had brooded him forth, a mouth split open like an egg. From the mouth came speech, and from speech fire.[37] [Cf. pl. xiiib.]

230   Here, then, speech becomes fire, but a little later on (2, 4) we are told that fire becomes speech. There is a similar connection between the two in Brihadaranyaka Upanishad:

"Yajñavalkya, what is the light of man?"
"The sun is his light," he answered. "It is by the light of the sun that a man rests, goes forth, does his work and returns."
"Quite so, Yajñavalkya. But when the sun is set, what then is the light of man?"
"The moon is his light," he answered. "It is by the light of the moon that a man rests, goes forth, does his work and returns."

[37] I, 3–4, trans. based on Hume, p. 294.

"Quite so, Yajñavalkya. But when the sun is set, and the moon is set, what then is the light of man?"

"Fire is his light," he answered. "It is by the light of the fire that a man rests, goes forth, does his work and returns."

"Quite so, Yajñavalkya. But when the sun is set, and the moon is set, and the fire has gone out, what then is the light of man?"

"Speech is his light," he answered. "It is by the light of speech that a man rests, goes forth, does his work and returns."

"Quite so, Yajñavalkya. But when the sun is set, and the moon is set, and the fire has gone out, and speech is hushed, what then is the light of man?"

"Self is his light," he answered. "It is by the light of the Self that a man rests, goes forth, does his work and returns." [38]

231   This association of mouth, fire, and speech is not as strange as it would seem: we speak of a man being "fired" or "inflamed" by another's words, of a "fiery" speech, "burning words," etc. In the language of the Old Testament mouth and fire are frequently connected, as in II Samuel 22:9: "There went up a smoke out of his nostrils, and fire out of his mouth. . . ." Isaiah 30:27: "The name of the Lord cometh from afar, burning with his anger . . . his lips are full of indignation, and his tongue as a devouring fire." Psalm 29:7 (RV): "The voice of the Lord scattereth flames of fire." Jeremiah 23:29: "Is not my word like as a fire?" And in Revelation 11:5 fire proceeds out of the mouth of the two prophetic witnesses.

232   Again and again fire is called "devouring," "consuming," a reminder of the function of the mouth, as in Ezekiel 15:4: "It is cast into the fire for fuel; the fire devoureth both the ends of it, and the midst of it is burned." Deuteronomy 4:24: "For the Lord thy God is a consuming fire, even a jealous God." Perhaps the best-known example is Acts 2:3-4: "And there appeared unto them cloven tongues [γλῶσσαι] like as of fire, and it sat upon each of them. And they were all filled with the Holy Ghost, and began to speak with other tongues [γλῶσσαις], as the Spirit gave them utterance." The γλῶσσα of the fire caused the glossolalia of the apostles. In a negative sense the Epistle of James 3:6 says: "And the tongue is a fire, a world of iniquity: so is the tongue among our members, that it defileth the whole body, and setteth on fire the course of nature; and it is set on

38 Trans. based on Hume, p. 133.

fire of hell." Proverbs 16:27 says likewise: "An ungodly man diggeth up evil: and in his lips there is as a burning fire." The dragons or horses of the Apocalypse (Rev. 9:17) breathe forth fire and smoke and brimstone, and as for Leviathan (Job 41:19f.): "Out of his mouth go burning lamps, and sparks of fire leap out."

233   The connection of the mouth with fire and speech is indubitable. Another fact to be considered is that the etymological dictionaries connect the Indo-European root *bhā with the idea of 'bright,' 'shining.' This root is found in Gr. φάω, φαίνω, φάος; in OIr. bàn, 'white'; and in the G. bohnen, 'to polish, make shining.' But the homonymous root *bhā also signifies 'speaking': it is found in Skr. bhan, 'to speak'; in Armen. ban, 'word'; in G. Bann, bannen, 'to ban, put a spell on'; in Gr. φα-μί, ἔφαν, φάτις, Lat. fā-ri, fātum.

234   The root la, 'to sound, to bark,' occurs in Skr. las lásati, 'to resound, reverberate,' and in las lásati, 'to radiate, shine.'

235   A similar archaic fusion of meanings occurs in a certain class of Egyptian words derived from the cognate roots ben and bel, duplicated into benben and belbel. The original meaning of these words was 'to burst forth, emerge, swell, well out,' with the associated idea of bubbling, boiling, roundness. Belbel, accompanied by the obelisk sign, meant a source of light. The obelisk itself had several names: teshenu, men, benben, and more rarely berber and belbel.[39] The Indo-European root *vel, meaning 'to wave about like fire,' occurs in Skr. ulunka, 'blaze,' Gr. Ϝαλέα, Att. ἀλέα, 'warmth of the sun,' Goth. vulan, 'undulate,' OHG. and MHG. Walm, 'warmth.' The related Indo-European root *vélkô, 'to lighten, glow,' occurs in Skr. ulka, 'firebrand,' Gr. Ϝελχᾱνος, 'Vulcan.' The same root *vel also means 'to sound'; in Skr. vāni, 'tone, song, music'; Czech volati, 'to call.' The root *svéno occurs in Skr. svan, svánati, 'to sound,' Zend qanañt, Lat. sonare, OIran. semn, Welsh sain, Lat. sonus, OE. svinsian. The related root *svénos, 'noise,' occurs in Ved. svánas, Lat. sonor, sonorus. A further related root is *svonós, OIran. son, 'word.' The root *své(n), locative *svéni, dative *sunéi, means 'sun'; in Zend qeng (cf. above, *svéno,

39 Cf. Brugsch, Religion und Mythologie der alten Aegypter, pp. 255f., and the Dictionnaire hiéroglyphique.

Zend *qanañt*); Goth. *sun-na, sunnô*.[40] Although the stars are only perceived by their light, we still talk of the music of the spheres and celestial harmony, just as Pythagoras did. Goethe opens his "Prologue in Heaven" in the same way:

> The day-star, sonorous as of old,
> Goes his predestined way along,
> And round his path is thunder rolled,
> While sister-spheres join rival song.[41]

Again, in Part II:

> Hearken to the storm of hours!
> Ringing out for spirits' ears
> Now the new-born day appears.
> Gates of rock grind back asunder,
> Phoebus comes with wheels of thunder,
> Light brings tumult in his train.
> Drums and trumpets far resounding,
> Dazzling, deafening, dumbfounding,
> A din the ears can scarce sustain.
> Into bells of blossom creep,
> Lie there quietly, as in sleep,
> Into rock and under leaf:
> If it strikes you, you are deaf.[42]

236   Nor should we forget the verses of Hölderlin:

> Where are you? Drunken with all your glory
> My soul dreams; yet even now I hearken,
> As full of golden tones the radiant sun-youth
> Raises his evening song on the heavenly lyre
> To the echoing woods and hills. . . .[43]

237   These images point back to the sun-god Apollo, whose lyre marks him out as the divine musician. The fusion of sound,

40 The word *swan* might also be mentioned here, because the swan sings when about to die. The swan, eagle, and phoenix occur in alchemy as related symbols. They signify the sun and thus the philosophical gold. Cf. also the verse from Heine (trans. by Todhunter):

> A swan on the lake sings lonely,
> He oars himself to and fro,
> Then faint and fainter singing,
> Sinks to his grave below.

41 Trans. by Wayne, p. 39.
42 Trans. based on MacNeice, p. 159, and on unpubl. trans. by Philip Wayne.
43 "Sunset." [Cf. trans. by Hamburger, p. 97.]

speech, light, and fire is expressed in an almost physiological way in the phenomenon of "colour-hearing," i.e., the perception of the tonal quality of colours and the chromatic quality of musical tones. This leads one to think that there must be a pre-conscious identity between them: the two phenomena have something in common despite their real differences. It is probably no accident that the two most important discoveries which distinguish man from all other living beings, namely speech and the use of fire, should have a common psychic background. Both are products of psychic energy, of libido or mana. In Sanskrit there is a term which expresses in all its nuances the preconscious situation I have suggested. This is the word *tejas,* and it combines the following meanings:

1. Sharpness, cutting edge.
2. Fire, brightness, light, ardour, heat.
3. Healthy appearance, beauty.
4. The fiery and colour-producing faculty of the human organism (located in the bile).
5. Strength, energy, vital force.
6. Passion.
7. Spiritual and magical power; influence, position, dignity.
8. Semen.[44]

238   *Tejas,* therefore, describes the psychological situation covered by the word "libido." It really denotes *subjective intensity.* Anything potent, any content highly charged with energy, therefore has a wide range of symbolic meanings. This is obvious enough in the case of language, which is capable of expressing practically anything. But it may not be out of place to say a few words about the symbolism of fire.

239   The Sanskrit word for fire is *agnis* (Lat. *ignis* [45]), personified as Agni, the god of fire, a divine mediator (cf. pl. xiiib) whose symbolism has certain affinities with Christian ideas.

240   An Iranian name for fire is *Nairyosagha,* 'masculine word.' (Cf. the Indian *Narasamsa,* 'wish of men.' [46]) Max Müller says of Agni:

It was a familiar idea with the Brahmans to look upon the fire both as the subject and the object of a sacrifice. The fire embraced the

44 [Cf. Macdonell, *Sanskrit Dictionary,* p. 112, s.v. "tégas."—EDITORS.]
45 Connected with *ag-ilis,* 'agile.' See Max Müller, *Origin and Growth of Religion,* p. 212.   46 Spiegel, *Eränische Altertumskunde,* II, p. 49.

offering, and was thus a kind of priest; it carried it to the gods, and was thus a kind of mediator between gods and men. But the fire represented also something divine, a god to whom honour was due, and thus it became both the subject and the object of the sacrifice. Hence the idea that Agni sacrifices himself, that he offers a sacrifice to himself, and likewise that he offers himself as a sacrifice.[47]

241   The affinity between this line of thought and the Christian symbol is obvious. Krishna expresses the same idea in the Bhagavad Gita:

All's then God!
The sacrifice is Brahm, the ghee and grain
Are Brahm, the fire is Brahm, the flesh it eats
Is Brahm, and unto Brahm attaineth he
Who, in such office, meditates on Brahm.[48]

242   The wise Diotima in Plato's *Symposium* has a rather different conception of the divine messenger and mediator. She teaches Socrates (ch. 23) that Eros is "the intermediary between mortals and immortals . . . a mighty daemon, dear Socrates; for everything daemonic is the intermediary between God and man." His function is to "interpret and convey messages to the gods from men and to men from the gods, prayers and sacrifices from the one, and commands and rewards from the other, thus bridging the gap between them, so that by his mediation the universe is at one with itself." Diotima gives an excellent description of Eros: "He is bold and forward and strenuous, always devising tricks like a cunning huntsman; he yearns after knowledge and is full of resource and is a lover of wisdom all his life, a skilful magician, an alchemist, a true sophist. He is neither mortal nor immortal; but on one and the same day he will live and flourish (when things go well with him), and also meet his death; and then come to life again through the force of his father's nature. Yet all that he wins is forever slipping away from him." [49]

243   In the Avesta and in the Vedas, fire is the messenger of the gods. In Christian mythology, too, there are points of contact

47 Max Müller, *Introduction to the Science of Religion*, pp. 164–65 n.
48 In Book IV, trans. by Arnold, pp. 25–26.
49 *Symposium* 202 E, 203 D – E, trans. by Hamilton, pp. 81f., modified.

with the Agni myth. Daniel 3 : 24f. speaks of the three men
in the burning fiery furnace:

> Then Nebuchadnezzar the king was astonied, and rose up in
> haste, and spake, and said unto his counsellors, Did we not cast three
> men bound into the midst of the fire? They answered and said unto
> the king, True, O king.
> He answered and said, Lo, I see four men loose, walking in the
> midst of the fire, and they have no hurt; and the form of the fourth
> is like the Son of God.

244   The *Biblia pauperum* (1471) makes the following comment:

> We read in the third chapter of the book of the prophet Daniel that
> Nabuchodonosor, the King of Babylon, caused three men to be
> placed in a glowing furnace, and that the king came to the furnace
> and looked in, and saw with the three a fourth, who was like the Son
> of God. The three signify for us the Holy Trinity of the person, and
> the fourth the unity of being. Thus Christ in his transfiguration
> signified the Trinity of the person and the unity of being.

245   According to this interpretation the legend of the three
men in the furnace is a magical procedure during which a
"fourth" is produced. The fiery furnace, like the fiery tripod in
Faust, is a mother-symbol. From the tripod come Paris and
Helen, the royal pair of alchemy, and in popular tradition children are baked in the oven. The alchemical athanor, or melting-
pot, signifies the body, while the alembic or *cucurbita,* the
Hermetic vessel, represents the uterus. The "fourth" in the fiery
furnace appears like a son of God made visible in the fire.[50]
Jehovah himself is a fire. Isaiah 10 : 17 (RSV) says of the saviour
of Israel: "And the light of Israel will become a fire, and his
Holy One a flame." A hymn of Ephraem the Syrian says of
Christ: "Thou who art all fire, have pity on me." This view is
based on the apocryphal saying of our Lord: "He who is near
unto me is near unto the fire."

246   Agni is the sacrificial flame, the sacrificer and the sacrificed.
Just as Christ left behind his redeeming blood, a true φάρμακον
ἀθανασίας, in the wine, so Agni is the *soma,* the holy drink of

---

[50] The alchemists, too, were interested in this story and regarded the "fourth" as
the *filius philosophorum.* Cf. *Psychology and Alchemy,* par. 449.

inspiration, the mead of immortality.[51] Soma and fire are identical in Vedic literature. The ancient Hindus saw fire both as a symbol of Agni and as an emanation of the inner libido-fire, and for them the same psychic dynamism was at work in the intoxicating drink ("fire-water," Soma-Agni as rain and fire). The Vedic definition of soma as "seminal fluid" [52] confirms this view. The "somatic" significance of Agni has its parallel in the Christian interpretation of the Eucharistic Blood as the body of Christ.

247   Soma is also the "nourishing drink." Its mythological characteristics coincide with those of fire, and so both are united in Agni. The drink of immortality, Amrita, was stirred by the Hindu gods like the fire. (Pl. xv.)

248   So far our exposition has been based on the *pramantha* component of the Agni sacrifice, and we have concerned ourselves with only one meaning of the word *manthāmi* or *mathnāmi*, namely with that which expresses the idea of rubbing. But as Kuhn has shown, the word can also mean 'to tear or break off,' 'to snatch,' and also 'to rob.' [53] In his view this meaning is apparent even in the early Vedic texts. Legend always conceives the discovery of fire as a *robbery,* and to that extent it is akin to the widespread motif of the "treasure hard to attain." In many myths fire-making is something forbidden, a criminal act of usurpation which can only be accomplished by cunning or violence, but mostly by cunning.[54] The religious laws of the ancient Hindus threatened with severe penalties anyone who prepared fire in an incorrect manner. It is the custom in the Catholic Church to light a new fire at Easter. So, even in the Occident, fire-making is an element in a religious mystery, which testifies to its symbolical and ambiguous character. The rules of the ritual must be scrupulously observed if it is to have its intended magical effect. Generally the rite has a prophylactic, apotropaic significance, and when incorrectly performed or used

[51] This side of Agni points to Dionysus, who exhibits parallels both with Christian and with Indian mythology.
[52] "Whatever is liquid he created from semen, and that is soma." Brih. Up. 1, 4, 6.
[53] The question is whether this meaning was only a secondary development. Kuhn seems to assume this; he says (*Mythol. Studien*, I, p. 18): "But, together with the meaning which the root *manth* had already developed, there also grew up in the Vedas, as a natural development of the procedure, the idea of tearing off or plucking."   [54] For examples see Frobenius, *Das Zeitalter des Sonnengottes.*

may conjure up the very danger it was intended to avert. Speech and fire-making represent primitive man's victory over his brutish unconsciousness and subsequently became powerful magical devices for overcoming the ever-present "daemonic" forces lurking in the unconscious. Both these applications of libido require attention, concentration, and inner discipline, thereby facilitating a further development of consciousness. On the other hand incorrect performance and use of the rite cause a retrograde movement of the libido, a regression which threatens to reproduce the earlier, instinctual, and unconscious state. The danger lies in those well-known "perils of the soul"— a splitting of the personality ("loss of a soul") and reduction of consciousness, both of which automatically increase the power of the unconscious. The consequences of this are a serious danger not only for primitives; in civilized man, too, they may give rise to psychic disturbances, states of possession, and psychic epidemics.

249   The blocking of libido leads to an accumulation of instinctuality and, in consequence, to excesses and aberrations of all kinds. Among them, sexual disturbances are fairly frequent, as we might expect. A particularly instructive example is the psychology of incendiarism: incendiarism is really a regressive act of fire-making, and in certain cases it is combined with masturbation. Schmid [55] tells of an imbecile peasant youth who started numerous fires. On one occasion he aroused suspicion by standing in the door of a house with his hands in his trouser-pockets, gazing with delight at the conflagration. Later, under examination, he admitted that he always masturbated while enjoying the spectacle of the fires he had started.

250   The preparation of fire is an immemorial custom, harmless enough in itself, which soon ceased to have anything very mysterious about it. But there was always a tendency to prepare fire in a mysterious ceremonial manner on special occasions— just as with ritual eating and drinking—and to do it according to prescribed rules from which no one dared to differ. This ritual serves to remind us of the original numinosity of fire-making, but apart from that it has no practical significance. The anamnesis of fire-making is on a level with the recollection of the ancestors among primitives and of the gods at a more civi-

55 "Zur Psychologie der Brandstifter," p. 80.

lized stage. From the psychological point of view the ceremony has the significance of a meaningful institution, inasmuch as it represents a clearly defined procedure for canalizing the libido. It has, in fact, the functional value of a paradigm, and its purpose is to show us how we should act when the libido gets blocked. What we call the "blocking of libido" is, for the primitive, a hard and concrete fact: his life ceases to flow, things lose their glamour, plants, animals, and men no longer prosper. The ancient Chinese philosophy of the *I Ching* devised some brilliant images for this state of affairs. Modern man, in the same situation, experiences a standstill ("I am stuck"), a loss of energy and enjoyment ("the zest—libido—has gone out of life"), or a depression. One frequently has to tell the patient what is happening to him, for modern man's powers of introspection leave much to be desired. If, even today, the new fire is kindled at Eastertide, it is in commemoration of the redemptive and saving significance of the first fire-boring. In this way man wrested a secret from nature—the Promethean theft of fire. He made himself guilty of an unlawful intervention, incorporating a fragment of the age-old unconscious into the darkness of his mind. With this theft he appropriated something precious and offended against the gods. Anyone who knows the primitive's fear of innovations and their unforeseen consequences can imagine the uncertainty and uneasy conscience which such a discovery would arouse. This primordial experience finds an echo in the widespread motif of robbery (sun-cattle of Geryon, apples of the Hesperides, herb of immortality). And it is worth remembering that in the cult of Diana at Aricia only he could become her priest who plucked the golden bough from the sacred grove of the goddess.

IV

THE ORIGIN OF THE HERO

251   The finest of all symbols of the libido is the human figure, conceived as a demon or hero. Here the symbolism leaves the objective, material realm of astral and meteorological images and takes on human form, changing into a figure who passes from joy to sorrow, from sorrow to joy, and, like the sun, now stands high at the zenith and now is plunged into darkest night, only to rise again in new splendour.[1] Just as the sun, by its own motion and in accordance with its own inner law, climbs from morn till noon, crosses the meridian and goes its downward way towards evening, leaving its radiance behind it, and finally plunges into all-enveloping night, so man sets his course by immutable laws and, his journey over, sinks into darkness, to rise again in his children and begin the cycle anew. The symbolic transition from sun to man is easily made, and the third and last creation of Miss Miller's follows this pattern. She calls it "Chiwantopel, A hypnagogic drama," and gives us the following information concerning its origin:

After an evening of trouble and anxiety, I had gone to bed at half past eleven. I felt restless; unable to sleep although very tired. I had the impression of being in a receptive mood. There was no light in the room. I closed my eyes, and had the feeling of waiting for something that was about to happen. Then I felt a great relaxation come over me, and I remained as completely passive as possible. Lines, sparks, and spirals of fire passed before my eyes, symptoms of nervousness and ocular fatigue, followed by a kaleidoscopic and fragmentary review of recent trivial events.

252   The reader will share my regret that we cannot know the cause of her worry and anxiety. It would have been of great

1 Hence the beautiful name of the sun-hero Gilgamesh, "The Man of Joy and Sorrow," in Jensen, *Das Gilgamesch-Epos*.

importance for what follows to have information on this point. This gap in our knowledge is the more regrettable because, between the first poem (1898) and the fantasy now to be discussed (1902), four whole years have passed. All information is lacking regarding this period, during which the problem was assuredly not slumbering in the unconscious. Maybe this lack has its advantages, in that our interest in the general validity of the fantasy now struggling to be born is not obscured by any sympathetic concern for the personal fate of the author. This obviates the difficulty which often prevents the doctor, in his daily

Fig. 17. The first three labours of Heracles
Classical sarcophagus relief

work, from turning his eyes away from the wearisome mass of petty detail to those wider relationships where every neurotic conflict is seen to be part of human fate as a whole.

253   The state of mind depicted by our author is very much like that which usually precedes a case of intentional somnambulism,[2] and has often been described by mediums. A certain willingness to give ear to these faint nocturnal voices must be there, otherwise these subtle and hardly perceptible inner experiences will pass unnoticed. We can discern in this listening attitude an inward-flowing current of libido, leading towards a still invisible and mysterious goal. It is as if the libido had suddenly discovered, in the depths of the unconscious, an object which exercises a powerful attraction. As our life is directed

2 Cf. the researches of Silberer, "Phantasie und Mythos," pp. 513ff.

outwards and does not normally allow of such introversions, we have to suppose a rather exceptional condition, for instance a lack of external objects, which forces the individual to seek a substitute in his own psyche. It is hard to believe that this teeming world is too poor to provide an object for human love— it offers boundless opportunities to everyone. It is rather the inability to love which robs a person of these opportunities. The world is empty only to him who does not know how to direct his libido towards things and people, and to render them alive and beautiful. What compels us to create a substitute from within ourselves is not an external lack, but our own inability to include anything outside ourselves in our love. Certainly the difficulties and adversities of the struggle for existence may oppress us, yet even the worst conditions need not hinder love; on the contrary, they often spur us on to greater efforts. Real difficulties alone will never drive the libido back to the point where a neurosis arises, because the conflict which is the precondition for every neurosis is lacking. Only a resistance, which opposes its obstinate "won't" to the "will," is capable of producing a regression that may become the starting-point for a pathogenic disturbance. Resistance to loving produces the inability to love, or else that inability acts as a resistance. Just as the libido may be compared to a steady stream pouring its waters into the world of reality, so a resistance, dynamically considered, resembles, not a rock that juts up from the river-bed and causes the stream to flow round it, but a flowing back towards the source. Part of the psyche really wants the external object, but another part of it strives back to the subjective world, where the airy and lightly built palaces of fantasy beckon. We can take this dichotomy of the human will, for which Bleuler has coined the term "ambitendency," [3] as a constant factor, bearing in mind that the most primitive motor impulses are essentially antithetical, since, even in a simple act like stretching, the flexor muscles must be innervated. Normally, however, this ambitendency never leads to the inhibition or prevention of the intended act, but is absolutely necessary for its co-ordination and execution. If, from this harmony of delicately balanced opposites, there should arise any resistance to the act, then it must be due to an abnormal plus or minus

[3] See Bleuler, "Zur Theorie des schizophrenen Negativismus."

quantity on one side or the other. The resistance springs from the intervention of this third factor. This is true also of the dichotomy of the will which is the cause of so many human problems. The abnormal "third factor" loosens the paired opposites which are normally bound tightly together and makes them appear as separate tendencies, as a genuine "won't" and "will" that get in each other's way.[4] Harmony thus turns into disharmony. This is not the place to investigate where the unknown third factor comes from and what it is. Freud sees the root complex in the incest problem, since in his view the libido that regresses to the parents produces not only symbols, but symptoms and situations that can only be regarded as incestuous. This is the source of all those incestuous relationships with which mythology swarms. The reason this regression is so easy seems to lie in the specific inertia of the libido, which will relinquish no object of the past, but would like to hold it fast forever. Stripped of its incestuous covering, Nietzsche's "sacrilegious backward grasp" is only a metaphor for a reversion to the original passive state where the libido is arrested in the objects of childhood. This inertia, as La Rochefoucauld says, is also a passion:

Of all the Passions we are exposed to, none is more concealed from our Knowledge than Idleness. It is the most violent, and the most mischievous of any, and yet at the same time we are never sensible of its Violence, and the damage we sustain by it is very seldom seen. If we consider its Power carefully, it will be found, upon all Occasions, to reign absolute over all our Sentiments, our Interests, and our Pleasures. This is a Remora that can stop the largest Ships, and a Calm of worse Consequence in our Affairs, than any Rocks, and Storms. The Ease and Quiet of Sloth is a secret Charm upon the Soul, to suspend its most eager Pursuits, and shake its most peremptory Resolutions. In a Word, to give a true image of this Passion, we must say that it is a supposed Felicity of the Soul, that makes her easie under all her Losses, and supplies the Place of all her Enjoyments and Advantages.[5]

254   This dangerous passion is what lies hidden beneath the hazardous mask of incest. It confronts us in the guise of the

---

[4] Cf. Krishna's exhortation to the hesitant Arjuna in the Bhagavad Gita: "But thou, be free of the pairs of opposites!" (Trans. by Arnold, p. 13.)
[5] La Rochefoucauld, *Moral Maxims*, No. DLX, p. 139.

Terrible Mother [6] (pl. xvi, cf. also pl. xxxviii), and is indeed the mother of innumerable evils, not the least of which are neurotic disturbances. For out of the miasmas arising from the stagnant pools of libido are born those baneful phantasmagorias which so veil reality that all adaptation becomes impossible. However, we shall not enquire further into the origin of incest fantasies; the bare mention of the incest problem must suffice. Here we are concerned only with the question whether the resistance which, in the case of our author, led to a regression, signifies a conscious external difficulty or not. If it were an external difficulty, then the libido would be violently dammed back, and would produce a flood of fantasies which could best be described as plans to overcome the obstacle: ideas that toy with solutions, perhaps even some hard thinking which might lead to anything rather than a hypnagogic poem. The passive state described above does not fit in with the idea of an external obstacle, but, through its very acquiescence, points to a tendency that scorns real solutions and prefers a fantastic substitute. In the last resort, therefore, we must be dealing with an internal conflict, somewhat after the style of those earlier experiences which resulted in the first two unconscious creations. We are thus forced to conclude that the external object simply *cannot* be loved, because an overwhelming proportion of the libido prefers an internal object that rises up from the unconscious as a substitute for the missing reality.

255   The visionary phenomena produced by the first stage of introversion can be classed among the well-known symptoms [7] of hypnagogic vision. They provide the basis for the actual visions or "self-perceptions" of the libido in the form of symbols.

256   Miss Miller continues:

Then an impression that something was on the point of being communicated to me. It seemed as if these words were repeating themselves in me—"Speak, Lord, for thy servant heareth — Open thou mine ears."

257   This passage describes the underlying intention very clearly; the word "communication" (*communiqué*) is actually a common expression in mediumistic circles. The Biblical words con-

6 Cf. the following chapters.
7 Cf. Müller, *Über die phantastischen Gesichtserscheinungen.*

tain an invocation or "prayer," that is, a wish addressed to God, a concentration of libido on the God-image. The prayer refers to I Samuel 3 : 1ff., where Samuel was called three times by God during the night, but thought it was Eli calling him, until Eli told him that it was God, and that if he was called again, he should answer: "Speak, Lord, for thy servant heareth." The dreamer uses these words in the opposite sense, in order to direct her wishes, her libido, into the depths of the unconscious.

258   We know that however much individuals differ from one another in the content of their conscious minds, they become all the more alike when regarded from the standpoint of the unconscious. The psychotherapist cannot fail to be impressed when he realizes how uniform the unconscious images are despite their surface richness. Differences only arise through individuation—a fact which provides the psychological justification for an essential portion of the philosophies of Schopenhauer, Carus, and von Hartmann, whose views have as their psychic basis the obvious uniformity of the unconscious. The unconscious consists, among other things, of remnants of the undifferentiated archaic psyche, including its animal stages. The reactions and products of the animal psyche have a uniformity and constancy of which we seem able to discover only sporadic traces in man. Man seems to us far more individual than the animals. This may perhaps be a delusion, since we have in us a convenient tendency to discern differences mainly in the things which interest us. Psychological adaptation makes this inevitable, for without the minute differentiation of impressions all adaptation would be impossible. So strong is this tendency that we have, in fact, the greatest difficulty in recognizing the common connection between the things we have to do with in everyday life. It is much easier to recognize the connection in things that are remote from us. For instance, it is almost impossible for a European to distinguish at first between the faces in a Chinese crowd, although the Chinese have just as individual a physiognomy as we Europeans; but what their faces have in common is much more evident to the outsider than their individual differences. If we live among the Chinese, the impression of uniformity gradually disappears, and in the end they too become individuals. Individuality is one of those conditioned factors which are greatly overrated on account of their

practical importance; it does not come into the category of those self-evident, universal truths upon which a science must be founded. The individual content of consciousness is therefore the most unfavourable object imaginable for psychology, precisely because it has differentiated the universal to the point of unrecognizability. The essence of conscious processes is adaptation, which takes place in a series of particulars. The unconscious, on the other hand, is universal: it not only binds individuals together into a nation or race, but unites them with the men of the past and with their psychology. Thus, by reason of its supra-individual universality,[8] the unconscious is the prime object of any real psychology that claims to be more than psychophysics.

259   Man as an individual is a very suspicious phenomenon whose right to exist could be questioned by the biologist, since from that point of view he is significant only as a collective creature or as a particle in the mass. The cultural point of view gives man a meaning apart from the mass, and this, in the course of centuries, led to the development of personality and the cult of the hero. The efforts of rationalistic theology to preserve the *personal* Jesus as the last and most precious remnant of a divinity whom we are no longer capable of imagining, are quite in keeping with this tendency. In this respect the Catholic Church proved more adaptable, since she met the universal need for a visible hero by recognizing God's vicar upon earth. The concrete reality of religious figures assists the canalization of libido into the equivalent symbols, provided that the worship of them does not get stuck at the outward object. But even if it does, it at least remains bound to the representative human figure and loses its original primitive form, even though it does not attain the desired symbolic form. This need for a visible reality has been secretly preserved in a certain personalistic brand of Protestant theology which insists on the historical Jesus. Not that men have ever loved the visible God: they do not love him for what he appears to be, a mere man, because if the pious want to love humanity they have only to turn to their neighbours or their enemies. The religious figure cannot be a mere man, for it has to represent what it actually is, namely the totality of all those primordial images which express the

8 In my later works, I therefore speak of the "collective" unconscious.

"extraordinarily potent," always and everywhere. What we seek in visible human form is not man, but the superman, the hero or god, that *quasi-human* being who symbolizes the ideas, forms, and forces which grip and mould the soul. These, so far as psychological experience is concerned, are the archetypal contents of the (collective) unconscious, the archaic heritage of humanity, the legacy left behind by all differentiation and development and bestowed upon all men like sunlight and air. But in loving this inheritance they love that which is common to all; they turn back to the mother of humanity, to the psyche, which was before consciousness existed, and in this way they make contact with the source and regain something of that mysterious and irresistible power which comes from the feeling of being part of the whole. It is the problem of Antaeus, who could only keep his giant strength through contact with mother earth. This temporary withdrawal into oneself seems, within certain limits, to have a favourable effect upon the psychic well-being of the individual. As one would expect, the two fundamental mechanisms of the psyche, extraversion and introversion, are also to a large extent the normal and appropriate ways of reacting to complexes—extraversion as a means of escaping from the complex into reality, introversion as a means of detaching oneself from external reality through the complex.

260   The story in I Samuel 3:1ff. illustrates how the libido can be directed inwards: the invocation expresses this introversion, and the explicit expectation that God will speak empties the conscious mind of activity and transfers it to the divine being constellated by the invocation, who, from the empirical point of view, must be regarded as a primordial image. It is a fact of experience that all archetypal contents have a certain autonomy, since they appear spontaneously and can often exercise an overwhelming compulsion. There is, therefore, nothing intrinsically absurd about the expectation that "God" will take over the activity and spontaneity of the conscious mind, for the primordial images are quite capable of doing precisely this.

261   Now that we have informed ourselves of the general purpose of the prayer, we are prepared to hear more about the visions of our dreamer. After the prayer, "the head of a sphinx in an Egyptian setting" appeared, only to disappear again immediately after. At this point the dreamer was disturbed, and

woke up for a moment. The vision recalls the fantasy of the Egyptian statue mentioned in the beginning, whose rigid gesture is entirely in place here as a functional phenomenon, the light stages of hypnosis being technically known as "engourdissement" (stiffening). The word "sphinx" suggests "enigma," an enigmatic creature who propounds riddles, like the Sphinx of Oedipus, and stands on the threshold of man's fate as though symbolically announcing the inevitable. The Sphinx is a semi-theriomorphic representation of the mother-imago, or rather of the Terrible Mother, who has left numerous traces in mythology. I shall be told that nothing except the word "Sphinx" justifies our allusion to the Sphinx of Oedipus. But, in the absence of any context, an individual interpretation of the vision is impossible. The "Egyptian" fantasy hinted at in Part I (par. 52) is far too vague to be used here. Therefore, in order to understand the vision at all, we have to turn boldly to the ethnological material, on the assumption that the unconscious coins its symbols today in much the same way as it did in the remote past. With regard to the Sphinx, I would remind the reader of what I said in Part I (par. 24) about theriomorphic representations of the libido. (Cf. pl. ɪᴠ*a*.) They are well known to the doctor from the dreams and fantasies of his patients, where instinct is often represented as a bull, horse, dog, etc. One of my patients, who had questionable relations with women, and who began the treatment with the fear that I would forbid him his adventures, dreamt that I had very skilfully speared a strange animal, half pig, half crocodile, to the wall. Dreams are full of these theriomorphic representations of libido. Hybrids and monsters, like the one found here, are not at all infrequent. Bertschinger [9] has given us a series of illustrations in which the lower (animal) half in particular is represented theriomorphically. The libido so represented is the "animal" instinct [10] that has got repressed. In the above-men-

[9] "Illustrierte Halluzinationen," pp. 69ff.

[10] In the Middle Ages, the sphinx was regarded as an "emblem" of pleasure. Thus Andrea Alciati says in his *Emblemata* (p. 801) that the sphinx signifies "corporis voluptas, primo quidem aspectu blandiens, sed asperrima, tristisque, postquam gustaveris. De qua sic . . . meretricius ardor egregiis iuvenes sevocat a studiis" (the pleasure of the body, attractive indeed at first sight, but very bitter and sad after you have tasted it. And . . . [name corrupt] says this about it: the love of whores lures young men away from lofty studies).

tioned case, one asks oneself in some bewilderment where the repression can lie in such a man, since he obviously lives out his instincts as much as possible. But we must remember that sex is not the only instinct, nor can instinct be identified outright with sex. It is therefore conceivable that my patient was damaging his instinct precisely through his manifest lack of sexual repression. His fear of my imposing some medical prohibition on him is reflected a little too faithfully in the dream for the latter to be altogether above suspicion. Dreams which repeat the real situation too emphatically, or insist too plainly on some anticipated reality, are making use of conscious contents as a means of expression. His dream is really expressing a projection: he projects the killing of the animal on to the doctor. That is the way it appears to him, because he does not know that he himself is injuring his instinct. The pointed instrument generally means the needle of the intellect, with which insects are pinned down and classified. He has "modern" ideas about sex, and does not know that he has an unconscious fear of my taking his pet theories away from him. This possibility is rightly feared, for if it were not in him he would hardly have had this dream. Thus the theriomorphic symbols always refer to unconscious manifestations of libido.

262   There are two main reasons why these instinctual impulses are unconscious: the first is the general unconsciousness which we all share to a greater or less degree; the other is a secondary unconsciousness due to the repression of incompatible contents. This is not a cause, but rather a symptom, of a neurotic attitude which prefers to overlook unpleasant facts, and unhesitatingly risks a whole chain of pathological symptoms for the sake of some small advantage in the present.

263   Repression, as we have seen, is not directed solely against sexuality, but against the instincts in general, which are the vital foundations, the laws governing all life. The regression caused by repressing the instincts always leads back to the psychic past, and consequently to the phase of childhood where the decisive factors appear to be, and sometimes actually are, the parents. But the inborn instincts of the child play a distinct role aside from the parents, as can be seen from the fact that the parents do not exercise a uniform influence on their children, who each react to them in a different way. They must,

therefore, possess individual determinants. Yet, to the empty consciousness of the child, it must seem as if all the determining influences came from outside, because children cannot distinguish their own instincts from the influence and will of their parents. This lack of discrimination in the child makes it possible for the animals which represent the instincts to appear at the same time as *attributes* of the parents, and for the parents to appear in animal form, the father as a bull, the mother as a cow (cf. pl. L*a*), and so on.[11]

264   If the regression goes still further back, beyond the phase of childhood to the preconscious, prenatal phase, then archetypal images appear, no longer connected with the individual's memories, but belonging to the stock of inherited *possibilities of representation* that are born anew in every individual. It is from them that there arise those images of "divine" beings, part animal, part human. The guise in which these figures appear depends on the attitude of the conscious mind: if it is negative towards the unconscious, the animals will be frightening; if positive, they appear as the "helpful animals" of fairytale and legend.[12] It frequently happens that if the attitude towards the parents is too affectionate and too dependent, it is compensated in dreams by frightening animals, who represent the parents just as much as the helpful animals did. The Sphinx is a fear-animal of this kind and still shows clear traces of a mother derivative. In the Oedipus legend the Sphinx was sent by Hera, who hated Thebes on account of the birth of Bacchus. Oedipus, thinking he had overcome the Sphinx sent by the mother-goddess merely because he had solved her childishly simple riddle, fell a victim to matriarchal incest and had to marry Jocasta, his mother, for the throne and the hand of the widowed queen belonged to him who freed the land from the plague of the Sphinx. This had all those tragic consequences which could easily have been avoided if only Oedipus had been sufficiently intimidated by the frightening appearance of the "terrible" or "devouring" Mother whom the Sphinx personified. (Cf. pls. XVI, XLVIII.) He was far indeed from the philosophical wonderment

11 The motif of the "helpful animals" may also be connected with the parental imago.
12 For relevant case material, see Gerhard Adler, *Studies in Analytical Psychology.*

of Faust: "The Mothers, the Mothers, it has a wondrous sound!" Little did he know that the riddle of the Sphinx can never be solved merely by the wit of man.

265   The genealogy of the Sphinx has manifold connections with the problem touched upon here: she was a daughter of Echidna, a monster with the top half of a beautiful maiden, and a hideous serpent below. This double being corresponds to the mother-imago: above, the lovely and attractive human half; below, the horrible animal half, changed into a fear-animal by the incest prohibition.[13] Echidna was born of the All-Mother, Mother Earth, Gaia, who conceived her with Tartarus, the personification of the underworld. Echidna herself was the mother of all terrors, of the Chimera, Scylla, the Gorgon (pl. xivb), of frightful Cerberus, of the Nemean lion, and of the eagle that devoured the liver of Prometheus. She also gave birth to a number of dragons. One of her sons was Orthrus, the dog of the monster Geryon, who was slain by Heracles. With this dog, her own son, Echidna incestuously begat the Sphinx. This should be sufficient to characterize the complex whose symbol is the Sphinx. It is evident that a factor of such magnitude cannot be disposed of by solving a childish riddle. The riddle was, in fact, the trap which the Sphinx laid for the unwary wanderer. Overestimating his intellect in a typically masculine way, Oedipus walked right into it, and all unknowingly committed the crime of incest. The riddle of the Sphinx was *herself* —the terrible mother-imago, which Oedipus would not take as a warning.

266   If, in spite of the lack of subjective material, we may venture an inference concerning the sphinx symbol in the case of Miss Miller, we may perhaps say that its meaning for her is approximately the same as it was for Oedipus, even though Oedipus was a man. We would almost expect a masculine sphinx, and as a matter of fact there are masculine as well as feminine sphinxes in Egypt. This may have been known to Miss Miller. (The Sphinx of Thebes was undoubtedly feminine.) If our expectations are correct, it would have to be a masculine monster, because the danger for a woman comes not from the mother, but from the father. We shall leave this question undecided for the moment, and turn back to the facts. After Miss Miller had

13 In Hellenistic syncretism, the Echidna became a cult-symbol of mother Isis.

concentrated her thoughts again, the vision continued as follows:

Suddenly, the apparition of an Aztec, complete in every detail: hand open, with large fingers, head in profile, armoured, with a head-dress resembling the plumed crests of the American Indians, etc. The whole is somewhat suggestive of the carvings on Mexican monuments.

267   Our conjecture that a masculine figure was hidden in the Sphinx is now confirmed. The Aztec is a primitive Indian, or rather a primitive American. On the personal level he represents the primitive side of the father, since Miss Miller was an American. I have frequently observed in the analysis of Americans that the inferior side of the personality, the "shadow," [14] is represented by a Negro or an Indian, whereas in the dream of a European it would be represented by a somewhat shady individual of his own kind. These representatives of the so-called "lower races" stand for the inferior personality component of the man. But Miss Miller is a woman. Therefore her shadow would have to be a feminine figure. But what we have here is a masculine figure which, in view of the role it plays in the Miller fantasies, must be regarded as a personification of the masculine component of the woman's personality. (Cf. pl. xvii.) In my later writings I have called this personification the "animus." [15]

268   The details of this vision are worth going into, because there are several things to be noticed. The head-dress of eagle's feathers has a magical significance. The Indian takes on something of the sun-like nature of this bird when he adorns himself with its feathers, just as he assimilates the courage and strength of his enemy when he eats the latter's heart or takes his scalp. At the same time the feather crest is a crown which is equivalent to the rays of the sun. (Pl. xxib.) The importance of the sun identification was made clear in Part I. Further proof of this is furnished not only by innumerable ancient customs, but by equally ancient religious figures of speech, as in the Wis-

[14] To the extent that the shadow is unconscious it corresponds to the concept of the "personal unconscious." Cf. "On the Psychology of the Unconscious," *Two Essays*, par. 103.
[15] Cf. Emma Jung, "Ein Beitrag zum Problem des Animus," pp. 296ff.

dom of Solomon 5:16: "Therefore shall they receive . . . a beautiful crown from the Lord's hand." There are countless other passages of this kind in the Bible. A hymn by J. L. K. Allendorf says of the soul:

> The soul is freed from all care and pain
> And in dying it has come
> To the crown of joy; she stands as bride and queen
> In the glitter of eternal splendour,
> At the side of the great king.

> It [the soul] sees a clear countenance [sun]:
> His [the sun's] joyful loving nature
> Now restores it through and through:
> It is a light in his light.
> Now the child can see the father.
> He feels the gentle emotion of love.
> Now he can understand the word of Jesus.
> He himself, the father, has loved you.
> An unfathomable sea of benefits,
> An abyss of eternal waves of blessing
> Is disclosed to the enlightened spirit:
> He beholds the countenance of God,
> And knows what signifies the inheritor
> Of God in light and the co-heir of Christ.
> The feeble body rests on the earth:
> It sleeps until Jesus awakens it.
> Then will the dust become the sun,
> Which now is covered by the dark cavern:
> Then shall we come together
> With all the pious, who knows how soon,
> And will be for eternity with the Lord.[16]

269   Another hymn, by Laurentius Laurentii (1660–1722), says:

> To the bride, because she conquers,
> Now is given the eternal crown.[17]

---

[16] Bunsen, *Gebetbuch*, No. 912, p. 789. [As trans. in the Hinkle (1916) edn.] The crown also plays a role in alchemy, perhaps as a result of cabalistic influence. (Cf. the compilation by Goodenough, "The Crown of Victory in Judaism," pp. 139ff.) The hermaphrodite is generally represented as crowned (pl. XVIII). For the alchemical material on the crown, see "Psychology of the Transference," par. 497, n. 14.
[17] Bunsen, No. 494, p. 271.

270   In a hymn by G. W. Sacer (1635–99) we find the passage:

Adorn my coffin with garlands
Just as a conqueror is adorned,
From those springs of heaven,
My soul has attained
The eternally green crown:
The true glory of victory,
Coming from the son of God
Who has so cared for me.[18]

271   Special importance seems to attach to the hand, which is described as "open," with "large" fingers. It is rather odd that the accent should fall on the hand, as one would rather have expected a description of the face and its expression. It is well known that the gesture of the hand is significant; unfortunately, further details are lacking here. Nevertheless, we might mention a parallel fantasy which also concerns the hand: a patient in a hypnagogic condition saw his mother painted on a wall, like a mural in a Byzantine church. She held one hand up, wide open, with splayed fingers. The fingers were very large, swollen at the ends into knobs, each surrounded by a small halo. The immediate association with this image was the fingers of a frog with suckers at the ends; then the resemblance to a phallus. The antiquated setting of the mother-image is also important. Presumably the hand in this fantasy had a spermatic and creative significance. This interpretation is borne out by other fantasies of the same patient: he saw what looked like a sky-rocket going up from his mother's hand, which on closer inspection proved to be a shining bird with golden wings—a golden pheasant, it then occurred to him. We have seen in the last chapter that the hand actually has a phallic meaning, and that it plays a corresponding role in the production of fire. Fire is bored with the hand; therefore fire comes from the hand; and Agni, fire, was worshipped as a golden-winged bird.[19]

272   Miss Miller says of the Aztec: "In my childhood I was particularly interested in Aztec remains and in the history of Peru and the Incas." Unfortunately, she tells us nothing more in this connection. We can, however, conclude from the sudden ap-

18 Ibid., No. 640, p. 348. [As trans. in the Hinkle (1916) edn.]
19 In popular German speech, incendiarism is called "putting a red cock on the roof."

pearance of the Aztec that the unconscious was willing to let itself be impressed by her reading, presumably because this material had a natural affinity with her unconscious contents or was able to give them satisfactory expression. Just as we surmised an aspect of the mother in the Sphinx, so the Aztec is probably an aspect of the father. The mother's influence is mainly on the Eros of her son, therefore it was only logical that Oedipus should end up by marrying his mother. But the father exerts his influence on the mind or spirit of his daughter—on her "Logos." This he does by increasing her intellectuality, often to a pathological degree which in my later writings I have described as "animus possession." These spiritual influences played a not unimportant part in the personal history of our author and, as I pointed out in the Foreword to the second edition of this volume, finally led to insanity. Although the Aztec is a masculine figure and thus clearly betrays the influence of the father, it was the feminine Sphinx that came first. In an American girl this might conceivably point to the preponderance of the feminine element. Mother complexes are extremely common in America and often very pronounced, probably because of the strong maternal influence in the home and the social position of women generally. The fact that more than half the capital in America is in women's hands gives one something to think about. As a result of this conditioning many American women develop their masculine side, which is then compensated in the unconscious by an exquisitely feminine instinct, aptly symbolized by a Sphinx.

273 The figure of the Aztec appears with all its "heroic" qualities: it represents the masculine ideal for the primitive, female side of our author. We have already met this ideal in the Italian naval officer, who "so softly and silently vanished away." Though, in certain respects, he came up to the unconscious ideal that floated before Miss Miller, he was not able to compete with this rival because he lacked the mysterious charm of the "demon lover," of the angel who takes a tender interest in the daughters of men, as angels sometimes seem inclined to do. (Hence the rule that women must cover up their hair in church, where the angels hover near!) We now understand what it was that turned against the naval officer: it was Miss Miller's spirituality, which, personified as the Aztec, was far too exalted for

her ever to find a lover among mortal men. However reasonable and unexacting the conscious attitude may be in such a case, it will not have the slightest effect on the patient's unconscious expectations. Even after the greatest difficulties and resistances have been overcome, and a so-called normal marriage is made, she will only discover later on what the unconscious wants, and this will assert itself either as a change of life style or as a neurosis or even a psychosis.

274   After this vision Miss Miller felt that a name was forming itself in her "bit by bit," a name that seemed to belong to this Aztec, who was the "son of an Inca of Peru." The name was "Chi-wan-to-pel." [20] The author says that it was somehow connected with her reminiscences. The act of naming is, like baptism, extremely important as regards the creation of personality, for a magical power has been attributed to the name since time immemorial. To know the secret name of a person is to have power over him. A well-known example of this is the tale of Rumpelstiltskin. In an Egyptian myth, Isis permanently robs the sun-god Ra of his power by compelling him to tell her his real name. Therefore, to give a name means to give power, to invest with a definite personality or soul.[21] Here the author remarked that the name reminded her very much of "Popo-catepetl," which as we all know belongs to the unforgettable memories of our school-days and, much to the indignation of patients under analysis, occasionally turns up in a dream or

---

20 In the mystery religions, there is no doubt about the identity of the divine hero with the celebrant. A prayer addressed to Hermes says: σὺ γὰρ ἐγὼ καὶ ἐγὼ σύ · τὸ σὸν ὄνομα ἐμὸν καὶ τὸ ἐμὸν σόν · ἐγὼ γὰρ εἰμι τὸ εἴδωλόν σου. (For you are I and I am you; your name is mine and my name is yours; for I am your image). Kenyon, *Greek Papyri in the British Museum*, p. 116, Pap. CXXII, 36–38; cited in Dieterich, *Mithrasliturgie*, p. 97. The hero as a libido-image is aptly portrayed in the head of Dionysus in Leiden (Roscher, *Lexikon*, I, 1128), where the hair is twisted up like a flame. Cf. Isaiah 10:17 (RSV): "The light of Israel will become a fire, and his Holy One a flame." Firmicus Maternus (*De errore*, XIX) reports that the god was greeted as the "bridegroom" and the "new light." He quotes the saying: νυμφίε χαῖρε νυμφίε χαῖρε νέον φῶς (Hail, bridegroom, hail, new light!), and contrasts it with the Christian: "Nullum aput te lumen est, nec est aliqui qui sponsus mereatur audire: unum lumen est, unus est sponsus. Nominum horum gratiam Christus accepit" (No light is with you, nor is there anyone who deserves the name of bridegroom: there is only one light, one bridegroom. The grace of these titles is reserved to Christ).
21 Hence the old custom of giving children the names of saints.

association. Although one might hesitate to regard this school-boy joke as of psychological importance, one must nevertheless inquire into the reasons for its existence. One must also ask: Why is it always Popocatepetl and not the neighbouring Ixtac-cihuatl, or the even higher and more beautiful Orizaba? The latter is a nicer name and is far easier to pronounce. Popo-catepetl, however, is impressive precisely because of its onoma-topoeic name. In English the onomatopoeia that comes to mind is *pop* or *pop-gun;* in German and French, the words *Hinter-pommern, Pumpernickel, Bombe, petarde* (*le pet* = flatus). The German word *Popo,* 'posterior,' does not exist in English,[22] but on the other hand to break wind is sometimes called *to pop* or *to poop,* and the act of defecation is commonly known as *to poop* or to *poo-poo* in childish speech. A jocular name for the posterior is *bum.* (*Poop* also means the rear end of a ship.) In French, *pouf!* is onomatopoeic; *pouffer,* 'explode,' *la poupe,* 'poop of a ship,' *le poupard,* 'baby in arms,' *la poupée,* 'doll.' *Poupon* is a pet name for a chubby-cheeked child. In Dutch, *pop* is 'doll'; in Latin, *puppis* means poop of a ship, though Plautus uses it jokingly for the backside of the body; *pupus,* 'child,' *pupula,* 'girl, little doll.' The Greek ποππύζω denotes a smacking, snapping, or blowing noise. It is used of kissing, but also (in Theocritus) of the subsidiary noises connected with flute-playing.

275   One of my patients, in his boyhood, always associated the act of defecation with the fantasy that his posterior was a volcano in full eruption, with violent explosions of gas and gushings forth of lava. The words for the elemental occurrences of nature are not, as a rule, very poetical: one thinks of a beautiful phenomenon like the meteor, which in German is called "Sternschnuppe" (smouldering wick of a star, which is "snuffed" out). Certain South American Indians call it "piss of the stars." The Voile de la Vierge waterfall in the Valais, famous for its beauty, has only recently been called by this poetic name. Formerly it was known as the Pissevache. One takes the name from the nearest source.

22 [The term is reported from the United States. In a popular song, "Feet Up, Pat Him on the Po-po," copyright 1952, a baby is being playfully patted on the buttocks. The term is said to occur in American Southern dialect and appears to be unrelated to German.—EDITORS.]

276   It seems very puzzling at first why the figure of Chiwantopel, whom Miss Miller awaited with positively mystical expectation and whom she herself compared, in a note, to a mediumistic control, should get into such a disreputable neighbourhood that his very essence—his name—appears to be bound up with those out-of-the-way regions of the body. In order to understand this, we have to realize that when something is produced from the unconscious, the first thing to come up is the infantile material that has long been lost to memory. We have, therefore, to adopt the point of view of that time, when this material was still on the surface. So if a much venerated object is related by the unconscious to the anal region, we have to conclude that this is a way of expressing respect and attention, such as the child feels for these forbidden functions. Naturally traces of this infantile interest still linger on in the adult. The only question is whether this interest corresponds to the psychology of the child. Before we attempt to answer this question, it must be said at once that the anal region is very closely connected with veneration. An Oriental fairy-tale relates that the Crusaders used to anoint themselves with the excrement of the Pope in order to make themselves more formidable. One of my patients, who had a special veneration for her father, had a fantasy in which she saw her father sitting on a commode in a dignified manner, while people filed past greeting him effusively. We might also mention the intimate connection between excrement and gold: [23] the lowest value allies itself to the highest. The alchemists sought their *prima materia* in excrement, one of the arcane substances from which it was hoped that the mystic figure of the *filius philosophorum* would emerge ("in stercore invenitur"). A very religiously brought-up young patient once dreamt that she saw the Crucifix formed of excrement on the bottom of a blue-flowered chamber-pot. The contrast is so enormous that one can only assume that the valuations of childhood are totally different from ours. And so, indeed, they are.

[23] De Gubernatis (*Zoological Mythology*) says that dung and gold are always associated in folklore, and Freud tells us the same thing on the basis of his psychological experience. Grimm reports the following magical practice: "If you want money in the house all the year round, you must eat lentils on New Year's Day." This singular association is very simply explained by the indigestibility of lentils, which reappear in the form of coins. In this manner one defecates money

Children bring to the act of defecation and its products an interest [24] such as is later evinced only by the hypochondriac. We can only begin to understand this interest when we realize that the young child connects defecation with a theory of propagation. This puts a somewhat different complexion on the matter. The child thinks: that is how things are produced, how they "come out."

277   The same child on whom I reported in my "Psychic Conflicts in a Child" and who had a well-developed anal birth theory, like Freud's "Little Hans," [25] later contracted the habit of sitting for hours on the toilet. On one occasion her father, growing impatient, went to the toilet and called: "Come out at once! Whatever are you doing?" Whereupon the answer came from within: "I'm doing a little cart and two ponies!" So the child was "making" a little cart and two ponies, things she particularly wanted at that moment. In this way one can make whatever one wishes. The child wishes passionately for a doll or, at heart, for a real baby—that is, she is practising for her future biological task; and in exactly the same way that things in general are produced, she makes the "doll" [26] that stands for the baby and all her other wishes. From a patient I got a parallel fantasy dating from her childhood: in the toilet there was a crack in the wall, and she used to imagine that a fairy would come out of this crack and give her everything she wished for. The toilet is well known as the place of dreams where much is created that would later be considered unworthy of this place of origin. Lombroso recounts a pathological fantasy of two insane artists, which is relevant here:

Each of them thought he was God Almighty and the ruler of the universe. They created or produced the world by making it come forth from the rectum, like a bird's egg from the oviduct (or cloaca). One of these artists was gifted with real artistic sense. He painted a picture of himself in the act of creation: the world came forth from his anus, his member was in full erection, he was naked, surrounded by women and by all the insignia of his power.[27]

[24] A French-speaking father, who naturally denied that his child had any such interests, nevertheless mentioned that whenever the child spoke of "cacao" (cocoa) he always added "lit" (bed), meaning "caca-au-lit."
[25] "Analysis of a Phobia in a Five-year-old Boy."
[26] See the etymological connections given above.
[27] Lombroso, *Genio e Follia*, p. 141.

278   It was only after I realized these connections that an observation I made many years ago, which kept on bothering me because I had never rightly understood it, finally became clear to me. The patient was an educated woman who was separated from her husband and child under tragic circumstances and taken to an asylum. She exhibited a typical apathy and slovenliness which were considered due to "affective deterioration." As I rather doubted this deterioration and was inclined to regard it more as a secondary phenomenon, I took great pains to find out how I could get at the blocked source of affect. Finally, after more than three hours' hard work, I hit upon a train of thought that suddenly produced a violent outburst of affect in the patient. Complete affective rapport was instantly established. This happened in the morning, and when I returned at the appointed time in the evening to see her in the ward, she had smeared herself with excrement from head to foot for my reception, and cried out laughingly: "How do you like me now?" She had never done this before; it was obviously a gesture intended for my benefit. The impression it made on me was so powerful that for years afterwards I was convinced of the affective deterioration of such cases. In reality this ceremony of welcome was a drastic attempt to ward off the transference—in so far as the patient acted as an adult. But in so far as she acted on the level of regressive infantilism, the ceremony denoted an outburst of positive feeling. Hence the equivocal "Do you like me now?"

279   The birth of Chiwantopel from Popocatepetl therefore means: "I make, produce, invent him out of myself." It is the creation or birth of man by the infantile route. The first men were made from earth or clay. The Latin *lutum*, which really means 'mud,' also had the metaphorical meaning of 'filth.' Plautus even uses it as a term of abuse, something like "You scum!" The idea of anal birth recalls the motif of throwing something behind one. A well-known example of this is the story of Deucalion and Pyrrha, the sole survivors of the Flood, who were told by the oracle to throw behind them the bones of the Great Mother. They thereupon threw stones behind them, from which mankind sprang. There is a similar legend that the Dactyls sprang from the dust which the nymph Anchiale threw behind her. In this connection one thinks of the humorous sig-

nificance that attaches to anal products: in popular humour excrement is often regarded as a monument or souvenir (which in the case of criminals plays an important part in the form of the *grumus merdae*). Everyone knows the joke about the man who wandered through labyrinthine passages looking for a hidden treasure, and who, after shedding all his clothing, deposited an excrementum as a last sign-post for the journey back. In the distant past no doubt such a sign possessed as great a significance as the droppings of animals to indicate a man's whereabouts or the direction taken. Stone monuments will later have replaced this more perishable memorial.

280 As a parallel to Chiwantopel's emergence into consciousness, Miss Miller mentions another instance of a name suddenly obtruding itself on her mind: "A-ha-ma-ra-ma," which, she felt, had something Assyrian about it. As a possible source there came into her mind the words: "Asurabama (who made cuneiform bricks)." This fact was unknown to me. We know that Assurbanipal left behind him the cuneiform library excavated at Kuyunjik, and it may be that "Asurabama" has something to do with "Assurbanipal." We must also consider the name "Aholibamah," which we met in Part I. The word "Ahama-rama" likewise has associations with Anah and Aholibamah, those daughters of Cain with the sinful passion for the sons of God. This possibility points to Chiwantopel as the longed-for son of God. Was Byron thinking, perhaps, of the two whorish sisters Aholah and Aholibah (Ezek. 23)? Aholibamah was the name of one of Esau's wives (Gen. 36:2 and 14), and another wife was called Adah. Dr. Riwkah Schärf has drawn my attention to a dissertation by Georg Mayn (1887) on Byron's "Heaven and Earth," in which the author points out that Anah was probably Adah in the original draft, but that Byron altered it to Anah because Adah had already occurred in his drama "Cain." So far as the meaning of the words is concerned, Aholibamah is reminiscent of Aholah and Aholibah: Aholah means "(she has) her (own) tabernacle," i.e., her own temple, and Aholibah means "my tabernacle is in her," i.e., in Jerusalem, just as Aholah is the name of Samaria (Ezek. 23:4). In Gen. 36:41 Aholibamah is also the name of one of the "dukes of Edom." The Canaanites worshipped on hills—*bamoth*—and a synonym for hill is *ramah*. Whether Miss Miller's neolo-

gism "Ahamarama" can legitimately be connected with this is open to question.

281   Miss Miller remarks that besides the name "Asurabama" she also thought of "Ahasuerus." This association points to a very different aspect of the problem of the unconscious personality. While the previous material told us something about the infantile theory of human birth, this association gives us a glimpse into the dynamics of the unconscious creation of personality. Ahasuerus is the Wandering Jew, whose main characteristic was that he had to wander restlessly over the earth till the end of the world. The fact that this particular name occurred to the author justifies us in following his trail.

282   The legend of Ahasuerus, whose first literary traces are to be found in the thirteenth century, appears to be of Occidental origin. The figure of the Eternal Jew has undergone even more literary elaboration than that of Faust, practically all of it dating from the last century. If the figure were not called Ahasuerus, it would still exist under another name, perhaps as the Comte de Saint-Germain, the mysterious Rosicrucian, whose immortality is assured and whose present whereabouts are supposed to be known.[28] Although the stories about Ahasuerus cannot be traced beyond the thirteenth century, the oral tradition may go much further back, and it is possible that a link with the Orient once existed. There the parallel figure is Khidr or El-Khadr, the "eternally youthful Chidher" celebrated in song by Friedrich Rückert. The legend is purely Islamic.[29] The strange thing is, however, that Khidr is not only regarded as a saint, but in Sufic circles even has the status of a deity. In view of the strict monotheism of Islam, one is inclined to think of him as a pre-Islamic, Arabian deity who, though not officially recognized by the new religion, was tolerated for reasons of expediency. But there is nothing to prove that. The first traces of Khidr are to be found in the commentaries on the Koran by al-Bukhari (d. 870) and al-Tabari (d. 923), and especially in the commentary on a noteworthy passage in the 18th Sura. This is entitled "The Cave," after the cave of the seven sleepers who, according to

[28] Popular belief refuses to give up its wandering sun-heroes. Cagliostro, for instance, is said to have driven out of the city of Basel from all the gates simultaneously, with four white horses!

[29] Cf. my paper "Concerning Rebirth," pars. 240ff.

legend, slept in it for 309 years, thus escaping the persecution, and woke up in a new age. It is interesting to see how the Koran, after lengthy moral reflections in the course of this same sura, comes to the following passage, which is especially important as regards the origin of the Khidr myth. I quote the Koran literally: [30]

And Moses said to his servant (Joshua the son of Nun): "I will not cease to wander until I have reached the place where the two seas meet, even though I journey for eighty years." But when they had reached the place where the two seas meet, they forgot their fish (which they had brought with them for food), and it took its way through a canal to the sea. And when they had gone past this place, Moses said to his servant: "Bring us our breakfast, for we are weary from our journey." But his servant answered: "See what has befallen me! When we were encamped there by the rock, I forgot the fish. Only Satan can have caused me to forget the fish and put it out of my mind, and in wondrous wise it took its way to the sea." Then Moses said: "That is the place we seek." And they went back the way they had come. And they found one of Our servants, whom We [31] had endowed with Our grace and wisdom. Moses said to him: "Shall I follow you, that you may teach me for my guidance some of the wisdom you have learnt?" But he answered: "You will not be able to endure me, for how should you have patience to bear with things you cannot comprehend?"

283   Moses now accompanies the mysterious servant of God, who does divers things which Moses cannot comprehend; finally the Unknown takes leave of him and speaks as follows:

The Jews will ask you about Dhulqarnein.[32] Say: I will tell you a story of him. We established his kingdom on earth and gave him the

[30] [The following passages are translated from the version used by the author, the source of which is not given. The material may also be found in Pickthall's trans., pp. 301ff., and Rodwell's, pp. 186ff.—TRANS.]   [31] Allah.
[32] The "two-horned." According to the commentators this refers to Alexander the Great, who in Arabian legend plays the same kind of role as Dietrich of Bern. The two-horned refers to the strength of the sun-bull. Alexander is often found on coins with the horns of Jupiter Ammon. (Pl. xxa.) This is one of the identifications of the legendary ruler with the spring sun in the sign of the Ram. There can be no doubt that mankind felt a great need to eliminate everything personal and human from its heroes so as to make them equal to the sun, i.e., absolute libido-symbols, through a kind of metastasis. If we think like Schopenhauer, we shall say "libido-symbol"; but if we think like Goethe, we say "sun." We exist because the sun sees us.

194

means of fulfilling all his wishes. He took his way until he came to the place where the sun sets, and it seemed to him as if it set in a black muddy spring. . . .

284   Now follows a moral reflection, then the story continues:

Then he took his way further, until he came to the place where the sun rises. . . .

285   If we wish to know who the unknown servant of God is, this passage tells us that he is Dhulqarnein, Alexander; he goes to the place of setting and the place of rising, like the sun. The commentators explain that the unknown servant of God is Khidr, "the Verdant One, the tireless wanderer, the teacher and counsellor of pious men, wise in divine knowledge, the immortal." [33] On the authority of al-Tabari, Khidr is connected with Dhulqarnein: Khidr, following the armies of Alexander, reached the "stream of life," and they both unwittingly drank of it, and so became immortal. Moreover, Khidr is identified by the old commentators with Elias (Elijah), who also did not die, but ascended to heaven in a fiery chariot, a feature he shares with Helios.[34] It has been conjectured that Ahasuerus owes his existence to an obscure passage in the Bible. This passage occurs in Matthew 16:28. First comes the scene where Christ appoints Peter as the rock of his Church and names him the holder of his power; then follows the prophecy of his death, ending with the words:

Verily I say unto you, There be some standing here, which shall not taste of death, till they see the Son of Man coming in his kingdom.

286   This is followed immediately by the Transfiguration:

And (he) was transfigured before them: and his face did shine as the sun, and his raiment was white as the light.

And, behold, there appeared unto them Moses and Elias talking with him.

Then answered Peter, and said unto Jesus, Lord, it is good for us to be here: if thou wilt, let us make here three tabernacles; one for thee, and one for Moses, and one for Elias.

[33] Vollers, "Chidher," pp. 234–84. This is my source for the Koran commentaries.
[34] Also with Mithras and Christ. See par 165, above.

287   From these passages it is clear that Christ is somehow equated with Elias without being identical with him,[35] although the people regarded him as Elias. The ascension, however, forms a parallel between Elias and Christ. Christ's prophecy shows that there are one or two immortals besides himself who shall not die until the Second Coming. According to John 21:21ff., John himself was considered to be one of these immortals, and in legend he is in fact not dead, but merely sleeping in the earth until the Second Coming, and his breath causes the dust to swirl around his grave.[36]

288   Another legend[37] says that Dhulqarnein brought his "friend" Khidr to the source of life, that he might drink of immortality.[38] Alexander himself bathed in the stream of life and performed the ritual ablutions. In the Arabian legend Khidr is the companion, or else he is accompanied (either by Dhulqarnein or by Elias, being "like unto" them or identical with them).[39] There are, therefore, two figures who resemble one another but are nevertheless distinct. The analogous situation in Christianity is the scene by the Jordan, where John leads Christ to the source of life. Christ, as the baptized, is here the subordinate, while John plays the superior role, as in the case of Dhulqarnein and Khidr, or Khidr and Moses, and Khidr and Elias. Vollers compares Khidr and Elias on the one hand with Gilgamesh and his primitive brother Eabani or Enkidu, and on the other hand with the Dioscuri, one of whom was mortal and the other immortal. This relation applies equally to Jesus and John the Baptist,[40] and Jesus and Peter. The last-named parallel can be explained only by comparison with the Mithraic mysteries, whose esoteric content is revealed to us in part by the surviving monuments. On the marble relief at Klagenfurt,[41] Mithras is shown crowning Helios with a crown of rays, as he kneels be-

---

[35] On the other hand, according to Matthew 17:13, Elias is to be understood as John the Baptist.

[36] Cf. the Kyffhäuser legend. [Referring to the Emperor Barbarossa, who is said to sleep inside a mountain.—EDITORS.]   [37] Vollers, "Chidher."

[38] There is also a legend that Alexander had been on the "mountain of Adam" in India, with his "minister" Khidr.

[39] These mythological equations follow the dream rule that the dreamer can be split up into several figures.

[40] John 3:30: "He must increase, but I must decrease."

[41] Cumont, *Textes*, I, pp. 172ff.

fore him or floats up to him from below. On the Osterburken monument, Mithras has in his right hand the shoulder of the mystic bull and holds it above the head of Helios, who stands bowed before him; his left hand rests on his sword hilt; a crown lies between them on the ground. Cumont[42] remarks that this scene probably represents the divine prototype of initiation into the degree of Miles, when a sword and crown were conferred on the neophyte. Helios is therefore appointed the Miles of Mithras. In general, Mithras seems to act in the capacity of patron to Helios. This recalls the bold attitude of Heracles towards the sun: on his way to fight the monster Geryon the sun burned too fiercely, so Heracles wrathfully threatened him with his invincible arrows. Helios was compelled to yield, and thereupon lent the hero the sun-ship which he used for crossing the sea. Thus Heracles came to Erythia, to the sun-cattle of Geryon.[43]

289   On the Klagenfurt monument, Mithras is also shown shaking Helios by the hand, either in farewell or in agreement. (Pl. xxiva.) In another scene he mounts the chariot of Helios for the ascension or sea-journey.[44] Cumont is of the opinion that Mithras performs a kind of ceremonial investiture: he consecrates the divine power of Helios by crowning him with his own hands.[45] This relationship corresponds to that between Christ and Peter. Peter's attribute, the cock, gives him a solar character. After Christ's ascension he becomes the visible representative of God; therefore he suffers the same death—crucifixion—as his master, replaces the chief deity of the Roman imperium, the *Sol invictus,* and becomes the head of the Church Militant and Triumphant. In the Malchus scene he already appears as the Miles of Christ, the holder of the sword. His successors all wear the triple crown. But the crown is a solar

42 Ibid., p. 173.

43 The parallel between Heracles and Mithras can be carried even further. Like Heracles, Mithras is an excellent archer. Judging from certain of the monuments, it would seem that not only Heracles, but Mithras too, was threatened in youth by a snake. The labours of Heracles have the same meaning as the conquest and sacrifice of the bull in the Mithraic mystery. (Cf. fig. 17.)

44 These three scenes are represented in a row on the Klagenfurt monument, so presumably there was some dramatic connection between them. Illustrated in Cumont, *Mysteries of Mithra,* fig. 24, p. 133.

45 Ibid. See also Roscher, II, 3048, 42ff.

attribute, hence the Pope is a symbolical "solis invicti comes" like the Roman Caesars. The setting sun appoints a successor whom he invests with his solar power. Dhulqarnein gives Khidr eternal life, Khidr imparts his wisdom to Moses; there is even a legend that Moses' forgetful servant Joshua unwittingly drank from the fountain of life, whereupon he became immortal and, as a punishment, was placed in a boat by Khidr and Moses and cast out to sea—another fragment of a sun-myth, the motif of the "sea-journey." [46]

290   The symbol for that portion of the zodiac in which the sun re-enters the yearly cycle at the time of the winter solstice is Capricorn, originally known as the "Goat-Fish" (αἰγόχερως, 'goat-horned'): the sun mounts like a goat to the tops of the highest mountains, and then plunges into the depths of the sea like a fish. The fish in dreams occasionally signifies the unborn child,[47] because the child before its birth lives in the water like a fish; similarly, when the sun sinks into the sea, it becomes child and fish at once. The fish is therefore a symbol of renewal and rebirth.

291   The journey of Moses with his servant Joshua is a life-journey (it lasted eighty years). They grow old together and lose the life-force, i.e., the fish, which "in wondrous wise took its way to the sea" (setting of the sun). When the two notice their loss, they discover at the place where the source of life is found (where the dead fish revived and sprang into the sea) Khidr wrapped in his mantle,[48] sitting on the ground. In another version he was sitting on an island in the midst of the sea, "in the wettest place on earth," which means that he had just been born from the maternal depths. Where the fish vanished Khidr, the Verdant One, was born as a "son of the watery deep," his head veiled, proclaiming divine wisdom, like the

[46] Cf. Frobenius, *Zeitalter des Sonnengottes.*

[47] This interpretation is still a bit mythological; to be more accurate, the fish signifies an autonomous content of the unconscious. Manu had a fish with horns. Christ was a fish, like Ἰχθύs, son of the Syrophoenician Derceto. Joshua ben Nun was called "son of the fish." The "two-horned" (Dhulqarnein = Alexander) turns up in the legend of Khidr. (Cf. pl. xxa.)

[48] The wrapping signifies invisibility, hence to be a "spirit." That is why the neophytes were veiled in the mysteries. (Cf. pl. ivb.) Children born with a caul over their heads are supposed to be particularly fortunate.

Babylonian Oannes-Ea (cf. fig. 18), who was represented in fish form and daily came out of the sea as a fish to teach the people wisdom.[49]

Fig. 18. Priest with a fish-mask, representing Oannes
Relief, Nimrud

292   Oannes' name was brought into connection with John's. With the rising of the reborn sun the fish that dwelt in darkness, surrounded by all the terrors of night and death,[50] becomes

[49] The Etruscan Tages, the boy who sprang from the freshly ploughed furrow, was also a teacher of wisdom. In the Litaolane myth of the Basuto (Frobenius, p. 105), we are told how a monster devoured all human beings and left only one woman alive, who gave birth to a son, the hero, in a cowshed (instead of a cave). Before she could prepare a bed of straw for the infant, he was already grown up and spoke "words of wisdom." The rapid growth of the hero, a recurrent motif, seems to indicate that the birth and apparent childhood of the hero are extraordinary because his birth is really a rebirth, for which reason he is able to adapt so quickly to his heroic role. For a more detailed interpretation of the Khidr legend, see my paper "Concerning Rebirth," pars. 240ff.

[50] Cf. Ra's fight with the night serpent.

the shining, fiery day-star. This gives the words of John the Baptist a special significance (Matthew 3 : 11):

I indeed baptize you with water unto repentance; but he that cometh after me is mightier than I . . . he shall baptize you with the Holy Ghost, and with fire.

293   Following Vollers, we may compare Khidr and Elias (or Moses and his servant Joshua) with Gilgamesh and his brother Eabani (Enkidu). Gilgamesh wanders through the world, driven by fear and longing, to find immortality. (Pl. xix.) His journey takes him across the sea to the wise Utnapishtim (Noah), who knows how to cross the waters of death. There Gilgamesh has to dive down to the bottom of the sea for the magical herb that is to lead him back to the land of men. On the return journey he is accompanied by an immortal mariner, who, banished by the curse of Utnapishtim, has been forbidden to return to the land of the blessed. But when Gilgamesh arrives home, a serpent steals the magic herb from him (i.e., the fish slips back into the sea). Because of the loss of the magic herb, Gilgamesh's journey has been in vain; instead he comes back in the company of an immortal, whose fate we cannot learn from the fragments of the epic. Jensen [51] believes that this banished immortal is the prototype of Ahasuerus.

294   Once again we meet the motif of the Dioscuri: mortal and immortal, the setting and rising sun. The Mithraic bull-sacrifice is often represented as flanked by the two dadophors, Cautes and Cautopates, one with a raised and the other with a lowered torch. (Cf. pl. xx*b*.) They form a pair of brothers whose characters are revealed by the symbolic position of the torches. Cumont not unjustly connects them with the sepulchral Erotes, who as genies with inverted torches have a traditional meaning. One would stand for death, the other for life. There are certain points of resemblance between the Mithraic sacrifice (where the bull in the centre is flanked on either side by dadophors) and the Christian sacrifice of the lamb (or ram). The Crucified

[51] *Gilgamesch-Epos*, I, p. 50. When revising this book, I left the above account, which is based mainly on Jensen, in its original form, though certain details could have been supplemented by the results of recent research. I refer the reader to Heidel, *The Gilgamesh Epic and Old Testament Parallels*; Schott, *Das Gilgamesch-Epos;* Speiser's version in Pritchard, ed., *Ancient Near Eastern Texts;* and especially to Thompson's remarkable trans., *The Epic of Gilgamish.*

is traditionally flanked by two thieves, one of whom ascends to paradise while the other descends to hell.[52] The Semitic gods were often flanked by two *paredroi;* for instance, the Baal of Edessa was accompanied by Aziz and Monimos (Baal being astrologically interpreted as the sun, and Aziz and Monimos as Mars and Mercury). According to the Babylonian view, the gods are grouped into triads. Thus the two thieves somehow go together with Christ. The two dadophors are, as Cumont has shown, offshoots [53] from the main figure of Mithras, who was supposed to have a secret triadic character. Dionysius the Areopagite reports that the magicians held a feast in honour of τοῦ τρι-πλασίου Μίθρου [54] (the threefold Mithras).[55]

295   As Cumont observes,[56] Cautes and Cautopates sometimes carry in their hands the head of a bull and of a scorpion respectively. Taurus and Scorpio are equinoctial signs,[57] and this is a clear indication that the sacrifice was primarily connected with the sun cycle: the rising sun that sacrifices itself at the summer solstice, and the setting sun. Since it was not easy to represent sunrise and sunset in the sacrificial drama, this idea had to be shown outside it.

296   We have already pointed out that the Dioscuri represent a similar idea in somewhat different form: one sun is mortal, the other immortal. As this whole solar mythology is psychology projected into the heavens, the underlying idea could probably be paraphrased thus: just as man consists of a mortal and an

52 The difference between this and the Mithraic sacrifice is significant. The dadophors are harmless gods of light who take no part in the sacrifice. The Christian scene is much more dramatic. The inner relation of the dadophors to Mithras, of which I will speak later, suggests that there was a similar relation between Christ and the two thieves.

53 For instance, there is the following dedication on a monument: "D[eo] I[nvicto] M[ithrae] Cautopati." One finds that "Deo Mithrae Caute" or "Deo Mithrae Cautopati" is interchangeable with "Deo Invicto Mithrae" or "Deo Invicto," or simply "Invicto." Sometimes the dadophors are equipped with knife and bow, the attributes of Mithras. From this we can conclude that the three figures represent three different states, as it were, of a single person. Cf. Cumont, *Textes*, I, pp. 208f.

54 Ibid., p. 208f.

55 The triadic symbolism is discussed in my "A Psychological Approach to the Dogma of the Trinity," pars. 172ff.

56 *Textes*, I, p. 210.

57 For the period from 4300 to 2150 B.C. So, although these signs had long been superseded, they were preserved in the cults until well into the Christian era.

immortal part, so the sun is a pair of brothers, one of whom is mortal, the other immortal. Man is mortal, yet there are exceptions who are immortal, or there is something immortal in us. Thus the gods, or figures like Khidr and the Comte de Saint-Germain, are our immortal part which continues intangibly to exist. The sun comparison tells us over and over again that the dynamic of the gods is psychic energy. This is our immortality, the link through which man feels inextinguishably one with the continuity of all life.[58] The life of the psyche is the life of mankind. Welling up from the depths of the unconscious, its springs gush forth from the root of the whole human race, since the individual is, biologically speaking, only a twig broken off from the mother and transplanted.

297   The psychic life-force, the libido, symbolizes itself in the sun [59] or personifies itself in figures of heroes with solar attributes. At the same time it expresses itself through phallic symbols. Both possibilities are found on a late Babylonian gem from Lajard's collection (fig. 19). In the middle stands an androgynous deity. On the masculine side there is a snake with a sun halo round its head; on the feminine side another snake with a sickle moon above it. This picture has a symbolic sexual nuance: on the masculine side there is a lozenge, a favourite symbol of the female genitals, and on the feminine side a wheel without its rim. The spokes are thickened at the ends into

[58] The Shvetashvatara Upanished (4, 6ff.) uses the following parable to describe the individual and the universal soul, the personal and transpersonal atman:

> Behold, upon the selfsame tree,
> Two birds, fast-bound companions, sit.
> This one enjoys the ripened fruit,
> The other looks, but does not eat.

> On such a tree my spirit crouched,
> Deluded by its powerlessness,
> Till seeing with joy how great its Lord,
> It found from sorrow swift release. . . .

> Hymns, sacrifices, Vedic lore,
> Past, future, all by him are taught.
> The Maya-Maker thinks the world
> In which by Maya we are caught.

(Trans. based on Hume, pp. 403f.)

[59] Among the elements composing man, the Mithraic liturgy lays particular stress on fire as the divine element, describing it as τὸ εἰς ἐμὴν κρᾶσιν θεοδώρητον (the divine gift in my composition). Dieterich, *Mithrasliturgie*, p. 58.

knobs, which, like the fingers we mentioned earlier, have a phallic meaning. It seems to be a phallic wheel such as was not unknown in antiquity. There are obscene gems on which Cupid is shown turning a wheel consisting entirely of phalli.[60] As to what the sun signifies, I discovered in the collection of antiquities at Verona a late Roman inscription with the following symbols: [61]

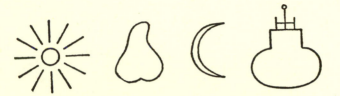

298   The symbolism is plain: sun = phallus, moon = vessel (uterus). This interpretation is confirmed by another monument from the same collection. The symbols are the same, except that the vessel [62] has been replaced by the figure of a woman. Certain symbols on coins can probably be interpreted in a similar manner. In Lajard's *Recherches sur la culte de Vénus* there is a coin from Perga, showing Artemis as a conical stone flanked by a masculine figure (alleged to be the deity Men) and a female figure (alleged to be Artemis). Men (otherwise called Lunus) appears on an Attic bas-relief with a spear, flanked by Pan with a club, and a female figure.[63] From this it is clear that sexuality as well as the sun can be used to symbolize the libido.

299   One further point deserves mention here. The dadophor Cautopates is often represented with a cock [64] and pine-cones. These are the attributes of the Phrygian god Men (pl. xxia), whose cult was very widespread. He was shown with the pileus [65] (or "Phrygian cap") and pine-cones, riding on the cock, and also

60 An illustration of the periodicity or rhythm expressed in sexuality.
61 Reproduced not from a photograph, but from a drawing I myself made.
62 In a myth of the Bakairi Indians, of Brazil, a woman appears who sprang from a corn mortar. A Zulu myth tells a woman to catch a drop of blood in a pot, then close the pot, put it aside for eight months, and open it again in the ninth month. She follows this advice, opens the pot in the ninth month, and finds a child inside it. (Frobenius, I, p. 237.)
63 Roscher, *Lexikon*, II, 2733/4, s.v. "Men."
64 A well-known sun-animal.   65 Like Mithras and the dadophors.

in the form of a boy, just as the dadophors were boyish figures. (This latter characteristic relates both them and Men to the Cabiri and Dactyls.) Now Men has affinities with Attis, the son and lover of Cybele. In Imperial times Men and Attis merged into one. Attis also wears the pileus like Men, Mithras, and the dadophors. As the son and lover of his mother he raises the incest problem. Incest leads logically to ritual castration in the Attis-Cybele cult; for according to legend the hero, driven mad by his mother, mutilates himself. I must refrain from going into

Fig. 19. Androgynous divinity
Late Babylonian gem
Fig. 20. Cybele and her son-lover Attis
Roman coin

this question more deeply at present, as I would prefer to discuss the incest problem at the end of this book. Here I would only point out that the incest motif is bound to arise, because when the regressing libido is introverted for internal or external reasons it always reactivates the parental imagos and thus apparently re-establishes the infantile relationship. But this relationship cannot be re-established, because the libido is an adult libido which is already bound to sexuality and inevitably imports an incompatible, incestuous character into the reactivated relationship to the parents.[66] It is this sexual character that now gives rise to the incest symbolism. Since incest must be avoided at all costs, the result is either the death of the son-lover or his self-castration as punishment for the incest he has

66 This explanation is not satisfactory, because I found it impossible to go into the archetypal incest problem and all its complications here. I have dealt with it at some length in my "Psychology of the Transference."

committed, or else the sacrifice of instinctuality, and especially of sexuality, as a means of preventing or expiating the incestuous longing. (Cf. fig. 20.) Sex being one of the most obvious examples of instinctuality, it is sex which is liable to be most affected by these sacrificial measures, i.e., through abstinence. The heroes are usually wanderers,[67] and wandering is a symbol of longing,[68] of the restless urge which never finds its object, of nostalgia for the lost mother. The sun comparison can easily be taken in this sense: the heroes are like the wandering sun, from which it is concluded that the myth of the hero is a solar myth. It seems to us, rather, that he is first and foremost a self-representation of the longing of the unconscious, of its unquenched and unquenchable desire for the light of consciousness. But consciousness, continually in danger of being led astray by its own light and of becoming a rootless will o' the wisp, longs for the healing power of nature, for the deep wells of being and for unconscious communion with life in all its countless forms. Here I must make way for the master, who has plumbed to the root of these Faustian longings:

> MEPHISTOPHELES: This lofty mystery I must now unfold.
>   Goddesses throned in solitude, sublime,
>   Set in no place, still less in any time,
>   At the mere thought of them my blood runs cold.
>   They are the Mothers!
>
> . . . .
>
>   Goddesses, unknown to mortal mind,
>   And named indeed with dread among our kind.
>   To reach them you must plumb earth's deepest vault;
>   That we have need of them is your own fault.

> FAUST: Where leads the way?

> MEPHISTOPHELES: There's none! To the untrodden,
>   Untreadable regions—the unforgotten
>   And unforgettable—for which prepare!
>   There are no bolts, no hatches to be lifted,
>   Through endless solitudes you shall be drifted.
>   Can you imagine Nothing everywhere?

. . . .

[67] Like Gilgamesh, Dionysus, Heracles, Mithras, etc.
[68] Cf. Graf, *Richard Wagner im Fliegenden Holländer.*

Supposing you had swum across the ocean
And gazed upon the immensity of space,
Still you would see wave after wave in motion,
And even though you feared the world should cease,
You'd still see something—in the limpid green
Of the calm deep are gliding dolphins seen,
The flying clouds above, sun, moon, and star.
But blank is that eternal Void afar.
You do not hear your footfall, and you meet
No solid ground on which to set your feet.

. . . .

Here, take this key.

. . . .

The key will smell the right place from all others:
Follow it down, it leads you to the Mothers.

. . . .

Then to the depths!—I could as well say height:
It's all the same. From the Existent fleeing,
Take the free world of forms for your delight,
Rejoice in things that long have ceased from being.
The busy brood will weave like coiling cloud,
But swing your key to keep away the crowd!

. . . .

A fiery tripod warns you to beware,
This is the nethermost place where now you are.
You shall behold the Mothers by its light,
Some of them sit, some walk, some stand upright,
Just as they please. Formation, transformation,
Eternal Mind's eternal recreation.
Thronged round with images of things to be,
They see you not, shadows are all they see.
Then pluck up heart, the danger here is great,
Approach the tripod, do not hesitate,
And touch it with the key.[69]

[69] Trans. based on MacNeice, pp. 175ff. Cf. also trans. by Wayne, Part II, pp. 76ff.

V

SYMBOLS OF THE MOTHER AND OF REBIRTH

300   The vision that follows the birth of the hero is described by Miss Miller as a "swarm of people." We know that this image symbolizes a secret,[1] or rather, the unconscious. The possession of a secret cuts a person off from his fellow human beings. Since it is of the utmost importance for the economy of the libido that his rapport with the environment should be as complete and as unimpeded as possible, the possession of subjectively important secrets usually has a very disturbing effect. It is therefore especially beneficial for the neurotic if he can at last disburden himself of his secrets during treatment. I have often noticed that the symbol of the crowd, and particularly of a streaming mass of people in motion, expresses violent motions of the unconscious. Such symbols always indicate an activation of the unconscious and an incipient dissociation between it and the ego.

301   The vision of the swarm of people undergoes further development: horses appear, and a battle is fought.

302   For the time being, I would like to follow Silberer and place the meaning of these visions in the "functional" category, because, fundamentally, the idea of the swarming crowd is an expression for the mass of thoughts now rushing in upon consciousness. The same is true of the battle, and possibly of the horses, which symbolize movement or energy. The deeper meaning of the horses will only become apparent in our treatment of mother-symbols. The next vision has a more definite character and a more significant content: Miss Miller sees a "dream-city." The picture is similar to one she had seen a short time before on the cover of a magazine. Unfortunately, further details are lacking. But one can easily imagine that this dream-city is something very beautiful and ardently longed for—a kind of

[1] Freud, *The Interpretation of Dreams*, pp. 245-46, 288.

heavenly Jerusalem, as the poet of the Apocalypse dreamt it.[2] (Cf. pl. xxiia.)

303   The city is a maternal symbol, a woman who harbours the inhabitants in herself like children. It is therefore understandable that the three mother-goddesses, Rhea, Cybele, and Diana, all wear the mural crown (pl. xxivb). The Old Testament treats the cities of Jerusalem, Babylon, etc. just as if they were women. Isaiah (47 : 1ff.) cries out:

> Come down, and sit in the dust, O virgin daughter of Babylon, sit on the ground: there is no throne, O daughter of the Chaldaeans: for thou shalt no more be called tender and delicate.
> Take the millstones, and grind meal: uncover thy locks, make bare the leg, uncover the thigh, pass over the rivers.
> Thy nakedness shall be uncovered, yea, thy shame shall be seen: I will take vengeance, and I will not meet thee as a man. . . .
> Sit thou silent, and get thee into darkness, O daughter of the Chaldaeans: for thou shalt no more be called, The lady of kingdoms.

304   Jeremiah (50 : 12) says of Babylon:

> Your mother shall be sore confounded; she that bare you shall be ashamed.

305   Strong, unconquered cities are virgins; colonies are sons and daughters. Cities are also harlots; Isaiah (23 : 16) says of Tyre:

> Take an harp, go about the city, thou harlot that hast been forgotten,

and (1 : 21):

> How is the faithful city become an harlot!

306   We find a similar symbolism in the myth of Ogyges, the prehistoric king of Egypt who reigned in Thebes, and whose wife was appropriately called Thebe. The Boeotian city of Thebes founded by Cadmus received on that account the cognomen "Ogygian." This cognomen was also applied to the great Flood, which was called "Ogygian" because it happened under Ogyges. We shall see later on that this coincidence can hardly be accidental. The fact that the city and the wife of Ogyges both have the same name indicates that there must be some relation between the city and the woman, which is not difficult to under-

2 Today we would call it a mandala symbol of the self.

stand because the city is identical with the woman. There is a similar idea in Hindu mythology, where Indra appears as the husband of Urvara. But Urvara means the "fertile land." In the same way the seizure of a country by the king was regarded as his marriage with the land. Similar ideas must also have existed in Europe. Princes at their accession had to guarantee a good harvest. The Swedish king Domaldi was actually killed as a result of failure of the crops (Ynglinga Saga, 18). In the Hindu Ramayana, the hero Rama marries Sita, the furrow. To the same circle of ideas belongs the Chinese custom of the emperor's having to plough a furrow on ascending the throne. The idea of the soil as feminine also embraces the idea of continuous cohabitation with the woman, a physical interpenetration. The god Shiva, as Mahadeva and Parvati, is both male and female: he has even given one half of his body to his wife Parvati as a dwelling-place (pl. XXIII). The motif of continuous cohabitation is expressed in the well-known lingam symbol found everywhere in Indian temples: the base is a female symbol, and within it stands the phallus.³ (Pl. XXV.) This symbol is rather like the phallic baskets and chests of the Greeks. The chest or casket is a female symbol (cf. fig. 21 and pl. LIII), i.e., the womb, a common enough conception in the older mythologies.⁴ The chest, barrel, or basket with its precious contents was often thought of as floating on the water, thus forming an analogy to the course of the sun. The sun sails over the sea like an immortal god who every evening is immersed in the maternal waters and is born anew in the morning.

307   Frobenius writes:

If, then, we find the blood-red sunrise connected with the idea that a birth is taking place, the birth of the young sun, the question immediately arises: Whose is the paternity? How did the woman become pregnant? And since this woman symbolizes the same idea as

³ Another form of the same motif is the Persian idea of the tree of life, which stands in the lake of rain, Vouru-Kasha. The seeds of this tree were mixed with the water and so maintained the fertility of the earth. The Vendidad, 5, 17ff. (trans. by Darmesteter, p. 54), says that the waters flow "to the sea Vouru-Kasha, towards the well-watered tree, whereon grow the seeds of my plants of every kind. . . . Those plants I, Ahura-Mazda, rain down upon the earth, to bring food to the faithful, and fodder to the beneficent cow." Another tree of life is the white haoma, which grows in the spring Ardvisura, the water of life. Spiegel, *Erānische Altertumskunde*, I, pp. 465ff.   ⁴ Examples in Rank, *Birth of the Hero*.

the fish, which means the sea (on the assumption that the sun descends into the sea as well as rises out of it), the strange primitive answer is that the sea has previously swallowed the old sun. The resulting myth is that since the sea-woman devoured the sun and now brings a new sun into the world, she obviously became pregnant in that way.[5]

308   All these sea-going gods are solar figures. They are enclosed in a chest or ark for the "night sea journey" (Frobenius), often in the company of a woman (pl. xxiib)—an inversion of the actual situation, but linking up with the theme of continuous cohabitation we met above. During the night sea journey the sun-god is shut up in the mother's womb, and often threatened by all kinds of dangers.

309   Instead of using numerous separate examples, I shall content myself with reproducing the diagram which Frobenius constructed from numberless myths of this sort:

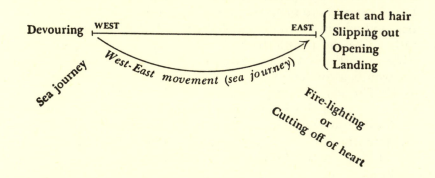

310   Frobenius gives the following legend by way of illustration:

A hero is devoured by a water-monster in the West (*devouring*). The animal travels with him to the East (*sea journey*). Meanwhile, the hero lights a fire in the belly of the monster (*fire-lighting*), and feeling hungry, cuts himself a piece of the heart (*cutting off of heart*). Soon afterwards, he notices that the fish has glided on to dry land (*landing*); he immediately begins to cut open the animal from within (*opening*); then he slips out (*slipping out*). It was so hot in the fish's belly that all his hair has fallen out (*heat and hair*). The hero may at the same time free all those who were previously devoured by the monster, and who now slip out too.[6]

[5] Frobenius, *Das Zeitalter des Sonnengottes*, p. 30.   [6] Ibid., p. 421.

311   A very close parallel is Noah's journey over the Flood that killed all living things; only he and his animals lived to experience a new Creation. A Polynesian myth [7] tells how the hero, in the belly of Kombili, the King Fish, seized his obsidian knife and cut open the fish's belly. "He slipped out and beheld a splendour. Then he sat down and began to think. 'I wonder where I am?' he said to himself. Then the sun rose up with a bound and threw itself from one side to the other." The sun had again slipped out. Frobenius cites from the Ramayana the story of the ape Hanuman, who represents the sun-hero:

The sun, travelling through the air with Hanuman in it, cast a shadow on the sea, a sea-monster seized hold of it and drew Hanuman down from the sky. But when Hanuman saw that the monster was about to devour him, he stretched himself out to enormous size, and the monster followed suit. Then Hanuman shrank to the size of a thumb, slipped into the huge body of the monster, and came out on the other side.[7a] Hanuman thereupon resumed his flight, and encountered a new obstacle in another sea monster, who was the mother of Rahu, the sun-devouring demon. She also drew Hanuman down to her by his shadow.[8] Once more he had recourse to his earlier stratagem, made himself small, and slipped into her body; but scarcely was he inside than he swelled up to gigantic size, burst her, and killed her, and so made his escape.[9]

We now understand why the Indian fire-bringer Matarisvan is called "he who swells in the mother." The ark (fig. 21), chest, casket, barrel, ship, etc. is an analogy of the womb, like the sea into which the sun sinks for rebirth. That which swells in the mother can also signify her conquest and death. Fire-making is a pre-eminently conscious act and therefore "kills" the dark state of union with the mother.

312   In the light of these ideas we can understand the mythological statements about Ogyges: it is he who possesses the mother, the city, and is thus united with the mother; therefore under him came the great flood, for it is typical of the sun myth that the hero, once he is united with the woman "hard to attain," is

---

[7] Ibid., pp. 6of.

[7a] Elsewhere in the poem we are told that he came out of the monster's right ear (like Rabelais' Gargantua, who was born from the ear of his mother).

[8] This probably means simply his soul. No moral considerations are implied.

[9] Frobenius, pp. 173f.

exposed in a cask and thrown out to sea, and then lands on a distant shore to begin a new life. The middle section, the night sea journey in the ark, is lacking in the Ogyges tradition. But the rule in mythology is that the typical parts of a myth can be fitted together in every conceivable variation, which makes it

Fig. 21. Noah in the Ark
Enamelled altar of Nicholas of Verdun, 1186,
Klosterneuburg, near Vienna

extraordinarily difficult to interpret one myth without a knowledge of all the others. The meaning of this cycle of myths is clear enough: it is the longing to attain rebirth through a return to the womb, and to become immortal like the sun. This longing for the mother is amply expressed in the literature of the Bible. I cite first the passage in Galatians 4 : 26ff. and 5 : 1:

212

But Jerusalem which is above is free, which is the mother of us all.

For it is written, Rejoice, thou barren that bearest not; break forth and cry, thou that travailest not: for the desolate hath many more children than she which hath an husband.

Now we, brethren, as Isaac was, are the children of promise.

But as then he that was born after the flesh persecuted him that was born after the Spirit, even so it is now.

Nevertheless what saith the scripture? Cast out the bondwoman and her son: for the son of the bondwoman shall not be heir with the son of the freewoman.

So then, brethren, we are not children of the bondwoman, but of the free.

Stand fast therefore in the liberty wherewith Christ hath made us free . . .

313   The Christians are children of the Higher City, not sons of the earthly city-mother, who is to be cast out; for those born after the flesh are opposed to those born after the spirit, who are not born from the fleshly mother but from a symbol of the mother. Here again one thinks of the American Indians who say that the first man was born from a sword-hilt and a shuttle. The symbol-creating process substitutes for the mother the city, the well, the cave, the Church, etc. (Cf. pls. xxiia, xxxa.) This substitution is due to the fact that the regression of libido reactivates the ways and habits of childhood, and above all the relation to the mother; [10] but what was natural and useful to the child is a psychic danger for the adult, and this is expressed by the symbol of incest. Because the incest taboo opposes the libido and blocks the path to regression, it is possible for the libido to be canalized into the mother analogies thrown up by the unconscious. In that way the libido becomes progressive again, and even attains a level of consciousness higher than before. The meaning and purpose of this canalization are particularly evident when the city appears in place of the mother: the infantile attachment (whether primary or secondary) is a crippling limitation for the adult, whereas attachment to the city fosters his civic virtues and at least enables him to lead a useful existence. In primitives the tribe takes the place of the city. We find a well-developed city symbolism in the Johannine Apocalypse, where two cities play a great part, one being cursed

10 And, of course, to the father, though the relation to the mother naturally takes first place, being on a deeper level.

and execrated, the other ardently desired. We read in the Revelation (17 : 1ff.):

> Come hither; I will show unto thee the judgement of the great whore that sitteth upon many waters:
> With whom the kings of the earth have committed fornication, and the inhabitants of the earth have been made drunk with the wine of her fornication.
> So he carried me away in the spirit into the wilderness: and I saw a woman sit upon a scarlet coloured beast, full of names of blasphemy, having seven heads and ten horns.
> And the woman was arrayed in purple and scarlet colour, and decked with gold and precious stones and pearls, having a golden cup in her hand full of abominations and filthiness of her fornication:
> And upon her forehead was a name written: Mystery, Babylon the Great, the Mother of Harlots and Abominations of the Earth.
> And I saw the woman drunken with the blood of the saints, and with the blood of the martyrs of Jesus: and when I saw her, I wondered with a great admiration. [Fig. 22.]

314   There now follows a barely intelligible interpretation of the vision, the main points of interest being that the seven heads of the dragon signify "seven mountains, on which the woman sitteth." This is probably a direct allusion to Rome, the city whose temporal power oppressed the world at that time. "The waters where the whore [the mother] sitteth" are "peoples, and multitudes, and nations, and tongues," and this too seems to refer to Rome, for she is the mother of peoples and possesses all lands. Just as colonies are called "daughters," so the peoples subject to Rome are like members of a family ruled over by the mother. In another scene the kings of the earth, i.e., the "sons," commit fornication with her. The Apocalypse continues (18 : 2ff.):

> Babylon the great is fallen, is fallen, and is become the habitation of devils, and the hold of every foul spirit, and a cage of every unclean and hateful bird.
> For all nations have drunk of the wine of the wrath of her fornication, and the kings of the earth have committed fornication with her.

315   This mother, then, is not only the mother of all abominations, but the receptacle of all that is wicked and unclean. The

Fig. 22. The Great Whore of Babylon
New Testament engraving by H. Burgkmaier, Augsburg, 1523

birds are soul-images,[11] by which are meant the souls of the damned and evil spirits. Thus the mother becomes the underworld, the City of the Damned. In this primordial image of the woman on the dragon [12] we recognize Echidna, the mother of

[11] In the Babylonian underworld, for instance, the souls wear feather-dresses like birds. Cf. the Gilgamesh Epic.
[12] In a 14th-century copy of the gospels, at Bruges, there is a miniature which shows the "woman," beautiful as the mother of God, standing with the *lower* half of her body in a dragon.

every hellish horror. Babylon is the symbol of the Terrible Mother, who leads the peoples into whoredom with her devilish temptations and makes them drunk with her wine (cf. fig. 22). Here the intoxicating drink is closely associated with fornication, for it too is a libido symbol, as we have already seen in the soma-fire-sun parallel.

316   After the fall and curse of Babylon, we find the hymn (Rev. 19 : 6ff.) which brings us from the lower half of the mother to the upper half, where everything that incest would have made impossible now becomes possible:

> Alleluia: for the Lord God omnipotent reigneth.
> Let us be glad and rejoice, and give honour to him: for the marriage of the Lamb [13] is come, and his wife hath made herself ready.
> And to her was granted that she should be arrayed in fine linen, clean and white: for the fine linen is the righteousness of saints.
> And he saith unto me, Write, Blessed are they which are called unto the marriage supper of the Lamb.

[13] The Greek text has τὸ ἀρνίον, 'little goat, kid,' a diminutive of the obsolete ἀρήν, 'ram.' (Theophrastus uses it in the sense of "young scion" of a family.) The related word ἄγνις characterizes a festival held annually in Argos in honour of Linus, where the so-called Linus lament was sung. Linus, the child of Psamathe and Apollo, was exposed at birth by his mother from fear of her father Crotopus, and was torn to pieces by dogs. In revenge Apollo sent a dragon, Poine, into the land of Crotopus, and the oracle at Delphi commanded a yearly lament by the women and maidens for the dead Linus. Honour was also paid to Psamathe. The Linus lament, as Herodotus shows (II, 79), was analogous to the lamentation for Adonis and Tammuz in Phoenicia, Cyprus, and Egypt. In Egypt, Linus was called Maneros. Brugsch thinks that the name Maneros comes from the Egyptian cry of lamentation *maa-n-chru,* 'come to the call.' The dragon Poine had the disagreeable habit of tearing children out of their mothers' wombs. All these motifs are to be found in Revelation 12 : 1f., where the child of the sun-woman was threatened by a dragon and afterwards "caught up" to God. Herod's massacre of the innocents is the "human" form of this primordial image. (Cf. Brugsch, *Adonisklage und Linoslied.*) Dieterich, in *Abraxas,* refers to the parallel myth of Apollo and Python, of which he gives the following version (based on Hyginus): Python, the son of the earth and a mighty dragon, had been told by an oracle that he would be slain by the son of Leto. Leto was with child by Zeus, but Hera arranged matters so that she could only give birth where the sun did not shine. When Python saw that Leto was near her time, he began to pursue her in order to compass her death; but Boreas carried her to Poseidon, who brought her to Ortygia and covered the island with waves. Python, unable to find Leto, went back to Parnassus, and Poseidon raised the island out of the sea. Here Leto brought forth. Four days later, Apollo took his revenge and killed Python.

317   The Lamb is the Son of Man who celebrates his nuptials with the "woman." Who the "woman" is remains obscure at first, but Rev. 21 : 9ff. shows us which "woman" is the bride, the Lamb's wife:

> Come hither, I will show thee the bride, the Lamb's wife.[14]
> And he carried me away in the spirit to a great and high mountain, and showed me that great city, the holy Jerusalem, descending out of heaven from God. [Cf. pl. xxiia.]

318   After all that has gone before, it is evident from this passage that the City, the heavenly bride who is here promised to the Son, is the mother or mother-imago.[15] In Babylon the impure maid was cast out, according to Galatians, in order that the mother-bride might be the more surely attained in the heavenly Jerusalem. It is proof of the most delicate psychological perception that the Church Fathers who compiled the canon did not allow the Apocalypse to get lost, for it is a rich mine of primitive Christian symbols.[16] The other attributes that are heaped on the heavenly Jerusalem put its mother significance beyond doubt (Rev. 22 : 1f.):

> And he showed me a pure river of water of life, clear as crystal, proceeding out of the throne of God and of the Lamb.

[14] Rev. 21 : 2: "And I John saw the holy city, new Jerusalem, coming down from God out of heaven, prepared as a bride adorned for her husband."

[15] The legend of Shaktideva, related by Somadeva Bhatta, tells how the hero, after he had escaped being devoured by a huge fish (terrible mother), finally sees the golden city and marries his beloved princess. (Frobenius, p. 175.)

[16] In the apocryphal *Acts of Thomas* (2nd century), the Church is thought of as the virgin mother-wife of Christ. One of the apostle's invocations says (trans. by Walker, p. 404): "Come, holy name of Christ, which is above every name; come, power of the Most High, and perfect compassion; come, grace most high; come, compassionate mother; come, thou that hast charge of the male child; come, thou who revealest secret mysteries. . . ." Another invocation says: "Come, perfect compassion; come, spouse of [lit. "communion with"] man; come, woman who knowest the mystery of the chosen one; come, woman who layest bare the hidden things, and makest manifest things not to be spoken, holy dove which hath brought forth twin nestlings; come, secret mother . . ." (trans. by Walker, modified). Cf. also Conybeare, "Die jungfräuliche Kirche und die jungfräuliche Mutter." The connection of the Church with the mother is beyond all doubt (cf. pl. xxxa), also the interpretation of the mother as the spouse. The "communion with man" points to the motif of continuous cohabitation. The "twin nestlings" refers to the old legend that Jesus and Thomas were twins, which was based on the Coptic idea of Jesus and his *ka*. See the *Pistis Sophia*.

In the midst of the street of it, and on either side of the river, was there the tree of life, which bare twelve manner of fruits, and yielded her fruit every month: and the leaves of the tree were for the healing of the nations.

And there shall be no more curse.

319   In this passage we meet the water-symbol which we found connected with the city in the case of Ogyges. The maternal significance of water (pl. XXVI) is one of the clearest interpretations of symbols in the whole field of mythology,[17] so that even the ancient Greeks could say that "the sea is the symbol of generation." From water comes life; [18] hence, of the two deities who here interest us most, Christ and Mithras, the latter is represented as having been born beside a river, while Christ experienced his "rebirth" in the Jordan. Christ, moreover, was born of the Πηγή,[19] the sempiternal *fons amoris* or Mother of God, whom pagan-Christian legend turned into a nymph of the spring. The spring is also found in Mithraism. A Pannonian dedication reads "Fonti perenni." An inscription from Apulum is dedicated to the "Fons aeternus." [20] In Persian, Ardvisura is the fount of the water of life. Ardvisura-Anahita is a goddess of water and love (just as Aphrodite is the "foam-born"). In the Vedas, the waters are called *matritamah*, 'most maternal.' All living things rise, like the sun, from water, and sink into it again at evening. Born of springs, rivers, lakes, and seas, man at death comes to the waters of the Styx, and there embarks on the "night sea journey." Those black waters of death are the water of life, for death with its cold embrace is the maternal womb, just as the sea devours the sun but brings it forth again. Life knows no death; as the Spirit says in *Faust:*

> In flood of life, in action's storm
> I ply on my wave
> With weaving motion
> Birth and the grave,
> A boundless ocean,

[17] Cf. Freud, *The Interpretation of Dreams,* pp. 399ff., and Abraham, *Dreams and Myths,* p. 23.
[18] Isaiah 48:1: "Hear ye this, O house of Jacob, which are called by the name of Israel, and are come forth out of the waters of Judah . . ."
[19] Wirth, *Aus orientalischen Chroniken.*   [20] Cumont, *Textes,* pp. 106f.

Ceaselessly giving
Weft of living,
Forms unending,
Glowing and blending. . . .[21]

320   The projection of the mother-imago upon water endows the
latter with a number of numinous or magical qualities peculiar
to the mother. A good example of this is the baptismal water
symbolism in the Church (pl. xxvii). In dreams and fantasies
the sea or a large expanse of water signifies the unconscious.
The maternal aspect of water coincides with the nature of the
unconscious, because the latter (particularly in men) can be
regarded as the mother or matrix of consciousness. Hence the
unconscious, when interpreted on the subjective level,[22] has
the same maternal significance as water.

321   Another equally common mother-symbol is the wood of life
(ξύλον ζωῆς), or tree of life. The tree of life may have been, in
the first instance, a fruit-bearing genealogical tree, and hence
a kind of tribal mother. Numerous myths say that human beings came from trees, and many of them tell how the hero was
enclosed in the maternal tree-trunk, like the dead Osiris in the
cedar-tree, Adonis in the myrtle, etc. (Cf. fig. 23.) Numerous
female deities were worshipped in tree form, and this led to the
cult of sacred groves and trees. Hence when Attis castrates himself under a pine-tree, he did so because the tree has a maternal
significance. Juno of Thespiae was a bough, Juno of Samos a
plank, Juno of Argos a pillar, the Carian Diana was an unhewn
block of wood, Athene of Lindus a polished column.[23] Tertullian called the Ceres of Pharos "rudis palus et informe lignum
sine effigie" (a rough and shapeless wooden stake with no face).
Athenaeus remarks that the Latona at Delos was ξύλινον ἄμορφον,
'an amorphous bit of wood.' Tertullian also describes an Attic
Pallas as a "crucis stipes" (cross-post). The naked wooden pole,
as the name itself indicates (φάλης, palus, Pfahl, pale, pile), is
phallic (cf. pl. xxviii). The φαλλός is a pole, a ceremonial lingam
carved out of figwood, as are all the Roman statues of Priapus.
Φάλος means the peak or ridge of a helmet, later called κῶνος,

21 Part I, trans. by Wayne, p. 48.
22 See my Psychological Types, Def. 50.
23 Cones were sometimes used instead of columns, as in the cults of Aphrodite,
Astarte, etc.

'cone.' Φάλληνος (from φαλλός) means 'wooden'; φαλ-άγγωμα is a cylinder; φάλαγξ, a round beam. The Macedonian shock-troops when drawn up in battle array were also known as a phalanx, and so is the finger-joint.[24] Finally, we have to consider φαλός, 'bright, shining.' The Indo-European root is *bhale, 'to bulge, swell.' [25] Who does not think of Faust's "It glows, it shines, increases in my hand!" [26]

322   This is "primitive" libido symbolism, which shows how direct is the connection between libido and light. We find much the same thing in the invocations to Rudra in the Rig-Veda:

> May we obtain favour of thee, O ruler of heroes, maker of bountiful water [i.e., urine]. . . .
> We call down for our help the fiery Rudra, who fulfils the sacrifice, the seer who circles in the sky. . . .
> He who yields sweetness, who hears our invocations, the ruddy-hued with the gorgeous helm, let him not deliver us into the power of jealousy.
> The bull of the Marut has gladdened me, the suppliant, with more vigorous health. . . .
> Let a great hymn of praise resound to the ruddy-brown bull, the white-shining (sun); let us worship the fiery god with prostrations; let us sing of the glorious being of Rudra.
> May the arrow of Rudra be turned from us; may the anger of the fiery god pass us by. Unbend thy firm bow (?) for the princes; thou who blessest with the waters of thy body, be gracious to our children and grandchildren.[27]

323   Here the various aspects of the psychic life-force, of the extraordinarily potent," the personified mana-concept, come together in the figure of Rudra: the fiery-white sun, the gorgeous helm, the puissant bull, and the urine (urere, 'to burn').

24 For the symbolism of the finger-joint, see my remarks on the dactyls, pars. 180–84. Here I would like to add the following from a Bakairi myth: "Nimaga-kaniro swallowed two Bakairi finger-bones. There were many of these lying about the house, because Oka used them for tipping his arrows, and killed many Bakairi and ate their flesh. From these finger-bones, and not from Oka, the woman became pregnant." (Frobenius, p. 236.)

25 Further evidence in Prellwitz, Wörterbuch.   26 [Cf. par. 180, above.]

27 Respectively, in I, 114: 3 and 4; in II, 33: 5, 6, 8, and 14. Trans. from Siecke, "Der Gott Rudra im Rigveda," pp. 237ff.

324   Not only the gods, but the goddesses, too, are libido-symbols, when regarded from the point of view of their dynamism. The libido expresses itself in images of sun, light, fire, sex, fertility, and growth. In this way the goddesses, as we have seen, come to possess phallic symbols, even though the latter are essentially masculine. One of the main reasons for this is that, just as the female lies hidden in the male (*pl.* xxix), so the male lies hidden in the female.[28] The feminine quality of the tree that represents the goddess (cf. pl. xxxi) is contaminated with phallic symbolism, as is evident from the genealogical tree that grows out of Adam's body. In my *Psychology and Alchemy* I have reproduced, from a manuscript in Florence, a picture of Adam showing the *membrum virile* as a tree.[29] Thus the tree has a bisexual character, as is also suggested by the fact that in Latin the names of trees have masculine endings and the feminine gender.[30]

325   The tree in the following dream of a young woman patient brings out this hermaphroditism: [31] *She was in a garden, where she found an exotic-looking tree with strange red fleshy flowers or fruits. She picked and ate them. Then, to her horror, she felt that she was poisoned.*

326   As a result of sexual difficulties in her marriage, the dreamer's fancy had been much taken by a certain young man of her acquaintance. The tree is the same tree that stood in Paradise, and it plays the same role in this dream as it did for our first parents. It is the tree of libido, which here represents the feminine as well as the masculine side, because it simply expresses the relationship of the two to one another.

327   A Norwegian riddle runs:

> A tree stands on the Billinsberg,
> Drooping over a lake.
> Its branches shine like gold.
> You won't guess that today.

[28] Cf. the anima/animus theory in my later writings.
[29] *Psychology and Alchemy*, fig. 131.
[30] The fig-tree is phallic. It is worth noting that Dionysus planted a fig-tree at the entrance to Hades, in the same way that phalloi were placed on graves. The cypress, sacred to Aphrodite, the Cyprian, became an emblem of death, and used to be placed at the door of houses where people were dying.
[31] Concerning hermaphroditism, see *Psychology and Alchemy*, index, s.v. "hermaphrodite."

328   In the evening the sun's daughter collects the golden branches that have dropped from the wonderful oak.

> Bitterly weeps the sun-child
> In the apple orchard.
> From the apple-tree has fallen
> The golden apple.
> Weep not, sun-child,
> God will make another
> Of gold or bronze,
> Or a little silver one.

329   The various meanings of the tree—sun, tree of Paradise, mother, phallus—are explained by the fact that it is a libido-symbol and not an allegory of this or that concrete object. Thus a phallic symbol does not denote the sexual organ, but the libido, and however clearly it appears as such, it does not mean *itself* but is always a symbol of the libido. Symbols are not signs or allegories for something known; they seek rather to express something that is little known or completely unknown. The *tertium comparationis* for all these symbols is the libido, and the unity of meaning lies in the fact that they are all analogies of the same thing. In this realm the fixed meaning of things comes to an end. The sole reality is the libido, whose nature we can only experience through its effect on us. Thus it is not the real mother who is symbolized, but the libido of the son, whose object was once the mother. We take mythological symbols much too concretely and are puzzled at every turn by the endless contradictions of myths. But we always forget that it is the unconscious creative force which wraps itself in images. When, therefore, we read: "His mother was a wicked witch," we must translate it as: the son is unable to detach his libido from the mother-imago, he suffers from resistances because he is tied to the mother.

330   The water and tree symbolism, which we found as further attributes of the symbol of the city, likewise refer to the libido that is unconsciously attached to the mother-imago. In certain passages of the Apocalypse we catch a clear glimpse of this longing for the mother.[32] Also, the author's eschatological expecta-

32 The relationship of the son to the mother was the psychological basis of numerous cults. Robertson (*Christianity and Mythology*, p. 322) was struck by Christ's relationship to the two Marys, and he conjectures that it probably points

tions end with the mother: "And there shall be no more curse."
There shall be no more sin, no more repression, no more disharmony with oneself, no guilt, no fear of death and no pain
of separation, because through the marriage of the Lamb the
son is united with the mother-bride and the ultimate bliss is
attained. This symbol recurs in the *nuptiae chymicae,* the
coniunctio of alchemy.[33]

331   Thus the Apocalypse dies away on that same note of radiant,
mystic harmony which was re-echoed some two thousand years
later in the last prayer of "Doctor Marianus":

> O contrite hearts, seek with your eyes
>   The visage of salvation;
> Blissful in that gaze, arise
>   Through glad regeneration.
> Now may every pulse of good
>   Seek to serve before thy face,
> Virgin, Queen of Motherhood,
>   Keep us, Goddess, in thy grace.[34]

332   The beauty and nobility of these feelings raises in our minds
a question of principle: is the causal interpretation of Freud
correct in believing that symbol-formation is to be explained
solely by prevention of the primary incest tendency, and is thus
a mere substitute product? The so-called "incest prohibition"
which is supposed to operate here is not in itself a primary phenomenon, but goes back to something much more fundamental,
namely the primitive system of marriage classes which, in its
turn, is a vital necessity in the organization of the tribe. So it
is more a question of phenomena requiring a teleological explanation than of simple causalities. Moreover it must be
pointed out that the basis of the "incestuous" desire is not cohabitation, but, as every sun myth shows, the strange idea of

to an old myth "in which a Palestinian God, perhaps named Joshua, figures in
the changing relations of lover and son towards a mythic Mary—a natural
fluctuation in early theosophy and one which occurs with a difference in the
myths of Mithras, Adonis, Attis, Osiris, and Dionysus, all of whom are connected
with Mother-Goddesses and either a consort or a female double, the mother and
consort being at times identified."

33 [Cf. "The Psychology of the Transference" and *Mysterium Coniunctionis,* ch. 6.
—Editors.]

34 *Faust,* Part II, Act 5, trans. by Wayne, p. 288.

becoming a child again, of returning to the parental shelter, and of entering into the mother in order to be reborn through her. But the way to this goal lies through incest, i.e., the necessity of finding some way into the mother's body. One of the simplest ways would be to impregnate the mother and beget oneself in identical form all over again. But here the incest prohibition intervenes; consequently the sun myths and rebirth myths devise every conceivable kind of mother-analogy for the purpose of canalizing the libido into new forms and effectively preventing it from regressing to actual incest. For instance, the mother is transformed into an animal, or is made young again,[35] and then disappears after giving birth, i.e., is changed back into her old shape. It is not incestuous cohabitation that is desired, but rebirth. The incest prohibition acts as an obstacle and makes the creative fantasy inventive; for instance, there are attempts to make the mother pregnant by means of fertility magic. The effect of the incest-taboo and of the attempts at canalization is to stimulate the creative imagination, which gradually opens up possible avenues for the self-realization of libido. In this way the libido becomes imperceptibly spiritualized. The power which "always desires evil" thus creates spiritual life. That is why the religions exalt this procedure into a system. It is instructive to see the pains they take to further the translation into symbols.[36] The New Testa-

[35] Rank (*Die Lohengrinsage*) has found some beautiful examples of this in the myth of the swan-maiden.

[36] Muther (*Geschichte der Malerei*, II, p. 355) says, in his chapter on "The First Spanish Classics": "Tieck once wrote: 'Sexuality is the great mystery of our being, sensuality the first cog in our machinery. It stirs our whole being and makes it alive and joyful. All our dreams of beauty and nobility have their source here. Sensuality and sexuality constitute the essence of music, of painting, and of all the arts. All the desires of mankind revolve round this centre like moths round a flame. The sense of beauty and artistic feeling are only other dialects, other expressions. They signify nothing more than the sexual urge of mankind. I regard even piety as a diverted channel for the sexual impulse.' This clearly expresses what one should never forget when judging the old ecclesiastical art, that the struggle to efface the boundaries between earthly and heavenly love, to blend them into each other imperceptibly, has always been the guiding thought, the most powerful impulse of the Catholic Church." To this I would add that it is hardly possible to restrict this impulse to sexuality. It is primarily a question of primitive instinctuality, of insufficiently differentiated libido which prefers to take a sexual form. Sexuality is by no means the only form of the "full feeling of life." There are some passions that cannot be derived from sex.

ment gives us an excellent example of this: in the dialogue about rebirth (John 3:4ff.), Nicodemus cannot help taking the matter realistically:

How can a man be born when he is old? Can he enter the second time into his mother's womb, and be born?

333   Jesus tries to purify the sensuous cast of Nicodemus' mind by rousing it from its dense materialistic slumbers, and translates the passage into the same, and yet not the same, words:

Verily, verily, I say unto thee, Except a man be born of water and of the Spirit, he cannot enter into the kingdom of God.
That which is born of flesh is flesh, and that which is born of the Spirit is spirit.
Marvel not that I said unto thee, Ye must be born again.
The wind bloweth where it listeth, and thou hearest the sound thereof, but canst not tell whence it cometh, and whither it goeth: so is every one that is born of the Spirit.

334   To be born of water simply means to be born of the mother's womb; to be born of the Spirit means to be born of the fructifying breath of the wind, as can be seen from the Greek text of the passages italicized above, where spirit and wind are expressed by the same word, πνεῦμα: "τὸ γεγεννημένον ἐκ τῆς σαρκὸς σάρξ ἐστιν, καὶ τὸ γεγεννημένον ἐκ τοῦ πνεύματος πνεῦμά ἐστιν. . . . Τὸ πνεῦμα ὅπου θέλει πνεῖ."

335   This symbolism arose from the same need as that which produced the Egyptian legend of the vultures: they were female only and were fertilized by the wind. The basis of these mythological statements is an ethical demand which can be formulated thus: you should not say that your mother is impregnated by a man in the ordinary way, but is impregnated in some extraordinary way by a spiritual being. As this stands in complete contrast to the empirical truth, the myth bridges over the difficulty by analogy: the son is said to have been a hero who died, was born again in a remarkable manner, and thus attained to immortality. The need responsible for this demand is evidently a desire to transcend reality. A son may naturally believe that a father begot him in the flesh, but not that he himself can impregnate his mother and so cause himself to be born young again. Such a thought is prohibited by the danger of regression, and is therefore replaced by the above demand that

one should, in certain circumstances, express the problem of
rebirth in symbolical terms. We see the same thing in Jesus'
challenge to Nicodemus: Do not think carnally, or you will be
flesh, but think symbolically, and then you will be spirit. It is
evident that this compulsion towards the symbolical is a great
educative force, for Nicodemus would remain stuck in banali-
ties if he did not succeed in raising himself above his concretism. Had he been a mere Philistine, he would certainly
have taken offence at the irrationality and unreality of this
advice and understood it literally, only to reject it in the end
as impossible and incomprehensible. The reason why Jesus'
words have such great suggestive power is that they express the
symbolical truths which are rooted in the very structure of the
human psyche. The empirical truth never frees a man from his
bondage to the senses; it only shows him that he was always so
and cannot be otherwise. The symbolical truth, on the other
hand, which puts water in place of the mother and spirit or
fire in place of the father, frees the libido from the channel of
the incest tendency, offers it a new gradient, and canalizes it
into a spiritual form. Thus man, as a spiritual being, becomes
a child again and is born into a circle of brothers and sisters:
but his mother has become the "communion of saints," the
Church (pl. xxxa), and his brothers and sisters are humanity,
with whom he is united anew in the common heritage of symbolical truth. It seems that this process was especially necessary
at the time when Christianity originated; for that age, as a result of the appalling contrast between slavery and the freedom
of the citizens and masters, had entirely lost consciousness of
the unity of mankind.

336   When we see how much trouble Jesus took to make the
symbolical view of things acceptable to Nicodemus, as if throwing a veil over the crude reality, and how important it was—and
still is—for the history of civilization that people should think
in this way, then one is at a loss to understand why the concern
of modern psychology with symbolism has met with such violent disapprobation in many quarters. It is as necessary today
as it ever was to lead the libido away from the cult of rationalism and realism—not, indeed, because these things have gained
the upper hand (quite the contrary), but because the guardians
and custodians of symbolical truth, namely the religions, have

been robbed of their efficacy by science. Even intelligent people no longer understand the value and purpose of symbolical truth, and the spokesmen of religion have failed to deliver an apologetic suited to the spirit of the age. Insistence on the bare concretism of dogma, or ethics for ethics' sake, or even a humanization of the Christ-figure coupled with inadequate attempts to write his biography, are singularly unimpressive. Symbolical truth is exposed undefended to the attacks of scientific thought, which can never do justice to such a subject, and in face of this competition has been unable to hold its ground. The truth, however, still remains to be proved. Exclusive appeals to faith are a hopeless *petitio principii,* for it is the manifest improbability of symbolical truth that prevents people from believing in it. Instead of insisting so glibly on the necessity of faith, the theologians, it seems to me, should see what can be done to make this faith possible. But that means placing symbolical truth on a new foundation—a foundation which appeals not only to sentiment, but to reason. And this can only be achieved by reflecting how it came about in the first place that humanity needed the improbability of religious statements, and what it signifies when a totally different spiritual reality is superimposed on the sensuous and tangible actuality of this world.

337   The instincts operate most smoothly when there is no consciousness to conflict with them, or when what consciousness there is remains firmly attached to instinct. This condition no longer applies even to primitive man, for everywhere we find psychic systems at work which are in some measure opposed to pure instinctuality. And if a primitive tribe shows even the smallest traces of culture, we find that creative fantasy is continually engaged in producing analogies to instinctual processes in order to free the libido from sheer instinctuality by guiding it towards analogical ideas. These systems have to be constituted in such a way that they offer the libido a kind of natural gradient. For the libido does not incline to *anything,* otherwise it would be possible to turn it in any direction one chose. But that is the case only with voluntary processes, and then only to a limited degree. The libido has, as it were, a natural penchant: it is like water, which must have a gradient if it is to flow. The nature of these analogies is therefore a serious problem because, as we have said, they must be ideas which attract the libido.

227

Their special character is, I believe, to be discerned in the fact that they are archetypes, that is, universal and inherited patterns which, taken together, constitute the structure of the unconscious. When Christ, for instance, speaks to Nicodemus of spirit and water, these are not just random ideas, but typical ones which have always exerted a powerful fascination on the mind. Christ is here touching on the archetype, and that, if anything, will convince Nicodemus, for the archetypes are the forms or river-beds along which the current of psychic life has always flowed.

338   It is not possible to discuss the problem of symbol-formation without reference to the instinctual processes, because it is from them that the symbol derives its motive power. It has no meaning whatever unless it strives against the resistance of instinct, just as undisciplined instincts would bring nothing but ruin to man if the symbol did not give them form. Hence a discussion of one of the strongest instincts, sexuality, is unavoidable, since perhaps the majority of symbols are more or less close analogies of this instinct. To interpret symbol-formation in terms of instinctual processes is a legitimate scientific attitude, which does not, however, claim to be the only possible one. I readily admit that the creation of symbols could also be explained from the spiritual side, but in order to do so, one would need the hypothesis that the "spirit" is an autonomous reality which commands a specific energy powerful enough to bend the instincts round and constrain them into spiritual forms. This hypothesis has its disadvantages for the scientific mind, even though, in the end, we still know so little about the nature of the psyche that we can think of no decisive reason against such an assumption. In accordance with my empirical attitude I nevertheless prefer to describe and explain symbol-formation as a natural process, though I am fully conscious of the probable one-sidedness of this point of view.

339   As we have said, sex plays an important part in this process, even when the symbols are religious. It is less than two thousand years since the cult of sex was in full bloom. In those days, of course, they were heathens and did not know any better, but the nature of the symbol-creating forces does not change from age to age. If one has any conception of the sexual content of those ancient cults, and if one realizes that the experience of

union with God was understood in antiquity as a more or less concrete coitus, then one can no longer pretend that the forces motivating the production of symbols have suddenly become different since the birth of Christ. The fact that primitive Christianity resolutely turned away from nature and the instincts in general, and, through its asceticism, from sex in particular, clearly indicates the source from which its motive forces came. So it is not surprising that this transformation has left noticeable traces in Christian symbolism. Had it not done so, Christianity would never have been able to transform libido. It succeeded in this largely because its archetypal analogies were for the most part in tune with the instinctual forces it wanted to transform. Some people profess to be very shocked when I do not shrink from bringing even the sublimest spiritual ideas into relation with what they call the "subhuman." My primary concern, however, is to *understand* these religious ideas, whose value I appreciate far too deeply to dispose of them with rationalistic arguments. What do we want, anyway, with things that cannot be understood? They appeal only to people for whom thinking and understanding are too much bother. Instead, we ask for blind faith and praise it to the skies. But that, in the end, only means educating ourselves to thoughtlessness and lack of criticism. What the "blind faith" so long preached from the pulpit was able to do in Germany, when that country finally turned its back on Christian dogma, has been bloodily demonstrated before our eyes by contemporary history. The really dangerous people are not the great heretics and unbelievers, but the swarm of petty thinkers, the rationalizing intellectuals, who suddenly discover how irrational all religious dogmas are. Anything not understood is given short shrift, and the highest values of symbolic truth are irretrievably lost. What can a rationalist do with the dogma of the virgin birth, or with Christ's sacrificial death, or the Trinity?

340   The medical psychotherapist today must make clear to his more educated patients the foundations of religious experience, and set them on the road to where such an experience becomes possible. If, therefore, as a doctor and scientist, I analyse abstruse religious symbols and trace them back to their origins, my sole purpose is to conserve, through understanding, the values they represent, and to enable people to think symbol-

ically once more, as the early thinkers of the Church were still able to do. This is far from implying an arid dogmatism. It is only when we, today, think dogmatically, that our thought becomes antiquated and no longer accessible to modern man. Hence a way has to be found which will again make it possible for him to participate spiritually in the substance of the Christian message.

341   At a time when a large part of mankind is beginning to discard Christianity, it may be worth our while to try to understand why it was accepted in the first place. It was accepted as a means of escape from the brutality and unconsciousness of the ancient world. As soon as we discard it, the old brutality returns in force, as has been made overwhelmingly clear by contemporary events. This is not a step forwards, but a long step backwards into the past. It is the same with individuals who lay aside one form of adaptation and have no new form to turn to: they infallibly regress along the old path and then find themselves at a great disadvantage, because the world around them has changed considerably in the meantime. Consequently, any one who is repelled by the philosophical weakness of Christian dogmatism or by the barren idea of a merely historical Jesus— for we know far too little about his contradictory personality and the little we do know only confuses our judgment—and who throws Christianity overboard and with it the whole basis of morality, is bound to be confronted with the age-old problem of brutality. We have had bitter experience of what happens when a whole nation finds the moral mask too stupid to keep up. The beast breaks loose, and a frenzy of demoralization sweeps over the civilized world.[37]

342   Today there are countless neurotics who are neurotic simply because they do not know why they cannot be happy in their own way—they do not even know that the fault lies with them. Besides these neurotics there are many more normal people, men and women of the better kind, who feel restricted and discontented because they have no symbol which would act as an outlet for their libido. For all these people a reductive analysis down to the primal facts should be undertaken, so that they can become acquainted with their primitive personality and learn how to take due account of it. Only in this way can cer-

37 [Cf. Jung's "Wotan."—EDITORS.]

tain requirements be fulfilled and others rejected as unreason-
able because of their infantile character. We like to imagine
that our primitive traits have long since disappeared without
trace. In this we are cruelly disappointed, for never before has
our civilization been so swamped with evil. This gruesome
spectacle helps us to understand what Christianity was up
against and what it endeavoured to transform. The transform-
ing process took place for the most part unconsciously, at any
rate in the later centuries. When I remarked earlier (par. 106)
that an unconscious transformation of libido was ethically
worthless, and contrasted it with the Christianity of the early
Roman period, as a patent example of the immorality and
brutalization against which Christians had to fight, I ought to
have added that mere faith cannot be counted as an ethical
ideal either, because it too is an unconscious transformation of
libido. Faith is a charisma for those who possess it, but it is no
way for those who need to understand before they can believe.
This is a matter of temperament and cannot be discounted
as valueless. For, ultimately, even the believer believes that God
gave man reason, and for something better than to lie and cheat
with. Although we naturally *believe* in symbols in the first
place, we can also *understand* them, and this is indeed the only
viable way for those who have not been granted the charisma
of faith.

343   The religious myth is one of man's greatest and most significant achievements, giving him the security and inner
strength not to be crushed by the monstrousness of the universe. Considered from the standpoint of realism, the symbol
is not of course an external truth, but it is psychologically true,
for it was and is the bridge to all that is best in humanity.[38]

344   Psychological truth by no means excludes metaphysical
truth, though psychology, as a science, has to hold aloof from all
metaphysical assertions. Its subject is the psyche and its contents.
Both are realities, because they *work*. Though we do not possess
a physics of the soul, and are not even able to observe it and
judge it from some Archimedean point "outside" ourselves, and
can therefore know nothing objective about it since all knowledge of the psyche is itself psychic, in spite of all this the soul

[38] For the functional significance of the symbol, see my "On Psychic Energy," sec.
III (d), on symbol formation (pars. 88ff.).

is the only experient of life and existence. It is, in fact, the only immediate experience we can have and the *sine qua non* of the subjective reality of the world. The symbols it creates are always grounded in the unconscious archetype, but their manifest forms are moulded by the ideas acquired by the conscious mind. The archetypes are the numinous, structural elements of the psyche and possess a certain autonomy and specific energy which enables them to attract, out of the conscious mind, those contents which are best suited to themselves. The symbols act as *transformers,* their function being to convert libido from a "lower" into a "higher" form. This function is so important that feeling accords it the highest values. The symbol works by suggestion; that is to say, it carries conviction and at the same time expresses the content of that conviction. It is able to do this because of the numen, the specific energy stored up in the archetype. Experience of the archetype is not only impressive, it seizes and possesses the whole personality, and is naturally productive of faith.

345   "Legitimate" faith must always rest on experience. There is, however, another kind of faith which rests exclusively on the authority of tradition. This kind of faith could also be called "legitimate," since the power of tradition embodies an experience whose importance for the continuity of culture is beyond question. But with this kind of faith there is always the danger of mere habit supervening—it may so easily degenerate into spiritual inertia and a thoughtless compliance which, if persisted in, threatens stagnation and cultural regression. This mechanical dependence goes hand in hand with a psychic regression to infantilism. The traditional contents gradually lose their real meaning and are only believed in as formalities, without this belief having any influence on the conduct of life. There is no longer a living power behind it. The much-vaunted "child-likeness" of faith only makes sense when the feeling behind the experience is still alive. If it gets lost, faith is only another word for habitual, infantile dependence, which takes the place of, and actually prevents, the struggle for deeper understanding. This seems to be the position we have reached today.

346   Since faith revolves round those central and perennially important "dominant ideas" which alone give life a meaning, the prime task of the psychotherapist must be to understand the

symbols anew, and thus to understand the unconscious, compensatory striving of his patient for an attitude that reflects the totality of the psyche.

347   After this digression, let us return to our author.

348   The vision of the city is immediately followed by that of a "strange conifer with knotty branches." This image no longer seems strange to us after what we have learned about the tree of life and its association with the mother, the city, and the water of life. The attribute "strange" probably expresses, as in dreams, a peculiar emphasis or numinosity. Unfortunately the author gives us no individual material in this connection. As the tree already suggested in the symbolism of the city is specially emphasized in the further development of the visions, I feel it necessary to discuss at some length the history of tree symbolism.

349   Trees, as is well known, have played a large part in religion and in mythology from the remotest times. (Pl. XXXI.) Typical of the trees found in myth is the tree of paradise, or tree of life; most people know of the pine-tree of Attis, the tree or trees of Mithras, and the world-ash Yggdrasill of Nordic mythology, and so on. The hanging of Attis, in effigy, on a pine-tree (cf. fig. 42), the hanging of Marsyas, which became a popular theme for art, the hanging of Odin, the Germanic hanging sacrifices and the whole series of hanged gods—all teach us that the hanging of Christ on the Cross is nothing unique in religious mythology, but belongs to the same circle of ideas. In this world of images the Cross is the Tree of Life and at the same time a Tree of Death—a coffin (cf. pl. XXXVI). Just as the myths tell us that human beings were descended from trees, so there were burial customs in which people were buried in hollow tree-trunks, whence the German *Totenbaum*, 'tree of death,' for coffin, which is still in use today. If we remember that the tree is predominantly a mother-symbol, then the meaning of this mode of burial becomes clear. *The dead are delivered back to the mother for rebirth.* (Cf. fig. 23 and pl. XLII.) We meet this symbol in the myth of Osiris as handed down by Plutarch.[39] Rhea was pregnant with Osiris and his twin sister Isis, and they mated together even in their mother's womb (night sea journey with

[39] *De Iside et Osiride*, in Babbitt trans., pp. 31–33.

incest). Their son was Arueris, later called Horus. Isis is said to have been "born in the All-Wetness" (ἐν πανύγροις γενέσθαι), and of Osiris it is related that a certain Pamyles of Thebes, whilst drawing water, heard a voice from the temple of Zeus which commanded him to proclaim that Osiris, "the great and beneficent king" (μέγας βασιλεὺς εὐεργέτης), was born. In honour of this Pamyles the Pamylia were celebrated, similar to the Phallophoria. Pamyles seems, therefore, to have been originally a phallic daimon, like Dionysus. In his phallic form he represents the creative power which "draws" things out of the unconscious (i.e., the water) and begets the god (Osiris) as a conscious content. This process can be understood both as an individual experience: Pamyles drawing water, and as a symbolic act or experience of the archetype: a drawing up from the depths. What is drawn up is a numinous, previously unconscious content which would remain dark were it not interpreted by the voice from above as the birth of a god. This type of experience recurs in the baptism in the Jordan, Matthew 3:17.

350 Osiris was killed in a crafty manner by the god of the underworld, Set (Typhon in Greek), who locked him in a chest. He was thrown into the Nile and carried out to sea. But in the underworld Osiris mated with his second sister, Nephthys. One can see from this how the symbolism is developed: already in his mother's womb, before his extra-uterine existence, Osiris commits incest; and in death, the second intra-uterine existence, he again commits incest, both times with a sister, for in remote antiquity brother-and-sister marriages were not only tolerated, but were a mark of the aristocracy. Zarathustra likewise recommended consanguineous marriages.

351 The wicked Set lured Osiris into the chest by a ruse, in other words the original evil in man wants to get back into the mother again, and the illicit, incestuous longing for the mother is the ruse supposedly invented by Set. It is significant that it is "evil" which lures Osiris into the chest; for, in the light of teleology, the motif of containment signifies the latent state that precedes regeneration. Thus evil, as though cognizant of its imperfection, strives to be made perfect through rebirth—"Part of that power which would / Ever work evil, but engenders good!" [40] The ruse, too, is significant: man tries to sneak into

40 *Faust*, Part I, trans. by Wayne, p. 75, modified.

rebirth by a subterfuge in order to become a child again. That is how it appears to the "rational" mind. An Egyptian hymn [41] even charges Isis with having struck down the sun god Ra by treachery: it was because of her ill will towards her son that she banished and betrayed him. The hymn describes how Isis fashioned a poisonous snake and set it in his path, and how the snake wounded the sun-god with its bite. From this wound he never recovered, so that he finally had to retire on the back of the heavenly cow. But the cow was the cow-headed mother-goddess (pl. xxx*b*), just as Osiris was the bull Apis. The mother is accused as though *she* were the cause of his having to fly to her in order to be cured of the wound she herself had inflicted. But the real cause of the wound is the incest-taboo,[42] which cuts a man off from the security of childhood and early youth, from all those unconscious, instinctive happenings that allow the child to live without responsibility as an appendage of his parents. There must be contained in this feeling many dim memories of the animal age, when there was as yet no "thou shalt" and "thou shalt not," and everything just happened of itself. Even now a deep resentment seems to dwell in man's breast against the brutal law that once separated him from instinctive surrender to his desires and from the beautiful harmony of animal nature. This separation manifested itself in the incest prohibition and its correlates (marriage laws, food-taboos, etc.). So long as the child is in that state of unconscious identity with the mother, he is still one with the animal psyche and is just as unconscious as it. The development of consciousness inevitably leads not only to separation from the mother, but to separation from the parents and the whole family circle and thus to a relative degree of detachment from the unconscious and the world of instinct. Yet the longing for this lost world continues and, when difficult adaptations are demanded, is forever tempting one to make evasions and retreats, to regress to the infantile

41 Erman, *Life in Ancient Egypt,* p. 265.
42 Here I must again remind the reader that I give the word "incest" a different meaning from that which properly belongs to it. Incest is the urge to get back to childhood. For the child, of course, this cannot be called incest; it is only for an adult with a fully developed sexuality that this backward striving becomes incest, because he is no longer a child but possesses a sexuality which cannot be allowed a regressive outlet.

past, which then starts throwing up the incestuous symbolism. If only this temptation were perfectly clear, it would be possible, with a great effort of will, to free oneself from it. But it is far from clear, because a new adaptation or orientation of vital importance can only be achieved in accordance with the instincts. Lacking this, nothing durable results, only a convulsively willed, artificial product which proves in the long run to be incapable of life. No man can change himself into anything from sheer reason; he can only change into what he potentially is. When such a change becomes necessary, the previous mode of adaptation, already in a state of decay, is unconsciously compensated by the archetype of another mode. If the conscious mind now succeeds in interpreting the constellated archetype in a meaningful and appropriate manner, then a viable transformation can take place. Thus the most important relationship of childhood, the relation to the mother, will be compensated by the mother archetype as soon as detachment from the childhood state is indicated. One such successful interpretation has been, for instance, Mother Church (cf. pl. xxxa), but once this form begins to show signs of age and decay a new interpretation becomes inevitable.

352   Even if a change does occur, the old form loses none of its attractions; for whoever sunders himself from the mother longs to get back to the mother. This longing can easily turn into a consuming passion which threatens all that has been won. The mother then appears on the one hand as the supreme goal, and on the other as the most frightful danger—the "Terrible Mother." [43]

353   After completing the night sea journey, the coffer containing Osiris was cast ashore at Byblos and came to rest in the branches of a cedar-tree, which shot up and enclosed the coffer in its trunk (cf. fig. 23). The king of the country, admiring the splendid tree, caused it to be cut down and made into a pillar supporting the roof of his house.[44] This period of Osiris' absence (the winter solstice) coincides with the age-old lament for

43 Frobenius, *Zeitalter*.
44 This recalls the phallic columns set up in the temples of Astarte. In fact, according to one version, the king's wife was named Astarte. This symbol is also reminiscent of the crosses which were aptly called ἐγκόλπια (pregnant), because they had a secret reliquary inside them.

the dead god, and his εὕρεσις (finding) was celebrated as a feast of joy.

354   Later on Set dismembered the body and scattered the pieces. We find this motif of dismemberment in numerous sun-myths [45] as a contrast to the putting together of the child in the mother's womb. Actually Isis collected the pieces together again with the help of the jackal-headed Anubis. Here the dogs and jackals,

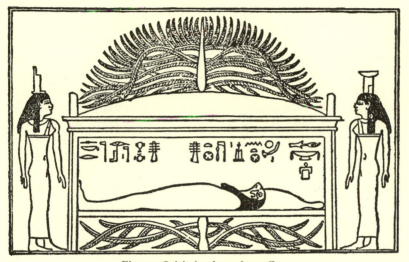

Fig. 23. Osiris in the cedar-coffin
Relief, Dendera, Egypt

devourers of corpses by night, assist in the reconstitution or reproduction of Osiris.[46] To this necrophagous function the Egyptian vulture probably owes its symbolic mother significance. In ancient times the Persians used to throw out their corpses for the dogs to devour, just as, today in Tibet, the dead are left to the vultures,[46a] and in Bombay, where the Parsis expose their corpses on the "towers of silence." The Persians had the custom

[45] Spielrein (pp. 358ff.) found numerous allusions to this motif in an insane patient. Fragments of different things and materials were "cooked" or "burnt." "The ashes can turn into a man," said the patient, and she also saw "dismembered children in glass coffins."

[46] Demeter collected the limbs of the dismembered Dionysus and put him together again.

[46a] [Cf. Harrer, *Seven Years in Tibet*, p. 61.—EDITORS.]

of leading a dog to the bedside of a dying man, who then had to give the dog a morsel to eat.[47] This custom suggests that the morsel should belong to the dog, so that he will spare the body of the dying man, just as Cerberus was pacified with the honey-cakes which Heracles gave him on his journey to hell. But when we consider the jackal-headed Anubis (pl. xxxiia) who rendered such good service in gathering together the remains of Osiris, and the mother significance of the vulture, the question arises whether this ceremony may not have a deeper meaning. This problem has been taken up by Creuzer,[48] who comes to the con-clusion that the deeper meaning is connected with the astral form of the dog ceremony, i.e., the appearance of the dog-star at the highest point of the solstice. Hence the bringing in of the dog would have a compensatory significance, death being made equal to the sun at its highest point. This is a thoroughly psychological interpretation, as can be seen from the fact that death is quite commonly regarded as an entry into the mother's womb (for rebirth). The interpretation would seem to be sup-ported by the otherwise enigmatic function of the dog in the Mithraic sacrifice. In the monuments a dog is often shown leap-ing upon the bull killed by Mithras. In the light of the Persian legend, and on the evidence of the monuments themselves, this sacrifice should be conceived as the moment of supreme fruit-fulness. This is most beautifully portrayed in the Mithraic relief at Heddernheim (pl. xxxiii). On one side of a large (formerly rotating) stone slab there is a stereotyped representa-tion of the overthrow and sacrifice of the bull, while on the other side stand Sol with a bunch of grapes in his hand, Mithras with the cornucopia, and the dadophors bearing fruits, in ac-cordance with the legend that from the dead bull comes all fruitfulness: fruits from his horns, wine from his blood, corn from his tail, cattle from his semen, garlic from his nostrils, and so forth. Over this scene stands Sylvanus, the beasts of the forest leaping away from him.

355   In this context the dog might very well have the significance suspected by Creuzer. Moreover the goddess of the underworld, Hecate, is dog-headed, like Anubis. As Canicula, she received dog sacrifices to keep away the pest. Her close relation to the

[47] Diodorus, III, 62 (cf. Oldfather and Geer trans., II, pp. 285ff.).
[48] *Symbolik und Mythologie der alten Völker.*

moon-goddess suggests that she was a promoter of growth. Hecate was the first to bring Demeter news of her stolen daughter, another reminder of Anubis. Dog sacrifices were also offered to Eileithyia, the goddess of birth, and Hecate herself (cf. pl. LVIII) is, on occasion, a goddess of marriage and birth. The dog is also the regular companion of Aesculapius, the god of healing, who, while still a mortal, raised a man from the dead and was struck by a thunderbolt as a punishment. These associations help to explain the following passage in Petronius:

I earnestly beseech you to paint a small dog round the foot of my statue . . . so that by your kindness I may attain to life after death.[49]

356   But to return to the myth of Osiris: although Isis had managed to collect the pieces of the body, its resuscitation was only partially successful because the phallus could not be found; it had been eaten by the fishes, and the reconstituted body lacked vital force.[50] The phantom Osiris lay once more with Isis, but the fruit of their union was Harpocrates, who was weak "in the lower limbs" (γυίον), i.e., in the feet. In the above-mentioned hymn, Ra was wounded in the foot by the serpent of Isis. The foot, as the organ nearest the earth, represents in dreams the relation to earthly reality and often has a generative or phallic significance.[51] The name Oedipus, 'Swell-foot,' is suspicious in this respect. Osiris, although only a phantom, now makes the young sun (his son Horus) ready for battle with Set, the evil spirit of darkness. Osiris and Horus represent the father-son symbolism mentioned at the beginning. Osiris is thus flanked by the comely Horus and the misshapen Harpocrates, who is mostly shown as a cripple, sometimes distorted to the point of

[49] *Satyricon*, ch. 71. [Cf. Heseltine trans., pp. 136–37.] ("Valde te rogo, ut secundum pedes statuae meae catellam pingas . . . ut mihi contingat tuo beneficio post mortem vivere.")

[50] Frobenius (*Zeitalter*, p. 393) observes that the fire-gods (sun-heroes) often have a limb missing. He gives the following parallel: "Just as the god wrenches out the ogre's arm, so Odysseus puts out the eye of the noble Polyphemus, whereupon the sun creeps mysteriously into the sky. Is there a connection between the twisting of the fire-sticks and the twisting out of the arm?" The main elements here are firstly a mutilation, and secondly a twisting movement, which Frobenius rightly connects with fire-boring. The mutilation is a castration in the case of Attis, and something similar in the case of Osiris.

[51] Cf. Aigremont, *Fuss- und Schuhsymbolik*.

freakishness. It is just possible that the motif of the unequal brothers has something to do with the primitive conception that the placenta is the twin-brother of the new-born child.

357 Osiris is frequently confused in tradition with Horus. The latter's real name is Horpi-chrud,[52] which is composed of *chrud* (child), and *Hor* (from *hri*, 'up, above, on top'). The name thus signifies the "up-and-coming child," the rising sun, as opposed to Osiris, who personifies the setting sun, the sun "in the Western Land." So Osiris and Horpi-chrud are one being, both husband and son of the same mother. Khnum-Ra, the sun-god of Lower Egypt, is a ram, and his consort, the female divinity of the nome, is Hatmehit, who wears the fish on her head. She is the mother and spouse of Bi-neb-did ('ram,' the local name for Khnum-Ra). In the hymn of Hibis, Amon-Ra is invoked as follows:

Thy Ram dwelleth in Mendes, united as the fourfold god Thmuis. He is the phallus, lord of the gods. The bull of his mother rejoiceth in the cow, and the husband maketh fruitful through his seed.[53]

358 In other inscriptions [54] Hatmehit is called the "mother of Mendes." (Mendes is the Greek form of Bi-neb-did.) She is also invoked as "The Good," with the subsidiary meaning of *ta-nofert,* "young woman." The cow as a mother-symbol (cf. pl. L*a*) appears in all the innumerable forms and variations of Hathor-Isis (cf. pl. xxx*b*), and also in the feminine aspect of Nun (whose parallel is the primitive goddess Nit or Neith), the primary substance—moisture—which is both masculine and feminine by nature. Nun is therefore invoked [55] as "Amon, the primordial waters,[56] which was in the beginning." He is also called the father of fathers, the mother of mothers. The corresponding invocation to Nun-Amon's feminine aspect, Nit or Neith, says:

Nit, the Ancient, the Mother of God, Mistress of Esne, Father of Fathers, Mother of Mothers, who is the Scarab and the Vulture, who was in the beginning.

[52] Brugsch, *Religion und Mythologie der alten Aegypter,* p. 354.
[53] Ibid., p. 310.   [54] Ibid., p. 310.   [55] Ibid., pp. 112ff.
[56] In Thebes the chief god Khnum, in his cosmogonic aspect, represented the wind-breath, from which the "spirit ($\pi\nu\epsilon\tilde{\upsilon}\mu\alpha$) of God moving over the waters" was later developed—the primitive idea of the World Parents lying pressed together until the son separates them.

Nit, the Ancient, the mother who bore Ra, the God of Light, who brought forth when there was nothing which brought forth.

The Cow, the Ancient, who bore the sun and set the seeds of gods and men.[57] [Cf. figs. 24, 25.]

Fig. 24. Nut giving birth to the Sun
Relief, Egypt

359   The word *nun* means 'young, fresh, new,' and also the new flood-waters of the Nile. In a metaphorical sense it is used for the chaotic waters of the beginning, and for the birth-giving primary substance,[58] which is personified as the goddess Naunet.

57 Brugsch, pp. 114f.   58 Ibid., pp. 128f.

From her sprang Nut, the sky-goddess, who is represented with a starry body or as a heavenly cow dotted with stars (figs. 24, 25).

360   So when the sun-god Ra retires on the back of the heavenly cow, it means that he is going back into the mother in order to rise again as Horus. In the morning the goddess is the mother, at noon she is the sister-wife, and at evening once more the mother who takes back the dead into her womb.

Fig. 25. The Divine Cow
From the tomb of Seti I, Egypt

361   Thus the fate of Osiris is explained: he enters into the mother's womb, into the coffer, the sea, the tree, the Astarte column; is dismembered, put together again, and reappears in his son Horpi-chrud.

362   Before we enter upon the other mysteries which this myth has in store for us, it will be as well to say a few words more about the symbol of the tree. Osiris comes to rest in the branches of a tree, which grow up round him.[59] The motif of embracing and entwining is often found in the sun myths and rebirth myths, as in the story of Sleeping Beauty, or the legend of the girl who was imprisoned between the bark and the wood of a tree.[60] A primitive myth tells of a sun-hero who has to be

59 Cf. the similar motif in the Egyptian "Tale of the Two Brothers": Erman, *Literature*, p. 156.
60 Serbian folksong, mentioned in Grimm, *Teutonic Mythology*, II, p. 653.

freed from a creeping plant.[61] The girl dreams that her lover has fallen into the water; she tries to rescue him, but first has to pull seaweed out of the water, then she catches him. In an African myth the hero, after his deed, has to be disentangled from the seaweed. In a Polynesian story the hero's canoe is caught in the tentacles of a giant polyp, just as Ra's barge was entwined by the nocturnal serpent on the night sea journey. The motif of entwining also occurs in Sir Edwin Arnold's poetic version of the story of Buddha's birth:

> Queen Maya stood at noon, her days fulfilled,
> Under a palsa in the palace-grounds,
> A stately trunk, straight as a temple-shaft,
> With crown of glossy leaves and fragrant blooms;
> And, knowing the time come—for all things knew—
> The conscious tree bent down its boughs to make
> A bower about Queen Maya's majesty:
> And Earth put forth a thousand sudden flowers
> To spread a couch; while, ready for the bath,
> The rock hard by gave out a limpid stream
> Of crystal flow. So brought she forth her child.[62]

363   There is a very similar motif in the cult-legend of the Samian Hera. Every year her image "disappeared" from the temple, attached itself to a lygos-tree somewhere on the seashore, and was entwined in its branches. There it was "found" and regaled with wedding-cakes. This festival was undoubtedly a *hieros gamos,* for in Samos there was a legend that Zeus had previously had a long-drawn-out clandestine love-affair with Hera. In Plataea and Argos a wedding procession was staged in their honour with bridesmaids, wedding feast, etc. The festival took place in the "wedding month" of Gamelion (beginning of February). The image was carried to a lonely spot in the woods, which is in keeping with Plutarch's story that Zeus kidnapped Hera and hid her in a cave on Mount Cithaeron. After our previous remarks we have to conclude that there is still another

---

61 Frobenius, *Zeitalter.*
62 *The Light of Asia,* p. 5. Cf. the birth of the Germanic king Aschanes, where there is a similar conjunction of rock, tree, and water. [Cf. par. 368, below.] Spitteler uses the same motif of the loving tree in his *Prometheus,* to describe how nature receives the "jewel" that was brought to earth. The idea is taken from Buddha's birth-story. Cf. "Om mani padme hum" (the jewel is in the lotus).

train of thought connected with the *hieros gamos,* namely, re-juvenation magic. The disappearance and hiding of the image in the wood, in the cave, on the seashore, its twining-about by the lygos-tree,[63] all this points to death and rebirth. The early springtime, Gamelion, fits in very well with this theory. In fact, Pausanias [64] tells us that the Argive Hera became a virgin again by taking a yearly dip in the fountain of Kanathos. The significance of this bath is further increased by the report that, in the Plataean cult of Hera Teleia, Tritonian nymphs appeared as water-carriers. The Iliad describes Zeus' conjugal couch on Mount Ida as follows:

As he spoke, the Son of Cronos took his wife in his arms; and the gracious earth sent up fresh grass beneath them, dewy lotus and crocuses, and a soft and crowded bed of hyacinths, to lift them off the ground. In this they lay, covered by a beautiful golden cloud, from which a rain of glistening dewdrops fell. . . . The Father lay peacefully on top of Gargarus with his arms round his wife, conquered by sleep and love. . . .[65]

364   Drexler sees in this description [66] an allusion to the garden of the gods on the extreme Western shore of the ocean—an idea which might have been taken from a pre-Homeric *hieros gamos* hymn.[67] The Western Land is the land of the setting sun; Heracles and Gilgamesh hasten thither, where the sun and the maternal sea are united in an eternally rejuvenating embrace. This seems to confirm our conjecture that the *hieros gamos* is connected with a rebirth myth. Pausanias mentions a related myth-fragment which says that the image of Artemis Orthia was also called *Lygodesma,* 'willow-captive,' [68] because it was found in a willow-tree. There seems to be some connection here with the popular Greek festival of the *hieros gamos* and its above-mentioned customs.

[63] Λύγος means 'willow,' or indeed any pliant twig or rod. λυγόω means 'to twist, plait, weave.'   [64] *Description of Greece,* II, 38, 2.
[65] Book XIV, 346–52, trans. by Rieu, p. 266.
[66] Curiously enough, near this point (XIV, 289–91) there is a description of Sleep sitting high up in a fir-tree: "There he perched, hidden by the branches with their sharp needles, in the form of a songbird of the mountains" (Rieu, p. 264, modified). It looks as if this motif belonged to the *hieros gamos.* Cf. also the magic net with which Hephaestus caught Ares and Aphrodite *in flagrante* and kept them there for the entertainment of the gods.
[67] See Roscher, *Lexikon,* I, 2102, 52ff.   [68] Pausanias, III, 16, 11.

365   The motif of "devouring" (pls. xxxii*b*, xxxiv), which Frobenius has shown to be one of the commonest components of the sun myth, is closely connected with embracing and entwining. The "whale-dragon" always "devours" the hero, but the devouring can also be partial. For instance, a six-year-old girl who hated going to school once dreamt that her leg was encircled by a large red worm. Contrary to what might be expected, she evinced a tender interest in the creature. Again, an adult patient who was unable to separate from an older woman friend on account of a strong mother transference to her, dreamt that she had to cross a broad stream. There was no bridge, but she found a place where she could step across. Just as she was about to do so, a large crab that lay hidden in the water seized hold of her foot and would not let go.[69]

366   This picture is borne out by etymology. There is an Indo-European root *vélu-*, with the meaning of 'encircling, enveloping, winding, turning.' From this are derived: Skr. *val, valati*, 'to cover, envelop, surround, encircle'; *valli*, 'creeping plant'; *ulūta*, 'boa-constrictor' = Lat. *volutus*; Lith. *velù, velti* = G. *wickeln*, 'to wind, wrap'; Church Slav. *vlina* = OHG. *wella*, 'a wave.' A related root is *vlvo*, 'covering, coil, membrane, womb.' Skr. *ulva, ulba*, has the same meaning; Lat. *volva, volvula, vulva*. *Vélu* is also cognate with *ulvora*, 'fruitful field, sheath or husk of a plant.' Skr. *urvárā*, 'sown field'; Zend *urvara*, 'plant.' The same root *vel* also has the meaning of G. *wallen*, 'boil, undulate.' Skr. *ulmuka*, 'conflagration'; Gr. ϝαλέα, ϝέλα, Goth. *vulan* = *wallen*. OHG. and MHG. *walm* = 'warmth.' [70] (It is typical that in the state of "involution" the hero's hair always falls out with the heat.) *Vel* is also found with the meaning 'to sound,' [71] and 'to will, wish.'

367   The motif of entwining is a mother-symbol.[72] The entwin-

---

69 See "On the Psychology of the Unconscious," pars. 123ff.

70 Fick, *Wörterbuch*, pp. 132f.

71 Cf. Goethe's "sonorous day-star," above, par. 235.

72 This motif also includes that of the "clashing rocks" (Frobenius, p. 405). The hero often has to steer his ship between two rocks that clash together. (A similar idea is that of the biting door or the snapping tree-trunk.) In its passage the stern of the ship (or the tail of the bird) is pinched off, another reminder of the mutilation motif (twisting out the arm). The 19th-cent. German poet J. V. von Scheffel uses this image in his poem "A herring loved an oyster." The poem ends with the oyster nipping off the herring's head in a kiss. The doves which bring

ing trees are at the same time birth-giving mothers (cf. pl. xxxix), as in the Greek myth where the μελίαι νύμφαι are ash-trees, the mothers of the men of the Bronze Age. The Bundahish symbolizes the first human beings, Mashya and Mashyoi, as the tree Rivas. According to a Nordic myth, God created man by breathing life into a substance called *tre* [73] (tree, wood).[74] Gr. ὕλη also means 'wood.' In the wood of the world-ash Yggdrasill a human pair hide themselves at the end of the world, and from them will spring a new race of men.[75] At the moment of universal destruction the world-ash becomes the guardian mother, the tree pregnant with death and life.[76] The regenerative function of the world-ash helps to explain the image in the chapter of the Egyptian Book of the Dead called "The Gate of Knowledge of the Souls of the East":

I am the pilot in the holy keel, I am the steersman who allows himself no rest in the ship of Ra.[77] I know the tree of emerald green from whose midst Ra rises to the height of the clouds.[78]

368   Ship and tree (i.e., the ship of death and tree of death) are closely related here. (Pl. xxxv.) The idea is that Ra rises up, born from the tree. The representations of the sun-god Mithras should probably be interpreted in the same way. In the Hed-

---

Zeus his ambrosia have to pass through the clashing rocks. Frobenius points out that these rocks are closely connected with the rocks or caves that only open at a magic word. The most striking illustration of this is a South African myth (p. 407): "You must call the rock by name and cry loudly: 'Rock Untunjambili, open, so that I may enter.'" But if the rock does not want to open, it answers: "The rock will not open to children, it opens to the swallows that fly in the air." The remarkable thing is that no human power can open the rock, only the magic word—or a bird. This formulation implies that opening the rock is an undertaking that can never be accomplished in reality, it can only be *wished*. *Wünschen* (wish) in Middle High German means the "power to do something extraordinary." The bird is a symbol of "wishful thinking."

73 Grimm, II, p. 571.

74 In Athens there was a family called Αἰγειρότομοι, 'hewn from the poplar.'

75 Herrmann, *Nordische Mythologie*, p. 589.

76 Certain Javanese tribes set up their idols in trees that have been artificially hollowed out. In Persian myth, the white haoma is a celestial tree growing in the lake Vouru-Kasha, while the fish Kar-mahi circles round it and protects it from the frog of Ahriman. The tree gives eternal life, children to women, husbands to girls, and horses to men. In the Mainyo-i-Khard it is called the "preparer of the corpse" (Spiegel, *Erānische Altertumskunde*, II, p. 115).

77 I.e., the sun-ship, which accompanies the sun and the soul over the sea of death towards the sunrise.   78 Brugsch, p. 177.

dernheim Relief (pl. XL) he is shown with half his body rising from the top of a tree, and in other monuments half his body is stuck in the rock, which clearly points to the rock-birth. Often there is a stream near his birthplace. This conglomeration of symbols [79] is also found in the birth of Aschanes, the first Saxon king, who grew from the Harz rocks in the middle of a wood near a fountain.[80] Here all the mother symbols are united—earth, wood, and water. So it is only logical that in the Middle Ages the tree was poetically addressed with the honorific title of "Lady." Nor is it surprising that Christian legend transformed the tree of death, the Cross, into the Tree of Life, so that Christ is often shown hanging on a green tree among the fruit (pl. XXXVI). The derivation of the Cross from the Tree of Life, which was an authentic religious symbol even in Babylonian times, is considered entirely probable by Zöckler,[81] an authority on the history of the Cross. The pre-Christian meaning of so universal a symbol does not contradict this view; quite the contrary, for its meaning is life. Nor does the existence of the cross in the sun-cult (where the regular cross and the swastika represent the sun-wheel) and in the cult of the love-goddesses in any way contradict its historical significance. Christian legend has made abundant use of this symbolism. The student of medieval art will be familiar with the representation of the Cross growing from Adam's grave (pl. XXXVII). The legend says that Adam was buried on Golgotha, and that Seth planted on his grave a twig from the tree of Paradise, which grew into Christ's Cross, the Tree of Death.[82] As we know, it was through Adam's guilt that sin and death came into the world, and Christ through his death redeemed us from the guilt. If we ask, In what did Adam's guilt consist? the answer is that the unpardonable sin to be punished by death was that he dared to eat of the tree of Paradise.[83] The

---

[79] Cf. Isaiah 51 : 1: ". . . look unto the rock whence ye are hewn, and to the hole of the pit whence ye are digged." Further evidence in Löwis of Menar, "Nordkaukasische Steingeburtssagen," pp. 509ff.

[80] Grimm, I, p. 474. [For Aschanes, see also Grimm, II, p. 572.—EDITORS.]

[81] *The Cross of Christ.*

[82] The legend of Seth is in Jubinal, *Mystères inédits du XV. siècle,* II, pp. 16ff. Cited in Zöckler, p. 225.

[83] The Germanic sacred trees were under an absolute taboo: no leaf might be plucked from them, and nothing picked from the ground on which their shadow fell.

consequences of this are described in a Jewish legend: one who was permitted to gaze into Paradise after the Fall saw the tree and the four streams, but the tree was withered, and in its branches lay a babe. The "mother" had become pregnant.[84]

369   This curious legend corresponds to the Jewish tradition that Adam, before he knew Eve, had a demon-wife called Lilith, with whom he strove for supremacy. But Lilith rose up into the air through the magic of God's name and hid herself in the sea. Adam forced her to come back with the help of three angels,[85] whereupon Lilith changed into a nightmare or lamia (pl. xxxviiia) who haunted pregnant women and kidnapped new-born infants. The parallel myth is that of the lamias, the nocturnal spectres who terrify children. The original legend is that Lamia seduced Zeus, but the jealous Hera caused her to bring only dead children into the world. Ever since then, the raging Lamia has persecuted children, whom she destroys whenever she can. This motif is a recurrent one in fairytales, where the mother often appears as a murderess [86] or eater of human flesh (cf. pl. xxxviiib); a well-known German paradigm is the story of Hansel and Gretel. Lamia is also the name of a large, voracious fish,[87] which links up with the whale-dragon motif worked out by Frobenius. Once again we meet the idea of the Terrible Mother in the form of a voracious fish, a personification of death.[88] In Frobenius there are numerous examples of

[84] According to German legend (Grimm, III, p. 969), the saviour will be born when he can be rocked in a cradle made from the wood of a tree that is now but a feeble shoot sprouting from a wall. The formula runs: "A limetree shall be planted, that shall throw out two *plantschen* [boughs] above, and out of their wood is a *poie* [buoy] to be made; the first child that therein lies is doomed to be brought from life to death by the sword, and then will salvation ensue." It is remarkable that in the German legends the heralding of the future event is connected with a *budding tree*. Christ was sometimes called a "branch" or a "rod."

[85] Here we may discern, perhaps, the motif of the "helpful bird"—angels are really birds. Cf. the feather-dress of the "soul-birds" in the underworld. In the Mithraic sacrifice the messenger of the gods—the "angel"—was a raven; the messenger is winged (Hermes). In Jewish tradition angels are masculine. The symbolism of the three angels is important because it signifies the upper, aerial, spiritual triad in conflict with the *one* lower, feminine power. Cf. my "Phenomenology of the Spirit in Fairytales," pars. 419ff.

[86] Frobenius, *Zeitalter.*   [87] Λαμός, 'gorge' = gullet; τὰ λαμία, 'gorge' = ravine.
[88] Note the close connection between δελφίς, 'dolphin,' and δελφύς, 'womb.' In Delphi there was the Delphic gorge and the δελφινίς, a tripod with feet in the form of dolphins. Cf. Melicertes on the dolphin and Melkarth's sacrifice by fire.

the monster devouring not only men (pl. xxxviiib), but animals, plants, and even an entire country, which are all delivered by the hero to a glorious rebirth.

370   The lamias (cf. pl. xxxviiia) are typical nightmares whose feminine nature is abundantly documented.[89] Their universal peculiarity is that they *ride* their victims. Their counterparts are the spectral horses who carry their riders away at a mad gallop. One can easily recognize in these symbols the typical anxiety dream which, as Laistner[90] has shown, holds an important clue to the interpretation of fairytales. The riding takes on a special aspect in the light of researches into child psychology: the two contributions of Freud and myself[91] have established the fear-significance of horses on the one hand, and the sexual meaning of riding fantasies on the other. The essential feature is the *rhythm,* which assumes a sexual significance only secondarily. If we take these factors into account, it will not surprise us to hear that the maternal world-ash Yggdrasill is called the *Schreckross* (terrible horse) in German. Cannegieter says of nightmares: "Even today the peasants drive away these female spirits (mother-goddesses, *moirae*) by throwing the bone of a horse's head upon the roof, and you can often see such bones on peasant houses hereabouts. But at night they are believed to ride at the time of the first sleep and to tire out the horses for long journeys."[92] At first sight, there seems to be an etymological connection between *nightmare* and *mare* (female horse)—G. *Mar* and *Mähre*. The Indo-European root for 'mare' is **mark;* cf. OIr. *marc. Mare* is akin to OHG. *meriha* (fem. of *marah,* 'stallion'), OE. *myre* (fem. of *mearh,* 'stallion'), ON. *merr.* The supposed source of *nightmare* is OE. and ON. *mara,* 'ogress, incubus, demon,' and, by extension, 'nightmare.' F. *cauchemar* comes from Lat. *calcare,* 'to tread,' in the reiterative sense of "treading" the grape; it is also used of the cock that "treads" the hen. This movement is equally typical of the nightmare; hence it was said of King Vanlandi: "Mara trað hann,"

89 Cf. Jones, *On the Nightmare.*   90 *Das Rätsel der Sphinx.*
91 Freud, "Phobia in a Five-year-old Boy," and my "Psychic Conflicts in a Child."
92 *Epistola de ara ad Noviomagum reperta,* p. 25. ("Abigunt eas nymphas (matres deas, moiras) hodie rustici osse capitis equini tectis injecto, cujusmodi ossa per has terras in rusticorum villis crebra est animadvertere. Nocte autem ad concubia equitare creduntur et equos fatigare ad longinqua itinera.") Cited from Grimm, III, p. 1246.

the Mara trod him to death in sleep.[93] A synonym for the nightmare is the troll or "treader." The treading movement has been
verified by the experience of Freud and myself with children,
which shows that a secondary sexual meaning attaches to stamping or kicking, though the rhythm is obviously primary. Like
the Mara, the "Stempe" treads.[94]

371   The Indo-European root *mer, *mor, means 'to die.' From
it also come Lat. mors, Gr. μόρος, 'fate,' and possibly Μοῖρα, the
goddess of fate.[95] The Norns who sit under the world-ash are
well-known personifications of fate, like Clotho, Lachesis, and
Atropos. With the Celts the conception of the Fates probably
passed into that of the matres and matronae,[96] who were considered divine by the Teutons. The divine significance of the
mothers comes out in Julius Caesar, where he says, "The
matrons should declare by lots and divinations whether it was
expedient to join battle or not." [97]

372   In connection with the etymology of Mar and (night)mare,
it should be added that F. mère has a strong phonetic resemblance to mare, although this, etymologically speaking, proves
nothing. In Slavonic, mara means 'witch'; in Polish, mora means
'nightmare.' Mor or More in Swiss-German means 'sow' (it
is also used as a swear-word). The Czech mura means both
'nightmare' and the Sphinx or hawk moth. This strange connection is explained by the fact that the butterfly is a symbol
and allegory of the psyche. The Sphingidae are evening moths—
they come, like the nightmare, in darkness. Finally, it should
be mentioned that the sacred olive-tree of Athene was called
μορία, which is derived from μόρος, 'fate.' Halirrhothios wanted
to cut down the tree, but killed himself with the axe in the
attempt.

[93] Ibid., III, p. 1246. [From the Ynglinga Saga, 16.]
[94] Ibid.; also I, pp. 277–78: "Eat fast tonight I pray, that the Stempe tread you
not." [The "Stempe," according to Grimm's citations, was an indeterminate nightmare figure that terrified children by trampling on them.—EDITORS.]
[95] Herrmann, Nordische Mythologie, p. 64, and Fick, Wörterbuch, I, p. 716. [In
more recent philology, a kinship of mors and μόρος is not assured. Not all the
etymological conjectures in this passage are now considered warranted.—EDITORS.]
[96] Grimm, I, p. 417.
[97] The Gallic War, I, 50, trans. by Edwards, pp. 82–83, slightly modified. ("Ut
matres familiae eorum sortibus et vaticinationibus declararent, utrum proelium
committi ex usu esset, necne.") Cf. the mantic significance of the Delphic gorge,
Mimir's fountain, etc.

373   The phonetic connection between G. *Mar*, F. *mère*, and the various words for 'sea' (Lat. *mare*, G. *Meer*, F. *mer*) is certainly remarkable, though etymologically accidental. May it perhaps point back to the great primordial image of the mother, who was once our only world and later became the symbol of the whole world? Goethe says of the Mothers that they are "thronged round with images of all creation." [98] Even the Christians could not refrain from reuniting their Mother of God with the water: "Ave maris stella" are the opening words of a hymn to Mary. It is probably significant that the infantile word *ma-ma* (mother's breast) is found in all languages, and that the mothers of two religious heroes were called Mary and Maya. That the mother is in fact the child's "horse" is apparent in the primitive custom of carrying the child on the back or riding it on the hip. And Odin hung upon the maternal world-ash, upon his "terrible horse."

374   As we have seen, Isis, the mother of the gods, played an evil trick on the sun-god with the poisonous snake, and, according to Plutarch, she behaved equally treacherously towards her son Horus. Horus vanquished the wicked Set who had murdered his father Osiris, but Isis set him free again. Outraged, Horus lifted his hand against his mother and snatched the royal diadem from her head,[99] in place of which Thoth gave her a cow's head (cf. pl. xxx*b*). Horus then vanquished Set for a second time. In the Greek legend, Typhon (Set) is a dragon. But even without this confirmation it is evident that Horus' fight is the typical fight of the sun-hero with the "whale dragon" who, as we know, is a symbol of the Terrible Mother, of the voracious maw, the jaws of death in which men are crunched and ground to pieces.[100] (Cf. pl. xxxviii*b*.) Whoever conquers this monster wins to eternal youth. But to this end, defying all danger, he must descend into the belly of the monster [101] ("journey to

98 Cf. p. 206, above.
99 Plutarch, *De Iside et Osiride*, 19, 6. [Cf. Babbitt trans., pp. 48–49.]
100 Cf. the exotic myths in Frobenius, where the belly of the whale is clearly the land of death.
101 One of the peculiarities of the Mara is that he can only get out through the hole by which he came in. [As Mephistopheles says (Wayne trans., p. 77): "All friends and phantoms must obey a law/ To use the way they entered in before."—TRANS.] This motif evidently belongs to the rebirth myth.

hell") and sojourn there for some time ("night sea imprisonment": Frobenius). (Cf. diagram, p. 210; pl. xxiib.)

375   The fight with the "nocturnal serpent" accordingly signifies conquest of the mother, who is suspected of an infamous crime, namely the betrayal of her son. Complete confirmation of all this is furnished by the fragments of the Babylonian Creation Epic discovered by George Smith, most of which come from the library of Assurbanipal. The text dates from about the time of Hammurabi (2000 B.C.). From this account of the Creation we learn that Ea, the son of the watery deep and god of wisdom,[102] has overthrown Apsu. Apsu is the progenitor of the great gods, so Ea has conquered the father. But Tiamat, the mother of the gods, plots revenge, and arrays herself for battle against them:

Mother Hubur, who created everything,
Procured invincible weapons, gave birth to giant snakes,
Sharp of tooth, unsparing of fang,
Filled their bodies with venom instead of blood,
Roaring dragons she clothed with terror,
Made them to swell with a terrible splendour, made them to prance,
So that he who beholds them shall perish of terror.
Their bodies shall rear up, and none shall turn them back.
She set up lizards, dragons, and sphinxes,
Hurricanes, mad dogs, scorpion-men,
Lion-demons, fish-men, and centaurs,
Bearing weapons that spare not, fearless in battle.
Mighty are Tiamat's commands, irresistible are they.

And when Tiamat had completed her handiwork,
She prepared for battle against the gods, her descendants.
To avenge Apsu, Tiamat did evil.

When Ea now heard this thing,
He was sore afraid, and he sat down sorrowfully.

He went to the father, his creator, Ansar,
To relate to him all that Tiamat plotted:
Tiamat, our mother, is incensed against us,
She has mustered a riotous throng, furiously raging.[103]

---

[102] For the abyss of wisdom, fount of wisdom, source of fantasies, see par. 640, below.

[103] Trans. of this and following passages based on Gressmann, *Altorientalische Texte*, I, pp. 4ff., and E. A. Speiser, in Pritchard, *Ancient Near Eastern Texts*, pp. 62–67.

376   Against the fearful hosts of Tiamat the gods finally put up
Marduk, the god of spring, who represents the victorious sun.
Marduk prepares himself for battle and forges his invincible
weapons:

He created the evil wind, Imhullu, the sou'wester, the hurricane,
The fourfold wind, the sevenfold wind, the whirlwind, and the
   harmful wind,
Then he let loose the winds he had brought forth, all seven of them:
To stir up confusion in Tiamat's vitals, they followed behind him.
Then the Lord raised up the cyclone, his mighty weapon;
For his chariot he mounted the storm-wind, matchless and terrible.

377   His chief weapons are the wind and a net with which he
hopes to catch Tiamat. He approaches Tiamat and challenges
her to single combat: [104]

Then Tiamat and Marduk, the wise one among the gods, joined
   issue,
Girding their loins for the fight, drawing near for battle.
Then the Lord spread out his net and caught her;
Imhullu, which followed behind, he let loose in her face,
When Tiamat opened her mouth, as wide as she could, to consume
   him,
He let Imhullu rush in and her lips could not close.
With the raging winds he filled her belly,
Her inward parts were seized and she opened wide her mouth.
He smote her with the spear, he hewed her in pieces,
He cut up her bowels and made mincemeat of her heart,
Vanquished her and put an end to her life,
Threw down her carcass and trampled upon it.

378   After Marduk had slain Tiamat, he sat down and planned
the creation of the world:

Then the Lord paused to contemplate her dead body,
That he might divide up the monster and do artful works.
He split her like a flat fish into two parts,[105]
One half he set up and with it he covered the sky.

379   In this manner Marduk created the world from the mother.
(Cf. fig. 41.) Evidently the killing of the mother-dragon here
takes the form of a negative wind-fertilization. The world is

104 "Then the Lord approached, looking for the inside of Tiamat."
105 Splitting of the mother; cf. Kaineus, pars. 439f., 460, 480, 638, below.

created from the mother, i.e., with the libido that is withdrawn from her through the sacrifice, and through prevention of the regression that threatened to overcome the hero. We shall have to examine this significant formula more closely in the final chapter. As Gunkel [106] has pointed out, the myth has interesting parallels in the literature of the Old Testament. Isaiah 51 : 9f. says: [106a]

> Awake, awake, put on strength, O arm of the Lord; awake, as in the days of old, the generations of long ago. Was it not thou that didst cut Rahab in pieces, that didst pierce the dragon?
> Was it not thou that didst dry up the sea, the waters of the great deep; that didst make the depths of the sea a way for the redeemed to pass over?

380   The name Rahab is frequently used for Egypt in the Old Testament (in Isaiah 30 : 7, Egypt is called "Rahab who sits still"), and also for dragon; it therefore meant something evil and hostile. Rahab appears here as the old dragon Tiamat, against whose evil power Marduk or Yahweh goes forth to battle. The term "the redeemed" refers to the children of Israel who were delivered from bondage; but it is also mythological, because the hero sets free those who had previously been devoured by the whale-dragon (Frobenius).

381   Psalm 89 : 10:

> Thou didst crush Rahab like a carcass. . . .

382   Job 26 : 12f.:

> By his power he stilled the sea,
> by his understanding he smote Rahab.
> By his wind the heavens were made fair,
> his hand pierced the fleeing serpent.

383   Gunkel equates Rahab with chaos, i.e., Tiamat. The dragon Rahab also appears as Leviathan, the monster of the deep and personification of the sea.

384   Psalm 74 : 13ff.:

> Thou didst divide the sea by thy might;
> thou didst break the heads of the dragons on the waters.
> Thou didst crush the heads of Leviathan,
> thou didst give him as food for the creatures of the wilderness.

106 *Schöpfung und Chaos*, p. 30ff.
106a [This and the next three passages are RSV.—TRANS.]

385   There is a further parallel in Isaiah 27 : 1:

In that day the Lord with his sore and great and strong sword shall punish Leviathan the piercing serpent, even Leviathan that crooked serpent; and he shall slay the dragon that is in the sea.

386   We come upon a special motif in Job 41 : 1f.:

Canst thou draw out Leviathan with an hook?
Or his tongue with a cord which thou lettest down?
Canst thou put an hook into his nose?
Or bore his jaw through with a thorn?

387   This motif has numerous parallels in the primitive myths collected by Frobenius, where the sea-monster was likewise fished for.

388   We have seen that the incest prohibition prevents the son from symbolically reproducing himself through the mother. It is not man as such who has to be regenerated or born again as a renewed whole, but, according to the statements of mythology, it is the hero or god who rejuvenates himself. These figures are generally expressed or characterized by libido-symbols (light, fire, sun, etc.), so that it looks as if they represented psychic energy. They are, in fact, personifications of the libido. Now it is a fact amply confirmed by psychiatric experience that all parts of the psyche, inasmuch as they possess a certain autonomy, exhibit a personal character, like the split-off products of hysteria and schizophrenia, mediumistic "spirits," figures seen in dreams, etc. Every split-off portion of libido, every complex, has or is a (fragmentary) personality. At any rate, that is how it looks from the purely observational standpoint. But when we go into the matter more deeply, we find that they are really archetypal formations. There are no conclusive arguments against the hypothesis that these archetypal figures are endowed with personality at the outset and are not just secondary personalizations. In so far as the archetypes do not represent mere functional relationships, they manifest themselves as δαίμονες, as personal agencies. In this form they are felt as actual experiences and are not "figments of the imagination," as rationalism would have us believe. Consequently, man derives his human personality only secondarily from what the myths call his descent from the gods and heroes; or, to put it in psychological terms, his

consciousness of himself as a personality derives primarily from the influence of quasi-personal archetypes.[107] Numerous mythological proofs could be advanced in support of this view.

389   It is, then, in the first place the god who transforms himself, and only through him does man take part in the transformation. Thus Khnum, "the maker, the potter, the builder," shapes his egg on the potter's wheel (pl. XLIb), for he is "immortal growth, his own generation and his own self-birth, the creator of the egg that came out of the primeval waters." The Egyptian Book of the Dead says: "I have risen like the mighty hawk [108] that comes forth from his egg," and: "I am the creator of Nun, who has taken up his abode in the underworld. My nest is not seen and my egg is not broken." Yet another passage speaks of "that great and glorious god in his egg, who created himself for that which came forth from him." [109] (Cf. fig. 36.) Therefore the god is also called Nagaga-uer, the "Great Cackler." (Book of the Dead 98 : 2: "I cackle like the goose, and whistle like the hawk.")

390   The canalization of regressive libido into the god justifies the mythological statement that it is the god or the hero who commits incest. On the primitive level no further symbolization is required. This only becomes necessary when the mythological statement begins to bring the god into discredit, which obviously only happens at a higher level of morality. Thus Herodotus reports:

I have already mentioned the festival of Isis at Busiris: it is here that everybody—tens of thousands of men and women—when the sacrifice is over, beat their breasts: in whose honour, however, I do not feel it is proper for me to say.

At Papremis there is a special ceremony in addition to the ordinary rites and sacrifices as practised elsewhere. As the sun draws towards setting, only a few of the priests continue to employ themselves about the image of the god, while the majority, armed with wooden clubs, take their stand at the entrance of the temple; opposite these is another crowd of men, more than a thousand strong, also armed with clubs and consisting of men who have vows to perform. The image of the god, in a little wooden gold-plated shrine, is

107 Represented in the human sphere by the quaternity composed of father, mother, godfather, godmother, the latter two corresponding to the divine pair.
108 I.e., the sun-god.   109 Brugsch, *Religion und Mythologie*, pp. 161ff.

conveyed to another sacred building on the day before the ceremony. The few priests who are left to attend to it put it, together with the shrine which contains it, in a four-wheeled cart, which they drag along towards the temple. The others, waiting at the temple gate, try to prevent it from coming in, while the votaries take the god's side and set upon them with their clubs. The assault is resisted, and a vigorous tussle ensues in which heads are broken and not a few actually die of the wounds they receive. That, at least, is what I believe, though the Egyptians told me that nobody is ever killed. The origin of this festival is explained locally by the story that the mother of Ares [110] once lived in the temple; Ares himself was brought up elsewhere, but when he grew to manhood he wished to get to know [111] his mother and for that purpose came to the temple where she was. Her attendants, however, not knowing him by sight, refused him admission, and succeeded in keeping him out until he fetched help from another town and forced his way in by violence. This, they say, is why the battle with clubs is part of the ceremony at the festival of Ares.[112]

391   A Pyramid Text, describing the dead Pharaoh's fight for supremacy in heaven, says:

The sky weeps, the stars shake, the keepers of the gods tremble and their servants flee, when they behold the King rising up as a spirit, as a god who lives on his fathers and possesses his mothers.[113]

392   It is clear that the votaries fight and even kill each other for their share in the mystery of divine incest.[114] In this way they participate in the action of the god.[115] The death of Baldur, by being wounded with the branch of mistletoe, is analogous to the death of Osiris and seems to require a similar

110 Ares probably means the Egyptian god Set.
111 [In the German text used by the author this word ($\sigma\upsilon\mu\mu\varepsilon\tilde{\iota}\xi\alpha\iota$) is translated as 'to have intercourse with.'—TRANS.]
112 Herodotus, Book II, 61ff., trans. by de Selincourt, pp. 126–27.
113 Cited in Dieterich, *Eine Mithrasliturgie*, p. 100.
114 The Polynesian myth of Maui says that the hero robbed his mother of her girdle. The theft of the veil in the myth of the swan-maiden means the same thing. In a myth of the Yoruba, of Nigeria, the hero simply ravishes his mother (Frobenius, *Zeitalter*).
115 The above-mentioned myth of Halirrhothios (par. 372), who killed himself in the attempt to cut down the sacred tree of Athens, the moria, expresses the same psychology, as also does the castration of the priests who serve the Great Mother. The ascetic tendency in Christianity (e.g., Origen's self-castration) is a similar phenomenon.

explanation. The legend says that all creatures had pledged themselves not to harm Baldur; only the mistletoe was forgotten, because she was supposed to be too young. Yet it was the twig of mistletoe that killed Baldur. The mistletoe is a parasite. The female fire-stick, the fire-mother, was obtained from the wood of a parasitic or creeping plant for the Indian fire-boring ceremony.[116] In Germanic legend the Mara, after its nightly jaunt, is said to rest on the "märentakken," which Grimm suggests is another name for mistletoe.[117] Mistletoe was also a sovereign remedy against barrenness.[118] In Gaul, it was only after offering sacrifice that the Druid was allowed, amid solemn ceremonies, to climb the sacred oak and cut the ritual branch of mistletoe. That which grows on the tree is the child (pl. xxxix), or *oneself* in renewed and rejuvenated form; and that is precisely what one cannot have, because the incest prohibition forbids it. We are told that the mistletoe which killed Baldur was "too young"; hence this clinging parasite could be interpreted as the "child of the tree." But as the tree signifies the origin in the sense of the mother, it represents the source of life, of that magical life-force whose yearly renewal was celebrated in primitive times by the homage paid to a divine son, a *puer aeternus*. The graceful Baldur is such a figure. This type is granted only a fleeting existence, because he is never anything but an anticipation of something desired and hoped for. This is so literally true that a certain type of "mother's son" actually exhibits all the characteristics of the flower-like, youthful god, and even dies an early death.[119] The reason is that he only lives on and through the mother and can strike no roots in the world, so that he finds himself in a state of permanent incest. He is, as it were, only a dream of the mother, an ideal which she soon takes back into herself, as we can see from the Near Eastern "son-gods" like Tammuz, Attis, Adonis, and Christ. The mistletoe, like Baldur, represents the "child of the mother," the

[116] Kuhn, *Mythol. Studien*, I.   [117] III, p. 1246. [Cf. par. 370, above.]
[118] Hence, in England, the custom of hanging mistletoe at Christmas. For mistletoe as the wand of life, see Aigremont, *Volkserotik und Pflanzenwelt*, II, p. 36.
[119] There is a beautiful description of the *puer aeternus* in an exquisite little book by the airman Antoine de Saint-Exupéry, *The Little Prince*. My impression that the author had a personal mother-complex was amply confirmed from first-hand information.

a. Expulsion of the demons
Anonymous engraving, 17th century

b. Sun-god
Shamanistic Eskimo idol, Alaska

Romulus and Remus with the She-Wolf
Painted wood, northern Italian, medieval

Christ in the Virgin's womb
Upper Rhenish Master, Germany, c. 1400

III

a. Boar-headed mother goddess: shakti of boar-headed Vishnu
Relief, northern India, 7th century

b. Scenes from the Eleusinian Mysteries
From a burial urn, Rome, 1st century A.D.

a. Veneration of the Buddha's teachings as a sun-wheel
Stupa of Amaravati, India, 2nd century A.D.

b. The Son of Man between the Seven Candlesticks
From the Beatus Commentary on the Apocalypse, late 12th century

V

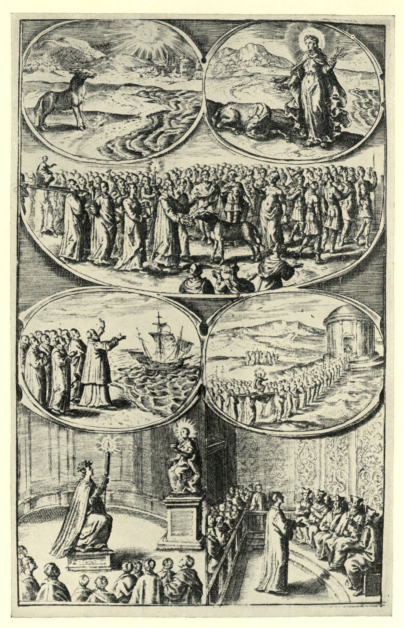

The initiation of Apuleius
From a 17th-century French edition of The Golden Ass

VI

The winged sun-disc, above the King
Throne of Tut-Ankh-Amon, 14th century B.C.

VII

The Overshadowing of Mary
Tempera painting on wood, Erfurt Cathedral, 1620–40

a. Winged sun-moon disc and tree of life
Hittite relief, Sakjegeuzi, northern Syria

b. Crucifixion, and the serpent lifted up
Thaler struck by the goldsmith Hieronymus Magdeburger of Annaberg

IX

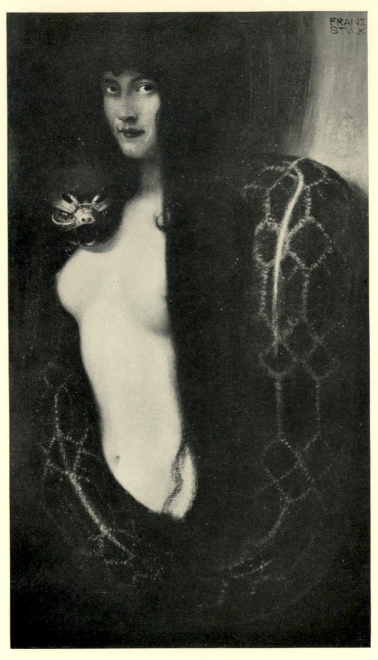

"Sin"
Painting by Franz Stuck (1863–1928), Germany

X

a. The King, attended, sacrifices to the sun-god
Stele of King Nabupaliddina, Babylon, 870 B.C.

b. The fertility god Frey
Bronze figure, Södermanland,
Sweden

XI

Phanes in the egg
Orphic relief, Modena

XII

a. The fire-god Tjintya
Wood carving, Bali

b. Agni on the ram, with fire-sticks
*Teak processional carving, southern
India*

XIII

a. The nourishing earth-mother (*below*)
Vault painting, Limburg Cathedral, c. 1235

b. Gorgon
Detail from a Greek vase

XIV

The Churning of the Milky Ocean
Miniature painting, Rajput School, India

XV

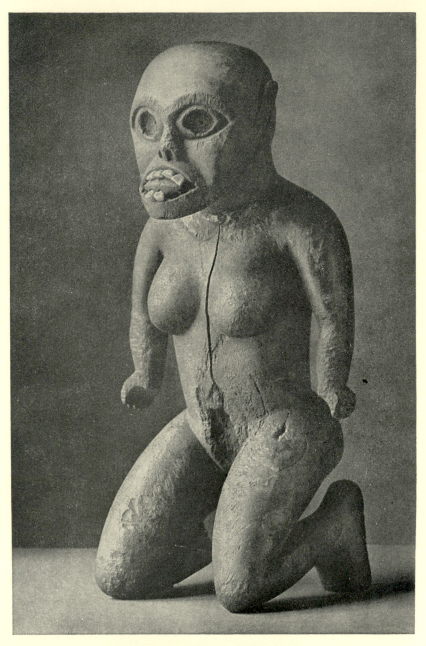

Kihe Wahine, goddess of goblins and lizards
Kou wood with human teeth, Hawaii

XVI

Female figure with head-dress symbolizing kingly power
King's incense bowl, Yoruba, West Africa

XVII

The crowned hermaphrodite
From a manuscript, "De alchimia," attributed to Thomas Aquinas, c. 1520

XVIII

Gilgamesh with the herb of immortality

Relief, palace of Assurnasirpal II (885–860 B.C.), Nimrud, Assyria

a. The horned Alexander
Coin of Lysimachus, 3rd century B.C.

b. The dadophors with raised and lowered torches
From a Mithraic marble bas-relief

XX

a. The god Men, on the cock
Attic wall-relief

b. Ceremonial head-dress of American Indian dancer
New Mexico

XXI

a. The New Jerusalem (Revelation, ch. 21)
Engraving from the Merian Bible, 1650

b. A man and woman devoured by the Terrible Mother
Shaman's amulet, walrus ivory, Tlingit Indians, Alaska, 19th century

XXII

Ardhanari: Shiva and Parvati united
Polychrome clay, India, 19th century

a. Mithras and Helios *(centre)*
*Fragment from the Mithraeum
near Klagenfurt*

b. Diana of Ephesus, with the mural crown
Alabaster and bronze, Roman, 2nd century A.D.

XXIV

Lingam with yoni
Angkor Wat, Cambodia, c. 12th century

The Fountain of Life
Icon, Constantinople School, 17th century

XXVI

Stoup, with arms encircling belly
Church at Kilpeck, Herefordshire, early 12th century

Hook for hanging
Painted wood, northern New Guinea

XXVIII

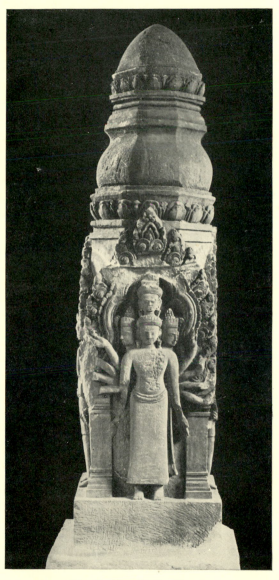

The Goddess in the Lingam
Cambodia, 14th century

XXIX

a. Mater Ecclesia
From the manuscript "Scivias" of
St. Hildegarde of Bingen, 12th century

b. The cow-headed Hathor
Bronze, Serapeum of
Sakkara, late period

The Tree of Life
Bronze vessel, Egypt, 7th–6th century B.C.

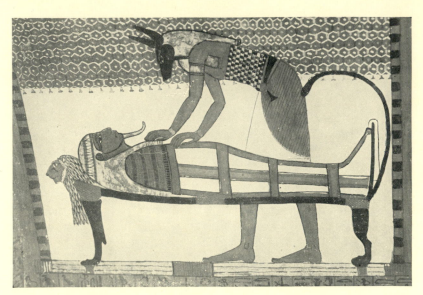

a. Jackal-headed Anubis bending over a mummy
From a tomb, Thebes, XX Dynasty

b. The sun-eating lion of alchemy
*From a manuscript, Library of St.
Gall, 17th century*

XXXII

The Mithraic sacrifice creating fruitfulness
The Heddernheim Relief, reverse

Demon eating the sun
Stone, eastern Java, 15th century

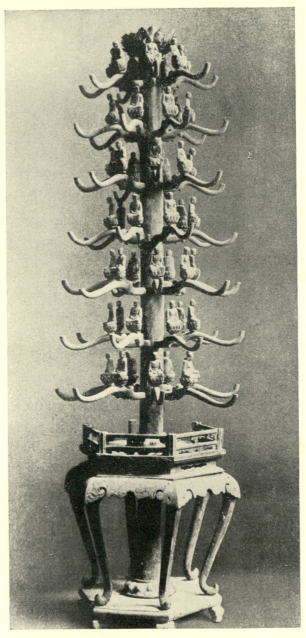

Buddhist tree of the dead
Wood carving, China

XXXV

Christ on the Tree of Life
Painting, Strasbourg

XXXVI

The Cross on Adam's grave
Detail over west door, Strasbourg Cathedral, c. 1280

XXXVII

a. Lamia bearing off a new-born babe
From the frieze "Tomb of the Harpies,"
Acropolis of Xanthos

b. The devouring mother
Shaman's amulet, walrus tusk,
Tlingit Indians, Alaska

The wak-wak tree with its human fruit

From a Turkish history of the West Indies, Constantinople, 1730

XXXIX

Mithras sacrificing the bull
The Heddernheim Relief

XL

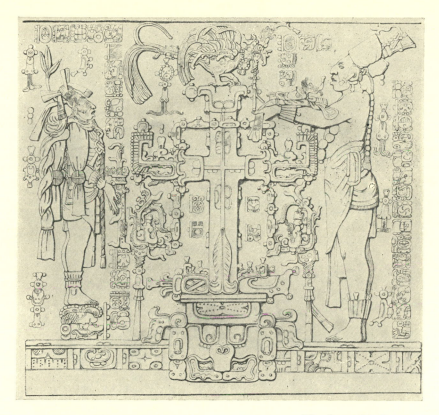

a. The Cross of Palenque
Mayan relief, Yucatán, Mexico

b. The shaping of the world-egg:
Ptah working on a potter's wheel
Egypt

Regeneration in the mother's body
Wooden figure, Nootka Indians, Vancouver Island, Canada

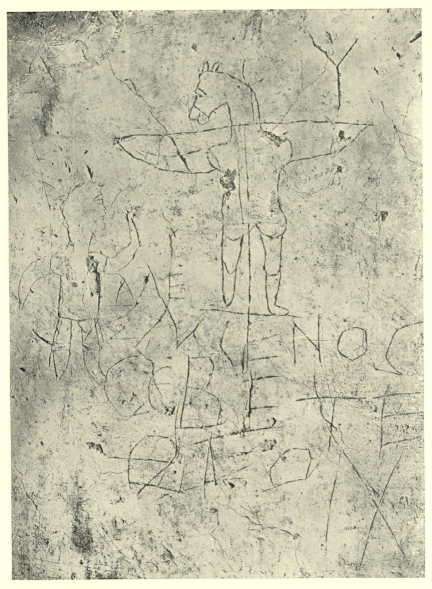

Mock crucifixion
Graffito, wall of the Imperial Cadet School, Palatine, Rome

Aion, with the signs of the zodiac
Rome, 2nd–3rd century

XLIV

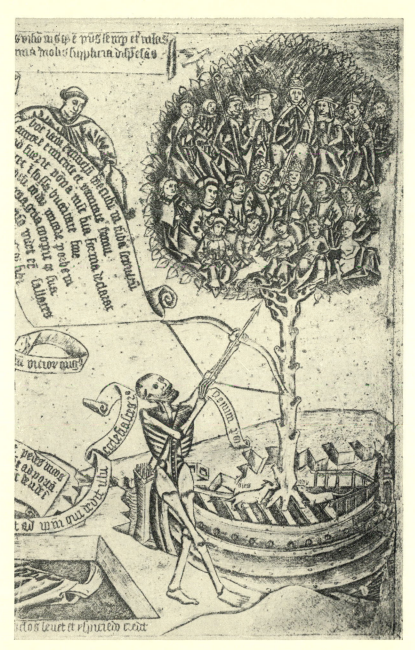

Death the archer
Detail from an engraving by the "Master of 1464," German School

a. The lotus growing out of Vishnu's navel, with Brahma inside
Relief, Vijayanagar, India

b. Ixion on the wheel
From a Cumaean vase

XLVI

Vishnu as a fish
Zinc figurine, India, 19th century

XLVII

The witch Rangda, thief of children
Painted wood, Bali

b. Queen Maya's dream of the Buddha's conception
Relief, Gandhara

XLIX

a. The Hathor Cow, suckling Queen Hatshepsut
Relief, Anubis Chapel, Temple of Der el-Bahri, XVIII Dynasty

b. The goddess Artio with a bear
*Bronze group, dedicated to the goddess of Licinia Sabinilla, from Muri,
near Bern*

L

The Mistress of the Beasts
Greek hydria, 600 B.C., found near Bern

A corn-god
Clay vessel, Chimbote culture, Peru

ISIDI·SACR

Basket of Isis, with snake
Marble altar from Caligula's temple of Isis, Rome

Matuta, an Etruscan Pietà
Fifth century B.C.

LIV

The Tree of Enlightenment
Pillar relief, stupa of Bharhut, India, 1st century B.C.

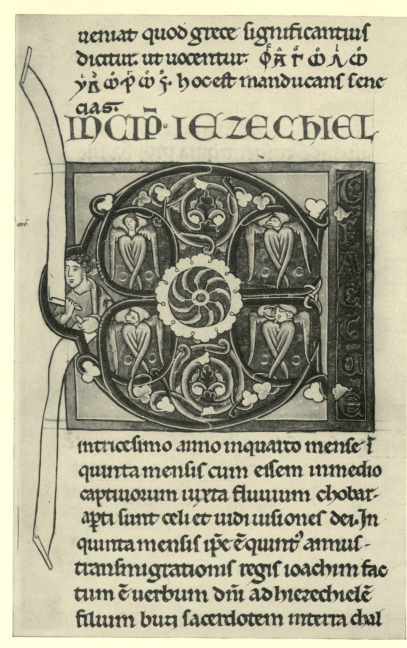

The Vision of Ezekiel
Bible of Manerius (French manuscript)

a. Cista and serpent
Silver coin, Ephesus, 57 B.C.

b. The sacrifice to the snake deity
Votive tablet, Sialesi (Eteonis), Boeotia

Triple-bodied Hecate
Roman

LVIII

a. The self-consuming dragon
.*From Lambsprinck's symbols in the* Musaeum hermeticum *(1678)*

b. Circle of gods
Bali

Christ surrounded by the Evangelists
Relief, Church at Arles-sur-Tech, Pyrénées-orientales, 11th century

a. The Serpent Mystery
Altar to the Lares, Pompeii

b. Priapus with snake
Roman

Devouring monster
Stone, Belahan, eastern Java, 11th century

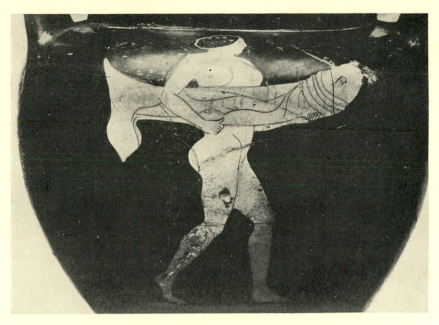

a. The regenerative symbol of the Haloa Festival
From a Greek vase, by the Pan Painter

b. Mixing-pot with lion and snake
Detail from the Heddernheim Relief (cf. Pl. XL)

Rubens: *The Last Judgment*
1618–20

LXIV

longed-for, revivified life-force that flows from her. But, separated from its host, the mistletoe dies. Therefore, when the
Druid cuts it, he kills it and by this act symbolically repeats
the fatal self-castration of Attis and the wounding of Adonis by
the boar's tusk. This is the dream of the mother in matriarchal
times, when there was as yet no father to stand by the side of
the son.

393   But why should the mistletoe kill Baldur, since it is, in a
sense, his sister or brother? The lovely apparition of the *puer
aeternus* is, alas, a form of illusion. In reality he is a parasite
on the mother, a creature of her imagination, who only lives
when rooted in the maternal body. In actual psychic experience
the mother corresponds to the collective unconscious, and the
son to consciousness, which fancies itself free but must ever
again succumb to the power of sleep and deadening unconsciousness. The mistletoe, however, corresponds to the shadow
brother, of whom E. T. A. Hoffmann gives such an excellent
description in his *Devil's Elixir,* and whom the psychotherapist
regularly meets as a personification of the personal unconscious.[120] Just as, at evening, the shadows lengthen and finally
engulf everything, so the mistletoe betokens Baldur's end.
Being an equivalent of Baldur himself, it is fetched down from
the tree like the "treasure hard to attain" (see the following
chapters). The shadow becomes fatal when there is too little
vitality or too little consciousness in the hero for him to complete his heroic task.

394   The "son of the mother," as a mere mortal, dies young, but
as a god he can do that which is forbidden and superhuman: he
commits the magical incest and thus obtains immortality. In
the myths the hero does not die; instead, he has to overcome
the dragon of death.

395   As the reader will long since have guessed, the dragon represents the negative mother-imago and thus expresses resistance
to incest, or the fear of it. Dragon and snake are symbolic representations of the fear of the consequences of breaking the taboo
and regressing to incest. It is therefore understandable that we
should come over and over again upon the motif of the tree and
the snake. Snakes and dragons are especially significant as guardians or defenders of the treasure. The black horse Apaosha

120 See "The Relations between the Ego and the Unconscious," par. 103.

also has this meaning in the old Persian *Song of Tishtriya,* where he blocks up the sources of the rain-lake. The white horse, Tishtriya, makes two futile attempts to vanquish Apaosha; at the third attempt he succeeds with the help of Ahura-Mazda.[121] Whereupon the sluices of heaven are opened and the fertilizing rain pours down upon the earth.[122] In this symbolism we can see very clearly how libido fights against libido, instinct against instinct, how the unconscious is in conflict with itself, and how mythological man perceived the unconscious in all the adversities and contrarieties of external nature without ever suspecting that he was gazing at the paradoxical background of his own consciousness.

396   The tree entwined by the snake may therefore be taken as the symbol of the mother who is protected against incest by fear. This symbol is frequently found on Mithraic monuments. The rock with a snake coiled round it has a similar meaning, for Mithras (and also Men) was born from a rock. The threatening of new-born infants by snakes (Mithras, Apollo, Heracles) is explained by the legend of Lilith and the Lamia. Python, the dragon of Leto, and Poine, who devastated the land of Crotopos, were sent by the father of the new-born. This fact points to the father as being the cause of the fear, which as we know prompted Freud to his famous aetiological myth of the primal horde with the jealous old patriarch at the top. The immediate model for this is obviously the jealous Yahweh, struggling to protect his wife Israel from whoredoms with strange gods. The father represents the world of moral commandments and prohibitions, although, for lack of information about conditions in prehistoric times, it remains an open question how far the first moral laws arose from dire necessity rather than from the family preoccu-

---

121 A variation of the same motif can be found in a legend from Lower Saxony: There was once a young ash-tree that grew unnoticed in a wood. Each New Year's Eve a white knight riding upon a white horse comes to cut down the young shoot. At the same time a black knight arrives and engages him in combat. After a lengthy battle the white knight overcomes the black knight and cuts down the tree. But one day the white knight will be unsuccessful, then the ash will grow, and when it is big enough for a horse to be tethered under it, a mighty king will come and a tremendous battle will begin: i.e., end of the world. (Grimm, III, p. 960.)

122 J. E. Lehmann, in Chantepie de la Saussaye, *Lehrbuch der Religionsgeschichte,* II, p. 185.

pations of the tribal father. At all events it would be easier to keep one's eye on a boxful of spiders than on the females of a primal horde. The father is the representative of the spirit, whose function it is to oppose pure instinctuality. That is his archetypal role, which falls to him regardless of his personal qualities; hence he is very often an object of neurotic fears for the son. Accordingly, the monster to be overcome by the son frequently appears as a giant who guards the treasure. An excellent example of this is the giant Humbaba in the Gilgamesh Epic, who guards the garden of Ishtar.[123] Gilgamesh conquers the giant and wins Ishtar, whereupon Ishtar immediately makes sexual advances to her deliverer.[124] These facts should be sufficient to explain the role played by Horus in Plutarch, and especially the violent treatment of Isis. By overpowering the mother the hero becomes equal to the sun: he renews himself. He wins the strength of the invincible sun, the power of eternal rejuvenation. We can now understand the series of pictures illustrating the Mithraic legend on the Heddernheim Relief (pl. XL). First we see the birth of Mithras from the top of the tree; the next picture shows him carrying the conquered bull (cf. pl. XLIXa). Here the bull has the same significance as the monster and may be compared with the bull that was conquered by Gilgamesh. He represents the father who—paradoxically—enforces the incest prohibition as a giant and dangerous animal. The paradox lies in the fact that, like the mother who gives life and then takes it away again as the "terrible" or "devouring" mother, the father apparently lives a life of unbridled instinct and yet is the living embodiment of the law that thwarts instinct. There is, however, a subtle though important distinction to be made here: the father commits no incest, whereas the son has tendencies in that direction. The paternal law is directed against incest with all the violence and fury of uninhibited instinct. Freud overlooks the fact that the spirit too is dynamic, as indeed it must be if the psyche is not to lose its self-regulating equilibrium. But as the "father," the representative of moral law, is not only an objective fact, but a subjective psychic factor in the son himself, the killing of the bull clearly denotes an overcoming of animal instinct, and at the same time

[123] Other examples in Frobenius, *passim*.
[124] Cf. Jensen, *Gilgamesch-Epos*, etc.

a secret and furtive overcoming of the power of the law, and hence a criminal usurpation of justice. Since the better is always the enemy of the good, every drastic innovation is an infringement of what is traditionally right, and may sometimes even be a crime punishable by death. As we know, this dilemma played an important part in the psychology of early Christianity, at the time when it came into conflict with Jewish law. In the eyes of the Jews, Christ was undoubtedly a law-breaker. Not unjustly is he called Adam Secundus; for just as the first Adam became conscious through sin, through eating of the tree of knowledge, so the second Adam broke through to the necessary relation with a fundamentally different God.[125]

397   The third picture shows Mithras reaching for the nimbus on the head of Sol. This act recalls the Christian idea that those who have conquered win the crown of eternal life.

398   In the fourth picture Sol kneels before Mithras. (Cf. pl. xxiva.) These last two pictures show that Mithras has arrogated to himself the strength of the sun and become its lord. He has conquered his animal nature (the bull). Animals represent instinct, and also the prohibition of instinct, so that man becomes human through conquering his animal instinctuality. Mithras has thus sacrificed his animal nature—a solution already anticipated in the Gilgamesh Epic by the hero's renunciation of the terrible Ishtar. In the Mithraic sacrifice the conquest of instinctuality no longer takes the archaic form of overpowering the mother, but of renouncing one's own instinctive desires. The primitive idea of reproducing oneself by entering into the mother's body has become so remote that the hero, instead of committing incest, is now sufficiently far advanced in the domestic virtues to seek immortality through the sacrifice of the incest tendency. This significant change finds its true fulfilment only in the symbol of the crucified God. In atonement for Adam's sin a bloody human sacrifice is hung upon the tree of

[125] This transformation of the God-image was clearly felt and expressed even in the Middle Ages (see *Psychology and Alchemy*, pars. 522ff.). The transformation had already begun in the Book of Job: Yahweh allows himself to be fooled by Satan, deals faithlessly with Job, misjudges the situation, and then has to admit his error. But although Job is obliged to bow to brute force he carries off the moral victory. In this conflict there lies a budding consciousness of the Johannine Christ: "I am the way, and the truth, and the life." [Cf. also Jung, "Answer to Job."—EDITORS.]

life.[126] (Cf. pl. XXXVI.) Although the tree of life has a mother significance, it is no longer the mother, but a symbolical equivalent to which the hero offers up his life. One can hardly imagine a symbol which expresses more drastically the subjugation of instinct. Even the manner of death reveals the symbolic content of this act: the hero suspends himself in the branches of the maternal tree by allowing his arms to be nailed to the cross. We can say that he unites himself with the mother in death and at the same time negates the act of union, paying for his guilt with deadly torment. This act of supreme courage and supreme renunciation is a crushing defeat for man's animal nature, and it is also an earnest of supreme salvation, because such a deed alone seems adequate to expiate Adam's sin of unbridled instinctuality. The sacrifice is the very reverse of regression—it is a successful canalization of libido into the symbolic equivalent of the mother, and hence a spiritualization of it.

399   As I have already pointed out, the hanging of the victim on a tree was a religious rite, of which numerous examples can be found in the Germanic sphere of culture.[127] It is also characteristic that the victims were pierced with a spear. Thus, in the Hovamol Edda, Odin says:

> I ween that I hung / on the windy tree,
> Hung there for nights full nine;
> With the spear I was wounded, / and offered I was
> To Odin, myself to myself.[128]

400   The hanging of the victims on crosses was a religious custom in Middle America. Müller [129] mentions the Fejérváry Manuscript (a Mexican hieroglyphic codex), which has, for a tailpiece, a cross with a gory divinity hanging in the centre. Equally significant is the Palenque Cross (pl. XLIa).[130] At the top is a bird, on either side two human figures facing the cross, one of them holding out a child for either sacrifice or baptism. The ancient Aztecs are said to have invoked the favour of Cinteotl, "the

126 Christ dies on the same tree against which Adam sinned. Zöckler, *The Cross of Christ*, p. 225.

127 The skins of animals were hung on the sacrificial trees and afterwards spears were thrown at them.   128 Trans. by Bellows, *The Poetic Edda*, p. 60.

129 J. G. Müller, *Geschichte der amerikanischen Urreligionen*, p. 498. [The codex, in the Liverpool Public Museum, is pre-Aztec, c. 11th–14th cents.—EDITORS.]

130 Stephens, *Travel in Central America*, II, p. 346.

daughter of heaven and goddess of the grain," by nailing a youth or maiden to the cross every spring and shooting the victim with arrows.[131] The name of the cross signifies "Tree of our life or flesh." [132] An effigy from the island of Philae represents Osiris in the form of a crucified god, mourned by Isis and Nephthys, his sister wives.[133]

401   The meaning of the cross is certainly not restricted to the tree of life, as has already been shown. Müller takes it as an emblem of rain and fertility.[134] We should also mention that it is a powerful charm for averting evil (e.g., making the sign of the cross).

402   In view of the fact that the cross resembles the human figure with arms outspread, it is worth noting that in early Christian art Christ is not nailed to the cross, but is shown standing before it with open arms.[135] Maurice interprets this as follows:

> It is a fact not less remarkable than well attested, that the Druids in their groves were accustomed to select the most stately and beautiful tree as an emblem of the deity they adored; and, having cut off the side branches, they affixed two of the largest of them to the highest part of the trunk, in such manner that those branches, extended on each side like the arms of a man, together with the body, presented to the spectator the appearance of a huge cross [cf. fig. 26]; and on the bark, in various places, was actually inscribed the letter "tau." [136]

403   The "tree of knowledge" of the Jains, of India, also has a human form; it is represented as an enormously thick trunk shaped like a human head, from the top of which grow two

---

131 Zöckler, p. 25.

132 Bancroft, *The Native Races of the Pacific States of North America*, II, p. 506. Cited in Robertson, *Christianity and Mythology*, p. 408.

133 Rossellini, *Monumenti dell' Egitto*, III, Pl. 23, cited in Robertson, p. 411.

134 Zöckler, pp. 6ff. In an Egyptian picture of the birth of a king, in Luxor, the bird-headed Thoth, the Logos and messenger of the gods, is shown announcing to the young queen Mautmes that she will give birth to a son. In the next scene Kneph and Hathor hold the *crux ansata* to her mouth, thus fertilizing her in a spiritual or symbolic manner. (Cf. fig. 27.) (Sharpe, *Egyptian Mythology*, pp. 18f., cited in Robertson, p. 328.)

135 Robertson, p. 409, mentions that in Mexico the sacrificial priest clothed himself in the skin of a newly killed woman and then stood before the war-god with arms stretched out like a cross.

136 Maurice, *Indian Antiquities*, VI, p. 68. By "tau" he means the primitive Egyptian form of the cross: ⊤.

long branches hanging down on either side, with a short, vertical branch sticking straight up, crowned with a bud-like knob.[137] Robertson tells us that in the Assyrian system God was represented in the form of a cross, the vertical standing for the

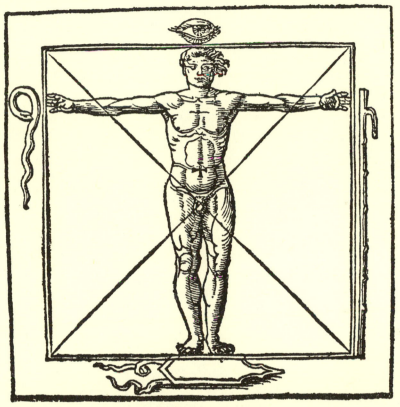

Fig. 26. The human cross
From Agrippa von Nettesheim, De occulta philosophia, *Cologne, 1533*

human figure, and the horizontal for a conventionalized pair of wings.[138] Archaic Greek idols, such as were found in large quantities in Aegina, have a similar character: an immoderately long head, wing-shaped arms slightly raised, and in front distinct breasts.[139]

137 Zöckler, p. 12.   138 Robertson, p. 133.
139 I am indebted for this information to Professor E. Fiechter, formerly of the Technical Institute, Stuttgart.

404   I must leave it an open question whether the symbol of the cross bears any relation to the two ceremonial fire-sticks used in fire-making, as has been claimed. But it seems very likely that the idea of "union" still lingers on in the cross, for underlying all fertility magic is the thought of renewal, which in turn is intimately connected with the cross. The idea of union expressed in the cross symbol is found in Plato's *Timaeus,* where the demiurge joins the parts of the world-soul together by means of two sutures, which form a X (chi). According to Plato, the world-soul contains the world in itself like a body, an image which cannot fail to remind us of the mother:

And in the centre he set a soul and caused it to extend throughout the whole and further wrapped its body round with soul on the outside; and so he established one world alone, round and revolving in a circle, solitary but by reason of its excellence able to bear itself company, needing no other acquaintance or friend but sufficient to itself. On all these accounts the world which he brought into being was a blessed god.[140]

405   This utter inactivity and desirelessness, symbolized by the idea of self-containment, amounts to divine bliss. Man in this state is contained as if in his own vessel, like an Indian god in the lotus or in the embrace of his Shakti. In accordance with this mythological and philosophical conception, the enviable Diogenes lived in a tub in order to give symbolical expression to the blissfulness and godlikeness of his freedom from desire. On the relation between the world-soul and the world-body Plato says:

Now this soul, though it comes later in the account we are now attempting, was not made by the god younger than the body; for when he joined them together, he would not have suffered the elder to be ruled by the younger. There is in us too much of the casual and random, which shows itself in our speech; but the god made soul prior to body and more venerable in birth and excellence, to be the body's mistress and governor.[141]

406   From other indications it appears that the image of the "soul" somehow coincides with the mother-imago.[142] The next

140 *Timaeus,* 34 B. This and the following passages trans. by Cornford, pp. 58f.
141 *Timaeus,* 34 B – C.
142 See *Psychological Types,* "soul" and "soul image," Defs. 48 and 49. The *anima* is the archetype of the feminine and plays a very important role in a

stage in the development of the world-soul takes place in a mysterious and rather controversial fashion.[143] When the operation was complete, the following was done:

> This whole fabric, then, he split lengthwise into two halves; and making the two cross one another at their centres in the form of the letter X, he bent each round into a circle and joined it up. . . .
> When the whole fabric of the soul had been finished to its maker's mind, he next began to fashion within the soul all that is bodily and brought the two together, fitting them centre to centre.[144]

407   A peculiar use is made of the cross symbol by the Muyscas Indians, of Peru; two ropes are stretched crosswise over the surface of the water (pool or stream), and fruits, oil, and precious stones are thrown in as a sacrifice at the point of intersection.[145] Here the divinity is evidently the water, not the cross, which only signifies the place of sacrifice. The symbolism is somewhat obscure. Water, and particularly deep water, usually has a maternal significance, roughly corresponding to "womb." The point of intersection of the two ropes is the point of union where the "crossing" takes place. (Note the double meaning of this word! According to all the analogies, the aim of fertility magic is to bring about the *increase* of the things marked for sacrifice.)

408   The cross in the form of the *crux ansata* frequently appears in the hand of the Egyptian Tum or Atum, the supreme god or hegemon of the Ennead. Its meaning is "life," which is to say that the god gives life. (Fig. 27.) It is important to know something about the attributes of this life-giving god. Tum of On-Heliopolis bears the name "the father of his mother," and his attendant goddess, Jusas or Nebit-Hotpet, is called sometimes the mother, sometimes the daughter, and sometimes the wife of the god. The first day in autumn is known in the Heliopolitan inscriptions as the "feast-day of the goddess Jusasit," as the arrival of the "sister who makes ready to unite herself with her father." It is the day on which "the goddess Mehnit completes

---

man's unconscious. See "The Relations between the Ego and the Unconscious," pars. 296ff. I have discussed the world-soul of Plato's *Timaeus* in "A Psychological Approach to the Dogma of the Trinity," pars. 186ff.
143 See my remarks ibid.   144 *Timaeus*, 36 B – E.   145 Zöckler, p. 24.

her work, so that the god Osiris may enter the left eye." [146] It is also called "the day for filling the sacred eye with what it needs." In the autumn equinox the heavenly cow with the moon-eye, Isis, receives the seed that begets Horus (the moon being the guardian of the seed).[147] The "eye" evidently stands

Fig. 27. The life-giving *crux ansata*
Egypt

for the female genitals, as is clear from the myth of Indra, who, as a punishment for his wantonness, was smitten with yonis all over his body, but was so far pardoned by the gods that the shameful yonis were changed into eyes. The little image reflected in the eye, the "pupilla," is a "child." The great god becomes a child again: he enters into the mother's womb for self-renewal.[148] (Cf. pl. XLII.) An Egyptian hymn says:

> Thy mother, the sky,
> Stretches forth her arms to thee.

[146] The "left eye" is the moon. See below, par. 487: the moon as the gathering-place of souls (cf. fig. 31).

[147] Brugsch, *Religion und Mythologie der alten Aegypter*, pp. 281ff.

[148] Cf. the retreat of Ra on the heavenly cow (par. 351). In one of the Hindu rites of purification the penitent has to crawl through an artificial cow in order to be reborn.

409   The hymn continues:

> Thou shinest, O father of the gods, upon the back of thy mother,
> daily thy mother taketh thee in her arms. When thou lightest up
> the habitation of the night, thou art one with thy mother, the sky.[149]

410   Tum of Pithum-Heroopolis not only carries the *crux ansata*
as a symbol, but even has this emblem as the commonest of his
titles, *ankh* or *ankhi*, which means 'life' or the 'Living One.'
He was chiefly worshipped as the Agathodaimon serpent (cf. fig.
37), of whom it was said: "The sacred Agathodaimon serpent
goes forth from the city of Nezi." The snake, because it casts
its skin, is a symbol of renewal, like the scarab beetle, a sun-
symbol, which was believed to be of masculine sex only and
to beget itself. "Khnum" (another name for Tum, but always
the sun-god is meant) comes from the verb *num*, 'to combine
or unite.' [150] Khnum appears as the potter and maker of his
own egg (cf. pl. XLIb).

411   It is clear from all this that the cross is a many-faceted symbol, and its chief meaning is that of the "tree of life" and the
"mother." Its symbolization in human form is therefore quite
understandable. The various forms of the *crux ansata* have the
meaning of "life" and "fruitfulness," and also of "union," which
can be interpreted as the *hieros gamos* of the god with his
mother for the purpose of conquering death and renewing
life.[151] This mythologem, it is plain, has passed into Christianity.
For instance, St. Augustine says:

> Like a bridegroom Christ went forth from his chamber, he went out
> with a presage of his nuptials into the field of the world. . . . He
> came to the marriage-bed of the cross, and there, in mounting it, he
> consummated his marriage. And when he perceived the sighs of the
> creature, he lovingly gave himself up to the torment in place of his
> bride, and he joined himself to the woman for ever.[152]

149 Cited in Schultze, *Psychologie der Naturvölker*, p. 338.
150 Brugsch, pp. 290ff.
151 This formula is not surprising, since it is the primitive man in us whose
animal forces appear in religion. From this point of view what Dieterich says
in his *Mithrasliturgie* (p. 108) is especially significant: "The old thoughts coming
from below gain a new strength in the history of religion. The revolution from
below creates new life in the old indestructible forms."
152 *Sermo Suppositus* 120, 8. ("Procedit Christus quasi sponsus de thalamo suo,
praesagio nuptiarum exiit ad campum saeculi; . . . pervenit usque ad crucis

412   The analogy is indeed so plain that it hardly requires further comment. It is, therefore, a very touching and, for all its naïveté, an extraordinarily profound piece of symbolism when Mary, in an Old English lament of the Virgin,[153] accuses the cross of being a false tree, which unjustly and insensately destroyed "the pure fruit of her body, her gentle birdling," with a poisonous draught, the draught of death, which was meant only for the guilty descendants of the sinner Adam. Her son was not to blame for their guilt. Mary laments:

> Tre unkynde, thou schalt be kud,
> mi sone step-moder I the calle:
> cros thou holdest him so heih on heigth,
> mi fruites feet I mai not kis;
> cros I fynde thou art my fo,
> thou berest my brid, beten blo. . . .

413   Whereupon the Holy Cross answers:

> Ladi to the I owe honour,
> thi brihte palmes nou I bere;
> thi fruit me florischeth in blod colour . . .
> that Blosme Blomed up in thi bour.
> ac not for the al-one,
> but for to winne all this world.

414   Concerning the relation of the two mothers to one another, the Cross says:

> thou art i-crouned hevene quene,
> thorw the burthe that thou beere.
> I am a Relyk that shineth shene,
> men wolde wite wher that I were,
> at the parlement wol I bene,
> on domes-day prestly a-pere;
> at the parlement shul puiten up pleynyng,
> hou Maydenes fruit on me gan sterve.[154]

---

torum et ibi firmavit ascendendo coniugium; ubi cum sentiret anhelantem in suspiriis creaturam commercio pietatis se pro coniuge dedit ad poenam; et copulavit sibi perpetuo iure matronam.") The "woman" is the Church. (Cf. pl. xxxa.)

153 "Dispute between Mary and the Cross," in Morris, *Legends of the Holy Rood,* pp. 134–35.

154 [In modern English: "Tree unkind thou shalt be known, my son's stepmother I call thee: Cross, thou holdest him so high in height, my fruit's feet I may not kiss; Cross, I find thou art my foe, thou bearest my bird, beaten

415   Thus the Mother of Death joins the Mother of Life in lamenting the dying god, and, as an outward token of their union, Mary kisses the cross and is reconciled.[155] In ancient Egypt this union of opposite tendencies was naïvely preserved in the Isis mother-imago. The separation of the son from the mother signifies man's leavetaking from animal unconsciousness. It was only the power of the "incest prohibition" [156] that created the self-conscious individual, who before had been mindlessly one with the tribe; and it was only then that the idea of the final death of the individual became possible. Thus through Adam's sin, which lay precisely in his becoming conscious, death came into the world. The neurotic who cannot leave his mother has good reasons for not doing so: ultimately, it is the fear of death that holds him there. It seems as if no idea and no word were powerful enough to express the meaning of this conflict. Certainly the struggle for expression which has continued through the centuries cannot be motivated by what is narrowly and crudely conceived as "incest." We ought rather to conceive the law that expresses itself first and last in the "incest prohibition" as the impulse to domestication, and regard the religious systems as institutions which take up the instinctual forces of man's animal nature, organize them, and gradually make them available for higher cultural purposes.

---

416   We will now return to Miss Miller's visions. Those that now follow do not require detailed discussion. First comes the image of a "bay of purple water." The symbolism of the sea links up

---

blue . . . / Lady, to thee I owe honour, thy bright palms now I bear; thy fruit flourisheth for me in blood colour . . . ; that blossom bloomed up in thy bower. And not for thee alone, but to win all this world. / Thou art crowned Heaven's queen, through the burden that thou barest. I am a Relic that shineth bright; men desire to know where I am. At the parliament [of the judgment day] shall I be, on doomsday appear suddenly; at the parliament I shall put up complaint, how a Maiden's fruit on me began to die."]

155 In Greece the stake on which criminals were executed or punished was known as the "hecate."

156 The incest-taboo is part of a complicated whole, i.e., the marriage class system, the most elementary form of which is the cross-cousin marriage. This is a compromise between the endogamous and exogamous tendencies. See my "Psychology of the Transference," pars. 433ff.

with what has gone before, and we could also refer back to the reminiscences of the bay of Naples in Part I. In the sequence of the whole we certainly ought not to overlook the significance of the bay, so it might be as well to cast a glance at the etymology of this conception. Generally speaking, *bay* denotes anything that stands open. F. *bayer* means 'to keep the mouth open, to gape.' Another word for the same thing is *gulf* (Lat. *sinus*), which, in F. *golfe,* is closely connected with *gouffre,* 'abyss' (cf. also Eng. *gap*). *Gulf* is related to κόλπος,[157] 'bosom, lap, womb'; also 'fold of a garment,' or 'pocket.' (In Swiss-German, *Buese* is 'pocket of a coat or skirt.') Κόλπος can also mean a deep hollow between two waves, or a valley between two high mountains. These significations point clearly to the underlying primitive ideas. They render intelligible Goethe's choice of words in the passage where Faust wishes to follow the sun with winged desire in order to drink its "streams of quenchless light":

> Then mountains could not check my godlike flight,
> With wild ravine or savage rocky ways;
> But lo, the sea, with warm and tranquil bays,
> Would hold its beauty to my wondering sight.[158]

417   Faust's desire, like that of every hero, is a yearning for the mystery of rebirth, for immortality; therefore his way leads out to sea and down into the maw of death, that frighteningly narrow "passage" which signals the new day:

> I hear a call towards the open main,
> My tide of soul is ebbing more and more;
> Lies at my feet the shining, glassy plain,
> A new day beckons to another shore.
> As if on wings, a chariot of fire
> Sweeps near me. I am ready to be free.
> Piercing the ether, new-born, I aspire
> To rise to spheres of pure activity.
>
> . . . .
>
> Now let me dare to open wide the gate
> Past which man's steps have ever flinching trod,
> The hour is come, as master of my fate,
> To prove in man the stature of a god,

157 Diez, *Wörterbuch der romanischen Sprachen,* p. 168.
158 Part I, trans. by Wayne, p. 66.

> Nor shrink before the cavern black and fell,
> Imagination's torment evermore,
> But *strive towards that passage,* at whose door
> —A narrow mouth—burn all the flames of hell.
> This step I take in cheerful resolution,
> Though I should plunge to death and dissolution.[159]

418   So it seems like a confirmation of this when in the very next vision Miss Miller sees "a perpendicular cliff." (Cf. *gouffre.*) This whole series of visions ends, so the author tells us, with a confusion of sounds, somewhat resembling "wa-ma, wa-ma." This strikes a very primitive, abysmal note. Since we learn nothing from Miss Miller about the subjective roots of this echo from the past, there is only one conjecture open to us: that it might, in the context as a whole, be considered a slight distortion of the well-known cry "Ma-ma."

[159] Ibid., p. 54.

THE BATTLE FOR DELIVERANCE FROM THE MOTHER

419   There now comes a short pause in the production of the visions; then the activity of the unconscious is energetically resumed.

420   A wood appears, with trees and bushes. After our discussion in the preceding chapter, we need only say that the meaning of the forest coincides essentially with that of the tabooed tree. The sacred tree is generally found in a wood or in a paradise-like garden. Sometimes the forbidden grove takes the place of the tabooed tree and is invested with all the attributes of the latter. The forest, like the tree, has a maternal significance. In the vision which now follows, the forest forms the setting for the dramatic representation of Chiwantopel's end. I will first give the beginning of the drama, i.e., the first attempt at sacrifice, as it appears in the original text. The reader will find the continuation, the monologue and sacrificial scene, at the beginning of the next chapter.

The figure of Chi-wan-to-pel comes up from the south, on horseback, wrapped in a blanket of bright colours, red, blue, and white. An Indian, dressed in buckskin, beaded and ornamented with feathers, creeps forward stealthily, making ready to shoot an arrow at Chi-wan-to-pel, who bares his breast to him in an attitude of defiance; and the Indian, fascinated by this sight, slinks away and disappears into the forest.

421   Chiwantopel appears on horseback. This fact seems to be of some importance because, as the next act of the drama will show, the horse does not play a neutral role, but suffers the same death as the hero, who even calls him his "faithful brother." This points to a curious similarity between horse and rider. There seems to be an intimate connection between the

two which leads them to the same fate. We have already seen that the libido directed towards the mother actually symbolizes her as a horse.[1] The mother-imago is a libido-symbol and so is the horse; at some points the meaning of the two symbols overlaps. But the factor common to both is the libido. In the present context, therefore, the hero and his horse seem to symbolize the

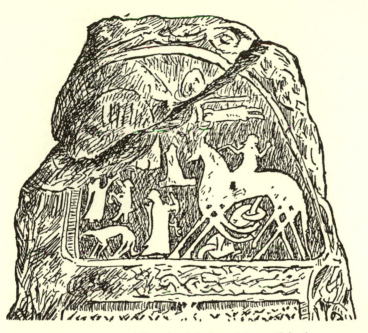

Fig. 28. Wotan riding the eight-legged horse Sleipnir
Tombstone, Götland, Sweden, c. A.D. *1000*

idea of man and the subordinate sphere of animal instinct. Parallel representations would be Agni on the ram (pl. XIII*b*), Wotan on Sleipnir (fig. 28), Ahura-Mazda on Angramainyu,[2]

---

[1] The goddess of the underworld, Hecate, is sometimes represented with a horse's head. Demeter and Philyra, wishing to escape the attentions of Kronos or Poseidon, change themselves into mares. Witches can easily change into horses, hence the nail-marks of the horseshoe may be seen on their hands. The devil rides on the witch's horse (fig. 29), and priests' housekeepers are changed after death into horses. (Negelein, "Das Pferd im Seelenglauben und Totenkult," XI, pp. 406ff.)

[2] In the same way the legendary king Tahmurath rides on Ahriman, the devil.

Christ on the ass,[3] Mithras on the bull, accompanied by his symbolic animals, the lion and the snake (pl. XL), Men on the human-footed horse, Frey on the boar with golden bristles, and so on. The steeds of mythology are always invested with great significance and very often appear anthropomorphized. Thus Men's horse has human forelegs, Balaam's ass human speech, and the bull upon whose back Mithras springs to deliver the death blow (*taurokathapsis:*[4] cf. pl. XL) is a life-giving deity.

Fig. 29. The Devil riding off with a witch
From Olaus Magnus, Historia, *Rome, 1555*

The mock crucifixion on the Palatine shows the Crucified with an ass's head (pl. XLIII), which may perhaps be a reference to the old legend that the image of an ass was worshipped in the temple at Jerusalem.[5] In the form of Drosselbart ('horse's beard') Wotan is half man, half horse. An old German riddle puts this unity of horse and rider [6] very nicely: "Who are the two that go to the Thing? Together they have three eyes,[7] ten

---

[3] The she-ass and her foal might derive from astrology, since the zodiacal sign Cancer, which rules at the summer solstice, was known in antiquity as the ass and its young. Cf. Robertson, *Christianity and Mythology*, p. 368.

[4] The image is probably taken from the Roman circus. The Spanish matador still has an heroic significance. Cf. Suetonius, *Opera*, trans. by Rolfe, II, pp. 40–43: "They drive wild bulls all over the arena, leaping upon them when they are tired out and throwing them to the ground by the horns."

[5] This legend is part of the astrological aspect of the Jewish god (Saturn), which I would rather not discuss here.

[6] Cf. the exhaustive account of this theme in Max Jähns, *Ross und Reiter*.

[7] Wotan is one-eyed. Cf. Schwartz, *Indogermanischer Volksglaube*, pp. 164ff.

feet and one tail,[8] and thus they travel over the land." Legend attributes properties to the horse which psychologically belong to the unconscious of man: there are clairvoyant and clairaudient horses, path-finding horses who show the way when the wanderer is lost, horses with mantic powers. In the Iliad (xix), the horse prophesies evil. They hear the words the corpse utters on its way to the grave—words which no human can hear. Caesar was told by his human-footed horse (probably derived from an identification of Caesar with the Phrygian Men) that he would conquer the world. An ass prophesied to Augustus the victory of Actium. Horses also see ghosts. All these things are typical manifestations of the unconscious. We can therefore see why the horse, as a symbol of the animal component in man, has numerous connections with the devil. The devil has a horse's hoof and sometimes a horse's form. At critical moments he shows the proverbial cloven hoof, just as, during the abduction of Hadding, Sleipnir suddenly looked out from behind Wotan's mantle.[9] The devil, like the nightmare, rides the sleeper; hence it is said that those who have nightmares are ridden by the devil. In Persian lore the devil is the steed of God. He represents the sexual instinct; consequently at the Witches' Sabbath he appears in the form of a goat or horse. The sexual nature of the devil is imparted to the horse as well, so that this symbol is found in contexts where the sexual interpretation is the only one that fits. Loki propagates in the form of a horse, and so does the devil, as an ancient god of fire. Lightning, too, is represented theriomorphically as a horse.[10] An uneducated hysterical patient once told me that as a child she was terrified of thunderstorms, because after each flash of lightning she saw a huge black horse rearing up to the sky. Indian legend tells of the black thunder-horse of Yama, the god of death, who dwells in the south, the mythical place of storms.[11] In German folklore the devil is a god of lightning who hurls the horse's hoof—lightning —on the rooftops. In accordance with the primitive idea that thunder fertilizes the earth, lightning and horses' hoofs both have a phallic meaning. An uneducated woman patient who had been violently forced by her husband to have coitus with him often dreamt that a wild horse leapt over her and kicked

8 Odin gives this riddle to King Heidhrekr (Hervarar Saga). Schwartz, p. 183.
9 Negelein, p. 412.   10 Ibid., p. 419.   11 Schwartz, p. 88.

her in the abdomen with his hind foot. Plutarch records the following words of a prayer from the Dionysian orgies:

Come, Dionysus, into thy temple at Elis, come with the Graces into thy holy temple, come with the bull's foot thundering, worthy bull, worthy bull! [12]

Pegasus struck the fountain of Hippocrene from the earth with his hoof. A Corinthian statue of Bellerophon, which was also a fountain, was made so that the water flowed from the hoof of the horse. Baldur's horse struck forth a spring with his kick. The horse's foot is therefore the dispenser of fruitful moisture.[13] A tale from lower Austria, recorded by Jähns,[14] says that a gigantic man on a white horse can sometimes be seen riding over the mountains, a sure sign of rain. In German legend, Mother Holle, the goddess of childbirth, comes on horseback. Pregnant women nearing confinement would often give oats to a white horse from their aprons and ask him for a speedy delivery. Originally it was the custom for the horse to nuzzle the woman's genitals. The horse, like the ass, has the significance of a priapic animal.[15] Hoof-marks were once worshipped as dispensers of blessings and fertility; they also established the right of possession and were of importance in determining boundaries, like the Priapic statues of Latin antiquity. It was a horse who, like the Dactyls, discovered the mineral wealth of the Harz Mountains with his hoof. The horse-shoe, an equivalent for the horse's foot,[16] brings luck and has an apotropaic meaning. In the Netherlands, a hoof is hung up in the stable to ward off sorcery. The analogous effect of the phallus is well known; hence the phalli on gates. The shank in particular is supposed to keep off lightning, on the principle that like cures like.

422   On account of their speed, horses signify wind, and here again the *tertium comparationis* is the libido-symbol. German legend knows the wind as the wild huntsman in lustful pursuit of the maiden. Wotan gallops along in a storm after the wind-bride (Frigg) fleeing before him.[17] Storm-centres often get

12 Preller, *Griechische Mythologie,* I, p. 432. [From Plutarch, *Quaestiones Graecae,* 36.]   13 For further examples see Aigremont, *Fuss- und Schuhsymbolik.*
14 *Ross und Reiter,* p. 27.
15 Aigremont, p. 17. [Cf. the erotic role of the horse in Robinson Jeffers' poem "Roan Stallion."—Editors.]
16 Negelein, XII, p. 386f.   17 Schwartz, p. 113.

their names from horses, e.g., the Schimmelberge ('white horse hills') on Lüneburg heath. The centaurs are, among other things, wind-gods.[18]

423   Horses also signify fire and light, like the fiery horses of Helios. Hector's horses were called Xanthos (yellow, glaring), Podargos (swift-footed), Lampos (shining), and Aithon (burning). Siegfried leaps over the wall of fire on the thunder-horse Grani, who was sired by Sleipnir and was the only one capable of taking the fiery hedge.[19] There is a distinct fire symbolism in the mystic quadriga mentioned by Dio Chrysostom:[20] the highest god always drives his chariot round in a circle. The chariot is drawn by four horses, and the outside horse moves very quickly. He has a shining coat, bearing on it the signs of the zodiac and the constellations.[21] The second horse goes more slowly and is illuminated on one side only. The third horse is slower still, and the fourth horse runs round himself. Once, however, the outside horse set the mane of the second horse on fire with his fiery breath, and the third horse drenched the fourth with streams of sweat. Then the horses dissolve and merge with the substance of the strongest and most fiery, which now becomes the charioteer. The horses represent the four elements. The catastrophe signifies world conflagration and the deluge, after which the division of God into Many ceases, and the divine One is restored.[22] There can be no doubt that the quadriga is meant as an astronomical symbol of Time. We saw in Part I that the Stoic conception of fate is a fire-symbol, so it is a logical continuation of this idea when the closely related conception of time exhibits the same libido symbolism.

[18] Evidence for the centaurs as wind-gods may be found in Meyer, *Indogermanische Mythen*, II, pp. 447ff.   [19] Schwartz, p. 141.

[20] *Opera*, XXXVI, 6. Cited in Cumont, *Mysteries of Mithra*, p. 25.

[21] This is a special motif which must have something typical about it. A schizophrenic patient ("The Psychology of Dementia Praecox," par. 290) declared that her horses had "half-moons" under their skins "like little curls." The *I Ching* is supposed to have been brought to China by a horse that had the magic signs (the "river map") on his coat. The skin of the Egyptian sky-goddess, the heavenly cow, is dotted with stars. (Cf. fig. 25.) The Mithraic Aion bears the signs of the zodiac on his skin (cf. pl. XLIV).

[22] This is the result of a world catastrophe. In mythology, too, the blossoming and withering of the tree of life denotes the turning point, the beginning of a new age.

424   The Brihadaranyaka Upanishad says:

> Dawn is the head of the sacrificial horse, the sun his eye, the wind
> his breath, the universal fire his open mouth. The year is the body
> of the sacrificial horse. The sky is his back, the air his belly, the
> earth the underpart of his belly. The poles are his flanks, the inter-
> mediate poles his ribs, the seasons his limbs, the months and half-
> months his joints, days and nights his feet, the stars his bones, the
> clouds his flesh. Sand is the food in his stomach, rivers are his en-
> trails. His liver and lungs are the mountains; plants and trees, his
> hair. The rising sun is his forepart, the setting sun his hindpart. . . .
> The ocean is his kinsman, the sea his cradle.[23]

425   Here the horse is undoubtedly conceived as a time-symbol,
besides being the whole world. In the Mithraic religion we meet
with a strange god, Aion (pl. XLIV), also called Chronos or *deus
leontocephalus* because he is conventionally represented as a
lion-headed human figure. He stands in a rigid attitude,
wrapped in the coils of a serpent whose head juts forward over
the head of the lion. In each hand he holds a key, on his breast
is a thunderbolt, on his back are the four wings of the wind,
and on his body are the signs of the zodiac. His attributes are
a cock and implements. In the Carolingian Utrecht Psalter,
which was based on classical models, Aion is shown as a naked
man bearing in his hand a snake.[24] As the name indicates, he is
a time-symbol, and is composed entirely of libido-images. The
lion, the zodiacal sign for the torrid heat of summer,[25] is the
symbol of *concupiscentia effrenata*, 'frenzied desire.' ("My soul
roars with the voice of a hungry lion," says Mechthild of Magdeburg.) In the Mithraic mysteries the snake is often shown as the
antagonist of the lion, in accordance with the myth of the sun's
fight with the dragon. In the Egyptian Book of the Dead, Tum
is addressed as a tom-cat, because in that form he fought the
Apophis-serpent. To be "entwined" or embraced is the same
as to be "devoured," which as we saw means entering into the
mother's womb. Time is thus defined by the rising and setting
sun, by the death and renewal of libido, the dawning and ex-

[23] Br. Up., 1, i, trans. by Hume, p. 73, modified.
[24] Cumont, *Textes*, I, p. 76.
[25] Therefore the lion was killed by Samson, who afterwards harvested honey from
the carcass. Summer's end is autumn's plenty. The legend of Samson is a parallel
of the Mithraic sacrifice. Cf. Steinthal, "Die Sage von Simson," pp. 129ff.

tinction of consciousness. The attribute of the cock again points to time, and the implements to creation through time (Bergson's "durée créatrice"). Oromazdes (Ahura-Mazda) and Ahriman came into being through *Zrwan akarana,* 'infinitely long duration.' So time, this empty and purely formal concept, is expressed in the mysteries through transformations of the creative force, libido, just as time in physics is identical with the flow of the energic process. Macrobius remarks: "By the lion's head the present time is indicated . . . because its condition is strong and fervent." [26] Philo Judaeus evidently knows better:

> Time is regarded as a god by evil men who wish to hide the Essential Being. . . . Vicious men think that Time is the cause of the world, but the wise and good think it is God.[27]

426   In Firdausi, time is often the symbol of fate.[28] The Indian text quoted above goes even further: its horse symbol contains the whole world, his kinsman and cradle is the sea, the mother, who is the equivalent of the world-soul. Just as Aion represents the libido in the "embrace" or state of death and rebirth, so here the cradle of the horse is the sea, i.e., the libido is in the "mother," dying and rising again in the unconscious.

427   We have already seen that the horse is connected through Yggdrasill with the symbolism of the tree. The horse too is a "tree of death"; for instance in the Middle Ages the bier was called "St. Michael's Horse," and the modern Persian word for coffin means 'wooden horse.' [29] The horse also plays the part of a psychopomp who leads the way to the other world—the souls of the dead are fetched by horsewomen, the Valkyries. Modern Greek songs speak of Charon as riding on a horse.

428   Finally, the symbol appears in yet another form: sometimes the devil rides on a *three-legged* horse. The goddess of death,

---

26 *Saturnaliorum Libri VII,* I, 20, 15, in *Opera,* II, p. 189. ("Leonis capite monstratur praesens tempus—quia conditio ejus . . . valida fervensque est.")

27 *In Genesim,* I, 100, in *Opera omnia,* VI, p. 338. Cited in Cumont, *Textes,* I, p. 82.

28 Spiegel, *Erānische Altertumskunde,* II, p. 193. In the treatise Περὶ φύσεως, which is ascribed to Zoroaster, Ananke, the goddess of fate, is symbolized by air. (Cumont, p. 87.)

29 Spielrein's patient (p. 394) speaks of horses who eat human beings and even exhumed corpses.

Hel, rides on a three-legged horse in time of pestilence.[30] In the Bundahish [31] there is a monstrous three-legged ass who stands in the heavenly rain-lake Vouru-Kasha; his urine purifies its waters, and at his cry all useful animals become pregnant and all harmful animals drop their young. The contrasting symbolism of Hel is fused into one image in the ass of Vouru-Kasha. The libido is fructifying as well as destructive.

429   In the Miller drama an Indian approaches the hero, preparing to shoot an arrow at him. But Chiwantopel, with a proud gesture, exposes his breast to the enemy. This image reminded the author of the scene between Cassius and Brutus in Shakespeare's *Julius Caesar*.[32] A misunderstanding has arisen between the two friends, Brutus accusing Cassius of withholding the money for the legions. Cassius breaks out in a peevish tirade:

> Come, Antony, and young Octavius, come,
> Revenge yourselves alone on Cassius,
> For Cassius is aweary of the world:
> Hated by one he loves: braved by his brother;
> Check'd like a bondman; all his faults observ'd,
> Set in a note-book, learn'd, and conn'd by rote,
> To cast into my teeth. O! I could weep
> My spirit from mine eyes! There is my dagger,
> And here my naked breast; within, a heart
> Dearer than Plutus' mine, richer than gold:
> If that thou be'st a Roman, take it forth;
> I, that denied thee gold, will give my heart.
> Strike, as thou didst at Caesar; for, I know,
> When thou didst hate him worst, thou lov'dst him better
> Than ever thou lov'dst Cassius.

430   Our material would not be complete if we did not mention that this speech of Cassius has several analogies with the agonized delirium of Cyrano, except that Cassius is far more theatrical. There is something childish and hysterical in his

30 Negelein, p. 416. Cf. my remarks on the three-legged horse in "The Phenomenology of the Spirit in Fairy Tales" (1954/55 edn., p. 28).
31 [Cf. *Psychology and Alchemy*, par. 535.—EDITORS.]   32 Act IV, scene III.

manner. Brutus has no intention of killing him; instead, he pours cold water on him in the following dialogue:

> Sheathe your dagger:
> Be angry when you will, it shall have scope;
> Do what you will, dishonour shall be humour.
> O Cassius! you are yoked with a lamb
> That carries anger as the flint bears fire,
> Who, much enforced, shows a hasty spark,
> And straight is cold again.

CASSIUS: Hath Cassius liv'd
> To be but mirth and laughter to his Brutus,
> When grief and blood ill-temper'd vexeth him?

BRUTUS: When I spoke that, I was ill-temper'd too.

CASSIUS: Do you confess so much? Give me your hand.

BRUTUS: And my heart too.

CASSIUS: O Brutus!

BRUTUS: What's the matter?

CASSIUS: Have you not love enough to bear with me,
> When that rash humour which my mother gave me
> Makes me forgetful?

BRUTUS: Yes, Cassius; and from henceforth
> When you are over-earnest with your Brutus,
> He'll think your mother chides, and leave you so.

431   Cassius's irritability is explained by the fact that he identifies with his mother and therefore behaves exactly like a woman, as his speech demonstrates to perfection.[33] His womanish yearning for love and his despairing self-abasement under the proud masculine will of Brutus fully justify the latter's remark that Cassius is "yoked with a lamb," in other words, has something feckless in his character, which is inherited from his mother. This can be taken as proof of an infantile disposition, which is

[33] A clear case of identity with the anima. The first carrier of the anima-image is the mother.

as always characterized by a predominance of the parental imago, in this case that of the mother. An individual is infantile because he has freed himself insufficiently, or not at all, from his childish environment and his adaptation to his parents, with the result that he has a false reaction to the world: on the one hand he reacts as a child towards his parents, always demanding love and immediate emotional rewards, while on the other hand he is so identified with his parents through his close ties with them that he behaves like his father or his mother. He is incapable of living his own life and finding the character that belongs to him. Therefore Brutus correctly surmises that "the mother chides" in Cassius, not he himself. The psychologically valuable fact to be elicited here is that Cassius is infantile and identified with the mother. His hysterical behaviour is due to the circumstance that he is still, in part, a "lamb," an innocent and harmless child. So far as his emotional life is concerned, he has not yet caught up with himself, as is often the case with people who are apparently so masterful towards life and their fellows, but who have remained infantile in regard to the demands of feeling.

432   Since the figures in the Miller drama are children of the author's imagination, they naturally depict those traits of character which belong to the author herself.[34] The hero Chiwantopel represents her ideal, who is here projected as a masculine figure; for Miss Miller is still youthful enough to see her ideal in a man. She has evidently received no salutary disappointments in this respect, but is still enjoying her illusions. She does not yet know that her ideal figure ought really to be feminine, because such a figure might touch her too closely. So long as the ideal is portrayed in the person of a man, it does not commit her to anything; it merely stimulates her fantastic demands. Were the ideal of her own sex, she might one day make the discovery that she does not quite come up to it. That would be uncomfortable, but salutary. Cyrano's gesture [35] is all very fine and impressive, but that of Cassius verges on the theatrical. Both heroes set about dying in the grand manner, and Cyrano actually succeeds in doing so. This yearning for death anticipates the inevitable end of the illusion that the *other* person is

[34] Because her fantasy is not a creation she consciously willed and formed, but an involuntary product.   [35] See par. 48, above.

the ideal. Miss Miller's ideal figure is evidently about to change his psychic localization—he might even take up his abode in the author herself. That would mark a very critical point in her career. For when such a vitally important figure as the ideal is about to change, it is as though that figure had to die. It then creates in the individual all sorts of unaccountable and apparently unfounded presentiments of death—a romantic world-weariness. These tendencies have already found expression in the "Song of the Moth," but now they become more sharply defined. Her infantile world wants to come to an end and be replaced by the adult phase. The wish of young girls to die is often only an indirect expression of this, but it remains a pose even if they really do die, for even death can be dramatized. Such an outcome merely makes the pose more effective. That the highest summit of life can be expressed through the symbolism of death is a well-known fact, for any growing beyond oneself means death. As an infantile person Miss Miller cannot realize what her task is in life; she cannot set herself any goal or standard for which she feels responsible. Therefore she is not yet prepared to accept the problem of love either, for this demands full consciousness and responsibility, circumspection and foresight. It is a decision in favour of life, at whose end death stands. Love and death have not a little to do with one another.

433 The proud gesture with which the hero offers himself to death may very easily be a manoeuvre for courting the sympathy of the other person, and it therefore invites the cool analysis which Brutus proceeds to give. The behaviour of Chiwantopel is equally suspicious, for the Cassius scene which serves as its model indiscreetly discloses the fact that the whole affair is merely infantile. When a gesture turns out to be too theatrical it gives ground for the suspicion that it is not genuine, that somewhere a contrary will is at work which intends something quite different.

434 In the ensuing drama the libido assumes a menacing activity that contrasts very strongly with the inactive nature of the preceding symbols, and a conflict develops in which one party threatens the other with murder. The hero, the ideal image of the dreamer, is ready to die; he has no fear of death. To judge from the infantile character of this hero, it is indeed high time for him to quit the stage. Death is to come for him in the form

of an arrow-shot. In view of the fact that many heroes are themselves mighty archers, or else are killed by arrows, it may not be superfluous to inquire what death by an arrow means. (Cf. pl. XLV.)

435   We read in the biography of Anna Catherina Emmerich, the hysterical German nun (1774–1824) who received the stigmata, the following account of her heart-trouble:

When only in her novitiate, she received as a Christmas gift from Christ a very painful heart-trouble, which lasted for the whole period of her ordained life. But God showed her inwardly its purpose: it was to atone for the decay of the spirit of the Order, and especially for the sins of her fellow sisters. But what made this trouble most painful to her was the gift which she had possessed from youth, of seeing with her mind's eye the inner nature of man as he really was. She felt the heart-trouble physically, as if her heart were continually pierced by arrows.[36] These arrows—and for her this was a far worse spiritual torment—she recognized as the thoughts, schemings, secret gossipings, misunderstandings, and uncharitable slanders with which her fellow sisters, wholly without reason and conscience, plotted against her and her God-fearing way of life.[37]

436   It is difficult to be a saint, because even a patient and long-suffering nature will not readily endure such a high degree of differentiation and defends itself in its own way. The constant companion of sanctity is temptation, without which no true saint can live. We know that these temptations can pass off unconsciously, so that only their equivalents reach consciousness in the form of symptoms. We know, too, that *Herz* traditionally rhymes with *Schmerz*.[38] It is a well-known fact that hysterics substitute a physical pain for a psychic pain which is not felt because repressed. Catherina Emmerich's biographer has understood this more or less correctly, but her own interpretation of the pain is based, as usual, on a projection: it is always the others who secretly say all sorts of wicked things about her, and this is the cause of her pains. The facts of the matter are rather different: the renunciation of all life's joys, this fading before the flower, is always painful, and especially painful are the un-

36 The heart of the mother of God is pierced by a sword, "that the thoughts of many hearts may be revealed." Luke 2 : 35.
37 Wegener, *Leben der Dienerin Gottes Anna Catherina Emmerich*, p. 63.
38 [German 'heart' and 'pain.'—EDITORS.]

fulfilled desires and the attempts of nature to break through the barrier of repression, without which no such differentiation would be possible. The gossip and sarcastic gibes of the sisters very naturally pick on these painful things, so that it must seem to the saint as if her difficulties came from there. She could hardly know that gossip is very apt to take over the role of the unconscious, and, like a skilled adversary, always aims at the chinks in our armour of which we know nothing.

437   The same idea is expressed in the following passage from the discourses of the Buddha:

But if those sensual pleasures fail the person who desires and wishes for them, he will suffer, pierced by the arrow of pain.[39]

438   The wounding and painful shafts do not come from outside, through gossip, which only pricks us on the surface, but from the ambush of our own unconscious. It is our own repressed desires that stick like arrows in our flesh.[40] On another occasion this became true for our nun, and in the most literal sense. It is a well-known fact that scenes of mystic union with the Saviour are strongly tinged with erotic libido.[41] Stigmatization amounts to an incubation with the Saviour, a slight modification of the ancient conception of the *unio mystica* as cohabitation with the god. The nun gives the following account of her stigmatization:

I had a contemplation of the sufferings of Christ, and I besought him to let me feel his sorrows with him, and prayed five paternosters in adoration of the five sacred wounds. Lying on my bed with arms outstretched, I entered into a great sweetness and into an endless thirst for the torments of Jesus. Then I saw a radiance descending towards me; it came slanting down from above. It was a crucified body, alive and transparent, the arms extended, but without the Cross. The wounds shone more brightly than the body; they were

39 *Sutta-Nipata,* trans. by Fausböll, p. 146.
40 Theocritus (27, 29), calls the pangs of birth the "darts of Eileithyia," as though the pain came from outside. [Cf. Edmonds trans., p. 337.] The same comparison is used for desire in Ecclesiasticus 19 : 2: "As an arrow that sticketh in the flesh of the thigh, so is a word in a fool's belly." That is to say, it gives him no peace until it is out.
41 This fact, however, does not prove that the experience of the *unio mystica* is exclusively erotic in origin. The upsurge of eroticism only proves that the canalization of libido has not been entirely successful, with the result that clear traces of the original form remain behind unassimilated.

five circles of glory emanating from the glory of the whole. I was enraptured, and my heart was moved with great pain and yet with great sweetness, from my longing to share the torments of my Saviour. And at the sight of the wounds my longing for the sufferings of the Redeemer increased more and more, as if streaming out of my breast, through my hands, side, and feet towards his holy wounds. Then from the hands, then from the side, then from the feet of the figure triple beams of shining red light shot forth into my hands, my side, and my feet, ending in an arrow.[42]

439   The beams are triple, terminating in an arrow-head.[43] Like Cupid, the sun has his quiver full of destroying or fertilizing arrows.[44] The arrow has a masculine significance; hence the Oriental custom of describing brave sons as the arrows or javelins of their father. "To make sharp arrows" is an Arabic expression for begetting valiant sons. To announce the birth of a son the Chinese used to hang a bow and arrow in front of the house. Accordingly the Psalms declare (127 : 4, RV): "As arrows in the hand of a mighty man, so are the children of youth." Thanks to this meaning of the arrow, we can see why the Scythian king Ariantes, wishing to prepare a census, demanded an arrow-head from each man.[45] A similar significance attaches to the lance: men are descended from the lance; the ash is the mother of lances; therefore the men of the Bronze Age are derived from her. Kaineus [46] commanded that his lance was to be worshipped. Pindar says of this Kaineus that, in the legend, "he descended into the depths, splitting the earth with a straight foot." [47] Originally he is supposed to have been a maiden

---

[42] Wegener, 77ff.

[43] Apuleius (The Golden Ass, II, 31, in Graves trans., p. 59) makes drastic use of the bow-and-arrow symbolism: "Since the first of Cupid's sharp arrows lodged in my heart this morning, I have been standing to arms all day, and now my bow is strung so tight that I'm afraid something will snap if the Advance isn't sounded pretty soon."

[44] And like the plague-bringing Apollo. In OHG., 'arrow' is strala.

[45] Herodotus, IV, 81. [Cf. Selincourt trans., p. 269.]

[46] Cf. Roscher, Lexikon, III, 894ff., s.v. "Kaineus."

[47] Pindar, fr. 166f. Spielrein's patient (p. 371) also had this idea of splitting the earth: "Iron is used for boring into the earth—With iron you can make men—The earth is split, burst open, man is divided—Man is cut up and put together again—In order to put a stop to being buried alive, Jesus told his disciples to bore into the earth." The motif of "splitting" is of world-wide significance. The Persian hero Tishtriya, taking the form of a white horse, split open the rain-lake

named Kainis, who, as a reward for her submissiveness, was changed by Poseidon into an invulnerable man. Ovid, describing the battle of the Lapithae with the invulnerable Kaineus, says that in the end they covered him completely with trees, because that was the only way they could get at him He continues:

His end is doubtful. Some say that his body was thrust down by the weight of the trees to the Tartarean pit, but the son of Ampycus denied this. For from the midst of the pile he saw a bird with golden wings fly up into the limpid air.[48]

440   Roscher[49] takes this bird to be the golden plover (*Charadrius pluvialis*), which gets its name from the fact that it lives in a χαράδρα, 'crack in the earth.' His song heralds the rain.

441   Once again we recognize the typical elements of a libido myth: original bisexuality, immortality (invulnerability) through entry into the mother (splitting the mother with the foot), resurrection as a soul-bird, and production of fertility (rain). When a hero of this type causes his lance to be worshipped, he probably does so because he thinks it a valid equivalent of himself.

442   From this standpoint the passage in Job, which we quoted in Part I, appears in a new light:

> He hath set me up for his mark.
> His archers compass me round about,
> He cleaveth my reins asunder, and doth not spare;
> He poureth out my gall upon the ground.
> He breaketh me with breach upon breach,
> He runneth upon me like a giant.[50]

443   Here Job is voicing the torment of soul caused by the onslaught of unconscious desires; the libido festers in his flesh, a cruel God has overpowered him and pierced him through with barbed thoughts that agonize his whole being.

---

and so made the earth fruitful. He is also called Tir, 'arrow.' He is sometimes represented as feminine, with bow and arrow. (Cumont, *Textes*, I, p. 136.) Mithras shoots water from the rock with his arrow in order to stop the drought. On Mithraic monuments the knife, otherwise used as the sacrificial instrument for killing the bull, is sometimes found stuck in the earth. (Ibid., pp. 115, 116, 165.)
48 *Metamorphoses*, trans. by Miller, II, pp. 216–17, modified.
49 In a review of Meyer's *Indogermanische Mythen*, in *Göttingische Gelehrte Anzeigen*, I (1884), p. 155.   50 Job 16:12ff.

444   The same image occurs in Nietzsche:

> Stretched out, shivering,
> Like one half dead whose feet are warmed,
> Shaken by unknown fevers,
> Shuddering from the icy pointed arrows of frost,
> Hunted by thee, O thought,
> Unutterable! veiled! horrible one!
> Thou huntsman behind the clouds.
> Struck to the ground by thee,
> Thou mocking eye that gazeth at me from the dark:
> Thus do I lie,
> Twisting, writhing, tortured
> With eternal tortures,
> Smitten
> By thee, cruel huntsman,
> Thou unknown—God!
>
> Smite deeper!
> Smite once more!
> Pierce, rend my heart!
> What meaneth this torturing
> With blunt-toothed arrows?
> Why gazest thou again,
> Never weary of human agony,
> With sardonic gods'-eyes, flashing lightning?
> Why wilt thou not kill,
> Only torture, torture? [51]

445   No long-drawn explanations are needed to see in this comparison the martyred and sacrificed god whom we have already met in the Aztec crucifixions and in the sacrifice of Odin.[52] We meet the same image in depictions of the martyrdom of St. Sebastian, where the glowing, girlishly tender flesh of the young saint betrays all the pain of renunciation which the sensibility of the artist projected into it. An artist cannot prevent his work from being coloured by the psychology of his time. This is true in even higher degree of the Christian symbol, the Crucified pierced by the lance. It is a true symbol of the man of the Christian era, tormented by his desires and crucified in Christ.

[51] *Thus Spake Zarathustra.* (*Werke,* VI, pp. 367f.) [Cf. trans. by Common, p. 293.]
[52] Spielrein's patient said that she too had been shot by God three times—"then came a resurrection of the spirit."

446   That the torment which afflicts mankind does not come from
outside, but that man is his own huntsman, his own sacrificer, his own sacrificial knife, is clear from another poem of
Nietzsche's, where the dualism is resolved into a psychic conflict
through the same symbolism:

> O Zarathustra,
> Most cruel Nimrod!
> Erstwhile hunter of God,
> Snare of all virtue,
> Arrow of evil!
> And now
> Self-hunted,
> Thine own quarry,
> Thyself pierced through . . .
>
> Now
> Alone with thyself,
> Split in thine own knowledge,
> Amidst a hundred mirrors
> To thine own self false,
> Amidst a hundred memories
> Uncertain,
> Languishing with each wound,
> Shivering with each frost,
> Strangled in thine own snares,
> Self-knower!
> Self-hangman!
>
> Why didst thou hang thyself
> With the noose of thy wisdom?
> Why hast thou enticed thyself
> Into the old serpent's Paradise?
> Why hast thou stolen
> Into thyself, thyself? [53]

447   The deadly arrows do not strike the hero from without;
it is himself who hunts, fights, and tortures himself. In him,
instinct wars with instinct; therefore the poet says, "Thyself
pierced through," which means that he is wounded by his own
arrow. As we know that the arrow is a libido-symbol, the mean-

---

[53] "Between Birds of Prey." (*Werke,* VIII, p. 414.) [Cf. trans. in *Ecce Homo and
Poetry* by Ludovici, Cohn, et al., p. 179.]

ing of this "piercing" is clear: it is the act of union with oneself, a sort of self-fertilization, and also a self-violation, a self-murder, so that Zarathustra can justly call himself his own hangman (like Odin, who sacrifices himself to Odin). One should not of course take this psychologem in too voluntaristic a sense: nobody deliberately inflicts such tortures on himself, they just happen to him. If a man reckons the unconscious as part of his personality, then one must admit that he is in fact raging against himself. But, in so far as the symbolism thrown up by his suffering is archetypal and collective, it can be taken as a sign that he is no longer suffering from himself, but rather from the spirit of the age. He is suffering from an objective, impersonal cause, from his collective unconscious which he has in common with all men.

448   Being wounded by one's own arrow signifies, therefore, a state of introversion. What this means we already know: the libido sinks "into its own depths" (a favourite image of Nietzsche's), and discovers in the darkness a substitute for the upper world it has abandoned—the world of memories ("Amidst a hundred memories"), the strongest and most influential of which are the earliest ones. It is the world of the child, the paradisal state of early infancy, from which we are driven out by the relentless law of time. In this subterranean kingdom slumber sweet feelings of home and the hopes of all that is to be. As Heinrich says of his miraculous work in Gerhart Hauptmann's *The Sunken Bell:*

> It sings a song, long lost and long forgotten,
> A song of home, a childlike song of love,
> Born in the waters of some fairy well,
> Known to all mortals, and yet heard of none.[54]

449   Yet "the danger is great," [55] as Mephistopheles says, for these depths fascinate. When the libido leaves the bright upper world, whether from choice, or from inertia, or from fate, it sinks back into its own depths, into the source from which it originally flowed, and returns to the point of cleavage, the navel, where it first entered the body. This point of cleavage is called the mother, because from her the current of life reached us. Whenever some great work is to be accomplished, before which a man

[54] Trans. by Meltzner, p. 75.   [55] *Faust,* Part II, "The Mothers."

recoils, doubtful of his strength, his libido streams back to the fountainhead—and that is the dangerous moment when the issue hangs between annihilation and new life. For if the libido gets stuck in the wonderland of this inner world,[56] then for the upper world man is nothing but a shadow, he is already moribund or at least seriously ill. But if the libido manages to tear itself loose and force its way up again, something like a miracle happens: the journey to the underworld was a plunge into the fountain of youth, and the libido, apparently dead, wakes to renewed fruitfulness. This idea is illustrated in an Indian myth: Vishnu sank into a profound trance, and in his slumber brought forth Brahma, who, enthroned on a lotus, rose out of Vishnu's navel, bringing with him the Vedas (pl. XLVIa), which he diligently read. (Birth of creative thought from introversion.) But through Vishnu's ecstatic absentmindedness a mighty flood came upon the world. (Devouring and destruction of the world through introversion.) Taking advantage of the general confusion, a demon stole the Vedas and hid them in the depths. Brahma then roused Vishnu, who, changing himself into a fish (pl. XLVII), plunged into the flood, fought the demon, conquered him, and recaptured the Vedas.

450   This is a primitive way of describing the libido's entry into the interior world of the psyche, the unconscious. There, through its introversion and regression, contents are constellated which till now were latent. These are the primordial images, the archetypes, which have been so enriched with individual memories through the introversion of libido as to become perceptible to the conscious mind, in much the same way as the crystalline structure latent in the saturated solution takes visible shape from the aggregation of molecules. Since these introversions and regressions only occur at moments when a new orientation and a new adaptation are necessary, the constellated archetype is always the primordial image of the need of the

[56] This is mythologically represented in the legend of Theseus and Peirithous, who wanted to abduct Persephone from the underworld. They entered a chasm in the grove of Colonus and descended into the bowels of the earth. When they got down below they wished to rest a little, but found they had grown fast to the rocks and could not rise. In other words, they remained stuck in the mother and were lost to the upper world. Later Theseus was rescued by Heracles, who appeared in the role of the death-conquering hero. The Theseus myth is therefore a representation of the individuation process.

moment. Although the changing situations of life must appear infinitely various to our way of thinking, their possible number never exceeds certain natural limits; they fall into more or less typical patterns that repeat themselves over and over again. The archetypal structure of the unconscious corresponds to the average run of events. The changes that may befall a man are not infinitely variable; they are variations of certain typical occurrences which are limited in number. When therefore a distressing situation arises, the corresponding archetype will be constellated in the unconscious. Since this archetype is numinous, i.e., possesses a specific energy, it will attract to itself the contents of consciousness—conscious ideas that render it perceptible and hence capable of conscious realization. Its passing over into consciousness is felt as an illumination, a revelation, or a "saving idea." Repeated experience of this process has had the general result that, whenever a critical situation arises, the mechanism of introversion is made to function artificially by means of ritual actions which bring about a spiritual preparation, e.g., magical ceremonies, sacrifices, invocations, prayers, and suchlike. The aim of these ritual actions is to direct the libido towards the unconscious and compel it to introvert. If the libido connects with the unconscious, it is as though it were connecting with the mother, and this raises the incest-taboo. But as the unconscious is infinitely greater than the mother and is only symbolized by her, the fear of incest must be conquered if one is to gain possession of those "saving" contents—the treasure hard to attain. Since the son is not conscious of his incest tendency, it is projected upon the mother or her symbol. But the symbol of the mother is not the mother herself, so in reality there is not the slightest possibility of incest, and the taboo can therefore be ruled out as a reason for resistance. In so far as the mother represents the unconscious, the incest tendency, particularly when it appears as the amorous desire of the mother (e.g., Ishtar and Gilgamesh) or of the anima (e.g., Chryse and Philoctetes), is really only the desire of the unconscious to be taken notice of. The rejection of the unconscious usually has unfortunate results; its instinctive forces, if persistently disregarded, rise up in opposition: Chryse changes into a venomous serpent. The more negative the attitude of the conscious towards the unconscious, the more dangerous does the latter become.[57] Chryse's curse was fulfilled so completely that Philoctetes, on approaching her altar, wounded himself in the foot with his own poison-tipped arrow, or, according to other versions [58] which are in fact better attested, was bitten in the foot by a poisonous snake,[59] and fell into a decline.[60]

[451]   This very typical injury also destroyed Ra, and is described as follows in an Egyptian hymn:

The mouth of the god twitched with age,
So that he dropped his spittle on the earth,
And what he spat fell on the ground.
Isis then kneaded it with her hands
Together with the earth which was there;
She fashioned from it a noble worm
And made it like a spear.

[57] When the Greeks set out on their expedition to Troy, they wished, like the Argonauts and Heracles before them, to offer sacrifice on the altar of Chryse, a nymph who lived on an island of the same name, in order to secure a happy end to their voyage. Philoctetes was the only one among them who knew the way to her hidden shrine. But there the disaster befell him which is described above. Sophocles treats of this episode in his *Philoctetes*. We learn from a scholiast that Chryse offered the hero her love, but, on being scorned, cursed him. Philoctetes, like his forerunner Heracles, is the prototype of the wounded and ailing king, a motif that is continued in the legend of the Grail and in alchemical symbolism (cf. *Psychology and Alchemy*, pars. 491ff. and fig. 149).

[58] Roscher, *Lexikon*, 2318, 15ff., s.v. "Philoctetes."

[59] When the Russian sun-hero Oleg approached the skull of the slain horse, a snake darted out and bit him in the foot, so that he fell sick and died. And when Indra, in the form of Shyena the falcon, stole the soma drink, Krishanu the herdsman wounded him in the foot with an arrow. De Gubernatis, *Zoological Mythology*, II, pp. 181–82.

[60] Like the Grail king who guards the chalice, symbol of the mother. The myth of Philoctetes comes from the wider context of the Heracles cycle. Heracles had two mothers, the helpful Alcmene and the vengeful Hera, from whose breast he drank the milk of immortality. Heracles conquered Hera's serpents while yet in the cradle; that is, he freed himself from the grip of the unconscious. But from time to time Hera sent him fits of madness, in one of which he killed his own children. This is indirect proof that she was a lamia. According to one tradition, Heracles perpetrated this deed after refusing to perform the labours for his task-master Eurystheus. As a consequence of his hanging back, the libido that was ready for the work regressed to the unconscious mother-imago, and this resulted in madness. In this state he identified with the lamia and killed his own children. The Delphic oracle told him that he was named Heracles because he owed his immortal fame to Hera, who through her persecutions drove him to his great deeds. It is evident that the great deed really means overcoming the mother and thus winning immortality. His characteristic weapon, the club, he cut from the

She did not wind it living about her face,
But threw it in a coil upon the path
Upon which the great god was wont to walk
At pleasure through his two countries.
The noble god stepped forth in his splendour,
The gods who served Pharaoh accompanied him,
And he walked as he did each day.
Then the noble worm stung him . . .
The divine god opened his mouth,
And the voice of his majesty rang through the heavens.
And the gods cried: Behold! Behold!
He could not answer them,
His jawbones chattered,
All his limbs trembled,
And the poison invaded his flesh
As the Nile invades his territory.[61]

452   In this hymn Egypt has preserved for us a primitive version of
the snake-sting motif. The aging of the autumn sun as a symbol
of human senility is traced back to poisoning by a serpent. The
mother is blamed for causing the death of the sun-god with her
mischievous arts. The serpent symbolizes the mysterious numen
of the "mother" (and of other daimonia) who kills, but who
is at the same time man's only security against death, as she is
the source of life.[62] Accordingly, only the mother can cure him
who is sick unto death, and the hymn goes on to describe how
the gods were called together to take counsel:

Then came Isis with her wisdom,
Whose mouth is full of the breath of life,
Whose decree banishes pain,
And whose word gives life to those who no longer breathe.

---

maternal olive-tree. Like the sun, he possessed the arrows of Apollo. He conquered the Nemean lion in its cave, whose meaning is the "grave in the mother's
womb" (see the end of this chapter). Then follows the fight with the Hydra (cf.
also fig. 17) and his other deeds, which were all wished on him by Hera. All of
them symbolize the fight with the unconscious. At the end of his career, however,
he became the slave of Omphale (ὀμφαλός = 'navel') as the oracle prophesied;
that is, he had to submit after all to the unconscious.

61 This and the following passages trans. from Erman, pp. 265–67, modified.

62 How concretely this mythologem is taken on the primitive level can be seen
from the description in Gatti, South of the Sahara (pp. 226ff.), of a medicine-
woman in Natal who had a twenty-foot boa constrictor as her familiar.

She said: What is it, what is it, divine Father?
Behold, a worm hath done thee this wrong.

Tell me thy name, divine Father,
For he whose name is spoken shall live.

453   Ra answers:

I am he who created heaven and earth, and piled up the mountains,
And made all living things.
I am he who made the water and caused the great flood,
Who made the Bull of his Mother,
Who is the Begetter.

The poison did not depart, it went further,
The great god was not healed.
Then said Isis to Ra:
That is not thy name which thou tellest me.
Tell me thy name, that the poison may depart,
For he whose name is spoken shall live.

454   Finally Ra decides to utter his true name. He was only partially cured, just as Osiris was only incompletely reconstituted,
and in addition he lost his power and finally had to retire on
the back of the heavenly cow.

455   The poisonous worm is a deadly instead of an animating
form of libido. The "true name" is Ra's soul and magic power
(his libido). What Isis demands is the transference of libido to
the mother. This request is fulfilled to the letter, for the aging
god returns to the heavenly cow, the symbol of the mother.

456   The meaning of this symbolism becomes clear in the light of
what we said earlier: the forward-striving libido which rules the
conscious mind of the son demands separation from the mother,
but his childish longing for her prevents this by setting up a
psychic resistance that manifests itself in all kinds of neurotic
fears—that is to say, in a general fear of life. The more a person
shrinks from adapting himself to reality, the greater becomes
the fear which increasingly besets his path at every point. Thus
a vicious circle is formed: fear of life and people causes more
shrinking back, and this in turn leads to infantilism and finally
"into the mother." The reasons for this are generally projected
outside oneself: the fault lies with external circumstances, or
else the parents are made responsible. And indeed, it remains

to be found out how much the mother is to blame for not letting the son go. The son will naturally try to explain everything by the wrong attitude of the mother, but he would do better to refrain from all such futile attempts to excuse his own ineptitude by laying the blame on his parents.

457   This fear of life is not just an imaginary bogy, but a very real panic, which seems disproportionate only because its real source is unconscious and therefore projected: the young, growing part of the personality, if prevented from living or kept in check, generates fear and changes into fear. The fear seems to come from the mother, but actually it is the deadly fear of the instinctive, unconscious, inner man who is cut off from life by the continual shrinking back from reality. If the mother is felt as the obstacle, she then becomes the vengeful pursuer. Naturally it is not the real mother, although she too may seriously injure her child by the morbid tenderness with which she pursues it into adult life, thus prolonging the infantile attitude beyond the proper time. It is rather the mother-imago that has turned into a lamia.[63] (Cf. pls. xxxviiia, xlviii.) The mother-imago, however, represents the unconscious, and it is as much a vital necessity for the unconscious to be joined to the conscious as it is for the latter not to lose contact with the unconscious. Nothing endangers this connection more in a man than a successful life; it makes him forget his dependence on the unconscious. The case of Gilgamesh is instructive in this respect: he was so successful that the gods, the representatives of the unconscious, saw themselves compelled to deliberate how they could best bring about his downfall. Their efforts were unavailing at first, but when the hero had won the herb of immortality (cf. pl. xix) and was almost at his goal, a serpent stole the elixir of life from him while he slept.

458   The demands of the unconscious act at first like a paralysing poison on a man's energy and resourcefulness, so that it may well be compared to the bite of a poisonous snake. (Cf. fig. 30.)

---

[63] The myth of Hippolytus has similar ingredients: His step-mother Phaedra falls in love with him, he repulses her, she accuses him of violation before her husband, who calls upon Poseidon to punish Hippolytus. Whereupon a monster comes out of the sea; Hippolytus' horses take fright and drag him to death. But he is restored to life by Aesculapius, and the gods convey him to the grove of the wise nymph Egeria, the counsellor of Numa Pompilius.

Apparently it is a hostile demon who robs him of energy, but in actual fact it is his own unconscious whose alien tendencies are beginning to check the forward striving of the

Fig. 30. Quetzalcoatl devouring a man
From the Codex Borbonicus, Aztec 16th century

conscious mind. The cause of this process is often extremely obscure, the more so as it is complicated by all kinds of external factors and subsidiary causes, such as difficulties in work, disappointments, failures, reduced efficiency due to age, depressing family problems, and so on and so forth. According to the myths

299

it is the woman who secretly enslaves a man, so that he can no longer free himself from her and becomes a child again.[64] It is also significant that Isis, the sister-wife of the sun-god, creates the poisonous serpent from his spittle, which, like all bodily secretions, has a magical significance, being a libido equivalent. She creates the serpent from the libido of the god, and by this means weakens him and makes him dependent on her. Delilah acts in the same way with Samson: by cutting off his hair, the sun's rays, she robs him of his strength. This demon-woman of mythology is in truth the "sister-wife-mother," the woman in the man, who unexpectedly turns up during the second half of life and tries to effect a forcible change of personality. I have dealt with certain aspects of this change in my essay on "The Stages of Life." It consists in a partial feminization of the man and a corresponding masculinization of the woman. Often it takes place under very dramatic circumstances: the man's strongest quality, his Logos principle, turns against him and as it were betrays him. The same thing happens with the Eros of the woman. The man becomes rigidly set in his previous attitude, while the woman remains caught in her emotional ties and fails to develop her reason and understanding, whose place is then taken by equally obstinate and inept "animus" opinions. The fossilization of the man shrouds itself in a smoke-screen of moods, ridiculous irritability, feelings of distrust and resentment, which are meant to justify his rigid attitude. A perfect example of this type of psychology is Schreber's account of his own psychosis, *Memoirs of My Nervous Illness.*[65]

459   The paralysis of progressive energy has in truth some very disagreeable aspects. It seems like an unwelcome accident or a positive catastrophe, which one would naturally rather avoid. In most cases the conscious personality rises up against the assault of the unconscious and resists its demands, which, it is clearly felt, are directed not only against all the weak spots in the man's character, but also against his chief virtue (the differentiated function and the ideal). It is evident from the myths of Heracles and Gilgamesh that this assault can become the

64 Cf. Heracles and Omphale.
65 The case was written up at the time by Freud in a very unsatisfactory way after I had drawn his attention to the book. See "Psycho-Analytical Notes upon an Autobiographical Account of a Case of Paranoia."

source of energy for an heroic conflict; indeed, so obvious is this impression that one has to ask oneself whether the apparent enmity of the maternal archetype is not a ruse on the part of Mater Natura for spurring on her favoured child to his highest achievement. The vengeful Hera would then appear as the stern "Mistress Soul," who imposes the most difficult labours on her hero and threatens him with destruction unless he plucks up courage for the supreme deed and actually becomes what he always potentially was. The hero's victory over the "mother," or over her daemonic representative (dragon, etc.), is never anything but temporary. What must be regarded as regression in a young person—feminization of the man (partial identity with the mother) and masculinization of the woman (partial identity with the father)—acquires a different meaning in the second half of life. The assimilation of contrasexual tendencies then becomes a task that must be fulfilled in order to keep the libido in a state of progression. The task consists in integrating the unconscious, in bringing together "conscious" and "unconscious." I have called this the individuation process, and for further details must refer the reader to my later works.[65a] At this stage the mother-symbol no longer connects back to the beginnings, but points towards the unconscious as the creative matrix of the future. "Entry into the mother" then means establishing a relationship between the ego and the unconscious. Nietzsche probably means something of the kind in his poem:

> Why hast thou enticed thyself
> Into the old serpent's Paradise?
> Why hast thou stolen
> Into thyself, thyself?
>
> A sick man now,
> Sick of the serpent's poison; [66]
> A captive now
> Who drew the hardest lot:
> Bent double
> Working in thine own pit,

[65a] [Cf. especially "A Study in the Process of Individuation."—EDITORS.]

[66] Spielrein's patient was also sick from "snake poison" (p. 385). Schreber said he was infected by "corpse poison," that "soul murder" had been committed on him, etc. (pp. 54ff.).

> Encaved within thyself,
> Burrowing into thyself,
> Heavy-handed,
> Stiff,
> A corpse—
> Piled with a hundred burdens,
> Loaded to death with thyself,
> A knower!
> Self-knower!
> The wise Zarathustra!
> You sought the heaviest burden
> And found yourself.[67]

460   Sunk in his own depths, he is like one buried in the earth;
a dead man who has crawled back into the mother;[68] a Kaineus
"piled with a hundred burdens" and pressed down to death,
groaning beneath the intolerable weight of his own self and his
own destiny. Who does not think here of Mithras, who, in the
Taurophoria, took his bull (or, as the Egyptian hymn says, "the
bull of his mother"), namely his love for his Mater Natura, on
his back, and with this heaviest burden set forth on the *via
dolorosa* of the Transitus?[69] The way of this passion leads to
the cave in which the bull is sacrificed. So, too, Christ had to
bear the Cross[70] to the place of sacrifice, where, according
to the Christian version, the Lamb was slain in the form of the

[67] "Between Birds of Prey." (*Werke*, VIII, p. 414.) [Cf. trans. in *Ecce Homo and
Poetry*, by Ludovici et al., p. 179.]
[68] Spielrein's patient (p. 336) uses the same images; she speaks of the "rigidity of
the soul on the cross," of "stone figures" who must be "melted."
[69] Gurlitt says: "The carrying of the bull [pl. XLIX*a*] is one of the difficult ἆθλα
which Mithras performed for the redemption of mankind; it corresponds roughly
—if we may compare small things with great—to Christ carrying the cross."
("Vorbericht über Ausgrabungen in Pettau"; cited in Cumont, *Textes*, I, p. 172.)
[70] Robertson (*Christianity and Mythology*, p. 401) makes an interesting contribution to the symbol of carrying the cross: Samson carried the gate-posts of the city
of Gaza, and died between the pillars of the temple of the Philistines. Heracles
carried his pillars to Gades (Cadiz), where, according to the Syrian version of the
legend, he died. The Pillars of Hercules mark the point in the west where the
sun sinks into the sea. "In ancient art," says Robertson, "he was actually represented carrying the two pillars in such a way under his arms that they form
exactly a cross. Here, probably, we have the origin of the myth of Jesus carrying
his own cross to the place of execution. Singularly enough, the three Synoptics
substitute for Jesus as cross-bearer one Simon, a man of Cyrene. Cyrene is in
Libya, the legendary scene, as we saw, of the pillar-carrying exploit of Heracles;

god, and was then laid to earth in the sepulchre.[71] The cross, or whatever other heavy burden the hero carries, is *himself,* or rather *the* self, his wholeness, which is both God and animal— not merely the empirical man, but the totality of his being, which is rooted in his animal nature and reaches out beyond the merely human towards the divine. His wholeness implies a tremendous tension of opposites paradoxically at one with themselves, as in the cross, their most perfect symbol. What seems like a poetic figure of speech in Nietzsche is really an age-old myth. It is as if the poet could still sense, beneath the words of contemporary speech and in the images that crowd in upon his imagination, the ghostly presence of bygone spiritual worlds, and possessed the capacity to make them come alive again. As Gerhart Hauptmann says: "Poetry is the art of letting the primordial word resound through the common word." [72]

461   The sacrifice, whose mysterious and manifold meanings we guess rather than understand, passes by the conscious mind of our author unrecognized and unconsummated. The arrow is not yet shot, the hero Chiwantopel is not yet fatally poisoned and ready for death through self-sacrifice. On the evidence before us we can say that this sacrifice means giving up the connection with the mother, relinquishing all the ties and limitations

and Simon (Simeon) is the nearest Greek name-form to Samson. . . . In Palestine, Simon, or Sem, was actually a god-name, representing the ancient sun-god Shemesh, identified with Baal, from whose mythus that of Samson unquestionably arose; and the God Simon was especially worshipped in Samaria." I give Robertson's words here, but must emphasize that the etymological connection between Simon and Samson is exceedingly questionable. The cross of Heracles may well be the sun-wheel, for which the Greeks used the symbol of the cross. The sun-wheel on the bas-relief of the Little Metropolis in Athens actually contains a cross which looks very like the Maltese cross. (Cf. Thiele, *Antike Himmelsbilder*, p. 59.) Here I must refer the reader to the mandala symbolism in *Psychology and Alchemy* and in *The Secret of the Golden Flower*.

71 The legend of Ixion (pl. XLVI*b*), who was "crucified on the four-spoked wheel" (Pindar), says the same thing. Ixion first murdered his father-in-law but was afterwards absolved from guilt by Zeus and blessed with his favour. Ixion, with gross ingratitude, then tried to seduce Hera, but Zeus tricked him by getting the cloud-goddess Nephele to assume Hera's shape. From this union the centaurs are said to have sprung. Ixion boasted of his deed, but as a punishment for his crimes Zeus cast him into the underworld, where he was bound on a wheel that turned forever in the wind.

72 Cited from the *Zentralblatt für Psychoanalyse*, II (1912), p. 365 [in a note by W. Stekel, quoting extracts from Hauptmann's published diary.—EDITORS].

which the psyche has taken over from childhood into adult life. From various hints of Miss Miller's it appears that at the time of these fantasies she was still living in the family circle, at an age when independence was an urgent necessity. It is therefore significant that the birth of her fantasies coincided with a journey abroad, i.e., with a breaking away from her childhood environment. It is not possible to live too long amid infantile surroundings, or in the bosom of the family, without endangering one's psychic health. Life calls us forth to independence, and anyone who does not heed this call because of childish laziness or timidity is threatened with neurosis. And once this has broken out, it becomes an increasingly valid reason for running away from life and remaining forever in the morally poisonous atmosphere of infancy.

462 The fantasy of the arrow-shot is part of this struggle for personal independence. As yet, however, the need for such a decision has not penetrated to the conscious mind of the dreamer: the fatal arrow of Cupid has not yet found its mark. Chiwantopel, playing the role of the author, is not yet wounded or killed. He is the bold adventurer who dares to do what Miss Miller obviously shrinks from doing: he offers himself, of his own free will, as a target for the fatal arrow-shot. The fact that this gesture of self-exposure is projected upon a masculine figure is direct proof that the dreamer is quite unconscious of its necessity. Chiwantopel is a typical animus-figure, that is to say, a personification of the masculine side of the woman's psyche. He is an archetypal figure who becomes particularly active when the conscious mind refuses to follow the feelings and instincts prompted by the unconscious: instead of love and surrender there is mannishness, argumentativeness, obstinate self-assertion, and the demon of opinion in every possible shape and form (power instead of love). The animus is not a real man at all; he is a slightly hysterical, infantile hero whose longing to be loved shows through the gaps in his armour. It is in this garb that Miss Miller has dressed the critical decisions of her life, or rather these decisions have not yet got beyond the stage of unconscious fantasy and are still not recognized by her conscious mind as her own decisions. (Cf. pl. XVII.)

463 The fact that the assassin allows himself to be scared away by Chiwantopel's heroics means that the impending death of this

pasteboard hero has been temporarily postponed: the conscious mind is not yet ready to come to a decision by itself, but prefers to adopt the ostrich policy of burying its head in unconsciousness. Chiwantopel must fall because the power of decision locked up in the unconscious, which is at present keeping the nerveless figure of the hero erect, is needed to strengthen the conscious mind, for without the co-operation of the unconscious and its instinctive forces the conscious personality would be too weak to wrench itself free from its infantile past and venture into a strange world with all its unforeseen possibilities. The whole of the libido is needed for the battle of life. The dreamer cannot bring herself to this decision, which would tear aside all sentimental attachments to childhood, to father and mother, and yet it must be taken if she wishes to follow the call of her individual destiny.

VII

THE DUAL MOTHER [1]

464   After his assailant has disappeared, Chiwantopel begins the
following monologue:

From the tip of the backbone [2] of these continents, from the farthest
lowlands, I have wandered for a hundred moons since quitting my
father's palace, forever pursued by my mad desire to find "her who
will understand." With jewels I tempted many beautiful women;
with kisses tried I to draw out the secrets of their hearts, with deeds
of daring I won their admiration. [He reviews one after another the
women he has known.] Chi-ta, the princess of my own race . . . she
was a fool, vain as a peacock, without a thought in her head except
trinkets and perfumes. Ta-nan, the peasant girl . . . bah! a perfect
sow, nothing but a bust and a belly, thinking of nothing but pleasure. And then Ki-ma, the priestess, a mere parrot, repeating the
empty phrases learnt from the priests, all for show, without real
understanding or sincerity, mistrustful, affected, hypocritical! . . .
Alas! Not one who understands me, not one who resembles me or
has a soul that is sister to mine. There is not one among them all
who has known my soul, not one who could read my thoughts—far
from it; not one capable of seeking the shining summits with me,
or of spelling out with me the superhuman word Love!

465   Here Chiwantopel admits that his travels and wanderings
are a search for the other, for the beloved, and for the meaning
of life that is to be found in union with her. This possibility
was merely hinted at in the first part of the book. The fact that
the seeker is masculine and the sought-for feminine is not so
very remarkable, since the prime object of unconscious desire
is the mother, as should be clear from what we have already
learnt. "She who understands" is, in infantile speech, the

1 [See p. 394, n. 1, concerning this chapter heading.—Editors.]
2 Probably an allusion to the Andes and the Rocky Mountains. [Note by
Flournoy.]

mother. The original concrete meaning of words like *comprehend, comprendre, begreifen, erfassen* (grasp, seize), etc., is literally to seize hold of something with the hands and hold it tight in the arms. That is just what the mother does with her child when it asks for help or protection, and what binds the child to its mother. But the older it grows, the greater becomes the danger of this kind of "comprehension" hindering its natural development. Instead of adapting itself, as is necessary, to its new surroundings, the libido of the child regresses to the sheltering ease of the mother's arms and fails to keep pace with the passing of time. This situation is described as follows in an old Hermetic text: "Being chained to the arms and breast of my mother, and to her substance, I cause my substance to hold together and rest, and I compose the invisible from the visible. . . ." [3] When a person remains bound to the mother, the life he ought to have lived runs away in the form of conscious and unconscious fantasies, which in the case of a woman are generally attributed to some hero-figure, or are acted out by him, as here. *He* is the one who then has the great longing for an understanding soul-mate, he is the seeker who survives the adventures which the conscious personality studiously avoids; he it is who, with a magnificent gesture, offers his breast to the slings and arrows of a hostile world, and displays the courage which is so sadly lacking to the conscious mind. It is all up with the man whom the whims of fortune bring into contact with this infantile woman: he will at once be made identical with her animus-hero and relentlessly set up as the ideal figure, threatened with the direst punishments should he ever make a face that shows the least departure from the ideal!

466   It is in this situation that our author now finds herself. Chiwantopel is the very devil of a fellow: a breaker of hearts by the dozen, all the women rave about him. He knows so many of them that he can pass them under review. Not one of them gets him, for he seeks one who (so she thinks) is known only to

---

[3] *Septem tractatus aurei* (1566), ch. IV, p. 24. ("Ego vinctus ulnis et pectori meae matris et substantiae eius continere et quiescere meam substantiam facio, et invisibile ex visibili compono.") The subject of this sentence (Mercurius or the arcane substance) can be interpreted as inner fantasy activity. The quotation naturally has a much more comprehensive, anagogic meaning in the original text, while making use of the primordial image of relationship to the mother. Cf. *Psychology and Alchemy*, par. 141.

our author. That is, she believes in her heart of hearts that he is looking for *her*. In this she is labouring under a delusion, for experience shows that this particular cat jumps quite differently. The animus, a typical "son"-hero, is not after her at all; true to his ancient prototype, he is seeking the mother. This youthful hero is always the son-lover of the mother-goddess and is doomed to an early death. (Cf. fig. 20.) The libido that will not flow into life at the right time regresses to the mythical world of the archetypes, where it activates images which, since the remotest times, have expressed the non-human life of the gods, whether of the upper world or the lower. If this regression occurs in a young person, his own individual life is supplanted by the divine archetypal drama, which is all the more devastating for him because his conscious education provides him with no means of recognizing what is happening, and thus with no possibility of freeing himself from its fascination. Herein lay the vital importance of myths: they explained to the bewildered human being what was going on in his unconscious and why he was held fast. The myths told him: "This is not you, but the gods. You will never reach them, so turn back to your human avocations, holding the gods in fear and respect." These ingredients can also be found in the Christian myth, but it is too veiled to have enlightened our author. Nor is anything said about these things in the catechism. The "shining heights" are beyond the reach of mere mortals, and the "superhuman word Love" betrays the divine nature of the *dramatis personae,* since even human love presents such a thorny problem to man that he would rather creep into the remotest corner than touch it with his little finger. The words we have quoted show how deeply our author has been drawn into the unconscious drama and how much she is under its spell. Looked at in this light, the pathos rings hollow and the heroics seem hysterical.

467   However, it looks somewhat different when viewed not from the personalistic standpoint, i.e., from the personal situation of Miss Miller, but from the standpoint of the archetype's own life. As we have already explained, the phenomena of the unconscious can be regarded as more or less spontaneous manifestations of autonomous archetypes, and though this hypothesis may seem very strange to the layman, it is amply supported by the fact the archetype has a numinous character: it exerts a fascina-

tion, it enters into active opposition to the conscious mind, and may be said in the long run to mould the destinies of individuals by unconsciously influencing their thinking, feeling, and behaviour, even if this influence is not recognized until long afterwards. The primordial image is itself a "pattern of behaviour" [4] which will assert itself with or without the co-operation of the conscious personality. Although the Miller case gives us some idea of the manner in which an archetype gradually draws nearer to consciousness and finally takes possession of it, the material is too scanty to serve as a complete illustration of the process. I must therefore refer my reader to the dream-series discussed in *Psychology and Alchemy,* where he will be able to follow the gradual emergence of a definite archetype with all the specific marks of its autonomy and authority.

468   From this point of view, then, the hero Chiwantopel represents a psychic entity which can only be compared to a fragmentary personality equipped with a relative degree of consciousness and a will to match. Such a conclusion is inevitable if our premise of the autonomy and purposiveness of the complex is correct. In that case the intentions both of Chiwantopel and of the mother-imago standing behind and above him can be subjected to closer scrutiny. He himself seems to find complete fulfilment in the role of the actor. As an ideal figure he attracts all our author's attention to himself, he gives voice to her most secret thoughts and desires, and, like Cyrano, he does so in a language which springs from Miss Miller's own heart. He is therefore sure of his success and cuts out all possible rivals. He wins the soul of the dreamer, not in order to lead her back to normal life, but to her spiritual destiny; for he is a bridegroom of death, one of the son-lovers who die young because they have no life of their own but are only fast-fading flowers on the maternal tree. Their meaning and their vitality begin and end in the mother-goddess. Therefore, when Chiwantopel, the "ghostly lover," [5] draws Miss Miller away from the path of life, he does so in a certain sense at the behest of the mother-imago, which in women personifies a special aspect of the unconscious. It does not, like the anima, stand for the chaotic life of the unconscious in all its aspects, but for the

4 See "On the Nature of the Psyche," Sec. VII.
5 Cf. Harding, *The Way of All Women.*

peculiarly fascinating background of the psyche, the world of primordial images. There is always a danger that those who set foot in this realm will grow fast to the rocks, like Theseus and Peirithous, who wanted to abduct the goddess of the underworld. It happens all too easily that there is no returning from the realm of the Mothers. As I have already hinted, this is the fate that has overtaken Miss Miller. But the danger could equally well prove to be her salvation, if only the conscious mind had some means of understanding the unconscious contents. This is certainly not the case with our author. For her these fantasies are "marvellous" products of an unconscious activity which she confronts more or less helplessly, although, as we shall see, the associations contain all the necessary clues that would enable her, with a little reflection, to guess what the fantasy-figures mean, and to use the symbols as a heavensent opportunity for assimilating her unconscious contents. Our culture, however, has neither eyes nor heart for these things. Anything that comes out of the psyche is regarded with suspicion at the best of times, and if it does not immediately prove its material value it goes for nothing.

469   The hero as an animus-figure acts vicariously for the conscious individual; that is to say, he does what the subject ought, could, or would like to do, but does not do. All the things that could happen in conscious life, but do not happen, are acted out in the unconscious and consequently appear in projection. Chiwantopel is characterized as the hero who leaves his family and his ancestral home in order to seek his psychic counterpart. He thus represents what in the normal course of events ought to happen. The fact that this appears as a fantasy-figure shows how little the author is doing it herself. What happens in fantasy is therefore compensatory to the situation or attitude of the conscious mind. This is also the rule in dreams.

470   How right we were in our supposition that what is going on in Miss Miller's unconscious is a battle for independence is now shown by her remark that the hero's departure from his father's house reminded her of the fate of the young Buddha, who renounced all the luxury of his home in order to go out into the world and live his destiny to the full.[6] The Buddha

6 Another source mentioned by Miss Miller, namely Samuel Johnson's *History of Rasselas* (1759), was not available to me at the time of writing.

set the same heroic example as Christ, who also cut himself off from his family and even spoke these bitter words (Matt. 10: 34f.):

Think not that I am come to send peace on earth: I came not to send peace, but a sword.

For I am come to set a man at variance against his father, and the daughter against her mother, and the daughter in law against her mother in law.

And a man's foes shall be they of his own household.

He that loveth father or mother more than me is not worthy of me. . . .

471 Horus snatches the head-dress from his mother, the emblem of her power. Nietzsche says:

We must suppose that a mind in which the ideal of the "free spirit" can grow to maturity and perfection has had its decisive crisis in some great act of emancipation, and that before this it was a spirit bound and apparently chained for ever to its corner and pillar. What binds it most tightly? What ties are the most unbreakable? For men of a superior and select type, it is the ties of duty: the reverence that befits youth, respect and tenderness for all the time-honoured and valued things, feelings of gratitude for the soil whence they grew, for the hand that guided them, for the shrine where they learnt to pray —their highest moments are the very ones that bind them most firmly, that put them under the most enduring obligations. The great emancipation comes suddenly for those who are so bound. . . .

"Better to die than live here," says the imperious voice of temptation; and this "here," this "at home," is all that the soul has hitherto loved! A sudden horror and mistrust of what it loved, a flash of contempt for its so-called "duty," a rebellious, wilful, volcanically impelling desire for travel, strangeness, estrangement, coldness, disillusion, glaciation; a hatred of love, perhaps a sacrilegious grasp and glance backwards [7] to everything it had worshipped and loved till then, perhaps a blush of shame over what it has just done and at the same time an exultation over having done it, an intoxicating,

---

[7] Cf. Horus's sacrilegious assault on Isis, which so horrifies Plutarch (*De Iside et Osiride,* trans. by Babbitt, V, pp. 48–49): "If they hold such opinions and relate such tales about the blessed and imperishable (in accordance with which our concept of the divine must be framed), as if such deeds and occurrences actually took place, then 'Much need there is to spit and cleanse the mouth,' as Aeschylus has it."

inner thrill of joy which signalizes victory—victory over what? over whom? an enigmatic, doubtful, questioning victory, but the first victory nonetheless. Of such evil and painful things is the history of the great emancipation composed. It is like a disease that can easily destroy the man, this first eruption of strength and will to self-determination. . . .[8]

472   The danger, as Nietzsche sees, lies in isolation within oneself:

Solitude surrounds and encircles him, ever more threatening, ever more constricting, ever more heart-strangling, that terrible goddess and *Mater saeva cupidinum.*[9]

473   The libido that is withdrawn so unwillingly from the "mother" turns into a threatening serpent, symbolizing the fear of death—for the relation to the mother must cease, *must die,* and this is almost the same as dying oneself. That is to say, the violence of the separation is proportionate to the strength of the bond uniting the son with the mother, and the stronger this broken bond was in the first place, the more dangerously does the "mother" approach him in the guise of the unconscious. This is indeed the *Mater saeva cupidinum,* 'savage mother of desire,' who in another form now threatens to devour the erstwhile fugitive. (Note the snake symbolism.)

474   Miss Miller now gives us a further reference, this time to something that influenced her fantasies in a more general way, namely Longfellow's great narrative poem, *The Song of Hiawatha.*[10] My reader must frequently have wondered at the number of times I adduce apparently very remote material for purposes of comparison and how I enlarge the basis upon which Miss Miller's creations rest. He must also have doubted whether it is justifiable, on the basis of such scanty suggestions,

[8] *Human, All Too Human,* trans. by Zimmern and Cohn, II, pp. 4f., modified.
[9] Ibid., II, p. 6.
[10] [Published 1855. It is based on American Indian legend, drawing its sources mainly from the work of Henry Rowe Schoolcraft, a pioneer of American Indian ethnology. Hiawatha was, historically, a 16th-century Iroquoian leader, but the terminology and legendary material of the poem are Algonquian. (Cf. *Standard Dictionary of Folklore,* s.v. "Hiawatha.") Longfellow derived the metre from the Finnish epic Kalevala.—EDITORS.]

to enter into fundamental discussions concerning the mythological foundations of these fantasies. For, he will say, we are not likely to find anything of the sort behind the Miller fantasies. I need hardly emphasize how hazardous these comparisons have seemed even to me. In this case I can at least plead that Miss Miller named her sources herself. So long as we stick to these clues we are moving on certain ground. The information we obtain from our patients, however, is seldom complete. We ourselves do not find it at all easy to remember where some of our own ideas and views come from. But, although instances of cryptomnesia are not uncommon, it is highly probable that not all our ideas are individual acquisitions, and that the ones whose origin we do not know are not necessarily cryptomnesias. It is rather different as regards the way in which our ideas are formed and the order in which they are arranged. Such things can undoubtedly be acquired and afterwards remembered. That need not always be the case, however, because the human mind possesses general and typical modes of functioning which correspond to the biological "pattern of behaviour." These pre-existent, innate patterns—the archetypes—can easily produce in the most widely differing individuals ideas or combinations of ideas that are practically identical, and for whose origin no individual experience can be made responsible. In the psychoses, for instance, there are very many ideas and images which impress the patient and his circle with their absolute strangeness, but which are quite familiar to the expert on account of the affinity of their motifs with certain mythologems. Because the basic structure of the psyche is everywhere more or less the same, it is possible to compare what look like individual dream-motifs with mythologems of whatever origin. So I have no hesitation in making comparisons between American Indian myth and the modern American psyche.

475   I had never read *Hiawatha* until I came to this point in my inquiry, when the continuation of my work made its perusal necessary. This poetical compilation of Indian myths proved to my satisfaction how justified were all my previous reflections, since it is unusually rich in mythological motifs. This fact should throw light on the wealth of associations in the Miller fantasies. It therefore behoves us to examine the contents of this epic more closely.

476   Nawadaha sings the songs of Hiawatha, the friend of man: [11]

> There he sang of Hiawatha,
> Sang the songs of Hiawatha,
> Sang his wondrous birth and being,
> How he prayed and how he fasted,
> How he lived, and toiled, and suffered,
> That the tribes of men might prosper,
> That he might advance his people.

477   The teleological significance of the hero as a symbolic figure who attracts libido to himself in the form of wonder and adoration, in order to lead it over the symbolic bridge of myth to higher uses, is already anticipated here. Thus we quickly become acquainted with Hiawatha as a saviour, and are prepared to hear all that is usually said about such a figure, about his miraculous birth, his mighty deeds in youth, and his sacrifice for his fellow men. The first canto opens with an "Evangelium": Gitche Manito, the "master of life," weary of the squabbles of his human children, calls his people together and makes known to them the joyous message:

> I will send a Prophet to you,
> A Deliverer of the nations,
> Who shall guide you and shall teach you,
> Who shall toil and suffer with you.
> If you listen to his counsels,
> You will multiply and prosper;
> If his warnings pass unheeded,
> You will fade away and perish!

478   Gitche Manito the Mighty, "the creator of the nations," [12] is shown standing erect "on the great Red Pipestone quarry":

> From his footprints flowed a river,
> Leaped into the light of morning,
> O'er the precipice plunging downward
> Gleamed like Ishkoodah, the comet.

---

[11] On the motif of the "friend," see my paper "Concerning Rebirth," pars. 240ff.
[12] The figure of Gitche Manito can be regarded as a kind of Original Man (Anthropos).

479   This image has a parallel in certain Coptic ideas. In the "Mysteries of Saint John and the Holy Virgin" we read:

[The Cherubim] answered and said unto me: "Seest thou that the water is under the feet of the Father? If the Father lifteth up His feet, the water riseth upwards; but if at the time when God is about to bring the water up, man sinneth against Him, He is wont to make the fruit of the earth to be little, because of the sins of men." [13]

By the water is meant the Nile, on which Egypt's fertility depended.

480   It is not only the feet themselves that have a fertility significance, it also seems to extend to their activity, treading. I observed that the dance-step of the Pueblo Indians consisted in a "calcare terram"—a persistent, vigorous pounding of the earth with the heels ("nunc pede libero pulsanda tellus": "with unfettered foot now we are to beat on the ground" [14]). Kaineus, as we saw, descended into the depths, "splitting the earth with a straight foot." Faust reached the Mothers by stamping on the ground: "Stamping descend, and stamping rise up again!" [15]

481   The heroes in the sun-devouring myths often stamp or kick in the gullet of the monster. Thor stamped clean through the bottom of the boat in his struggle with the monster and touched the bottom of the sea. The regression of libido makes the ritual act of treading out the dance-step seem like a repetition of the infantile "kicking." The latter is associated with the mother and with pleasurable sensations, and recapitulates a movement that was already practised inside the mother's womb. The foot and the treading movement are invested with a phallic significance,[16] or with that of re-entry into the womb, so that the rhythm of the dance transports the dancer into an unconscious state. The Dancing Dervishes and other primitive dancers offer confirmation of this. The comparison of the water flowing from Gitche Manito's footprints with a comet means that it is a light- or libido-symbol for the fertilizing moisture (sperma). According to a note in Humboldt's *Cosmos*,[17] certain South American Indian tribes call meteors the "piss of the stars." We should also mention that Gitche Manito is a fire-maker: he

13 Budge, *Coptic Apocrypha in the Dialect of Upper Egypt*, p. 243.
14 [Horace, *Odes*, I, xxxvii, 1–2.]   15 [Cf. MacNeice trans., p. 179.]
16 See evidence in Aigremont, *Fuss- und Schuhsymbolik*.
17 Humboldt, *Cosmos*, I, p. 99, n.

blows upon a forest so that the trees rub against one another and burst into flame. Hence this god too is a libido-symbol, since he produces not only water but fire.

482   After this prologue there follows in the second canto the story of the hero's antecedents. His father, the great warrior Mudjekeewis, has overcome by stealth the great bear, "the terror of the nations," and stolen from him the magic "belt of wampum," a girdle of shells. Here we meet the motif of the "treasure hard to attain," which the hero wrests from the monster. The "mystic" identity of the bear comes out in the poet's comparisons: Mudjekeewis smites the bear on the head after robbing him of the treasure:

> With the heavy blow bewildered
> Rose the great Bear of the mountains;
> But his knees beneath him trembled,
> And he whimpered like a woman.

483   Mudjekeewis tells him mockingly:

> Else you would not cry and whimper
> Like a miserable woman! . . .
> But you, Bear! sit here and whimper,
> And disgrace your tribe by crying,
> Like a wretched Shaugodaya,
> Like a cowardly old woman!

484   These three comparisons with a woman occur on the same page. What Mudjekeewis slays is his feminine component, the anima-image, whose first carrier is the mother. Like a true hero, he has snatched life from the jaws of death, from the all-devouring Terrible Mother. This deed, which as we have seen is also depicted as the journey to hell, the night sea journey (cf. pars. 308f.), or the conquest of the monster from within, signifies at the same time entry into the mother's womb, a rebirth that has notable consequences for Mudjekeewis. As in the Zosimos vision, so here the entrant becomes the pneuma, a wind-breath or spirit: Mudjekeewis becomes the West Wind, the fertilizing breath, the father of the winds.[18] His sons become the other

---

[18] Porphyry (*De antro nympharum*, p. 190), says that, according to Mithraic doctrine, the ancients "very reasonably connected winds with souls proceeding into generation, and again separating themselves from it [i.e., at birth and death], because, as some think, souls attract spirit, and have a pneumatic nature."

winds. An intermezzo tells of them and their loves, of which I will mention only the courtship of Wabun, the East Wind, because the wind's wooing is described in particularly graphic language. Every morning he sees a beautiful girl in the meadow, whom he eagerly courts:

> Every morning, gazing earthward,
> Still the first thing he beheld there
> Was her blue eyes looking at him,
> Two blue lakes among the rushes.

485   The comparison with water is not irrelevant, because from "wind and water" man shall be born anew.

> And he wooed her with caresses,
> Wooed her with his smile of sunshine,
> With his flattering words he wooed her,
> With his sighing and his singing,
> Gentlest whispers in the branches,
> Softest music, sweetest odors.

486   The caressing courtship of the wind is beautifully expressed in the lilting onomatopoeia.[19]

487   The third canto gives us the antecedents of Hiawatha's two mothers. We are told that as a girl his grandmother lived in the moon. One day when she was swinging on a grape-vine, a jealous lover cut it down, and Nokomis, Hiawatha's grandmother, fell to earth. The people who saw her fall thought she was a shooting-star. The wonderful origin of Nokomis is explained more fully in the course of the same song. Young Hiawatha asks his grandmother what the moon really is. She tells him that the moon is the *body of a grandmother* who had been thrown up there by one of her warlike grandchildren in a fit of rage. (Cf. fig. 32.)[20] According to the ancient belief, the moon is the gath-

19 In the Mithraic liturgy, the generating breath of the spirit comes from the sun, presumably from the "sun-tube" (cf. Part I, pars. 149–54). There is a similar idea in the Rig-Veda, where the sun is called "one-footed." Cf. the Armenian prayer that the sun may let its foot rest on the face of the worshipper. Abeghian, *Der armenische Volksglaube*, p. 43.
20 [The Haida myth upon which the depiction in fig. 32 is based tells of a woman who offended the moon and was removed thence, together with her water-pail and a berry-bush she grasped in trying to save herself. Cf. Swanton, *Ethnology of the Haida*, p. 142.—EDITORS.]

ering-place of departed souls [21] (fig. 31), a guardian of the seed, and hence a source of life with a feminine significance. The remarkable thing is that Nokomis, when she fell to earth, gave birth to a daughter, Wenonah, who afterwards became the mother of Hiawatha. The throwing upward of the mother, her fall and birth-pangs, seem to be something altogether typical. A seventeenth-century story relates that a raging bull tossed a pregnant woman "as high as a house" and tore open her body, and the child fell to earth without injury. This child, on account of his wonderful birth, was supposed to be a hero or

Fig. 31. The moon as the abode of souls
Chalcedon gem, 1st century B.C.

Fig. 32. The woman in the moon
Tattoo pattern, Haida Indians,
Northwest America

miracle-worker, but he died young. There is a widespread belief among primitives that the sun is feminine and the moon masculine. Among the Namaqua Hottentots, the sun is thought to consist of clear bacon-fat. "Those who travel on boats," we read,[22] "draw it down by magic every evening, and after cutting off a sizeable piece, kick it up again into the sky." In infancy, food comes from the mother. In the fantasies of the Gnostics there is a legend about the origin of man which may be of some

[21] Firmicus Maternus (*Matheseos libri octo,* I, 5, 9, in edn. of Kroll, etc., pp. 16–17): "Cui [animo] descensus per orbem solis tribuitur, per orbem vero lunae praeparatur ascensus" (The soul is believed to descend through the disc of the sun, but its ascent is prepared through the disc of the moon). Lydus (*De mensibus,* IV, 1, 2, in Wunsch edn., p. 66) reports the saying of the hierophant Praetextus that Janus "sends the diviner souls to the lunar throng." Epiphanius (*Adversus octoginta haereses,* LXVI, 52): "the disc of the moon is filled with souls." It is the same in exotic myths. Cf. Frobenius, *Zeitalter,* pp. 352ff.
[22] Waitz, *Anthropologie der Naturvölker,* II, p. 342.

relevance here. The female archons who were bound to the vault of heaven were unable, on account of its rapid rotation, to keep their young within them, but let them fall to earth, where they grew into human beings. (This may be connected with certain barbarous obstetric methods, in which women in labour were dropped or thrown to the ground.) The assault on the mother begins with the Mudjekeewis episode and is continued in the violent treatment of Grandmother Nokomis, who, as a result of the cutting of the grape-vine and her fall to earth, seems to have become pregnant in some way. The "plucking of the branch" hints, as we have already seen, at an infringement of the incest-taboo. The song about "Saxonland, where beautiful maidens grow upon trees," or proverbs like "stolen fruits are sweetest," point to a similar idea. The fall of Nokomis deserves comparison with a poetical figure in Heine:

> A star, a star is falling
> Out of the glittering sky!
> The star of Love! I watch it
> Sink in the depths and die.
>
> The leaves and buds are falling
> From many an apple-tree;
> I watch the mirthful breezes
> Embrace them wantonly.[23]

Wenonah is later wooed by the caressing West Wind and is made pregnant by him. Being a young moon-goddess, she is as beautiful as the moonlight. Nokomis warns her of the dangerous courtship of Mudjekeewis, but Wenonah allows herself to become infatuated and conceives from the breath of the West Wind a son, our hero:

> And the West Wind came at evening . . .
> Found the beautiful Wenonah
> Lying there among the lilies,
> Wooed her with his words of sweetness,
> Wooed her with his soft caresses,
> Till she bore a son in sorrow,
> Bore a son of love and sorrow.

[23] Trans. by Untermeyer, p. 78.

489   The star or comet plainly belongs to the birth-scene; Nokomis, too, comes to earth as a falling star. Mörike's poetic fancy
imagined another such divine conception:

> And she who bore me in her womb,
>   And gave me food and clothing,
> She was a maid, a wild, brown maid,
>   Who looked on men with loathing.
>
> She fleered at them and laughed aloud,
>   And bade no suitor tarry;
> "I'd rather be the Wind's own bride
>   Than have a man and marry."
>
> Then came the Wind and held her fast,
>   His captive, love-enchanted;
> And lo, by him a merry child
>   Within her womb was planted.[24]

490   The same idea can be seen in the story of Buddha's marvellous birth, as told by Sir Edwin Arnold:

> Maya the queen . . .
> Dreamed a strange dream; dreamed that a star from heaven—
> Splendid, six-rayed, in colour rosy-pearl,
> Whereof the token was an Elephant
> Six-tusked, and white as milk of Kamadhuk—
> Shot through the void; and, shining into her,
> Entered her womb upon the right.[25] [Pl. XLIXb.]

491   During the conception

> A wind blew
> With unknown freshness over lands and seas.

492   After the birth the four genies of the East, West, North, and
South come to offer their services as palanquin-bearers. (Cf. the
coming of the Wise Men at the birth of Christ.) To complete
the symbolism, there is in the Buddha myth, besides the fertilization by star and wind, fertilization by a theriomorphic sym-

24 [As trans. in the Hinkle edn. (1916), pp. 254f.]
25 *The Light of Asia*, Book I, p. 2. The elephant is shown penetrating Maya's
side with his trunk. According to a medieval tradition, Mary's conception of
Jesus took place through the ear.

bol, the elephant, who, as Bodhisattva, begets the Buddha. In Christian picture-language the unicorn, as well as the dove, is a symbol of the spermatic Word or Spirit.[26] (Cf. pl. VIII.)

493   At this point we might ask ourselves why the birth of a hero always has to take place under such extraordinary circumstances. One would think it possible for a hero to be born in the normal manner, and then gradually to grow out of his humble and homely surroundings, perhaps with a great effort and in face of many dangers. (This motif is by no means uncommon in the hero-myths.) As a general rule, however, the story of his origins is miraculous. The singular circumstances of his procreation and birth are part and parcel of the hero-myth. What is the reason for these beliefs?

494   The answer to this question is that the hero is not born like an ordinary mortal because his birth is a rebirth from the mother-wife. That is why the hero so often has two mothers. As Rank [27] has shown with a wealth of examples, the hero is frequently exposed and then reared by foster-parents. In this way he gets two mothers. An excellent example of this is the relation of Heracles to Hera. In the Hiawatha epic, Wenonah dies after giving birth, and her place is taken by Nokomis.[28] Buddha, too, was brought up by a foster-mother. The foster-mother is sometimes an animal, e.g., the she-wolf of Romulus and Remus, etc. (pls. II, La). The dual mother may be replaced by the motif of dual birth, which has attained a lofty significance in various religions. In Christianity, for example, baptism represents a rebirth, as we have already seen. Man is not merely born in the commonplace sense, but is born again in a mysterious manner, and so partakes of divinity. Anyone who is reborn in this way becomes a hero, a semi-divine being. Thus Christ's redemptive death on the cross was understood as a "baptism," that is to say, as rebirth through the second mother, symbolized by the tree of death. (Cf. pls. XXXVI, XXXVII.) Christ himself said (Luke 12 : 50): "But I have a baptism to be baptized with; and how am I straitened till it be accomplished!" He therefore

26 Cf. *Psychology and Alchemy*, pars. 518ff.
27 *The Myth of the Birth of the Hero.*
28 The rapid death of the mother, or separation from the mother, is an essential part of the hero-myth. The same idea is expressed in the myth of the swan-maiden, who flies away again after the birth of the child, her purpose fulfilled.

interprets his own death-agony symbolically as the pangs of re-birth.

495   The dual-mother motif suggests the idea of a dual birth. One of the mothers is the real, human mother, the other is the symbolical mother; in other words, she is distinguished as being divine, supernatural, or in some way extraordinary. She can also be represented theriomorphically. In certain cases she has more human proportions, and here we are dealing with projections of archetypal ideas upon persons in the immediate environment, which generally brings about complications. For instance the rebirth symbol is liable to be projected upon the step-mother or mother-in-law (unconsciously, of course), just as, for her part, the mother-in-law often finds it difficult not to make her son-in-law her son-lover in the old mythological manner. There are innumerable variations on this motif, especially when we add individual elements to the collective mythological ones.

496   He who stems from two mothers is the hero: the first birth makes him a mortal man, the second an immortal half-god. That is what all the hints in the story of the hero's procreation are getting at. Hiawatha's father first conquers the mother under the terrifying symbol of the bear; [29] then, having become a god himself, he begets the hero. What the hero Hiawatha then has to do is suggested to him by Nokomis, when she tells him the story of the origin of the moon: he is to throw his mother up into the sky, whereupon she will become pregnant and give birth to a daughter. This rejuvenated mother would, according to the Egyptian fantasy, be given as a daughter-wife to the sun-god, the "father of his mother," for purposes of self-reproduction. What Hiawatha does in this respect we shall see presently. We have already examined the behaviour of the dying and re-surgent gods of the Near East. In regard to the pre-existence of Christ, the gospel of St. John is, as we know, the crowning witness to this idea. One has only to think of the words of the Baptist (John 1 : 30): "After me cometh a man which is preferred before me: for he was before me." The opening words are equally significant: "In the beginning was the Word, and the Word was with God, and the Word was God. The same was

29 The bear is associated with Artemis and is thus a "feminine" animal. Cf. also the Gallo-Roman Dea Artio (pl. L*b*), and my "Psychological Aspects of the Kore," pars. 340ff.

in the beginning with God. All things were made by him; and without him was not any thing made that was made." Then follows the annunciation of the Light, of the rising sun—the *Sol mysticus* which was before and will be afterwards. In the baptistry at Pisa, Christ is shown bringing the tree of life to mankind, his head surrounded by a sun-wheel. Over this relief stand the words "INTROITUS SOLIS."

497   Because the reborn is his own begetter, the story of his procreation is veiled beneath strange symbolical events which conceal and reveal at the same time. Quite in keeping with this is the extraordinary assertion about the virgin conception. The idea of supernatural conception can, of course, be taken as a metaphysical fact, but psychologically it tells us that a content of the unconscious ("child") has come into existence without the natural help of a human father (i.e., consciousness). (Cf. pl. VIII.) It tells us, on the contrary, that some god has begotten the son and further that the son is identical with the father, which in psychological language means that a central archetype, the God-image, has renewed itself ("been reborn") and become "incarnate" in a way perceptible to consciousness. The "mother" corresponds to the "virgin anima," who is not turned towards the outer world and is therefore not corrupted by it. She is turned rather towards the "inner sun," the archetype of transcendent wholeness—the self.[30]

498   As is consistent with the birth of the hero and renewed god from the ocean of the unconscious, Hiawatha passes his childhood between land and water, by the shores of the great lake:

> By the shores of Gitche Gumee,
> By the shining Big-Sea-Water,
> Stood the wigwam of Nokomis,
> Daughter of the moon, Nokomis.
> Dark behind it rose the forest,
> Rose the black and gloomy pine-trees,
> Rose the firs with cones upon them;
> Bright before it beat the water,
> Beat the clear and sunny water,
> Beat the shining Big-Sea-Water.

499   In these surroundings he was reared by Nokomis. Here she taught him the first words and told him the first fairytales, and

[30] Cf. Layard, "The Incest Taboo and the Virgin Archetype," pp. 254ff.

the sounds of the water and the forest mingled with them, so that the child learned to understand not only the language of men, but the language of nature:

> At the door on summer evenings
> Sat the little Hiawatha;
> Heard the whispering of the pine-trees,
> Heard the lapping of the water,
> Sounds of music, words of wonder:
> "Minne-wawa!" said the pine-trees,
> "Mudway-aushka!" said the water.

500   Hiawatha hears human speech in the sounds of nature; thus he understands nature's language. The wind says "wawa." The goose cries "wawa." "Wah-wah-taysee" is the name of the little glow-worm that enchants him. Thus the poet describes the gradual drawing in of external nature into the world of the subject, and the contamination of the primary object, the mother, to whom those first lisping words were addressed and from whom the first sounds were learned, with the secondary object, nature, which imperceptibly usurps the mother's place and takes over the sounds first heard from her, together with all those feelings we later rediscover in ourselves in our warm love for Mother Nature. The subsequent blending, whether pantheistic or aesthetic, of the sensitive, civilized man with nature [31] is, looked at retrospectively, a reblending with the mother, who was our first object, with whom we were truly and wholly one. She was our first experience of an *outside* and at the same time of an *inside:* from that interior world there emerged an image, apparently a reflection of the external mother-image, yet older, more original and more imperishable than this—a mother who changed back into a Kore, into an eternally youthful figure. This is the anima, the personification of the collective unconscious. So it is not surprising if we see the old images rising up again in the graphic language of a

---

[31] Karl Joël (*Seele und Welt*, pp. 153f.) says: "Life is not lessened in artists and prophets, but is enhanced. They are our guides into the Lost Paradise, which only becomes Paradise through being found again. It is not the old, mindless unity that the artist strives for, but a felt reunion; not empty unity, but full unity; not the oneness of indifference, but the oneness attained through differentiation. . . . All life is a loss of balance and a struggling back into balance. We find this return home in religion and art."

modern philosopher, Karl Joël, symbolizing this oneness with the mother and the merging of subject and object in the unconscious. Joël gives the following account of this "Primal Experience": [32]

I lie on the seashore, the sparkling flood blue-shimmering in my dreamy eyes; light breezes flutter in the distance; the thud of the waves, charging and breaking over in foam, beats thrillingly and drowsily upon the shore—or upon the ear? I cannot tell. The far and the near become blurred into one; outside and inside merge into one another. Nearer and nearer, friendlier, like a homecoming, sounds the thud of the waves; now, like a thundering pulse, they beat in my head, now they beat over my soul, wrapping it round, consuming it, while at the same time my soul floats out of me as a blue waste of waters. Outside and inside are one. The whole symphony of sensations fades away into one tone, all senses become one sense, which is one with feeling; the world expires in the soul and the soul dissolves in the world. Our little life is rounded by a great sleep. Sleep our cradle, sleep our grave, sleep our home, from which we go forth in the morning, returning again at evening; our life a short pilgrimage, the interval between emergence from original oneness and sinking back into it! Blue shimmers the infinite sea, where the jelly-fish dreams of that primeval existence to which our thoughts still filter down through aeons of memory. For every experience entails a change and a guarantee of life's unity. At that moment when they are no longer blended together, when the experient lifts his head, still blind and dripping, from immersion in the stream of experience, from flowing away with the thing experienced; when man, amazed and estranged, detaches the change from himself and holds it before him as something alien—at that moment of estrangement the two sides of the experience are substantialized into subject and object, and at that moment consciousness is born.[33]

501   Joël describes here, in unmistakable symbolism, the merging of subject and object as the reunion of mother and child. The symbols agree with those of mythology even in their details. There is a distinct allusion to the encircling and devouring motif. The sea that devours the sun and gives birth to it again

[32] By "primal experience" is meant that first human differentiation between subject and object, that first conscious objectivation which is psychologically inconceivable without an inner division of the human animal against himself—the very means by which he separated himself from the oneness of nature.
[33] *Seele und Welt.*

is an old acquaintance. The moment of the rise of consciousness, of the separation of subject and object, is indeed a birth. It is as though philosophical speculation hung with lame wings on a few primordial figures of human speech, beyond whose simple grandeur no thought can fly. The image of the jelly-fish is far from accidental. Once when I was explaining to a patient the maternal significance of water, she experienced a very disagreeable sensation at this contact with the mother-complex. "It makes me squirm," she said, "as if I'd touched a *jelly-fish*." The blessed state of sleep before birth and after death is, as Joël observes, rather like an old shadowy memory of that unsuspecting state of early childhood, when there is as yet no opposition to disturb the peaceful flow of slumbering life. Again and again an inner longing draws us back, but always the life of action must struggle in deadly fear to break free lest it fall into a state of sleep. Long before Joël, an Indian chieftain had expressed the same thing in the same words to one of the restless white men: "Ah, my brother, you will never know the happiness of thinking nothing and doing nothing. This is the most delightful thing there is, next to sleep. So we were before birth, and so we shall be after death." [34]

502   We shall see from the later destinies of Hiawatha how important his early childhood impressions were in his choice of a wife. Hiawatha's first deed was to kill a roebuck with his arrow:

> Dead he lay there in the forest
> By the ford across the river. . . .

503   This is typical of Hiawatha's deeds. Whatever he kills generally lies by or in the water, or better still, half in water and half on land.[35] His subsequent adventures will explain why this is so. Further, the roebuck was no ordinary animal, but a magic one with an unconscious (i.e., symbolical) significance. Hiawatha made himself gloves and moccasins from its hide: the gloves gave such power to his arms that he could crumble rocks

---

[34] Crèvecoeur, *Voyage dans la haute Pensylvanie*, I, p. 362. I heard much the same thing from a chief of the Pueblo Indians, who told me the Americans were mad because they were so restless.

[35] The dragons of Greek (and Swiss) legend also live in or near springs or other waters, of which they are often the guardians. This links up with the motif of the "struggle by the ford."

to dust, and the moccasins had the virtue of seven-leagued boots. By clothing himself in the hide he became a sort of giant. Therefore the roebuck killed at the ford[36] was a "doctor animal," a magician who had changed his shape, or a daemonic being—a symbol, that is to say, which points to the "animal" and other such powers of the unconscious. That is why it was killed at the ford, i.e., at the crossing, on the border-line between conscious and unconscious. The animal is a representative of the unconscious, and the latter, as the matrix of consciousness, has a maternal significance, which explains why the mother was also represented by the bear. All animals belong to the Great Mother (pl. LI), and the killing of any wild animal is a transgression against the mother. Just as the mother seems a giantess to the small child, so the attribute of size passes to the archetypal Great Mother, Mother Nature. Whoever succeeds in killing the "magic" animal, the symbolic representative of the animal mother, acquires something of her gigantic strength. This is expressed by saying that the hero clothes himself in the animal's skin and in this way obtains for the magic animal a sort of resurrection. At the Aztec human sacrifices criminals played the part of gods: they were slaughtered and flayed, and the priests then wrapped themselves in the dripping pelts in order to represent the gods' resurrection and renewal.[37]

504   In killing his first roebuck, therefore, Hiawatha was killing the symbolic representative of the unconscious, i.e., his own *participation mystique* with animal nature, and from that comes his giant strength. He now sallies forth to do battle with Mudjekeewis, the father, in order to avenge his mother Wenonah. (Cf. Gilgamesh's fight with the giant Humbaba.) In this fight the father may also be represented by some sort of magic animal which has to be overcome, but he can equally well be represented by a giant or a magician or a wicked tyrant. *Mutatis mutandis* the animals can be interpreted as the "mother," as the "mater saeva cupidinum," or again as that

36 Where one can wade through the water—cf. what we said above about the encircling and devouring motif. Water as an obstacle in dreams seems to indicate the mother, or a regression of libido. Crossing the water means overcoming the obstacle, i.e., the mother as symbol of man's longing for the condition of sleep or death. See my "On the Psychology of the Unconscious," pars. 132ff.
37 Cf. the Attic custom of stuffing a bull in spring; also the Lupercalia, Saturnalia, etc.

amiable Isis who laid a horned viper in her husband's path—in short, they can be interpreted as the Terrible Mother who devours and destroys, and thus symbolizes death itself.[38] (I remember the case of a mother who kept her children tied to her with unnatural love and devotion. At the time of the climacteric she fell into a depressive psychosis and had delirious states in which she saw herself as an animal, especially as a wolf or pig, and acted accordingly, running about on all fours, howling like a wolf or grunting like a pig. In her psychosis she had herself become the symbol of the all-devouring mother.)

505   Interpretation in terms of the parents is, however, simply a *façon de parler*. In reality the whole drama takes place in the individual's own psyche, where the "parents" are not the parents at all but only their imagos: they are representations which have arisen from the conjunction of parental peculiarities with the individual disposition of the child.[39] The imagos are activated and varied in every possible manner by an energy which likewise pertains to the individual; it derives from the sphere of instinct and expresses itself as instinctuality. This dynamism is represented in dreams by theriomorphic symbols. All the lions, bulls, dogs, and snakes that populate our dreams represent an undifferentiated and as yet untamed libido, which at the same time forms part of the human personality and can therefore fittingly be described as the *anthropoid psyche*. Like energy, the libido never manifests itself as such, but only in the form of a "force," that is to say, in the form of something in a definite energic state, be it moving bodies, chemical or electrical tension, etc. Libido is therefore tied to definite forms or states. It appears as the *intensity* of impulses, affects, activities, and so on. But these phenomena are never impersonal; they manifest themselves like parts of the personality. The same is true of complexes: they too behave like parts of the personality.

506   It is this anthropoid psyche which will not fit into the ra-

[38] This fact led my pupil Dr. Spielrein to develop her idea of the death-instinct, which was then taken up by Freud. In my opinion it is not so much a question of a death-instinct as of that "other" instinct (Goethe) which signifies spiritual life.

[39] An essential part of this disposition is the *a priori* existence of "organizing factors," the archetypes, which are to be understood as inborn modes of functioning that constitute, in their totality, man's nature. The chick does not learn how to come out of the egg—it possesses this knowledge *a priori*.

tional pattern of culture—or only very unsatisfactorily and with extreme reluctance—and resists cultural development to the utmost. It is as though its libido were constantly striving back to the original unconscious state of untamed savagery. The road of regression leads back to childhood and finally, in a manner of speaking, into the mother's body. The intensity of this retrospective longing, so brilliantly depicted in the figure of Enkidu in the Gilgamesh Epic, becomes quite unbearable with the heightened demands made by adaptation. These may be due either to external or to internal causes. If the demand comes from "inside," the main difficulty lies not so much in unfavourable external circumstances as in an enhanced "subjective" demand that seems to increase with the years, and in the ever-stronger emergence of the inner, and hitherto hidden, "real" personality. The source of this change is to all appearances the anthropoid psyche, and the anthropoid psyche is also the aim and end of every regression, which immediately sets in whenever there is the least hesitation to adapt—not to speak of cases where the demands of life cannot be met at all.

507 Scenting the dangers in this situation, religious and conventional morality joins forces with Freudian theory in consistently devaluing the regression and its ostensible goal—reversion to infantilism—as "infantile sexuality," "incest," "uterine fantasy," etc. Reason must here call a halt, for it is hardly possible to go farther back than the maternal uterus. At this point concretism comes up against a brick wall; what is more, moral condemnation seizes upon the regressive tendency and tries by every trick of devaluation to prevent this sacrilegious return to the mother, surreptitiously aided and abetted by the one-sided "biological" orientation of the Freudian school. But anything that exceeds the bounds of a man's personal consciousness remains unconscious and therefore appears in projection; that is to say, the semi-animal psyche with its regressive demands against which he struggles so desperately is attributed to the mother, and the defence against it is seen in the father. Projection, however, is never a cure; it prevents the conflict only on the surface, while deeper down it creates a neurosis which allows him to escape into illness. In that way the devil is cast out by Beelzebub.

508 As against this, therapy must support the regression, and continue to do so until the "prenatal" stage is reached. It must

be remembered that the "mother" is really an imago, a psychic image merely, which has in it a number of different but very important unconscious contents. The "mother," as the first incarnation of the anima archetype, personifies in fact the whole unconscious. Hence the regression leads back only apparently to the mother; in reality she is the gateway into the unconscious, into the "realm of the Mothers." Whoever sets foot in this realm submits his conscious ego-personality to the controlling influence of the unconscious, or if he feels that he has got caught by mistake, or that somebody has tricked him into it, he will defend himself desperately, though his resistance will not turn out to his advantage. For regression, if left undisturbed, does not stop short at the "mother" but goes back beyond her to the prenatal realm of the "Eternal Feminine," to the immemorial world of archetypal possibilities where, "thronged round with images of all creation," slumbers the "divine child," patiently awaiting his conscious realization. This son is the germ of wholeness, and he is characterized as such by his specific symbols.

509   When Jonah was swallowed by the whale, he was not simply imprisoned in the belly of the monster, but, as Paracelsus tells us,[40] he saw "mighty mysteries" there. This view probably derives from the *Pirkê de Rabbi Elieser,* which says:

Jonah entered its mouth just as a man enters the great synagogue, and he stood there. The two eyes of the fish were like windows of glass giving light to Jonah. R. Meir said: One pearl was suspended inside the belly of the fish and it gave illumination to Jonah, like this sun which shines with all its might at noon; and it showed to Jonah all that was in the sea and in the depths.[41]

510   In the darkness of the unconscious a treasure lies hidden, the same "treasure hard to attain" which in our text, and in many other places too, is described as the shining pearl, or, to quote Paracelsus, as the "mystery," by which is meant a *fascinosum* par excellence. It is these inherent possibilities of "spiritual" or "symbolic" life and of progress which form the ultimate, though unconscious, goal of regression. By serving as a means of expression, as bridges and pointers, symbols help to

40 *Liber Azoth,* ed. by Sudhoff, XIV, p. 576.
41 Trans. by Friedlander, ch. 10, p. 69.

prevent the libido from getting stuck in the material corporeality of the mother. Never has the dilemma been more acutely formulated than in the Nicodemus dialogue: on the one hand the impossibility of entering again into the mother's womb; on the other, the need for rebirth from "water and spirit." The hero is a hero just because he sees resistance to the forbidden goal in all life's difficulties and yet fights that resistance with the whole-hearted yearning that strives towards the treasure hard to attain, and perhaps unattainable—a yearning that paralyses and kills the ordinary man.

511   Hiawatha's father is Mudjekeewis, the West Wind: the battle therefore is fought in the West. From that quarter came life (fertilization of Wenonah) and death (Wenonah's). Hence Hiawatha is fighting the typical battle of the hero for rebirth in the Western Sea. The fight is with the father, who is the obstacle barring the way to the goal. In other cases the fight in the West is a battle with the devouring mother. As we have seen, the danger comes from both parents: from the father, because he apparently makes regression impossible, and from the mother, because she absorbs the regressing libido and keeps it to herself, so that he who sought rebirth finds only death. Mudjekeewis, who had acquired his godlike nature by overcoming the maternal bear, is himself overcome by his son:

> Back retreated Mudjekeewis,
> Rushing westward o'er the mountains,
> Stumbling westward down the mountains,
> Three whole days retreated fighting,
> Still pursued by Hiawatha
> To the doorways of the West Wind,
> To the portals of the Sunset,
> To the earth's remotest border,
> Where into the empty spaces
> Sinks the sun, as a flamingo
> Drops into her nest at nightfall.

512   The "three days" are a stereotyped expression for the "night sea imprisonment" (December 21 to 24). Christ, too, spent three days in the underworld. During this struggle in the West the hero wins the treasure hard to attain. In Hiawatha's case the father is forced to make a great concession to the son: he gives

him his divine nature,[42] that very wind-nature whose incorporeality alone protected Mudjekeewis from death.[43] He says to his son:

> I will share my kingdom with you,
> Ruler shall you be henceforward
> Of the Northwest Wind, Keewaydin,
> Of the home-wind, the Keewaydin.

513   Hiawatha's being appointed the ruler of the home-wind has its exact parallel in the Gilgamesh Epic, where Gilgamesh obtains from the wise old Utnapishtim, who dwells in the West, the magic herb which brings him safely over the sea to his native land (cf. pl. XIX), but which is stolen from him by a serpent on his arrival home. As a reward for his victory Hiawatha receives a "pneumatic" body, a breath-body or subtle body not subject to corruption. On the return journey he stops with a skilled arrowsmith who has a lovely daughter:

> And he named her from the river,
> From the waterfall he named her,
> Minnehaha, Laughing Water.

514   When Hiawatha, in his early childhood reveries, felt the sounds of wind and water crowding upon his ears, he recognized in the phonetics of nature the speech of his own mother. "Minnewawa" said the murmuring pines on the shore of the great lake. And once again, through the murmuring of the wind and the lapping of the water, he discovers his childhood reveries in the girl of his choice, "Minnehaha," the laughing water. For the hero, even more than the rest of mankind, finds his mother in the woman he loves, so that he can become a child again and win to immortality. The archetype of the Feminine, the anima, first appears in the mother and then transfers itself to the beloved.

515   The fact that Minnehaha's father is a skilled arrowsmith tells us that he is a protagonist in the unconscious drama, namely the father of the hero (just as the beloved is his mother). The archetype of the wise old man first appears in the father, being a personification of meaning and spirit in its procreative

[42] In the Gilgamesh Epic, too, immortality is the goal of the hero.
[43] Cf. "The Visions of Zosimos," par. 86: ". . . by compelling necessity I am sanctified as a priest and now stand in perfection as a spirit." (Also in Berthelot, *Alch. grecs*, III, i, 2.)

sense.[44] The hero's father is often a master carpenter or some kind of artisan. According to an Arabian legend, Terah, the father of Abraham, was a master craftsman who could cut a shaft from any bit of wood, which means in Arabic usage that he was a begetter of excellent sons.[45] In addition, he was a maker of images. Tvashtri, the father of Agni, was the cosmic architect, a smith and carpenter, and the inventor of fire-boring. Joseph, the father of Jesus, was a carpenter, and so was Cinyras, the father of Adonis, who was supposed to have invented the hammer, the lever, roof-building, and mining. The father of the many-faced Hermes, Hephaestus, was a cunning technician and sculptor. In fairytales, the hero's father is, more modestly, the traditional woodcutter. In the Rig-Veda the world is hewn from a tree by the cosmic architect, Tvashtri. To say that Hiawatha's father-in-law was an arrowsmith means, therefore, that the mythological attribute otherwise characteristic of the hero's father has been transferred to the father-in-law. This corresponds to the psychological fact that the anima always stands in the relationship of a daughter to the wise old man.[46] Nor is it uncommon to find the father-in-law so much emphasized that he replaces the real father. The reason for this is the archetypal relationship we have just discussed.

516   Finally, father-attributes may occasionally fall to the son himself, i.e., when it has become apparent that he is of one nature with the father. The hero symbolizes a man's *unconscious self*, and this manifests itself empirically as the sum total of all archetypes and therefore includes the archetype of the father and of the wise old man. To that extent the hero is his own father and his own begetter. This combination of motifs can be found in the legend of Mani. He performs his great deeds as a religious teacher, then goes into hiding for years in a cave, dies, and is skinned, stuffed, and hung up. Besides that, he is an artist and has a crippled foot. There is a similar combination of motifs in Wieland the Smith.

44 Cf. my "Phenomenology of the Spirit in Fairytales," pars. 400ff.

45 Sepp, *Das Heidentum und dessen Bedeutung für das Christentum*, III, p. 82, cited in Drews, *The Christ Myth*, p. 116, n.

46 An excellent example of this is the love-story of Sophia, reported by Irenaeus, *Adversus Haereses*, Roberts and Rambaut trans., I, p. 7.

517   Hiawatha kept silent, on his return to Nokomis, about what he had seen at the old arrowsmith's house, and did nothing further to win Minnehaha. But now something happens which, if it were not in an Indian epic, we might rather have expected to find in the anamnesis of a neurosis. Hiawatha introverts his libido, puts up the most dogged resistance to the natural course of events, and builds himself a hut in the forest in order to fast and have dreams and visions. For the first three days he wanders through the forest as in his boyhood, looking at all the animals and plants:

> Master of Life! he cried, desponding,
> Must our lives depend on these things?

518   This question, as to whether our lives must depend on "these things," is very strange. It sounds as if Hiawatha found it unendurable that life should come from "these things," i.e., from the world of nature. Nature seems suddenly to have taken on an alien meaning. The only possible explanation for this is that a considerable quantity of libido which till now was unconscious has suddenly been either transferred to nature or withdrawn from it. At any rate, some crucial change has taken place in the general direction of feeling, consisting apparently in a regression of libido. Hiawatha returns home to Nokomis without having undertaken anything; but there again he is driven away, because Minnehaha is already standing in his path. So he withdraws himself still further, back into the time of early boyhood when he learnt to hear the mother-sounds in the sounds of nature, whose undertones now fill his mind with memories of Minnehaha. In this reactivation of the impressions of nature we can see a revival of those very early and powerful impressions which are only surpassed by the still stronger impressions the child received from its mother. The glamour of this feeling for her is transferred to other objects in the child's environment, and from them there emanate in later years those magical, blissful feelings which are characteristic of the earliest memories of childhood. When, therefore, Hiawatha hides himself again in the lap of nature, what he is doing is to reawaken the relationship to the mother, and to something older than the mother, and it is therefore to be expected that he will emerge reborn in some other form.

519　　Before we turn to this new creation born of introversion, there is still another meaning to be considered in this question of whether life must depend on "these things." Life can depend on "these things" in the quite simple sense that, without them, man must perish of hunger. In that case we would have to conclude that the question of nourishment has suddenly come to lie close to the hero's heart. The question of nourishment has to be considered here because regression to the mother is bound to revive the memory of the "alma mater," [47] the mother as the nourishing source. Incest is not the only aspect characteristic of regression: there is also the hunger that drives the child to its mother. Whoever gives up the struggle to adapt and regresses into the bosom of the family, which in the last resort is the mother's bosom, expects not only to be warmed and loved, but also to be fed. If the regression has an infantile character, it aims—without of course admitting it—at incest and nourishment. But when the regression is only apparent, and is in reality a purposive introversion of libido directed towards a goal, then the endogamous relationship, which is in any case prohibited by the incest-taboo, will be avoided, and the demand for nourishment replaced by intentional fasting, as was the case with Hiawatha. Such an attitude compels the libido to switch over to a symbol or to a symbolic equivalent of the "alma mater," in other words, to the collective unconscious. Solitude and fasting have from time immemorial been the best-known means of strengthening any meditation whose purpose is to open the door to the unconscious.

520　　On the fourth day of his fast Hiawatha ceases to address himself to nature; he lies on his couch exhausted, his eyes half-closed, sunk in his dreams, a picture of extreme introversion. We have already seen that in such states inner experiences take the place of external life and reality. Hiawatha then has a vision:

> And he saw a youth approaching,
> Dressed in garments green and yellow,
> Coming through the purple twilight,
> Through the splendour of the sunset;
> Plumes of green bent o'er his forehead,
> And his hair was soft and golden.

[47] *Almus* means 'nourishing, refreshing, kind, bountiful.' (Cf. pl. xiva.)

521   This singular personage addresses Hiawatha as follows:

> From the Master of Life descending,
> I, the friend of man, Mondamin,
> Come to warn you and instruct you,
> How by struggle and by labour
> You shall gain what you have prayed for.
> Rise up from your bed of branches,
> Rise, O youth, and wrestle with me!

522   Mondamin is the maize, the Indian corn. Hiawatha's introversion gives birth to a god who is eaten. His hunger—in the
twofold sense described above—his longing for the nourishing
mother, calls forth from the unconscious another hero, an edible god, the maize, son of the Earth Mother. The Christian
parallel is obvious. It is hardly necessary to suppose any Christian influence here, since Fray Bernardino de Sahagún had
already described the eucharist of Huitzilopochtli among the
Aztecs early in the sixteenth century.[48] This god, too, was cere-
monially eaten. Mondamin, the "friend of man," [49] challenges
Hiawatha to single combat in the glow of evening. In the "purple twilight" of the setting sun (i.e., in the western land) there
now ensues the mythological struggle with the god who has
sprung out of the unconscious like a transformed reflection of
Hiawatha's introverted consciousness. As a god or god-man he is
the prototype of Hiawatha's heroic destiny; that is to say, Hiawatha has in himself the possibility, indeed the necessity, of con-
fronting his daemon. On the way to this goal he conquers the
parents and breaks his infantile ties. But the deepest tie is to
the mother. Once he has conquered this by gaining access to her
symbolical equivalent, he can be born again. In this tie to
the maternal source lies the strength that gives the hero his extraordinary powers, his true genius, which he frees from the
embrace of the unconscious by his daring and sovereign independence. Thus the god is born in him. The mystery of the
"mother" is divine creative power, which appears here in the
form of the corn-god Mondamin. (Cf. pl. LII.) This view is cor

---

[48] Bernardino de Sahagún, *General History of the Things of New Spain*, Book 3,
pp. 5f. [Cf. "Transformation Symbolism in the Mass," pars. 339ff.]

[49] For the "friend," see my discussion of Khidr in "Concerning Rebirth," pars.
240ff. [Cf. also *Psychology and Alchemy*, pars. 155–57. The account of Khidr is in
the Koran, Sura 18.—EDITORS.]

roborated by a legend of the Cherokee Indians, "who invoke it [the corn] under the name of 'the old woman,' in allusion to a myth that it sprang from the blood of an old woman killed by her disobedient sons." [50]

> Faint with famine, Hiawatha
> Started from his bed of branches,
> From the twilight of his wigwam
> Forth into the flush of sunset,
> Came and wrestled with Mondamin;
> At his touch he felt new courage
> Throbbing in his brain and bosom,
> Felt new life and hope and vigour
> Run through every nerve and fibre.

523   The battle in the sunset with the corn-god gives Hiawatha new strength—necessarily so, because the fight against the paralysing grip of the unconscious calls forth man's creative powers. That is the source of all creativity, but it needs heroic courage to do battle with these forces and to wrest from them the treasure hard to attain. Whoever succeeds in this has triumphed indeed. Hiawatha wrestles with himself in order to create himself.[51] The struggle again lasts for the mythical three days; and on the fourth day, as Mondamin prophesied, Hiawatha conquers him, and Mondamin, yielding up his soul, sinks to the ground. In accordance with the latter's wish, Hiawatha buries him in the earth his mother, and soon afterwards, young and fresh, the corn sprouts from his grave for the nourishment of mankind. (Cf. pl. LII.) Had Hiawatha not succeeded in conquering him, Mondamin would have "killed" him and usurped his place, with the result that Hiawatha would have become "possessed" by a demon.[52]

524   Now the remarkable thing here is that it is not Hiawatha who passes through death and emerges reborn, as might be expected, but the god. It is not man who is transformed into a god, but the god who undergoes transformation in and through

50 Frazer, *The Golden Bough*, IV, p. 297.
51 "You sought the heaviest burden, and found yourself."—Nietzsche. [Cf. par. 459, above.]
52 Christ successfully resisted the temptations of the power-devil in the wilderness. Whoever prefers power is therefore, in the Christian view, possessed by the devil. The psychologist can only agree.

man. It is as though he had been asleep in the "mother," i.e., in Hiawatha's unconscious, and had then been roused and fought with so that he should not overpower his host, but should, on the contrary, himself experience death and rebirth, and reappear in the corn in a new form beneficial to mankind. Consequently he appears at first in hostile form, as an assailant with whom the hero has to wrestle. This is in keeping with the violence of all unconscious dynamism. In this manner the god manifests himself and in this form he must be overcome. The struggle has its parallel in Jacob's wrestling with the angel at the ford Jabbok. The onslaught of instinct then becomes an experience of divinity, provided that man does not succumb to it and follow it blindly, but defends his humanity against the animal nature of the divine power. It is "a fearful thing to fall into the hands of the living God," and "whoso is near unto me, is near unto the fire, and whoso is far from me, is far from the kingdom"; for "the Lord is a consuming fire," the Messiah is "the Lion of the tribe of Judah":

> Judah is a lion's whelp;
> from the prey, my son, thou art gone up.
> He stooped down, he couched as a lion,
> and as an old lion; who shall rouse him up? [53]

525   The devil, too, "as a roaring lion, walketh about seeking whom he may devour." [54] These well-known examples suffice to show that this idea is very much at home even in the Judaeo-Christian teachings.

526   In the Mithraic mysteries, the cult-hero has to fight the bull; in the "transitus" he carries it into the cave, where he kills it. From its death comes all fruitfulness, especially things to eat.[55] (Cf. pl. XXXIII.) The cave is the equivalent of the grave. The same idea is expressed in the Christian mystery, but in a more

---

53 Hebrews 10 : 31; Origen, *In Jeremiam,* 3, 3 [see James, *Apocryphal New Testament,* p. 35]; Hebrews 12 : 29; Revelation 5 : 5; Genesis 49 : 9.
54 I Peter 5 : 8.
55 It is an almost invariable feature of the dragon-whale myth that the hero begins to feel very hungry in the belly of the monster and cuts off bits of the innards for food. He is, in fact, inside the "nourishing mother." His next act is to make a fire in order to get out of the monster. In an Eskimo myth from the Bering Strait, the hero finds a woman in the whale's belly, who is its soul. Cf. Frobenius, *Zeitalter.*

beautiful and humane form. The struggle in Christ's soul in Gethsemane, where he wrestles with himself in order to complete his work; then the "transitus," the carrying of the cross,[56] when he takes on his shoulders the symbol of the deadly mother and in so doing carries himself to the grave, from which he will rise again after three days—all these images express the same fundamental thought: that Christ is a divinity who is eaten in the Lord's Supper. His death transforms him into bread and wine, which we relish as mystical food.[57] The relation of Agni to the soma-drink and of Dionysus to the wine [58] should not pass without mention here. Another parallel is Samson's strangling of the lion, and the subsequent inhabitation of the dead lion by a swarm of bees, which gave rise to the riddle: "Out of the eater came forth meat, and out of the strong came forth sweetness." [59] These ideas seem to have played a role in the Eleusinian mysteries, too. (Cf. also pl. ivb.) Besides Demeter

---

[56] The carrying of the tree ($\theta\alpha\lambda\lambda o\phi o\rho\iota a$), as we know from Strabo, played an important part in the cults of Dionysus and Ceres (Demeter).

[57] A Pyramid text dealing with the arrival of the dead Pharaoh in heaven describes how he overpowers the gods in order to assimilate their divine nature and become their lord. "His servants have caught the gods with lassoes, and have taken them and dragged them away, they have bound them, they have cut their throats and taken out their entrails, they have cut them up and cooked them in hot cooking-pots. And the king consumes their strength and eats their souls. He devours the great gods for breakfast, the middle gods for dinner, and the little gods for supper . . . The king devours everything that comes his way. He consumes all things in his greed, and his magic power becomes greater than all magic power. He becomes an heir of power greater than all heirs, he becomes the lord of heaven, he eats all the crowns and bracelets, he eats the wisdom of all the gods." (Wiedemann, in *Der Alte Orient*, II (1900), p. 50; i.e., no. 2, p. 18.) This ravenous hunger ($\beta o\upsilon\lambda\iota\mu\iota a$) aptly describes man's repressive instinctuality at the stage where the parents have a predominantly nutritive significance.

[58] The sacrifice of Dionysus-Zagreus and the eating of the sacrificial meat produced the $\nu\epsilon o s \Delta\iota\delta\nu\upsilon\sigma o s$, the resurrection of the god, as is apparent from the Cretan fragment of Euripides quoted by Dieterich (*Mithrasliturgie*, p. 105):

ἀγνὸν δὲ βίον τείνων, ἐξ οὗ
Διὸς Ἰδαίου μύστης γενόμην
καὶ νυκτιπόλου Ζαγρέως βούτας
τοὺς ὠμοφάγους δαῖτας τελέσας.

(Leading a holy life since I have been initiated into the mysteries of Idaean Zeus, and have eaten raw the flesh of Zagreus, the night-roaming shepherd.) Through eating the raw flesh the initiates assimilated the essence of the god. Cf. the Mexican rite of Teoqualo, "god-eating," in my "Transformation Symbolism in the Mass," pars. 339ff. [59] Judges 14 : 14.

and Persephone, Iacchus was one of the chief gods in the Eleusinian cult; he was a *puer aeternus,* the eternal boy, whom Ovid apostrophizes as follows:

For thine is unending youth, eternal boyhood: thou art the most lovely in the lofty sky; thy face is virgin-seeming, if without horns thou stand before us.[60]

527   The image of Iacchus was carried at the head of the great Eleusinian procession. It is not easy to say exactly what god Iacchus is, but he was probably a boy or a new-born son, similar perhaps to the Etruscan Tages, who bore the epithet "the fresh-ploughed boy," because, according to legend, he sprang out of a furrow behind a peasant ploughing his fields. This image illustrates the Mondamin motif very clearly: the plough has a well-known phallic meaning (cf. fig. 15), and the furrow, as in India, stands for woman. Psychologically this image is a symbolical equivalent of copulation, the son being the edible fruit of the field. The lexicographers called him "Demeter's daimon." He was identified with Dionysus, especially with the Thracian Dionysus-Zagreus, who is supposed to have undergone the typical fate of being reborn. Hera, we are told, had stirred up the Titans against Zagreus, who tried to escape them by changing into various shapes. In the end they caught him when he had taken on the form of a bull. They then killed him, cut him in pieces, and threw the pieces into a cauldron; but Zeus slew the Titans with a thunderbolt and swallowed the still-throbbing heart of Zagreus. In this manner he was regenerated, and Zagreus stepped forth again as Iacchus.

528   Another thing carried in the Eleusinian procession was the winnowing-basket (cf. also pl. ivb), the cradle of Iacchus (λίκνον, *mystica vannus Iacchi*). The Orphic legend[61] relates that Iacchus was reared by Persephone in the underworld, where, after slumbering for three years, he awoke in the λίκνον. The 20th of Boedromion (the month of Boedromion lasted from about September 5 to October 5) was called Iacchus, in honour of the hero. On the evening of this day a great torchlight pro-

---

[60] *Metamorphoses,* IV, 18–20, trans. by Miller, I, p. 181.
[61] Orphic Hymn 46, trans. by Taylor, p. 100. Cf. Roscher, *Lexikon,* s.v. "Iakchos."

cession was held on the sea-shore, where the search and lament of Demeter were re-enacted. The part of Demeter, who, abstaining from food and drink, wanders over the face of the earth seeking her lost daughter, has, in the American Indian epic, been taken over by Hiawatha. He turns to all creatures, but receives no answer. Just as Demeter first gets news of her daughter from the moon-goddess Hecate, so Hiawatha only finds the one he is looking for—Mondamin [62]—through profound introversion, by a descent into the darkness of night, to the Mothers. As to the content of the mysteries, we have the following testimony from Bishop Asterius (c. A.D. 390): "Is not there [in Eleusis] the dark descent, and is not the solemn communion of hierophant and priestess between him and her alone? Are not the torches doused, and does not the great multitude see their salvation in that which is consummated by the two in the darkness?" [63] This clearly points to a *hieros gamos* which was celebrated underground. The priestess of Demeter seems to have represented the earth-goddess, or possibly the ploughed furrow.[64] The descent into the earth is a piece of womb symbolism and was widespread in the form of cave worship. Plutarch says that the Magi offered sacrifices to Ahriman "in a sunless place." [65] In Lucian, the magician Mithrobarzanes descends into the bowels of the earth "at a desolate spot, marshy and sunless." [66] According to the testimony of Moses of Chorene, the Armenians worshipped "Sister Fire" and "Brother Spring" in a cave. Julian records the Attis legend of a "descent into the

---

62 An exact parallel is the legend of Izanagi, the Japanese Orpheus, who followed his dead wife down to the underworld and begged her to return with him. She was willing to do so but besought him not to look at her. Izanagi then made a light with one of the "masculine" prongs of his comb and immediately lost his wife. (Frobenius, *Zeitalter*, p. 343.) For "wife" read "mother," "anima," "unconscious." Instead of the mother, the hero brings back fire, just as Hiawatha produced the corn, Odin the runes, etc.

63 Cited from De Jong, *Das antike Mysterienwesen*, p. 22. [For Asterius, bishop of Amasea, see his *Homilia X in sanctos martyres*, in Migne, *P.G.*, vol. 40, 323–24.—EDITORS.]

64 A son-lover from the Demeter myth was Iasion, who lay with Demeter on a thrice-ploughed cornfield, and was struck with lightning by Zeus. (Ovid, *Metamorphoses*, IX.)

65 εἰς τόπον ἀνήλιον.—*De Iside et Osiride*, 369. [Cf. Babbitt trans., V, p. 113.]

66 εἰς χωρίον ἔρημον καὶ ὑλῶδες καὶ ἀνήλιον.—*Menippus*. [Cf. Harman trans., IV, p. 89.]

cave," from which Cybele brings back her son-lover.[67] The cave where Christ was born in Bethlehem ("The House of Bread") is said to have been an Attis spelaeum.

529   A further piece of Eleusinian symbolism relating to the celebration of the *hieros gamos* is the mysterious baskets (pl. LVIIa), which, according to the testimony of Clement of Alexandria, contained pastries, salt-offerings, and fruit. But the *synthema* (confession) of the neophyte, as handed down by Clement, points to other things besides:

I have fasted, I have drunk the mixed drink, I have taken from the cista, and after working with it I have laid it back in the basket and from the basket into the cista.[68]

530   The question of what was in the cista has been elucidated by Dieterich.[69] The "working" he interprets as some phallic activity which the neophyte had to perform. And there are in fact representations of the magic basket with a phallus lying in it surrounded by fruits.[70] On the so-called Lovatelli funeral urn, carved with scenes supposedly taken from the Eleusinian mysteries, there is a picture of a neophyte fondling the snake entwined about Demeter. The fondling or kissing of the "fear-animal" symbolizes the ceremonial conquest of incest. According to Clement of Alexandria, there was a snake in the mystical basket.[71] This snake signifies the danger that comes from the regressive movement of libido. Rohde [72] mentions that, at the Arrhetophoria festival, pastries shaped like phalli and serpents were thrown into a pit near the Thesmophorion, to invoke the blessing of children and good harvests.[73] The snake

---

[67] κατάβασις εἰς ἄντρον.—Oratio V. [Cf. Wright trans., I, p. 463.] Here cited from Cumont, *Textes*, I, p. 56.

[68] *Protrepticus*. [Cf. the Wilson trans., I, p. 13.] Ἐνήστευσα, ἔπιον τὸν κυκεῶνα, ἔλαβον ἐκ κίστης, ἐργασάμενος ἀπεθέμην εἰς κάλαθον καὶ ἐκ καλάθου εἰς κίστην.   Instead of ἐργασάμενος Lobeck suggests ἐγγευσάμενος, 'after I have tasted.' Dieterich (*Mithrasliturgie*, p. 125) keeps to the traditional reading.

[69] Dieterich, pp. 123ff.

[70] As, for instance, in a Campana bas-relief in Caetani-Lovatelli, *Antichi monumenti*, Pl. IV, fig. 5. [The "Lovatelli urn" is described and depicted, also, in this work.—EDITORS.] Similarly, the Verona Priapus holds a basket filled with phalli. (Cf. pl. LXIb.)   [71] Wilson trans., I, p. 17.   [72] "ΣΚΙΡΑ," p. 124.

[73] The mother is the giver of nourishment. St. Dominic was nourished at the breasts of the mother of God, and so was the adept in alchemy. The sun-woman of the Namaquas, of South Africa, is made of bacon-fat. Cf. the megalomaniac

also played a large part in the initiation ceremonies, under the strange title "ὁ διὰ χόλπου θεός" (the god through the lap). Clement says that the symbol of the Sabazius mysteries was "The god through the lap: and that is a snake which is dragged through the laps of the initiates." [74] From Arnobius we learn: "A golden snake is let down into the lap of the initiates and is drawn out again from below." [75] In the 52nd Orphic hymn, Bacchus is invoked by the name of ὑποκόλπιε (lying in the lap), which suggests that the god entered his devotees as if through the female genitals.[76] At the Eleusinian mysteries the hierophant proclaimed in a loud voice: "The great goddess has borne a divine boy, Brimo has borne Brimos!" [77] This Christmas message "Unto us a son is born" is further elucidated by the tradition [78] that the Athenians "silently held up before the celebrants the great, the wonderful, the supreme epoptic mystery—a mown ear of corn." [79] (Cf. pl. iv*b*.)

531   The parallel to the motif of dying and rising again is that of being lost and found again. It appears ritually at exactly the same place, in connection with the *hieros-gamos*-like spring festivities, where the image of the god was hidden and then found again. There is an uncanonical tradition that Moses left his father's house at the age of twelve in order to instruct man-

---

ideas of my patient: "I am Germania and Helvetia made of exclusively sweet butter" ("Psychology of Dementia Praecox," par. 201).

74 *Protrepticus*, II, 16. Cited in Dieterich, p. 123. (ὁ διὰ κόλπου θεός, δράκων δέ ἐστι καὶ οὗτος διελκόμενος τοῦ κόλπου τῶν τελουμένων.)

75 *Adversus Gentes*, V, 21. ("aureus coluber in sinum demittitur consecratis et eximitur rursus ab inferioribus partibus atque imis.") [Cf. Bryce and Campbell trans., p. 244.]

76 Cf. Nietzsche's images: "thyself pierced through," "working in thine own pit," etc. [pars. 446 and 459, above]. A prayer to Hermes in a papyrus says: ἐλθέ μοι, κύριε Ἑρμῆ, ὡς τὰ βρέφη εἰς τὰς κοιλίας τῶν γυναικῶν (Come to me, O Hermes, as children come into the womb of women).—Kenyon, *Greek Papyri in the British Museum*, I, p. 116: Pap. CXXII, ll. 2ff.; cited in Dieterich, p. 97.

77 ἔτεκε πότνια κοῦρον, Βριμὼ Βριμόν.—Brimo = Demeter. Jupiter is said to have had intercourse with his mother Deo (Demeter) in the form of a bull. This made the goddess so furious that, to pacify her, he pretended to castrate himself. Roscher, *Lexikon*, IV, s.v. "Sabazios," 253, 5.

78 De Jong, *Das antike Mysterienwesen*, p. 22.

79 The corn-god of antiquity was Adonis, whose death and resurrection were celebrated annually. He was the son-lover of the mother, for the corn is the son and fructifier of the earth's womb, as Robertson (*Christianity and Mythology*, p. 318) has already pointed out.

kind. Similarly, Christ was lost by his parents, and they found him teaching wisdom in the temple, just as in the Mohammedan legend Moses and Joshua lose the fish and find in its stead Khidr, the teacher of wisdom. So, too, does the corn-god, lost and believed dead, suddenly spring from the earth in the splendour of youth.

532   We can see from these accounts how comforting the Eleusinian mysteries were for the celebrant's hopes of a world to come. One epitaph says:

> Truly the blessed gods have proclaimed a most beautiful secret:
> Death comes not as a curse, but as a blessing to men!

533   The Homeric hymn to Demeter says the same thing of the mysteries:

> Happy is he among men upon earth who has seen these mysteries; but he who is uninitiate and has no part in them, never has lot of like good things once he is dead, down in the darkness and gloom.[80]

534   And we find the same symbolism in a nineteenth-century hymn by Samuel Preiswerk:

> The world is yours, Lord Jesus,
> The world, on which we stand,
> Because it is thy world
> It cannot perish.
> Only the wheat, before it comes
> Up to the light in its fertility,
> Must die in the womb of the earth
> First freed from its own nature.
> Thou goest, O Lord, our chief,
> To heaven through thy sorrows,
> And guide him who believes
> In thee on the same path.
> Then take us all equally
> To share in thy sorrows and kingdom,
> Guide us through thy gate of death,
> Bring thy world into the light.[81]

535   Firmicus says of the Attis mystery:

> On a certain night the image is laid on its back in a litter, and the people bewail it with rhythmical laments. And when they have had

80 Trans. by Evelyn-White, p. 323.
81 [As trans. in the Hinkle edn. (1916), p. 378.]

their fill of this pretended lamentation, a light is brought in. Then the priest anoints the throats of all who wept, and this having been done, the priest whispers softly: "Take courage, ye initiates, for the god is saved, and you too shall have salvation out of sorrow." [82]

536   These parallels show how little there is of the human and personal in the Christ-image, and how strong is the universal and mythological element. The hero is an extraordinary being who is inhabited by a daemon, and it is this that makes him a hero. That is why the mythological statements about heroes are so typical and so impersonal. Christ was a divine being, as the early Christian interpretation tells us at first hand. All over the earth, in the most various forms, each with a different time-colouring, the saviour-hero appears as a fruit of the entry of libido into the maternal depths of the unconscious. The Bacchic consecrations depicted on the Farnese stucco-relief contain a scene in which a neophyte, wrapped in a mantle drawn over his head, is being led before Silenus, who holds the λίκνον, which is covered with a cloth. The covering of the head signifies invisibility, that is, death.[83] Among the Nandi, of East Africa, the newly-circumcised, the initiates, have to go about for a long time dressed in queer cone-shaped grass hats, which envelop them completely and reach to the ground. The circumcised have become invisible, i.e., spirits. The veil has the same significance among nuns. The neophyte dies like the seed-corn, springs up again and gets into the winnowing-basket. Proclus reports that the neophytes were buried in the ground up to their necks.[84] The Church is, in a sense, the hero's grave (cf. the catacombs). The believer descends into the grave in order to rise again from the dead with the hero. It can scarcely be doubted that the underlying meaning of the Church is the mother's womb. The Tantric texts interpret the interior of the temple as the interior of the body, and the *adyton* is called "garbha griha," the seeding-place or uterus. We can see this quite plainly in the worship of the Holy Sepulchre, a good

---

82 ("Nocte quadam simulacrum in lectica supinum ponitur, et per numeros digestis fletibus plangitur; deinde cum se ficta lamentatione satiaverint, lumen infertur: tunc a sacerdote omnium qui flebant fauces unguentur, quibus peruncti sacerdos hoc lento murmure susurrat: Θαρρεῖτε μύσται τοῦ θεοῦ σεσωσμένου, ἔσται γὰρ ἡμῖν ἐκ πόνων σωτηρία").—*De errore profanarum religionum*, XXII, I, p. 57.
83 Dieterich, p. 167.   84 Ibid.

example being the Holy Sepulchre of San Stefano in Bologna. The church itself, an extremely ancient polygonal building, was built from the remains of a temple to Isis. Inside, there is an artificial spelaeum, known as the Holy Sepulchre, into which one creeps through a tiny door. Worshippers in such a spelaeum could hardly help identifying themselves with him who died and rose again, i.e., with the reborn. Similar initiations seem to have been performed in the neolithic caves of Hal Saflieni in Malta. An Etruscan ossuary in the archaeological museum at Florence serves at the same time as a statue of Matuta (pl. LIV), the goddess of death: the clay figure of the goddess is hollowed out inside as a receptacle for ashes. It is clear from the accompanying illustration that Matuta is the mother. Her chair is adorned with sphinxes, a fitting symbol of the mother of death. (Cf. the Oedipus myth.)

537 Of the further deeds of Hiawatha only a few can interest us here. The battle with Mishe-Nahma, the fish-king, in the eighth canto, deserves mention as a typical battle of the sun-hero. Mishe-Nahma is a monster fish who lives at the bottom of the waters. Challenged to battle by Hiawatha, he swallows the hero together with his boat:

> In his wrath he darted upward,
> Flashing leaped into the sunshine,
> Opened his great jaws, and swallowed
> Both canoe and Hiawatha.
>
> Down into that darksome cavern
> Plunged the headlong Hiawatha,
> As a log on some black river
> Shoots and plunges down the rapids,
> Found himself in utter darkness,
> Groped about in helpless wonder,
> Till he felt a great heart beating,
> Throbbing in that utter darkness.
>
> And he smote it in his anger,
> With his fist, the heart of Nahma,
> Felt the mighty king of fishes
> Shudder through each nerve and fibre . . .
> Crosswise then did Hiawatha
> Drag his birch-canoe for safety,

> Lest from out the jaws of Nahma,
> In the turmoil and confusion,
> Forth he might be hurled and perish.

538   This is the almost worldwide myth of the typical deed of the hero. He journeys by ship, fights the sea monster, is swallowed, struggles against being bitten and crushed to death (kicking or stamping motif), and having arrived inside the "whale-dragon," seeks the vital organ, which he proceeds to cut off or otherwise destroy. Often the monster is killed by the hero lighting a fire inside him—that is to say, in the very womb of death he secretly creates life, the rising sun. Thus the fish dies and drifts to land, where with the help of a bird the hero once more sees the light of day.[85] The bird probably signifies the renewed ascent of the

[85] As an example, I will quote here the Polynesian myth of Rata (Frobenius, *Zeitalter*, pp. 64–66): "The boat was sailing along merrily over the ocean under a favourable wind, when one day Nganaoa called out: 'O Rata! A fearful enemy is rising up from the sea!' It was a giant clam, wide open. One of its shells was in front of the boat, the other behind, and the vessel lay in between. The next moment the horrible clam would have snapped shut and ground the boat and all its occupants to pulp. But Nganaoa was prepared for this possibility. Seizing his long spear, he thrust it quickly into the creature's belly, so that instead of snapping shut it sank instantly to the bottom of the sea. After escaping from this danger they continued on their way. Yet soon the voice of the ever watchful Nganaoa was heard again: 'O Rata! Another fearful enemy is rising up from the sea!' This time it was a mighty octopus, whose giant tentacles were already wrapped round the boat to destroy it. At this critical moment Nganaoa seized his spear and plunged it into the head of the octopus. The tentacles sank down limply, and the dead monster floated away on the surface of the ocean. Once more they continued on their journey, but a still greater danger awaited them. One day the valiant Nganaoa cried out: 'O Rata! Here is a great whale!' Its huge jaws were wide open, the lower jaw was already under the boat, the upper one was over it. Another moment and the whale would have swallowed them. Then Nganaoa, the 'slayer of monsters,' broke his spear in two, and just as the whale was about to crush them he stuck the two pieces in his enemy's gullet, so that he could not close his jaws. Then Nganaoa leapt into the maw of the great whale (devouring of the hero) and peered down into his belly, and what did he see? There sat his two parents, his father Tairitokerau and his mother Vaiaroa, who had been swallowed by this monster of the deep when out fishing. The oracle had come true. The voyage had reached its goal. Great was the joy of the parents of Nganaoa when they beheld their son, for they were now persuaded that their liberation was at hand. And Nganaoa, too, was bent upon vengeance. Taking one of the two sticks from the animal's gullet—the other was enough to prevent the whale from closing his jaws and to keep the passage clear for Nganaoa and his parents—he broke it into two pieces for use as fire-sticks. He told his father to

sun, the rebirth of the phoenix, and is at the same time one of those "helpful animals" who render supernatural aid during the birth: birds, as aerial beings, symbolize spirits or angels. Divine messengers frequently appear at these mythological births, as can be seen from the use we still make of *god-parents*. The sun-symbol of the bird rising from the water is preserved etymologically in the idea of the singing swan. "Swan" derives from the root *sven,* like 'sun' and "sound." [86] This ascent signifies rebirth, the bringing forth of life from the mother,[87] and the ultimate conquest of death, which, according to an African Negro myth, came into the world through the carelessness of one old woman: when the season of universal skin-casting came round again (for in those days people renewed themselves by casting their skins like snakes), she was absent-minded enough to put on her old skin instead of the new one, and in consequence died.

539   It is easy to see what the battle with the sea monster means: it is the attempt to free the ego-consciousness from the deadly grip of the unconscious. The making of a fire in the monster's belly suggests as much, for it is a piece of apotropaic magic aimed at dispelling the darkness of unconsciousness. The rescue of the hero is at the same time a sunrise, the triumph of consciousness. (Cf. fig. 33.)

540   Unfortunately, however, this heroic deed has no lasting effects. Again and again the hero must renew the struggle, and always under the symbol of deliverance from the mother. Just as Hera, in her role of the pursuing mother, is the real source of the mighty deeds performed by Heracles, so Nokomis allows Hiawatha no rest, but piles up new difficulties in his path,

---

hold one piece firmly below, while he himself manipulated the upper one until the fire began to glimmer (fire-lighting). Then, blowing it into a flame, he hastened to heat the fatty parts inside the belly (i.e., the heart) with the fire. The monster, writhing with pain, sought relief by swimming to land (sea journey). As soon as it reached the sandbank (landing), father, mother and son stepped ashore through the open gullet of the dying whale (slipping out of the hero)." See diagram on p. 210.   86 [Cf. par. 235, above.]

87 In the Maori myth of Maui (Frobenius, pp. 66ff.) the monster to be overcome is Grandmother Hine-nui-te-po. Maui, the hero, says to the birds who help him: "My little friends, when I creep into the jaws of the old woman, you must not laugh, but once I have been in and have come out of her mouth again, you may welcome me with shouts of laughter." Then Maui creeps into the mouth of the old woman as she sleeps.

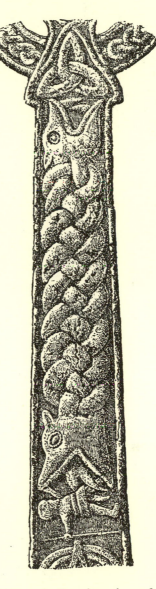

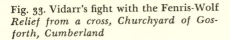
Fig. 33. Vidarr's fight with the Fenris-Wolf
Relief from a cross, Churchyard of Gos-forth, Cumberland

hazardous adventures in which the hero may be victorious, but may also meet with his death. Man with his consciousness is always a long way behind the goals of the unconscious; unless his libido calls him forth to new dangers he sinks into slothful inactivity, or in the prime of life he is overcome with longing for the past and is paralysed. But if he rouses himself and follows the

349

dangerous urge to do the forbidden and apparently impossible thing, then he must either go under or become a hero. The mother is thus the daemon who challenges the hero to his deeds and lays in his path the poisonous serpent that will strike him. Accordingly Nokomis, in the ninth canto, calls Hiawatha, points with her hand to the West, where the sun sets in purple splendour, and says to him:

> Yonder dwells the great Pearl-Feather,
> Megissogwon, the Magician,
> Manito of Wealth and Wampum,
> Guarded by his fiery serpents,
> Guarded by the black pitch-water.
> You can see his fiery serpents . . .
> Coiling, playing in the water.

541   The danger that dwells in the West is death, whom none, not even the mightiest, escapes. The magician, we are told, had killed the father of Nokomis. Now she sends her son forth to avenge her father. From the symbols assigned to the magician we can see what he symbolizes. Snake and water are mother attributes. The snake coils protectingly round the maternal rock, lives in the cave, twines itself round the mother-tree, and guards the precious hoard, the secret "treasure." The black Stygian water, like the muddy spring of Dhulqarnein, is the place where the sun sinks down for rebirth, the maternal sea of death and night. On his journey thither Hiawatha takes with him the magic oil of Mishe-Nahma, which helps his canoe through the waters of death (hence it is an immortality philtre, as was the dragon's blood for Siegfried). Thus Hiawatha makes the "night sea journey" over the Stygian waters:

> All night long he sailed upon it,
> Sailed upon that sluggish water,
> Covered with its mould of ages,
> Black with rotting water-rushes,
> Rank with flags and leaves of lilies,
> Stagnant, lifeless, dreary, dismal,
> Lighted by the shimmering moonlight
> And by will-o'-the-wisps illumined,
> Fires by ghosts of dead men kindled
> In their weary night encampments.

350

542   This description clearly shows that they are the waters of death. The rotting water-plants point to the entwining and devouring motif already mentioned. The dream-book of Jagaddeva [88] says: "Whoever dreams that his body is wrapped round with bast, creepers or cords, with snake-skins, threads or webs, will certainly die."

543   There is no doubt that the above description refers to the realm of the Terrible Mother, represented in this case by the magician, a negative father-figure, or by a masculine principle in the mother herself, just as the secret *spiritus rector* who impels Hiawatha to his task is represented by Nokomis, the mother, who is a feminine principle in the breast of the hero. The latter is Hiawatha's anima, and the former would correspond to the animus of the Terrible Mother.

544   Arrived in the Western Land, the hero challenges the magician to battle, and a terrible struggle begins. Hiawatha is powerless because Megissogwon is invulnerable. In the evening Hiawatha, wounded and despairing, retires for a short rest:

> Paused to rest beneath a pine-tree,
> From whose branches trailed the mosses,
> And whose trunk was coated over
> With the Dead Man's Moccasin-leather,
> With the fungus white and yellow.

545   This sheltering tree is described as "coated" with fungus. Tree-anthropomorphism is an important factor wherever tree-worship prevails, as for instance in India, where every village has its sacred tree (pl. LV), which is clothed and treated exactly like a human being. The trees are anointed with sweet-smelling waters, sprinkled with powder, adorned with garlands and draperies. And just as the people pierce their ears as an apotropaic charm against death, so they pierce the sacred tree. "Of all the trees in India there is none more sacred to the Hindus than the peepul or aswatha (*Ficus religiosa*). It is known to them as Vriksha Raja (king of trees). Brahma, Vishnu, and Maheswar live in it, and the worship of it is the worship of the Triad. Almost every Indian village has an aswatha." [89]

546   This well-known "village linden-tree" is clearly character-

88 Negelein, ed., *Der Traumschlüssel des Jaggadeva*, p. 256.
89 Cited from Negelein, p. 256.

ized as a mother-symbol: it contains the three gods. So when Hiawatha retires to rest under the pine-tree,[90] he is taking a dangerous step, for he is seeking refuge with the mother whose garment is the garment of death. As in the battle with the whale-dragon, so here the hero needs the help of a bird, of one of those helpful animals who represent the stirrings or intuitions of the unconscious, the helpful mother:

> Suddenly from the boughs above him
> Sang the Mama, the woodpecker:
> Aim your arrows, Hiawatha,
> At the head of Megissogwon,
> Strike the tuft of hair upon it,
> At their roots the long black tresses;
> There alone can he be wounded!

547   So "Mama"—an amusing touch this, one must own—hastens to his aid. Oddly enough, the woodpecker also happened to be the "mama" of Romulus and Remus, for he put food into their mouths with his beak.[91] The woodpecker owes his special significance to the fact that he hammers holes in trees. Hence we can understand why he was honoured in Roman legend as an ancient king of the country, who was the possessor or ruler of the sacred tree, and the prototype of the *pater familias*. An old fable relates that Circe, the wife of king Picus, changed him into *Picus martius,* the woodpecker. She killed and magically transformed him into a soul-bird. Picus was also regarded as a wood demon and incubus,[92] and a soothsayer.[93] He was sometimes equated with Picumnus, the inseparable companion of Pilumnus, both of whom were called *infantium dii,* 'gods of small children.' Pilumnus especially was said to protect new-born infants from the wicked attacks of the wood-imp Sylvanus. This helpful little bird now counsels our hero to aim under the

[90] It is the pine-tree that speaks the significant word "Minne-wawa!"
[91] In the story of Cinderella, the helpful bird appears on the tree that grows out of her mother's grave.
[92] Roscher, *Lexikon,* s.v. "Picus," III, 2, 2496, 30.
[93] The father of Picus was called Sterculus or Sterculius, a name which is obviously derived from *stercus,* 'excrement.' He is also said to have invented manure. The original Creator who fashioned the mother did so in the infantile manner, as we saw earlier. This supreme god laid an egg, his mother, from which he hatched himself out. Excrement in alchemy signifies the *prima materia.*

magician's topknot, the only vulnerable spot. It is situated on the crown of the head, at the point where the mythical "head-birth" takes place, which even today figures among the birth-theories of children. There Hiawatha shoots in three arrows [94] and so makes an end of Megissogwon. He then steals the magic belt of wampum which makes him invisible; the dead magician he leaves lying in the water:

> On the shore he left the body,
> Half on land and half in water,
> In the sand his feet were buried,
> And his face was in the water.

548 The situation is therefore the same as with the fish-king, for the magician is the personification of the water of death, which in its turn stands for the devouring mother. This great deed of Hiawatha's, when he conquers the Terrible Mother and death-bringing daemon in the guise of the negative father, is followed by his marriage with Minnehaha. He can only turn to his human side after he has fulfilled his heroic destiny: firstly the transformation of the daemon from an uncontrolled force of nature into a power that is his to command; secondly the final deliverance of ego-consciousness from the deadly threat of the unconscious in the form of the negative parents. The first task signifies the creation of will-power, the second the free use of it.

549 We might mention, from a later canto (the twelfth), a little fable which the poet has interpolated: an old man is changed back into a youth by crawling through a hollow oak-tree.[95] The fourteenth canto describes how Hiawatha invents writing. I must confine myself here to the description of two hieroglyphs:

> Gitche Manito the Mighty,
> He, the Master of Life, was painted

---

94 Spielrein's patient received three arrow wounds from God, through her head, breast, and eye, "then came a resurrection of the spirit" (p. 376). In the Tibetan legend of Bogda Gesser Khan, the sun-hero shoots his arrow into the forehead of the demoniacal old woman, who then eats him and spits him out again. In a legend of the Kalmucks, from Siberia, the hero shoots the arrow into the "bull's-eye" that grows on the bull's forehead and "emits rays."

95 This is synonymous with entering into the mother, becoming immersed in oneself, crawling through something, boring, picking the ear, driving in nails, swallowing snakes, etc.

> As an egg, with points projecting
> To the four winds of the heavens.
> Everywhere is the Great Spirit,
> Was the meaning of this symbol.

550   The world is enclosed in the egg (cf. fig. 36) which surrounds it on all sides; it is the cosmic birth-giver, a symbol used by Plato and by the Vedas. This "mother" is omnipresent, like the air. But air is spirit, so the world-mother is a spirit, the *anima mundi*. The hieroglyph is at the same time a quaternity-symbol, which psychologically always points to the self.[96] It therefore depicts the uttermost circumference and the innermost centre, the infinite and the infinitesimal, corresponding to the Indian idea of the atman, which encompasses the whole world and dwells, "no bigger than a thumb," in the heart of man. The second hieroglyph is as follows:

> Mitche Manito the Mighty,
> He the dreadful Spirit of Evil,
> As a serpent was depicted,
> As Kenabeek, the great serpent.

551   The spirit of evil is fear, negation, the adversary who opposes life in its struggle for eternal duration and thwarts every great deed, who infuses into the body the poison of weakness and age through the treacherous bite of the serpent; he is the spirit of regression, who threatens us with bondage to the mother and with dissolution and extinction in the unconscious. (Cf. fig. 35 and pl. LXII.) For the hero, fear is a challenge and a task, because only boldness can deliver from fear. And if the risk is not taken, the meaning of life is somehow violated, and the whole future is condemned to hopeless staleness, to a drab grey lit only by will-o'-the-wisps.

552   The fifteenth canto describes how Chibiabos, Hiawatha's best friend, the amiable player and singer, the incarnation of all life's joys, was enticed into an ambush by evil spirits, fell through the ice, and was drowned. Hiawatha mourned him so long that, with the help of magicians, he succeeded in calling him back again. But he comes back only as a spirit, and is made master of the Land of Spirits. More battles follow, and then comes the loss of a second friend, Kwasind, the embodiment of

[96] Cf. "Psychology and Religion," par. 97.

354

physical strength. These events are omens of the end, like the
death of Eabani in the Gilgamesh Epic. In the twentieth canto
comes the famine, followed by the death of Minnehaha, which
is foretold by two taciturn guests from the Land of the Dead;
and in the twenty-second canto Hiawatha prepares for the final
journey to the Western Land:

> I am going, O Nokomis,
> On a long and distant journey,
> To the portals of the Sunset,
> To the regions of the home-wind,
> Of the Northwest Wind, Keewaydin.
>
> One long track and trail of splendour,
> Down whose stream, as down a river,
> Westward, westward, Hiawatha
> Sailed into the fiery sunset,
> Sailed into the purple vapours,
> Sailed into the dusk of evening.
>
> Thus departed Hiawatha,
> Hiawatha the Beloved,
> In the glory of the sunset,
> In the purple mists of evening,
> To the regions of the home-wind,
> Of the Northwest Wind, Keewaydin,
> To the Islands of the Blessed,
> To the kingdom of Ponemah,
> To the land of the Hereafter!

553   The sun, rising triumphant, tears himself from the enveloping womb of the sea, and leaving behind him the noonday
zenith and all its glorious works, sinks down again into the
maternal depths, into all-enfolding and all-regenerating night.
(Cf. figs. 3, 24.) This image is undoubtedly a primordial one,
and there was profound justification for its becoming a symbolical expression of human fate: in the morning of life the son
tears himself loose from the mother, from the domestic hearth,
to rise through battle to his destined heights. Always he imagines his worst enemy in front of him, yet he carries the enemy
within himself—a deadly longing for the abyss, a longing to
drown in his own source, to be sucked down to the realm of
the Mothers. His life is a constant struggle against extinction, a
violent yet fleeting deliverance from ever-lurking night. This

death is no external enemy, it is his own inner longing for the stillness and profound peace of all-knowing non-existence, for all-seeing sleep in the ocean of coming-to-be and passing away. Even in his highest strivings for harmony and balance, for the profundities of philosophy and the raptures of the artist, he seeks death, immobility, satiety, rest. If, like Peirithous, he tarries too long in this abode of rest and peace, he is overcome by apathy, and the poison of the serpent paralyses him for all time. If he is to live, he must fight and sacrifice his longing for the past in order to rise to his own heights. And having reached the noonday heights, he must sacrifice his love for his own achievement, for he may not loiter. The sun, too, sacrifices its greatest strength in order to hasten onward to the fruits of autumn, which are the seeds of rebirth. The natural course of life demands that the young person should sacrifice his childhood and his childish dependence on the physical parents, lest he remain caught body and soul in the bonds of unconscious incest. This regressive tendency has been consistently opposed from the most primitive times by the great psychotherapeutic systems which we know as the religions. They seek to create an autonomous consciousness by weaning mankind away from the sleep of childhood. The sun breaks from the mists of the horizon and climbs to undimmed brightness at the meridian.[97] Once this goal is reached, it sinks down again towards night. This process can be allegorized as a gradual seeping away of the water of life: one has to bend ever deeper to reach the source. When we are feeling on top of the world we find this exceedingly disagreeable; we resist the sunset tendency, especially when we suspect that there is something in ourselves which would like to follow this movement, for behind it we sense nothing good, only an obscure, hateful threat. So, as soon as we feel ourselves slipping, we begin to combat this tendency and erect barriers against the dark, rising flood of the unconscious and its enticements to regression, which all too easily takes on the deceptive guise of sacrosanct ideals, principles, beliefs, etc. If we wish to stay on the heights we have reached, we must struggle all the time to consolidate our consciousness and its attitude. But we soon discover that this praiseworthy and apparently unavoid-

---

[97] Cf. the Μεσουράνισμα ἡλίου, position of the sun at midday as symbol of the initiate's illumination, in "The Visions of Zosimos," pars. 86 and 95.

able battle with the years leads to stagnation and desiccation of soul. Our convictions become platitudes ground out on a barrel-organ, our ideals become starchy habits, enthusiasm stiffens into automatic gestures. The source of the water of life seeps away. We ourselves may not notice it, but everybody else does, and that is even more painful. If we should risk a little introspection, coupled perhaps with an energetic attempt to be honest for once with ourselves, we may get a dim idea of all the wants, longings, and fears that have accumulated down there—a repulsive and sinister sight. The mind shies away, but life wants to flow down into the depths. Fate itself seems to preserve us from this, because each of us has a tendency to become an immovable pillar of the past. Nevertheless, the daemon throws us down, makes us traitors to our ideals and cherished convictions—traitors to the selves we thought we were. That is an unmitigated catastrophe, because it is an *unwilling* sacrifice. Things go very differently when the sacrifice is a voluntary one. Then it is no longer an overthrow, a "transvaluation of values," the destruction of all that we held sacred, but transformation and conservation. Everything young grows old, all beauty fades, all heat cools, all brightness dims, and every truth becomes stale and trite. For all these things have taken on shape, and all shapes are worn thin by the working of time; they age, sicken, crumble to dust—unless they change. But change they can, for the invisible spark that generated them is potent enough for infinite generation. No one should deny the danger of the descent, but it *can* be risked. No one *need* risk it, but it is certain that some one will. And let those who go down the sunset way do so with open eyes, for it is a sacrifice which daunts even the gods. Yet every descent is followed by an ascent; the vanishing shapes are shaped anew, and a truth is valid in the end only if it suffers change and bears new witness in new images, in new tongues, like a new wine that is put into new bottles.

554   *The Song of Hiawatha* contains material that is well suited to bring into play the vast potentialities for archetypal symbolization latent in the human mind and to stimulate the creation of images. But the products always contain the same old human problems, which rise up again and again in new symbolic guise from the shadowy world of the unconscious.

555   Thus it is that Chiwantopel puts Miss Miller in mind of

another hero, who makes his entry in the form of Wagner's Siegfried. Chiwantopel cries out in his monologue: "Alas! Not one who understands me, not one who resembles me or has a soul that is sister to mine." Miss Miller declares that the sentiments expressed in this passage have the greatest analogy with Siegfried's feelings for Brünhilde. This analogy prompts us to cast a glance at the relations between Siegfried and Brünhilde in Wagner. It is well known that Brünhilde, the Valkyrie, looked with favour on the brother-sister incest that gave birth to Siegfried. But whereas Sieglinde is the human mother, Brünhilde acts the part of the symbolic mother, the "spirit-mother" (mother-imago), not as a persecutor, like Hera with the infant Heracles, but as a helper. The sin of incest, of which she makes herself guilty by her complicity, is the reason for her banishment by Wotan. Siegfried's birth from the sister-wife characterizes him as a Horus, the reborn sun, a reincarnation of the aging sun-god. The birth of the young sun, the god-man, stems from human partners, but they are really only vehicles for cosmic symbols. The spirit-mother therefore lends it her protection; she sends Sieglinde forth, with the child in her womb,[98] on the night sea journey to the East:

> Away then, hasten;
> Turn to the East! . . .
> Woman, you cherish
> The noblest hero in the world
> In your sheltering womb! [99]

556   The motif of dismemberment recurs in the broken sword of Siegmund, which was kept for Siegfried. Life is put together again from the broken pieces (miracle of Medea). Just as a blacksmith welds the broken pieces together, so the dismembered corpse is reconstituted. This comparison also occurs in Plato's *Timaeus:* the world's parts are joined together with pegs. In the Rig-Veda the world creator Brahmanaspati is a blacksmith:

> This world Brahmanaspati
> Welded together like a blacksmith.[100]

[98] Cf. Mary's flight into Egypt, the persecution of Leto, etc.
[99] *Die Walküre*, li. 1782–83, 1792–94.
[100] Rig-Veda, X, 72, trans. from the German of Deussen, *Allgemeine Geschichte der Philosophie*, I, p. 145.

557   The sword denotes solar power, therefore a sword goes out from the mouth of Christ in the Apocalypse (cf. pl. v*b*), namely the procreative fire, speech, or the spermatic Word. In the Rig-Veda, Brahmanaspati is the prayer-word, which is accorded a pre-worldly, creative significance:

> And this prayer of the singer, continually expanding,
> Became a cow that was there before the beginning of the world.
> The gods are foster-children of the same brood,
> Dwelling together in the womb of this god.[101]

558   The Logos becomes a cow, i.e., a mother who bears the gods in her womb. The transformation of Logos into mother is not really surprising, since in the *Acts of Thomas* the Holy Ghost is addressed as the mother, and it is always the mother-imago which proves to be the hero's greatest danger but is for that very reason the prime source of his deeds and of his ascent. His ascent signifies a renewal of the light and hence a rebirth of consciousness from the darkness, i.e., from regression to the unconscious.

559   The persecution motif is not connected here with the mother, but with Wotan, as in the Linus legend, where the father is the vengeful pursuer. Brünhilde stands in a peculiar relation to her father Wotan. She says to him:

> You speak to the will of Wotan
> When you tell me what you wish.
> Who am I
> If I am not your will?

> WOTAN: I take counsel with myself alone
> When I speak with you . . .[102]

560   Brünhilde is a sort of "split-off" from Wotan, part of his personality, just as Pallas Athene was an emanation of Zeus. She is, as it were, Wotan's emissary or agent, and therefore corresponds to the angel of Yahweh, to the "eye of Ahura" or Vohu Manah, God's good thought in Persian legend, or to the Babylonian Nabu, the word of fate, or to Hermes, the messenger of the gods, whom the philosophers equated with Reason and Logos. In Assyria the role of Logos falls to the fire god, Gibil.

[101] Rig-Veda, X, 31, trans. from ibid., p. 140.
[102] *Die Walküre,* li. 900–903, 907–908.

That Wagner should have put the designs of so martial a god as Wotan into the hands of a feminine agent is somewhat remarkable, despite the Greek precedent of Pallas Athene. A very similar figure is the Kore in the *Acts of Thomas*, of whom Thomas sings:

Maiden, daughter of the light,
In whom there abides the majestic splendour of kings . . .
On the crown of her head the king is seated,
Feeding with his own ambrosia those seated beside him.
Truth rests upon her head . . .
Her tongue is like the curtain of a door
Which is drawn back for them who go in.
Her neck rises up like a stairway,
And the first builder of the world created it.
Her two hands signify and proclaim the dance of the blessed ages,
And her fingers the gates of the city . . .[103]

561   This maiden, according to the *Acts of Thomas*, is the "Mother of Wisdom." Conversely, the Holy Ghost is worshipped in feminine form in one of the Eucharistic prayers:

Come, thou that knowest the secrets of the chosen;
Come, thou that partakest in all the combats of the noble combatant . . .
Come, peace,
That revealest the great things of all greatness;
Come, thou that layest bare the hidden things,
And makest manifest things not to be spoken;
Come, holy dove,
Which hast brought forth the twin nestlings;
Come, secret mother . . .[104]

562   This Eucharistic feast is celebrated at a characteristic moment, immediately after Thomas had delivered a "beautiful woman" from an "unchaste demon" who had been plaguing her for years. This is probably no accident, because the therapeutic meaning of the hymn is the transformation of a sexual obsession into a recognition of the positive qualities of the feminine spirit.

563   In line with the *Acts of Thomas* is the Ophite view that the Holy Ghost is the "first word," the "Mother of All Living," and the Valentinian idea that the Third Person is the "Word ot

[103] Trans. by Walker, p. 392, modified.   [104] Ibid., p. 416, modified.

the Mother from Above." It is clear from all this that Wagner's Brünhilde is one of the numerous anima-figures who are attributed to masculine deities, and who without exception represent a dissociation in the masculine psyche—a "split-off" with a tendency to lead an obsessive existence of its own. This tendency to autonomy causes the anima to anticipate the thoughts and decisions of the masculine consciousness, with the result that the latter is constantly confronted with unlooked-for situations which it has apparently done nothing to provoke. Such is the situation of Wotan, and indeed of every hero who is unconscious of his own intriguing femininity.

564   Something of the sort must have been in Wagner's mind when he wrote Wotan's lament for Brünhilde:

> None knew as she my innermost thoughts;
> None knew as she the source of my will;
> She herself was
> The creating womb of my wish;
> And now she has broken
> That happy bond! [105]

565   Brünhilde's sin was her support of Siegmund, but behind that lies the incest which was projected into the brother-sister pair Siegmund and Sieglinde. The symbolical meaning, however, is that Wotan, the father, has entered into his own daughter in order to rejuvenate himself. This archaic fact is expressed here in a rather veiled way. In the legend of the "Entkrist" it is expressed openly by the devil, the father of the Anti-Christ. Wotan is justly indignant with Brünhilde, for she has taken over the role of Isis and through the birth of a son has deprived the old man of his power. Wotan beats off the first herald of doom, Siegmund, and smashes his sword, but Siegmund rises again in the grandson, Siegfried. And the instrument of fate is always the woman, who knows and reveals his secret thoughts; hence the impotent rage of Wotan, who cannot bring himself to recognize his own contradictory nature.

566   At Siegfried's birth Sieglinde dies, as is proper. The foster-parent [106] who brings him up is not a woman, but a chthonic god, Mime, a crippled dwarf who belongs to a race that has

---

[105] Die Walküre, li. 1867–74.
[106] Grimm mentions the legend that Siegfried was suckled by a doe.

abjured love.[107] Similarly, the god of the Egyptian underworld, the crippled shadow of Osiris (who underwent a sorry resurrection in Harpocrates), brings up the infant Horus to avenge the death of his father.

567   Meanwhile Brünhilde lies in enchanted slumber [108] on the mountain where Wotan has put her to sleep with the magic thorn (Edda), surrounded by a curtain of fire that keeps off all who approach and at the same time symbolizes the fiery longing of the hero for the forbidden goal.[109] Mime, however, becomes Siegfried's enemy and wills his death through Fafner. Here Mime's dynamic nature is revealed: he is a masculine representative of the Terrible Mother who lays the poisonous worm in her son's path.[110] Siegfried's longing for the mother-

107 Cf. Grimm, *Teutonic Mythology*, I, pp. 379ff. Mime or Mimir is a gigantic being of great wisdom, an "elder nature god" with whom the Norse gods associate. Later fables make him a forest spirit and skilful smith. Like Wotan, who goes to the wise woman for advice, Odin goes to the fountain of Mimir in which wisdom and cunning lie hidden. There he asks for a drink (the drink of immortality), but no sooner does he receive it than he sacrifices his eye to the fountain. The fountain of Mimir is an obvious allusion to the mother-imago. Mimir and his fountain are a condensation of mother and embryo (dwarf, subterranean sun, Harpocrates); but at the same time he is, as the mother, the source of wisdom and art. Just as Bes, the dwarf and teacher, is associated with the Egyptian mother goddess, so Mimir is associated with the maternal fountain. In Barlach's play, *Der tote Tag* (1912), the demonic mother has a familiar house-spirit called "Steissbart" (Rumpbeard), who is a dwarfish figure like Bes. These are all mythological animus-figures. Concerning the animus see "The Relations between the Ego and the Unconscious," pars. 328ff.

108 The enchanted sleep also occurs in Homer's celebration of the *hieros gamos*.

109 Cf. Siegfried's words (li. 2641–50):

> Through burning fire
> I sped toward you;
> Neither shield nor buckler
> Guarded my body:
> The flames have broken
> Through to my breast;
> My blood races
> Hot through my veins;
> A raging fire
> Is kindled within me.

110 The dragon in the cave is the Terrible Mother. In German legend the maiden in distress often appears as a snake or dragon that has to be kissed; then it changes into a beautiful woman. Certain wise women are supposed to have a fish's or a serpent's tail. A king's daughter was immured in the Golden Mount as a

imago drives him away from Mime:

> Away with the imp!
> Let me see him no more.
> If only I knew
> What my mother was like!
> But that will my thought never tell me!
> Her eyes' tender light
> Surely did shine
> Like the soft eyes of the doe.[111]

568   Siegfried wants to part from the "imp" who was his mother in the past, and longingly he reaches out for the other mother. For him, too, nature acquires a hidden maternal significance ("doe"); he, too, discovers in the sounds of nature a hint of his mother's voice and his mother's speech:

> Sweet little bird!
> Never yet have I heard you;
> Do you live here in the forest?
> Could I but follow your sweet warbling!
> Surely it would tell me
> Something of my dear mother?[112]

569   But his conversation with the bird lures Fafner out of the cave. Siegfried's longing for the mother-imago has unwittingly exposed him to the danger of looking back to his childhood and to the human mother, who immediately changes into the death-dealing dragon. He has conjured up the evil aspect of the unconscious, its devouring nature (cf. pls. xxxii*b*, xxxiv), personified by the cave-dwelling terror of the woods. Fafner is the guardian of the treasure; in his cave lies the hoard, the source of life and power. The mother apparently possesses the libido of the son (the treasure she guards so jealously), and this is in fact true so long as the son remains unconscious of himself.[113] In psychological terms this means that the "treasure hard to attain" lies hidden in the mother-imago, i.e., in the unconscious. This symbol points to one of life's secrets which is expressed in countless symbolical ways in mythology. When such symbols occur in

---

snake. In Oselberg, near Dinkelsbühl, there is a snake with a woman's head and a bunch of keys round the neck. Grimm, III, p. 969.
111 *Siegfried*, li. 1462–70.   112 Ibid., li. 1482–87.
113 This problem is dealt with in Barlach's *Der tote Tag*, which gives a brilliant description of the mother complex.

individual dreams, they will be found on examination to be pointing to something like a centre of the total personality, of the psychic totality which consists of both conscious and unconscious. Here I must refer the reader to my later works, where I deal at some length with the symbol of the self.[114] The rewards of this battle with Fafner are glowingly described in the Siegfried legend. According to the Edda, Siegfried eats Fafner's heart,[115] the seat of life. He wins the magic cap through whose power Alberich had changed himself into a serpent—an allusion to the motif of rejuvenation by casting the skin. Another lucky cap is the caul that is occasionally found over the heads of new-born children. In addition, by drinking the dragon's blood Siegfried learns to understand the language of birds, and thus enjoys a peculiar relationship to nature, which he now dominates by knowledge. Last but not least, he wins the hoard.

570   *Hort* is a Middle High German and Old High German word meaning 'collected and guarded treasure'; Goth. *huzd;* OIcel. *hodd;* Germanic **hozda,* from the pre-Germanic **kuzdho*—for *kudtho*—'hidden.' Kluge [116] associates it with Gr. κεύθω, ἔκυθον, 'to hide, conceal'; also with G. *Hütte,* 'hut,' *Hut,* 'custody,' E. *hide,* Germanic root **hud,* from IEur. **kuth* (possibly related to κεύθω and κύσθος, 'cavity, female genitals.' Prellwitz [117] also relates Goth. *huzd,* OE. *hyde,* E. *hide* and *hoard* to κεύθω. Stokes [118] relates E. *hide,* OE. *hydan,* G. *Hütte,* Lat. *cūdo,* 'helmet,' Skr. *kuhara,* 'hollow'(?), to Celt. *koudo,* 'concealment,' Lat. *occultatio.* In this connection we might also mention the report of Pausanias:

There was in Athens a sacred precinct [a temenos] dedicated to Gaia and surnamed Olympia. Here the ground is torn open to the width of a cubit; and they say that the water flowed off here after the flood at the time of Deucalion; and every year they cast into the fissure wheatmeal kneaded with honey.[119]

571   We have already seen that pastries in the form of snakes and phalli were flung into a pit at the Arrhetophoria. We men-

---

114 *Psychological Types;* Jung and Wilhelm, *The Secret of the Golden Flower; Psychology and Alchemy; Aion.*
115 Cf. Schlauch, trans., *The Saga of the Volsungs,* p. 101.
116 *Etymologisches Wörterbuch der deutschen Sprache,* s.v. "Hort."
117 *Etymologisches Wörterbuch der griechischen Sprache.*
118 *Urkeltischer Sprachschatz,* p. 89.   119 *Description of Greece,* I, 18, 7.

tioned this in connection with the earth fertilization ceremonies. It is significant that the deadly flood flowed off into the fissure, back into the mother again, for it was from the mother that death came into the world in the first place. The Deluge is simply the counterpart of the all-vivifying and all-producing water, of "the ocean, which is the origin of all things." [120] Honey-cakes are offered to the mother that she may spare one from death. In Rome money-offerings were thrown every year into the *lacus Curtius,* formerly a chasm that had been closed through the sacrificial death of Curtius. He was the hero who went down to the underworld in order to conquer the danger that threatened the Roman state after the opening of the chasm. In the Amphiaraion at Oropos those healed through incubation in the temple threw their money-offerings into the sacred well. Pausanias says:

If anyone is cured of a sickness through a saying of the oracle, it is customary for him to throw a silver or gold coin into the well; for they say that this was where Amphiaraos rose up as a god.[121]

572　　Presumably this Oropian well was also the scene of his *katabasis.* There were any number of entrances to Hades in antiquity. Thus, near Eleusis, there was a gorge through which Aidoneus came up and into which he descended after kidnapping the Kore. There were crevasses in the rocks where the souls could ascend to the upper world. Behind the temple of Chthonia in Hermione lay a spot sacred to Pluto, with a chasm through which Heracles came up with Cerberus. There was also an "Acherusian" lake.[122] This chasm, therefore, was the entrance to the place where death had been conquered. The chasm on the Areopagus in Athens was believed to be the seat of the dwellers in the underworld.[123] Similar ideas are suggested by an old Greek custom: [124] girls used to be sent for a virginity test to a cave where there lived a poisonous serpent. If they were bitten, it was a sign that they were no longer chaste. We find the same motif in the Roman legend of St. Sylvester, dating from the end of the fifth century:

There used to be a huge dragon inside the Tarpeian Hill, where the Capitol stands. Once a month magicians and wanton girls went

120 Iliad, XIV, 246.　　121 Ibid. I, 34, 4.　　122 Rohde, *Psyche,* p. 162.
123 Ibid.　　124 Maehly, *Die Schlange im Mythus und Kultus,* p. 13.

down the 365 steps to this dragon, as though into the underworld, bearing with them sacrifices and purificatory offerings from which the great dragon could be given his food. Then the dragon would suddenly rise up, and though he did not come out he poisoned the air with his breath, so that men died and much sorrow was occasioned by the deaths of children. When, therefore, St. Sylvester was fighting the pagans in defence of truth, the pagans challenged him, saying: Sylvester, go down to the dragon, and in the name of thy God make him desist, if only for a year, from this slaughter of human lives.[125]

573   St. Peter then appeared to Sylvester in a dream, and counselled him to close this door to the underworld with a chain, as in the vision of the Apocalypse:

And I saw an angel come down from heaven, having the key of the bottomless pit and a great chain in his hand.

And he laid hold on the dragon, that old serpent, which is the Devil, and Satan, and bound him a thousand years, and cast him into the bottomless pit, and shut him up, and set a seal upon him.[126]

574   Writing at the beginning of the fifth century, the anonymous author of a treatise entitled "De promissionibus" mentions a very similar legend:

Near the city of Rome there was a certain cavern in which could be seen a frightful and terrible dragon of marvellous size, a mechanical contrivance that brandished a sword in its mouth [127] and had shin-

[125] "Erat draco immanissimus in monte Tarpeio, in quo est Capitolium collocatum. Ad hunc draconem per CCCLXV gradus, quasi ad infernum, magi cum virginibus sacrilegis descendebant semel in mense cum sacrificiis et lustris, ex quibus esca poterat tanto draconi inferri. Hic draco subito ex improviso ascendebat et licet non egrederetur vicinos tamen aeres flatu suo vitiabat. Ex quo mortalitas hominum et maxima luctus de morte veniebat infantum. Sanctus itaque Silvester cum haberet cum paganis pro defensione veritatis conflictum, ad hoc venit ut dicerent ei pagani: Silvester descende ad draconem et fac eum in nomine Dei tui vel uno anno ab interfectione generis humani cessare." Duchesne, *Liber Pontificalis*, I, p. cxi; cited in Cumont, *Textes*, I, p. 351.

[126] Revelation 20: 1–2.

[127] Cf. Revelation 20: 3. We find the same motif of the armed dragon who pierces the women with a sword in a myth of the Oyster Bay tribe, of Tasmania: "A devilfish lay hidden in the hollow of a rock—a huge devilfish! The devilfish was enormous and he had a very long spear. From his hole he espied the women; he saw them dive into the water, he pierced them with his spear, he killed them, he carried them away. For a time they were no longer to be seen." The monster was then killed by the two heroes. They made a fire and brought the women back to life again. Frobenius, *Zeitalter*, p. 77.

ing red jewels for eyes.[128] Every year girls were consecrated and adorned with flowers, and then given to the dragon in sacrifice. For, as they descended with their gifts, they unwittingly touched the step to which this devilish mechanism of a dragon was attached, and were instantly pierced through with the sword that sprang out, so that innocent blood was shed. A certain monk, who was known to Stilicho the patrician on account of his good deeds, destroyed the dragon in the following manner: he carefully examined each step with a rod and with his hand until he discovered the diabolical fraud. Then, stepping over it, he went down, smote the dragon and cut it to pieces, thus showing that they are not true gods who are made by the hands of men.[129]

575   The hero has much in common with the dragon he fights—or rather, he takes over some of its qualities, invulnerability, snake's eyes, etc. Man and dragon might be a pair of brothers, even as Christ identified himself with the serpent which—*similia similibus*—conquered the plague of fiery serpents in the wilderness (John 3 : 14 and Numbers 21 : 6f.). As a serpent he is to be "lifted up" on the cross; that is to say, as a man with merely human thoughts and desires, who is ever striving back to childhood and the mother, he must die on the mother-tree, his gaze fixed on the past. This formulation is not to be taken as anything more than a psychological interpretation of the crucifixion symbol, which, because of its long-lasting effects over the centuries, must somehow be an idea that accords with the nature of the human soul. If this were not so, the symbol would long since have perished. Here, as everywhere else in this book when discussing the psychology of religious figures, I am not concerned with the theological point of view. I would like to state this categorically, for I am aware that my comparative

128 The eyes of the Son of Man are like a "flame of fire." Rev. 1 : 14.
129 "Apud urbem Romam specus quidam fuit in quo draco mirae magnitudinis mechanica arte formatus, gladium ore gestans, oculis rutilantibus gemmis metuendus ac terribilis apparebat. Huic annuae devotae virgines floribus exornatae, eo modo in sacrificio dabantur, quatenus inscias munera deferentes gradum scalae, quo certe ille arte diaboli draco pendebat, contingentes impetus venientis gladii perimeret, ut sanguinem funderet innocentem. Et hunc quidam monachus, bene ob meritum cognitus Stiliconi tunc patricio, eo modo subvertit; baculo, manu, singulos gradus palpandos inspiciens, statim ut illum tangens fraudem diabolicam repperit, eo transgresso descendens, draconem scidit, misitque in partes; ostendens et hic deos non esse qui manu fiunt."—Cited in Cumont, *Textes*, I, p. 351.

procedure often juxtaposes figures which from another point of view can hardly be compared at all. It is clear to me that such comparisons might easily give offence to the newcomer to psychology. On the other hand, anyone who has to do with the phenomena of the unconscious knows with what hair-raising irrationalism and with what shocking tactlessness and ruthlessness the unconscious "mind" dismisses our logical concepts and moral values. The unconscious, it appears, does not obey the same laws as the conscious—indeed, if it did, it would not be able to fulfil its compensatory function.

576   Christ, as a hero and god-man, signifies psychologically the self; that is, he represents the projection of this most important and most central of archetypes. (Cf. pl. LX.) The archetype of the self has, functionally, the significance of a ruler of the inner world, i.e., of the collective unconscious.[130] The self, as a symbol of wholeness, is a *coincidentia oppositorum,* and therefore contains light and darkness simultaneously. (Cf. pl. LVI, also fig. 39.) In the Christ-figure the opposites which are united in the archetype are polarized into the "light" son of God on the one hand and the devil on the other. The original unity of opposites is still discernible in the original unity of Satan and Yahweh. Christ and the dragon of the Anti-Christ lie very close together so far as their historical development and cosmic significance are concerned.[131] The dragon legend concealed under the myth of the Anti-Christ is an essential part of the hero's life [132] and is therefore immortal. Nowhere in the latter-day myths are the paired opposites so palpably close together as in the figures of Christ and Anti-Christ. (Here I would refer the reader to Merezhkovsky's admirable account of this problem in his novel *Leonardo da Vinci.*) It is a convenient rationalistic conceit to say that the dragon is only "artificial," thus banishing the mysterious gods with a word. Schizophrenic patients often make use of this mechanism for apotropaic purposes. "It's all a fake," they say, "all artificially made up." The following dream of a

130 Cf. "The Psychology of Eastern Meditation," pars. 943ff.
131 Cf. Bousset, *The Antichrist Legend.*
132 How very much Christ is the archetypal hero can be deduced from Cyril of Jerusalem (d. 386), who was of the opinion that Christ's body was a bait for the devil. On swallowing the bait, however, the devil found it so indigestible that he had to yield it up again, as the whale spewed forth Jonah.

schizophrenic is typical: *He is sitting in a dark room which has only one small window, through which he can see the sky. The sun and moon appear, but they are made of oiled paper.* Sun and moon, as divine equivalents of the parent archetype, possess a tremendous psychic power that has to be weakened apotropaically, because the patient is already far too much under the power of the unconscious.

577   The descent of the 365 steps refers to the course of the sun, and hence to the cavern of death and rebirth. That this cavern is in fact related to the subterranean mother of death can be seen from a note in Malalas, the historian of Antioch,[133] who says that in that city Diocletian dedicated a crypt to Hecate, with 365 steps leading down to it. Cave mysteries in her honour seem also to have been celebrated in Samothrace. The Hecate mysteries flourished in Rome towards the end of the fourth century, so that the two legends quoted above might well refer to her cult. Hecate [134] is a real spook-goddess of night and phantoms, a nightmare; she is sometimes shown riding a horse, and in Hesiod she is counted the patron goddess of riders. It is she who sends that horrible and fearful night-time apparition, the Empusa, which Aristophanes says comes wrapped in a bladder swollen with blood. According to Libanius, the mother of Aischines was also called Empusa, because she ἐκ σκοτεινῶν τόπων τοῖς παισὶν καὶ ταῖς γυναιξὶν ὡρμᾶτο—"rushed out upon women and children from dark places." The Empusa had peculiar feet: one foot was of brass, the other of ass's dung. In Tralles, Hecate appears side by side with Priapus; there is also a Hecate Aphrodisias. Her symbols are the key,[135] the whip,[136] the dagger, and the torch (pl. LVIII). As the deadly mother, her attributes are dogs, whose significance we have already discussed at some length. As guardian of the gate of Hades and as the triple-bodied goddess of dogs, she is more or less identical with Cerberus. Thus, in bringing up Cerberus, Heracles was really bringing the vanquished mother of death to the upper world.

---

133 Cited in Cumont, *Textes*, I, p. 352.   134 Cf. Roscher, *Lexikon*, I, 1885ff.
135 *Faust*, Part II, "The Mothers." The key belongs to Hecate as the guardian of Hades and divine psychopomp. Cf. Janus, Peter, and Aion.
136 An attribute of the Terrible Mother. Ishtar "chastised the horse with goad and whip and tortured him to death." Jensen, *Gilgamesch-Epos*, p. 18. [Cf. Speiser trans., in Pritchard, p. 84.]

As the "spirit-mother" she sends madness, the moonsickness. This idea is perfectly sensible, because most forms of lunacy consist of affections which amount to an invasion by the unconscious and an inundation of the conscious mind. In the Hecate mysteries a wand, named the λευκόφυλλος ('white-leaved'), was broken. This wand protected the purity of virgins and caused madness in anyone who touched it. We recognize here the motif of the sacred tree, the mother who might not be touched. Only a madman would attempt to do so. As an incubus or vampire she appears in the form of Empusa, or as a man-eating lamia (cf. pl. xxxviiia), or again in that more beautiful guise, the "Bride of

Fig. 34. Hecate of Samothrace
Gnostic gem

Corinth." She is the mother of all witchcraft and witches, the patron goddess of Medea, because the power of the Terrible Mother is irresistible, coming as it does from the unconscious. She plays an important part in Greek syncretism, being confused with Artemis, who was also called ἑκάτη, the 'far-hitting,' or 'she who hits at will,' a name that once more reveals her superordinate power. Artemis is the huntress with hounds, and Hecate too is the wild huntress prowling at night. She has her name in common with Apollo: ἕκατος, ἑκάεργος. The identification of Hecate with Brimo as the underworldly mother is understandable, also her identification with Persephone and Rhea, the primitive All-Mother. Her maternal significance also explains her confusion with Eileithyia, the goddess of childbirth. Hecate is a birth-goddess (κουροτρόφος), the multiplier of cattle and goddess of marriage. In Orphic cosmogony she occupies the centre of the world as Aphrodite and Gaia, if not as the world-soul itself. On a carved gem she is shown with a cross on her head (fig. 34). The pillory where criminals were scourged was also known as the ἑκάτη; and to her, as to the Roman Trivia, were dedicated junctions of three roads, forked roads, and crossroads. Where the roads branch off or meet, dog-sacrifices were offered to her, and there too were thrown the bodies of the executed: the sacrifice occurs at the point of union. Where the roads *cross* and enter into one another, thereby symbolizing the union of opposites, there is the "mother," the object and epitome of all union. Where the roads *divide,* where there is parting, separation, splitting, there we find the "division," the cleft [137]—the symbol of the mother and at the same time the essence of what the mother means for us, namely cleavage and farewell. Accordingly, the meaning of a sacrifice on this spot would be: propitiation of the mother in both senses. The temenos of Gaia, the fissure and the well, can easily be understood as the doors of life and death,[138] "past which man's steps have ever flinching trod," [139] sacrificing there his obolus or his πελανοί instead of his body, just as Heracles pacified Cerberus with the honey-cakes. Thus the crevice at Delphi with the Castalian spring was the habitation of the chthonic Python who was vanquished by the sun-hero Apollo. The Python, incited by Hera, had pursued Apollo's mother, Leto, when he was still in her womb; but she fled to the floating island of Delos on a "night sea journey" and was there safely delivered of her child,

137 [The relation of these words to one another and to the "mother" is etymologically apparent in the German: *Scheidung,* 'parting' in the sense of 'division'; *Abschied,* 'parting' in the sense of 'farewell'; *Scheide,* 'parting' in the sense of 'line of separation,' as in *Wasserscheide,* 'watershed'; hence 'sheath, scabbard.' *Scheide* also means 'vagina.'—TRANS.]

138 Cf. the symbolism in the Melk hymn to Mary (12th century):

> Sancta Maria,
> Closed gate
> Opened at God's command—
> Sealed fountain,
> Locked garden,
> Gate of Paradise. (Cf. Song of Solomon 4 : 12.)

There is the same symbolism in the erotic verse:

> Maiden, let me enter with you
> Into your rose garden
> Where the red rosebuds grow,
> Those delicate and tender rosebuds,
> With a tree nearby
> Rustling to and fro,
> And the deep cool well
> That lies below.

139 *Faust;* cf. above, p. 272.

who later slew the Python. In Hierapolis (Edessa) a temple was built over the crack in the earth where the flood subsided, and in Jerusalem the foundation-stone of the temple was laid over the great abyss,[140] in the same way that Christian churches are often built over caves, grottoes, wells, etc. We find the same motif in the Grotto of Mithras[141] and the various other cave-cults, including the Christian catacombs, which owe their importance not to legendary persecutions but to the cult of the dead.[142] Even the burial of the dead in consecrated ground ("garden of the dead," cloisters, crypts, etc.) is a rendering back to the mother with the hope of resurrection which such burials presuppose. In olden times, the dragon in the cave who represented the devouring mother had to be propitiated with human sacrifices, later with gifts. Hence the Attic custom of giving the dead man the μελιτοῦττα (same as μᾶζα, honey-cakes), with which to pacify the hound of hell, the three-headed monster guarding the door of the underworld. A substitute for the gifts seems to have been the obolus given to Charon, which is why Rohde calls him the second Cerberus, akin to the jackal-headed Anubis of the Egyptians.[143] (Cf. pl. xxxiia.) The dog and the underworld serpent are identical. In the Greek tragedies the Erinyes are serpents as well as dogs; the monsters Typhon and Echidna are parents of the Hydra, of the dragon of the Hesperides, and of the Gorgon (cf. pl. xivb); they also spawned the dogs Cerberus, Orthros, and Scylla.[144] Snakes and dogs are guardians of the treasure. The chthonic god was in all probability a snake that was housed in a cave and was fed with πέλανοι (pl. lviib). In the Asclepieia of the later period the sacred snakes were hardly ever visible, so they may have existed only figuratively.[145] Nothing was left but the hole in which the snake was said to dwell. There the πέλανοι were placed and the obolus thrown in. The sacred cave in the temple at Cos consisted of a rectangular pit covered by a stone slab with a square hole in it. This arrange-

---

140 Herzog, "Aus dem Asklepieion von Kos," pp. 219ff.

141 A Mithraic sanctuary was, whenever possible, an underground grotto, and the cave was often only an imitation one. It is possible that the Christian crypts and underground churches had a similar meaning. (Cf. pl. xxxiii.)

142 Cf. Schultze, *Die Katakomben*, pp. 9ff.

143 Rohde, *Psyche*, p. 247. Further evidence in Herzog, p. 224.

144 Further evidence in ibid., p. 225.

145 Sacred snakes were, however, kept for display and other purposes.

ment served the purpose of a treasure-house: the snake-pit had become a slot for money, a "poor-box," and the cave a "hoard." That this development is fully in accord with the archaeological evidence is proved by a discovery in the temple of Aesculapius and Hygeia at Ptolemaïs:

A coiled granite snake with an arched neck was found. In the middle of the coils there is a narrow slit, polished by use, just large enough to allow a coin of at most 4 cm. diameter to drop through. At the sides are holes for handles to lift this heavy object, the lower half of which could be inserted as a lid.[146]

578 Here the serpent lies on the treasury as protector of the hoard. Fear of the deadly maternal womb has become the guardian of the treasure of life. That the snake really is a death-symbol is evident from the fact that the souls of the dead, like the chthonic gods, appear as serpents, as dwellers in the kingdom of the deadly mother.[147]

579 The development of this symbol, showing how the crevice in the earth, interpreted on the primitive level as the "mother," came to signify the place of the treasure, therefore corresponds to the etymology of G. *Hort,* 'hoard,' as suggested by Kluge. Κεύθος (from κεύθω) means the innermost womb of the earth (Hades), and κύσθος, which he associates with it, has a similar meaning: 'cavity' or 'womb.' Prellwitz makes no mention of this connection. On the other hand, Fick[148] connects *Hort,* Goth. *huzd,* with Armen. *kust* (Lat. *venter,* 'belly'), Slav. *cista,* Ved. *kostha,* 'abdomen,' from the IEur. root **koustho-s,* 'viscera, abdomen, chamber, storeroom.'[149] Prellwitz connects κύσθος with κύστις and κύστη, 'bladder, bag,' Skr. *kustha-s,* 'hollow of the loins'; also with κύτος, 'cavity, vault'; κυτίς, 'casket,' from κύειν, 'to be pregnant.' Whence also κύτος, 'hollow vessel, skin'; κύαρ, 'hole'; κύαθος, 'cup'; κύλα, 'depression under the eye'; κῦμα, 'swelling, wave, billow.' The basic IEur. root[150] is **kevo,* 'to swell, be strong'; whence the above-mentioned κυεῖν, κύαρ and Lat. *cavus,* 'hollow, arched, cave, hole'; *cavea,* 'cavity, enclosure,

---

146 Herzog, p. 212.   147 Rohde, *Psyche,* p. 163.
148 *Vergleichendes Wörterbuch der indogermanischen Grundsprache,* I, p. 28.
149 Also Lat. *cuturnium,* the vessel into which wine was poured for sacrifice.
150 Fick, I, p. 424.

cage, scene, stage, assembly'; *caulae,* 'cavity, aperture, stable'; [151]
IEur. **kuéyô,* 'I swell,' part. **kueyonts,* 'swelling'; **en-kueyonts,*
'enceinte'; ἐγκυέων, Lat. *inciens,* 'pregnant'; cf. Skr. *vi-śvàyan,*
'swelling.' [152]

580   The treasure which the hero fetches from the dark cavern
is *life:* it is himself, new-born from the dark maternal cave of
the unconscious where he was stranded by the introversion or
regression of libido. Hence the Hindu fire-bringer is called
Matarisvan, he who swells in the mother. The hero who clings
to the mother is the dragon, and when he is reborn from the
mother he becomes the conqueror of the dragon. (Pl. LIX*a.*) He
shares this paradoxical nature with the snake. According to
Philo the snake is the most spiritual of all creatures; it is of a
fiery nature, and its swiftness is terrible. It has a long life and
sloughs off old age with its skin.[153] In actual fact the snake is a
cold-blooded creature, unconscious and unrelated. It is both
toxic and prophylactic, equally a symbol of the good and bad
daemon (the Agathodaemon), of Christ and the devil. Among
the Gnostics it was regarded as an emblem of the brain-stem
and spinal cord, as is consistent with its predominantly reflex
psyche. It is an excellent symbol for the unconscious, perfectly
expressing the latter's sudden and unexpected manifestations,
its painful and dangerous intervention in our affairs, and its
frightening effects. Taken purely as a psychologem the hero
represents the positive, favourable action of the unconscious,
while the dragon is its negative and unfavourable action—not
birth, but a devouring; not a beneficial and constructive deed,

151 Cf. the cleaning of the Augean stables. The stable, like the cave, is a place of
birth; e.g., the cave and stable in which Christ was born. (See Robertson, *Christ
and Krishna.*) Birth in a stable is also found in a Basuto myth (Frobenius,
Zeitalter). It belongs to the sphere of animal fables; hence the story of how the
barren Sarah conceived is prefigured in the Egyptian fable of the Apis bull.
Herodotus says: "This Apis—or Epaphus—is the calf of a cow which is never afterwards able to have another. The Egyptian belief is that a flash of light descends
upon the cow from heaven, and this causes her to conceive Apis." (III, 28; trans.
by Selincourt, p. 186.) Apis is the sun, and his distinguishing marks are a white
patch on the forehead, on his back the figure of an eagle, and on his tongue a
beetle.
152 Some authorities connect κῦρος, 'supreme power,' κύριος, 'lord,' with OIran.
caur, cur, 'hero,' Skr. *śura-s,* 'strong, hero.' But the connection is regarded as
doubtful or improbable.
153 Maehly, *Die Schlange im Mythus und Kultus,* p. 7.

but greedy retention and destruction. (Fig. 35; cf. also pl. XXXIV and fig. 30.)

581   Every psychological extreme secretly contains its own opposite or stands in some sort of intimate and essential relation to it.[154] Indeed, it is from this tension that it derives its peculiar

Fig. 35. The assault by the dragon
From Vitruvius, De architectura, *Venice, 1511*

dynamism. There is no hallowed custom that cannot on occasion turn into its opposite, and the more extreme a position is, the more easily may we expect an enantiodromia, a conversion of something into its opposite. The best is the most threatened with some devilish perversion just because it has done the most to suppress evil. This peculiar relationship to the opposite

154 A good example of this is the Yang-Yin doctrine in classical Chinese philosophy.

375

can also be seen in the vagaries of language, as for instance in the comparison of 'good, better, best.' 'Better,' however, derives from the old word *bass*, meaning 'good.' The related English word is 'bad'; its comparative would therefore be 'better' (badder!). What happens everywhere in language happens also in mythology: in one version of a fairytale we find God, in another the devil.[155] And how often has it happened in the history of religion that its rites, orgies and mysteries degenerate into vicious debauches![156] Thus a blasphemer who arose at the beginning of the nineteenth century says of the Communion:

The communion of the devil is in the brothels. Everything that they sacrifice there they sacrifice to the devil and not to God. There they have the devil's cup and the devil's board; there they have sucked the head of the snake,[157] there they have fed on the bread of iniquity and drunk the wine of fornication.

582   Anton Unternährer, as this man was called, fancied himself a sort of priapic divinity. He says of himself:

Black-haired, very charming withal and of handsome countenance, everyone enjoys listening to thee because of the graceful speeches which flow from thy mouth; therefore do the virgins love thee.[158]

155 [Etymologically, 'devil' and 'divinity' are both related to Skr. *deva*, 'demon.' —TRANS.]

156 Cf. the account of the orgies practised by certain Russian sects in Merezhkovsky, *Peter and Alexis*. The orgiastic cult of Anahita or Anaitis, the Asiatic goddess of love, is still practised among the Ali Illahija, the self-styled "extinguishers of the light," and the Yezidis and Dushik Kurds, who indulged nightly in religious orgies ending in a wild sexual debauch during which incestuous unions occur. (Spiegel, *Erānische Altertumskunde*, II, p. 64.) Further examples in Stoll, *Das Geschlechtsleben in der Völkerpsychologie*.

157 Concerning the snake-kiss, see Grimm, *Teutonic Mythology*, III, p. 969. By this means a beautiful woman was set free. Spielrein's patient (pp. 344f.) says: "Wine is the blood of Jesus.—The water must be blessed and was blessed by him.—He who is buried alive becomes a vineyard.—That wine turns to blood.—The water is mingled with childishness because God says 'Become like children.' —There is also a spermatic water that can be steeped in blood. Maybe that is the water of Jesus." This hotch-potch of ideas is characteristic. Wiedemann ("Die Toten und ihre Reiche," p. 51, cited from Dieterich, p. 101) documents the Egyptian idea that man could drink immortality by sucking the breast of a goddess. Cf. the myth of Heracles, who became immortal after a single sip at the breast of Hera.

158 From the *Geheimes Reskript* (1821) of Unternährer. I have to thank the Rev. O. Pfister for calling my attention to this document.

583   He continues:

> Ye fools and blind men, behold God has created man in his own image, as male and female, and has blessed them and said: "Be fruitful and multiply, and replenish the earth, and subdue it." Therefore has he given the greatest honour to these poor members, and placed them naked in the garden . . .
>
> Now are the fig-leaves and the covering removed, because ye have turned to the Lord, for the Lord is Spirit, and where the Spirit of the Lord is, there is liberty,[159] there is the brightness of the Lord mirrored with uncovered countenance. This is precious before God, and is the glory of the Lord and the adornment of our God, when ye stand in the image and honour of God as God created you, naked and unashamed.
>
> Who shall ever praise sufficiently in the sons and daughters of the living God those members of the body which are appointed for procreation?
>
> In the lap of the daughters of Jerusalem is the gate of the Lord, and the righteous shall there go into the temple, even to the altar. And in the lap of the sons of the living God is the water-pipe of the upper part, which is a tube, like a rod with which to measure the temple and the altar. And underneath the water-pipe are erected the sacred stones, as a sign and testimony [160] of the Lord, who has taken to himself the seed of Abraham.
>
> Out of the seed in the chamber of the mother God creates with his hand a man, formed in his own image. Then is the house of the mother and the chamber of the mother opened for the daughters of the living God, and God himself brings forth the child through them. Thus God creates children from stones, for the seed comes from the stones.

584   History has numerous examples of how easily the mystery can turn into a sexual orgy just because it grew out of the opposite of the orgy. It is characteristic that this fanatic should return again to the symbol of the snake, which in the mystery religions entered into the faithful, fecundating and spiritualizing them, though all the time keeping its phallic significance. In the mysteries of the Ophites, the festival was celebrated with

---

159 Nietzsche: "And this parable I also give unto you: not a few who sought to cast out their devil, themselves entered into the swine" (*Zarathustra*).

160 *Testis* originally had the double meaning of 'testicle' and 'testimony.' [Cf. the Biblical custom of swearing an oath by placing the hand "under the thigh"; Genesis 24:2f and 47:29f.—EDITORS.]

live snakes, and the creatures were even kissed. (Cf. the kissing of the Demeter serpent in the Eleusinian mysteries.) This kiss plays a not unimportant part in the sexual orgies of certain modern Christian sects.

585   One of my patients dreamt that a snake shot out of a cave and bit him in the genital region. This dream occurred at the moment when the patient was convinced of the truth of the analysis and was beginning to free himself from the bonds of his mother-complex. He felt that he was making progress and that he had more control over himself. But the moment he felt the impulse to go forward he also felt the pull of the bond to the mother. Being bitten in the genital region by a snake (cf. pls. LXIb, LXIV), reminds us of Attis, whose self-castration was occasioned by his mother's jealousy. Another patient had the following dream after a relapse into neurosis: she was completely filled inside with an enormous snake. Only the end of its tail stuck out from her arm. She tried to seize hold of it, but it slithered away. A third patient complained that a snake was stuck in her throat.[161] Nietzsche uses this symbolism in his "vision" of the shepherd and the snake:

> And verily, what I saw was like nothing I ever saw before. I saw a young shepherd, writhing, choking, twitching, with distorted countenance, and with a heavy black serpent hanging out of his mouth.
> Did ever I see so much loathing and pale horror on a human countenance?[162] Perhaps he had been asleep, and the serpent had crawled into his mouth—and bitten fast.
> My hand tugged at the serpent, and tugged in vain. I could not pull the serpent out of his throat. Then a cry broke from me: "Bite —its head off! Bite hard!" My horror, my hatred, my loathing, my pity, all my good and bad broke from me in one cry.
> You valiant ones about me . . . , you lovers of mysteries, solve me the riddle I then saw, interpret for me the vision of the loneliest man!
> For a vision it was, and a foresight: *what* did I then see in a semblance? And *who* is it that is to come?

161 Cf. Nietzsche's poem: "Why hast thou enticed thyself / Into the old serpent's Paradise?" [Cf. par. 459, above.]
162 Nietzsche himself seems to have shown at times a certain predilection for loathsome animals. Cf. Bernoulli, *Franz Overbeck und Friedrich Nietzsche*, I, p. 166.

Who is the shepherd into whose mouth the serpent crawled? *Who* is the man into whose throat all the heaviest and blackest must crawl? [163]

But the shepherd bit, as my cry bade him—he bit with a strong bite! Far off he spat the head of the serpent and leapt to his feet.

No longer a shepherd, no longer a man, but a transfigured being with light all about him, who *laughed*! Never yet on earth did a human being laugh as *he* laughed!

O my brothers, I heard a laughter which was no human laughter —and now a thirst consumes me, a longing that is never allayed.

My longing for that laughter consumes me: O how can I bear to live, and how could I bear to die! [164]

586   The experience described here by Nietzsche can be interpreted as follows with the help of what we said above: the snake represents the unconscious psyche which, like the snake-god in the Sabazios mysteries, crawls into the mouth of the celebrant, i.e., Nietzsche himself as the ποιμήν or ποιμάνδρης, the shepherd of souls and preacher, firstly to stop him from talking too much, and secondly to make him ἔνθεος—' "enthused," filled with God.' The snake had already bitten fast, but fear was swifter and more violent: it bit off the snake's head and spat it out. If you want the snake to bruise your heel you have only to tread on its head. The shepherd laughed on getting rid of the snake—a wild hysterical laughter, because he had dished the compensation from the unconscious. He could now reckon without his host, and with the well-known consequences: one has only to read the passages in *Zarathustra* where Nietzsche speaks of laughing and laughter. Unfortunately, everything happened afterwards just as if the whole German nation had paid heed to Nietzsche's sermon.

587   The unconscious insinuates itself in the form of a snake if the conscious mind is afraid of the compensating tendency of the unconscious, as is generally the case in regression. But if the compensation is accepted in principle, there is no regression, and the unconscious can be met half-way through introversion.

163 Cf. Nietzsche's dream, quoted at p. 34, n. 1, above.
164 *Thus Spake Zarathustra* (in *Werke*, VI, pp. 233f.). This image is reminiscent of the myth of Dietrich of Bern: he was wounded in the forehead by an arrow, and because a piece remained lodged there, he was called the "immortal." Similarly, half of Hrungnir's stone club embedded itself in Thor's skull. Grimm, I, pp. 371–72.

It must be admitted, however, that the problem as it presented itself to Nietzsche was insoluble, for nobody could expect the shepherd to swallow down a snake under such circumstances. We are confronted here with one of those fatal cases, by no means uncommon, where the compensation appears in a form that cannot be accepted and could only be overcome by something that is equally impossible for the patient. Cases of this kind occur when the unconscious has been resisted for too long on principle, and a wedge violently driven between instinct and the conscious mind.

588   Through introversion, as numerous historical witnesses testify, one is fertilized, inspired, regenerated, and reborn. In Indian philosophy this idea of creative spiritual activity has even acquired a cosmogonic significance. According to the Rig-Veda (X, 121), the unknown creator of all things is Prajapati, "Lord of Creation." His cosmogonic activity is described as follows in the various Brahmanas:

Prajapati desired: I will propagate myself, I will be many. He practised *tapas,* and after he had practised *tapas* he created these worlds.[165]

589   The term *tapas* is to be translated, according to Deussen,[166] as "he heated himself with his own heat," [167] in the sense that "he brooded his own brooding," brooder and brooded being conceived not as separate, but as one and the same thing. As Hiranyagarbha (the Golden Germ), Prajapati is the self-begotten egg, the cosmic egg from which he hatches himself (fig. 36). He creeps into himself, becomes his own womb, makes himself pregnant with himself in order to hatch forth the world of multiplicity. Thus Prajapati transforms himself by introversion into something new, into the multiplicity of the world. It is particularly interesting to note the gradual approximation of widely divergent ideas. Deussen says:

Just as, in a hot country like India, the idea of *tapas* became the symbol of strenuous effort and suffering, so the idea of *tapo atapyata* gradually acquired the meaning of self-castigation, and became associated with the view . . . that creation is an act of self-abnegation on the part of the creator.[168]

[165] Rig-Veda, X, 121, trans. from Deussen, *Geschichte,* I, p. 181.
[166] Ibid., pp. 181f.   [167] *Sa tapo atapyata.*   [168] *Geschichte,* I, p. 182.

590   Self-incubation,[169] self-castigation, and introversion are closely
related ideas. Immersion in oneself (introversion) is a penetration into the unconscious and at the same time asceticism. The
result, for the philosophy of the Brahmanas, is the creation of
the world, and for the mystic the regeneration and spiritual rebirth of the individual, who is born into a new world of the

Fig. 36. Prajapati with the world-egg
India

spirit. Indian philosophy also assumes that creativity as such
springs from introversion. Rig-Veda X, 129 says:

Then the One, that was hidden in the shell,
Was born through the force of fiery torment.

[169] The Stoic conception of creative heat, which we have already recognized as
libido (p. 67, n. 51, above), is a kindred idea, like the birth of Mithras from
a stone "through the sole heat of libido."

From it there arose in the beginning love,[170]
Which is the germ and the seed of knowledge.
The wise found the root of being in not-being
By investigating the impulses of the human heart.[171]

591   This philosophical view conceives the world as an emanation of libido. When therefore the insane Schreber brought
about the end of the world through his introversion, he was
withdrawing libido from the world about him, thereby making
it unreal.[172] Schopenhauer tried in exactly the same way to
abolish through negation (the equivalent of holiness and asceticism) the cardinal error of the Primal Will in creating the world
at all. Does not Goethe also say: "Is not the core of nature in
the heart of man?"

592   The hero who sets himself the task of renewing the world
and conquering death personifies the world-creating power
which, brooding on itself in introversion, coiled round its own
egg like a snake, threatens life with its poisonous bite, so that
the living may die and be born again from the darkness. The
same idea is found in Nietzsche:

How long already have you sat on your misfortune?
Give heed, lest you hatch me
An egg,
A basilisk egg
From your long travail.[173]

593   The hero is himself the snake, himself the sacrificer and the
sacrificed, which is why Christ rightly compares himself with
the healing Moses-serpent (cf. pl. IXb), and why the saviour of
the Christian Ophites was a serpent, too. It is both Agathodaimon (fig. 37) and Cacodaimon. In German legend we are
told that the heroes have snake's eyes. [174]

594   Clear traces of the original identity of hero and snake are
to be found in the myth of Cecrops. Cecrops was half snake,
half man. In primitive times he was probably the snake of the
Athenian citadel itself. As a buried god he was, like Erechtheus,
a chthonic snake-deity. Above his subterranean dwelling rose

170 Kama = Eros, and = the libido.   171 Trans. from Deussen, I, p. 123.
172 *Memoirs of My Nervous Illness.*
173 "Glory and Eternity" ("Ruhm und Ewigkeit," in *Werke*, VIII, I, p. 425).
174 Grimm, IV, p. 1395. Sigurd was called "Ormr î Auga" (Snake's Eyes).

the Parthenon, the temple of the virgin goddess. The flaying of the god, which we have already touched on in connection with the flaying-ceremonies of the Aztecs, is intimately bound up with the snake-like nature of the hero. It is reported of Mani, the founder of Manichaeism, that he was killed, flayed, stuffed, and hung up.[175] The hanging up of the god has an unmistakable symbolic value, since suspension is the symbol of unfulfilled longing or tense expectation ("suspense"). Christ, Odin, Attis, and others all hung upon trees. Jesus ben Pandira suffered such

Fig. 37. Agathodaimon serpent
Antique gem

a death on the eve of the feast of the Passover, in the reign of Alexander Jannaeus (106–79 B.C.). This Jesus is supposed to have been the founder of the Essene sect,[176] which had certain links with the Christianity that came afterwards. The Jesus ben Stada who was identified with the earlier Jesus but was later supposed to have lived in the second century A.D., was also hanged. Both were first stoned, a punishment which was, so to speak, a bloodless one like hanging. This may not be without significance in the light of a strange ceremony reported from Uganda:

When a king of Uganda wished to live for ever, he went to a place in Busiro, where a feast was given by the chiefs. At the feast the Mamba clan[177] was especially held in honour, and during the

175 Galatians 3 : 27 contains an allusion to this primitive idea: "For as many of you as were baptized into Christ have put on Christ" (RSV). The word used here, ἐνδύειν (*induere*), means literally to 'put on, clothe oneself, insinuate oneself into.'   176 Cf. Robertson, *Christianity and Mythology*, p. 395.
177 The mamba is the African cobra.

festivities a member of this clan was secretly chosen by his fellows, caught by them, and beaten to death with their fists; no stick or other weapon might be used by the men appointed to do the deed. After death, the victim's body was flayed and the skin made into a special whip. . . . After the ceremony of the feast in Busiro, with its strange sacrifice, the king of Uganda was supposed to live for ever, but from that day he was never allowed to see his mother again.[178]

595   Marsyas, who seems to have been a substitute for Attis, the son-lover of Cybele, was also skinned.[179] Whenever a Scythian king died, his slaves and horses were slaughtered, skinned, and stuffed, and then set up again.[180] In Phrygia, the representatives of the father-god were killed and skinned. The same was done in Athens with an ox, which was skinned and stuffed and afterwards hitched to the plough. In this way the renewal of the earth's fertility was celebrated.[181]

596   The god-hero, symbolized by the spring zodion (Aries, Taurus), descends to the lowest point in winter, overcomes it, and having passed beyond the summer solstice is himself overcome as if by an unconscious longing for death. Nevertheless he is divided within himself, and his descent and approaching end therefore seem to him like evil designs of the sinister mother who secretly lays a poisonous snake in his path to undo him. The mysteries, however, hold out the consoling promise that there is no contradiction [182] and no disharmony when life changes into death: "The bull is the father of the dragon and the dragon is the father of the bull." [183]

[178] Frazer, *The Golden Bough*, Part IV, p. 405.
[179] Ibid., p. 242.   [180] Ibid., p. 246.
[181] Ibid., p. 249. Concerning the flaying motif, see my "Transformation Symbolism in the Mass," par. 348.
[182] Another attempt at a solution seems to be the Dioscuri motif: two brothers who resemble one another, one mortal, the other immortal. This motif is found in Indian mythology as the two Asvins, though here they are not differentiated. It appears very clearly in Shvetashvatara Upanishad (4, 6) as the companion birds who "clasp the selfsame tree," i.e., as the personal and suprapersonal atman. In the Mithraic cult, Mithras is the father, Sol the son, and yet both are one as ὁ μέγας θεὸς Ἥλιος Μίθρας: "the great god Helios Mithras." (Cf. Dieterich, p. 68.) That is to say, man does not change at death into his immortal part, but is mortal and immortal even in life, being both ego and self.
[183] ταῦρος δράκοντος καὶ ταύρου δράκων πατήρ.—Firmicus Maternus, *De errore profanarum religionum*, XXVI, 1, p. 67.

597 Nietzsche voices the same mysterious truth:

> Here I sit,
> Or rather,
> Here I am swallowed down
> By this smallest oasis.
> Yawning it opened
> Its lovely lips—
> All hail to that whale
> If he provides thus
> For his guest's welfare!
>
> Hail to his belly,
> If it is
> Such a lovely oasis belly!
>
> The desert grows; woe to him who hides deserts!
> Stone grinds on stone, the desert gulps and strangles.
> Monstrous Death, glowing under his tan,
> Stares and chews . . . his life is his chewing . . .
> O man burnt out by lust, do not forget:
> You are the stone, the desert, the death's-head! [184]

598 After slaying the dragon, Siegfried meets father Wotan, who is plagued by gloomy cares because the earth-mother Erda has laid the old serpent in his path in order to enfeeble him. He says to Erda:

> All-knowing one,
> Care's piercing sting
> By thee was planted
> In Wotan's dauntless heart:
> With fear of shameful
> Ruin and downfall
> Thy knowledge filled him;
> The fearful tidings
> Choked his breast!
> Art thou the world's wisest woman?
> Then tell me:
> How may a god conquer his care?
>
> ERDA: Thy name
> Is not as thou sayest!

[184] *Werke*, VIII, p. 413.

599   With poisoned sting the mother has robbed her son of the joy of life and deprived him of the power which lies in the secret name. Just as Isis demanded the secret name of Ra, so Erda says: "Thy name is not as thou sayest!" But the Wanderer has found a way to conquer the fatal charm of the mother:

> The gods' downfall
> No more dismays me
> Since I willed their doom!
>
> To the loveliest Wälsung
> I leave my heritage;
> To the eternally young
> Joyously yields the god! [185]

600   These wise words contain in fact the saving thought: it is not the mother who lays the poisonous worm in our path, but life itself, which wills itself to complete the sun's course, to mount from morn to noon, and then, crossing the meridian, to hasten towards evening, no more at odds with itself, but desiring the descent and the end.[186]

601   Nietzsche's Zarathustra says:

I praise my death, the free death which comes to me because *I* desire it.

[185] Wagner, *Siegfried,* li. 2088–2101, 2117–19, 2126–27, 2248–49.

[186] It is a striking fact that the lion-killing heroes Samson and Heracles fight *without weapons.* (Cf. fig. 17.) The lion is a symbol of the fierce heat of midsummer; astrologically he is the *domicilium solis.* Steinthal ("Die Sage von Simson," p. 133) reasons as follows: "When, therefore, the sun-god fights the summer heat, he is fighting himself; if he kills it, he kills himself. . . . The Phoenicians and Assyrians and Lydians believed that their sun-god was committing suicide, for only as suicide could they comprehend how the sun's heat could grow less. Therefore, when the sun stood at its height in summer and burnt everything with its scorching rays, they thought: thus the god burns himself, but he does not die, he only rejuvenates himself. . . . Heracles burns himself too, but mounts to Olympus in the flames. This is the contradiction in the pagan gods: as forces of nature they are both helpful and harmful to men. So, in order to do good and rescue mankind, they must work against themselves. The contradiction is mitigated if each of the two sides of the force of nature is personified as a separate god, or if both are conceived as a single divine person, the beneficent and injurious sides each being assigned a separate symbol. The symbol becomes more and more autonomous and in the end becomes a god itself; and whereas originally the god worked against himself and destroyed himself, now symbol fights against symbol, god against god, or the god against the symbol." The hero has no weapons precisely because he fights himself.

And when shall I desire it?
He who has a goal and an heir desires death at the proper time
for the goal and the heir.[187]

602   Nietzsche's *amor fati* is somewhat overdone, and like an ailing Superman he tries to be always one jump ahead of fate.
Siegfried is more cautious: he conquers father Wotan and sets
out to win Brünhilde. The first thing he sees is her horse; then
he thinks he espies a man sleeping in armour. He cuts off the
coat of mail, and when he sees that it is a woman he is seized
with terror:

> My heart doth faint and falter!
> On whom shall I call for help?
> Mother! Mother!
> Remember me . .
> Can this be fear?
> O Mother, Mother!
> Thy dauntless child!
> A woman lies sleeping
> And she has taught him to fear!
>
> Awake, awake!
> Holiest maid!
> So shall I suck life
> From sweetest lips,
> Even though I die in a kiss!

603   In the duet which immediately follows the mother is invoked:

> O mother, hail,
> Who gave me birth.

604   Brünhilde's avowal is particularly significant:

> Didst thou but know,
> O joy of the world,
> How I have ever loved thee!
> Thou wert my gladness,
> Thou wert my care!
> Thy tender life I sheltered
> Before it was thine;

[187] "Voluntary Death," in *Zarathustra*. [Cf. trans. by Common, p. 125.]

387

Before thou wert born
My shield was thy guard.[188]

605   Brünhilde, standing to Wotan in a daughter-anima relationship, is clearly revealed here as the symbolical or spiritual
mother of Siegfried, thus confirming the psychological rule that
the first carrier of the anima-image is the mother. Siegfried says:

Then death took not my mother?
Was the loved one but sleeping?

606   The mother-imago, at first identical with the anima, represents the feminine aspect of the hero himself. Brünhilde tells
him as much in the words:

Thine own self am I
In the bliss of thy love!

607   As the anima she is the mother-sister-wife, and as the pre-
existent archetype she has always loved him:

O Siegfried, Siegfried!
Conquering light!
Always I have loved thee,
For I alone divined
Wotan's hidden thought-
The thought which I never
Dared to name,
Which I dared not think,
Which I only felt,
For which I fought,
Struggled and strove,
For which I defied
Him who conceived it. . . .
Canst thou not guess?
It was naught but my love for thee!

608   The anima-image brings with it still other aspects of the
mother-imago, amongst others those of water and submersion:

A glorious flood
Before me rolls.
With all my senses

188 *Siegfried,* li. 2478–82, 2496–2500, 2511–16, 2542–43, 2552–59. It was an Etruscan
custom to bury the cinerary urn of the dead man in the earth and cover it with
a shield.

I only see
Its buoyant, gladdening billows. . . .
I long to plunge
My burning heat
In the water's balm;
Just as I am
To sink in the flood.
O that its billows
Might drown me in bliss!

609   The water represents the maternal depths and the place of
rebirth; in short, the unconscious in its positive and negative
aspects. But the mystery of regeneration is of an awe-inspiring
nature: it is a deadly embrace. There is an allusion to the terrible mother of heroes, who teaches them fear, in the words of
Brünhilde, the horse-woman who conducts the dead to the other
side:

Fearest thou, Siegfried?
Fearest thou not
The wild, raging woman?

610   The orgiastic "Occide moriturus" from the love-scene in the
metamorphosis of Apuleius resounds in Brünhilde's words:

Laughing let us be lost,
Laughing go down to death!

611   And in the cry

Light-giving love,
Laughing death! [189]

we find the same significant contrast. These orgiastic frenzies
and barbaric extremes are in the very nature of the *Mater saeva
cupidinum* and determine the fate of the hero. Luck must
stand unbidden and unforeseen at his side if he is not to perish
of exaggerated self-confidence at the very first undertaking. But
his mother-anima is blind, and his fate overtakes him sooner or
later regardless of his luck—in most cases sooner. The subsequent fate of Siegfried is the fate of every archetypal hero: the
spear of the one-eyed Hagen, the Dark One, strikes his vulnerable spot. In the shape of Hagen the one-eyed Wotan slays the
son. The hero is the ideal masculine type: leaving the mother,

[189] *Siegfried*, li. 2561–62, 2565–66, 2571–90, 2738–50, 2797–99, 2818–19, 2862–63.

the source of life, behind him, he is driven by an unconscious desire to find her again, to return to her womb. Every obstacle that rises in his path and hampers his ascent wears the shadowy features of the Terrible Mother, who saps his strength with the poison of secret doubt and retrospective longing; and in every conquest he wins back again the smiling, loving and life-giving mother. This image, taken as a kind of musical figure, a contrapuntal modulation of feeling, is extremely simple and its meaning is obvious. To the intellect, however, it presents an almost insuperable difficulty, particularly as regards logical exposition. The reason for this lies in the fact that no part of the hero-myth is single in meaning, and that, at a pinch, all the figures are interchangeable. The only certain and reliable thing is that the myth exists and shows unmistakable analogies with other myths. Myth-interpretation is a tricky business and there is some justification for looking at it askance. Hitherto the myth-interpreter has found himself in a somewhat unenviable position, because he only had exceedingly doubtful points for orientation at his disposal, such as astronomical and meteorological data. Modern psychology has the distinct advantage of having opened up a field of psychic phenomena which are themselves the matrix of all mythology—I mean dreams, visions, fantasies, and delusional ideas. Here the psychologist not only finds numerous points of correspondence with myth-motifs, but also has an invaluable opportunity to observe how such contents arise and to analyse their function in a living organism. We can in fact discover the same multiplicity of meanings and the same apparently limitless interchangeability of figures in dreams. On the other hand we are now in a position to establish certain laws, or at any rate rules, which make dream interpretation rather more certain. Thus, we know that dreams generally compensate the conscious situation, or supply what is lacking to it.[190] This very important principle of dream-interpretation also applies to myths. Furthermore, investigation of the products of the unconscious yields recognizable traces of archetypal structures which coincide with the myth-motifs,

190 Although the unconscious is, in general, complementary to consciousness, the complementing is not of a mechanical nature that can be clearly predicted, but acts in each case purposively and intelligently, so that it is better to think of it as compensation.

among them certain types which deserve the name of domi-
nants. These are archetypes like the anima, animus, wise old
man, witch, shadow, earth-mother, etc., and the organizing domi-
nants, the self, the circle, and the quaternity, i.e., the four functions or aspects of the self (cf. pls. LVI, LX) or of consciousness. It

Fig. 38. World plan
From an Aztec codex

is evident (figs. 38 and 39; pl. LIX*b*) that knowledge of these
types makes myth interpretation considerably easier and at the
same time puts it where it belongs, that is, on a psychic basis.

612   Looked at in this light, the hero myth is an unconscious
drama seen only in projection, like the happenings in Plato's
parable of the cave. The hero himself appears as a being of more
than human stature. He is distinguished from the very beginning by his godlike characteristics. Since he is psychologically

391

an archetype of the self, his divinity only confirms that the self is numinous, a sort of god, or having some share in the divine nature. In this mythologem may lie the root of the argument in favour of "homoousia." For psychology it makes a vast difference whether the self is to be considered "of the same nature" as the Father (ὁμοούσιος), or merely "of a similar nature" (ὁμοιούσιος). The decision in favour of homoousia was of great psychological importance, for it asserted that Christ is of the same nature as

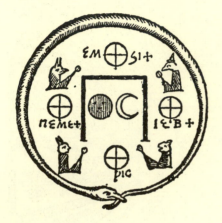

Fig. 39. The four corners of the zodiac: sun and moon in centre *Coptic emblem*

God. But Christ, from the point of view of psychology and comparative religion, is a typical manifestation of the self. For psychology the self is an *imago Dei* and cannot be distinguished from it empirically. (Cf. pl. LX.) The two ideas are therefore of the same nature. The hero is the protagonist of God's transformation in man; he corresponds to what I call the "mana personality." [191] The latter has such an immense fascination for the conscious mind that the ego all too easily succumbs to the temptation to identify with the hero, thus bringing on a psychic inflation with all its consequences. For this reason the repugnance felt by certain ecclesiastical circles for the "inner Christ" is understandable enough, at least as a preventive measure against the danger of psychic inflation which threatens the Christian European. Although the religion and philosophy of India are largely dominated by the idea of homoousia,[192] there

[191] See "The Relations between the Ego and the Unconscious," pars. 374ff.
[192] Identity of the personal and the suprapersonal atman.

is less danger in this direction because the Indian has an equally homoousian idea of God (Brahman), which is very definitely not the case with the Christian. The latter has far too little introspection to be able to realize what modifications in his present conception of God the homoousia of the self (Atman) would involve. I hope my reader will pardon these reflections, which may seem very remote from our theme. I add them here only to put the numinosity of the hero archetype in the right perspective.[193]

[193] Cf. *Psychological Types* (1923 edn., pp. 245ff.), and *Aion*, the chapters on the symbolism of the self.

VIII

THE SACRIFICE [1]

613   Let us now turn back to the Miller fantasies and watch the last act of the drama. Chiwantopel cries out with painful emotion:

"In all the world there is not a single one! I have searched among a hundred tribes. I have aged a hundred moons since I began. Will there never be anyone who will know my soul?—Yes, by almighty God, yes!—But ten thousand moons will wax and wane before her pure soul is born. And it is from another world that her parents will come to this one. She will be fair of skin and fair-haired. She will know sorrow even before her mother bears her. Suffering will be her companion; she too will seek—and will find no one who understands her. Many a suitor will wish to pay court to her, but not one of them will know how to understand her. Temptation will often assail her soul, but she will not yield. . . . In her dreams I shall come to her, and *she will understand*. I have kept my body inviolate. I have come ten thousand moons before her time, and she will come ten thousand moons too late. *But she will understand!* It is but once in ten thousand moons that a soul like hers is born!"

(A lacuna.)—A green viper darts out of the bushes, glides towards him, and stings him in the arm; then it attacks his horse, which is the first to succumb. Then Chi-wan-to-pel says to his horse: "Farewell, faithful brother! Enter into your rest! I have loved you and you have served me well. Farewell, I shall rejoin you soon!" Then to the serpent: "Thanks, little sister, you have put an end to my wanderings!" Now he shrieks with pain and calls out in prayer, "Almighty God, take me soon! I have sought to know thee and to keep thy law. Oh, suffer not my body to fall into corruption and decay, and become carrion for the eagles!" A smoking volcano appears in the distance, the rumbling of an earthquake is heard,

1 [In the Swiss edition, Ch. VII, "Das Opfer" ("The Sacrifice"), embraces all of the text composing Chs. VII and VIII of the present edition. It contains a break in the text at this point, but no heading. The present arrangement corresponds to that of the original Swiss edition and its English trans.—EDITORS.]

followed by a landslide. Chi-wan-to-pel cries out in an extremity of anguish as the earth closes over his body: "Ah, she will understand! Ja-ni-wa-ma, Ja-ni-wa-ma, thou that understandest me."

614 Chiwantopel's prophecy is an echo from Longfellow's *Hiawatha*, where, at the end of the hero's career, the poet could not resist the sentimentality of dragging in the white man's Saviour in the guise of the supreme representative of Christianity and Christian morals. (One thinks ruefully of the work of salvation accomplished by the Spaniards in Mexico and Peru, and of the Indian wars in North America.) With this prophecy the personality of our author is again brought into closest relationship with the hero as the real object of Chiwantopel's longing. The hero would undoubtedly have married her had she only lived in his time, but unfortunately she comes too late—ten thousand moons too late. This very considerable time-gap points to a gap in another sense: Miss Miller's ego is separated by a gulf from the figure of Chiwantopel. He is wholly "on the other side." She will seek him in vain, just as he seeks her; in other words, there will never be any possibility of a meeting or union of conscious and unconscious, the one thing needful to compensate the conscious attitude and create wholeness. She or he will be able at most to dream of such a meeting, and only so will their souls be able to understand one another, to love and embrace. But this love will never become a conscious fact. In this respect the situation holds no favourable prognosis for Miss Miller; for every real love-relationship consists ultimately in the girl finding her hero, and the hero his soul, not in dreams, but in palpable reality.

615 The next passage runs: "I have kept my body inviolate." This proud sentence, which naturally only a woman could utter, since a man is not given to boasting about such matters, confirms yet again that all enterprises have remained but dreams. The hero's assertion that he is inviolate refers back to the abortive attempt on his life in the preceding chapter and explains what exactly it meant. He tells us in the words: "Temptation will often assail her soul—but she will not yield." This statement expresses the "touch me not" attitude of our author, which is as it were dictated by her "ghostly lover." [2] At all

2 Cf. Harding, *The Way of All Women*.

events the awakening of this hero-figure—the animus—usually has some such consequences for the conscious mind. It is as if a new instinct were aroused, and the soul were seized by a hitherto unknown longing: the image of earthly love pales before that of the heavenly, which turns the heart and mind away from their "natural" destination. I use the word "natural" here in the sense given it by the Age of Enlightenment. In reality of course the world-spurning passion of the "spirit" is just as natural as the marriage-flight of insects. Love for the "heavenly bridegroom" or for Sophia is a phenomenon that is by no means confined to the sphere of Christianity. It is in fact that "other," equally natural instinct to cleave to the realities of the soul. These are not makeshift inventions, as certain theories would have us believe, but facts and figures which can fill a man with passion and enchantment, and turn his head as easily as the creatures of this world. "You are conscious only of the single urge," [3] says Faust to Wagner. But Miss Miller seems to be on the point of forgetting this urge for the sake of the other. By so doing she does not escape the danger of one-sidedness, but only changes its sign. Whoever loves the earth and its glory, and forgets the "dark realm," or confuses the two (which is mostly what happens), has spirit for his enemy; and whoever flees from the earth and falls into the "eternal arms" has life for an enemy. This is what happens to the hero Chiwantopel, who personifies Miss Miller's otherworldliness: he falls foul of the green snake.[4] Green is the colour of the vegetation numen ("green is life's golden tree"), and the snake is the representative of the world of instinct, especially of those vital processes which are psychologically the least accessible of all. Snake dreams always indicate a discrepancy between the attitude of the conscious mind and instinct, the snake being a personification of the threatening aspect of that conflict. The appearance of the green viper therefore means: "Look out! Danger ahead!"

616   We know from the rest of the story that Chiwantopel is eliminated very thoroughly indeed: first he is fatally bitten by the snake, then the snake kills his horse, his animal vitality, and finally he is engulfed in a volcanic eruption. This solution of the problem represents an attempt on the part of the unconscious

[3] [Cf. MacNeice trans., p. 40.]
[4] Cf. Jaffé's study of E. T. A. Hoffmann's "Golden Bowl."

to compensate and help the dangerous situation of the conscious mind. So far this situation has only been hinted at. But if it requires so drastic an annihilation of the hero, in contradiction to his usual mythological role, we may justifiably conclude that the human personality of the author is threatened in the highest degree by an invasion from the unconscious (euphemistically conceived as a "creative fantasy"). If only the fascinating Chiwantopel could be got out of the way, then there would at least be some hope of her interest turning again to the earth and its greenness, the other way being barred by the death of her lover. An invasion from the unconscious is very dangerous for the conscious mind when the latter is not in a position to understand and integrate the contents that have irrupted into it. One certainly does not have the feeling that Miss Miller is the "one who understands," though it is perfectly plain that "she who will understand" is meant for her. Since she has in fact not the slightest idea of what is happening, her situation is critical, because in these circumstances there is a very good chance of the conscious being overwhelmed by the unconscious, as indeed actually happened a little later, with fatal results.[5]

617   When such an invasion happens, we are often faced with a situation in which the unconscious overtakes or "takes over" the conscious mind. The latter has somehow got stuck, with the result that the unconscious takes over the forward-striving function, the process of transformation in time, and breaks the deadlock. The contents then pouring into consciousness are archetypal representations of what the conscious mind should have experienced if deadlock was to be avoided. The tendency to stand still can easily be seen from the special emphasis laid on the inviolateness of the body, as well as from the wish to preserve it from corruption in the grave. She wants to stop the turning wheel that rolls the years along with it—wants to hang on to childhood and eternal youth rather than die and rot in the earth. But although we can forget, in the long-cherished feelings of youth, in the dreamy recollection of memories stubbornly hung on to, that the wheel rolls onward, yet the greying hair, the lax skin, the lined face are pitiless reminders that whether or not we expose ourselves to the destructive forces of life, the poison of the stealthily creeping serpent of time con-

5 See my foreword to the 2nd (1925) edn. of the present work.

sumes our bodies nonetheless. Flight from life does not exempt us from the law of age and death. The neurotic who tries to wriggle out of the necessity of living wins nothing and only burdens himself with a constant foretaste of aging and dying, which must appear especially cruel on account of the total emptiness and meaninglessness of his life. If it is not possible for the libido to strive forwards, to lead a life that willingly accepts all dangers and ultimate decay, then it strikes back along the other road and sinks into its own depths, working down to the old intimation of the immortality of all that lives, to the old longing for rebirth.

618   Hölderlin follows this path in his poetry and in his life. I will let the poet speak for himself:

To a Rose

In the mother-womb eternal,
     Sweetest queen of every lea,
Still the living and supernal
     Nature carries thee and me.

Little rose, the tempest dire
     Strips our petals, ages us;
Yet the deathless seeds aspire
     To new blooms, miraculous.[6]

619   The following comments may be made on the imagery of this poem. The rose is a symbol of the beloved.[7] So when the poet dreams that he and the rose are in the womb of nature, it means psychologically that he is still in the mother. There he finds eternal germination and renewal, a potential life that has everything before it, containing in itself all possibilities of realization without his having to submit to the labour of giving them shape. Plutarch records the same motif in the naïve myth of Osiris and Isis mating in their mother's womb. Hölderlin likewise feels that it is the enviable prerogative of the gods to enjoy everlasting infancy. He says in "Hyperion's Song of Fate":

---

6 *Gedichte*, p. 53. [As trans. in the Hinkle (1916) edn.]

7 It is, indeed, the essence of the beloved and a designation for the Virgin Mary (mystical rose). Cf. Jung and Wilhelm, *The Secret of the Golden Flower* (1962 edn.), pp. 101f., and the mandala symbolism in *Psychology and Alchemy*, pars. 99 and 139; also Hartlaub, *Giorgiones Geheimnis*.

> Fateless, like the sleeping
> Infant, breathe the heavenly ones,
> Chastely guarded
> In modest bud;
> Their spirits
> Blossom eternally,
> And the quiet eyes
> Gaze out in placid
> Eternal serenity.[8]

620   This quotation shows what he means by heavenly bliss. Hölderlin was never able to forget this first and greatest happiness whose haunting presence estranged him from real life. The motif of the twins in the mother's womb is found in the African legend, recorded by Frobenius,[9] of the Big Snake, which grew out of a little snake in a hollow tree ("stretching forth of the serpent"), and which devoured all human beings (devouring mother = death) until only one pregnant woman remained. She dug a ditch, covered it with a stone, and there gave birth to twins who afterwards became dragon-killers. The mating in the mother also occurs in the following West African legend: "In the beginning, Obatala the Sky and Odudua the Earth, his wife, lay pressed close together in a calabash." [10] Being "guarded in modest bud" is an image that is found in Plutarch, where it is said that the sun is born at dawn from a flower bud. Brahma, too, comes out of a bud (cf. pl. xlvia), and in Assam a bud gave birth to the first human pair.

Man

> Scarcely had the ancient mountain tops
> Sprouted from the waters, O earth,
> And the first green islands, redolent
> With young saplings, breathed delight
> Through the May air over the ocean,
> And the joyful eye of the sun-god
> Looked down on his firstlings, the trees and flowers,
> Laughing children of his youth, your offspring:
> When, on the fairest of those islands,
> Born after a warm night, in the dawn-light long ago,
> Earth's most beautiful child

8 *Gedichte*, p. 315. [Based on the trans. in the Hinkle (1916) edn.]
9 *Zeitalter*, p. 68.   10 Ibid., p. 269.

Lay under clustering grapes. And the boy
Looked up to Father Helios, who knew him,
And tasting the sweet berries, he chose
The sacred vine for his nurse.
And soon he is grown; the beasts
Fear him, for he is other than they,
A Man. He is not like you and not
Like the father, for boldly the high
Soul of the father in him is united
With your joys and your sadness for always,
O earth. Rather would he resemble
Eternal nature, mother of gods, the terrible.

Therefore, O earth, his presumption
Drives him away from your breast, and your tender
Gifts are in vain; ever and ever too high
Does the proud heart beat!

Leaving the sweet meadow of his shores
Man must go out into flowerless waters,
And though his orchards shine like the starry night
With golden fruit, yet he digs

Caves for himself in the mountains and grubs in the pit
Far from the sacred ray of his father,
Faithless also to the sun-god, who
Loves not toilers and mocks at cares.

Ah! the birds of the wood breathe freer, and though
The breast of man more wildly and proudly heaves,
His arrogance turns to fear, and the delicate
Flowers of tranquillity bloom not for long.[11]

621   This poem contains the first hint of discord between the poet and nature; he begins to feel estranged from reality. Note that the little child chooses the "vine for his nurse." This Dionysian allusion reminds us of Judah in Jacob's blessing (Genesis 49 : 11): "binding his foal unto the vine, and his ass's colt unto the choice vine."

622   There is a Gnostic gem showing a she-ass suckling her foal, surmounted by the sign of Cancer and the inscription "D.N.-IHV.XPS.": *Dominus noster Jesus Christus*, to which is added,

[11] *Gedichte*, p. 115.

"Dei filius." [12] As Justin Martyr indignantly observes, the connections between the Christian legend and that of Dionysus are unmistakable (e.g., the miracle of the wine). In the Dionysus legend the ass plays an important part as the steed of Silenus. The ass pertains to the "second sun," Saturn, who was the star of Israel and is therefore to some extent identical with Yahweh. The mock crucifixion on the Palatine, with an ass's head (cf. pl. XLIII), is an allusion to the tale that an ass's head was worshipped in the temple at Jerusalem.[13] The difference between Christians and Jews was at that time not very clear to an outsider.

623   Hölderlin is mainly concerned with the Dionysian nature of man: the vine is his nurse, and his ambition is to "resemble eternal Nature, mother of gods, the terrible." The "terrible Mother" is the *mater saeva cupidinum,* unbridled and unbroken Nature, represented by the most paradoxical god of the Greek pantheon, Dionysus, who significantly enough was also Nietzsche's god, although actually Nietzsche's original experience suggests rather the sinister huntsman, Wotan. Wagner was more explicit on this point.

624   "Presumption" drives man away from the mother and from the earth, and estranges him from the "sacred ray of his father," until his defiance changes into fear. As a child of nature he falls into discord with her, precisely because he tries to resemble the "mother of gods." No reason guides him, only the Dionysian *libido effrenata:*

To Nature

While about thy veil I lingered, playing,
    And, like any bud, upon thee hung,[14]
Still I felt thy heart in every straying
    Sound about my heart that shook and clung.
While I groped with faith and painful yearning
    To your picture, glowing and unfurled,
Still I found a place for all my burning
    Tears, and for my love I found a world!

---

12 Robertson, *Christianity and Mythology,* p. 369.
13 [Cf. Tacitus, *Historiae,* V, III, 4, and Josephus, *Against Apion,* II, 4.—EDITORS.]
14 After our discussion of Hölderlin's last poem, it will be clear that Nature is to be understood as the mother. (Cf. fig. 1.) Here the poet imagines the mother as a tree upon which the child hangs like a bud. (Cf. pl. XXXIX.)

To the sun my heart before all others
    Turned as though he heard my every cry,
And it called the stars its little brothers,[15]
    As it called the spring God's melody;
And each breeze in groves or woodlands fruity
    Held thy spirit, and that same sweet joy
Moved the well-springs of my heart with beauty—
    Those were golden days without alloy.

Where the spring is cool in every valley,[16]
    And the youngest bush and twig is green,
And about the rocks the grasses rally,
    And the branches show the sky between,
There I lay, imbibing every flower
    In a rapt, intoxicated glee,
And, surrounded by a golden shower,
    From their heights the clouds sank down to me.[17]

Often, as a weary, wandering river
    Longs to join the ocean's placid mirth,
I have wept and lost myself forever
    In the fulness of thy love, O earth!

[15] In connection with his calling the stars his "brothers," I would remind the reader of what I said in Part I (par. 130) about the mystic identification with the stars: "I am a star wandering together with you," etc. Separation and differentiation from the mother, "individuation," produces that confrontation of subject and object which is the foundation of consciousness. Before this, man was one with the mother; that is to say, he was merged with the world as a whole. He did not yet know the sun was his brother; only after the separation did he begin to realize his affinity with the stars. This is a not uncommon occurrence in psychosis. For instance, in the case of a young labouring-man who developed schizophrenia, the first symptoms of his illness consisted in the feeling that he had a special relation to the sun and the stars. The stars became full of meaning for him, he thought they had something to do with him personally, and the sun gave him all sorts of strange ideas. One finds this apparently quite novel feeling for Nature very often in this disease. Another patient began to understand the language of the birds, who brought him messages from his sweetheart. (Cf. Siegfried!)

[16] Springs, fountains, etc. are images of totality.

[17] This image expresses the state of divine or infantile beatitude, as in Hölderlin's "Hyperion's Song of Fate" (trans. by Hamburger, p. 113):
    "You walk above in the light
    On soft floors, O blessed genii!
    Shining breezes of gods
    Touch you lightly."

Then, with every other joyful being,
    Forth I rushed from Time's captivity,
Like a pilgrim home from travel, fleeing
    To the arms of rapt Eternity.

Blest be childhood's golden dreams, their power
    Hid from me life's dismal poverty;
All the heart's good seeds ye brought to flower,
    Things I could not reach, ye gave to me!
In thy beauty and thy light, O Nature,
    Of all effort and compulsion free,[18]
Fruitful love attained a kingly stature,
    Rich as harvests reaped in Arcady.

That which brought me up is dead and riven,
    Dead the youthful world which was my shield,
And this breast, which used to harbour heaven,
    Dead and dry as any stubble field.
Though the songs of springtime sound as ever,
    Bringing friendly comfort to my smart,
Yet the morning of my life is over
    And the spring has faded from my heart.

Shadows are the things that once we cherished,
    Love itself must fade and cannot bide;
Since the golden dreams of youth have perished
    Even friendly Nature's self has died.
Heart, poor heart, those days could never show it—
    How far-off thy home, and where it lies;
Now, alas, thou nevermore wilt know it
    If a dream of it does not suffice.[19]

Palinode

What gathers about me, Earth, in your dusky, friendly green?
What do you waft me, airs, what do you bring me again?
There is a rustling in all the tree-tops . . .

[18] This passage is specially significant: in childhood everything came as a gift, and he is unable to attain this state again, because it is won only through "effort and compulsion"—even love costs effort. In childhood the spring runs over in bubbling fulness, but in later life it needs a lot of hard work to keep it flowing at all, because the older we get the more it tends to flow back to its source.

[19] *Gedichte*, p. 57. [As trans. in the Hinkle (1916) edn., slightly modified.]

Why do you wake my soul? why stir up
The past in me, ye kindly ones?
Spare me and let them rest, do not mock
The ashes of my joy. Pass on,
Ye fateless gods, let your youthfulness
Flower upon those grown old.
If you would deign to come down to mortals,
Young girls will blossom for you,
Young heroes, and sweeter than ever
Morning will play round the cheeks of the happy,
And ravishing sound
The songs of those without care . . .

Ah, once the fountain of song
So easily rushed from my bosom, when heavenly
Joy still shone from my eyes . . .[20]

625   The separation from youth has even taken away the golden glamour of Nature, and the future appears hopeless and empty. But what robs Nature of its glamour, and life of its joy, is the habit of looking back for something that used to be outside, instead of looking inside, into the depths of the depressive state. This looking back leads to regression and is the first step along that path. Regression is also an involuntary introversion in so far as the past is an object of memory and therefore a psychic content, an endopsychic factor. It is a relapse into the past caused by a depression in the present. Depression should therefore be regarded as an unconscious compensation whose content must be made conscious if it is to be fully effective. This can only be done by consciously regressing along with the depressive tendency and integrating the memories so activated into the conscious mind—which was what the depression was aiming at in the first place.

Empedocles

You seek life, and a godly fire
Gushes and gleams for you out of the deeps of earth,
As, with shuddering longing, you
Hurl yourself down to the flames of Etna.

So by a queen's wanton whim
Pearls were dissolved in wine—heed her not!

20 Ibid., p. 156.

What folly, O poet, to cast your riches
Into that bright and bubbling cup!

Yet still you are holy to me, as the might of earth
That bore you away, audaciously perishing!
And I would follow the hero into the depths
Did not love hold me.[21]

626　　This poem reveals the poet's secret longing for the maternal depths and for the regenerating womb. (Cf. fig. 40.) He would

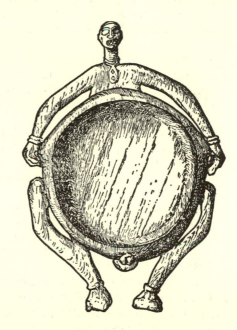

Fig. 40. The womb of the World Mother
Wooden bowl, Congo

like to be melted like pearls in wine, to be sacrificed in the chalice, the "krater" of rebirth. He longs to imitate Empedocles, of whom Horace says: "Empedocles, eager to be thought a god immortal, coolly leapt into burning Aetna." [22]

627　　He wants to go the way of the hero, the ideal figure that floats before him, and to share his fate. Yet love still holds him back in the light of day. The libido still has an object which makes life worth living. If this object were abandoned, then the

21 Ibid., p. 142. [Cf. Leishman trans., p. 55.]
22 *Ars poetica,* trans. by Fairclough, pp. 488–89.

libido would sink down to the subterranean mother for rebirth:

In Memoriam

Daily I go a different path, sometimes
Into the green wood, sometimes to bathe in the spring,
Or to the rock where the roses bloom.
From the top of the hill I look over the land,

Yet nowhere, O lovely one, nowhere in the light do I find you,
And in the breezes my words die away,
The sacred words we once had . . .

Aye, you are far removed, holy countenance!
And the melody of your life is kept from me,
No longer overheard. And where are
The magical songs that once

Soothed my heart with the peace of the heavenly ones?
How long it is, how long! the youth is
Grown old, the earth itself, which then
Smiled upon me, has grown different.

Farewell! each day the soul departs,
Turns back to you, and over you weeps
The eye that with brighter shining
Gazes across again, there where you tarry.[23]

628   This distinctly suggests a renunciation, an envy of one's own
youth, of that time of "effortlessness" which one would so gladly
cling on to. But the final stanza portends disaster: a gazing towards the other land, the distant coast of sunrise or sunset. Love
no longer holds the poet fast, the bonds with the world are
broken, and loudly he calls for help to the mother:

Achilles

Lordly son of the gods! Because you had lost your beloved,
You went to the rocky coast and cried aloud to the flood,
Till the depths of the holy abyss heard you and echoed your grief
In the stillness, where far from the clamour of ships,
Deep under the waves, in a peaceful cave, the beautiful

[23] *Gedichte,* p. 157.

Thetis dwells, your protectress, goddess and nymph of the sea.
Mother she was to the youth, for the powerful goddess
Had once, on the rocky shore of his island, lovingly
Nursed the boy at her breast, had made him a hero
With the might of her strengthening bath and the powerful song of
    the waves.
And the mother, lamenting, heard the cry of her child,
And rose like a cloud from the gloomy bed of the sea,
Quieted with tender embraces the pains of her darling.
And he listened while she, caressing him, promised to help him.
Son of the gods! O were I like you, I could trustingly
Pour out my secret grief to one of the Heavenly Ones.
This I shall never see, but must bear the disgrace, as though I
No more belonged to her who still thinks of me, even with tears.
Beneficent gods, who disdain not men's prayers, then hear me!
How raptly and fervently have I not loved you, holy light,
Since I have lived, the earth and your fountains and woodlands,
Father Aether—this heart has felt you about me too ardent and pure.
O soften, ye kind ones, my sorrows, that my soul be not silenced too
    early,
That I may live and thank you, heavenly powers in the highest,
With joyful song till the last, hurrying day,
Thank you for gifts gone by, for the joys of lost youth,
Then take me out of my loneliness up to yourselves.[24]

629   These songs describe more vividly than one could hope to
do in plain language the poet's steady withdrawal and increasing estrangement from life, his gradual submersion in the abyss
of memory. After these nostalgic longings the apocalyptic vision
of Patmos bursts upon us like a mysterious visitor from another
world, a vision swirled round by mists from the abyss, by the
gathering clouds of insanity bred by the mother. Mythological
ideas again flash forth, symbolic intimations of death and the
resurrection of life.

630   I give here some significant fragments from "Patmos":

    Near is God
    And hard to apprehend.
    But where danger is, there
    Arises salvation also.[25]

24 Ibid., p. 244.
25 Ibid., pp. 335ff. [For passages up to par. 642, from "Patmos," cf. Hamburger
trans., pp. 217ff.]

631 These words show that the libido has now sunk to a depth where "the danger is great" (*Faust*, "The Mothers"). There God is near, there man would find the maternal vessel of rebirth, the seeding-place where he could renew his life. For life goes on despite loss of youth; indeed it can be lived with the greatest intensity if looking back to what is already moribund does not hamper your step. Looking back would be perfectly all right if only it did not stop at externals, which cannot be brought back again in any case; instead, it ought to consider where the fascination of the past really springs from. The golden haze of childhood memories arises not so much from the objective facts as from the admixture of magical images which are more intuited than actually conscious. The parable of Jonah who was swallowed by the whale reproduces the situation exactly. A person sinks into his childhood memories and vanishes from the existing world. He finds himself apparently in deepest darkness, but then has unexpected visions of a world beyond. The "mystery" he beholds represents the stock of primordial images which everybody brings with him as his human birthright, the sum total of inborn forms peculiar to the instincts. I have called this "potential" psyche the collective unconscious. If this layer is activated by the regressive libido, there is a possibility of life being renewed, and also of its being destroyed. Regression carried to its logical conclusion means a linking back with the world of natural instincts, which in its formal or ideal aspect is a kind of *prima materia*. If this *prima materia* can be assimilated by the conscious mind it will bring about a reactivation and reorganization of its contents. But if the conscious mind proves incapable of assimilating the new contents pouring in from the unconscious, then a dangerous situation arises in which they keep their original, chaotic, and archaic form and consequently disrupt the unity of consciousness. The resultant mental disturbance is therefore advisedly called schizophrenia, since it is a madness due to the splitting of the mind.

632 In his poem, Hölderlin describes the experience of entering into that wonderland of primordial images:

> In darkness dwell
> The eagles, and fearless across the abyss
> Go the sons of the Alps
> On lightly built bridges.

633   With these words the dark fantastic poem sweeps on. The
eagle, the sun-bird, dwells in darkness—the libido has hidden
itself, but high overhead pass the dwellers in the mountains,
probably the gods ("Ye wander above in the light"), symbols of
the sun travelling across the sky like an eagle flying over the
depths.

> Therefore, since all round are upheaped
> The summits of time,
> And those that dwell nearest in love
> Must languish on uttermost mountains,
> Give us then innocent water,
> O pinions give us, to pass
> Over with constant minds and again return.

634   The first image is a sombre one of mountains and time,
probably called up by the sun wandering over the mountains;
the next image, visualizing the simultaneous nearness and
separation of the lovers, seems to hint at life in the underworld,[26] where one is united with everything that was dear to
one and yet cannot enjoy the happiness of reunion because it
is all shadowy, unreal and devoid of life. There the descending
soul drinks the "innocent" water, the drink of rejuvenation,[27]
that he may grow wings and soar up again into life, like the
winged sun-disc (cf. pls. VII, IXa) which rises swan-like from the
water.

> So I spoke, when swifter
> Than I had fancied, and far
> Whither I never had thought to come,
> A Genius bore me away

[26] Cf. the passage in Odysseus' journey to Hades, where he meets his mother:
"As my mother spoke, there came to me out of the confusion in my heart the
one desire, to embrace her spirit, dead though she was. Thrice, in my eagerness
to clasp her to me, I started forward with my hands outstretched. Thrice, like a
shadow or a dream, she slipped through my arms and left me harrowed by an
even sharper pain." (Odyssey, XI, 204–8, trans. by Rieu, p. 181.)

[27] Spielrein's patient (p. 345), in connection with the significance of the communion, speaks of "water mingled with childishness," "spermatic water," "blood
and wine." On p. 368 she says: "The souls fallen in the water are saved by God:
they fall on deeper ground. Souls are saved by the sun-god." Cf. also the miraculous properties of the alchemical *aqua permanens* (*Psychology and Alchemy*, pars.
94 and 336f.).

> From my house. In the twilight
> The shadowy woods darkened as I went
> And the yearning brooks of my home;
> No more did I know these lands.

635   After the dark and enigmatic prelude, which is like a premonition of what is to come, the poet begins the journey to the East, towards the sunrise, towards the mystery of eternity and rebirth, of which Nietzsche also dreams:

O how should I not burn for eternity and for the nuptial ring of rings—the ring of return! Never yet did I find the woman from whom I desired children, unless it be this woman whom I love: for I love thee, O Eternity.[28]

636   Hölderlin puts this same longing into a magnificent image, whose main features we know already:

> Yet soon in fresh radiance,
> Mysterious
> In the golden smoke,
> Swiftly sprung up
> With the tread of the sun,
>
> Asia bloomed out before me,
> Fragrant with a thousand peaks, and dazzled
> I sought one that I knew, for I was
> A stranger to the broad streets
> Where the gold-flecked Pactolus
> Rushes down from Tmolus,
> And Taurus stands and Messogis,
> And full of flowers the garden,
> A quiet fire. But high in the light
> Blossoms the silver snow,
> And, witness to life everlasting,
> On attainless walls
> The immemorial ivy [29] grows, and upborne
> Upon living columns of cedars and laurels
> Are the solemn,
> The divinely built palaces.

[28] *Thus Spake Zarathustra:* "The Seven Seals," trans. by Common, p. 272, modified.

[29] The φάρμακον ἀθανασίας, the soma-drink, the haoma of the Persians, may have been made from *Ephedra vulgaris.* Spiegel, *Erānische Altertumskunde,* I, p. 433.

637   The vision is apocalyptic: the mother-city in the land of
eternal youth, surrounded by the flowery verdure of imperishable spring.[30] (Cf. pl. xxiia.) The poet identifies himself here
with John, who lived on Patmos and consorted with the "Son of
the Highest" and saw him face to face:

> As at the mystery of the vine
> They sat together at the hour of the banquet,
> And quietly prescient in his great soul
> The Lord spake death and the last love . . .
>
> Thereon he died. Of that
> There were much to be said. And the friends saw
> How he gazed forth victorious,
> The most joyful of all, at the last . . .
>
> Therefore he sent them
> The Spirit, and the house
> Solemnly trembled,
> And the storm of God
> Rolled far-thundering over their visionary heads,
> Where brooding
> The heroes of death were assembled,
> As he now, in departure,
> Once more appeared before them.
> For now was put out
> The day of the sun, the kingly one,
> And himself, divinely suffering,
> Shattered the straight-rayed sceptre,
> For it shall come again
> At the proper time . . .

[30] Like the heavenly city in Hauptmann's *Hannele* (trans. by Meltzer, pp. 91–92):
> "The Realm of Righteousness is filled with light and joy,
> God's everlasting peace reigns there without alloy,
> Its mansions are marble, its roofs are of gold,
> Through its rivulets ripple wines ruddy and old.
> In its silver-white streets blow the lily and rose,
> In its steeples the chiming of joy-bells grows.
> The beautiful butterflies frolic and play
> On its ramparts, rich-robed in the mosses of May . . .
> The blessed below, in the regions of Light,
> Wander on, hand in hand, and rejoice in their flight.
> In the depths of the radiant, the ruby-red waves,
> Swan dives after swan, as its plumage it laves.
> So they wash themselves clean in the clear, deep red
> Of the blood that their Lord, their dear Saviour, had shed."

638   The underlying images are the sacrificial death and resurrection of Christ, conceived as the self-sacrifice of the sun, which voluntarily breaks its rayed sceptre in the certain hope of resurrection. Concerning the substance of the rayed sceptre the following may be noted: Spielrein's patient said that "God pierces the earth with his ray." For her the earth was a woman; she also regarded the sunbeam in mythological fashion as something solid: "Jesus Christ has shown me his love by tapping at the window with a sunbeam." I have come across the same idea of the solid substance of the sunbeam in other insane patients. Thor's hammer, which split the earth and penetrated deep into it, may be compared with Kaineus' foot. Inside the earth the hammer comports itself like the treasure, for in the fulness of time it comes to the surface again, i.e., is born again from the earth. At the place where Samson threw away the jawbone of the ass the Lord caused a fountain to gush forth.[31] Springs also come from hoof-marks, footprints, horse's hooves. Magic wands and sceptres in general come into this category of meanings. Gr. σκῆπτρον is related to σκᾶπος, σκηπάνιον, σκήπων = 'staff'; σκηπτός = 'storm-wind'; Lat. *scapus,* 'shaft, stalk'; OHG. *scaft,* 'spear, lance.' [32] (Cf. pl. XLV.) So once again we meet in this context the connections already known to us as libido-symbols. The breaking of the sceptre therefore signifies the sacrifice of power as previously exercised, i.e., of the libido which had been organized in a certain direction.

639   That Hölderlin's poem should pass from Asia to Patmos and thence to the Christian mystery may seem like a superficial association of ideas, but actually it is a highly significant train of thought: it is the entry into death and the land beyond, seen as the self-sacrifice of the hero for the attainment of immortality. At this time, when the sun has set and life seems extinguished, man awaits in secret expectancy the renewal of all life:

> And it was joy
> From now on
> To dwell in loving night and maintain
> Steadfast in simple eyes
> Abysses of wisdom.

31 Judges 15 : 17f.
32 Prellwitz, *Wörterbuch der griechischen Sprache,* s.v. σκήπτω.

640   Wisdom dwells in the depths, the wisdom of the mother; being one with her means being granted a vision of deeper things, of the primordial images and primitive forces which underlie all life and are its nourishing, sustaining, creative matrix. Hölderlin, in his pathological ecstasy, senses the grandeur of the things seen, but unlike Faust he does not care to bring into the light of day all that he has found in the depths:

> And no evil it is if something
> Is lost and the living sound
> Fades from our speech,
> For heavenly labour is like to our own.
> The Highest would not have
> All at one time.
> So long as the pit bears iron
> And Etna fiery resin,
> So I have riches
> To fashion an image and see
> The Spirit [33] as ever it was.

641   What the poet beholds in his Vulcan's pit is in truth the "Spirit" as ever it was, namely the totality of primary forms from which the archetypal images come. In this world of the collective unconscious spirit appears as an archetype which is endowed with supreme significance and is expressed through the figure of the divine hero, whose counterpart in the West is Christ.

> He wakens the dead,
> Who are not yet bound
> By the grossness of death . . .

> And if the heavenly ones,
> As I believe, so love me. . . .

> Quiet is his [34] sign
> In the thunderous sky. And One stands beneath it
> His life long. For Christ lives yet.

642   But, as once Gilgamesh, bringing back the magic herb from the Western Land (cf. pl. xix), was robbed of his treasure by

---

[33] When writing this book I used an old edition of Hölderlin. Modern editions have "Christ" for "Geist." I have retained the old reading, because, on the internal evidence of the poem, I gathered that it meant Christ even before I saw the modern reading.   [34] I.e., the Father's.

the demon-serpent, so Hölderlin's poem dies away in a painful lament, which tells us that his descent to the shadows will be followed by no resurrection in this world:

> . . . shamefully
> A mighty force wrenches the heart from us,
> For the heavenly each demand sacrifice.

643   This recognition, that one must give up the retrospective longing which only wants to resuscitate the torpid bliss and effortlessness of childhood, *before* the "heavenly ones" wrench the sacrifice from us (and with it the entire man), came too late to the poet.

644   I therefore take it as a wise counsel which the unconscious gives our author, to let her hero die, for he was really not much more than the personification of a regressive and infantile reverie, having neither the will nor the power to make good his aversion from this world by fishing up another from the primeval ocean of the unconscious, which would truly have been an heroic act. Such a sacrifice can only be accomplished through whole-hearted dedication to life. All the libido that was tied up in family bonds must be withdrawn from the narrower circle into the larger one, because the psychic health of the adult individual, who in childhood was a mere particle revolving in a rotary system, demands that he should himself become the centre of a new system. That such a step includes the solution, or at least some consideration, of the sexual problem is obvious enough, for unless this is done the unemployed libido will inevitably remain fixed in the unconscious endogamous relationship to the parents and will seriously hamper the individual's freedom. We must remember that Christ's teaching means ruthlessly separating a man from his family, and we saw in the Nicodemus dialogue how he took especial pains to give regression a symbolic meaning. Both tendencies serve the same goal, namely that of freeing man from his family fixations, from his weakness and uncontrolled infantile feelings. For if he allows his libido to get stuck in a childish milieu, and does not free it for higher purposes, he falls under the spell of unconscious compulsion. Wherever he may be, the unconscious will then recreate the infantile milieu by projecting his complexes, thus reproducing

all over again, and in defiance of his vital interests, the same dependence and lack of freedom which formerly characterized his relations with his parents. His destiny no longer lies in his own hands: his Τύχαι καί Μοῖραι (fortunes and fates) fall from the stars. The Stoics called this condition Heimarmene, compulsion by the stars, to which every "unredeemed" soul is subject. When the libido thus remains fixed in its most primitive form it keeps men on a correspondingly low level where they have no control over themselves and are at the mercy of their affects. That was the psychological situation of late antiquity, and the saviour and physician of that time was he who sought to free humanity from bondage to Heimarmene.[35]

645   Miss Miller's vision seems at first sight to treat the problem of sacrifice as a purely individual problem, but if we examine the way it is worked out we shall see that it is something that must be a problem for humanity in general. For the symbols employed—the snake that kills the horse, and the hero who sacrifices himself of his own free will—are mythological figures born of the unconscious.

646   To the extent that the world and everything in it is a product of thought, the sacrifice of the libido that strives back to the past necessarily results in the creation of the world. For him who looks backwards the whole world, even the starry sky, becomes the mother who bends over him and enfolds him on all sides, and from the renunciation of this image, and of the longing for it, arises the picture of the world as we know it today. This simple thought is what constitutes the meaning of the cosmic sacrifice, a good example being the slaying of Tiamat (fig. 41), the Babylonian mother-dragon, from whose body heaven and earth were made.[36] But perhaps the fullest expres-

---

[35] This was the real purpose of all the mystery religions. They created symbols of death and rebirth (cf. pl. LXIa). As Frazer points out in *The Golden Bough* (Part III: "The Dying God," pp. 214ff.), even primitive peoples have in their initiation mysteries the same symbolism of dying and being born again as Apuleius records in connection with the initiation of Lucius into the Isis mysteries (*The Golden Ass*, XI, 23, trans. by Graves, p. 286): "I approached the very gates of death and set one foot on Proserpine's threshold, yet was permitted to return, rapt through all the elements." The rites of initiation "approximate to a voluntary death" from which Lucius was "born again" (p. 284). (Cf. pl. VI.)

[36] From the sacrifice of the dragon in alchemy comes the microcosm of the philosophers' stone (*Psychology and Alchemy*, par. 404).

sion of this idea is to be found in Indian philosophy of the oldest date, in the Vedic hymns. The Rig-Veda asks:

> What was the wood, what was the tree,
> From which heaven and earth were hewn?
> Let the sages inquire within their minds.[37]

Fig. 41. Marduk fighting Tiamat
Assyrian cylinder seal

647   Vishvakarman, the All-Creator, who made the world from the unknown tree, did so as follows:

> Sacrificing as a wise sacrificer,
> Our Father entered into all these beings;
> Striving for blessings through prayer,
> Hiding his origin, he went into the lower world.
> Yet what and who has served him
> As a resting-place and a support?

648   The Rig-Veda proceeds to answer these questions: **Purusha** (Man, Anthropos) was the primal being who

> Encompassed the earth on all sides
> And ruled over the ten-finger place
> (the highest point of heaven).[38]

649   Purusha is evidently a sort of Platonic world-soul who surrounds the earth from outside:

> Being born he overtopped the world
> Before, behind, and in all places.

[37] Rig-Veda, X, 81, 4. This passage, and those in pars. 647 and 649, trans. from Deussen, *Geschichte*, pp. 136 and 156.
[38] Rig-Veda, X, 90. This passage, and those in pars. 650, 651, 656, trans. by W. Norman Brown, in the *Journal of the American Oriental Society*, LI (1931).

650   As the all-encompassing world-soul Purusha has a maternal character, for he represents the original "dawn state" of the psyche: he is the encompasser and the encompassed, mother and unborn child, an undifferentiated, unconscious state of primal being. As such a condition must be terminated, and as it is at the same time an object of regressive longing, it must be sacrificed in order that discriminated entities—i.e., conscious contents—may come into being:

Him, Purusha, born at the beginning, they besprinkled on the straw; the gods sacrificed with him, and the saints and the sages.

651   The passage is very remarkable. If one attempted to put this mythologem on the Procrustean bed of logic sore violence would be done to it. How on earth ordinary "sages" come to be sacrificing the primal being side by side with the gods is an utterly fantastic conception, quite apart from the fact that in the beginning (i.e., before the sacrifice) nothing existed except the primal being! But if this primal being means the great mystery of the original psychic state, then everything becomes clear:

From that sacrifice when it was fully offered the speckled (clotted) butter was collected; it constituted the birds and the wild and domestic animals.

From that sacrifice when it was fully offered the hymns were born, and the chants; the metres were born from it, and from it the prose formula was born. . . .

The moon was born from his mind; from his eye was born the sun; from his mouth Indra and Agni; from his breath Vayu was born.

From his navel grew the atmosphere; from his head the sky; from his feet the earth; from his ear the directions. Thus the worlds are made.

652   It is evident that by this is meant not a physical, but a psychological cosmogony. The world comes into being when man discovers it. But he only discovers it when he sacrifices his containment in the primal mother, the original state of unconsciousness. What drives him towards this discovery is conceived by Freud as the "incest barrier." The incest prohibition blocks the infantile longing for the mother and forces the libido along the path of life's biological aim. The libido, driven back from the mother by the incest prohibition, seeks a sexual object in

place of the forbidden mother. Here the terms "incest prohibition," "mother," etc. are used metaphorically, and it is in this sense that we have to interpret Freud's paradoxical dictum: "To begin with we knew only sexual objects." [39] This statement is not much more than a sexual allegory, as when one speaks of male and female electrical connections, screws, etc. All it does is to read the partial truths of the adult into infantile conditions which are totally different. Freud's view is incorrect if we take it literally, for it would be truer to say that at a still earlier stage we knew nothing but nourishing breasts. The fact that the infant finds pleasure in sucking does not prove that it is a sexual pleasure, for pleasure can have many different sources. Presumably the caterpillar finds quite as much pleasure in eating, even though caterpillars possess no sexual function whatever and the food instinct is something quite different from the sex instinct, quite unconcerned about what a later sexual stage may make of these earlier activities. Kissing, for instance, derives far more from the act of nutrition than from sexuality. Moreover the so-called "incest barrier" is an exceedingly doubtful hypothesis (admirable as it is for describing certain neurotic conditions), because it is a product of culture which nobody invented and which grew up naturally on the basis of complex biological necessities connected with the development of "marriage classes." The main purpose of these is not to prevent incest but to meet the social danger of endogamy by instituting the "cross-cousin marriage." The typical marriage with the daughter of the maternal uncle is actually implemented by the same libido which could equally well possess the mother or the sister. So it is not a question of avoiding incest, for which incidentally there are plenty of opportunities in the frequent fits of promiscuity to which primitives are prone, but of the social necessity of spreading the family organization throughout the whole tribe.[40]

653   Therefore it cannot have been the incest-taboo that forced mankind out of the original psychic state of non-differentiation. On the contrary, it was the evolutionary instinct peculiar to man, which distinguishes him so radically from all other ani-

[39] "The Dynamics of the Transference," p. 105.
[40] Cf. my "Psychology of the Transference," pars. 433ff. and Layard, "The Incest Taboo and the Virgin Archetype," pp. 254ff.

mals and forced upon him countless taboos, among them the incest-taboo. Against this "other urge" the animal in us fights with all his instinctive conservatism and misoneism—hatred of novelty—which are the two outstanding features of the primitive and feebly conscious individual. Our mania for progress represents the inevitable morbid compensation.

654   Freud's incest theory describes certain fantasies that accompany the regression of libido and are especially characteristic of the personal unconscious as found in hysterical patients. Up to a point they are infantile-sexual fantasies which show very clearly just where the hysterical attitude is defective and why it is so incongruous. They reveal the shadow. Obviously the language used by this compensation will be dramatic and exaggerated. The theory derived from it exactly matches the hysterical attitude that causes the patient to be neurotic. One should not, therefore, take this mode of expression quite as seriously as Freud himself took it. It is just as unconvincing as the ostensibly sexual traumata of hysterics. The neurotic sexual theory is further discomfited by the fact that the last act of the drama consists in a return to the mother's body. This is usually effected not through the natural channels but through the mouth, through being devoured and swallowed (pl. LXII), thereby giving rise to an even more infantile theory which has been elaborated by Otto Rank. All these allegories are mere makeshifts. The real point is that the regression goes back to the deeper layer of the nutritive function, which is anterior to sexuality, and there clothes itself in the experiences of infancy. In other words, the sexual language of regression changes, on retreating still further back, into metaphors derived from the nutritive and digestive functions, and which cannot be taken as anything more than a *façon de parler*. The so-called Oedipus complex with its famous incest tendency changes at this level into a "Jonah-and-the-Whale" complex, which has any number of variants, for instance the witch who eats children, the wolf, the ogre, the dragon, and so on. Fear of incest turns into fear of being devoured by the mother. The regressing libido apparently desexualizes itself by retreating back step by step to the presexual stage of earliest infancy. Even there it does not make a halt, but in a manner of speaking continues right back to the intra-uterine, pre-natal condition and, leaving the sphere

of personal psychology altogether, irrupts into the collective psyche where Jonah saw the "mysteries" ("représentations collectives") in the whale's belly. The libido thus reaches a kind of inchoate condition in which, like Theseus and Peirithous on their journey to the underworld, it may easily stick fast. But it can also tear itself loose from the maternal embrace and return to the surface with new possibilities of life.

655   What actually happens in these incest and womb fantasies is that the libido immerses itself in the unconscious, thereby provoking infantile reactions, affects, opinions and attitudes from the personal sphere, but at the same time activating collective images (archetypes) which have a compensatory and curative meaning such as has always pertained to the myth. Freud makes his theory of neurosis—so admirably suited to the nature of neurotics—much too dependent on the neurotic ideas from which precisely the patients suffer. This leads to the pretence (which suits the neurotic down to the ground) that the *causa efficiens* of his neurosis lies in the remote past. In reality the neurosis is manufactured anew every day, with the help of a false attitude that consists in the neurotic's thinking and feeling as he does and justifying it by his theory of neurosis.

656   After this digression, let us turn back to our Vedic hymn. Rig-Veda X, 90 closes with a significant verse which is also of the greatest importance as regards the Christian mystery:

With the sacrifice the gods sacrificed to the sacrifice; these were the first ordinances. These powers (arising from the sacrifice) reach the sky where are the saints and the gods.[41]

657   Sacrifice brings with it a plenitude of power that is equal to the power of the gods. Even as the world is created by sacrifice, by renouncing the personal tie to childhood, so, according to the teaching of the Upanishads, will be created the new state of man, which can be described as immortal. This new state beyond the human one is again attained through a sacrifice, the horse-sacrifice, which has cosmic significance. What the sacrificed horse means we learn from the Brihadaranyaka Upanishad:

Om!
    1. Verily, dawn is the head of the sacrificial horse, the sun his eye, the wind his breath, universal fire his open mouth. The year is the

41 Trans. by W. Norman Brown.

body of the sacrificial horse, the sky his back, the atmosphere his belly, the earth the underpart of his belly, the quarters his flanks, the intermediate quarters his ribs, the seasons his limbs, the months and half-months his joints, days and nights his feet, the stars his bones, the clouds his flesh. Sand is the food in his stomach, rivers are his entrails. His liver and lungs are the mountains, plants and trees his hair. The rising sun is his forepart, the setting sun his hindpart. When he shows his teeth, that is lightning. When he shakes himself, then it thunders. When he urinates, then it rains. His voice is speech.

2. Verily, day was created for the horse as the sacrificial dish which stands before him; its place is the world-ocean towards the east. Night was created for the sacrificial horse as the sacrificial dish which stands behind him; its place is the world-ocean towards the west.

Verily, these two surround the horse on both sides as the two sacrificial vessels.

As a steed he carried the gods, as a charger the Gandharvas, as a racer the demons, as a horse men. The ocean is his kinsman, the sea his cradle.[42]

658   As Deussen remarks, the horse-sacrifice signifies a renunciation of the world. When the horse is sacrificed the world is sacrificed and destroyed—a train of thought that also suggested itself to Schopenhauer. The horse stands between two sacrificial vessels, passing from one to the other, just as the sun passes from morning to evening. (Cf. fig. 3.) Since the horse is man's steed and works for him, and energy is even measured in terms of "horse power," the horse signifies a quantum of energy that stands at man's disposal. It therefore represents the libido which has passed into the world. We saw earlier on that the "mother-libido" must be sacrificed in order to create the world; here the world is destroyed by renewed sacrifice of the same libido, which once belonged to the mother and then passed into the world. The horse, therefore, may reasonably be substituted as a symbol for this libido because, as we saw, it has numerous connections with the mother.[43] The sacrifice of the horse can only produce another phase of introversion similar to that which

42 Trans. by Hume, *The Thirteen Principal Upanishads*, pp. 73–74, modified.
43 The Bundahish (XV, 37) says that the bull Sarsaok will be sacrificed at the end of the world. Sarsaok helped to distribute the human race: he carried nine of the fifteen races on his back through the sea to the most distant parts of the earth. The primordial bull of Gayomart has, as we saw earlier, a maternal significance on account of his fertility.

prevailed before the creation of the world. The position of the horse between the two vessels, which represent the birth-giving and the devouring mother, hints at the idea of life enclosed in the ovum; consequently the vessels are destined to "surround" the horse. That this is in fact so can be seen from the Brihada-ranyaka Upanishad 3, 3 ("Where the offerers of the horse sacrifice go"):

"What has become of the Parikshitas? I ask you, Yajñavalkya, what has become of the Parikshitas?"
Yajñavalkya said: ". . . Doubtless they have gone whither the offerers of the horse sacrifice go."
"And where, pray, do the offerers of the horse sacrifice go?"
"This inhabited world is as broad as thirty-two days' journeys of the sun-god's chariot. The earth, which is twice as broad, surrounds it on all sides. The ocean, which is twice as broad, surrounds the earth on all sides. There [44] is a gap as broad as the edge of a razor or the wing of a mosquito. Indra, taking the form of a falcon, delivered the Parikshitas to the wind, and the wind took them and bore them to the place where the offerers of the horse sacrifice were . . .
"Therefore the wind is the most individual thing (*vyashti*) and the most universal (*samashti*). He who knows this wards off repeated death." [45]

659   As the text says, the offerers of the horse-sacrifice go to that narrowest of gaps between the shells of the world-egg, the point where they are at once united and divided. Indra, who in the form of a falcon has stolen the soma (the treasure hard to attain), is the psychopomp who delivers the souls to the wind, to the generating pneuma, the individual and universal *prana* (life-breath),[46] to save them from "repeated death." This line of thought summarizes the meaning of innumerable myths and is at the same time an excellent example of how far Indian philosophy is, in a certain sense, nothing more than refined and sublimated mythology.[47] In the Miller drama the first to die is the

44 Deussen says (*Sechzig Upanishads*, III, p. 434): " 'There,' on the horizon where the sky and the sea meet, between the two shells of the world egg, is a narrow crack through which one can get out onto 'the back of the sky,' where . . . union with Brahman takes place."
45 Trans. by Hume, p. 111, modified.   46 Symbol of Brahman (Deussen).
47 If mythological symbolism is for Silberer ("Über die Symbolbildung," III, pp. 664ff.) a cognitional process on the mythological level, then there is complete agreement between his view and mine.

horse, the animal brother of the hero (corresponding to the early death of the half-bestial Enkidu, friend and brother of Gilgamesh). His sacrificial death brings to mind the whole category of animal-sacrifices in mythology. The animal-sacrifice, where it has lost its original meaning as an offered gift and has taken on a higher religious significance, has an inner relationship to the hero or god. The animal represents the god himself; thus the bull represents Dionysus Zagreus and Mithras, the

Fig. 42. The sacred tree of Attis
Relief from an altar to Cybele

lamb Christ, etc.[48] The sacrifice of the animal means, therefore, the sacrifice of the animal nature, the instinctual libido. This is expressed most clearly in the cult legend of Attis. Attis was the son-lover of Agdistis-Cybele, the mother of the gods. Driven mad by his mother's insane love for him, he castrated himself under a pine-tree. The pine-tree played an important part in his cult (fig. 42); every year a pine-tree was decked with garlands, an effigy of Attis was hung upon it and then it was cut down. Cybele then took the pine-tree into her cave and lamented over it. The tree obviously signifies the son—according to one version Attis was actually changed into a pine-tree—whom the mother takes back into her "cave," i.e., the maternal womb. At the

[48] The following interesting Sumerian-Assyrian fragment (Gressmann, *Altorientalische Texte*, I, p. 101) comes from the library of Assurbanipal: "To the wise man he said: A lamb is a substitute for a man. He gives the lamb for his life, he gives the head of a lamb for the head of a man."

same time, the tree also has a maternal significance, since the hanging of the son or his effigy on the tree represents the union of mother and son. Common speech employs the same image: a person is said to "hang on his mother." Again, the felling of the pine-tree parallels the castration and is a direct reminder of it. In that case the tree would have more of a phallic meaning. But since the tree is primarily significant of the mother, its felling has the significance of a mother-sacrifice. These intricate overlappings of meaning can only be disentangled if we reduce them to a common denominator. This denominator is the libido: the son personifies the longing for the mother which exists in the psyche of every individual who finds himself in a similar situation. The mother personifies the (incestuous) love for the son. The tree personifies the mother on the one hand and the phallus of the son on the other. The phallus in its turn stands for the son's libido. The felling of the pine, i.e., castration, denotes the sacrifice of this libido, which seeks something that is as incongruous as it is impossible. The myth therefore depicts, through the arrangement and nature of the protagonists, the typical fate of a libido regression that is played out mainly in the unconscious. At the same time the dramatis personae appear in consciousness as in a dream, but in essence they are only envisagings of the currents and tendencies of the libido. The actuating principle of all the figures is the libido, which by its own unity binds its products so closely together that certain attributes or activities may easily pass from one figure to the next—a fact which presents no difficulties to intuitive understanding, but vastly complicates the task of logical exposition.

660   The impulse to sacrifice proceeds in the above instance from the *mater saeva cupidinum,* who drives the son to madness and self-mutilation. As a primal being the mother represents the unconscious; hence the myths tell us that the impulse to sacrifice comes from the unconscious. This is to be understood in the sense that regression is inimical to life and disrupts the instinctual foundations of the personality, and is consequently followed by a compensatory reaction taking the form of violent suppression and elimination of the incompatible tendency. It is a natural, unconscious process, a collision between instinctive tendencies, which the conscious ego experiences in most cases

passively because it is not normally aware of these libido movements and does not consciously participate in them.

661 Ovid, by the way, says of the pine-tree that it is "pleasing to the mother of the gods, because Cybelean Attis here put off his human form and stiffened into a tree-trunk." [49]

662 Transformation into the pine-tree amounts to burial in the mother, just as Osiris was overgrown by the cedar. (Cf. fig. 23.) On the Coblenz bas-relief,[50] Attis is shown growing out of a tree. This is interpreted by Mannhardt as the indwelling vegetation numen, but it is probably simply a tree-birth, as with Mithras. (Cf. the Heddernheim Relief, pl. XL.) As Firmicus Maternus notes, tree and effigy played an important part in the Isis and Osiris cult and also in that of Kore-Persephone.[51] Dionysus bore the name of Dendrites, and in Boeotia he was supposed to have been called ἔνδενδρος, 'he in the tree.' [52] In the legend of Pentheus, which is bound up with the Dionysus myth, there is a striking counterpart to the death of Attis and the subsequent lamentation: Pentheus,[53] curious to see the orgies of the Maenads, climbed up into a pine-tree but was spotted by his mother; the Maenads cut down the tree, and Pentheus, taken for a wild animal, was torn to pieces by them in their frenzy,[54] his own mother being the first to hurl herself upon him.[55] In this legend the phallic meaning of the tree (felling = castration), its maternal nature (the tree "bears" Pentheus), and its identity with the son (felling = slaying of Pentheus), are all present; at the same time we have here the counterpart and complement of the Pietà, namely the Terrible Mother. The feast of Attis was celebrated first as a lamentation and then as a festival of joy in the spring. (Good Friday and Easter.) The

[49]   "Grata deum matri, siquidem Cybeleius Attys
    Exuit hac hominem, truncoque induruit illo."
       Metamorphoses, X, 104. [Cf. Miller trans., II, pp. 70–71.]

[50] Roscher, *Lexikon*, s.v. "Attis," I, 722, 10.

[51] Firmicus Maternus, *De errore profanarum religionum*, XXVII, p. 69: "Per annos singulos arbor pinea caeditur, et in media arbore simulacrum iuvenis subligatur" (Each year a pine-tree is felled, and an effigy of a youth is tied to the middle of the tree).

[52] Preller, *Griechische Mythologie*, I, p. 555. Cited in Robertson, *Christianity and Mythology*, p. 407.

[53] Another hero with a serpent nature; his father was Echion, the adder.

[54] The typical sacrificial death in the Dionysus cult.

[55] Roscher, *Lexikon*, s.v. "Dionysus," I, 1054, 56ff.

priests of the Attis-Cybele cult were eunuchs, and were called Galloi.[56] The *archigallos* was called Atys.[57] Instead of the annual castration the priests merely scratched their arms till they bled. (Arm as substitute for phallus; twisting out the arms.[58]) There is a similar instinct-sacrificing symbolism in the Mithraic religion, where the essential portions of the mystery consisted in the catching and subduing of the bull. A parallel figure to Mithras is the Original Man, Gayomart. He was created together with his ox, and the two lived in a state of bliss for six thousand years. But when the world entered the aeon of Libra (the seventh zodiacal sign), the evil principle broke loose. In astrology, Libra is known as the "Positive House" of Venus, so the evil principle came under the dominion of the goddess of love, who personifies the erotic aspect of the mother. Since this aspect, as we have seen, is psychologically extremely dangerous, the classical catastrophe threatened to overtake the son. As a result of this constellation, Gayomart and his ox died only thirty years later. (The trials of Zarathustra also lasted for thirty years.) Fifty-five species of grain and twelve kinds of healing plants came from the dead ox. His seed entered into the moon for purification, but the seed of Gayomart entered into the sun. This seems to suggest that the bull has a hidden feminine significance. Gosh or Drvashpa was the bull's soul and it was worshipped as a female divinity. At first she was so faint-hearted that she refused to become the goddess of cattle until, as a consolation, the coming of Zarathustra was announced to her. This has its parallel in the Purana where the earth received the promise of Krishna's coming.[59] Like Ardvisura, the goddess of love, Gosh rides in a chariot. So the bull-anima appears to be decidedly feminine. In astrology Taurus, too, is a House of Venus. The myth of Gayomart repeats in modified form the primitive "closed circle" of a self-reproducing masculine and feminine divinity.

[56] For the festal processions they wore women's clothes.
[57] In Bithynia, Attis was called πάπας (papa, pope) and Cybele, Mā. The Cybele cults of the Near and Middle East worshipped at the fish, and fish-eating was taboo for the priests of the mother-goddess. It is also worth knowing that the son of Atargatis, who is identical with Astarte, Cybele, etc., was called Ἰχθύς. Roscher, s.v. "Ichthys."   [58] Cf. Frobenius, *Zeitalter, passim*.
[59] Spiegel, *Erānische Altertumskunde*, II, p. 76.

663   Like the sacrificial bull, fire—whose sacrifice we have already discussed in Chapter III—has a feminine nature in Chinese philosophy, according to one of the commentators [60] on the Chuang-tzu (350 B.C.): "The hearth spirit is called Chi. He is dressed in bright red, resembling fire, and in appearance is like a lovely, attractive maiden." The Book of Rites says: "Wood is burnt in the flames for the Au spirit. This sacrifice to Au is a sacrifice to the old women who are dead." These hearth and fire spirits are the souls of departed cooks and are therefore referred to as "old women." The god of kitchens grew out of this pre-Buddhistic tradition and later, as a man, became the ruler of the family and the link between it and heaven. In this way the original female fire-spirit became a sort of Logos and mediator.

664   From the seed of the bull sprang the first progenitors of cattle, as well as 272 kinds of useful animals.[61] According to the Mainyo-i-Khard,[62] Gayomart destroyed Dev Azur, the demon of evil desires. Azhi, another evil demon, remained the longest on earth despite the activities of Zarathustra, but was finally destroyed at the Resurrection (like Satan in the Apocalypse). Another version says that Angramainyu and the serpent were left until the last so as to be destroyed by Ahura-Mazda himself.[63] Kern suggests that Zarathustra may mean "Golden Star" and may be identical with Mithras.[64] The name Mithras is related to Modern Persian *mihr*, meaning 'love' and 'sun.'

665   In the case of Zagreus, we saw that the bull is identical with the god and that the bull-sacrifice is a divine sacrifice. But the animal is, as it were, only a part of the hero; he sacrifices only his animal attribute, and thus symbolically gives up his instinctuality. His inner participation in the sacrificial act [65] is perfectly expressed in the anguished and ecstatic countenance of the bull-slaying Mithras. He slays it willingly and unwillingly

[60] Nagel, "Der chinesische Küchengott (Tsau-kyun)," pp. 23ff.
[61] Spiegel, I, p. 510.
[62] Spiegel, *Grammatik der Parsisprache*, pp. 135, 166. [Cf. West trans., *Mainyo-i-Khard*, XXVII, 15 (p. 157).]
[63] Spiegel, *Altertumskunde*, II, p. 164. [Cf. West trans., VIII, 15 (p. 142).]
[64] Ibid., I, p. 708.
[65] Porphyry (*De antro nympharum*, 24, in Taylor trans., p. 190) says: "For Mithras, as well as the bull, is the demiurge and lord of generation." (Cited in Dieterich, *Mithrasliturgie*, p. 72.)

at once,[66] hence the rather pathetic expression on certain monuments, which is not unlike the somewhat mawkish face of Christ in Guido Reni's *Crucifixion*. Benndorf says of Mithras:

The features, which . . . especially in the upper portion have an absolutely ideal character, wear an extremely sickly expression.[67]

666   Cumont likewise stresses the facial expression of the Tauroctonos:

The face, which can be seen in the best reproductions, is that of a young man of almost feminine beauty; a mass of curly hair rising up from the forehead surrounds it as with an aureole; the head is slightly tilted backwards, so that his glance is directed towards the heavens, and the contraction of the brows and lips gives a strange expression of sorrow to the face.[68]

667   The head from Ostia (cf. frontispiece), supposed by Cumont to be that of Mithras Tauroctonos,[69] certainly wears an expression which we know all too well from our patients as one of sentimental resignation. It is a fact worth noting that the spiritual transformation that took place in the first centuries of Christianity was accompanied by an extraordinary release of feeling, which expressed itself not only in the lofty form of charity and love of God, but in sentimentality and infantilism. The lamb allegories of early Christian art fall in this category.

668   Since sentimentality is sister to brutality, and the two are never very far apart, they must be somehow typical of the period between the first and third centuries of our era. The morbid facial expression points to the disunity and split-mindedness of the sacrificer: he wants to, and yet doesn't want to. This conflict tells us that the hero is both the sacrificer and the sacrificed. Nevertheless, it is only his animal nature that Mithras sacrifices, his instinctuality,[70] always in close analogy to the course of the sun.

[66] The death of the bull, too, is voluntary and involuntary. As Mithras stabs the bull a scorpion nips it in the testicles (cf. pl. XL). (Autumn equinox of the Taurus aeon.)

[67] Benndorf and Schöne, *Bildwerke des Lateranischen Museums*, No. 547.

[68] *Textes*, I, p. 182. In another passage (p. 183) Cumont speaks of the "sorrowful and almost morbid grace of the hero's features."

[69] [It has also been identified as Attis.—EDITORS.]

[70] The libido nature of the sacrificed is indubitable. In Persia it was a ram that induced the first man to commit the first sin (cohabitation); it is also the first

669   We have learned in the course of this investigation that the libido which builds up religious structures regresses in the last analysis to the mother, and thus represents the real bond through which we are connected with our origins. When the Church Fathers derive the word *religio* from *religare* (to reconnect, link back), they could at least have appealed to this psychological fact in support of their view.[71] As we have seen, this regressive libido conceals itself in countless symbols of the most heterogeneous nature, some masculine and some feminine —differences of sex are at bottom secondary and not nearly so important psychologically as would appear at first sight. The essence and motive force of the sacrificial drama consist in an unconscious transformation of energy, of which the ego becomes aware in much the same way as sailors are made aware of a volcanic upheaval under the sea. Of course, when we consider the beauty and sublimity of the whole conception of sacrifice and its solemn ritual, it must be admitted that a psychological formulation has a shockingly sobering effect. The dramatic concreteness of the sacrificial act is reduced to a barren abstraction, and the flourishing life of the figures is flattened into two-dimensionality. Scientific understanding is bound, unfortunately, to have regrettable effects—on one side; on the other side abstraction makes for a deepened understanding of the phenomena in question. Thus we come to realize that the figures in the mythical drama possess qualities that are interchangeable, because they do not have the same "existential" meaning as the concrete figures of the physical world. The latter suffer tragedy, perhaps, in the real sense, whereas the others

---

animal they sacrifice (Spiegel, I, p. 511). The ram is therefore equivalent to the serpent in the Garden of Eden, which, according to the Manichaean view, was Christ. Melito of Sardis (2nd cent.) taught that Christ the Lamb was comparable to the ram caught in the thicket that Abraham sacrificed in place of his son, and that the thicket represented the Cross. (Fr. V, cited in Robertson, p. 412.)

71 The original derivation from *religere* (to go through again, think over, recollect) is the more probable. (Cicero, *De inventione*, 2, 53, and *De natura deorum*, 1, 42.) Lactantius (*Divinae Institutiones*, 4, 28; in Fletcher trans., I, p. 282, modified) derives it from *religare:* "Hoc vinculo pietatis obstricti Deo et religati sumus" (We are bound and tied to God by this link of piety). Similarly St. Jerome and St. Augustine. See Walde, *Lateinisches Wörterbuch*, p. 233, "diligo." The crucial contrast is between *religo* and *neglego.*

merely enact it against the subjective backcloth of introspective consciousness. The boldest speculations of the human mind concerning the nature of the phenomenal world, namely that the wheeling stars and the whole course of human history are but the phantasmagoria of a divine dream, become, when applied to the inner drama, a scientific probability. The essential thing in the mythical drama is not the concreteness of the figures, nor is it important what sort of an animal is sacrificed or what sort of god it represents; what alone is important is that an act of sacrifice takes place, that a process of transformation is going on in the unconscious whose dynamism, whose contents and whose subject are themselves unknown but become visible indirectly to the conscious mind by stimulating the imaginative material at its disposal, clothing themselves in it like the dancers who clothe themselves in the skins of animals or the priests in the skins of their human victims.

670   The great advantage of scientific abstraction is that it gives us a key to the mysterious processes enacted behind the scenes, where, leaving the colourful world of the theatre behind us, we enter into the ultimate reality of psychic dynamism and psychic meaningfulness. This knowledge strips the unconscious processes of all epiphenomenality and allows them to appear as what our whole experience tells us that they are—autonomous quantities. Consequently, every attempt to derive the unconscious from the conscious sphere is so much empty talk, a sterile, intellectual parlour-game. One suspects this wherever writers cheerfully talk of the "subconscious," without apparently realizing what an arrogant prejudice they are presuming to express. How do they know, forsooth, that the unconscious is "lower" and not "higher" than the conscious? The only certain thing about this terminology is that consciousness deems itself higher —higher than the gods themselves. One day, let us hope, its "god-almightiness will make it quiver and quake"!

671   The annual sacrifice of a maiden to the dragon is perhaps the ideal sacrifice on a mythological level. In order to mollify the wrath of the Terrible Mother the most beautiful girl was sacrificed as a symbol of man's concupiscence. Milder forms were the sacrifice of the first-born and of various domestic animals. The alternative ideal is self-castration, of which a milder form is circumcision. Here at least only a modicum is sacrificed,

which amounts to replacing the sacrifice by a symbolical act.[72] By sacrificing these valued objects of desire and possession, the instinctive desire, or libido, is given up in order that it may be regained in new form. Through sacrifice man ransoms himself from the fear of death and is reconciled to the demands of Hades. In the late cults the hero, who in olden times conquered evil and death through his labours, has become the divine protagonist, the priestly self-sacrificer and renewer of life. Since he is now a divine figure and his sacrifice is a transcendental mystery whose meaning far exceeds the value of an ordinary sacrificial gift, this deepening of the sacrificial symbolism is a reversion to the old idea of human sacrifice, because a stronger and more total expression is needed to portray the idea of *self-sacrifice*. The relation of Mithras to his bull comes very close to this idea. In Christianity it is the hero himself who dies of his own free will. On the Mithraic monuments we often come across a strange symbol: a krater [73] (mixing-bowl) with a snake coiled round it, and a lion facing the snake like an antagonist.[74] (Pl. LXIII*b*.) It looks as if they were fighting for the krater. The krater symbolizes the maternal vessel of rebirth, the snake fear and resistance, and the lion raging desire.[75] The snake almost always assists at the bull-sacrifice by gliding towards the blood flowing from the wound. It seems to follow from this that the bull's life—its blood—is offered to the snake, that it is a sacrificial offering to the powers of the underworld, like the blood drunk by the shades in the nekyia of Odysseus. We have already pointed out the reciprocal relationship between bull and snake, and we saw that the bull symbolizes the living hero, whereas the snake symbolizes the dead, buried, chthonic hero. But as the hero, when dead, is back in the mother, the snake also

---

72 Cf. Zipporah's words to her son after she had circumcised him (Exodus 4 : 25): "Surely a bloody husband art thou to me." [AV; RSV has "bridegroom of blood." —Trans.] Joshua 5 : 2ff. says that Joshua reintroduced circumcision for the benefit of the children born in the wilderness. "In this way he replaced the child sacrifices, which it had been customary to offer to Yahweh in early days, by the offering of the foreskin of the male" (Drews, *The Christ Myth*, p. 83).

73 We learn from Porphyry (*De antr. nymph.*) that "instead of a fountain a mixing-bowl [κρατήρ] is placed near Mithras." (Cited in Cumont, *Textes*, I, p. 101.) This is of some importance in interpreting the krater. Cf. also the krater of Zosimos (Berthelot, *Alchimistes grecs*, III, p. 235).

74 Cumont, I, p. 100.   75 As the zodiacal sign for the sun's greatest heat.

stands for the devouring mother. The combination of the bull's blood and the snake therefore looks like a union of opposites, and the lion and snake fighting for the krater may mean the same thing. This is probably the cause of the miraculous fertility that results from the sacrifice of the bull. Even on the primitive level, among the Australian blackfellows, we meet with the idea that the life-force wears out, turns "bad" or gets lost, and must therefore be renewed at regular intervals. Whenever such an *abaissement* occurs the rites of renewal must be performed. There is an infinite number of these rites, but even on a much higher level they retain their original meaning. Thus the Mithraic killing of the bull is a sacrifice to the Terrible Mother, to the unconscious, which spontaneously attracts energy from the conscious mind because it has strayed too far from its roots, forgetting the power of the gods, without whom all life withers or ends catastrophically in a welter of perversity. In the act of sacrifice the consciousness gives up its power and possessions in the interests of the unconscious. This makes possible a union of opposites resulting in a release of energy. At the same time the act of sacrifice is a fertilization of the mother: the chthonic serpent-demon drinks the blood, i.e., the soul, of the hero. In this way life becomes immortal, for, like the sun, the hero regenerates himself by his self-sacrifice and re-entry into the mother. After all this we should have no difficulty in recognizing the son's sacrifice to the mother in the Christian mystery. Just as Attis unmans himself for the sake of his mother, and his effigy was hung on the pine-tree in memory of this deed, so Christ hangs [76] on the tree of life, on the wood of martyrdom, the 'Εκάτη and mother (cf. pl. xxxvi), and ransoms creation from death. By entering again into the womb of the mother,

---

[76] The end of Prometheus is a similar sacrificial death: he was chained to the rocks. In another version his chains were drawn through a pillar. He suffered as a punishment the fate that Christ took upon himself willingly. The fate of Prometheus is therefore reminiscent of the misfortune that befell Theseus and Peirithous, who grew fast to the rocks, the chthonic mother. According to Athenaeus, Jupiter, on setting Prometheus free again, commanded him to wear a willow crown and an iron ring, thus symbolizing his captivity and bondage. Robertson (p. 397) compares the crown of Prometheus to Christ's crown of thorns. The devout wear crowns in honour of Prometheus, in order to represent his bondage. In this connection, therefore, the crown has the same meaning as the betrothal ring: the worshippers are κάτοχοι τοῦ θεοῦ, 'captives of the god.'

432

he pays in death [77] for the sin which the Protanthropos Adam committed in life, and by that deed he regenerates on a spiritual level the life which was corrupted by original sin. St. Augustine, as we have already remarked, actually interprets Christ's death as a *hieros gamos* with the mother, similar to the feast of Adonis, where Venus and Adonis were laid upon the bridal couch:

Like a bridegroom Christ went forth from his chamber, he went out with a presage of his nuptials into the field of the world. . . . He came to the marriage-bed of the cross, and there, in mounting it, he consummated his marriage. And when he perceived the sighs of the creature, he lovingly gave himself up to the torment in place of his bride, and he joined himself to the woman [*matrona*] for ever.[78]

672   *Matrona* in the language of St. Augustine means the Church, the bride of the Lamb. The feeling-tone of the classical *hieros gamos* has here changed into its opposite: torment instead of lust, and the martyr's stake instead of the mother and mistress. What was once felt as pleasurable—i.e., the union of the masculine consciousness with the feminine unconscious—is now felt as painful; the symbol of the *hieros gamos* is no longer experienced concretely on the bodily level, but on a higher, psychic one as the union of God with his congregation (the *corpus mysticum*). To put it in modern psychological language, this projection of the *hieros gamos* signifies the conjunction of conscious and unconscious, the transcendent function characteristic of the individuation process. Integration of the unconscious invariably has a healing effect.[79]

673   Comparison between the Mithraic and the Christian sacrifice should show just where the superiority of the Christian symbol lies: it lies in the frank admission that not only has

[77] The spear wound given by Longinus takes the place of the dagger thrust in the Mithraic bull-sacrifice. Aeschylus says that the "jagged tooth of the brazen wedge" was driven through the breast of the enchained Prometheus (*Prometheus*, trans. by Smyth, I, pp. 220–21). Odin and Huitzilopochtli were pierced by the spear, Adonis was killed by the boar's tusk.

[78] *Sermo Suppositus* 120, 8. [Cf. par. 411, above.]

[79] The same idea is found in Nordic mythology: through hanging on the tree of life Odin obtained knowledge of the runes and of the inspiriting drink that gave him immortality. People are inclined to trace this mythologem back to Christian influence. But what about Huitzilopochtli?

man's animal instinctuality (symbolized by the bull) to be sacrificed, but the entire natural man, who is more than can be expressed by his theriomorphic symbol. Whereas the latter represents animal instinctuality and utter subjection to the law of the species, the natural man means something more than that, something specifically human, namely the ability to deviate from the law, or what in theological language is known as the capacity for "sin." It is only because this variability in his nature has continually kept other ways open that spiritual development has been possible for *Homo sapiens* at all. The disadvantage, however, is that the absolute and apparently reliable guidance furnished by the instincts is displaced by an abnormal learning capacity which we also find in the anthropoid apes. Instead of instinctive certainty there is uncertainty and consequently the need for a discerning, evaluating, selecting, discriminating consciousness. If the latter succeeds in compensating the instinctive certainty, it will increasingly substitute reliable rules and modes of behaviour for instinctive action and intuition. There then arises the opposite danger of consciousness being separated from its instinctual foundations and of setting up the conscious will in the place of natural impulse.

674   Through the sacrifice of the natural man an attempt is made to reach this goal, for only then will the dominating ideal of consciousness be in a position to assert itself completely and mould human nature as it wishes. The loftiness of this ideal is incontestable and should indeed not be contested. Yet it is precisely on this lofty height that one is beset by a doubt whether human nature is capable of being moulded in this way, and whether our dominating idea is such that it can shape the natural material without damaging it. Only experience will show. Meanwhile, the attempt must be made to climb these heights, for without such an undertaking it could never be proved that this bold and violent experiment in self-transformation is possible at all. Nor could we ever estimate or understand the powers that favour the attempt or make it utterly impossible. Only then shall we be in a position to see whether the self-sacrifice of the natural man, as the Christian understands it, is a final solution or a view capable of further modification. Whereas the Mithraic sacrifice was still symbolized by the archaic slaughter of an animal and aimed only at domesticating and disciplin-

ing the instinctual man,[80] the Christian idea of sacrifice is symbolized by the death of a human being and demands a surrender of the whole man—not merely a taming of his animal instincts, but a total renunciation of them and a disciplining of his specifically human, spiritual functions for the sake of a spiritual goal beyond this world. This ideal is a hard schooling which cannot help alienating man from his own nature and, to a large degree, from nature in general. The attempt, as history has shown, was entirely possible and led in the course of a few centuries to a development of consciousness which would have been quite out of the question but for this training. Developments of this kind are not arbitrary inventions or mere intellectual fantasies; they have their own inner logic and necessity. The barrage of materialistic criticism that has been directed against the physical impossibility of dogma ever since the age of enlightenment is completely beside the point. Dogma *must* be a physical impossibility, for it has nothing whatever to say about the physical world but is a symbol of "transcendental" or unconscious processes which, so far as psychology can understand them at all, seem to be bound up with the unavoidable development of consciousness. Belief in dogma is an equally unavoidable stop-gap which must sooner or later be replaced by adequate understanding and knowledge if our civilization is to continue.

675   In Miss Miller's fantasy, too, there is an inner necessity that compels it to go on from the horse-sacrifice to the sacrifice of the hero. Whereas the former symbolizes the renunciation of biological drives, the latter has the deeper and ethically more valuable meaning of a human self-sacrifice, a renunciation of egohood. In her case, of course, this is true only in a metaphorical sense, since it is not the author of the story but its hero, Chiwantopel, who offers himself and is voluntarily sacrificed. The morally significant act is delegated to the hero, while Miss Miller only looks on admiringly and applaudingly, without, it seems, realizing that her animus-figure is constrained to do what she herself so signally fails to do. The advance from the animal sacrifice to the human sacrifice is therefore only an idea, and when Miss Miller plays the part of a pious spectator

[80] Mithraism was the religion of the Roman legionaries and admitted only men as initiates.

435

of this imaginary sacrificial act, her participation is without ethical significance. As is usual in such cases, she is totally unconscious of what it means when the hero, the vehicle of the vitally important magical action, perishes. When that happens, the projection falls away and the threatening sacrificial act recoils upon the subject herself, that is, upon the personal ego of the dreamer. In what form the drama will then run to an end it is impossible to predict. Nor, in the case of Miss Miller, owing to the lack of material and my ignorance of her personality, did I foresee, or venture to assume, that it would be a psychosis which would form the companion piece to Chiwantopel's sacrifice. It was, in fact, a κατοχή—a total surrender, not to the positive possibilities of life, but to the nocturnal world of the unconscious, a débâcle similar to the one that overtook her hero.

676   Chiwantopel is killed by a snake. We have already found abundant evidence for the snake as an instrument of sacrifice (the legend of St. Sylvester, the virginity test, wounding of Ra and Philoctetes, lance and arrow symbolism). It is the knife that kills, but also the phallus as symbol of the regenerative power of the grain, which, buried in the earth like a corpse, is at the same time the inseminator of the earth. (Pl. LXIIIa.) The snake symbolizes the numen of the transformative act as well as the transformative substance itself, as is particularly clear in alchemy. As the chthonic dweller in the cave she lives in the womb of mother earth, like the Kundalini serpent who lies coiled in the abdominal cavity, at the base of the spine. Alchemy has the legend of Gabricus and Beya, the royal brother-sister pair. During the *hieros gamos,* Gabricus gets right inside the body of his sister and disappears completely; he is buried in her womb, where, dissolved into atoms, he changes into the soul-snake, the *serpens mercurialis.*[81] (Cf. fig. 6.) Such fantasies are not uncommon among patients. Thus one patient of mine had the fantasy that she was a snake which wound itself round her mother and finally crawled right into her.

677   The snake that killed the hero is *green.* So was the snake of another patient,[82] who said: "Then a little green snake came up to my mouth, it had the finest, loveliest feeling—as if

[81] Cf. *Psychology and Alchemy,* par. 436: "Visio Arislei."
[82] "The Psychology of Dementia Praecox," par. 284.

it had human reason and wanted to tell me something—just as if it wanted to kiss me." Spielrein's patient said of her snake: "It is God's animal, it has such wonderful colours: green, blue, and white. The rattlesnake is green; it is very dangerous. . . . The snake can have a human mind, it can have divine judgment; it is a friend of children. It would save the children who are needed to preserve human life." [83] The significance of the snake as an instrument of regeneration is unmistakable. (Cf. fig. 37.)

678   As the horse is the brother, so the snake is the sister of Chiwantopel ("my little sister"). Rider and horse form a centaur-like unit,[84] like man and his shadow, i.e., the higher and lower man, ego-consciousness and shadow, Gilgamesh and Enkidu. In the same way the feminine belongs to man as his own unconscious femininity, which I have called the anima. She is often found in patients in the form of a snake. Green, the life-colour, suits her very well; it is also the colour of the Creator Spiritus. I have defined the anima as the *archetype of life itself*.[85] Here, because of the snake symbolism, she must also be thought of as having the attribute of "spirit." This apparent contradiction is due to the fact that the anima personifies the total unconscious so long as she is not differentiated as a figure from the other archetypes. With further differentiations the figure of the (wise) old man becomes detached from the anima and appears as an archetype of the "spirit." He stands to her in the relationship of a "spiritual" father, like Wotan to Brünhilde or Bythos to Sophia. Classic examples are to be found in the novels of Rider Haggard.

679   When Chiwantopel calls the snake his "little sister," this is not without significance for Miss Miller, because the hero is in fact her brother-beloved, her "ghostly lover," the animus. She herself is his life-snake which brings death to him. When the hero and his horse die, the green snake remains, and the snake is nothing other than the unconscious psyche of the author herself who now, as we have seen, will suffer the same fate as Chiwantopel, that is, she will be overpowered by her unconscious.

680   The conflict between horse and snake or bull and snake

83 Spielrein, p. 366.
84 For case material, cf. Gerhard Adler, *Studies*, Ch. V, "Consciousness and Cure."
85 See my "Archetypes of the Collective Unconscious," par. 66.

represents a conflict within the libido itself, a striving forwards and backwards at one and the same time.[86] It is as if the libido were not only a ceaseless forward movement, an unending will for life, evolution, creation, such as Schopenhauer envisaged in his cosmic Will, where death is a mishap or fatality coming from outside; like the sun, the libido also wills its own descent, its own involution. During the first half of life it strives for growth; during the second half, softly at first and then ever more perceptibly, it points towards an altered goal. And just as in youth the urge for limitless expansion often lies hidden under veiling layers of resistance to life, so that "other urge" often hides behind an obstinate and purposeless cleaving to life in its old form. This apparent contradiction in the nature of the libido is illustrated by a statue of Priapus in the archaeological museum at Verona: Priapus, with a sidelong smile, points with his finger to a snake biting his phallus (pl. LXI*b*).

681   A similar motif can be found in a Rubens' *Last Judgment* (pl. LXIV), where, in the foreground, a man is being castrated by a serpent. This motif illustrates the meaning of the end of the world.[87] The fantasy of world conflagration, of the cataclysmic end of the world in general, is the projected primordial image of the great transformation, the enantiodromia of life into death, which Rubens represents as emasculation by the serpent. The image of the consuming change that dissolves the phenomenal world of individual psychic existence originates in the unconscious and appears before the conscious mind in dreams and shadowy premonitions. And the more unwilling the latter is to heed this intimation, the more frightening become the symbols by which it makes itself known. The snake plays an important role in dreams as a fear-symbol. Because of

[86] Bleuler called this "ambivalence" or "ambitendency," and Stekel "the bipolarity of all psychic phenomena" (*Die Sprache des Traumes*, pp. 535f.).

[87] The role played by the serpent in mythology is analogous to the end of the world. It is said in the Völuspa that the deluge would begin when the Midgard Serpent rises up for universal destruction. The name of the Serpent is Jormungandr, which means literally 'monstrous dragon' [Paul, *Grundriss der germanischen Philologie*—EDITORS]. The world-destroying Fenris-Wolf likewise has connections with the sea. *Fen* is found in Fensalir (Meersäle), the dwelling-place of Frigga; originally it meant 'sea' (Frobenius, *Zeitalter*, p. 179). In the story of Red Riding Hood, the serpent or fish is replaced by a wolf, because he is the typical destroyer.

its poisonousness, its appearance is often an early symptom of physical disease. As a rule, however, it expresses an abnormally active or "constellated" unconscious and the physiological symptoms—mainly abdominal—associated therewith. Interpretation in any given case depends as always on individual circumstances and must be modified accordingly. In youth it denotes fear of life; in age, fear of death. In the case of Miss Miller the fatal significance of the green snake is obvious enough in the light of subsequent events. But it is not so easy to say what was the real cause of the unconscious gaining the upper hand. The necessary biographical material is lacking. I can only say that I have very often noticed in such cases a singularly narrow consciousness, an apprehensive stiffness of attitude, and a spiritual and emotional horizon bounded by childish naïveté or pedantic prejudice. To judge from the little we know of Miss Miller, it seems to be more a case of emotional naïveté: she underestimated the possibilities in her and leapt too lightly into dangerously deep waters where some knowledge of the shadow would have been in place. Such people should be given as much psychological knowledge as possible. Even if it doesn't protect them from the outbreak of psychosis, it nevertheless makes the prognosis look more hopeful, as I have often observed. In border-line cases such as this a real psychological understanding is often a matter of life and death.

682   As at the beginning of our investigation the name of the hero obliged us to speak of the symbolism of Popocatapetl as the "creative" part of the body, so now at the end of the Miller drama we again have an opportunity to see how the volcano assists at the death of the hero and, by means of an earthquake, causes him to disappear into the bowels of the earth. Just as the volcano gave birth and name to the hero, so at the end it swallows him back again.[88] We learn from his last words that the longed-for beloved who alone understands him is called

[88] Cf. Hölderlin's longing in his poem "Empedocles," also Zarathustra's journey to Hades through the mouth of a volcano. I have shown elsewhere ("On the Psychology of Occult Phenomena," pars. 140ff.; "Cryptomnesia," 181ff.) that this passage in Nietzsche is a cryptomnesia. Death is a re-entry into the mother. Hence the Egyptian king Men-kau-Re (Mykerinos) had his daughter buried in a gilded wooden cow, as a guarantee of rebirth. The cow was placed in a gorgeous apartment and offerings were made to it. In an adjoining apartment were the images of the king's concubines. Herodotus, II, 129, in Selincourt trans., p. 153.

"Ja-ni-wa-ma." In this name we find those sweet lispings already known to us from the babyhood of Hiawatha: *wawa, wama, mama*. The only one who really understands us is the mother. For *ver-*, in *vcrstehen*, 'to understand' (OHG. *firstân*), may be derived from a primitive Germanic prefix *fri-*, which is identical with περί, 'round,' 'about.' The OHG. *antfristôn*, 'to interpret,' is considered to be identical with *firstân*. Hence the fundamental meaning of *verstehen* would be to 'stand round about something.' [89] *Comprehendere* and κατασυλλαμβάνειν both express an image similar to the German *erfassen*, 'to grasp, comprehend.' The factor common to all these terms is the idea of surrounding, embracing. And there is no doubt at all that nothing in the world ever embraces us so completely as the mother. When the neurotic complains that the world does not understand him, he is telling us in a word that he wants his mother. Paul Verlaine has given beautiful expression to this thought in his poem "Mon Rêve familier":

> Je fais souvent ce rêve étrange et pénétrant
> D'une femme inconnue, et que j'aime, et qui m'aime,
> Et qui n'est, chaque fois, ni tout à fait la même
> Ni tout à fait une autre, et m'aime et me comprend.
>
> Car elle me comprend, et mon cœur, transparent
> Pour elle seule, hélas! cesse d'être un problème
> Pour elle seule, et les moiteurs de mon front blême,
> Elle seule les sait rafraîchir, en pleurant.
>
> Est-elle brune, blonde ou rousse?—Je l'ignore.
> Son nom? Je me souviens qu'il est doux et sonore
> Comme ceux des aimés que la Vie exila.
>
> Son regard est pareil au regard des statues,
> Et, pour sa voix, lointaine, et calme, et grave, elle a
> L'inflexion des voix chères qui se sont tues.[90]

[89] Kluge, *Wörterbuch*.   [90] *Poèmes saturniens* (1866).

EPILOGUE

683   So end the Miller fantasies. Their melancholy outcome is
due largely to the fact that they break off at the critical moment
when the threat of invasion by the unconscious is plainly apparent. It is hardly to be supposed that Miss Miller, who evidently had not the faintest clue as to the real meaning of her
visions—which even Théodore Flournoy, despite his fine feeling
for values, could do nothing to explain—would be able to meet
the next phase of the process, namely the assimilation of the
hero to her conscious personality, with the right attitude. In
order to do so she would have had to recognize what fate
demanded of her, and what was the meaning of the bizarre
images that had broken in upon her consciousness. That there
was already some degree of dissociation is obvious, since the
unconscious went ahead independently and kept on churning
out images which she had not consciously produced herself and
which she felt as strange and portentous. To the objective ob-
server it is perfectly clear that the fantasies were products of a
psychic energy not under the control of the conscious mind.
They were longings, impulses, and symbolic happenings which
it was quite unable to cope with either positively or negatively.
The instinctual impulse that was trying to rouse the dreamer
from the sleep of childhood was opposed by a personal pride
that was distinctly out of place, and also, one must suppose, by
a correspondingly narrow moral horizon, so that there was nothing to help her understand the spiritual content of the symbols.
Our civilization has long since forgotten how to think symbolically, and even the theologian has no further use for the
hermeneutics of the Church Fathers. The cure of souls in
Protestantism is in an even more parlous condition. Who ever
would go to the trouble, nowadays, of patching together the
basic ideas of Christianity from a "welter of pathological fan-

441

tasies"? For patients in this situation it is a positive life-saver when the doctor takes such products seriously and gives the patient access to the meanings they suggest. In this way he makes it possible for the patient to assimilate at least part of the unconscious and to repair the menacing dissociation by just that amount. At the same time the assimilation guards against the dangerous isolation which everyone feels when confronted by an incomprehensible and irrational aspect of his personality. Isolation leads to panic, and that is only too often the beginning of a psychosis. The wider the gap between conscious and unconscious, the nearer creeps the fatal splitting of the personality, which in neurotically disposed individuals leads to neurosis, and, in those with a psychotic constitution, to schizophrenia and fragmentation of personality. The aim of psychotherapy is therefore to narrow down and eventually abolish the dissociation by integrating the tendencies of the unconscious into the conscious mind. Normally these promptings are realized unconsciously or, as we say, "instinctively," and though their spiritual content remains unnoticed, it nevertheless insinuates itself into the conscious spiritual life of the patient, mostly in disguised form, without his being aware of it. All this passes off smoothly and without difficulty provided that his consciousness contains certain ideas of a symbolic nature—"for those who have the symbol the passage is easy," say the alchemists. If, on the other hand, there is already a tendency to dissociation, perhaps dating back to youth, then every advance of the unconscious only increases the gap between it and consciousness. As a rule outside help is needed to bridge the gap. Had I treated Miss Miller I would have had to tell her some of the things of which I have written in this book, in order to build up her conscious mind to the point where it could have understood the contents of the collective unconscious. Without the help of these "représentations collectives," which have psychotherapeutic value even for primitives, it is not possible to understand the archetypal associations of the products of the unconscious. It is in no sense sufficient to try to do so with nothing but a personalistically oriented psychology. Anyone who wants to treat serious dissociations must know something of the anatomy and evolutionary history of the mind he is setting out to cure. The physician who treats physical diseases is required to have some knowledge of anatomy, physiology, embryology, and comparative evolution. Neurotic dissociations can, up to a point, be remedied with the help of purely personalistic psychology, but not the problem of transference, which crops up in the majority of cases and always hides collective contents.

684   The Miller case is a classic example of the unconscious manifestations which precede a serious psychic disorder. Their presence does not by any means prove that a disorder of this kind is bound to occur. That, as I have already said, depends among other things on whether the conscious attitude towards them is positive or negative. The Miller case suited my book very well because I had nothing to do with it personally and could thus refute the oft-repeated charge that I had "influenced" the patient. Had the case come up for treatment at the very first sign of spontaneous fantasy creations, the later episode of Chiwantopel, for instance, might have taken a very different turn, and the end, so we will hope, would have been less calamitous.

685   With these remarks we come to the end of our programme. We set ourselves the task of examining an individual fantasy system in relation to its sources, and in the course of our inquiry have stumbled upon problems of such enormous proportions that our attempts to understand their full scope and complexity cannot of necessity amount to much more than a superficial survey. I do not take kindly to the argument that because certain working hypotheses may not possess eternal validity or may possibly be erroneous, they must be withheld from the public. Certainly I have done my best to guard against error, which can be particularly pernicious on such treacherous ground, by keeping myself fully conscious of the dangers that beset an investigation of this kind. We doctors are not so happily placed as research workers in other fields. We cannot choose our assignment or mark off the territory to be investigated, for the sick man who comes to us for treatment confronts us with unforeseeable problems and expects us to fulfil a therapeutic task for which we cannot but feel inadequate. The strongest incentive to unceasing research has always come to me from my practice, and it consisted in the simple question which no man can ignore: "How can you treat something that you do not under-

stand?" Dreams, visions, fantasies, and delusions are expressive of a situation. If I do not understand the dreams, neither do I understand the situation of the patient, and of what use is my treatment then? It was never my intention to justify my theories by my patients; it seemed to me far more important to understand their situation in all its aspects, which naturally include the compensatory activity of the unconscious. Such was the case with Miss Miller. I have tried to understand her situation to the best of my ability and have set down the results of my efforts as an example of the nature and extent of the problems about which any doctor who wants to practise psychotherapy should have scientific knowledge. He needs a science of the psyche, not a theory about it. I do not regard the pursuit of science as a bickering about who is right, but as an endeavour to augment and deepen human knowledge. The present work is addressed to those who think and feel about science in the same way.

Fig. 43. Antique cameo

APPENDIX:

THE MILLER FANTASIES

[Translated from "Quelques Faits d'imagination créatrice sub-consciente," in *Archives de psychologie* (Geneva), V (1906), 36–51. The article contains an introduction of five pages signed by Théodore Flournoy, which is not translated here. In it, Flournoy speaks of the Miller material as a "traduction"; it is therefore evident that Miss Miller wrote her memoir in English and it was translated (by Flournoy?) into French. Flournoy describes her as "a young American who studied for a semester at our [Geneva] university and who today pursues a distinguished career as a journalist and lecturer in the United States." The original of the Miller memoir has never come to light, and accordingly a double translation has been necessary both in the present edition and in the Hinkle translation of 1916 (where, however, the full Miller text was not given, as here). Professor Jung based his study on the French version, and therefore certain words and phrases that he considered of special point are here given in French, in brackets. Likewise, indication is given of words and passages that the Flournoy publication left in English.
—EDITORS.]

SOME INSTANCES OF SUBCONSCIOUS CREATIVE IMAGINATION

by Miss Frank Miller
of New York

I. PHENOMENA OF TRANSITORY SUGGESTION OR OF INSTANTANEOUS AUTOSUGGESTION

What I mean by this, in default of a better term, is a curious phenomenon that I have observed in myself and that occurs in different forms. It consists in this, that at certain moments and for a few seconds only, the impressions or feelings of another person are so strongly suggested to me that they seem to be *mine*, although, as soon as the suggestion is over, I am perfectly sure that this was not the case. Here are some examples:

1. I am passionately fond of caviar, the odour and taste of which are, on the contrary, very repellent to certain members of my family. But if one of them, just as I am about to eat it, begins to express her disgust, this disgust is at once suggested to me so clearly that, for a few moments, I feel complete repugnance for the smell and the taste of caviar. It takes, however, only a minute's effort for me to dispel this impression and to find the caviar as delectable as ever.

2. Here, on the other hand, is an example of the transmission of a pleasing impression. There are certain perfumes and essences that affect me disagreeably because they smell too strong, so much so as to give me nausea and make me almost ill. Yet if a lady begins to smell her eau-de-Cologne, recommending it to me for its strength and exquisite perfume, her pleasure for an instant becomes mine—probably not for more than three to five seconds—after which it disappears and gives place to my usual aversion to strong odours. It is much easier for me, it seems, to

447

dismiss the agreeable suggestion and return to my real feeling of distaste than to do the reverse.

3. When I am following a story with great interest, either reading or listening, I often have the illusion, which may last up to a minute, of really taking part in the action, instead of merely reading or hearing it. This is especially marked at fine theatrical productions (for example, performances by Sarah Bernhardt, Duse, or Irving). The illusion becomes so complete in certain very moving scenes that in *Cyrano,* for instance, when Christian is killed and Sarah Bernhardt throws herself upon him to stanch the bleeding of his wound, I have felt a real, piercing pain in my own breast, just where Christian is supposed to have received the blow. This kind of suggestion may last a minute, or a second.

4. Such momentary suggestions sometimes take on very curious aspects, in which the part played by imagination is accentuated. For example, I have enjoyed my sea voyages enormously, and I retain a particularly vivid memory of crossing the Atlantic. Now, someone lately showed me a beautiful photograph of a steamship in mid ocean; and instantly—the illusion was of an arresting power and beauty—I felt the throb of the engines, the heave of the waves, the roll of the ship. It can hardly have lasted for more than a second, but during that barely appreciable instant it was as though I were once more at sea. The same phenomenon recurred, though less clearly, on seeing the same photograph again some days later.

5. Here is an example proceeding evidently from creative fantasy. One day when I was taking a bath and was preparing to use the shower, I was in the act of winding a towel round my head to protect my hair from the water. The towel, of a thick material, had taken a conical shape, and I was standing in front of a mirror to pin it firmly in place. This conical form was, no doubt, a striking reminder of the pointed head-dress of the ancient Egyptians; be that as it may, it seemed to me, for one moment and with an almost breath-taking clarity, that I was on a pedestal, a veritable Egyptian statue with all its details; stiff-limbed, one foot forward, holding insignia in my hand, etc. This indeed was superb, and it was with regret that I felt the impression fading away like a rainbow; like a rainbow, too, it returned again faintly before it disappeared altogether.

6. Yet another phenomenon. An artist of some reputation very much wished to illustrate some of my publications. But in this matter I have my own ideas and am difficult to please. However, I succeeded in making him draw landscapes, such as those of Lake Geneva, where he had never been, and he used to pretend that I could make him depict things that he had never seen and give him the sense of a surrounding atmosphere that he had never felt; in short, that I was using him as he himself used his pencil; that is, simply as an instrument.

I do not attach much importance to the various things I have just described—they are so fugitive and nebulous!—and I think that all persons with a nervous temperament and imagination, who react with a lively sympathy towards external impressions, experience analogous phenomena. They do not seem to me to be of much consequence in themselves, unless they can help us to understand other things, less elementary. I believe that this sympathic or sympathizing (sympathetic [1]) temperament, in people whose health is quite normal, plays a large part in the creation or the possibility of such "suggested" images and impressions. Now, may it not be that, under certain favourable conditions, something quite new, different from anything that one knows, may come over the mental horizon, something as dazzling and splendid as a rainbow and yet as natural in its origin and cause? For, surely, these queer little experiences (I mean the last of those above) differ as much from the ordinary, everyday course of life as a rainbow differs from blue sky.

The aim of the few preceding observations is to serve as an introduction to two or three further, more important ones which, in their turn, seem to me of a nature that throws some light on the even more complex and mystifying phenomena experienced by other persons, who are carried away by them because they are unable—or unwilling—to analyse the abnormal, subliminal, or subconscious working of their minds.

1 [In English in Flournoy's publication.]

II. "GLORY TO GOD": A DREAM POEM

1. One could imagine nothing more delightful than the voyage from Odessa to Genoa in winter, with brief but entrancing landings at Constantinople, Smyrna, Athens, at the ports of Sicily and the west coast of Italy. . . . One must be a philistine indeed, devoid of any aesthetic feeling, not to be carried away with admiration by the glory of the Bosporus, or not to respond with all one's soul to the remembrance of the past in Athens. . . . That was the voyage on which I was privileged to go at the age of twenty, with my family, in 1898.

After the long and rough voyage from New York to Stockholm, then to St. Petersburg and Odessa, it was a real pleasure [*une véritable volupté*] to leave the world of cities, of roaring streets, of business—in short, of the earth—and enter the world of waves, sky, and silence. . . . I spent hours on end on the deck of the ship, dreaming, stretched out in a deck chair. All the histories, legends, and myths of the different countries I saw in the distance came back to me confusedly, dissolved in a kind of luminous mist in which real things seemed to lose their being, while dreams and ideas took on the aspect of the only true reality. At first I even avoided all company and kept to myself, lost in my reveries, where everything I had ever known that was truly great, beautiful, and good came back to mind with renewed life and vigour. I also spent a good part of my days writing to absent friends, reading, or scribbling little bits of poetry in remembrance of the various places we visited. Some of these poems were of a rather serious character. But as the voyage drew near its end, the ship's officers outdid themselves in kindness and amiability [*se montrèrent tout ce qu'il y a de plus empressés et aimables*], and I passed many an amusing hour teaching them English.

Off the coast of Sicily, in the port of Catania, I wrote a seachanty, which, however, was little more than an adaptation of a well-known song about the sea, wine, and love ("Brine, wine and damsels fine" [2]). The Italians are all good singers, as a rule; and one of the officers, singing at night as he stood watch on

[2] [In English.]

deck, had made a great impression on me and had given me the idea of writing some words that could be fitted to his melody.

Soon afterwards, I nearly did as the old proverb says, "See Naples and die," for in the port of Naples I began by being very ill (though not dangerously so); then I recovered sufficiently to go ashore and visit the principal sights of the city in a carriage. This outing tired me extremely; and as we were intending to visit Pisa the next day, I soon returned on board and went to bed early, without thinking of anything more serious than the good looks of the officers and the ugliness of Italian beggars.

2. From Naples to Leghorn is one night by boat, during which I slept moderately well—my sleep is rarely deep or dreamless—and it seemed to me that my mother's voice woke me up just at the end of the following dream, which must, therefore, have taken place immediately before waking.

First, I was vaguely conscious of the words "when the morning stars sang together," [3] which served as the prelude, if I may so put it, to an involved idea of creation and to mighty chorales reverberating through the universe. But, with the confusion and strange contradiction characteristic of dreams, all this was mixed up with choruses from oratorios given by one of the leading musical societies of New York, and with indistinct memories of Milton's *Paradise Lost*. Then, slowly, out of this medley, words appeared, and a little later they arranged themselves in three stanzas, in my handwriting, on a sheet of ordinary blue-lined writing-paper, in a page of my old poetry album that I always carry about with me: in short, they appeared to me exactly as they did in reality, a few minutes later, in my book.

That was the moment when my mother called to me: "Now then, wake up! You can't sleep all day and see Pisa too!" This made me jump down from my bunk, crying out, "Don't speak to me! Not a word! I've just had the most beautiful dream in my life, a real poem! I have seen and heard the words, the verses, even the refrain. Where is my notebook? I must write it down at once before I forget any of it."—My mother, quite accustomed to see me writing at all hours, took my whim in good part and even admired my dream, which I told her as quickly as I could put it into sentences. It took me some minutes to find my notebook and a pencil and slip on a garment; but, short

3 [In English.]

though it was, this delay was enough for my immediate recollection of the dream to have begun to fade a little; so that, when I was ready to write, the words had lost something of their clearness. However, the first verse came easily enough; the second was harder to recollect, and it cost me a great effort to re-memorize the last, distracted as I was by the feeling that I cut a rather ridiculous figure, perched on the upper bunk of the cabin, and scribbling away, half-dressed, while my mother made fun of me. Thus, the first version left something to be desired. My duties as a guide absorbed me after this, until the end of our long voyage; and it was not until some months later, when I was installed at Lausanne for my studies, that the thought of this dream came back to haunt me in the calm of loneliness. Then I produced a second version of my poem, more exact than the first, I mean much closer to the original dream. I give it here in both forms.

FIRST VERSION [4]

When God had first made Sound,
A myriad ears sprang into being
And throughout all the Universe
Rolled a mighty echo:
"Glory to the God of Sound!"

When beauty (light) first was given by God,
A myriad eyes sprang out to see
And hearing ears and seeing eyes
Again gave forth that mighty song:
"Glory to the God of Beauty (Light)!"

When God has first given Love,
A myriad hearts lept up;
And ears full of music, eyes all full of Beauty,
Hearts all full of love sang:
"Glory to the God of Love!"

SECOND VERSION (more exact) [4]

When the Eternal first made Sound
A myriad ears sprang out to hear,
And throughout all the Universe
There rolled an echo deep and clear:
"All glory to the God of Sound!"

When the Eternal first made Light,
A myriad eyes sprang out to look,
And hearing ears and seeing eyes,
Once more a mighty choral took:
"All glory to the God of Light!"

When the Eternal first gave Love,
A myriad hearts sprang into life;
Ears filled with music, eyes with light,
Pealed forth with hearts with love all rife:
"All glory to the God of Love!"

4 [Both versions in English.]

3. Never having been an adept in spiritualism or the contra-natural (which I distinguish from the supernatural), I set to work, some months afterwards, trying to find out the probable causes and the necessary conditions for such a dream.

What struck me most, and still seems to me like an unex-plained fantasy, is that, contrary to the Mosaic account, in which I had always believed, my poem put the creation of light in the second place instead of the first. It may be of interest to recall that Anaxagoras, too, makes the cosmos arise out of chaos by means of a whirlwind—which does not normally occur with-out producing a noise. But at that time I had not yet made a study of philosophy and I knew nothing either of Anaxagoras or of his theories about the νοῦς which I found I had been uncon-sciously following. I was in equally complete ignorance of the name of Leibniz and consequently of his doctrine "dum Deus calculat fit mundus." But let us come to what I have discovered concerning the probable sources of my dream.

In the first place, there is Milton's *Paradise Lost,* of which we had a fine edition at home, illustrated by Gustave Doré, and which I have known well since childhood. Then the Book of Job, which has been read aloud to me ever since I can remem-ber. Now, if you compare my first line with the first words of *Paradise Lost,* you find it is in the same metre (‿—/ ‿—/ ‿—/ ‿—):

> Of man's first disobedience . . .
> When the Eternal first made sound.

Moreover, the general idea of my poem is slightly reminiscent of various passages in Job, and also of one or two places in Handel's oratorio *The Creation* [5] (which appeared in the con-fusion at the beginning of the dream).

I remember that, at the age of fifteen, I was very much excited by an article my mother had read to me, about "the Idea spon-taneously creating its own object," and I passed almost the whole night without sleep, wondering what it could all mean.—From the age of nine to sixteen, I used to go on Sundays to a Presbyterian church, where the pastor was a highly cultivated man, now president of a well-known college. And in one of the

[5] [Probably Haydn's *Creation* is meant.—C. G. J.]

earliest memories I have of him, I see myself, still quite a little girl, sitting in our large pew in church and struggling to keep myself awake, without being able to understand what in the world he meant when he spoke to us of "Chaos," "Cosmos," and "the Gift of Love."

With regard to dreams, I recollect that once, at the age of fifteen, while I was preparing for an examination in geometry, and had gone to bed without being able to solve a problem, I awoke in the middle of the night, sat up in bed, repeated to myself a formula that I had just discovered in a dream, and then went to sleep again, and in the morning everything had become clear in my mind.—Something very similar happened to me with a Latin word I was trying to remember.—I have also dreamed, many times, that friends far away have written to me, and this just before the actual arrival of letters from them; the explanation of which is, very simply, that while I was asleep I calculated approximately the time they would be likely to write to me, and that the idea of the letter's actual arrival was substituted, in the dream, for the expectation of its probable arrival. I draw this conclusion from the fact that I have several times had dreams of receiving letters that were not followed by their arrival.

To sum up, when I reflect upon the foregoing, and upon the fact that I had just composed a number of poems at the time of this dream, the dream does not seem to me so extraordinary as it did at first. It seems to me to result from a mixture in my mind of *Paradise Lost, Job,* and *The Creation,* with notions like the "Idea spontaneously creating its own object," the "Gift of Love," "Chaos," and "Cosmos." Just as the little bits of coloured glass in a kaleidoscope form marvellous and rare patterns, so, in my opinion, the fragments of philosophy, aesthetics, and religion in my mind were blended together—under the stimulation of the voyage and of countries fleetingly seen, coupled with the vast silence and impalpable charm of the sea—to produce this beautiful dream. There was only this and nothing more. [*Ce ne fut que cela et rien de plus.*] "Only this and nothing more!" 6

6 [Quoted in English, preceded by the French.]

III. "THE MOTH AND THE SUN": A HYPNAGOGIC POEM

The day before I left Geneva for Paris had been extremely exhausting. I had made an excursion up the Salève, and on my return I found a telegram that obliged me to pack my bags, settle my affairs, and depart within the space of two hours. My fatigue on the train was such that I hardly slept an hour. It was horribly hot in the ladies' compartment. Towards four o'clock I lifted my head from the bag that had served me for a pillow, sat up, and stretched my swollen limbs. A tiny butterfly, or moth, was fluttering towards the light that shone through the glass panel behind a curtain that was swinging with the motion of the train. I lay down and tried to sleep again, and almost succeeded; that is to say, I found myself as nearly asleep as possible without completely losing self-consciousness. It was then that the following piece of poetry suddenly came into my mind. It was impossible to drive it away in spite of my repeated efforts. I took a pencil and wrote it down straight away.

The Moth to the Sun [7]

I longed for thee when first I crawled to consciousness.
My dreams were all of thee when in the chrysalis I lay.
Oft myriads of my kind beat out their lives
Against some feeble spark once caught from thee.
And one hour more—and my poor life is gone;
Yet my last effort, as my first desire, shall be
But to approach thy glory: then, having gained
One raptured glance, I'll die content,
For I, the source of beauty, warmth and life
Have in his perfect splendor once beheld!

This little poem made a profound impression on me. I could not at first find a sufficiently clear and direct explanation of it.

[7] [Title and poem in English.] Miss Miller has shown me her original draft, in pencil, written very irregularly on account of the movement of the train. It shows one or two crossings-out, or corrections of detail, in the same kind of scrawl as all the rest, which she had made immediately upon re-reading the piece as soon as it was completed. The only one that is noteworthy concerns the first line, which was first written as "I longed for thee when consciousness first woke": the last three words are crossed out with a big stroke leading right down to the bottom of the page, where the variant is written—"first I crawled to consciousness."—T.F.

But a few days afterwards, having again taken up a philosophical article that I had read in Berlin the previous winter, which had delighted me extremely, and reading it aloud to a friend, I came upon these words: "The same passionate longing of the moth for the star, of man for God. . . ." I had completely forgotten them, but it seemed to me quite obvious that these were the words that had reappeared in my hypnagogic poem. Moreover, a play entitled *The Moth and the Flame*,[8] which I saw a few years ago, also came back to me as another possible source of my poem. You see how often the word *Moth* has been impressed upon me!—I would add that, in the spring, I had been reading a selection of Byron's poems that pleased me greatly and that I often dipped into. Moreover, there is a great similarity of rhythm between my two last lines, "For I, the source, etc." and these two of Byron's:

> Now let me die as I have lived in faith
> Nor tremble tho' the Universe should quake!

It is possible that my having so often read this book had an influence on me, and contributed towards my inspiration, as much from the point of view of meaning as of rhythmical form.

[8] [A comedy, in three acts, by the American playwright Clyde Fitch, produced in New York on Apr. 11, 1898. The following synopsis of its plot (from a review in the *New York Dramatic Mirror*, Apr. 16, 1898), is given here *in extenso* because of the interesting pertinence of its heroine's character and problems.

"*The Moth and the Flame* begins at a children's party given by Mr. and Mrs. Wolton at their New York home. Their daughter, Marion, has rejected the love of Douglas Rhodes to become betrothed to Ned Fletcher, a man of somewhat shady record, whom she expects to reform. The children's party is at its merriest moment when a thud above and a clattering chandelier announce the suicide of the host in his room. Wolton, knowing Fletcher to be a swindler and dreading the disgrace that must befall by Marion's marriage to Fletcher, has killed himself. Yet the guests know not, and the fun goes on. Marion falters into the room after discovering the horrible thing, and falls into her mother's arms, sobbing out the awful truth while a dozen unsuspecting revelers dance and sing about the stricken women. The family are threatened with terrible distress, and Fletcher, as Marion's affianced lover, announces his purpose to stand by the Woltons.

"The next act presents St. Hubert's Chapel, wherein is to occur the wedding of Fletcher and Marion, to which society has been invited by Mrs. Wolton. The ceremony is rudely interrupted by a woman who demands that Fletcher shall marry her and give his name to her child. Fletcher repudiates the woman's story, and Marion believes him. But the interloper persists and steps between the bridal couple. Then Fletcher fells her with a cruel blow. Marion, horrified, cries

Comparing this poem, which came to me in a half-waking dream-state, with, on the one hand, those written when wide awake and, on the other hand, the previous poem [Sec. ɪɪ, above] that came when I was fast asleep, it seems to me that these three categories form a perfectly natural series. The intermediate state establishes a simple and easy transition between the two extremes, and thus dispels any suspicion of an intervention of the "occult" that one might have had about the poem I produced while asleep.

ɪᴠ. "CHIWANTOPEL.": A HYPNAGOGIC DRAMA

Borderland phenomena—or, if you prefer it, the productions of the brain in the half-dreaming state—are of particular interest to me, and I believe that a detailed and intelligent examination of them would do much to clear up the mystery of so-called "spirits" and dispel superstition concerning them. It is with this idea in mind that I am sending you an observation which, in the hands of someone less careful of the exact truth, or less scrupulous about indulging in embroideries or amplifications, might very well give rise to some fantastic romance that would outdo the fictitious ramblings of your mediums. I have re-written the following observation as faithfully as possible from the notes I made immediately after the half-dream in question, and have limited myself to the insertion between brackets [ ] of one or two remarks and of letters referring to the explanatory notes that follow.

Observation of 17 March, 1902. Half an hour after midnight.

1st Phase.—After an evening of trouble and anxiety, I had gone to bed at half past eleven. I felt restless; unable to sleep

---

'Coward!' and, flinging the wedding bouquet at his feet, rushes from the chapel.
"In the last act, Fletcher seeks to frighten Marion into marrying him, telling her that her father had owed his respected position to the fact that his (Fletcher's) money had preserved the honor of the Wolton name in the world's eyes. But she rejects his advances and espouses the still faithful Rhodes. Fletcher, in contrition, vows to marry the woman he had scorned, and so ends the play."—Eᴅɪᴛᴏʀs.]

although very tired. I had the impression of being in a receptive mood. There was no light in the room. I closed my eyes, and had the feeling of waiting for something that was about to happen. Then I felt a great relaxation come over me, and I remained as completely passive as possible. Lines, sparks, and spirals of fire passed before my eyes, symptoms of nervousness and ocular fatigue, followed by a kaleidoscopic and fragmentary review of recent trivial events. Then an impression that something was on the point of being communicated to me. It seemed as if these words were repeating themselves in me—"Speak, Lord, for thy servant heareth—Open thou mine ears." The head of a sphinx suddenly appeared in the field of vision, in an Egyptian setting: then it faded away. At that moment my parents called to me, and I immediately answered them in a perfectly coherent way, a proof that I was not asleep.

2nd Phase.—Suddenly, the apparition of an Aztec, complete in every detail: hand open, with large fingers, head in profile, armoured, with a head-dress resembling the plumed crests of the American Indians, etc. The whole is somewhat suggestive of the carvings on Mexican monuments [note A].[8a]—The name "Chi-wan-to-pel" forms itself bit by bit, and it seems to belong to the previous personage, son of an Inca of Peru [note B].—Then a swarm of people. Horses, a battle, the view of a *dream-city* [note C].—A strange conifer with knotty branches, lateen sails in a bay of purple water, a perpendicular cliff. A confusion of sounds resembling Wa-ma, Wa-ma, etc.

(A lacuna.)—The scene changes to a wood. Trees, undergrowth, bushes, etc. The figure of Chi-wan-to-pel comes up from the south, on horseback, wrapped in a blanket of bright colours, red, blue, and white. An Indian, dressed in buckskin, beaded and ornamented with feathers [note D], creeps forward stealthily, making ready to shoot an arrow at Chi-wan-to-pel, who bares his breast to him in an attitude of defiance [note E]; and the Indian, fascinated by this sight, slinks away and disappears into the forest. Chi-wan-to-pel sinks down upon a mound, leaves his horse to graze on the tether, and delivers himself of the following soliloquy, all in English: [9] "From the tip of the backbone of these continents [probably an allusion to the Andes and the Rocky Mountains], from the farthest lowlands, I have wandered

8a [See p. 461.]   9 [But given by Flournoy here in French.]

for a hundred moons since quitting my father's palace [note F], forever pursued by my mad desire to find 'her who will understand.' With jewels I tempted many beautiful women; with kisses tried I to draw out the secrets of their hearts, with deeds of daring I won their admiration. [He reviews one after another the women he has known.] Chi-ta, the princess of my own race . . . she was a fool, vain as a peacock, without a thought in her head except trinkets and perfumes. Ta-nan, the peasant girl . . . bah! a perfect sow, nothing but a bust and a belly, thinking of nothing but pleasure. And then Ki-ma, the priestess, a mere parrot, repeating the empty phrases learnt from the priests, all for show, without real understanding or sincerity, mistrustful, affected, hypocritical! . . . Alas! Not one who understands me, not one who resembles me or has a soul that is sister to mine [note G]. There is not one among them all who has known my soul, not one who could read my thoughts—far from it; not one capable of seeking the shining summits with me, or of spelling out with me the superhuman word Love!"

(A lacuna.)—He cries mournfully: "In all the world there is not a single one! I have searched among a hundred tribes. I have aged a hundred moons since I began. Will there never be anyone who will know my soul?—Yes, by almighty God, yes!—But ten thousand moons will wax and wane before her pure soul is born. And it is from another world that her parents will come to this one. She will be fair of skin and fair-haired. She will know sorrow even before her mother bears her. Suffering will be her companion; she too will seek—and will find no one who understands her. Many a suitor will wish to pay court to her, but not one of them will know how to understand her. Temptation will often assail her soul, but she will not yield. . . . In her dreams I shall come to her, and *she will understand* [note H]. I have kept my body inviolate [note I]. I have come ten thousand moons before her time, and she will come ten thousand moons too late. *But she will understand!* It is but once in ten thousand moons that a soul like hers is born!"

(A lacuna.)—A green viper darts out of the bushes, glides towards him, and stings him in the arm; then it attacks his horse, which is the first to succumb. Then Chi-wan-to-pel says to his horse: "Farewell, faithful brother! Enter into your rest! I have loved you and you have served me well. Farewell, I shall

459

rejoin you soon!" Then to the serpent: "Thanks, little sister, you have put an end to my wanderings!" Now he shrieks with pain and calls out in prayer, "Almighty God, take me soon! I have sought to know thee and to keep thy law. Oh, suffer not my body to fall into corruption and decay, and become carrion for the eagles!" A smoking volcano appears in the distance [note K], the rumbling of an earthquake is heard, followed by a landslide. Chi-wan-to-pel cries out in an extremity of anguish as the earth closes over his body: "Ah, she will understand! Ja-ni-wa-ma, Ja-ni-wa-ma, thou that understandest me!"

Remarks and Explanatory Notes

You will agree, I think, that as a work of imagination, this hypnagogic fantasy is well worth a little attention. It is certainly not wanting in complexity and strangeness of form, and one may even claim a certain originality for its combination of themes. One might even be able to make it into a kind of melodrama in one act. If I were personally inclined to exaggerate the purport of compositions of this kind, and were not able to recognize many familiar elements in this phantasmagoria, I might let myself go so far as to regard Chi-wan-to-pel as my "control," my spirit-guide, after the manner of so many mediums. I need hardly tell you that I do no such thing. So let us look for the probable sources of this little account.

First, as to the name Chi-wan-to-pel: one day, when I was fully awake, there suddenly came into my mind the word A-ha-ma-ra-ma, surrounded by an Assyrian decoration, and I had only to compare it with other names I already knew, such as Ahasuerus, Asurabama (who made cuneiform bricks), to detect its origin. Similarly here; compare Chi-wan-to-pel with Po-po-cat-a-pel,[10] the name of a volcano in Central America as we have been taught to pronounce it: the similarity of construction is striking.

I note also that, on the previous day, I had received a letter from Naples, on the envelope of which there was a view of Vesuvius smoking in the distance [K].—In my childhood I was particularly interested in Aztec remains and in the history of Peru and the Incas. [A and B].—I had recently visited a fasci-

10 [Sic. Regularly Popocatepetl; it is actually in central Mexico.]

460

nating exhibition of Indians, with their costumes, etc., which have found a quite appropriate place in the dream [D].—The well-known passage in Shakespeare [11] where Cassius bares his breast to Brutus furnishes me with an easy explanation of scene [E]; and scene [F] recalls to me the story of Buddha leaving his father's home, or equally, the story of Rasselas, prince of Abyssinia, by Samuel Johnson.—There are many details, too, which make one think of the Song of Hiawatha, Longfellow's Indian epic, whose rhythm has been unconsciously followed in several passages of Chi-wan-to-pel's soliloquy. And his burning need for someone who resembles himself [G] presents the greatest analogy with Siegfried's feelings for Brunhild, so marvellously expressed by Wagner.—Finally [I] I had recently heard a lecture by Felix Adler, on the Inviolable Personality (The inviolate Personality [12]).

In the feverish life one leads in New York, a thousand different elements are often mixed in the total impression of a single day. Concerts, lectures, books, reviews, theatrical performances, etc., there is enough to put your brain in quite a whirl. It is said that nothing of what enters into your mind is ever completely lost; that some association of ideas, or a certain conjunction of circumstances, may be enough to re-animate even the slightest impression. It seems that this may apply in many cases. For example here, the details of the *dream-city* [C] reproduced almost exactly those on the cover of one of the reviews I had lately been reading. So it is possible, after all, that this whole affair may be nothing more than a mosaic of the following elements:

    A.—Aztec remains and history of the Incas of Peru.

    B.—Pizarro in Peru.

    C.—Engravings and illustrations, recently seen in various magazines.

    D.—Exhibition of Indians with their costumes, etc.

    E.—Recollection of a passage from Shakespeare's *Julius Caesar*.

    F.—Departure of Buddha and of Rasselas.

    G. and H.—Siegfried sighing after Brunhild.

    I.—Memory of a lecture on the Inviolable Personality.

    K.—View of Vesuvius on the envelope of a letter.

[11] *Julius Caesar*, Act IV, scene 3.   [12] [*Sic*, in English.]

And now, if I add that, for days before, I had been in quest of "an original idea," not much effort is required to see that this mosaic may have formed itself out of the multitude of impressions that are necessarily encountered in a very busy life, and may have taken on this fantastic, oneiric form. This was about midnight, and it may be that my fatigue and torment of mind had to some degree disturbed or deformed the current of my thoughts.

P.S.—I fear that my concern for exactitude may have induced me to give my observations rather too personal a turn. But I hope—and this is my excuse—that they may help others to free their minds from things of the same kind that are worrying them and do something to clear up the more complex phenomena that are often presented by mediums.

BIBLIOGRAPHY

BIBLIOGRAPHY

ABEGHIAN, MANUK. *Der armenische Volksglaube.* Leipzig, 1899.

ABRAHAM, KARL. *Dreams and Myths.* Translated by William Alanson White. (Nervous and Mental Disease Monograph Series, 15.) New York, 1913.

Acts of Thomas. In: *Apocryphal Gospels, Acts, and Revelations.* Translated by Alexander Walker. (Ante-Nicene Christian Library, 16.) Edinburgh, 1870. (Pp. 389–422.)

ADLER, GERHARD. *Studies in Analytical Psychology.* London and New York, 1948.

AESCHYLUS. *Prometheus.* In: *Aeschylus.* [*Plays*]. With an English translation by Herbert Weir Smyth. 2 vols. (Loeb Classical Library.) London and New York, 1922–26.

AGRIPPA, HEINRICH CORNELIUS, of Nettesheim. *De occulta philosophia Libri tres.* Cologne, 1533.

AIGREMONT, DR., pseud. (Siegmar Baron von Schultze-Galléra). *Fuss- und Schuhsymbolik und -Erotik.* Leipzig, 1909.

——. *Volkserotik und Pflanzenwelt.* 2 vols. Halle, 1908–9.

ALCIATI, ANDREA. *Emblemata cum Commentariis.* Padua, 1621.

APULEIUS, LUCIUS. *The Golden Ass, being the Metamorphoses of Lucius Apuleius.* With an English translation by William Adlington (1566) revised by Stephen Gaselee. (Loeb Classical Library.) London and New York, 1915.

——. *Les Metamorphoses ou l'Asne Dor de L. Apulée, Philosophe Platonique.* Paris, 1648.

——. *The Transformations of Lucius, known as the Golden Ass.* Translated by Robert Graves. (Penguin Classics.) London, 1950.

Archäologische Zeitung. (Gerhards Denkmäler, Forschungen und Berichte.) Berlin.

465

ARCHAEOLOGISCHES INSTITUT DES DEUTSCHEN REICHES (Rome). *Annali.*

ARNOBIUS. *Disputationum adversus Gentes libri septem.* See Migne, *P.L.*, vol. 5, cols. 713–1290.

——. *The Seven Books of Arnobius Adversus Gentes.* Translated by A. H. Bryce and H. Campbell. (Ante-Nicene Christian Library, 19.) Edinburgh, 1871.

ARNOLD, SIR EDWIN. *The Light of Asia, or The Great Renunciation.* London, 1906 (1st edn., 1879).

——. See also Bhagavad Gita.

ASTERIUS, BISHOP OF AMASEA. *Homilia X in sanctos martyres.* See Migne, *P.G.*, vol. 40, cols. 323–24.

AUGUSTINE, SAINT. *Confessiones.* See Migne, *P.L.*, vol. 32. For translation, see:

[——.] *The Confessions of St. Augustine.* Translated by Francis Joseph Sheed. New York and London, 1943.

——. *De Civitate Dei.* See Migne, *P.L.*, vol. 41.

——. *Sermo Suppositus* 120. (*In Natali Domini* IV, 8.) See Migne, *P.L.*, vol. 39, cols. 1984–87.

——. *Tractatus in Johannis Evangelium.* See Migne, *P.L.*, vol. 35.

BACHOFEN, J. J. *Versuch über die Gräbersymbolik der Alten.* Basel. 1859.

BAILLET, LOUIS. "Les Miniatures du Scivias de Ste Hildegarde," *Monuments et Mémoires publiés par l'Académie des Inscriptions et Belles-Lettres* (Paris), XIX (1911), 49–149.

BALDWIN, JAMES MARK. *Thought and Things: A Study of the Development and Meaning of Thought, or Genetic Logic.* (Library of Philosophy.) London, 1906–11. 3 vols.

BANCROFT, HUBERT HOWE. *The Native Races of the Pacific States of North America.* New York and London. 1875–76. 5 vols.

BARCHUSEN, JOHANN KONRAD. *Elementa chemiae.* Lugdunum Batavorum [Leiden], 1718.

BARLACH, ERNST. *Der tote Tag.* Berlin, 1912; 2nd edn., 1918.

BELLOWS, HENRY ADAMS (trans.). *The Poetic Edda*. New York, 1923.

BENNDORF, OTTO, and SCHÖNE, RICHARD. *Die antiken Bildwerke des Lateranischen Museums*. Leipzig, 1867.

BERNARDINO DE SAHAGÚN. *General History of the Things of New Spain (Florentine Codex)*. Book 3: *The Origin of the Gods*. Translated by Arthur J. O. Anderson and Charles E. Dibble. (Monographs of the School of American Research, 14, Part IV.) Santa Fe, 1952.

BERNOULLI, CARL ALBRECHT. *Franz Overbeck und Friedrich Nietzsche: Eine Freundschaft*. Jena, 1908. 2 vols.

BERNOULLI, JOHANN JACOB. *Die erhaltenen Darstellungen Alexanders des Grossen*. Munich, 1905.

BERTHELOT, MARCELLIN. *Collection des anciens alchimistes grecs*. Paris, 1887–88. 3 vols.: Introduction, Textes, Traductions.

BERTSCHINGER, H. "Illustrierte Halluzinationen," *Jahrbuch für psychoanalytische und psychopathologische Forschungen* (Leipzig and Vienna), III (1912), 69–100.

[Bhagavad Gita.] *The Song Celestial, or Bhagavad-Gita*. Translated by Sir Edwin Arnold. London, 1930.

Bible. The following versions are cited textually:
    [AV] Authorized ("King James") Version (cited unless otherwise indicated).
    [DV] Douay-Reims Version.
    [RSV] Revised Standard Version (1952).
    [ZB] Zürcher Bibel (first trans. 16th cent.; cited in English trans. from a 1932 edn. published by the Consistory of Canton Zurich on the order of the Zurich Church Synod, being the German version generally used by the author).

[——.] *Bybel printen* . . . [by] Matthaeus Merian. Amsterdam, [1650?].

BLAKE, WILLIAM. *Europe*. London, 1794.

——. *Jerusalem*. London, 1804.

BLEULER, EUGEN. "Zur Theorie des schizophrenen Negativismus." *Psychiatrisch-neurologische Wochenschrift* (Halle), XII (1910), nos. 18–21.

[BÖHME, JAKOB.] *Auslese aus den mystisch-religiösen Schriften Jakob Böhmes.* Newly edited, after the original Amsterdam edn. of 1700, by A. von den Linden. (Geheime Wissenschaften, 16.) Berlin, 1918.

BOTHO, CONRAD. *Sachsisch Chronicon . . . continuirt bis vff den Monat Maium . . . . 1596 . . . durch Mattheum Dresserum.* Magdeburg, 1596.

BOUSSET, WILHELM. *The Antichrist Legend.* Translated by A. H. Keane. London, 1896.

BROWN, W. NORMAN. "The Sources and Nature of pūruṣa in the Pūruṣasukta (Rigveda 10.91)," *Journal of the American Oriental Society* (New Haven), LI (1931), 108–18.

BRUGSCH, HEINRICH. *Die Adonisklage und das Linoslied.* Berlin, 1852.

——. *Dictionnaire hiéroglyphique (Hieroglyphisch-demotisches Wörterbuch).* Leipzig, 1867–82 (lithographed). 7 vols.

——. *Religion und Mythologie der alten Ägypter.* Leipzig, 1885–88. 2 parts.

BUBER, MARTIN (ed.). *Ekstatische Konfessionen.* Jena, 1909.

BÜCHER, KARL. *Arbeit und Rhythmus.* Leipzig, 1899; 3rd edn., 1902.

——. *Die Aufstände der unfreien Arbeiter 143 bis 129 vor Christus.* Frankfort, 1874.

BUDGE, SIR ERNEST ALFRED THOMPSON WALLIS. *Coptic Apocrypha in the Dialect of Upper Egypt.* London, 1913.

——. *The Gods of the Egyptians.* London, 1904. 2 vols.

——. *Osiris and the Egyptian Resurrection.* London, 1911. 2 vols.

Bundahish. In: E. W. WEST (tr.). *Pahlavi Texts.* (Sacred Books of the East, 5.) Oxford, 1880.

BUNSEN, CHRISTIAN CARL JOSIAS, BARON VON. *Versuch eines allgemeinen Gesang- und Gebetbuchs.* Hamburg, 1833.

BURCKHARDT, JACOB. *The Civilization of the Renaissance [in Italy].* London and New York (Phaidon Press), 1944.

[——.] *The Letters of Jacob Burckhardt.* Selected, edited, and translated by Alexander Dru. London and New York, 1955.

Byron, George Gordon, Lord. *Poetical Works.* Oxford, 1945.

Caesar, Caius Julius. *The Gallic War.* With an English translation by H. J. Edwards. (Loeb Classical Library.) London and New York, 1917.

Caetani-Lovatelli, Ersilia, Countess. *Antichi monumenti illustrati.* Rome, 1889.

Cannegieter, Hendrik. *Epistola ad comitem Ottonem de Lynden, de ara ad Noviomagum Gelriae reperta, aliisque inscriptionibus nuper effossis.* Arnhem, 1766.

Carlyle, Thomas. "On Heroes and Hero-Worship" [1841]. In: *Sartor Resartus; On Heroes, Hero-Worship, and the Heroic in History.* (Everyman's Library.) London and New York, 1948.

Chamberlain, Houston Stewart. *The Foundations of the 19th Century.* Translated by John Lees. London and New York, 1911 [1910]. 2 vols.

Chantepie de la Saussaye, Pierre Daniel. *Lehrbuch der Religionsgeschichte.* Tübingen, 1905. 2 vols.

Chapouthier, Fernand. *Les Dioscures au service d'une déesse.* (Bibliothèque des Écoles françaises d'Athènes et de Rome, fasc. 137.) Paris, 1935.

Cicero, Marcus Tullius. *De inventione, etc.* With an English translation by H. M. Hubbell. (Loeb Classical Library.) London and New York, 1949.

——. [*De natura deorum.*] In: *Academica.* With an English translation by H. Rackham. (Loeb Classical Library.) London and New York, 1933.

——. *Pro Quinctio, etc.* With an English translation by J. H. Freese. (Loeb Classical Library.) London and New York, 1930.

——. *The Tusculan Disputations.* With an English translation by J. E. King. (Loeb Classical Library.) London and New York, 1927.

Claparède, Édouard. "Quelques mots sur la définition de l'hystérie," *Archives de psychologie* (Geneva), VII (1908), 169–93.

CLEMEN, PAUL. *Die romanischen Wandmalereien des Rheinlands.* (Publikationen der Gesellschaft für rheinische Geschichtskunde, 25.) Düsseldorf, 1905.

CLEMENT OF ALEXANDRIA. *Protrepticus.* In: *The Writings of Clement of Alexandria.* Translated by the Rev. William Wilson. (Ante-Nicene Christian Library, 4, 12.) Edinburgh, 1877–79.

CLEMENT OF ROME, SAINT. *Homilies.* See Migne, *P.G.,* vol. 2. Translation: *The Clementine Homilies.* Translated by the Rev. Alexander Roberts and James Donaldson. (Ante-Nicene Christian Library, 17.) Edinburgh, 1870.

COHN, WILLIAM. *Buddha in der Kunst des Ostens.* Leipzig, 1925.

COLERIDGE, SAMUEL TAYLOR. *The Poems.* Edited by E. H. Coleridge. London, 1935.

COLONNA, FRANCESCO. *Hypnerotomachia Poliphili.* . . . Venice, 1499. See also FIERZ-DAVID.

CONYBEARE, F. C. C. "Die Jungfräuliche Kirche und die jungfräuliche Mutter," *Archiv für Religionswissenschaft* (Freiburg i. B.), IX (1906), 73–86.

CORNFORD, W. F. (trans.). *Plato's Cosmology; The Timaeus of Plato.* New York and London, 1937.

CREUZER, [GEORG] FRIEDRICH. *Symbolik und Mythologie der alten Völker.* Leipzig and Darmstadt, 1810–23. 6 vols.

[CRÈVECOEUR, MICHEL GUILLAUME JEAN DE.] *Voyage dans la Haute Pensylvanie.* Paris, 1801. 3 vols.

CUMONT, FRANZ. *The Mysteries of Mithra.* Translated from the 2nd revised French edn. by Thomas J. McCormack. London, 1903.

——. *Textes et monuments figurés relatifs aux mystères de Mithra.* Brussels, 1896–99. 2 vols.

CYPRIAN, SAINT, pseud. *De Pascha Computus.* In: Migne, *P.L.,* vol. 4, cols. 939–68.

DANZEL, THEODOR WILHELM. "Altmexikanische Symbolik." *Eranos-Jahrbuch 1937* (Zurich, 1938).

——. *Mexiko I.* (Kulturen der Erde, 11.) Hagen i. W. and Darmstadt, 1922.

——. *Symbole, Dämonen und heilige Türme.* Hamburg, 1930.

DARESSY, GEORGES. "Statues de divinités," *Catalogue générale des antiquités égyptiennes du Musée du Caire,* nos. 38001–39384 (1905–6).

DE GUBERNATIS, ANGELO. *Zoological Mythology.* London, 1872. 2 vols.

DE JONG, KAREL HENDRIK EDUARD. *Das antike Mysterienwesen.* Leiden, 1909.

DEUBNER, LUDWIG. *Attische Feste.* Berlin, 1932.

DEUSSEN, PAUL. *Allgemeine Geschichte der Philosophie.* Leipzig, 1894–1917. 2 vols.

——. *Sechzig Upanishad's des Veda.* Leipzig, 1897; 3rd edn., 1938.

DIETERICH, ALBRECHT. *Abraxas: Studien zur Religionsgeschichte des späteren Altertums.* Leipzig, 1891.

——. *Eine Mithrasliturgie.* Leipzig, 1903; 2nd edn., 1910.

——. *Mutter Erde.* Leipzig, 1905; 2nd edn., 1913.

DIEZ, FRIEDRICH CHRISTIAN. *Etymologisches Wörterbuch der romanischen Sprachen.* 5th edn., Bonn, 1887.

DIO CHRYSOSTOM. [*Works.*] With an English translation by J. W. Cohoon and H. Lamar Crosby. (Loeb Classical Library.) London and New York, 1932–51. 5 vols.

DIODORUS. [*Works.*] Edited with an English translation by C. H. Oldfather and Russel M. Geer. (Loeb Classical Library.) London and New York, 1935– . 12 vols. (vols. 1–4 and 9 published).

DIOSCORIDES. *Pedanii Dioscuridis de materia medica libri quinque.* Edited by Max Wellmann. Berlin, 1907–14. 3 vols.

DREWS, ARTHUR. *The Christ Myth.* Translated [from the 3rd edn.] by C. Delisle Burns. London and Leipzig, [1910].

——. *Plotin und der Untergang der antiken Weltanschauung.* Jena, 1907.

DREXEL, FRIEDRICH. "Das Kastell Stockstadt," *Der obergermanisch-raetische Limes des Römerreiches* [pub. at Heidelberg by the Reichs-Limeskommission], XXXIII (1910), 1–136.

DUCHESNE, LOUIS. *Le Liber Pontificalis.* Texte, Introduction et Commentaire. (Bibliothèque des Écoles françaises d'Athènes et de Rome, 2nd series, III.) Paris, 1886–92, 2 vols.

EBBINGHAUS, HERMANN. "Psychologie." In: WILHELM DILTHEY and others. *Die Kultur der Gegenwart.* Berlin and Leipzig, 1907.

EBERSCHWEILER, A. "Untersuchungen über die sprachliche Komponente der Assoziation." In: *Allgemeine Zeitschrift für Psychiatrie* (Berlin), LXV (1908), 240–71.

EHRENSTEIN, THEODOR. *Das Alte Testament im Bilde.* Vienna, 1923.

ELIEZER, BEN HYRCANUS, pseud. *Pirkê de Rabbi Elieser.* Translated and annotated . . . by Gerald Friedlander. London, 1916.

EMERSON, RALPH WALDO. *The Conduct of Life.* In: *The Complete Works of Ralph Waldo Emerson.* Edited by Edward Waldo Emerson. (Centenary Edition.) Boston, 1903–4. 16 vols. (Vol. VI.)

EPIPHANIUS, SAINT. *Adversus octoginta haereses, vel Panarium.* See Migne, *P.G.*, vol. 41, col. 173, to vol. 42, col. 832.

ERMAN, ADOLF. *Life in Ancient Egypt.* Translated by H. M. Tirard. London and New York, 1894.

——. *Literature of the Ancient Egyptians.* Translated by A. M. Blackman. London, 1927.

——. *Die Religion der Ägypter.* Berlin and Leipzig, 1934.

EVELYN-WHITE, H. G. (trans.). *Hesiod, the Homeric Hymns and Homerica.* (Loeb Classical Library.) London and New York, 1920.

FERENCZI, SANDOR. "Introjection and Transference." In: *First Contributions to Psycho-Analysis.* Translated by Ernest Jones. London, 1952.

FERRERO, GUGLIELMO. *Les Lois psychologiques du symbolisme.* Paris, 1895. (Original: *I Simboli in rapporto alla storia e filosofia del diritto.* Turin, 1893.)

FICHTE, IMMANUEL HERMANN VON. *Psychologie.* Leipzig, 1864–73. 2 vols.

FICK, FRIEDRICH CHRISTIAN AUGUST. *Vergleichendes Wörterbuch der indogermanischen Grundsprache.* 4th edn., Göttingen, 1890–1909. 3 vols. See also STOKES.

472

[FIERZ-DAVID, LINDA.] *The Dream of Poliphilo*. Related and interpreted by Linda Fierz-David. Translated by Mary Hottinger. (Bollingen Series XXV.) New York, 1950. See also COLONNA.

FIRMICUS MATERNUS, JULIUS. *De errore profanarum religionum*. Edited by Konrad Ziegler. Leipzig, 1907.

———. *Matheseos libri octo*. Edited by W. Kroll, F. Skutsch, and K. Ziegler. Leipzig, 1897–1913. 2 vols.

FLOURNOY, THÉODORE. *From India to the Planet Mars*. Translated by D. B. Vermilye. New York and London, 1900.

———. See also MILLER.

FRANCE, ANATOLE. *Le Jardin d'Épicure*. 4th edn., Paris, 1895.

FRAZER, SIR JAMES GEORGE. *The Golden Bough*. Part III: "The Dying God"; Part IV: "Adonis, Attis, Osiris." London, resp. 1911 and 1907 (2nd edn.).

FREUD, SIGMUND. "Analysis of a Phobia in a Five-year-old Boy." In: Standard Edition,* X. London, 1955. (Pp. 3–149.)

———. "Creative Writers and Day-Dreaming." In: Standard Edition, IX. London, 1959. (Pp. 143–153.)

———. "The Dynamics of the Transference." In: Standard Edition, XII. London, 1958. (Pp. 99–108.)

———. "The Future of an Illusion." In: Standard Edition, XXI. London, 1961. (Pp. 5–56.)

———. *The Interpretation of Dreams*. In: Standard Edition, IV and V. London, 1953.

———. "Leonardo da Vinci and a Memory of His Childhood." In: Standard Edition, XI. London, 1957. (Pp. 63–137.)

* Complete title: *The Standard Edition of the Complete Psychological Works of Sigmund Freud*, translated from the German under the general editorship of James Strachey in collaboration with Anna Freud, assisted by Alix Strachey and Alan Tyson.

——. "Psycho-Analytic Notes on an Autobiographical Account of a Case of Paranoia (Dementia Paranoides)." In: Standard Edition,* XII. London, 1958. (Pp. 9–82.)

——. "Three Essays on the Theory of Sexuality." In: Standard Edition, VII. London, 1953. (Pp. 123–243.)

FRIEDLÄNDER, S. " 'Veni Creator!' Zehn Jahre nach dem Tode Friedrich Nietzsche's," *Jugend* (Munich), II (1910) : 35, 823.

FROBENIUS, LEO. *Das Zeitalter des Sonnengottes.* Vol. I (no more published). Berlin, 1904.

FUHRMANN, ERNST. *Reich der Inka.* (Kulturen der Erde, 1 and 2.) Hagen i. W., 1922. 2 vols.

GATTI, ATTILIO. *South of the Sahara.* London, 1946.

GIVRY, G. DE. *Le Musée des Sorciers.* Paris, 1929.

[GOETHE.] *Goethe's Faust, Parts I and II.* An abridged version translated by Louis MacNeice. London and New York, 1951.

——. *Faust, Part One* and *Part Two.* Translated by Philip Wayne. (Penguin Classics.) Harmondsworth, 1949, 1959.

GOODENOUGH, ERWIN R. "The Crown of Victory in Judaism," *Art Bulletin* (New York), XXVIII (Sept., 1946), 139–59.

GÖRRES, JOHANN JOSEPH VON. *Die Christliche Mystik.* Regensburg and Landshut, 1836–42. 4 vols.

GRAF, MAX. *Richard Wagner im Fliegenden Holländer.* (Schriften zur angewandten Seelenkunde, 9.) Leipzig and Vienna, 1911.

GRAY, LOUIS HERBERT, and MACCULLOCH, JOHN ARNOTT (eds.). *The Mythology of All Races.* Boston, 1916–28. 13 vols.

GRESSMANN, HUGO. *Altorientalische Texte und Bilder zum alten Testamente.* Tübingen, 1909. 2 vols.

* Complete title: *The Standard Edition of the Complete Psychological Works of Sigmund Freud,* translated from the German under the general editorship of James Strachey in collaboration with Anna Freud, assisted by Alix Strachey and Alan Tyson.

——. *Die orientalischen Religionen im hellenistisch-römischen Zeitalter.* Berlin and Leipzig, 1930.

GRIMM, JAKOB LUDWIG KARL. *Teutonic Mythology.* Translated from the 4th edn. by James Steven Stallybrass. London, 1883–88. 4 vols.

GUÉNON, RENÉ. *Man and His Becoming according to the Vedānta.* London, 1945.

GUIRAND, FÉLIX (ed.). *Mythologie générale.* Paris, 1935.

GUNKEL, JOHANN FRIEDRICH HERMANN. *Schöpfung und Chaos in Urzeit und Endzeit.* Göttingen, 1895.

GURLITT, W. "Vorbericht über Ausgrabungen in Pettau," *Jahreshefte des österreichischen archäologischen Institutes in Wien,* II (1899), col. 101.

HAHN, EDUARD. *Demeter und Baubo.* Lübeck, [1896].

HAMANN, JOHANN GEORG. *Schriften.* Edited by Friederich Roth. Berlin, 1821–43. 8 vols.

HARDING, MARY ESTHER. *The Way of All Women.* London and New York, 1933.

HARRER, HEINRICH. *Seven Years in Tibet.* London, 1954.

HARTLAUB, GUSTAV FRIEDRICH. *Giorgiones Geheimnis.* Munich, 1925.

HARTMANN, KARL ROBERT EDUARD VON. *Die Weltanschauung der modernen Physik.* Leipzig, 1902.

HAUPTMANN, GERHART. *Hannele.* Translated by Charles Henry Meltzer. London and New York, 1908.

——. *The Sunken Bell.* Translated by Charles Henry Meltzer. London and New York, 1900.

HEIDEL, ALEXANDER. *The Gilgamesh Epic and Old Testament Parallels.* Chicago, 1946.

[HEINE, HEINRICH.] *Heine's Book of Songs.* Translated by John Todhunter. Oxford, 1907.

[——.] *Heinrich Heine, Paradox and Poet: The Poems.* Translated by Louis Untermeyer. New York, 1937.

HERODOTUS. *The Histories.* Translated by Aubrey de Selincourt. (Penguin Classics.) Harmondsworth, 1953.

HERRMANN, PAUL. *Nordische Mythologie in gemeinverständlicher Darstellung.* Leipzig, 1903.

HERZOG, RUDOLF. "Aus dem Asklepieion von Kos," *Archiv für Religionswissenschaft* (Freiburg i. B.), X (1907), 201–28.

HESIOD. See EVELYN-WHITE.

HIPPOCRATES. In: *Hippocrates and the Fragments of Heracleitus.* Translated by W. H. S. Jones and E. T. Withington. (Loeb Classical Library.) London and New York, 1923–31. 4 vols.

HIPPOLYTUS. *Elenchos.* In: *Hippolytus' Werke.* Edited by Paul Wendland. Vol. III. Leipzig, 1916.

HIRT, HERMANN. *Etymologie der neuhochdeutschen Sprache.* Munich, 1909.

HOFFMANN, ERNEST THEODOR WILHELM. *The Devil's Elixir.* Edinburgh, 1824. 2 vols.

HÖLDERLIN, JOHANN CHRISTIAN FRIEDRICH. *Gedichte.* Edited by Franz Zinkernagel. Leipzig, 1922.

[——.] *Hölderlin: His Poems.* Translated by Michael Hamburger. 2nd edn., London and New York, 1952.

——. *Selected Poems.* Translated by J. B. Leishman. London, 1944.

HOMER. *The Iliad.* Translated by E. V. Rieu. (Penguin Classics.) Harmondsworth, 1950.

——. *The Odyssey.* Translated by E. V. Rieu. (Penguin Classics.) Harmondsworth, 1946.

Homeric Hymns. See EVELYN-WHITE.

HORACE. *Ars poetica.* In: *Horace: Satires, Epistles, and Ars poetica.* With an English translation by H. Rushton Fairclough. (Loeb Classical Library.) London and New York, 1926.

——. *Odes and Epodes.* Translated by C. E. Bennett (Loeb Classical Library.) London and New York, 1914.

HUGH OF ST. VICTOR. *De laude caritatis.* In Migne, *P.L.,* vol. 176, cols. 969–76.

476

HUMBOLDT, FRIEDRICH HEINRICH ALEXANDER, BARON VON. *Cosmos.* Translated by E. C. Otté, B. H. Paul, and W. S. Dallas. (Bohn's Scientific Library.) London, 1849–58. 5 vols.

HUME, ROBERT ERNEST (trans.). *The Thirteen Principal Upanishads.* Oxford, 1921.

I Ching. The German translation by Richard Wilhelm rendered into English by Cary F. Baynes. New York (Bollingen Series XIX) and London, 1950. 2 vols.

INTERNATIONAL CHALCOGRAPHICAL SOCIETY. *Publications.* [*Veröffentlichungen der Internationalen chalkographischen Gesellschaft.*] 1888.

[IRENAEUS.] *The Writings of Irenaeus.* Translated by Alexander Roberts and W. H. Rambaut. (Ante-Nicene Christian Library, 5, 9.) Edinburgh, 1868. 2 vols.

JAFFÉ, ANIELA. "Bilder und Symbole aus E. T. A. Hoffmanns Märchen 'Der goldne Topf.'" In: C. G. JUNG. *Gestaltungen des Unbewussten.* Zurich, 1950.

JÄHNS, MAX. *Ross und Reiter in Leben und Sprache, Glauben und Geschichte der Deutschen.* Leipzig, 1872. 2 vols.

JAMES, M. R. (trans.). *The Apocryphal New Testament.* Oxford, 1924.

JAMES, WILLIAM. *Principles of Psychology.* London, 1907. 2 vols.

JANET, PIERRE. *Les Névroses.* Paris, 1909.

JEFFERS, ROBINSON. *Roan Stallion, Tamar, and Other Poems.* New York, 1925.

JENSEN, PETER. *Das Gilgamesch-Epos in der Weltliteratur.* Strasbourg, 1906– (in progress).

JEREMIAS, ALFRED. *Das Alte Testament im Lichte des alten Orients.* 4th edn., Leipzig, 1930.

JEROME, SAINT. *Adversus Jovinianum.* In Migne, *P.L.,* vol. 23, cols. 211–338.

——. *Epistola 58 ad Paulinum.* In Migne, *P.L.,* vol. 22, col. 581.

JODL, FRIEDRICH. *Lehrbuch der Psychologie.* 5th and 6th edn., Stuttgart and Berlin, 1924. 2 vols.

JOËL, KARL. *Seele und Welt.* Jena, 1912.

JOHN CHRYSOSTOM, SAINT, pseud. *De solstitiis et aequinoctiis.* In Cumont, *Textes* (q.v.), p. 355.

JOHNSON, SAMUEL. *The History of Rasselas, Prince of Abissinia.* London, 1759.

JONES, ERNEST. "On the Nightmare." In: *American Journal of Insanity* (Baltimore), LXVI (1910), 383–417. (As a book, augmented: International Psycho-Analytical Library, 20. London, 1931.)

JONES, H. STUART (ed.). *A Catalogue of the Ancient Sculptures Preserved in the Municipal Collections of Rome: The Sculptures of the Palazzo dei Conservatori.* (British School at Rome.) Oxford, 1926.

JOSEPHUS, FLAVIUS. *Against Apion.* In: *Josephus.* Translated by H. Thackeray and Ralph Marcus. (Loeb Classical Library.) London and New York, 1926–43. 9 vols. (Vol. I.)

JUBINAL, MICHEL LOUIS ACHILLE. *Mystères inédits du XV. siècle.* Paris, 1837. 2 vols.

[JULIAN.] *The Works of the Emperor Julian.* Translated by Wilbur Cave Wright. (Loeb Classical Library.) London and New York, 1913–23. 3 vols.

JUNG, C. G. *Aion: Researches into the Phenomenology of the Self. Collected Works,* * Vol. 9, part ii. 1959; 2nd edn., 1968.

——. "Answer to Job." In: *Collected Works,* Vol. 11. 1958; 2nd edn., 1969.

——. "The Archetypes of the Collective Unconscious." In: *Collected Works,* Vol. 9, part i. 1959; 2nd edn., 1968.

——. Commentary on "The Secret of the Golden Flower." In: *Collected Works,* Vol. 13. 1967.

——. "The Concept of the Collective Unconscious." In: *Collected Works,* Vol. 9, part i. 1959; 2nd edn., 1968.

——. "Concerning Rebirth." In: *Collected Works,* Vol. 9, part i. 1959.

* For details of the *Collected Works of C. G. Jung,* see the list at the end of this volume.

——. "The Content of the Psychoses." In: *Collected Works,* Vol. 3. 1960.

——. "Cryptomnesia." In: *Collected Works,* Vol. 1. 1957; 2nd edn., 1970.

——. "General Aspects of Dream Psychology." In: *Collected Works,* Vol. 8. 1960; 2nd edn., 1969.

——. *Gestaltungen des Unbewussten.* Zurich, 1950.

——. *Mysterium Coniunctionis. Collected Works,* Vol. 14. 1963; 2nd edn., 1970.

——. "On the Nature of Dreams." In: *Collected Works,* Vol. 8. 1960; 2nd edn., 1969.

——. "On the Nature of the Psyche." In: *Collected Works,* Vol. 8. 1960; 2nd edn., 1969.

——. "On the Psychology and Pathology of So-called Occult Phenomena." In: *Collected Works,* Vol. 1. 1957; 2nd edn., 1970.

——. "On the Psychology of the Unconscious." In: *Collected Works,* Vol. 7. 1953; 2nd edn., 1966.

——. "Paracelsus as a Spiritual Phenomenon." In: *Collected Works,* Vol. 13. 1967.

——. "The Phenomenology of the Spirit in Fairytales." In: *Collected Works,* Vol. 9, part i. 1959; 2nd edn. 1968.

——. "Psychic Conflicts in a Child." In: *Collected Works,* Vol. 17. 1954; 2nd edn., 1964.

——. "A Psychological Approach to the Dogma of the Trinity." In: *Collected Works,* Vol. 11. 1958; 2nd edn., 1969.

——. "The Psychological Aspects of the Kore." In: *Collected Works,* Vol. 9, part i. 1959; 2nd edn., 1968.

——. *Psychological Types. Collected Works,* Vol. 6. 1970.

——. *Psychology and Alchemy. Collected Works,* Vol. 12. 1953; 2nd edn., 1968.

——. "Psychology and Religion." In: *Collected Works,* Vol. 11. 1958; 2nd edn., 1969.

——. "The Psychology of the Child Archetype." In: *Collected Works,* Vol. 9, part i. 1959; 2nd edn., 1968.

———. "The Psychology of Dementia Praecox." In: *Collected Works,* Vol. 3. 1960.

———. "The Psychology of Eastern Meditation." In: *Collected Works,* Vol. 11. 1958; 2nd edn., 1969.

———. "The Psychology of the Transference." In: *Collected Works,* Vol. 16. 1954; 2nd edn., 1966.

———. "The Relations between the Ego and the Unconscious." In: *Collected Works,* Vol. 7. 1953; 2nd edn., 1966.

———. "A Review of the Complex Theory." In: *Collected Works,* Vol. 8. 1960; 2nd edn., 1969.

———. "Studies in Word Association." In: *Collected Works,* Vol. 2. (Alternative source: *Studies in Word-Association* . . . under the direction of C. G. Jung, translated by M. D. Eder, London, 1918, New York, 1919.)

———. "A Study in the Process of Individuation." In: *Collected Works,* Vol. 9, part i. 1959; 2nd edn., 1968.

———. "Transformation Symbolism in the Mass." In: *Collected Works,* Vol. 11. 1958; 2nd edn., 1969.

———. *Two Essays on Analytical Psychology. Collected Works,* Vol. 7. 1953; 2nd edn., 1966.

———. "The Visions of Zosimos." In: *Collected Works,* Vol. 13. 1967.

———. "Wotan." In: *Collected Works,* Vol. 10. 1964.

——— and KERÉNYI, C. *Essays on a Science of Mythology.* Translated by R. F. C. Hull. (Bollingen Series XXII.) New York, 1949; reissued 1969. (Also pub. as *Introduction to a Science of Mythology,* London 1950.)

JUNG, EMMA. "Ein Beitrag zum Problem des Animus." In: C. G. JUNG. *Wirklichkeit der Seele.* Zurich, 1934.

JUNG, ERICH. *Germanische Götter und Helden in Christlicher Zeit.* Munich and Berlin, 1939.

KALTHOFF, ALBERT. *The Rise of Christianity.* Translated by Joseph McCabe. London, 1907.

KENYON, SIR FREDERIC GEORGE. *Greek Papyri in the British Museum.* London, 1893–1917. 5 vols.

KERÉNYI, KARL (C.). *Die Geburt der Helena.* (Albae Vigiliae, new series, 3.) Zurich, 1945.

——. "Die Göttin Natur," *Eranos-Jahrbuch* (Zurich), XIV (1946), 39–86.

——. "The Mysteries of the Kabeiroi." In: *The Mysteries,* q.v.

——. *Prometheus: Archetypal Image of Human Existence.* Translated by Ralph Manheim. New York (Bollingen Series LXV : 1) and London, 1963.

KERNER, JUSTINUS. *The Seeress of Prevorst.* Translated by Mrs. [Catherine] Crowe. New York, 1859. (Original: *Die Seherin von Prevorst.* Stuttgart and Tübingen, 1829. 2 vols.)

KIRCHER, ATHANASIUS. *Oedipus Aegyptiacus.* Rome, 1652–54. 3 parts in 4 vols.

KLEINPAUL, RUDOLF. *Das Leben der Sprache und ihre Weltstellung.* Leipzig, 1893. 3 vols.

KLUGE, FRIEDRICH. *Etymologisches Wörterbuch der deutschen Sprache.* 2nd edn., Strassburg, 1883.

KOCH-GRÜNBERG, THEODOR. *Südamerikanische Felszeichnungen.* Berlin, 1907.

Koran. Translated by J. M. Rodwell. (Everyman's Library.) London, 1909.

[——.] *The Meaning of the Glorious Koran.* Translated by Marmaduke Pickthall. London, 1930.

KUELPE, OSWALD. *Outlines of Psychology.* Translated by Edward Bradford Titchener. London, 1895.

KUHN, FRANZ FELIX ADALBERT. *Mythologische Studien,* Vol. I: *Die Herabkunft des Feuers und des Göttertranks.* Gütersloh, 1886.

——. "Die Sprachvergleichung und die Urgeschichte der indogermänischen Völker," *Zeitschrift für vergleichende Sprachforschung* (Berlin), IV (1854), 81–124.

——. "Über die durch Nasale erweiterten Verbalstämme," ibid., II (1853), 392–98.

481

LABRUNIE DE NERVAL, GÉRARD. *Aurelia,* etc. Translated by Richard Aldington. [London], 1932. (Original: 1855.)

LACTANTIUS, FIRMIANUS. *Divinae Institutiones.* In: *The Works of Lactantius.* Translated by William Fletcher. (Ante-Nicene Christian Library, 21, 22.) Edinburgh, 1871. 2 vols.

LAISTNER, LUDWIG. *Das Rätsel der Sphinx.* Berlin, 1889. 2 vols.

LAJARD, JEAN BAPTISTE FÉLIX. *Mémoire sur une représentation figurée de la Vénus orientale androgyne.* (Nouvelles annales de l'Institut Archéologique.) Rome, 1873.

LANZONE, RIDOLFO V. *Dizionario di Mitologia Egizia.* Turin, 1881–85. 2 vols.

[LA ROCHEFOUCAULD, FRANÇOIS, DUC DE.] *The Moral Maxims and Reflections of the Duke de La Rochefoucauld.* With an introduction and notes by George N. Powell. London, 1903.

LAYARD, JOHN WILLOUGHBY. "The Incest Taboo and the Virgin Archetype," *Eranos-Jahrbuch* (Zurich), XII (1945), 254–307.

LE BLANT, EDMOND. *Les Sarcophages chrétiens de la Gaule.* Paris, 1886.

LE COQ, ALBERT VON. *Die Buddhistische Spätantike in Mittelasien.* Berlin, 1922–33. 7 vols.

LIEPMANN, HUGO. *Über Ideenflucht: Begriffsbestimmung und psychologische Analyse.* Halle, 1904.

LOMBROSO, CESARE. *Genio e Follia.* Turin, 1882.

LONGFELLOW, HENRY WADSWORTH. *The Song of Hiawatha.* Boston, 1855.

LOTZE, RUDOLF HERMANN. *Logik.* (System der Philosophie, 1.) Leipzig, 1874.

LÖWIS OF MENAR, A. VON. "Nordkaukasische Steingeburtsagen," *Archiv für Religionswissenschaft* (Freiburg i. B.), XIII (1910), 509–524.

LUCIAN. *Menippus.* In: *Lucian.* With an English translation by A. M. Harman. (Loeb Classical Library.) London, 1913ff. 8 vols.

LUCRETIUS. *De rerum natura.* With an English translation by W. H. D. Rouse. (Loeb Classical Library.) London and New York, 1924.

LYDUS, JOHANNES. *De mensibus.* Edited by Richard Wünsch. Leipzig, 1898.

MACARIUS, JOANNES. *Abraxas.* Antwerp, 1657.

MACDONELL, ARTHUR ANTHONY. *A Practical Sanskrit Dictionary.* New edn., London, 1924.

MACROBIUS, AMBROSIUS THEODOSIUS. *Saturnaliorum Libri VII.* In: *Opera quae supersunt.* Edited by Ludovicus Janus. Quedlinburg and Leipzig, 1848–52. 2 vols.

MAEDER, A. "Die Symbolik in den Legenden, Märchen, Gebräuchen und Träumen," *Psychiatrisch-Neurologische Wochenschrift* (Halle), X (1908).

MAEHLY, JACOB A. *Die Schlange in Mythus und Kultus der klassischen Völker.* Basel, 1867.

MAETERLINCK, MAURICE. *The Blue Bird.* Translated by Alexander Teixeira de Mattos. London, 1924.

——. *Wisdom and Destiny.* Translated by Alfred Sutro. London, 1898.

[Mainyo-i-Khard.] *Book of the Mainyo-i-Khard.* Translated by E. W. West. London, 1871.

MANNHARDT, WILHELM. *Antike Wald- und Feldkulte.* Berlin, 1875–77. 2 vols.

Manuscripts.
Leiden. Rijksuniversiteit Bibliotheek. Codex Vossianus Chymicus 29. Thomas Aquinas, pseud. "De Alchimia." c. 1520.
Paris. Bibliothèque nationale. MS. Lat. 11534. Bible of Manerius.
——. Library of the Palais Bourbon. Codex Borbonicus. 16th cent.
St. Gall. Bibliothek. Alchemical MS. 17th cent.
Tübingen. Universitätsbibliothek. MS. Theol. Lat. fol. 561. Beatus Commentary. Mid 12th cent.
Wiesbaden. Nassauische Landesbibliothek. St. Hildegarde of Bingen, "Scivias." 12th cent.

MAUDSLAY, A. P. *Biologia Centrali-Americana: Archaeology*. (Biologia Centrali-Americana, ed. by F. D. Godman and Osbert Salvin, 55–59.) London, 1896–99. 4 vols.

MAURICE, THOMAS. *Indian Antiquities*. London, 1796. 7 vols.

MAUTHNER, FRIEDRICH. *Sprache und Psychologie*. (Beiträge zur Kritik der Sprache.) Stuttgart, 1901.

MAX MÜLLER, FRIEDRICH. *Introduction to the Science of Religion*. London, 1882.

——. *Lectures on the Origin and Growth of Religion*. London, 1891.

—— (trans.). *The Upanishads*. Parts I and II. (Sacred Books of the East, 1 and 15.) Oxford, 1879 and 1884.

MAYN, GEORG. *Über Byrons "Heaven and Earth."* Breslau (dissertation), 1887.

MEAD, GEORGE ROBERT STOW. *A Mithraic Ritual*. (Echoes of the Gnosis Series.) London, 1907.

MECHTHILD OF MAGDEBURG, SAINT. *Das fliessende Licht der Gottheit*. Translated into modern German and explained by Mela Escherich. Berlin, 1909.

——. *The Revelations*. Translated by Lucy Menzies. London and New York, 1953.

MELITO OF SARDIS. *Fragmentum ex catena in Genesim*. In Migne, *P.G.*, vol. 5, cols. 1215–18. Also in Pitra, *Spicilegium solesmense* (q.v.), II, p. lxiii.

MEREZHKOVSKY, DMITRY SERGYEEVICH. *Peter and Alexis*. London, 1905. (Original: 1905.)

——. *The Romance of Leonardo da Vinci*. Translated by Bernard Guilbert Guerney. London and New York, 1938. (Original: 1901.)

MERIAN, MATTHAEUS. See Bible.

MERINGER, R. "Wörter und Sachen." *Indogermanische Forschungen* (Strassburg), XVI (1904), 101–96.

MEYER, ELARD HUGO. *Indogermanische Mythen*. Berlin, 1883–87. 2 vols.

MIGNE, JACQUES PAUL (ed.). *Patrologiae cursus completus*.
[*P.L.*] Latin Series. Paris, 1844–64. 221 vols.
[*P.G.*] Greek Series. Paris, 1857–66. 166 vols.

(These works are cited as "Migne, *P.L.*" and "Migne, *P.G.*" respectively. References are to columns, not to pages.)

MILLER, MISS FRANK, pseud. "Quelques faits de l'imagination créatrice subconsciente." [Translated?] with an introduction by Théodore Flournoy. *Archives de psychologie* (Geneva), V (1906), 36–51.

[MONTELIUS, OSCAR.] *Opuscula archaeologica Oscari Montelio septuagenario dicata*. Stockholm, 1913.

MÖRIKE, EDUARD. *Werke*. Edited by Harry Maync. Leipzig and Vienna, 1914. 3 vols.

MORRIS, RICHARD. *Legends of the Holy Rood*. (Early English Text Society Series, 46.) London, 1871.

MÜLLER, JOHANN GEORGE. *Geschichte der amerikanischen Urreligionen*. 2nd edn., Basel, 1867.

MÜLLER, JOHANNES. *Über die phantastischen Gesichtserscheinungen*. Coblenz, 1826.

MÜLLER, NIKLAS. *Glauben, Wissen und Kunst der alten Hindus*. . . . Mainz, 1822.

Musaeum Hermeticum reformatum et amplificatum . . . continens tractatus chimicos XXI. Frankfurt a. M., 1678.

MUTHER, RICHARD. *Geschichte der Malerei*. 3rd edn., Berlin, 1920. 3 vols.

The Mysteries. Translated by Ralph Manheim and R. F. C. Hull. (Papers from the Eranos Yearbooks, 2.) New York (Bollingen Series XXX), 1955; London, 1956.

NAGEL, A. "Der chinesische Küchengott (Tsau-kyun)," *Archiv für Religionswissenschaft* (Freiburg i. B.), XI (1907–8), 23–43.

NAZARI, ORESTE. "Spizzico di etimologie latine e greche," *Rivista di Filologia* (Turin), XXXVI (1908), 567–78.

NEGELEIN, JULIUS VON. "Das Pferd im Seelenglauben und Totenkult," *Zeitschrift des Vereins für Volkskunde* (Berlin), XI (1901), 406–20; XII (1902), 14–25, 377–90.

———. *Der Traumschlüssel des Jagaddeva*. (Religionsgeschichtliche Versuche und Vorarbeiten, 11, part 4, edited by A. Dieterich and R. Wünsch.) Giessen, 1912.

Nerval, Gérard de. See Labrunie de Nerval.

Neumann, Erich. *The Great Mother.* Translated by Ralph Manheim. New York (Bollingen Series XLVII) and London, 1955.

——. *The Origins and History of Consciousness.* Translated by R. F. C. Hull. New York (Bollingen Series XLII) and London, 1954.

——. *Umkreisung der Mitte.* Zurich, 1953–54. 3 vols. (Vol. 3 translated in: *Art and the Creative Unconscious.* New York (Bollingen Series LXI) and London, 1959.)

Nietzsche, Friedrich Wilhelm. *Ecce Homo and Poems.* Translated by Anthony M. Ludovici, poetry by Paul V. Cohn and others. (Complete Works, 17.) Edinburgh, London and New York, 1911.

——. *Human, All-too-Human.* Translated by Helen Zimmern and Paul V. Cohn. (Complete Works, 6, 7.) London and New York, 1909, 1911. 2 vols.

——. *Thus Spake Zarathustra.* Translated by Thomas Common. (Complete Works, 11.) London and New York, 1909.

——. *Werke.* Leipzig, 1899–1913. 19 vols.

Norden, Eduard. *Die Geburt des Kindes.* (Studien der Bibliothek Warburg, 3.) Leipzig and Berlin, 1924.

Orientalistische Literaturzeitung. Leipzig, 1898–

[Orphic Hymns.] *The Mystical Hymns of Orpheus.* Translated from the Greek by Thomas Taylor. London, 1896.

Ovid (Publius Ovidius Naso). *Metamorphoses.* With an English translation by Frank Justus Miller. (Loeb Classical Library.) London and New York, 1916. 2 vols.

Paracelsus. *Liber Azoth.* In: Sudhoff, Karl (ed.). *Theophrast von Hohenheim genannt Paracelsus Sämtliche Werke.* First Section: Medizinische Schriften (in 14 vols.), 14. Munich and Berlin, 1933. (Pp. 547–95.)

Paul, Hermann. *Grundriss der germanischen Philologie.* Strassburg, 1889–93. 2 vols.

——. *Prinzipien der Sprachgeschichte.* 4th edn., Halle, 1909.

Pausanias. *Description of Greece.* With an English translation by W. H. S. Jones. (Loeb Classical Library.) London and New York, 1918–35. 5 vols.

486

PETRONIUS ARBITER, TITUS. *Satyricon.* With an English translation by Michael Heseltine. (Loeb Classical Library.) London and New York, 1913.

PFISTER, OSKAR. *Die Frömmigkeit des Grafen Ludwig von Zinzendorf.* (Schriften zur angewandten Seelenkunde, 8.) Leipzig and Vienna, 1910.

PHILO JUDAEUS. *De somniis.* In: [*Works.*] Translated by F. H. Colson and G. H. Whitaker. (Loeb Classical Library.) New York and London, 1929–   . 10 vols. (Vol. 5, pp. 285ff.)

——. *Quaestiones et solutiones in Genesim.* In: *Philonis Judaei Opera omnia.* (Editio Stereotypa.) Leipzig, 1893. (Translated from Armenian into Latin by J. B. Aucher.)

[PINDAR.] *The Odes of Pindar.* With an English translation by Sir John Sandys. (Loeb Classical Library.) London and New York, 1915.

Pistis Sophia. Translated by G. R. S. Mead. [London], 1921.

PITRA, JEAN BAPTISTE, CARDINAL (ed.). *Analecta sacra spicilegio Solesmensi parata.* Paris, 1876–91. 8 vols.

——. *Spicilegium solesmense.* . . . Paris, 1852–58. 4 vols.

[PLATO.] *Plato's Cosmology; the Timaeus of Plato.* Translated by F. M. Cornford. New York and London, 1937.

——. *The Symposium.* Translated by W. Hamilton. (Penguin Classics.) Harmondsworth, 1951.

[PLINY.] *The Natural History of Pliny.* Translated by John Bostock and H. Riley. (Bohn's Classical Library.) London, 1855–56. 6 vols.

PLOTINUS. [*Enneads.*] *Complete Works.* Translated by Kenneth Sylvan Guthrie. Alpine, New Jersey, [1918]. 4 vols.

PLUTARCH. *De Iside et Osiride.* In: *Plutarch's Moralia.* With an English translation by Frank Cole Babbitt. (Loeb Classical Library.) London and New York, 1927 ff. 14 vols. (Vol. 5, pp. 6–191.)

——. *Quaestiones Graecae.* In: Ibid. (Vol. 4, pp. 173–249.)

POE, EDGAR ALLAN. *The Raven and Other Poems.* New York, 1845.

PÖHLMANN, ROBERT VON. *Geschichte des antiken Kommunismus und Sozialismus.* Munich, 1893, 1901. 2 vols.

PORPHYRY. *De antro nympharum.* In: *Select Works of Porphyry.* Translated by Thomas Taylor. London, 1823.

PRAMPOLINI, GIACOMO. *La Mitologia nella vita dei popoli.* Milan, 1937–38. 2 vols.

PRELLER, LUDWIG. *Griechische Mythologie.* Leipzig, 1854. 2 vols.

PRELLWITZ, WALTHER. *Etymologisches Wörterbuch der griechischen Sprache.* 2nd edn., Göttingen, 1905.

PREUSS, K. T. "Der Ursprung der Religion und Kunst." *Globus* (Brunswick), LXXXVI (1904), 355–63.

PRITCHARD, JAMES B. (ed.). *Ancient Near Eastern Texts Relating to the Old Testament.* Princeton, 1950.

PUROHIT SWAMI, SHREE, and YEATS, WILLIAM BUTLER (trans.). *The Ten Principal Upanishads.* New York and London, 1937.

RANK, OTTO. *Der Künstler: Ansätze zu einer Sexualpsychologie.* (Imago-Bücher, 1.) 4th edn., Leipzig, Vienna, Zurich, 1925.

——. *Die Lohengrinsage.* (Schriften zur angewandten Seelenkunde, 13.) Leipzig and Vienna, 1911.

——. *The Myth of the Birth of the Hero.* Translated by William Alanson White. (Nervous and Mental Disease Monograph Series, 18.) New York, 1914.

——. "Ein Traum, der sich selbst deutet," *Jahrbuch für psychoanalytische und psychopathologische Forschungen* (Leipzig and Vienna), II (1910), 465–540.

REITZENSTEIN, RICHARD. *Die hellenistischen Mysterienreligionen.* Leipzig and Berlin, 1910.

RENAN, JOSEPH ERNEST. *Dialogues et fragments philosophiques.* Paris, 1876.

Revue archéologique. Paris.

[Rig-Veda.] *The Hymns of the Rigveda.* Translated with a popular commentary by Ralph T. H. Griffith. Benares, 1889–92. 4 vols. See also BROWN, W. NORMAN; DEUSSEN, PAUL.

488

RIKLIN, FRANZ. *Wishfulfilment and Symbolism in Fairy Tales*. Translated by William Alanson White. (Nervous and Mental Disease Monograph Series, 21.) New York, 1915.

ROBERT, CARL. *Die antiken Sarkophag-Reliefs*. Berlin, 1897.

ROBERTSON, JOHN MACKINNON. *Christ and Krishna*. London, 1889.

——. *Christianity and Mythology*. London, 1900.

ROHDE, ERWIN. *Psyche*. Translated from the 4th German edn. by W. B. Hillis. London, 1925.

——. "Σκιρα· ἐπι Σκιρῳ ἱεροποιια," *Hermes* (Berlin), XXI (1886), 124.

[Rome. Archaeological Commission.] *Bullettino della Commissione Archeologica Comunale di Roma*.

ROSCHER, WILHELM HEINRICH. *Ausführliches Lexikon der griechischen und römischen Mythologie*. Leipzig, 1884–1937. 6 vols.

ROSSELLINI, NICCOLA FRANCESCO IPPOLITO BALDASSARE. *I Monumenti dell' Egitto e della Nubia*. Pisa, 1842–44. 3 vols.

ROSTAND, EDMOND. *Cyrano de Bergerac*. Translated by Gladys Thomas and Mary F. Guillemard. New York and London, 1898.

RUSKA, JULIUS FERDINAND. *Tabula Smaragdina: ein Beitrag zur Geschichte der hermetischen Literatur*. Heidelberg, 1926.

SAINT-EXUPÉRY, ANTOINE JEAN BAPTISTE MARIE ROGER DE. *The Little Prince*. Translated by Katherine Woods. New York and London, 1944.

SALLUST. [*Works*.] With an English translation by J. C. Rolfe. (Loeb Classical Library.) London and New York, 1920.

SANDERS, DANIEL HENDEL. *Das Volksleben der Neugriechen*. Mannheim, 1844.

SCHAEFER, HEINRICH. *Von ägyptischer Kunst*. 3rd edn., Leipzig, 1930.

SCHÄRF, RIWKAH. "Die Gestalt des Satans im Alten Testament." In: C. G. JUNG. *Symbolik des Geistes*. Zurich, 1948.

SCHELLING, FRIEDRICH WILHELM JOSEPH VON. *Philosophie der Mythologie*. Part II, vol. 2 of: *Sämmtliche Werke*. Stuttgart and Augsburg, 1856–61.

SCHILLER, FRIEDRICH. *Die Piccolomini.* In: *Sämmtliche Werke.* Stuttgart and Tübingen, 1840.

SCHLAUCH, MARGARET (trans.). *The Saga of the Volsungs.* (Scandinavian Classics, 35.) New York and London, 1930.

SCHMID, HANS. "Zur Psychologie der Brandstifter." In: C. G. JUNG (ed.). *Psychologische Abhandlungen,* I. Zurich, 1914.

SCHOPENHAUER, ARTHUR. *The World as Will and Idea.* Translated by R. B. Haldane and J. Kemp. (English and Foreign Philosophical Library, 22–24.) London, 1883–86. 3 vols.

SCHOTT, ALBERT. *Das Gilgamesch-Epos.* Leipzig, [1934].

SCHREBER, DANIEL PAUL. *Memoirs of My Nervous Illness.* Translated by Ida Macalpine and Richard A. Hunter. (Psychiatric Monograph Series, 1.) London, 1955. (Original: *Denkwürdigkeiten eines Nervenkranken.* Leipzig, 1903.)

SCHULTZ, WOLFGANG. *Dokumente der Gnosis.* Jena, 1910.

SCHULTZE, FRITZ. *Psychologie der Naturvölker.* Leipzig, 1900.

SCHULTZE, VIKTOR. *Die Katakomben.* Leipzig, 1882.

SCHWARTZ, W. *Indogermanischer Volksglaube.* Berlin, 1885.

SCHWEITZER, ALBERT. *The Quest of the Historical Jesus.* Translated by W. Montgomery. London, 1910.

SCOTT, WALTER (ed.). *Hermetica.* Oxford, 1924–36. 4 vols.

SENECA. *Ad Lucilium epistulae morales.* With an English translation by Richard M. Gummere. (Loeb Classical Library.) London and New York, 1917–25. 3 vols.

SEPP, JOHANN NEPOMUK. *Das Heidentum und dessen Bedeutung für das Christentum.* Regensburg, 1853. 3 vols.

Septem tractatus seu capitula Hermetis Trismegisti aurei ["Tractatus aureus"]. In: *Ars chemica.* . . . Argentorati [Strasbourg], 1566. (Pp. 7–31.)

SHAKESPEARE, WILLIAM. *Julius Caesar.* In: *The Complete Works of William Shakespeare.* Edited by W. J. Craig, Oxford, 1947.

SHARPE, SAMUEL. *Egyptian Mythology and Egyptian Christianity.* London, 1863.

SIECKE, ERNST. "Der Gott Rudra im Rigveda," *Archiv für Religionswissenschaft* (Freiburg i. B.), I (1898), 209–59.

SILBERER, HERBERT. "Phantasie und Mythos," *Jahrbuch für psychoanalytische und psychopathologische Forschungen* (Leipzig and Vienna), II (1910), 541–622.

——."Über die Symbolbildung," ibid., III (1912), 661–723.

SOPHOCLES. *Philoctetes.* In: [*Works.*] Translated by F. Storr. (Loeb Classical Library.) London and New York, 1912–13. 2 vols. (Vol. 2.)

SPIEGEL, FRIEDRICH. *Erānische Altertumskunde.* Leipzig, 1871–78. 3 vols.

——. *Grammatik der Parsisprache nebst Sprachproben.* Leipzig, 1851.

SPIELREIN, S. "Über den psychologischen Inhalt eines Falls von Schizophrenie," *Jahrbuch für psychoanalytische und psychopathologische Forschungen* (Leipzig and Vienna), III (1912), 329–400.

SPIESS, KARL VON. *Marksteine der Volkskunst.* (Jahrbuch für historische Volkskunde, 5–6, 8–9.) Berlin, 1937–42. 2 vols.

Spirit and Nature. Translated by Ralph Manheim and R. F. C. Hull. (Papers from the Eranos Yearbooks, 1.) New York (Bollingen Series XXX), 1954; London, 1955.

SPITTELER, CARL. *Imago.* Jena, 1919.

——. *Prometheus and Epimetheus.* Translated by James Fullarton Muirhead. London, 1931.

Standard Dictionary of Folklore, Mythology and Legend. Edited by Maria Leach. New York, 1949–50. 2 vols.

STEINTHAL, H. "Die Sage von Simson." *Zeitschrift für Völkerpsychologie und Sprachwissenschaft* (Berlin), II (1861), 129–78.

——. "Die ursprüngliche Form der Sage von Prometheus," ibid., II, 1–29.

STEKEL, WILHELM. Note on "Aus Gerhart Hauptmanns Diarium," *Zentralblatt für Psychoanalyse* (Wiesbaden), II (1912), 365–66.

——. *Die Sprache des Traumes.* Wiesbaden, 1911.

STEPHENS, JOHN LLOYD. *Incidents of Travel in Central America etc.* London, 1841. 2 vols.

STOKES, WHITLEY. *Urkeltischer Sprachschatz.* Göttingen, 1894. (Vol. II of FICK, *Vergleichendes Wörterbuch,* q.v.)

STOLL, OTTO. *Das Geschlechtsleben in der Völkerpsychologie.* Leipzig, 1908.

SUETONIUS. [*Opera.*] With an English translation by J. C. Rolfe. (Loeb Classical Library.) London and New York, 1914. 2 vols.

Sutta-Nipata. Translated by Victor Fausböll. (Sacred Books of the East, 10, part 2.) Oxford, 1881.

SWANTON, JOHN R. *Contributions to the Ethnology of the Haida.* (American Museum of Natural History Memoir.) Leiden, 1905–9.

Tabula smaragdina. See RUSKA.

TACITUS, CORNELIUS. *The Histories,* etc. Translated by Clifford H. Moore. (Loeb Classical Library.) London and New York, 1925–37. 4 vols.

TA'RIKH AL-HIND AL-GHARBI. ["History of the West Indies," in Arabic.] Constantinople, 1730.

TERTULLIAN (Quintus Septimus Tertullianus). [*Apologia.*] *Apologeticus adversus gentes pro Christianis.* See Migne, *P.L.,* vol. I, cols. 257–536. For translation, see: *The Writings of Quintus Septimus Tertullianus.* Vol. I. Translated by S. Thelwall. (Ante-Nicene Christian Library, 11.) Edinburgh, 1869. (Pp. 53–140.)

Theatrum chemicum. Strasbourg, 1602–61. 6 vols. (*Platonis liber quartorum* in V, pp. 114–208.)

THEOCRITUS. In: *The Greek Bucolic Poets.* With an English translation by J. M. Edmonds. (Loeb Classical Library.) London and New York, 1912.

THIBOUT, GABRIELLE. *La Cathédrale de Strasbourg.* With photographs by Marc Foucault. Paris. 1939.

THIELE, GEORG. *Antike Himmelsbilder.* Berlin, 1898.

THOMPSON, REGINALD CAMPBELL (trans.). *The Epic of Gilgamish.* London, 1928.

TISCHNER, HERBERT. *Oceanic Art.* With photographs by Friedrich Hewicker. London and New York, 1954.

UNTERNÄHRER, ANTON. *Geheimes Reskript der bernischen Regierung an die Pfarr- und Statthalterämter.* n.p., 1821.

Upanishads. See GUENON; HUME; MAX MÜLLER; PUROHIT SWAMI.

USENER, HERMANN. *Das Weihnachtsfest.* (Religionsgeschichtliche Untersuchungen, Part I.) 2nd edn., Bonn, 1911.

[Vendidad.] *The Zend-Avesta.* Part I: *The Vendidad.* Translated by James Darmesteter. (Sacred Books of the East, 4.) Oxford, 1880.

VERLAINE, PAUL. *Poèmes saturniens.* Paris, 1866.

VIRGIL (PUBLIUS VERGILIUS MARO). [*Works.*] With an English translation by H. Rushton Fairclough. (Loeb Classical Library.) London and New York, 1929. 2 vols.

VITRUVIUS POLLIO, MARCUS. *De architectura.* Edited by Fra G. Giocondo. Venice, 1511.

VOLLERS, KARL. "Chidher," *Archiv für Religionswissenschaft* (Freiburg i. B.), XII (1909), 234–84.

WACHLMAYR, ALOIS. *Das Christgeburtsbild der frühen Sakralkunst.* Munich, 1939.

WAGNER, WILHELM RICHARD. *Gesammelte Schriften.* Ed. Julius Kapp. Leipzig, n.d. 14 vols. (*Siegfried:* IV, pp. 141–222. *Walküre:* IV, pp. 71–140.)

WAITZ, THEODOR. *Anthropologie der Naturvölker.* Leipzig, 1859–72. 6 vols.

WALDE, ALOIS. *Lateinisches etymologisches Wörterbuch.* 2nd edn., Heidelberg, 1910.

WEBER, ALBRECHT. *Indische Studien.* Berlin, 1850–63. 8 vols.

WEGENER, THOMAS A VILLANOVA. *Das wunderbare innere und äussere Leben der Dienerin Gottes Anna Catherina Emmerich.* Dülmen, 1891.

WIEDEMANN, ALFRED. "Die Toten und ihre Reiche im Glauben der alten Ägypter," *Der Alte Orient* (Leipzig), II (1900), 33–68.

[WILHELM, RICHARD.] *The Secret of the Golden Flower; a Chinese Book of Life.* Translated and explained by Richard Wilhelm, with a foreword and commentary by C. G. Jung. Translated from the German by Cary F. Baynes. Revised edn., London and New York, 1962.

WIRTH, ALBRECHT (ed.). *Aus orientalischen Chroniken*. Frankfurt a. M., 1894.

WIRTH, HERMANN FELIX. *Der Aufgang der Menschheit*. Vol. I (no more pub.). Jena, 1928.

WOLFF, CHRISTIAN. *Psychologia empirica methodo scientifica pertractata*. Frankfurt a. M. and Leipzig, 1732.

WOLTERS, PAUL H. A., and BRUNS, GERDA (eds.). *Das Kabirenheiligtum bei Theben,* Vol. I. (Archaeologisches Institut des Deutschen Reiches.) Berlin, 1940.

WORRINGER, WILHELM. *Die altdeutsche Buchillustration*. Munich, 1919 (3rd edn., 1921).

WUNDT, WILHELM. *Grundriss der Psychologie*. 6th edn., Leipzig, 1904.

——. *Philosophische Studien*. Vol. XIII. Leipzig, 1898.

YEATS, WILLIAM BUTLER. See PUROHIT SWAMI.

Zeitschrift des Vereins für Volkskunde. Berlin.

ZÖCKLER, OTTO. *The Cross of Christ*. Translated by Maurice J. Evans. London, 1877.

ZOSIMOS. "Sur l'art." In Berthelot, *Alchimistes grecs* (q.v.), III, 1, 2.

LINGUISTIC ABBREVIATIONS

Armen.	Armenian	Lith.	Lithuanian
Att.	Attic	MHG.	Middle High German
Celt.	Celtic	OBulg.	Old Bulgarian
Church		OE.	Old English (Anglo-Saxon)
Slav.	Church Slavonic	OHG.	Old High German
E., Eng.	English	OIcel.	Old Icelandic
F.	French	OInd.	Old Indic
G.	German	OIr.	Old Irish
Goth.	Gothic	OIran.	Old Iranian
Gr.	Greek	ON.	Old Norse
Icel.	Icelandic	Skr.	Sanskrit
IEur.	Indo-European	Slav.	Slavonic
Lat.	Latin	Ved.	Vedic

* indicates a hypothetical form

INDEX

INDEX

A page reference with asterisk indicates a text figure. For sources of both plates and text figures, see the lists of these in the front part of the book.

betrayal of the hero, motif of, 30
betrothal ring, meaning of, 432*n*
Bhagavad Gita, 166, 174*n*
Bhrigu, 146
Bible: association of hero's name with parallels in, 192; cities as women, 213; longing for the mother, 212*f;* of Manerius, pl. LVI; of Merian, pl. XXII*a;* mouth, fire, and speech symbolism, 162*f;* *see also* New Testament; Old Testament
Biblia pauperum, 167
bier, name for, 281
Big Snake, African legend of, 399
Bi-neb-did, 240
biological phenomena, changes in original sexual character of, 136
bird(s): with golden wings, 289; helpful, 248*n,* 347*f,* 352*f;* language of, 402*n;* as soul-images, 215; symbol of wishful thinking, 246*n*
birth: anal, 191; dual, of the hero, motif of, 321*ff;* extraordinary, of the hero, 318; goddess of, 370; mythological conjunction of rock, tree, and water, 243; myths, ethical basis of, 225; pangs of, 287*n;* in a stable, 199*n,* 374*n;* theories, of children, 353; of water and spirit, 225
birth-giving primary substance, 241
bisexuality: of gods and goddesses, 221; in libido myth, 289; *see also* hermaphrodite
Bithynia: Attis-Cybele cult, 426*n*
Blackfoot, *see* Melampus
blacksmith, 358
Bleuler, Eugen, 40*n;* on "ambitendency," 173*f;* on "ambivalence," 109, 173*f,* 438*n;* on schizophrenic group, 18*n*
bliss: in childhood memories, 334; divine, 266, 402*n*
blood: of dragon, 364; Eucharistic, 168; sacrificial offering, 431; vestments dipped in, 104

boa constrictor, 296*n*
Bodhisattva, 321
body: exploration of, in child's rhythmic activity, 144; inviolate, 395*ff,* 459; motif of dismemberment and reassembly, 237*f,* 239; mutilation of parts of, 239, 245*n;* "pneumatic," or subtle, 332; protruding parts and cavities, 147*n;* secretions as libido equivalents, 300; *see also* deformity
Boedromion, month of, 340
Boeotia, sacrifice to snake deity in, pl. LVII
Bogda Gesser Khan, 353*n*
Böhme, Jakob, 91*
Bologna: Holy Sepulchre of San Stefano, 346
Bombay, 237
Book of the Dead (Egyptian), 280; self-creation of the gods in, 256; tree-image in, 246
Book of Rites, 427
borderland phenomena, 457
"bore/born," etymology, 147–48*n*
Boreas, 216*n*
boring: associated with fire and procreation, 153; etymology, 147*n;* finger gesture, 142*ff;* and fire-making, 145*ff;* masturbatory, 160
Botho, Conrad, 96*
Bousset, Wilhelm, 368*n*
bow-and-arrow symbolism, 287*n; see also* arrow
Brahma, 122*f,* 351; emergence from Vishnu, 293, 399, pl. XLVI*a*
Brahman, 393, 422*n*
Brahmanaspati, 358*f*
Brahman ideas of fire and sacrifice, 165*f*
brain, inherited structure and functioning, 29
Brazil: Bakairi Indians, 203*n,* 220*n*
breast: as "mama," 23*n,* 251; drink of immortality from, 376*n;* exposed to arrow-shot, 282*ff*
breast-beating, 256
Brenner, Albert, 32*n*

and speech, 13*f;* symbolic, in dreams, 7; and thinking, 11

Lanzone, R. V., 123*

Laodonia, cattle of, 149

lap: entrance of the god through, 343; procreative symbol, 377

La Rochefoucauld, François, Duc de, on idleness, 174

Last Judgment (Rubens), pl. LXIV

Latona, at Delos, 219

laughter: and death, 389; of God, 45; inhuman, 379

Laurentius Laurentii, 184

law of the species, 434

Layard, J. W., 323*n,* 418*n*

Le Blant, Edmond, 107*n*

Le Coq, Albert von, pl. XLIX*b*

Lehmann, J. E., 260*n*

Leibniz, G. W., 453; "dum Deus calculat fit mundus," 46

Leiden Papyrus, 45

Lenclos, Ninon de, 4

lentils, magical practice *re,* 189*n*

Leo, zodiacal sign, 121; *see also* lion

Leonardo da Vinci, Freud's study of, 5

Leto, 216*n,* 260; night sea journey of, 371

Leviathan, 55*ff,* 116, 254*f*

Lévy-Bruhl, Lucien, on *participation mystique,* 141, 327

Liber, Italian god of procreation, 131*n*

"libidine," (Italian) word, 130*n*

libido: adult, bound to sexuality, 204; affluxes, 132; as appetite, 135*ff;* attracted to hero, 314; attributes, 125; bodily secretions as equivalents, 300; canalization of, *see following;* cathexes, projection of, 128*n;* characterization of, 97; of child, regression of, 307; classical authors on, 129*f;* and collective unconscious, 335; compared with sun and fire, 96; compulsion of, 67*ff;* concept of, 132–41; conflict within, 260, 438; con-

version and transformation of, 152, 232; and creation of world, 253*f,* 382, 415; creative power of man's soul, 121; and cult of rationalism and realism, 226; daemonic nature of, 112; death and renewal of, 280*f;* displacement onto a symbolical object, 54; effect of blocking of, 169; effect of immersion in unconscious, 420; *effrenata,* 401; *vs.* ego, 64*f;* as an energy-value, 137; erotic, and mystic union with Christ, 287; etymological context, 131; first manifestation of, in infants, 143; fixation in childhood milieu, 414*f;* and forward-striving, 398, 438; freed from instinctuality by psychic systems, 227; Freud's theory of, 128*f;* fructifying and destructive, 282; God as projection of, 56*f;* gradient of, 227; heat of, 101*n,* 381*n;* human figure as symbol of, 171; -images, 99, 115*n;* and light, 115*n,* 220; and incest prohibition, 417*f;* and incest-taboo, 294; instinctual, sacrifice of, 423–25; intensification of impressions, 38; and internal object as substitute for external object, 175; introversion of, 88*f,* 172*f,* 204, 292*f,* 334*f,* 374; as intuitive faculty, 125; love-object of, 405*f;* manifestations of, and personality, 328; meaning of, 165; menacing activity of, 285; myth, typical elements of, 289; progression of, 301; psychic object, 85; psychology *re,* 131; and rapport with environment, 207; regressive, *see following;* and release from underworld, 293; religious structures of, and regression, 429; reversion to presexual stage, 159; sacrifice of, 412, 415, 431; search for sexual object, 417*f;* and sexuality, 134, 224*n;* speech and fire-making as appli-

THE COLLECTED WORKS OF
C. G. JUNG

T HE PUBLICATION of the first complete edition, in English, of the works of C. G. Jung was undertaken by Routledge and Kegan Paul, Ltd., in England and by Bollingen Foundation in the United States. The American edition is number XX in Bollingen Series, which since 1967 has been published by Princeton University Press. The edition contains revised versions of works previously published, such as *Psychology of the Unconscious*, which is now entitled *Symbols of Transformation*; works originally written in English, such as *Psychology and Religion*; works not previously translated, such as *Aion*; and, in general, new translations of virtually all of Professor Jung's writings. Prior to his death, in 1961, the author supervised the textual revision, which in some cases is extensive. Sir Herbert Read (d. 1968), Dr. Michael Fordham, and Dr. Gerhard Adler compose the Editorial Committee; the translator is R. F. C. Hull (except for Volume 2) and William McGuire is executive editor.

The price of the volumes varies according to size; they are sold separately, and may also be obtained on standing order. Several of the volumes are extensively illustrated. Each volume contains an index and, in most cases, a bibliography; the final volume will contain a complete bibliography of Professor Jung's writings and a general index to the entire edition.

In the following list, dates of original publication are given in parentheses (of original composition, in brackets). Multiple dates indicate revisions.

* Published 1957; 2nd edn., 1970.　　　† Published 1960.

On the Importance of the Unconscious in Psychopathology (1914)
On the Problem of Psychogenesis in Mental Disease (1919)
Mental Disease and the Psyche (1928)
On the Psychogenesis of Schizophrenia (1939)
Recent Thoughts on Schizophrenia (1957)
Schizophrenia (1958)

*4. FREUD AND PSYCHOANALYSIS
Freud's Theory of Hysteria: A Reply to Aschaffenburg (1906)
The Freudian Theory of Hysteria (1908)
The Analysis of Dreams (1909)
A Contribution to the Psychology of Rumour (1910–11)
On the Significance of Number Dreams (1910–11)
Morton Prince, "The Mechanism and Interpretation of Dreams": A
    Critical Review (1911)
On the Criticism of Psychoanalysis (1910)
Concerning Psychoanalysis (1912)
The Theory of Psychoanalysis (1913)
General Aspects of Psychoanalysis (1913)
Psychoanalysis and Neurosis (1916)
Some Crucial Points in Psychoanalysis: A Correspondence between
    Dr. Jung and Dr. Loÿ (1914)
Prefaces to "Collected Papers on Analytical Psychology" (1916, 1917)
The Significance of the Father in the Destiny of the Individual
    (1909/1949)
Introduction to Kranefeldt's "Secret Ways of the Mind" (1930)
Freud and Jung: Contrasts (1929)

†5. SYMBOLS OF TRANSFORMATION (1911–12/1952)
    PART I
Introduction
Two Kinds of Thinking
The Miller Fantasies: Anamnesis
The Hymn of Creation
The Song of the Moth
    PART II
Introduction
The Concept of Libido
The Transformation of Libido
The Origin of the Hero   (continued)

* Published 1961.
† Published 1956; 2nd edn., 1967. (65 plates, 43 text figures.)

* Published 1953; 2nd edn., 1966.
† Published 1960; 2nd edn., 1969.

* Published 1959; 2nd edn., 1968. (Part I: 79 plates, with 29 in colour.)

* Published 1964; 2nd edn., 1970. (8 plates.)
† Published 1958; 2nd edn., 1969.

* Published 1953; 2nd edn., completely revised, 1968. (270 illustrations.)
† Published 1968. (50 plates, 4 text figures.)
‡ Published 1963; 2nd edn., 1970. (10 plates.)

The Significance of the Unconscious in Individual Education (1928)
The Development of Personality (1934)
Marriage as a Psychological Relationship (1925)

18. MISCELLANY
Posthumous and Other Miscellaneous Works

19. BIBLIOGRAPHY AND INDEX
Complete Bibliography of C. G. Jung's Writings
General Index to the Collected Works